Beginning Japanese

REVISED EDITION

AN INTEGRATED APPROACH TO LANGUAGE AND CULTURE

Michael L. Kluemper • Lisa Berkson • Nathan Patton • Nobuko Patton

TUTTLE Publishing

Tokyo | Rutland, Vermont | Singapore

We would like to dedicate this book to the never-ending support, inspiration, and patience of our families and friends, sensei and students—past and present.

Special thanks for the generous cooperation given by Heizaburou and Natsuko Ebata, and Hisaho Onodera in recording the audio. Special acknowledgement of Paul and Miriam Ash, Yuko Betsukawa, Rick Britton, Rebecca Evans, Sakino Imaruoka, Kaede Kato, Fumiko Kikuchi, Kaori Miyashita, John Sparks, Akiko and Calder Miyamoto, Manami Imaoka, Morgan Mulberry, Amy Noblitt, Paul Gatchell, Miki Sawaoka, friends in Omonogawa, and the many others who have assisted in so many ways in this endeavor.

Published by Tuttle Publishing, an imprint of Periplus Editions (HK) Ltd.

www.tuttlepublishing.com

Illustrations by Boya Sun and Keiko Murakami

Library of Congress Control Number: 2009933853

ISBN 978-0-8048-4528-1 (2016 edition)
ISBN 978-0-8048-4132-0 (hardcover edition)

Distributed by

North America, Latin America & Europe
Tuttle Publishing
364 Innovation Drive
North Clarendon, VT 05759-9436 U.S.A.
Tel: 1 (802) 773-8930
Fax: 1 (802) 773-6993
info@tuttlepublishing.com
www.tuttlepublishing.com

Japan
Tuttle Publishing
Yaekari Building, 3rd Floor
5-4-12 Osaki Shinagawa-ku Tokyo 141 0032
Tel: (81) 3 5437-0171
Fax: (81) 3 5437-0755
sales@tuttle.co.jp
www.tuttle.co.jp

Asia Pacific
Berkeley Books Pte. Ltd.
61 Tai Seng Avenue #02-12 Singapore 534167
Tel: (65) 6280-1330
Fax: (65) 6280-6290
inquiries@periplus.com.sg
www.periplus.com

First edition
20 19 18 5 4 3 1801RR
Printed in China

To the Learner

Welcome to *Beginning Japanese*. This first step on your journey to Japanese language proficiency will set you well on your way. This book will teach you how to:

- read and write all hiragana and katakana
- read and recognize 151 kanji
- use Japanese to describe basic details of your own life, including family, school, hobbies, likes and dislikes, and daily activities
- answer questions in Japanese about your daily life with low-level to mid-level fluency
- use Japanese to ask a friend about his/her family and daily life, and invite them to join you in an activity such as shopping
- describe a person or a situation using a variety of adjectives in Japanese
- skim and scan written Japanese passages for important content and meaning
- respond to short written communications, such as e-mail messages, in Japanese
- make a short oral presentation in Japanese about a hobby or a recent event
- talk at a basic level about Japanese geography, history, and culture

Be sure your seatbelt is on, and get ready to enjoy the journey of a lifetime as you learn this exciting language and experience the culture from which it comes!

The Authors

Contents

To the Learner 3
Goals and Guidelines 6
Introduction 9

1 Introductions and Getting Started 15

1-1 東京(とうきょう)へ いきます! Going to Tokyo! 16
1-2 日本(にほん) Land of the Rising Sun. 22
1-3 私(わたし)は キアラ(きあら) です。 I am Kiara. 26
1-4 こちらは母(はは) です。 This is my mother. 33
1-5 こんばんは。 Good evening. 38
1-6 よく できました。 Well done! 44
New Word Checklist 46

2 Family and Friends in Tokyo 48

2-1 それは 何(なん) ですか。 What is that? 49
2-2 こちらは ベン君(べんくん)の お母(かあ)さん です。 This is Ben's mother. 57
2-3 この バッグ(ばっぐ)に おみやげが あります。どうぞ。 The souvenirs are in this bag. Here you go. 64
2-4 その えんぴつと けしゴム(ごむ)を 二(ふた)つ 下(くだ)さい。 Please give me that pencil and two erasers. 69
2-5 お母(かあ)さん、晩(ばん)ご飯(はん)は 何(なん) ですか。 Mom, what's for dinner? 74
New Word Checklist 79

3 The Ins and Outs of Schools in Japan 81

3-1 いいえ、小学校(しょうがっこう)は ありません。 No, there is no elementary school. 82
3-2 社会(しゃかい)と 音楽(おんがく)と 英語(えいご)が あります。 You will have social studies, music and English. 91
3-3 次(つぎ)は 何時間目(なんじかんめ) ですか。 What period is next? 100
3-4 今日(きょう)、宿題(しゅくだい)は ありません。 There is no homework today. 106
3-5 むし暑(あつ)い ですね。 It's muggy, isn't it. 110
New Word Checklist 116

4 People and Places of Nagasaki 118

4-1 何人(なにじん)ですか。 Where are you from? 119
4-2 何語(なにご)を 話(はな)しますか。 What language do you speak? 126
4-3 私は ここで 食(た)べません。 I won't eat here. 131
4-4 私は 江戸(えど)に 行(い)きます。 I will go to Edo. 137
4-5 この 寿司(すし)を 食(た)べて 下(くだ)さい。 Please eat this sushi. 142
New Word Checklist 148

5 Time in Nara 150

5-1 毎週(まいしゅう) 月曜日(げつようび)の 12時に 私に、電話(でんわ)して 下さい。 Please telephone me every Monday at 12:00. 151
5-2 私も、アメリカ(あめりか) で、漢字(かんじ)を ちょっと 勉強(べんきょう)しました。 I also studied some kanji in the U.S. 158
5-3 朝(あさ)から、晩(ばん)まで、ずっと 食べます。 I eat from morning all the way until night. 165

5-4 先週も、あちこちに 行きました。 Last week too, we went here and there. 171
5-5 Verb Review 176
New Word Checklist 177

6 Body Parts and Clothing in Hiraizumi 179

6-1 頭が とても いい です。 You are very smart. 180
6-2 弁慶さんは、とても 背が 高い ですね。 Benkei is very tall, isn't he! 188
6-3 お茶を 飲んでも いい ですか。 May I drink some green tea? 197
6-4 私達は 洋服を 着ています。 We are wearing Western clothing. 203
6-5 弁慶さんに 会って、たくさん 話して、歴史を 勉強しました。
We met Benkei, talked a lot, and studied history. 209
New Word Checklist 213

7 Hobbies in the Ancient City of Heian-kyou 215

7-1 僕の 趣味は 食べる事です。 My hobby is eating. 216
7-2 キアラさんは、日本が 大好きですね。 Kiara, you really love Japan, don't you? 224
7-3 キアラさんは、日本語が とても 上手です。 Kiara's Japanese is very good. 230
7-4 友さんの 銀色の 着物も、かっこいいですよ。 Tomo's silver-colored kimono also looks great! 236
7-5 僕も、雅楽は とてもかっこいいと 思います。 I also think that gagaku is really cool! 241
New Word Checklist 245

8 Adjectives in Amanohashidate 246

8-1 海が きれい ですね。 The ocean is beautiful, isn't it? 247
8-2 この海は もっと きれいでした。 This ocean used to be prettier. 254
8-3 これは 美味しくありません。 This is not delicious. 262
8-4 漬け物は、美味しくありませんでした。 The pickles were not tasty! 269
New Word Checklist 273

9 Purchasing and Giving Gifts in Edo 274

9-1 買い物を します。 I'm going shopping. 275
9-2 はい、一冊 1,025円 です。 Yes, one volume is 1,025 yen. 282
9-3 もっと 大きい スリッパは ありますか。 Are there bigger slippers? 290
9-4 私は ベン君に、おせんべいと 漫画を あげます。 I will give senbei and a comic book to Ben. 295
9-5 これは、私の 妹が くれました。 My younger sister gave me this. 301
New Word Checklist 305

10 Meeting Basho in Kanazawa 307

10-1 明日も 晴れ でしょう。 Probably tomorrow will also be sunny. 308
10-2 「ここで 一緒に、食事をしませんか。」 "Won't you have a meal here with us?" 315
10-3 日本語を、もっと 勉強したい です。 I want to study Japanese more. 322
10-4 まだ 起きたく ない です。 I do not want to wake up yet. 326
10-5 食べ物も、飲み物も、たくさん 持って行きましょう。 Let's take a lot of food and drinks. 332
New Word Checklist 338

Kanji List 339
Appendix 1: **Grammar References** 342
Verb Conjugation Summary / Verbs by Chapter / Counting Basic Numbers / Counters / Question Words / Adjectives & Adjective Conjugation Summary / Adverbs & Time Words / Particles / Noun Categories
Appendix 2: **Japanese Names** 348
Appendix 3: **Food and Drinks** 348
Appendix 4: **Classroom Objects** 349
Japanese-English Glossary 350
English-Japanese Glossary 367

Goals and Guidelines

	Performance Goals	Language Points	Kanji
Chapter 1: Introductions and Getting Started	• pronounce Japanese vowels and syllabary • recognize the difference between Chinese characters and hiragana • introduce yourself politely • make simple statements and questions • use greetings appropriately • understand classroom commands	• particles は, か • は～です statements • relative pronouns • じゃ　ありません **Culture** • showing respect • name order	木日本東京語私父母気元人休
Chapter 2: Family and Friends in Tokyo	• describe your family and the families of others • count up to 900 and count objects • specify relative location of people and objects • make polite requests and offers	• particles の, と, を, and も • counters • verbs of existence: あります/います • use of ください/どうぞ **Culture** • lucky and unlucky numbers • Tokyo neighborhoods	何家兄姉弟妹一二三四五六七八九十百犬
Chapter 3: The Ins and Outs of Schools in Japan	• talk about daily class schedules • tell time • make contrasting statements using でも • engage in small talk about the weather	• negative verb endings • particles を, に, and で (*by means of*), and the sentence ending particles よ, ね and ねえ • use of the conjunction でも (*but*) **Culture** • the Japanese school system and calendar • school club activities • Shinto shrine torii	高小中大学校年先生山英国音楽今分書寺時門間下暑寒神社風友

	Performance Goals	Language Points	Kanji
Chapter 4: People and Places of Nagasaki	• inquire about nationality • discuss languages spoken in various countries • talk about eating and drinking • use the verbs for going, coming, and returning	• non-past and non-past negative of verbs • summary of verb forms introduced and used at this point • particle で for place of action • particles へ and に for place of direction **Culture** • Tokugawa period • geography of Kyushu • foreign trade and influence in early 17th-century Japan	言外話食 飲物車行 来帰見聞
Chapter 5: Time in Nara	• make affirmative and negative past tense statements and questions • use a variety of time and date words to talk about past, present, and future schedules • state your birth date	• affirmative and negative past tense of verbs • particle に to indicate a specific time • the から〜まで pattern **Culture** • Nara, its history, and historic sites • imperial reign periods and dating • Japanese festivals and holidays	前午後良 月火水金 土曜千万 末毎週電 達
Chapter 6: Body Parts and Clothing in Hiraizumi	• name basic body parts and describe someone's physical features • inquire about someone's health • request, grant, and deny permission • talk about wearing clothes and accessories • ask what someone is doing and respond with a series of actions	• adverbs • the ~て form of verbs • particle で (*by means of*) • the ~て います • (present progressive [~ing]) form of verbs **Culture** • geography, history, and products of Hiraizumi, Iwate Prefecture, and Tohoku • Yoshitsune and his retainer Benkei • Chinese and Japanese medicine	体目口耳 手足心持 待強平和 低太医者 薬着
Chapter 7: Hobbies in the Ancient City of Heian-kyou	• discuss your hobbies, and your likes and dislikes • state what you are good at and what you are poor at • point out different colors • state your opinion using "I think..."	• the particle が • dictionary form • negative adverbs • ". . . と 思います" **Culture** • Heian period culture • Murasaki Shikibu and *The Tale of Genji* • waka	花池趣味 事好上色 白黒赤青 歌思

	Performance Goals	Language Points	Kanji
Chapter 8: Adjectives in Amanohashidate	• describe objects and scenes using い and な adjectives in the present, past and negative conjugation	• adjective conjugation **Culture** • geography and history of Amanohashidate • Japanese folk tales, including *Urashima Tarou* • onomatopoeic words	美長短海 安悪面天 立昔々有 広島暗明
	Performance Goals	**Language Points**	**Kanji**
Chapter 9: Purchasing and Giving Gifts in Edo	• go shopping, ask prices, and purchase goods • understand and use common shopping expressions • talk about what you gave someone, and what sort of present you received	• noun + SHIMASU expressions • もっと (comparative) • use of の to replace nouns • verbs of giving and receiving **Culture** • hanga and ukiyoe • Hokusai and other famous ukiyoe artists • Japanese bathing rituals • gift-giving practices	買売店全 部円
Chapter 10: Meeting Basho in Kanazawa	• talk about and predict the weather • politely invite a friend to do something • accept, or decline, an invitation • say that you want, or don't want, to do something • note that something has not happened yet • talk about bringing someone, or taking something, somewhere	• DESHO • the ~たい form • まだ + negative verb **Culture** • history and attractions of Kanazawa • the poet Basho • hanami (cherry blossom viewing) • the song "Sakura"	春夏秋冬 石使作当 桜

Please visit **TimeForJapanese.com** for detail on how *Beginning Japanese* aligns with the standards set forth by organizations such as the Japanese National Standards Task Force, ACTFL (American Council on the Teaching of Foreign Languages), and others.

Introduction

In *Beginning Japanese* some of the characters you meet are learning Japanese along with you. You will be able to interact with them, learn what they learn, and have a great time exploring Japanese language, history, and culture. The first person that you will meet is Kiara. She's about to arrive in Japan from the U.S. and will be attending a Japanese high school for the next year, maybe longer. That is, until a sudden change of plans occurs.

Many of you will be using this text to study a foreign language for the first time. Some of you already speak one or two other languages. Either way, as you go through this text, you will find some hints and techniques that will help the learning process. You might have heard people say that Japanese is a hard language to learn. The authors and characters of this textbook say that if you are interested in Japan and the Japanese language, Japanese will definitely be the easiest language for you to learn! It is going to take some time before you can consider yourself fluent, but the doors that are about to open for you will reveal fantastic treasures. Be ready for them!

This series is designed to help students take their language learning experience to the next level: *Beginning Japanese* will help you improve your understanding of the language and how this language, specific to this culture, developed and exists today. Historical aspects of Japan, its people, traditions, society, and culture are embedded into this series. This is done to give you, the learner, a clearer understanding of this unique language and the contexts in which it is used.

Using This Book

Beginning Japanese is based on "natural language acquisition" principles. When learning a language "naturally," the learner is exposed to much more information than he/she actually needs to answer questions, meet personal needs, or to accomplish tasks. Thus, when using this series, it is important for teachers to reinforce the fact that students do not need to understand every word to participate in a conversation, glean necessary information from signage, a passage, or print news, or function in a foreign situation. With this in mind, the manga, dialogues, and journal entries in *Beginning Japanese* are designed to complement each other. Material has deliberately been included that is not explicitly explained or defined. This is because that information is not necessary for comprehension of the main ideas and details of the section (it may be explained in a subsequent lesson). This mimics the natural learning process in that the learner often grasps the general outline of material before examining it carefully and sequentially.

Anyone who experiences a new language can testify that you don't have to be fluent in a language to express yourself on a basic level or to understand general meaning. Conversations about when a train leaves, where the restroom is, or how much a t-shirt costs happen every day between people who do not share a common language. If the person speaking and the person listening are good communicators, information can be shared and understood. In fact, this sort of exchange often makes for a memorable experience. Skill with another language, however, allows you to delve much deeper into a culture and to more easily make new friends across cultures. Both the disc included with *Beginning Japanese* and the website **TimeForJapanese.com** include additional listening practices and should be utilized by teachers as they see fit.

Beginning Japanese is the first step in a language learning series designed to give you a more natural experience in Japanese language acquisition. Aspects of this book and the accompanying web and audio resources include language beyond what is expected of you at any given point in your learning process. Through exposure to words, characters, sights, and sounds provided through this text and its supplementary materials, you will come to have a deeper understanding not only of Japanese language, but also of its culture, sights, sounds, and history.

This series is different from other learning sources in that:

1. KANJI characters (non-phonetic) are taught from the first lessons. In traditional materials, often students are expected to master the two phonetic "alphabets," *hiragana* and *katakana*, prior to the introduction of kanji.

   The kanji characters include FURIGANA, phonetic guides below each kanji to help you read the new characters and to give assistance where needed. To challenge yourself, don't just rely on the furigana guides; rather, consciously cover up the furigana readings with your hand or a piece of paper while reading. This will help your reading skills improve enormously. Eventually, the furigana disappear from the text; if you have been weaning yourself off of them as you progress, you will not even miss them and will realize that it's much easier to read Japanese without this aid. For many, learning to read kanji and exploring ways to use them and learn vocabulary through them can be a very enjoyable part of the process.
2. Visuals are presented in a manga format and in photographs. The manga bring the characters in the story to life and help you interact with historical figures for a contextualized learning experience on a wide range of topics. The photographs provide authentic exposure to what Japan really "looks" like. They provide a source for conversation and contribute to your mastery of the vocabulary.
3. An engaging story is woven through the pages of the book and website. The story provides information about Japan's culture, history, and historical figures, and it offers a level of language learning that increases in difficulty as your language skills improve. This increase in difficulty challenges you and offers opportunities for practicing real-life skills.

Learning Strategies

For Western language speakers, the study of Japanese is generally a more abstract process than learning a European language. It may be difficult, at first, to make any intuitive leaps in your learning. Therefore, it is important to find constructive ways to organize the new information you will be learning. This organization process is useful not just for learning Japanese, but when studying any new language or content area.

Since new material, including language, can be learned in a variety of ways, it is crucial that you, the learner, find the most effective method for you to memorize vocabulary and other unfamiliar information. Try to use as many of your senses as you can. For example, writing down and saying out loud what you write lets you use more than one sense: you are moving your hand, you are seeing the words on paper, you are speaking, and you are hearing. Learning strategies like this will help you retain the information in a more intuitive way and speed up your learning so that you can naturally use new vocabulary and grammatical structures in your repertoire of linguistic tools. Here are some ideas for studying material effectively and producing it from memory when needed.

- Figure out what type of learner you are: visual, auditory, kinesthetic, or verbal. Then make your strengths work for you.
- Use flashcards. Flashcards for the vocabulary in this book can be downloaded on the **TimeForJapanese.com** website.
- Print out and use the kanji and vocabulary learning charts found on **TimeForJapanese.com**.
- Type your vocabulary words in Japanese, including their English meanings. Typing a word in Japanese helps you better understand unique Japanese language characteristics like long and short vowels and double consonants.

Hiragana and Katakana

Beginning Japanese hiragana and katakana learning booklets are available on the disc ("Kana Booklet") and at **TimeFor Japanese.com**. These are the basic phonetic character sets used in Japanese and are necessary to learn as you begin your study. Your goal should be to complete the kana booklet as quickly as possible so that your progress through the textbook will be smoother and more efficient. This edition does not contain romaji (Roman-letter) pronunciations for the Japanese. However, the first two chapters with romaji pronunciation guides are available on the "Beginning" page of **TimeForJapanese.com.**

Graphic Organizers

Use graphic organizers to organize your new Japanese vocabulary in different ways. When you place linguistic parts into different sorts of categories, it helps you remember vocabulary and sentence patterns.

Again, it is important for you as a beginning Japanese learner to find ways of organizing new material so that you can quickly locate, and use, the appropriate vocabulary word, kana, or kanji as you need it. A few graphic organizers you might try include grouping by:

- first, end, or overall sounds
- a-i-u-e-o order
- part of speech (verbs, adjectives, nouns, etc.)
- meaning (things that move, that you eat, that you drink, that are blue, etc.)
- mapping (making a story map on paper)
- making charts or graphs
- making up songs

Visit **TimeForJapanese.com** regularly for additional downloads, practice exercises, review games, and other activities. Be sure to send in ideas which you've found particularly helpful in your study, as well.

The Components

Beginning Japanese is made up of several component parts designed to assist you in gaining proficiency in the four competencies of language: speaking, listening, reading, and writing. Each chapter includes:

■ 漫画(まんが) Japanese Comics

Each section begins with a manga. These manga generally include a dialogue or conversation between characters designed to help give context to the conversations through visual clues. The dialogue is designed to be adaptable to situations that you may experience in your own Japanese language learning. It is important to realize that you will not know all of the words you read and hear in this section however, this mimics real life and will help you develop your communication skills as it is a more natural way of learning language. The meanings of all words can be found in the glossary in the back. Audio for manga and dialogues can be found on the **TimeForJapanese.com** website.

■ 会話(かいわ) Dialogue

The dialogue from the manga characters is presented in this component as straight text, allowing you to view the conversation from a more literary perspective. Again, it is important to realize that you will not know all of the words you read and hear in this section however, this mimics real life and will help you develop your communication skills as it is a more natural way of learning language. The meanings of all words can be found in the glossary in the back. Audio for manga and dialogues can be found on the **TimeForJapanese.com** website.

■ 単語 New Words
たんご

Beginning Japanese vocabulary items are introduced through pictures as much as possible. There are two reasons for this: 1) to take advantage of the brain's tendency to more easily associate images with meanings; and 2) to limit the amount of "translating" done by students when internalizing meaning. Our hope is that beginning students will make associations between the new vocabulary and the objects, ideas, and actions they represent rather than relying on translation. More advanced learners often have developed more sophisticated memorization techniques and are better able to internalize vocabulary meanings and need less visual support. The glossary in the *Beginning Japanese* textbook contains words taught as "Vocabulary." There are additional words in the Dialogue and Journal sections that do not appear in the New Words section, but have been included in the glossary as supplemental vocabulary (denoted by an "s" after their Chapter/Section code).

Kanji characters (see below) introduced in that section or prior ones are shown in gray in New Words sections.

■ 漢字 Kanji
かんじ

Beginning Japanese includes more kanji for students to learn than most introductory-level textbooks. One rationale for this is the belief that the more exposure learners have to characters in contextual situations, the deeper the learning. Beginning with Chapter 1, *Beginning Japanese* includes kanji that you will see and read in authentic Japanese materials such as websites, books, products, and manga. It is uncommon to teach kanji such as 東 and 京 in the first chapter of a Japanese textbook, however. There are several reasons for including kanji from the beginning.

1. These two kanji (東 and 京) mean "Tokyo" when placed together. Tokyo is the setting for the first three chapters of this text and as such, appears often in these chapters. Furthermore, introducing these two kanji is an opportunity to teach other aspects of kanji learning.
2. Learning kanji requires different skills than learning vocabulary, sentence structure, and even hiragana/katakana. It often appeals to a student's creative nature and can be an exciting learning experience.
3. Learning kanji in conjunction with culture and language helps bring the language to life in a much more deep and real way.

Pronunciation sub-scripts (guides below) rather than super-scripts (guides above) are provided to help you develop your reading skills. Commonly used kanji characters, many of which originated as pictograms, are specifically taught to you from the first lesson. As you advance through this series, you will learn how and when it is appropriate to use kanji, and strategies to help you guess at their meaning from context. The way that written Japanese is used continually changes. As is the case with English and other languages today, much written Japanese is created with the aid of electronic devices, including computers and cell phones. *Beginning Japanese* takes these technological developments and changes into account as far as expectations for passive and active kanji knowledge and reading abilities are concerned. The degree to which you are required to use kanji increases gradually as you progress through the series. Written workbook exercises and tests where kanji are to be produced will include kanji banks where needed, allowing you to choose the necessary characters. Kanji that you see and write often will become very familiar to you, while you will probably refer to the kanji banks for those kanji less commonly used by you personally. Gradually, though, as you work your way through *Beginning Japanese*, you will be able to produce these kanji from memory.

Each kanji is introduced first by a large-sized example, with the stroke order numbered. In the box just to the right of this large example is a guide to common pronunciations. This includes the most common and useful pronunciations of kanji as well as others, which might prove to help you learn the kanji and vocabulary better. Kanji pronunciations can vary depending on the context in which the kanji is used. The first examples are written in katakana (ex.: ホン). These pronunciations are called ON-YOMI, or "Chinese readings." They are based on the original pronunciations of the kanji used in medieval China. The pronunciations following the on-yomi are written in hiragana and are known as the KUN-YOMI, or the pronunciations native to Japanese (ex.: もと).

To the right of the pronunciation guides the kanji is shown stroke by stroke. Learning and using the proper stroke order when writing is very important as it later will help you more clearly understand new kanji and how to use a kanji dictionary.

The box below the pronunciation offers some common usages of that kanji in vocabulary words. The most efficient way to study kanji is in the context of vocabulary words where they appear, as opposed to studying kanji independently of existing vocabulary.

The final portion of each kanji section is a short story or mnemonic device to help you remember the kanji. We encourage you to think of even better and more creative ways to help remember each kanji. Please share your ideas with **TimeForJapanese.com** so learning kanji can become even more fun and creative.

The workbook pages contain writing practice exercises that will help you fix each kanji into your memory. Of course, you are welcome to do more kanji writing practice on your own—all over your notebook, for instance, or when you write notes to your friends!

■ 言葉の探索 Language Detection

Unlike many other language books, this component is not limited to grammatical explanations. It also offers contextual, social, and cultural cues for how, when, and why the words and phrases being introduced are used. This component also includes several examples of each pattern. Bonus Sheets providing expanded or additional structural information can be found on **www.TimeForJapanese.com.**

■ 自習 Self Check

This component is designed as a quick-check test for you to complete orally by yourself, to confirm your understanding of the patterns covered in the Language Detection section above. Doing this check orally allows you not only to read Japanese, but also to say and hear the words, helping you better learn the pattern being practiced. Examine the tasks and test yourself. If you are unsure of some point, reexamine the Language Detection section and ask your instructor for clarification. Do this section out loud by yourself to see if you can complete the task before moving on to the next component, which involves practice with a partner, in small groups, or as a class.

■ 練習の時間 Time for Practice

This practice area provides an opportunity to apply the material introduced in the Language Detection component with a partner, in a small group, or as a class. By the time you have completed this component, you should have a good understanding of the material covered in the Language Detection component and the new vocabulary in this section. If you are unclear about any aspect of the new material, ask your instructor for clarification or additional examples.

■ 文化箱 Culture Chest

The Culture Chest offers additional information related to the setting or historical background of each section. More information, including photographs and video links, can be found on the **TimeForJapanese.com** website. Click on the link for the appropriate chapter. Teacher submissions and suggestions are invited.

■ キアラのジャーナル Kiara's Journal

きあら じゃーなる

In the first section of this text you meet Kiara, the main character of this text. She is an American student who has studied Japanese for less than a year and who is embarking on her journey, just as you are, to learn more about Japanese language and culture. Through her journals and the writings of other characters, you will learn, review, and be challenged to use a variety of language strategies to understand and, to some extent, participate in the experiences on this very atypical journey.

When you travel to Japan as a non-native speaker, you are bombarded with visual and auditory stimuli that must be decoded into something comprehensible to you. Essentially, this decoding happens through strengthening your translating and interpreting skills. Sifting through all of the authentic sights and sounds you experience to comprehend the core elements required to meet your needs is the process through which language is internalized and learned. As would happen in an actual experience in Japan, you will probably not understand everything you see and hear in this book or this series, but you will develop coping skills and learn to sort out the main points, ideas, and details that you need.

These journal entries and other writings are designed to simulate what you might experience in Japan as a non-native speaker of Japanese. Reading these, and searching for the "gist" of the passage, will develop and reinforce your interpretive skills. Kiara's story actually extends beyond the boundaries of this text. More details of her journey can be found at **TimeForJapanese.com.**

The manga images and journal entries found in this text are designed to provide insight into Japanese history, culture, and historical figures. The Japanese language, like all languages, has been constantly changing and evolving throughout its long history. Some liberties have been taken in order to present language as it's spoken in modern times, and to meld past and present to give you, the learner, an engaging story in which you can learn with the characters.

■ 単語チェックリスト New Word Checklist

たんごちぇっくりすと

Each chapter contains a comprehensive glossary where new words from that chapter are listed in the Japanese alphabetical (a-i-u-e-o) order by section. You will learn this alphabetical system in Chapter 1. If you have a question about the English meaning of a vocabulary word, you can quickly find a translation in this section of each chapter. A complete glossary for all the words in the New Word Checklists is also included in the back of the book.

Workbook and Supplemental Materials

The workbook, **TimeForJapanese.com**, and disc material that accompany this book are designed to help check your understanding and to practice and apply previously learned and new material. Audio files for the text and activities can be found in the disc material. All audio files (including updates), review activities, downloadable files, assessment activities, and links for other content are available on **TimeForJapanese.com**.

TimeForJapanese.com

The web-based resource for this series, **TimeForJapanese.com**, contains additional learning content and practice tools. **TimeForJapanese.com** is continually being updated and enhanced. Bookmark or save it to your favorites list on your computer and visit it often.

Introductions and Getting Started

第 1 課

Learning and Performance Goals

This chapter will enable you to:

A) introduce yourself and others in Japanese
B) greet a person in Japanese appropriately
C) respond correctly to classroom commands
D) use a variety of learning strategies to facilitate your study of Japanese
E) say things such as *This is sushi* or *That is a book*
F) read and write at least half of the hiragana and 13 kanji
G) use the "can-do" chart found on **TimeForJapanese.com** to chart your progress for what you "can-do" for each chapter

Narita Airport, Tokyo's international airport

第1課の1 東京(とうきょう)へ　いきます! Going to Tokyo!

■ キアラのジャーナル　Kiara's Journal

Dear Journal,

I've been thinking about some things that my Japanese teacher told me before I left. I was only in Japanese class for part of the semester before I had to leave, but I think that I got a pretty good start. She said that when learning Japanese, there are several things to think about. One of these is to be careful to practice good pronunciation. I really want to sound as much like a native Japanese speaker as possible, so I paid a lot of attention to this part. Japanese pronunciation didn't take me long to learn, because there are only five basic vowels and nearly every other sound uses the same vowels, but with a consonant or hard sound in front of them. The only sound that does not end in a vowel sound is the sound of the letter N. My teacher said that vowels should not be drawn out when pronounced, but instead should be "short and clear."

Here is a pronunciation guide:

あ or **a** as in f<u>a</u>ther
い or **i** as in <u>ea</u>t
う or **u** as in b<u>oo</u>t
え or **e** as in g<u>e</u>t
お or **o** as in g<u>o</u>

Once you master these five vowel sounds, all of the remaining sounds (except for the "n" sound) are consonant/vowel combinations. The chart below shows the sounds of Japanese. It is written vertically starting on the right side, and reading from top to bottom. Japanese language can be written both horizontally like English (left to right) and vertically, as seen in the charts below, writing from the top down and starting on the right side and moving left. There are two charts because Japanese uses two writing styles: the hiragana is used for Japanese words, and the katakana is used for foreign and scientific words as well as onomatopoetic or mimetic words.

1A. Hiragana Chart

ん N	わ WA	ら RA	や YA	ま MA	は HA*	な NA	た TA	さ SA	か KA	あ A
		り RI		み MI	ひ HI	に NI	ち CHI	し SHI	き KI	い I
		る RU	ゆ YU	む MU	ふ FU	ぬ NU	つ TSU	す SU	く KU	う U
		れ RE		め ME	へ HE*	ね NE	て TE	せ SE	け KE	え E
	を WO*	ろ RO	よ YO	も MO	ほ HO	の NO	と TO	そ SO	こ KO	お O

2. Katakana Chart

ン N	ワ WA	ラ RA	ヤ YA	マ MA	ハ HA*	ナ NA	タ TA	サ SA	カ KA	ア A
		リ RI		ミ MI	ヒ HI	ニ NI	チ CHI	シ SHI	キ KI	イ I
		ル RU	ユ YU	ム MU	フ FU	ヌ NU	ツ TSU	ス SU	ク KU	ウ U
		レ RE		メ ME	ヘ HE*	ネ NE	テ TE	セ SE	ケ KE	エ E
	ヲ WO*	ロ RO	ヨ YO	モ MO	ホ HO	ノ NO	ト TO	ソ SO	コ KO	オ O

* **HA:** particle **WA**; **HE:** particle **E**; **WO:** particle **O**

Many of my friends have the impression that Japanese is difficult, but the pronunciation is actually quite simple. This is one of the things that I really like about Japanese! Most sounds are pronounced just like they look. Here are a few sounds that you have to be a little careful with:

す (su) as in soup
ち (chi) as in cheese
つ (tsu) similar to the "ts" in cats
ふ (fu) is pronounced not with an "f," but like the sound you make when you blow out a candle.

The "ra" line, ら(RA)、り(RI)、る(RU)、れ(RE)、and ろ(RO), is different from the "r" sound in English, but is close to the "r" sound in some other languages, such as Spanish. My sensei said that it was more like a combination of the letters R/L/D all rolled up into one. It really isn't difficult at all if you just concentrate on trying to sound just like your teacher or like the voice on the audio files.

There are a few other things you should know about Japanese pronunciation.

1B. Hiragana: Other Syllables

ぱ PA	ば BA	だ DA	ざ ZA	が GA
ぴ PI	び BI	ぢ JI	じ JI	ぎ GI
ぷ PU	ぶ BU	づ ZU	ず ZU	ぐ GU
ぺ PE	べ BE	で DE	ぜ ZE	げ GE
ぽ PO	ぼ BO	ど DO	ぞ ZO	ご GO

When you add two marks ("), called TEN TEN, or a small circle (°), called MARU, to the top right of a character (for example, (for example, か KA → が GA or は HA → ぱ PA), the sound of the consonant changes.

The sounds above make up the building blocks of all sounds in Japanese. There are a few combinations that change them slightly, but they don't add to the length of the syllables at all when they are placed together. They merely change the sounds. For example the KI and YO sounds following each other would be きよ (KIYO), two syllables. When the second character is "half-sized" or smaller, though, the sounds are combined, turning it into the one-syllable きょ (KYO).

1C. Hiragana: Combined Sounds

りゃ RYA	みゃ MYA	ぴゃ PYA	びゃ BYA	ひゃ HYA	にゃ NYA	ちゃ CHA	じゃ JA	しゃ SHA	ぎゃ GYA	きゃ KYA
りゅ RYU	みゅ MYU	ぴゅ PYU	びゅ BYU	ひゅ HYU	にゅ NYU	ちゅ CHU	じゅ JU	しゅ SHU	ぎゅ GYU	きゅ KYU
りょ RYO	みょ MYO	ぴょ PYO	びょ BYO	ひょ HYO	にょ NYO	ちょ CHO	じょ JO	しょ SHO	ぎょ GYO	きょ KYO

Other important pronunciation points:

Some vowels are elongated sounds, which means they are held for twice as long. The difference between the two is like this: いえ I E means *house* while いいえ I I E, which has an elongated vowel, means *no*. With katakana words, the elongated vowel sound is shown by a straight line after the katakana character. For example, the first "A" sound in the word ジャーナル JA A NARU (*journal*) is pronounced twice as long as the second "A" sound.

One other type of sound found in Japanese is the "doubled consonant." To make this sound, you pause, or freeze your mouth, for just a brief extra second between the sounds just before and after the small TSU (っ). The small TSU (っ) is about half the size of the normal つ TSU and does not have a specific sound of its own. Here are a few words with doubled consonants: いっぱい I P PA I (a lot) and きっさてん KI S SA TE N (coffee shop). This isn't hard to do. Just pay attention when your teacher explains how to pronounce the doubled consonant and listen carefully to the audio files that come with this book.

■ 単語(たんご) New Words

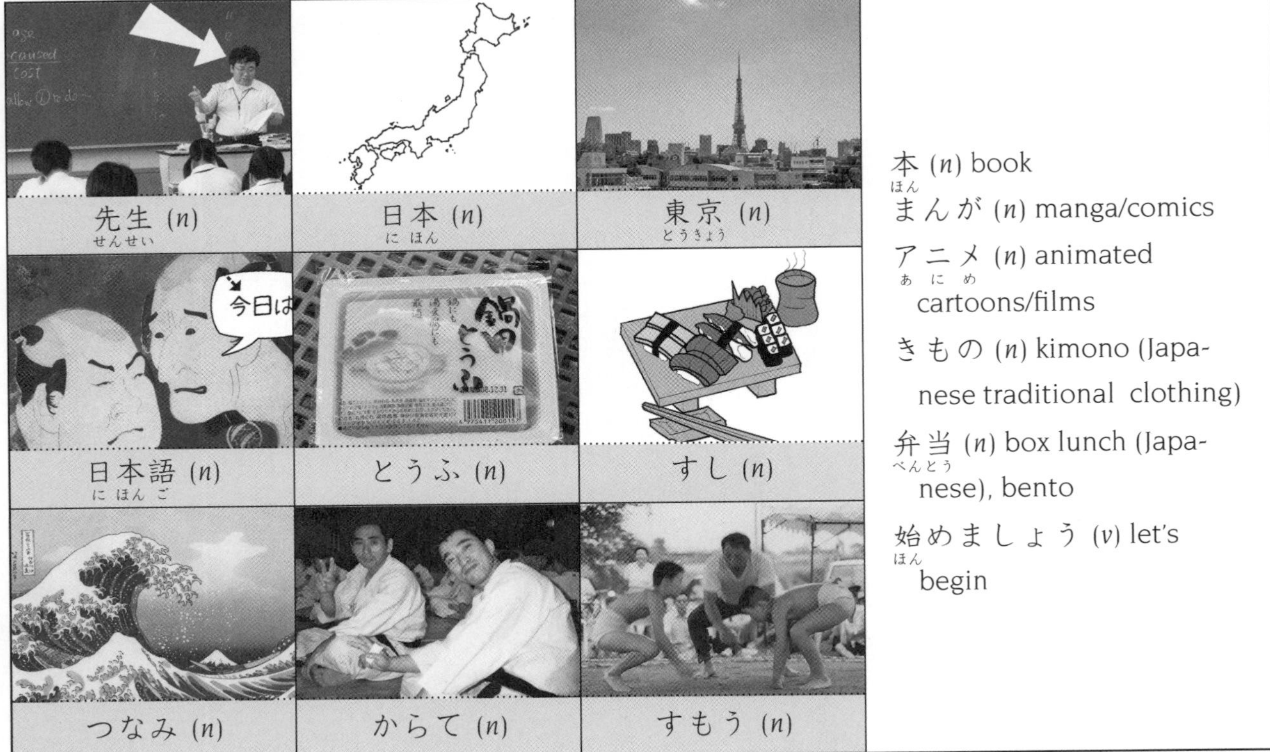

先生(せんせい) (n)
日本(にほん) (n)
東京(とうきょう) (n)
今日は
日本語(にほんご) (n)
とうふ (n)
すし (n)
つなみ (n)
からて (n)
すもう (n)
本(ほん) (n) book
まんが (n) manga/comics
アニメ(あにめ) (n) animated cartoons/films
きもの (n) kimono (Japanese traditional clothing)
弁当(べんとう) (n) box lunch (Japanese), bento
始(ほん)めましょう (v) let's begin

Vocabulary Learning Hints

There are several methods of learning vocabulary words. The trick is finding out which method works best for you. When learning anything new, the more of your senses that you use during the learning process the better, and the longer you will retain the information. An example of this is how we use flash cards. Flash cards are one of the best ways for the beginning learner to remember vocabulary. Many students make flashcards (you can also download flashcards from this book's website, TimeForJapanese.com) and think about the meanings in their heads. A more efficient way of using them is to say each word out loud as you review it. This method has you reading, speaking, AND hearing each vocabulary word. And if you've already written the word down, you have now used all four aspects of language learning and communication!

When learning vocabulary, cramming for a test might seem like a good way to learn the words quickly in the short term, but as with other things, it's easier and more efficient to learn words gradually and to build on them. Each word has to be memorized and incorporated into your long-term memory. Associating words with pictures or with other words that you already know is an excellent way to cement vocabulary into your knowledge base. This is the reason this book, when possible, gives interpretations of Japanese words in pictorial form rather than translating. Then, when you need that vocabulary word later, you can pull the picture out of your memory.

Finally, based on the "use it or lose it" concept, the more you use new words, the better you will remember them. Try to use new Japanese words with your teacher, classmates, family, Japanese speakers, and anybody else who will listen to you! If your goal is to memorize new vocabulary, do not worry whether your spoken Japanese is perfect or not, just try to use the new words as much as possible even if you have a hard time making complete sentences. Study partners are great for getting lots of focused practice as well. Find someone who wants to learn as much as you do!

■ キアラ（きあら）のジャーナル（じゃーなる） Kiara's Journal

Dear Journal,

I have been on this airplane for nearly 12 hours and am just about ready to land in 成田空港（なりたくうこう）, Narita International Airport, the main international airport in 東京（とうきょう）. I'm really excited about living in 日本（にほん） for the first time. I have wanted to go there for so long that I can't believe that it's really happening! My host brother Jun and his parents are coming to the airport by train to take me back to their house in Tokyo. I have a couple of days until I start school, which I am also a bit nervous about. But I'm excited, too, because this is going to be such a cool adventure!

This airplane is huge. There are 10 seats from side to side and it's full of people from all over the world. The nice woman next to me is on her way to Japan, too. She lives in Sendai, a city in northern Japan, and the person on the other side of her is going to the Philippines.

I always thought that the flight path to Japan would cross the U.S. and then the Pacific, but instead we flew north over Canada and then Alaska. When I asked the flight attendant, he said that our path was actually the shortest route. I also can't believe how cold it is outside! The screen on the back of the seat in front of me shows that the outside temperature at this altitude is REALLY cold. I can use the same screen to watch movies, or look at a map of where we are, the current time at home and in Japan, how far we've come, and how far we have yet to go to our destination. I think I've figured out which line on this screen tells the speed of the airplane. Which one do you think it is?

I think that I've packed enough clothes for the entire year, but Jun told me not to worry about that because there are some really good stores near his house. He says I'll be able to get what I need there if I forgot something. Jun is going to take me shopping for school supplies before school starts, so I didn't bring anything like that.

I did bring some candy, pencils and other things with my school's name on them to give to the kids in my class, and some Western food for my new host family. I've heard that it's important to bring gifts called OMIYAGE, but I'm not sure if what I brought is appropriate or not. My teacher gave me some good recommendations, though. I know one of the most important things is to welcome opportunities and enjoy new experiences. A lot of my friends think I'm a bit crazy to do this, but I think it's going to be the best experience of my life. Here goes. The captain just said that we're landing in 20 minutes!!

第1課の2

日本（にほん）
Land of the Rising Sun

■ キアラのジャーナル(きあら じゃーなる) Kiara's Journal

Dear Journal,

こんにちは！ I've got to practice writing what I've learned, so I don't forget. Writing Japanese is challenging, but I think it's very interesting. Japan had no written language of its own until the 4th century C.E., when Japan began interacting with China. After that, manuscripts, mostly religious, began to arrive in Japan, via Korea, and the Japanese adopted more and more Chinese institutions, including its writing system. Japanese monks and scholars adopted these characters from Chinese writing to write down their own Japanese language. Japanese call characters of Chinese origin 漢字(かんじ). The process was difficult in the beginning, because the two languages don't sound at all alike, but it works for the Japanese today. Besides, the writing system is a lot of fun to learn.

Some KANJI resemble pictures, so it is really easy to guess what they mean. Studying kanji is fun. I already have a stack of flash cards that I look at regularly. The more kanji you learn, the easier it is to learn additional ones, because the characters build on each other. For example, the kanji for tree is 木(き). It looks a little like a tree with branches that stretch out and droop down. If you put two trees together, you have the start of a small woods, 林(はやし); if you combine three trees, you get a forest 森(もり). When a line is drawn across the bottom of the vertical stroke in 木(き), like this 本(ほん), the bottom part, or what's underground, that is, the roots, is emphasized. 本(ほん) means *book* or *origin root/source* as in the "source" of knowledge.

The kanji for *sun* looks like this: 日(にち). The origin of this character is harder to guess. The character started out as a circle with a dot in it = ⨀ but the shape changed over time into something more square, like 日. Note that modern kanji do not have circles in them. When you put together the *sun* (日) and *origin* (本), that is, the *origin* of the *sun*, or the place where the sun rises, you get 日本(にほん), or Japan, the "land of the rising sun."

Although the origins of the writing system called HIRAGANA are unclear, some believe hiragana were invented by a Buddhist monk named Koubou Daishi (774-835), who had traveled to China. Hiragana were created by simplifying some of the characters of Chinese origin and creating a group of phonetic syllables, similar to an alphabet. This was a system that could be used to write all spoken Japanese. They were useful because nearly anyone could learn to read them. It had taken years to learn to read all of the characters of Chinese origin. During the Heian Period (794-1185 C.E.), women in the emperor's court wrote with hiragana, and it came to be called "女手(おんなで)", or *women's hand*. There was a separate group of simplified characters for the 46 basic Japanese sounds developed later called KATAKANA, which is currently used to write foreign words and names in Japanese, such as ベースボール(べーすぼーる)

(*baseball*). Katakana is also used for scientific names of plants and animals, and onomatopoeia (such as ワンワン (わんわん) = *bark bark* and トントン (とんとん) = *knock knock*). HIRAGANA and KATAKANA together are often called "KANA."

I would really like the chance to meet someone like Koubou Daishi, but of course he's been dead for nearly 1,200 years, so that would be impossible ... right?

■ 漢字 (かんじ) Kanji

Below are the kanji that you will have to learn for this section. When kanji are presented as they are below, you will need to learn how to read and write them. Be sure to pay attention to the numbers corresponding to the stroke order for each character. Stroke order is a very important aspect of kanji writing and is critical information when using kanji dictionaries.Learning correct stroke order might not seem that important at the beginning, but you will eventually understand why it is so crucial.

Notice that most kanji strokes start in the upper left corner and eventually end in the bottom right corner. The basic rule is to write strokes from left to right and from top to bottom. Make mental notes of exceptions to this rule when they come up, such as in the first stroke of the kanji 千 (せん) (1,000), which is written at a downward angle from right to left.

Soon you will notice that kanji are made up of parts called radicals. The more you can mentally break down a kanji into its parts, the easier it will be to memorize it. It will be easier to learn new kanji as well, since the new kanji contain some of the same parts (radicals). The kanji hints provided underneath each new kanji identify the parts that make up the new kanji while also offering mental images to help you learn that new kanji. For instance, it will be much easier down the road for you to memorize a potentially difficult new kanji such as "cherry tree." 桜 (さくら) is made up of parts which easily help explain the overall meaning of the kanji. The left side (木 (き)) is a tree; the right side has a woman (女 (おんな)) sitting with three cherry petals floating down as she admires the spring display.

Here are your three KANJI for this section:

木 (4 strokes)	モク (もく); き – tree	一	十	才	木			
	木 (き) – tree; 木曜日 (もくようび) – Thursday							
	This kanji is a picture of a TREE, with a trunk and long sweeping branches.							

日 (4 strokes)	ニ (に); ひ, か – day; sun	丨	冂	月	日			
	(日 (に)) 本 (ほん) – Japan; 日 (ひ) – sun, day							
	This was originally a picture of the SUN that has been simplified over the years. It came to also mean DAY. This character appears as a part of many kanji related to time.							

本	ホン(ほん) – book, origin; もと – origin	一	十	才	木	本		
	本(ほん) – book; (日)本(にほん) – Japan; (日)本(語)(にほんご) – Japanese language; (松)本(まつもと) – family/place name							
5 strokes	The origin of all BOOKS is one (一) piece of a tree (木). 本 is also a tree (木) where the roots or ORIGIN at the bottom is emphasized. The term for Japan (日本) means "land where the sun originates."							

■ キアラのジャーナル Kiara's Journal

Dear Journal,

We just landed, but we're still sitting in the airplane. Taxiing toward the terminal seems to be taking forever. The plane trip from Chicago took about 12 hours. It was really cool to fly over Alaska. I could see snow-covered mountains and glaciers and then nothing but blue water, water, and more water, until the green rice fields of Japan appeared.

My host family should be at the airport waiting to pick me up. They said that I have to go through Immigration to get my passport stamped and then through Customs where they sometimes check your luggage. My sensei told me not to wrap any of my OMIYAGE because customs agents might open them.

I really must practice introducing myself to my host family. I'm kind of nervous about meeting them. Besides Jun, there is his mother Mayumi, his father Tarou, his older brother Ichirou, and his little sister Aiko. We have been e-mailing messages back and forth, and we did one videoconference, but it was early in the morning at home and they were going to bed in Japan. We talked in both English and in Japanese. I'm just going to try to remember what my parents always say, about how good communication means being open to listening and not being afraid to respond. Well, we're at the gate and people are unbuckling their seat belts and getting up. HAJIMEMASHITE, HAJIMEMASHITE, HAJIMEMASHITE...

第1課の3 私は キアラ です。

わたし　きあら

I am Kiara.

■ 会話(かいわ) Dialogue

REMINDER: You may see some kanji / vocabulary you do not recognize. Use the context to try to understand the meanings of those parts of the dialogue.

1. Male agent : 日本語(にほんご)が　わかりますか。
2. Kiara : はい、わかります。
3. Female agent : いい　ですね。*Can you introduce yourself?*
4. Kiara : 初(はじ)めまして。私(わたし)は　キアラ(きあら)　です。どうぞ　よろしく。

■ 単語(たんご) New Words

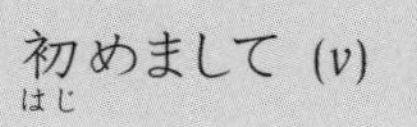

初(はじ)めまして (*v*)	私(わたし) (*pron.*)	私達(わたしたち) (*pron.*)	僕(ぼく) (*pron.*) (note: used by males only)

きょうかしょ (*n*) – textbook
おねがいします (*exp*)– please
よろしく　おねがいします (*exp*) – best regards, treat me favorably

どうぞよろしく　おねがいします (*exp*) – polite for よろしく　おねがいします

どうぞよろしく (*exp*) – best regards, treat me favorably (same meaning as よろしく　おねがいします)

名前(なまえ) (*n*) – name

～先生(せんせい) (*n, suffix*) – used immediately AFTER a teacher's, lawyer's, or doctor's name

～さん (*suffix*) – used immediately AFTER a name (never use with your own name)

～くん (*suffix*) – used immediately AFTER a boy's name (never use with your own name)

は (*part.*) – particle that denotes the sentence topic. Pronounced WA (not HA) when used as a particle.

です (*copula*) – similar to "is" or "am"

Classroom Commands and Questions

The top row of each command below is a simple command form of the verb ("Stand!", for example), the second row is a polite request ("Please stand."), and the third row asks permission to do the action ("May I stand?").

 たって	 すわって	 みて
たってください	すわってください	みてください
たっても いいですか。	すわっても いいですか。	みても いいですか。
 きょうかしょを だして	 ひらいて	 とじて
きょうかしょを だしてください	ひらいて ください	とじて ください
きょうかしょを だしても いいですか。	ひらいても いいですか。	とじても いいですか。
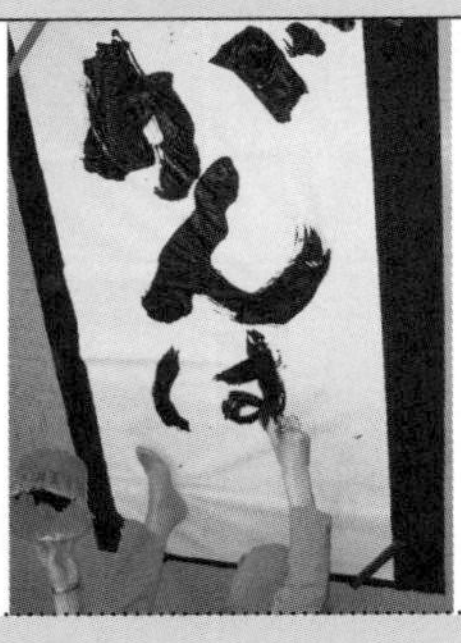 かいて	 きいて	 よんで
かいてください	きいてください	よんでください
かいても いいですか。	きいても いいですか。	よんでも いいですか。

■ 漢字(かんじ) Kanji

When you get up in the morning and see the sun (日) behind a tree (木) like this (東), you are looking east at the sunrise. 東(ひがし) means *east*.

Historically, large walls surrounded cities in China, where kanji originated. Each of the four city walls had a large 門(もん) or gate for people entering and leaving the city. This character for MON (門) looks like a gate, doesn't it? On either side of the gate stood large lanterns, often made of stone, similar to the one shown in the picture here. When you saw the large lanterns on either side of a gate, you knew you were approaching the capital. The kanji for *capital* is pronounced KYOU (京). Can you see the three legs and the small hole in the middle for candle light to shine through?

The second capital of Japan was the city of 京都(きょうと). Later, the capital was moved to the east (東) where it is now. The present-day capital is written 東京(とうきょう), or *eastern capital*. Can you understand the meaning by looking at these characters together?

Below you will find a list of kanji that you must learn for this section. Pay careful attention to the stroke order of each kanji. Following along with the examples in the next several chapters and paying close attention to the samples will help you understand exactly how to write other kanji. Be sure to use the kanji practice space in your workbook as instructed.

東 8 strokes	トウ(とう); ひがし – east 東(京)(とう きょう) – (eastern) capital of Japan; 東(ひがし) – east (direction)	Think of the sun rising in the EAST behind a tree.
京 8 strokes	キョウ(きょう) – capital (東)京(とう きょう) – capital city of Japan	Think of the picture of the lantern described above. Imagine the top two strokes as a top hat, the next three strokes as a mouth (ロ), and the last three strokes as the kanji for small (小). Here is a person with a top hat talking loudly to politicians in the CAPITAL.
語 14 strokes	ゴ(ご) – language (日本)語(に ほん ご) – the Japanese language	The left side is the kanji means *to say* (言); the right side includes the kanji for 5 (五), which is pronounced ご(GO) and the kanji for mouth (ロ). If at least five people can use their mouths to say something in common, it must be a LANGUAGE.

■ 言葉の探索 Language Detection

(ことば　たんさく)

1. Japanese grammar is relatively simple. Small parts of speech called "particles" show the "relationship" between the words they connect. Imagine that particles are like the hitches that hold train cars together: nearly every word (train car) has a particle (hitch) that connects it to the following word. Check the appendix at the back of this book for a list of common particles and their uses.

2. The particle は and です

- は is often called a "topic marker." The topic of a sentence is what is being spoken about, and it is followed by the particle は (pronounced WA).
- です is known as a copula. It acts like the English verbs of being (is, am, was). Japanese verbs usually come at the end of the sentence.

When these two are together, the は usually connects two words (these words can be nouns, pronouns, adjectives or some combination) and gives the sentence an A = B meaning.

WATASHI wa KIARA DESU	= I am Kiara.
A　は　B　です。	= A is B.

例 (れい) EXAMPLE

A. 「山川(やまかわ)さんは　先生(せんせい)　です。 = (Mr. *or* Ms.) Yamakawa is a teacher.

B. ここは　日本(にほん)　です。 = This place is Japan.

C. おすしは　おいしい　です。 = Sushi is delicious.

3. ～たち

For most nouns, Japanese does not distinguish between singular and plural. For instance, 名前(なまえ) can mean *name* or *names*, depending on the context. Certain terms used for people, however, can be pluralized by adding the suffix "～たち".* Can you guess what these examples mean?

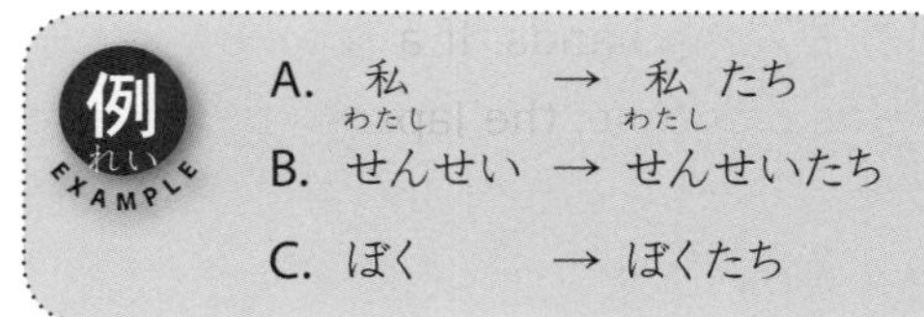

例 れい EXAMPLE
A. 私(わたし) → 私(わたし)たち
B. せんせい → せんせいたち
C. ぼく → ぼくたち

*The tilde (～) is used from time to time to let you know that something precedes or follows the word.

■ 練習の時間 Time for Practice

(れんしゅう　じかん)

1. Pair Practice

Use the example dialogue below to take turns introducing yourself to others nearby and letting them introduce themselves to you. When introducing yourself or when someone introduces himself or herself to you, it is proper to bow. With your arms at your sides, bow from the waist, letting your eyes move toward the ground with your head and shoulders. There are different degrees of bowing depending on the situation, but for beginners a good generic depth of your bow would be about 45 degrees. A good time to bow is when either of you says the word 初(はじ)めまして.

A-SAN : 初(はじ)めまして。 僕(ぼく) は アダム(あだむ) (Adam) です。 どうぞ よろしく 。
B-SAN : 初(はじ)めまして。 私(わたし) は パメラ(ぱめら) (Pamela) です。 どうぞ よろしく。

2. Pair Practice

Use all the Classroom Commands and Questions on page 28 to practice your new Japanese by playing the roles of student and sensei. First the "sensei" will give commands and the student will act them out. Then the student will ask for permission and the sensei will grant it. Take turns being the sensei.

NOTE: When granting permission, you can just take off the か from the end of the sentence.

例 れい EXAMPLE

A-SENSEI	:	本(ほん)を 出(だ)してください。	= Please take out your textbook.
STUDENT	:	(takes out textbook)	
B-STUDENT	:	たっても いいですか。	= May I stand up?
SENSEI	:	はい、たってもいいです。	= Yes, you may stand up.
STUDENT	:	ありがとうございます。	= Thank you. (Student then stands up.)

■ 文化箱(ぶんかばこ) Culture Chest

1. Showing Respect

Japanese society is traditionally considered very polite and respectful. There are many ways that the Japanese people show respect to each other. One example of this is the tradition of bowing. When Japanese people first meet, they usually bow, rather than shaking hands. If a Japanese person is meeting a Westerner for the first time, the Japanese person may wait until the Westerner extends his or her hand before deciding whether to shake hands or to bow. Japanese teachers may nod their heads and make a slight bow when meeting their students in the hallway. Deep and extended bowing is an inherent part of other Japanese rituals such as the tea ceremony.

There are many different subtle and not so subtle ways that Japanese vary their bowing techniques depending on the social situation. Observing all the intricacies of the ways Japanese bow can be a fascinating spectator sport for foreigners in Japan. It is said that in a random mix of people from Asia, you can identify the Japanese from a distance because they are the ones bowing the most. Sometimes Japanese even bow when they are talking on the telephone!

Other ways to show respect are built into the language. You may have noticed that Kiara does not use the suffix さん after her own name. You should not use this or any other ending after your own name, either, when speaking Japanese. However, when talking to others, it is polite to use their proper names (not the pronoun "you") followed by one of the following endings:

～さん which is similar to Mr. or Ms. or Mrs. in English. It is the most common suffix attached to the end of a name.

～せんせい can be used alone and means *teacher.* It is a respectful term used immediately *after* the names of teachers and some professionals such as doctors, lawyers, and politicians.

～くん is used after boys' names.

～ちゃん is used for babies, elementary school age children, girls who are younger than the speaker in informal situations, and sometimes with family members or close friends.

～さま is used when addressing someone in a letter or when showing extreme politeness as a service person would with a patron.

Can you tell which of the following people are older and which are younger? Notice the order of the family name and the given name in Japanese vs. English.

A. ➲ 山本（やまもと）　明先生（あきらせんせい）　Mr. Akira Yamamoto (Teacher)
B. ➲ 山田（やまだ）　道夫（みちお）さん　Mr. Michio Yamada
C. ➲ 高橋（たかはし）　花子（はなこ）さん　Mrs. Hanako Takahashi
D. ➲ 山口（やまぐち）　愛子（あいこ）ちゃん　Aiko Yamaguchi
E. ➲ 中山（なかやま）　けいたくん　Keita Nakayama

2. Saying and Writing Your Name

East Asian names are usually written with KANJI; non-East Asian names, however, are written with KATAKANA. When saying and writing your name in Japanese, keep in mind that it won't necessarily sound the same as it does in English because not all English sounds are the same in Japanese (for instance, Rs and Ls) or even exist (for instance, the *th* sound and many English vowel sounds do not exist in Japanese). Can you guess what English names these are?

A. ➲ キャシー（きゃしー）
B. ➲ トム（とむ）
C. ➲ ベン（べん）
D. ➲ エミリー（えみりー）
E. ➲ レオナルド（れおなるど）
F. ➲ マイケル（まいける）
G. ➲ キム（きむ）
H. ➲ ジャック（じゃっく）

第1課の4 こちらは 母(はは) です。This is my mother.

■ 会話(かいわ) Dialogue

REMINDER: You may see some kanji / vocabulary you do not recognize. Use the context to try to understand the meanings of those parts of the dialogue.

(At the airport)

1. キアラ(きあら)：初(はじ)めまして。 私(わたし)は キアラ(きあら) です。
よろしく おねがいします。じゅん君(くん) ですか。

2. じゅん：はい、そう です。僕(ぼく)は じゅん です。ようこそ！
よろしく おねがいします。こちらは 母(はは) です。こちらは 父(ちち) です。

3. まゆみ：初(はじ)めまして。

4. 太郎(たろう)：じゅんの父(ちち)です。どうぞよろしくおねがいします。

■ 単語(たんご) New Words

ようこそ (*exp.*)	こちら (*pron.*)	母(はは) (*n*)	父(ちち) (*n*)

日本人(にほんじん) (*n*) – Japanese person

太郎(たろう) (*n*) – a male name

はい (*interj.*) – yes, OK, here (roll call)

いいえ (*interj.*) – no

はい、そう です – yes it is

いいえ、ちがいます – no, it is not/different

か (*part.*) – particle signifying a question

■ 漢字(かんじ) Kanji

私 (7 strokes)								
わたくし – I, me (polite); わたし – I, me	丿	二	千	禾	禾	私	私
私(わたくし) – I, me (formal); 私(わたし) – I, me							
It's probably going to be easy to remember that this kanji means I or ME, since you'll be writing about yourself a lot! Just remember to keep the first stroke slanted and not straight across and note that it is written from right to left.							

父 (4 strokes)							
フ(ふ)；ちち；(お)とう(さん) – father	ノ	ハ	父	父			
父(ちち) – (my) father; (お)父(とう)(さん) – father; 祖父(そふ) – grandfather							
Here you see a picture of a FATHER's face with a mustache, mouth, and the top of a beard.							

母 (5 strokes)	ボ(ぼ); はは; (お)かあ(さん) – mother							
	母(はは) – (my) mother; (お)母(かあ)(さん) – mother; 祖母(そぼ) – grandmother							
	This is actually an ancient pictograph of a woman with two breasts, symbolizing a MOTHER. Be sure to give her two arms and two legs when you write MOTHER.							

■ 言葉(ことば)の探索(たんさく) Language Detection

1. 〜か - Questions

Forming a question in Japanese is easy. Simply add the particle か to the end of the sentence.

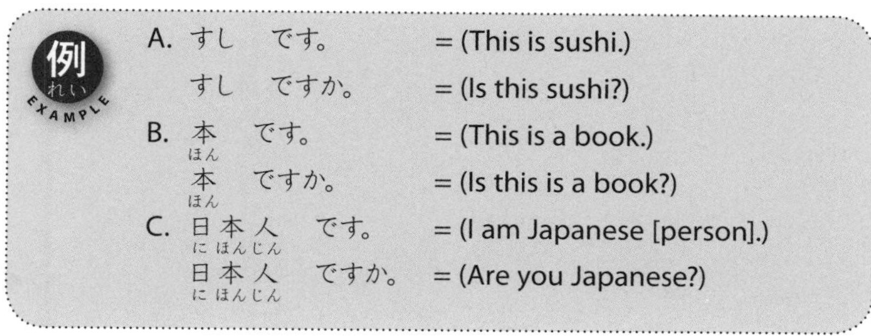

A. すし　です。 = (This is sushi.)
すし　ですか。 = (Is this sushi?)
B. 本(ほん)　です。 = (This is a book.)
本(ほん)　ですか。 = (Is this is a book?)
C. 日本人(にほんじん)　です。 = (I am Japanese [person].)
日本人(にほんじん)　ですか。 = (Are you Japanese?)

2. A は B ではありません。- Making a negative statement

To change an affirmative 〜です(日本(にほん)です。) statement to a negative statement, replace the です with では　ありません or じゃ　ありません. じゃありません is less formal.

Affirmative:	A	は	B	です。		= A is B.
	私(わたし)	は	じゅん	です。		= I am Jun.
Negative:	A	は	B	では	ありません。	= A is not B.
	私(わたし)	は	じゅん	では	ありません。	= I am not Jun.
	私(わたし)	は	じゅん	じゃ	ありません。	= I am not Jun. (less formal)

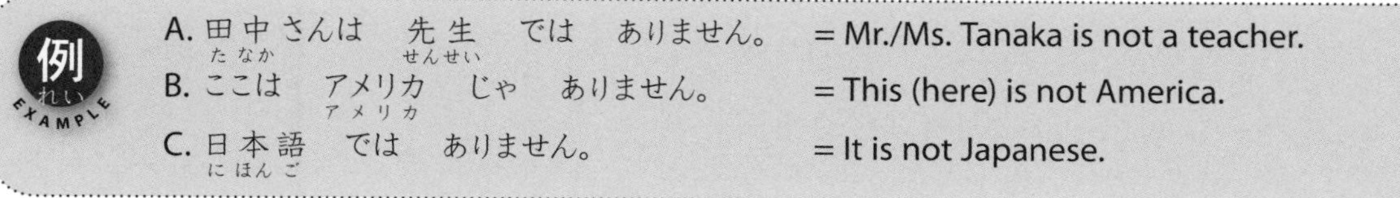

A. 田中(たなか)さんは　先生(せんせい)　では　ありません。 = Mr./Ms. Tanaka is not a teacher.
B. ここは　アメリカ(アメリカ)　じゃ　ありません。 = This (here) is not America.
C. 日本語(にほんご)　では　ありません。 = It is not Japanese.

NOTE: じゃ is the abbreviation of では. As with English, abbreviations tend to be less formal and are used more in spoken than in written Japanese.

3. Punctuation

Japanese punctuation is not too complicated. Written Japanese uses periods (。), commas (、), and quotation marks (「　」). All sentences, whether statements or questions, end in periods in normal Japanese writing. Manga, signs, and advertising sometimes use English question marks, exclamation marks, and other symbols as well. Questions end with the particle か followed by the Japanese period (。). Commas may be used wherever writers feel a pause would be appropriate, or to convey meaning, however they are not regulated as much as they are in English.

■ 自習(じしゅう) Self Check

1. First, cover up the "Question" column below and make each statement into a question by adding か to the end. Check your answers. Next, cover up the "Negative Statement" column below and answer each question in the negative by changing the です to では　ありません or じゃ　ありません. Check your answers.

Statement	Question	Negative Statement
こちらは　先生(せんせい)　です。	こちらは　先生(せんせい)　ですか。	こちらは　先生(せんせい)　では　ありません/ じゃ　ありません。
東京(とうきょう)　です。	東京(とうきょう)　ですか。	東京(とうきょう)　では　ありません / じゃ　ありません。
なりたくうこう　です。	なりたくうこう　ですか。	なりたくうこう　では　ありません / じゃ　ありません。
これは　とうふ　です。	これは　とうふ　ですか。	これは　とうふ　では　ありません / じゃ　ありません。
けいこさん　です。	けいこさん　ですか。	けいこさん　では　ありません / じゃ　ありません。

■ 練習(れんしゅう) の時間(じかん) Time for Practice

1. Small Group Practice (sets of pairs)

Use the dialogue below to ask your partner his/her name. Next, introduce your partner to another group of classmates. Take turns, each person introducing their partner to the others.

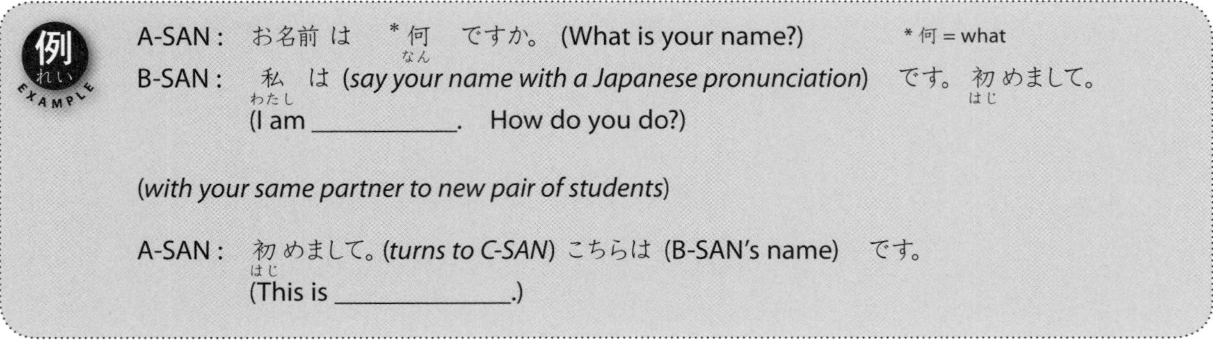

例(れい) EXAMPLE

A-SAN : お名前 は　*何(なん)　ですか。 (What is your name?)　　* 何 = what

B-SAN : 私(わたし)　は (*say your name with a Japanese pronunciation*)　です。 初(はじ)めまして。
(I am ____________.　How do you do?)

(*with your same partner to new pair of students*)

A-SAN : 初(はじ)めまして。(*turns to C-SAN*) こちらは (B-SAN's name)　です。
(This is ______________.)

2. Small Group Activity (sets of pairs)

Choose a Japanese name for yourself from the list in Appendix 2 in the back of the book. Note that family names come first in Japanese. Using your new Japanese name, repeat the 1. Small Group Practice above.

3. Pair Practice

Take turns asking and answering the names of your classmates. Intentionally get some names wrong to allow your partner to practice making negative statements using either じゃ　ありません or では　ありません until they can say these smoothly.

例 れい EXAMPLE

You : John くんですか。(*pointing to a classmate:* Is that John?)
Your partner : はい、 John くんです。(Yes, that is John.)
-OR- いいえ、John くん　じゃ　ありません。(No, that is not John.)
-OR- いいえ、John くん　では　ありません。(No, that is not John.)
This is slightly more formal than the previous example.

■ 文化箱（ぶんかばこ） Culture Chest

よろしく　おねがいします

This phrase is often translated into English as "Pleased to meet you." It really has a broader implication and is useful in situations other than first meeting someone. よろしく　おねがいします is used a great deal in everyday Japanese conversation. For instance, a high school baseball team will use this term when they bow in unison to their opponents before beginning a game. In this case you would translate よろしく　おねがいします roughly as "please, keep me in your good favor." You are establishing a relationship with someone new and that relationship, in Japanese culture, is taken very seriously. You may or may not meet this person again, but when and if you do, you want them to remember you favorably just in case you might need to make a request of them at some point. Most classes in Japan begin with students standing up and everyone, including the teacher, saying this phrase in unison, to remind everyone of the importance of group cooperation. よろしく　おねがいします！

第1課の5 こんばんは。Good evening.

■ 会話(かいわ) Dialogue

REMINDER: You may see some kanji / vocabulary you do not recognize. Use the context to try to understand the meanings of those parts of the dialogue.

1. 愛子(あいこ)　：じゅん君(くん)、ただいま。キアラ(きあら)さんは　どこですか。
2. じゅん：おかえりなさい。キアラ(きあら)さんは　へやに　*います。
3. 愛子(あいこ)　：こんばんは。
4. キアラ(きあら)：こんばんは。
5. 愛子(あいこ)　：初(はじ)めまして。あいこです。
6. キアラ(きあら)：初(はじ)めまして。キアラ(きあら)です。どうぞよろしく。
7. まゆみ：これは　おすし　です。
8. まゆみ：これは　おはしです。どうぞ。
9. キアラ(きあら)：しょうゆは　どれ　ですか。
10. まゆみ：あれ　です。それは　わさび　です。
11. キアラ(きあら)：たまごは　それ　ですか。
12. じゅん：はい、そう　です。

* います to exist (animate beings)

■ 単語(たんご) New Words

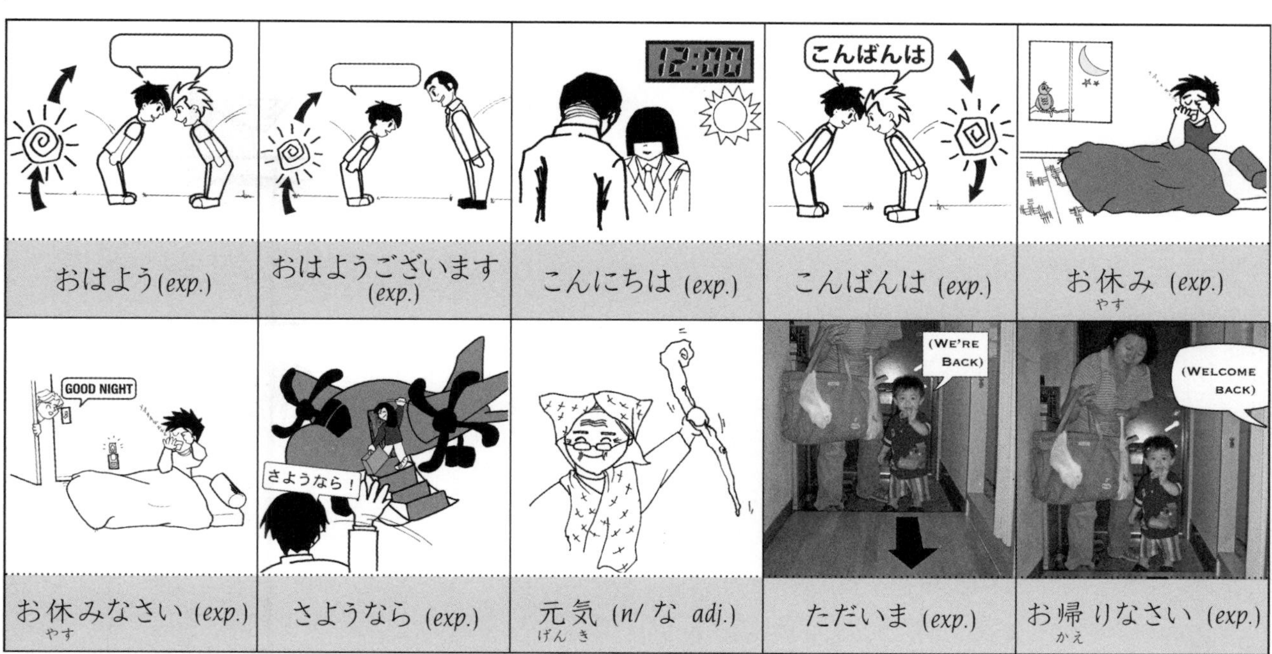

おはよう (exp.)	おはようございます (exp.)	こんにちは (exp.)	こんばんは (exp.)	お休(やす)み (exp.)
お休(やす)みなさい (exp.)	さようなら (exp.)	元気(げんき) (n/ な adj.)	ただいま (exp.)	お帰(かえ)りなさい (exp.)

じゃあ　また (*exp.*) – see you later (informal)

どうぞ (*exp.*) – please (here you go), by all means

では　また (*exp.*) – see you later (formal)

バイバイ (ばいばい) (*exp.*) – bye-bye, good-bye (informal)

に (*part.*) – particle after a location word denoting where someone/something exists

■ 漢字 (かんじ) Kanji

気 (6 strokes)								
	き – spirit; energy	ノ	𠂉	𠂉	气	気	気	
	気 (き) – spirit; energy							
	A person's SPIRIT, marked with an "X," is kept between several layers that consist of flesh and bone. But there is always a key (the first stroke) to unbridling that SPIRIT.							

元 (4 strokes)								
	ゲン (げん) – an ancient currency; もと – origin	一	二	テ	元			
	元(気) (げんき) – healthy, in good spirits							
	The top two strokes make up the kanji for two (二), and the bottom two strokes can be thought of as legs. The ORIGIN of modern humans began when we started to walk on two legs.							

人 (2 strokes)								
	~ジン (じん); ~ニン (にん); ひと — person	ノ	人					
	人 (ひと) person; (三)人 (さんにん); ひと — three (people) (counter for people); (日本)人 (にほんじん) (Japanese) people							
	This is the shape of a PERSON standing up.							

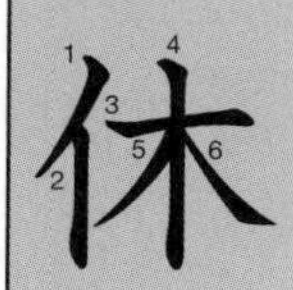

休 6 strokes	やす(む) – to rest, take a break, a vacation	ノ	イ	仁	什	休	休	
	休(む) – to rest, take a break, a vacation; (お)休(み) – good night							
	The left side represents a person (人) and appears in many kanji that have something to do with people. The right side is a tree (木). This kanji represents a person RESTING against a tree.							

■ 言葉の探索 Language Detection

1. じゅん君、ただいま。 **- Jun, I'm home.**

As in the examples below, it is common in Japanese to say the name of the person or their title before the greeting.

A) 山本先生、おはようございます。 = Good morning Mr. Yamamoto.
B) 愛子さん、こんにちは。 = Hello Aiko.
C) まゆみさん、お元気ですか。 = How are you Mayumi?
D) 山本先生、さようなら。 = Goodbye Mr. Yamamoto.

2. これ, それ, あれ, どれ

これ = this (one)
それ = that (one) near the listener
あれ = that (one over there) away from the speaker and listener
どれ = which one?

A) これは　しょうゆ　です。 = This is soy sauce.
B) わさびは　どれ　ですか。 = Wasabi is which one?
NOTE: it is also common to use this pattern when using どれ:
どれが　わさび　ですか。 = Which is wasabi?

The use of each of these pronouns depends on the location of an object and the relative locations of the speaker and the listener. これ is used for objects near you, the speaker. それ refers to object(s) near the listener and away from the speaker. あれ is used when the object is away from both the speaker and the listener. どれ is only used for questions.

3. お is placed in front of some nouns, especially words related to food or drink, to make these references more polite. For example, people in the past were often lucky to get fresh water or rice so お was placed in front of those words to show gratitude. お is not used in front of proper names or words for other animate things. Some examples include:

おはし (chopsticks)　おすし (sushi)　おみず (water)　おちゃ (green tea)

4. **Bonus Sheet - I like tofu, I dislike celery.**

Go to the Web Activities on **www.TimeforJapanese.com** for this chapter and section to download this Bonus Sheet.

■ 自習(じしゅう) Self Check

1. What is the appropriate greeting to use in each situation? The first one is done for you.
   A. 7:00 A.M. (greet your teacher) = おはようございます
   B. 9:00A.M. (greet your friend)
   C. Noon (greet your friend or teacher)
   D. 8:00 P.M. (greet your friend or teacher)
   E. 10:00 P.M. (what do you say to your host brother before going to sleep)
   F. 10:00 P.M. (what do you say to your parents before going to sleep)
   G. What do you say to your Japanese boyfriend/girlfriend when breaking up for the final time?

2. Try saying the sentences below in Japanese using the pronouns これ, それ あれ, and どれ. Test yourself to make sure you know which pronoun to use in which situation.
   A. This is a book.
   B. That (near a partner) is a pencil. (えんぴつ)
   C. This is an eraser. (けしゴム(ごむ))
   D. Which one is a notebook? (ノート(のーと))
   E. That one (over there) is a window. (まど)
   F. That one (over there) is a car. (くるま)
   G. That one (near a partner) is a cat. (ねこ)

3. Restate the following in English.
   A. ねこが　へやに　います。
   B. 私(わたし)の　本(ほん)は　家(うち)に　あります。
   C. キアラ(きあら)さんの　先生(せんせい)は　犬(いぬ)の　となりに　います。
   D. 北海道(ほっかいどう)は　本州(ほんしゅう)の　北(きた)に　あります。 (see map inside the front cover)

   Restate the following in Japanese:
   A. The sushi is in the bag.
   B. My father is in Tokyo.
   C. The chopsticks are between the egg and the soy sauce.
   D. Kyushu is to the west of Shikoku. (see map inside the front cover)

■ 練習(れんしゅう)の時間(じかん) Time for Practice

1. Pair Practice

Place some of your hiragana or vocabulary flash cards (face up) near you, some near your partner, and some far away from both of you. Take turns asking and answering questions about the location of each of the cards using the correct pronoun. For example, if the flash card for あ is near you, you would say:

例 れい EXAMPLE

You :	これは "あ" ですか。	= Is this "A"?
Your partner :	はい、それは "あ" です。	= Yes, that (near you) is "A."

NOTE: If you do not have flashcards or if you want extra practice, use the list of Classroom Objects in Appendix 4 at the back of the book to do the same pair practice using これ、それ、あれ、どれ.

2. Pair Practice

Point to one of the items pictured below and ask your partner a question. If the object seems near you, use これ. If the object seems near the speaker, use それ. If the object seems distant from both of you, use あれ.

NOTE: Try to ask your questions in a way that lets your partner practice both affirmative and negative responses.

You : *(pointing to map of Japan)*	これは 日本(にほん)ですか。	= Is this Japan?
Your partner :	*(if it is correct)* はい、そうです。	= Yes, that is correct.
-OR-	*(if it is incorrect)* いいえ、ちがいます。	= No, that is wrong.

アメリカ (あめりか)

キアラ (きあら)

先生(せんせい)

おすし

なりたくうこう

日本(にほん)

3. Pair Practice

Point to one of the pictures below. Your partner will say the appropriate greeting in 日本語. Take turns.

You :	*(pointing to picture of the student greeting teacher early in the day)*
Your partner :	おはよう ございます。

第1課の6 よく　できました。 Well done!

■ 単語(たんご) New Words

Useful Classroom Commands and Expressions			
よく　出来(でき)ました。	 ちょっと　待(ま)って下(くだ)さい。	 ゆっくり　おねがいします。	もう一度(いちど)　言(い)って下(くだ)さい。
 (はい、) 分(わ)かります。	いいえ、分(わ)かりません。	静(しず)かに　して　下(くだ)さい。	英語(えいご)で　言(い)って　下(くだ)さい。
X (*object*) を　貸(か)して下(くだ)さい。	X は (英語(えいご) / 日本語(にほんご)) で何(なん)と　言(い)いますか。	 (お) 手洗(てあら)いへ　行(い)ってもいいですか	ロッカー(ろっかー)へ　行(い)ってもいいですか。
(お) 水(みず)を　飲(の)んでもいいですか。	きりつ	れい	ちゃくせき

■ 練習(れんしゅう)の時間(じかん) Time for Practice

1. Pair Practice

Verbally order your partner to do one of the commands from the list of expressions in Chapter 1-3. Your partner will act it out. Switch roles and do it again until you have both gone through all the commands in that section. If your partner does a particularly good job, you can praise him or her by saying 良(よ)く出来(でき)ました。

2. Pair Practice

Look at the list of classroom objects in Appendix 4. Ask your partner to loan you one. Take turns.

A-さん： けしゴム(ごむ)を　貸(か)して下(くだ)さい。 = Please lend me an eraser.

B-さん： (*Handing, or pretending to hand over, object*)

はい、どうぞ。 = Here, please (take it).

3. Class Practice

Play *Sensei Says* using the classroom commands you have learned. Students take turns being the "Sensei."

Caller says : 「Sensei says, たって　下(くだ)さい。」(*all students stand up*)

Caller says : 「すわって　下(くだ)さい。」(*no one should sit down*)

Caller says : 「Sensei says, 本(ほん)を　開(ひら)いて　下(くだ)さい。」(*everyone should open their textbooks*)

■ 単語チェックリスト New Word Checklist

1-1

あにめ・アニメ *n* animated cartoons/films
からて・空手 *n* karate (martial art)
きもの・着物 *n* kimono (Japanese traditional clothing)
すし・寿司 *n* sushi
すもう・相撲 *n* Japanese sumo wrestling
せんせい・先生 *n* teacher
つなみ・津波 *n* exceptionally large ocean wave
とうきょう・東京 *pn* Tokyo (place name)
とうふ・豆腐 *n* tofu
にほん・日本 *pn* Japan (place name)
にほんご・日本語 *n* Japanese language
はじめましょう・始めましょう *exp.* Let's begin.
べんとう・弁当 *n* box lunch (Japanese), bento
ほん・本 *n* book
まんが・漫画 *n* Japanese comics

1-3

おねがい・お願い/おねがいします・お願いします *exp.* please
かく・書く/かきます・書きます *v* to write
かく・描く/かきます・描きます *v* to draw
きく・聞く/ききます・聞きます *v* to listen
きょうかしょ・教科書 *n* textbook
くん・〜君 *suff.* suffix AFTER a boy's name
さん・〜さん *suff.* suffix AFTER a name
すわる・座る/すわります・座ります *v* to sit
せんせい・〜先生 *n, suff.* suffix AFTER a teacher's, lawyer's, or doctor's name
だす・出す/だします・出します *v* to take (it) out
たつ・立つ/たちます・立ちます *v* to stand
です *copula* helping verb/linking verb used similarly to "is" or "am"
どうぞ よろしく *exp.* best regards, treat me favorably (same meaning as よろしく おねがいします)
どうぞ よろしく おねがいします・ お願いします *exp.* polite for よろしくお願いします
とじる・閉じる/とじます・閉じます *v* to close; to shut [bound paper objects]
なまえ・名前 *n* name
は *part.* denotes a sentence topic
はじめまして・初めまして *exp.* How do you do?
ひらく・開く/ひらきます・開きます *v* to open [book/bound object]
ぼく・僕 *pron.* I, me (used by males only)
みる・見る/みます・見ます *v* to look/see
よむ・読む/よみます・読みます *v* to read
よろしく おねがいします・お願いします *exp.* best regards, treat me favorably
わたし・私 *pron.* I, me
わたしたち・私達 *pron.* we, us

Classroom Commands and Questions

かいて・書いて *v* to write
かいて ください。・書いて下さい。 Write please.
かいても・書いてもも いいですか。 Is it OK to write?
きいて・聞いて *v* to listen
きいてください。・聞いて下さい Listen please.
きいても・聞いても いいですか。 Is it OK to listen?
きょうかしょ・教科書 *n* textbook
すわって・座って *v* sit
すわって ください。・座って 下さい。 Sit please.
すわっても・座っても いいですか。 Is it OK to sit?
だして・出して *v* to take (it) out
だして ください。・出して 下さい。 Take (it) out please.
だしても・出しても いいですか。 Is it OK to take out (it)?
たって・立って *v* to stand
たって ください・立って 下さい。 Stand please.
たっても・立っても いいですか。 Is it OK to stand?
とじて・閉じて *v* to close; shut
とじてください。・閉じて下さい。 Close/shut (it) please.
とじても・閉じても いいですか。 Is it OK to close/shut (it)?
ひらいて・開いて *v* to open (book)
ひらいて ください。・開いて下さい。 Open (book) please.
ひらいても・開いても いいですか。 Is it OK to open?
みて・見て *v* to look/watch
みて ください。・見て 下さい Look/watch please.
みても・見ても いいですか。 Is it OK to see/watch?
よんで 読んで *v* to read
よんで ください。・読んで 下さい。 Read please.
よんでも・読んでも いいですか。 Is it OK to read?

1-4

いいえ　no

いいえ、ちがいます。・違います。 *exp.* No, it is not/different.

か *part.* signifies a question

こちら *pron.* this person (polite)

たろう・太郎 *pn* Tarou (male name)

ちち・父 *n* father, dad

にほんじん・日本人 *n* Japanese (person)

はい　yes, OK, here (roll call)

はい、そう　です。 *exp.* yes it is

はは・母 *n* mother, mom

ようこそ *exp.* Welcome!, Nice to see you.

1-5

あれ *pron.* that (over there)

おかえりなさい・お帰りなさい *exp.* welcome home

おはよう *exp.* good morning (informal)

おはよう　ございます *exp.* good morning (formal)

おやすみ・お休み *exp.* good night (informal)

おやすみなさい・お休みなさい *exp.* good night (formal)

げんき・元気 *n/なadj.* healthy, energetic

ごはん・ご飯 *n* cooked rice, a meal

これ *pron.* this (one)

こんにちは・今日は *exp.* hello

こんばんは・今晩は *exp.* good evening

さようなら *exp.* goodbye

じゃあ　また *exp.* see you later (informal)

しょうゆ・醤油 *exp.* soy sauce

それ *pron.* that (one)

ただいま *exp.* I'm home

たまご・卵 *n* egg

ではまた *exp.* see you later (formal)

どうぞ *adv.* please (here you go), by all means

どれ *inter.* which (one)

に *part.* in; at; used after a location or time word

ばいばい・バイバイ　bye-bye

(お)はし・(お)箸 *n* chopsticks

へや・部屋 *n* room (a)

わさび *n* wasabi, Japanese horseradish

1-6

Useful Classroom Commands and Expressions

よく　できました。・出来ました。 Well done.

ちょっと　まって　ください。・待って　下さい。 Wait a minute please.

ゆっくり　おねがいします。・お願い　します。 Please say it more slowly.

もういちど　いって　ください。・もう一度　言って　下さい。 Say it again please.

わかりますか。・分かりますか。 Do you understand?

はい、わかります。・分かります。 Yes, I understand.

いいえ、わかりません。・分かりません。 No, I don't understand.

しりません。・知りません。 I don't know.

しずかに　してください。・静かに　して下さい。 Please be quiet.

えいごで　いってください。・英語で　言って　下さい。 Please say it in English.

X (object)を　かしてください。・貸して　下さい。 Please lend me X.

X (object)は (えいご/にほんご)で　なんと　いいますか。・X は (英語/日本語)で　何と　言いますか。 What is X in English/Japanese?

おてあらいへ　いっても　いいですか。・お手洗いへ　行っても　いいですか。 May I go to the restroom/W.C.?

ロッカーへ　いっても・行っても　いいですか。 May I go to my locker?

おみずを　のんでも・お水を　飲んでも　いいですか。 May I drink (some) water?

きりつ・起立 *n* stand up

れい・礼 *n* bow

ちゃくせき・着席 *n* sit down

Family and Friends in Tokyo

第 2 課

Learning and Performance Goals

This chapter will enable you to:

A) learn and use vocabulary and kanji for talking about family members

B) learn some methods of counting, including general counting and using counter endings for people and objects from 1 to 900

C) learn and use vocabulary for talking about basic locations of people and objects

D) talk in general about location of objects and people, and specifically about this one, that one, which one, etc.

E) master the rest of the hiragana if you haven't finished them and learn 18 additional kanji

F) use the "can-do" chart found on **TimeForJapanese.com** to chart your progress for what you "can-do" for each chapter

第2課の1

それは 何(なん) ですか。

What is that?

1)それは 何 ですか。

2)これは 私の バッグ です。

3)このなかに、しゃしんが あります。 これは 私の 家族 です。 家族は 六人 です。

4)こちらは 父と 母 です。

5)妹が 二人 です。こちらの 二人が 妹 です。

6)こちらは 兄 です。

7)犬の なまえは こま です。

■ 会話 Dialogue

REMINDER: You may see some kanji / vocabulary you do not recognize. Use the context to try to understand the meanings of those parts of the dialogue.

1. じゅん： それは　何　ですか。
2. キアラ： これは　私の　バッグ　です。
3. キアラ： この　なかに　しゃしんが　あります。これは私の　家族　です。
   家族は　六人　です。
4. キアラ： こちらは　父と　母　です。
5. キアラ： 妹が　二人　います。こちらの二人が　妹　です。
6. キアラ： こちらは　兄　です。
7. キアラ： 犬の　名前は　こま　です。

■ 単語 New Words

家族 (*n*) | 何 (*inter.*) | だれ (*inter.*) | しゃしん (*n*) | 犬 (*n*) | ねこ (*n*) | 電話 (*n*)

ご家族 (*n*) – (someone else's family)

しょうかい　します (*v*) – to make an introduction

じこしょうかい（を）する / します (*v*) – to introduce oneself

しょうかい（を）　して下さい (*v*) – please introduce (someone/something)

姉 (*n*) – (my) older sister

兄 (*n*) – (my) older brother

弟 (*n*) – (my) younger brother

妹 (*n*) – (my) younger sister

兄弟 (*n*) – siblings

祖父 (*n*) – (my) grandfather

祖母 (*n*) – (my) grandmother

いる / います (*v*) – to exist (animate beings)

ある / あります (*v*) – to exist (inanimate things)

の (*part.*) – possession; replaces a noun (similar to 's in English)

Other words you might like to know:

一番上(いちばんうえ)の 兄(あに)/姉(あね)	my oldest brother/sister
二番目(にばんめ)の 兄(あに)/姉(あね)	my second oldest brother/sister
すぐ下(した)の 弟(おとうと)/妹(いもうと)	my next youngest brother/sister
一番下(いちばんした)の 弟(おとうと)/妹(いもうと)	my youngest brother/sister
ぎりの〜	step-, or in-law, a non-"blood" relative

	1	2	3	4	5	6	7	8	9	10	how many?
Counting	一 いち	二 に	三 さん	四 よん/し	五 ご	六 ろく	七 しち/なな	八 はち	九 く/きゅう	十 じゅう	いくつ
Counting People	一人 ひとり	二人 ふたり	三人 さんにん	四人 よにん	五人 ごにん	六人 ろくにん	七人 しち/ななにん	八人 はちにん	九人 く/きゅうにん	十人 じゅうにん	何人 なんにん
Counting Small Animals	一匹 いっぴき	二匹 にひき	三匹 さんびき	四匹 よんひき	五匹 ごひき	六匹 ろっぴき	七匹 ななひき	八匹 はっぴき	九匹 きゅうひき	十匹 じゅう/じっぴき	何匹 なんびき

■ 漢字(かんじ) Kanji

何 (7 strokes)	
なに；なん – what	ノ イ 仁 仃 何 何 何
何(なに/なん) – what; 何人(なんにん) – how many people?	
The first two strokes are a person. The 3rd and 7th strokes are a nail, and the center three strokes are a mouth. Imagine seeing a person striking a nail with his head; you will want to open your mouth and yell "WHAT?"	

家 (10 strokes)	
カ(か)，いえ – house; it is also sometimes pronounced as うち – house (home)	丶 丶 宀 宀 宁 宇 家 家 家 家
家(いえ/うち) – house; home; 家(か)(族(ぞく)) – family	
The first 3 strokes represent a roof; the remaining 7 strokes are the right side of pig 豚 (imagining these 7 strokes as pork ribs may help). Imagine the three little piggies hiding under the roof of their HOUSE.	

兄 (5 strokes)	
キョウ(きょう)；あに；(お)にい(さん) – older brother	丨 冂 口 尸 兄
兄(あに) – older brother (informal); お兄(にい)さん – polite term for someone else's older brother	
This kanji consists of a big mouth (ロ) with two long legs. Think of some tall big-mouthed OLDER BROTHER that you might know!	

姉 8 strokes	あね ;(お)ねえ(さん) – older sister
	姉(あね) – older sister (informal); (お)姉(ねえ)(さん) – older sister (polite term for someone else's older sister)
	The left side of this kanji (女) is the kanji for female while the right side (市) means city and the combo could represent an OLDER SISTER who lives in the city.

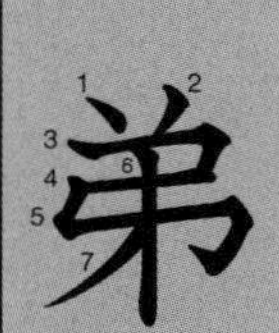

弟 7 strokes	ダイ(だい) ; おとうと – younger brother
	弟(おとうと) – younger brother (informal); 弟(おとうと)(さん) – younger brother (polite term for someone else's younger brother); (兄)弟(きょうだい) – siblings
	Does this look like a YOUNGER BROTHER wearing a scary mask? If not, send your better idea to TimeForJapanese.com

妹 8 strokes	いもうと – younger sister
	妹(いもうと) – younger sister (informal); 妹(いもうと)(さん) – younger sister (polite)
	The left side of this kanji (女) again is the kanji for female, while the right side (未) is a tree with an extra horizontal line across representing the floor of a tree house the YOUNGER SISTER's father is making for her.

■ 言葉(ことば)の探索(たんさく) Language Detection

1. います and あります "to exist"

Both of these verbs mean "to exist." However, the difference is that います is used for animate beings and あります is used for inanimate objects. Both います and あります are often translated as "to have" or "there is."

です, which you learned previously, generally means "is" or "am" in the sense of pointing out the *identity* of someone/something, as in: "私はせいとです。" (I am a student.) or "それはえんぴつです。" (That is a pencil.)

います and あります generally mean "is" or "have" in the sense of pointing out the *existence* of someone/something, as in: "せいとがいます。" (There is a student.) or "えんぴつがあります。" (I have a pencil.)

The particle が is usually used in statements with います and あります. When います or あります are used in questions, you can use the particle は after the topic being asked about.

A) 先生(せんせい)が　います。 = I have a teacher./There is a teacher.
B) すずきさんは　先生(せんせい)です。 = Mr. Suzuki is a teacher.
C) 兄(あに)が　います。 = I have an older brother./There is an older brother.
D) 犬(いぬ)が　います。 = I have a dog./There is a dog.
E) 家族(かぞく)の　しゃしんが　あります。 = I have family pictures./There is a family picture.
F) 私(わたし)の　おはしが　あります。 = I have chopsticks./My chopsticks are (here).
G) たまごは　ありますか。 = Do you have any eggs?/Are there eggs?
H) ご家族(かぞく)の　しゃしんは　ありますか。 = Do you have a picture of your family?

Remember, to help you distinguish between います and あります and the previously-learned です, focus on the fact that the first are used to talk about the *existence* of someone/something, whereas です is used to point out the *identity* of someone/something (that is, to say who or what something is).

Look at Example A above; whether you are saying "I have a teacher" or "There is a teacher", you are pointing out the *existence* of a teacher. In Example B, you are *identifying* Mr. Suzuki as a teacher, using です.

2. The particle の

Two uses of the particle の are to show possession, and to show a relationship of one noun to another, one noun being "of" the kind/type of another.

To show possession, の is placed between two nouns with the first one "possessing" the second.

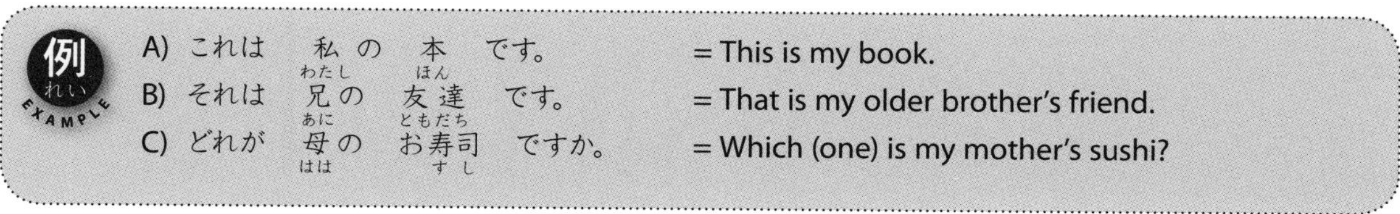

The particle の is used to show the relationship of one noun to another as in *Japanese book*, *Japanese sushi*, etc. The noun being described (*book* or *sushi* in these examples) is second and の comes after the first noun (the one doing the describing).

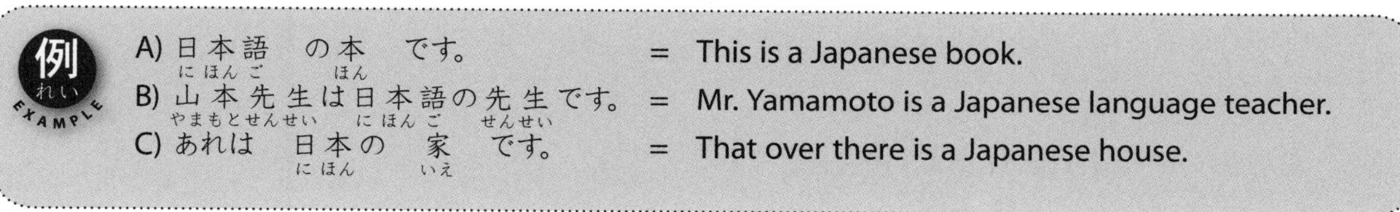

3. Pointing Out Location

Go to **www.TimeforJapanese.com** for the Web Activities for this chapter and section to download this Bonus Sheet.

■ 自習(じしゅう) Self Check

1. Use the words from these two lists to make complete sentences. Use the particle の to say what belongs to whom. First use です. Remember that using です at the end of sentences like the examples implies "there is" or "there are". Follow examples A and B, and say them out loud to yourself in Japanese. Then choose words from the lists to make sentences or questions using います and あります as in examples C and D. Remember that using います and あります can also mean "there is" or "there are", but also can mean "(to) have".

例 (れい) EXAMPLE

A) 父(ちち) + 写真(しゃしん) → これは　父(ちち)の　写真(しゃしん)　です。
= This is my father's photo.

B) それは　じゅんさん　の　はし　です。
= Those are Jun's chopsticks.

C) 父(ちち)の + 写真(しゃしん)が　あります。
= There is my father's photo./My father's photo is here.

D) 先生(せんせい)が　います。
= There is a teacher.

List 1	List 2
父(ちち)	写真(しゃしん)
僕(ぼく)	漫画(まんが)
妹(いもうと)	へや
英語(えいご)	先生(せんせい)
弟(おとうと)	ごはん
じゅん	はし
キアラ(きあら)	(free choice)

2. How would you respond to the following?

A) ➲ ご家族(かぞく)は　何人(なんにん)　ですか。　B) ➲ ご家族(かぞく)を　しょうかい (introduce) して　ください。

3. Look at a variety of objects around you. Practice saying which object belongs to whom. Refer to Appendix 4, Classroom Objects.

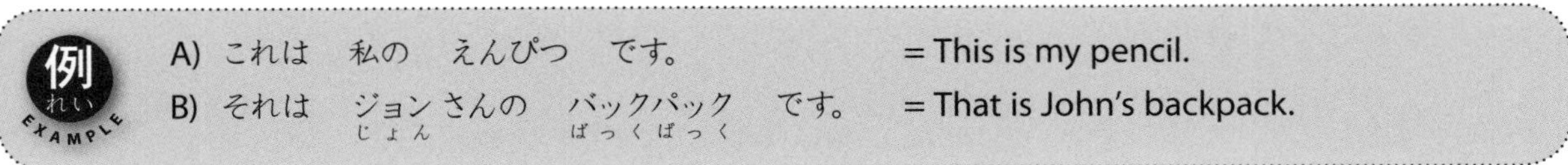

例 (れい) EXAMPLE

A) これは　私の　えんぴつ　です。　= This is my pencil.

B) それは　ジョン(じょん)さんの　バックパック(ばっくぱっく)　です。　= That is John's backpack.

■ 練習(れんしゅう)の時間(じかん) Time for Practice

1. Pair Practice

Alternating between using あります and います, point out everyone and everything in the classroom using only Japanese. Use Appendix 4 at the back of the book when you run out of objects you can say in Japanese.

A) 本が　あります。　= There is a book. (There are books.)

B) 先生(せんせい)が　います。　= There is a teacher.

C) 電話(でんわ)が　あります。　= There is a telephone. (There are telephones.)

D) ナオミ(なおみ)さんが　います。　= There is Naomi.

2. Pair Practice

As you did in the previous pair practice, point out things and people around you, but this time add の to show possession or to give more information about the people and things you point out.

A) 私(わたし)の　本(ほん)が　あります。 = There is my book. (I have my book.)
B) 日本語(にほんご)の先生(せんせい)が　います。 = There is a Japanese language teacher.
C) 先生(せんせい)の　電話(でんわ)が　あります。 = There is the teacher's telephone.
D) ナオミ(なおみ)さんの　バッグ(ばっぐ)が　あります。 = There is Naomi's bag.

3. Pair Practice

Following the example, ask your partner about his/her family. After you've both introduced your families including pets, draw a picture of your partner's family, properly labeling individual names and the Japanese family words for mother, older brother, etc. After you have finished, show your picture to your partner to confirm that you got all the information correct since you will use this picture again in section 2.2.

NOTE: do not forget that in Japanese you count yourself in the number of family members.

A-さん：ご家族(かぞく)は　何人(なんにん)ですか。 = How many members are there in your family?
B-さん：家族(かぞく)は　五人(ごにん)　です。 = My family has five members.
A-さん：紹介(しょうかい)して　ください。 = Please introduce (them).
B-さん：母(はは)と　父(ちち)と　兄(あに)と　妹(いもうと)　が　います。 = I have a mother, father, older brother, and younger sister.
B-さん：母(はは)の　名前(なまえ)は　けいこ　です。 = My mother's name is Keiko.

4. Group Work

Using the vocabulary and grammar from Language Detection 3 in this section, describe where the section 1.1 New Words pictures (page 20) are in relation to each other as in the examples:

A) 先生(せんせい)の　写真(しゃしん)は　日本(にほん)の　左(ひだり)に　あります。 = The teacher's photo is to the left of "Japan."
B) すしの　写真(しゃしん)は　東京(とうきょう)の　下(した)に　あります。 = The photo of sushi is below "Tokyo."
C) 豆腐(とうふ)の　写真(しゃしん)は　日本(にほん)と　からての　間(あいだ)に　あります。 = The photo of tofu is between "Japan" and "karate."

■ 文化箱(ぶんかばこ) Culture Chest

Humility

Outward signs of pride are frowned upon in Japan. Therefore, the use of humble terms when talking about yourself and your own family members is the rule. That is why Kiara uses the humble form of mother 母(はは) when she talks about her own mother to others but the polite term お母(かあ)さん when she speaks directly to her own mother. Polite family terms take the suffix –さん– and sometimes the honorific お–, while the humble terms do not. The suffix –さん roughly means Mr. or Ms. and thus would be too polite when talking about one's own family (just as it would be strange to use Mr. and Ms. when talking about your own parents in English).

Since the Japanese people consider family members an extension of themselves, it is not uncommon for Japanese mothers to say rather negative things about their children or spouses as a natural way of being humble. For instance, some mothers may talk about how their children are unintelligent or lazy. It is wise NOT to agree with mothers when they say such things, as the opposite is quite often true!

■ キアラのジャーナル Kiara's Journal 

Dear Journal,

I landed in Tokyo today. There were two nice people at the immigration desk at 成田空港 who were very helpful. After I showed them my passport, they asked me several questions about why I was coming to Japan, where I was staying, and how long I would be here. I was a bit nervous, but they smiled and welcomed me to 日本. Once I finished with Customs, I went out into the huge and noisy arrival lobby. Jun-kun stood among all the other greeters, with his お父さん and お母さん. Jun-san's お父さん、holding up a sign with my name on it, was easy to spot. I'm so glad they are as friendly as I imagined. I was pretty nervous about whether or not we would like each other, but it looks like we'll get along fine. じゅん君 is a little taller than I am and he is very thin. He's a really friendly guy but he does seem a little geeky. Once we left Narita Airport, we boarded the train for 東京. The train was amazing. By pushing a lever, you could turn the seats around 180° to adjust to the new direction of the train or to be able to face your friends or family members. There were even vending machines selling drinks, telephone cards, and disposable cameras in one of the cars. I've never seen anything like that. The train ride seemed long, about an hour. And that wasn't all: then we had to ride a bus for 15 minutes from 東京 Station to じゅん君の家. じゅん君 brought along a manga and read almost the entire book before we reached his 家. I was excited, but exhausted too. I remember seeing rice fields and temples, then lots of cars and buildings.

I was a bit nervous about finally meeting the rest of じゅん君のご家族. Once we got to his house, his mother went out to get 天ぷら for dinner while I went to my room to unpack.

I almost forgot my おみやげ, but I grabbed it out of my bags at the last minute and brought it downstairs. They seemed to appreciate the gifts. After we ate the delicious 天ぷら, they gave me some green tea and cookies and let me take a bath and rest. I was more tired than I realized and nearly fell asleep in the bathtub.

第2課の2

こちらは　ベン君の　お母さん　です。

べんくん　かあ

This is Ben's mother.

1.

1) ここは
友達の 家 です。
しつれい します。

2)はいはい。

2.

3) じゅん君、
こんにちは。

4) こんにちは。こちらは
ベン君の お母さん です。

3.

5) 私はキャシーです。

4.

6) こんにちは。I'm Kiara.
I'm staying with Jun's family.
日本語で 話してもいい ですか。

7) いい ですよ。日本ですから。
がんばって 下さい！どうぞ
上がって 下さい。

5.

8) こちらは ベン君の お兄さんです。
ジャックさん です。こちらは妹さん達
です。ケーラさんとセーラさん です。

9) 初めまして。

(ジャック)

ケーラ
and
セーラ

■ 会話(かいわ) Dialogue

REMINDER: You may see some kanji / vocabulary you do not recognize. Use the context to try to understand the meanings of those parts of the dialogue.

1. じゅん　：　ここは　友達(ともだち)の　家(いえ)　です。[knock knock] しつれいします。

2. ベン(べん)の母(はは)：　はいはい。

3. 　　じゅん君(くん)、こんにちは。

4. じゅん　：　こんにちは。こちらは　ベン君(べんくん)の　お母(かあ)さん　です。

5. ベン(べん)の母(はは)：　私(わたし)は　キャシー(きゃしー)　です。

6. キアラ(きあら)　：　こんにちは。I'm Kiara. I'm staying with Jun's family. 日本語で　話(はな)しても　いい　ですか。

7. ベン(べん)の母(はは)：　いい　ですよ。日本　です　から。がんばって　下(くだ)さい！
どうぞ　上(あ)がって　下(くだ)さい。

8. じゅん　：　こちらは　ベン君(べんくん)の　お兄(にい)さん　です。ジャック(じゃっく)さん　です。
こちらは　妹(いもうと)さん達(たち)　です。*ケーラ(けーら)さんと　*セーラ(せーら)さん　です。

9. キアラ(きあら)　：　初(はじ)めまして。

* ケーラ(けーら) - Kara (proper name in English)　* セーラ(せーら) - Sarah (proper name in English)

■ 単語(たんご) New Words 

お父(とう)さん (*n*) – (someone else's) father
お母(かあ)さん (*n*) – (someone else's) mother
お兄(にい)さん (*n*) – (someone else's) older brother
お姉(ねえ)さん (*n*) – (someone else's) older sister
弟(おとうと)さん (*n*) – (someone else's) younger brother
妹(いもうと)さん (*n*) – (someone else's) younger sister
おばあさん (*n*) – (someone else's) grandmother
おばさん (*n*) – aunt or woman quite a bit older than you
おじいさん (*n*) – (someone else's) grandfather
おじさん (*n*) – uncle or man quite a bit older than you
家(いえ/うち) (*n*) – house/home
人(ひと) (*n*) – person
と (*part.*) – particle used for "and"
しつれいします (*exp.*) – excuse me; I'm sorry to bother you

 友達(ともだち) (*n*)	十一(じゅういち) – 11	十八(じゅうはち) – 18	六十(ろくじゅう) – 60	四百(よんひゃく) – 400
	十二(じゅうに) – 12	十九(じゅうく/きゅう) – 19	七十(ななじゅう) – 70	五百(ごひゃく) – 500
	十三(じゅうさん) – 13	二十(にじゅう) – 20	八十(はちじゅう) – 80	六百(ろくひゃく) – 600
	十四(じゅうし) – 14	二十一(にじゅういち) – 21	九十(きゅうじゅう) – 90	七百(ななひゃく) – 700
	十五(じゅうご) – 15	三十(さんじゅう) – 30	百(ひゃく) – 100	八百(はちひゃく) – 800
	十六(じゅうろく) – 16	四十(よんじゅう) – 40	二百(にひゃく) – 200	九百(きゅうひゃく) – 900
	十七(じゅうなな/しち) – 17	五十(ごじゅう) – 50	三百(さんびゃく) – 300	

■ 漢字(かんじ) Kanji

Kanji	Readings / Meaning	Stroke order
一 (1 stroke)	イチ(いち); ひと(つ) – one 一(いち) – one; 一(ひと)(つ) – one (thing)	一
二 (2 strokes)	ニ(に); ふた(つ) – two 二(に) – two; 二(ふた)(つ) – two (things)	一 二
三 (3 strokes)	サン(さん); みっ(つ) – three 三(さん) – three; 三(みっ)(つ) – three (things)	一 二 三
四 (5 strokes)	シ(し); よん; よっ(つ) – four 四(よん/し) – four; 四(よっ)(つ) – four (things) The two legs are thinking, "What did I do to deserve being trapped inside these FOUR walls?"	丨 冂 門 四 四
五 (4 strokes)	ゴ(ご); いつ(つ) – five 五(ご) – five; 五(いつ)(つ) – five (things) The middle two strokes were originally a cross and this character represented a crossroads. Since Japanese count to ten with one hand, FIVE represents the crossroads when the direction of counting changes from right to left.	一 丆 万 五
六 (4 strokes)	ロク(ろく); むっ(つ) – six 六(ろく) – six; 六(むっ)(つ) – six (things) The first two strokes are a top hat and the bottom two strokes are straight legs. Imagine SIX of these freaky characters with no heads or torsos trying to put you SIX feet under, and you will never forget SIX.	丶 亠 亣 六
七 (2 strokes)	シチ(しち); なな／なな(つ) — seven 七(なな/しち) – seven; 七(なな)(つ) – seven (things) Imagine a boy sitting down with outstretched hands to collect the money that falls from the sky. Talk about lucky SEVEN!	一 七

八 2 strokes	ハチ(はち) — eight; やっ(つ) – eight things	ノ	八					
	八(はち) – eight; 八(やっ)(つ) – eight (things)							
	This kanji is made up of two strokes that look somewhat like a volcano. Volcanoes can reach at least a level EIGHT on a scale of hotness!							

九 2 strokes	キュウ(きゅう); く; ここの(つ) – nine	ノ	九					
	九(きゅう/く) – nine; 九(ここの)(つ) – nine (things)							
	The two strokes of the kanji for NINE intersect at a NINEty degree angle with the second stroke starting at what would be NINE o'clock.							

十 2 strokes	ジュウ(じゅう); とお – ten	一	十					
	十(じゅう) – ten; 十(とお) – ten (things)							
	This looks like a "T," the first letter of TEN and TOU (TEN things).							

百 6 strokes	ヒャク(ひゃく) – hundred	一	丆	丆	百 (partial)	百 (partial)	百	
	百(ひゃく) – one hundred							
	This character looks like a large tray holding 100 glasses of water on top of a hot sun.							

■ 言葉(ことば)の探索(たんさく) Language Detection

1. Counters

In English, we have "counter" words such as *flocks, loaves, packs, slices, herds,* etc. to differentiate the numbers of various objects or animals. The Japanese language also uses different word endings (counters) to count various types of animate and inanimate objects. For example, one person is 一人(ひとり), one tree is 一本(いっぽん), and one car is 一台(いちだい). When counting people, place the number in front of the kanji ～人(にん) (person). The pronunciations for *one person* (一人(ひとり)) and *two people* (二人(ふたり)) are based on an old Japanese counting system. Counting up from three people and higher is simple: use the numbers you have already learned and add the counter 人(にん) after each number.

For a list of other counters, see Appendix 1.

2. と "and"

One use of と is as a particle that connects two or more nouns just like the word "and." Unlike English, however, と is used between every noun in a list, even if you are listing three or more things. Note that the particle と can only be used to connect nouns (people, places, and things) and not verbs, adverbs, and adjectives.

A) すしと　わさびと　しょうゆが　あります。 = There is sushi and wasabi and soy sauce.

B) お父(とう)さんと　お母(かあ)さんが　います。 = He/she has a father and mother.

C) キアラ(きあら)と　じゅんは　いますか。 = Are Kiara and Jun (here)?

■ 自習(じしゅう) Self Check

1. The first column contains family words for your own family. The second column contains words for someone else's family. See how well and quickly you can fill in the blanks, without using your book. Then check your answers. The first one is done for you.

My family	**Someone else's family**
1. 妹(いもうと)	妹(いもうと)さん
2. ____________	お兄(にい)さん
3. ____________	おばあさん
4. 母(はは)	____________
5. 弟(おとうと)	____________
6. ____________	お父(とう)さん
7. 姉(あね)	____________
8. 祖父(そふ)	____________

2. Count from one to ten, three times, as quickly as you can. Use hand motions. Then count backwards. Then take turns with your partner, each of you counting off one number.

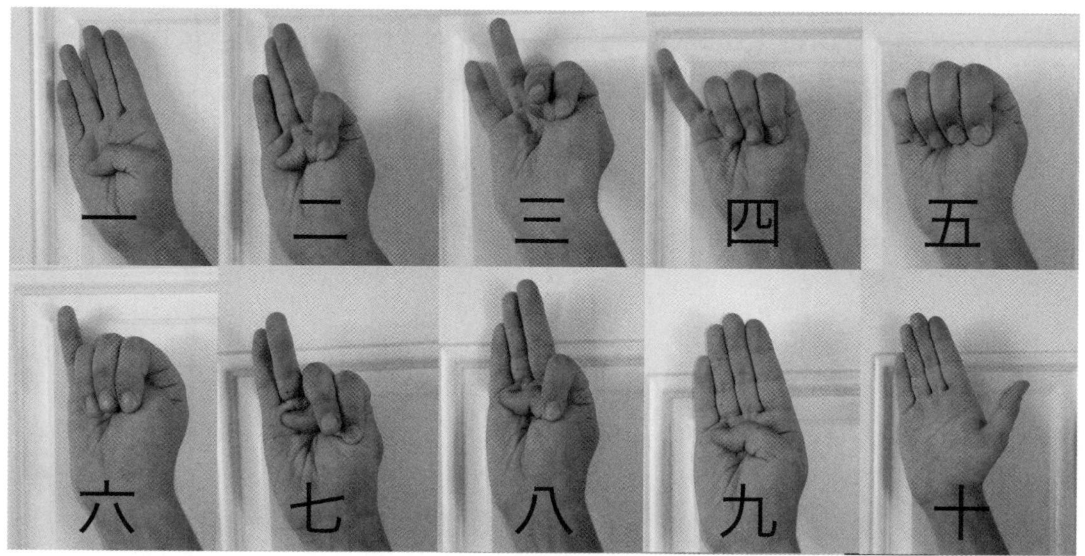

■ 練習(れんしゅう)の時間(じかん) Time for Practice

1. Pair Practice

Introducing someone else's family

Look at the 練習(れんしゅう)の時間(じかん) in Chapter 2-1 and use the drawing you did for that section, or find another online. Introduce your partner's family to a new partner, as in the example, including the names of all family members. Take turns.

A- さん：	こちらは　いちろうさんの　ご家族(かぞく)です。	= This is Ichirou's family.
B- さん：	家族(かぞく)は　何人(なんにん)ですか。	= How many people are in the family?
A- さん：	四人(よにん)です。	= Four people.
A- さん：	お母(かあ)さんと　お父(とう)さんと　弟(おとうと)さんが　います。	= He has a mother, father, and younger brother.
A- さん：	お母(かあ)さんのお名前(なまえ)は　久美子(くみこ)さんです。	= His mother's name is Kumiko.

2. Small Group Practice

Form groups of 4 students. In pairs, find out how many people are in your partner's family, and who they are. Share that information with your group. Take turns.

A- さん： ご家族(かぞく)は　何人(なんにん)　ですか。 = How many people are there in your family?

B- さん： 四人(よにん)　です。 父(ちち)と　母(はは)と　妹(いもうと)　が　います。
= Four people. My father, mother, and my younger sister.

A- さん： (to group) B- さんの　ご家族(かぞく)は　四人(よにん)　です。 お父(とう)さんと　お母(かあ)さんと　妹(いもうと)さんと B- さんの　四人(よにん)　です。
= Mr./Ms. B's family has four people. His/her father, mother, younger sister, and himself/herself equals four people.

Follow up by asking your partner the names of their family members and then sharing those names with the group.

A- さん：	お母(かあ)さんの　名前(なまえ)は　何(なん)　ですか。	= What is your mother's name?
B- さん：	母(はは)の　名前(なまえ)は　さとみ　です。	= My mother's name is Satomi.
A- さん：	*(to other)* B- さん の　お母(かあ)さんの　名前(なまえ)は　さとみさん　です。	= Mr./Ms. B's mother's name is Satomi.

3. Class Practice

Your sensei will hold up between 1 and 10 fingers. Quickly and silently form groups with as many people as the teacher holds up fingers. Upon the sensei's cue, call out the counter for that many people. For example, if your teacher holds up three fingers, you quickly form groups of three and, upon cue, call out 三人(さんにん). Repeat, when your sensei holds up another group of fingers.

■ 文化箱 Culture Chest

It's all in the numbers...

In Japan some numbers are considered unlucky. し, one of two pronunciations for *four* (四), is often considered the unluckiest number because し can also mean *death* (死). Hospitals in Japan rarely have a fourth floor (floors skip from three to five), and some hospitals intentionally omit the number four in room numbers. Many times the alternate pronunciation よん is used. Nine is also an unlucky number, since the sound KU can also mean *suffering* in both the words 苦 and 苦労. There are even unlucky ages. For men, it is well known in Japan that 42 is the unluckiest age, since the kanji 四二 can be pronounced SHI NI, which is close to 死に or "to the death." Less well known is that 33 is the unluckiest age for women because one way you can read these kanji 三三 is SANZAN, which can also mean "to have a terrible time."

■ キアラのジャーナル Kiara's Journal

Read these questions and then read Kiara's journal entry to answer them.

1. How many people are in Jun's family?
2. Compare Japanese naming traditions with how you received your name. Are there any similarities?
3. How many people are in Ben's family?
4. What is Ben's older brother studying?

Dear Journal,

じゅん君の　ご家族は　四人　です。お父さんの　名前は　太郎さん　です。お母さんの名前は　まゆみさん　です。妹さんは　愛子ちゃん　です。

I didn't know that all Japanese names have meaning. For instance, 愛 means love. So 愛子 actually means "love child"! Can you guess what his older brother's name means? Parents put a lot of time and consideration into choosing names for their children. The meanings and even the stroke count are important and so parents often consult family members (especially grandparents) when naming a child.

Tonight I met Jun's 友達. 友達の名前はベンです。　家は　広尾に　あります。広尾 is an upscale part of 東京. オーストラリア大使館は (Embassy) very close. ベン君はオーストラリア人です。ベン君のお母さん works at the オーストラリア大使館 and his お父さん works for a Japanese export company.

ベン君は　お父さんと　お母さんと　お兄さん　一人と　双子の　妹さんが　います。犬２匹と　ねこも　一匹　います。お兄さんは studying 日本語 at 東京国際大学, Tokyo International University.

第2課の3

この　バッグに　おみやげが　あります。どうぞ。

The souvenirs are in this bag. Here you go.

1. 1) この バッグに 皆さんの おみやげが あります。どうぞ。

2) あらっ・・・ どうも ありがとう。

2. 3) どう いたしまして。

4) その 本は お母さんへの おみやげ です。その ぼうしは お父さんの です。

3. 5) この T-シャツは じゅん君のです。この キャンディは お兄さんと妹さんのです。

6) どうも ありがとう。

7) じゅん君、クラスには 何人 いますか。クラスの 皆にも おみやげが あります。

8) 四十人です。

4.

■ 会話(かいわ) Dialogue

REMINDER: You may see some kanji / vocabulary you do not recognize. Use the context to try to understand the meanings of those parts of the dialogue.

1. キアラ(きあら)：この　バッグ(ばっぐ)に　皆(みな)さんの　おみやげが　あります。どうぞ。
2. まゆみ：あらっ…　どうも　ありがとう。
3. キアラ(きあら)：どう　いたしまして。
4. キアラ(きあら)：その　本(ほん)は　お母(かあ)さんへの　おみやげ　です。その　ぼうしは　お父(とう)さんの　です。
5. キアラ(きあら)：この　Tシャツ(てぃーしゃつ)は　じゅん君(くん)の　です。この　キャンディ(きゃんでぃ)は　お兄(にい)さんと　妹(いもうと)さんの　です。
6. じゅん：どうも　ありがとう。
7. キアラ(きあら)：じゅん君(くん)、クラス(くらす)には　何人(なんにん)　いますか。クラス(くらす)の　皆(みんな)にも　おみやげが　あります。
8. じゅん：四十人(よんじゅうにん)　です。

* 皆(みな)さん - (polite for) everyone

■ 単語(たんご) New Words

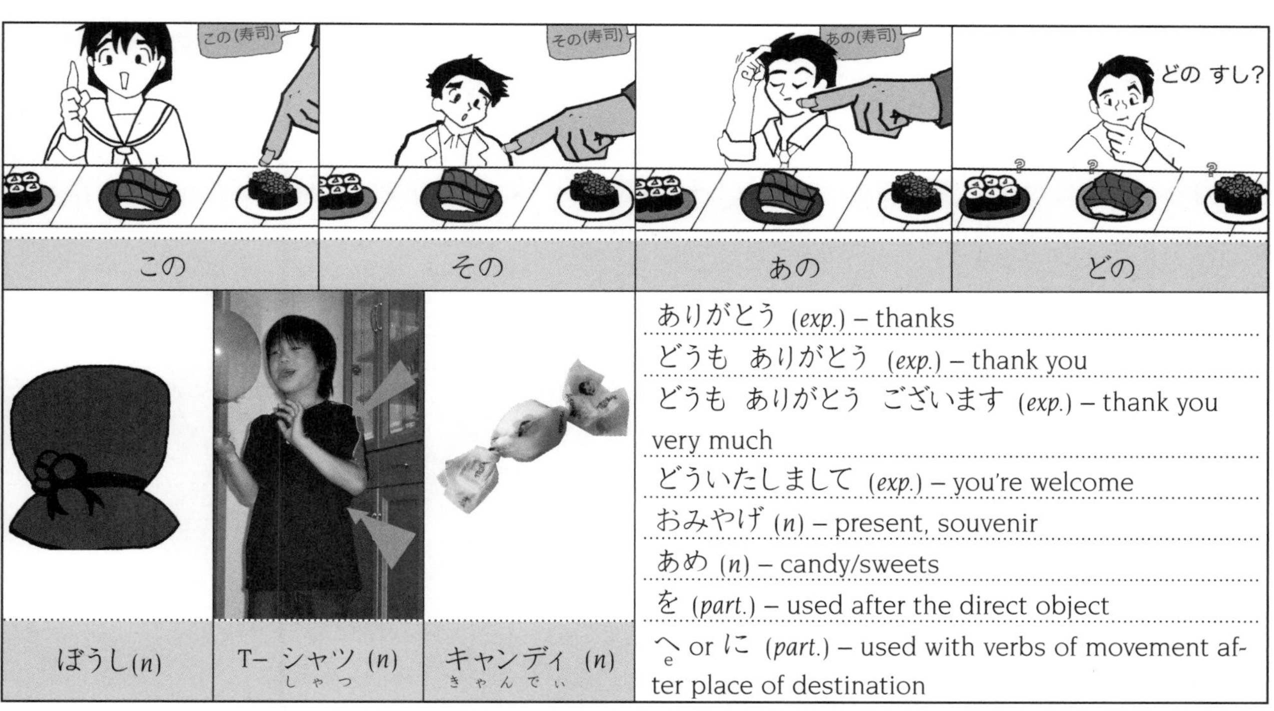

ありがとう (*exp.*) – thanks
どうも　ありがとう (*exp.*) – thank you
どうも　ありがとう　ございます (*exp.*) – thank you very much
どういたしまして (*exp.*) – you're welcome
おみやげ (*n*) – present, souvenir
あめ (*n*) – candy/sweets
を (*part.*) – used after the direct object
へ(e) or に (*part.*) – used with verbs of movement after place of destination

■ 漢字 Kanji

犬 4 strokes	ケン；いぬ – dog	一	ナ	大	犬			
	犬 – dog							
	This is the kanji for DOG. 大 means big, and if you can picture the top right corner of this as a big DOG's mouth and the last stroke as a bone being thrown into the DOG's mouth, you should be able to remember this kanji.							

■ 言葉の探索 Language Detection

1. この、その、あの、どの

These words have similar meaning to これ、それ、あれ、どれ. The only difference is that この、その、あの、どの come before a noun in ALL cases. これ、それ、あれ、どれ are not attached to nouns since they are pronouns that replace nouns.

これ	= this one	あれ	= that one (over there)
この　すし	= this sushi	あの　しょうゆ	= that soy sauce (over there)
それ	= that one (near the listener)	どれ	= which one
その　わさび	= that wasabi (near the listener)	どの　へや	= which room?

2. を

The particle を follows the direct object of a sentence. The direct object is the noun that receives the action of the verb, that is, what is eaten, what is written, what is played, etc. This particle will be explained in more detail in Chapter 3. Here are some English sentences that contain direct objects. The direct objects are bolded and underlined here.

I ate the **hamburger**.　　Jose watches **TV**.
Please write the **report**.　　Timmy did not kick the **ball**.

A. Object を　下さい.　⇨　This phrase is used to ask someone to give you something.

例 れい EXAMPLE
A) しょうゆを　下さい。 = Please give me the soy sauce.
B) 本を　下さい。 = Please give me a/the book.
C) まんがを　下さい。 = Please give me a/the manga.

B. Object を　どうぞ.　⇨　This phrase is used to offer something to someone.

例 れい EXAMPLE
A) お水を　どうぞ。 = Have some water.
B) ケーキを　どうぞ。 = Have some cake.
C) ティッシュを　どうぞ。 = Please have a tissue.

The word どうぞ, when used by itself, can often be translated as "go ahead" or "here you are."

■ 自習(じしゅう) Self Check

1. Count the number of students in the classroom, using the proper counter words for people.

2. What words best fit in the blanks below?

A) __________すし = this sushi

B) __________犬(いぬ) = that dog near you

C) __________ごはん = that bowl of rice over there

D) __________たまご = which egg?

3. Translate the following into English, out loud, to yourself.

A) そのすしを　どうぞ。

B) しゃしんを　下(くだ)さい。

4. Translate the following into Japanese, out loud, to yourself.

A) Please give me the chopsticks.

B) Here you are. (go ahead)

■ 練習(れんしゅう)の時間(じかん) Time for Practice

1. Pair Practice

Use the classroom objects in Appendix 4 for vocabulary. Ask your partner to give you as many different items as he or she can. Your partner responds.

A- さん：　えんぴつ　を　下(くだ)さい。　= Please give me a pencil.

B- さん：　えんぴつ　を　どうぞ。　= Here is a pencil.

2. Pair Practice

Do the same pair practice as above, but this time, point and insert the words この、その、あの、どの into the sentences. Remember, you will use a different word depending on where the object is located IN RELATION to the speaker.

A- さん：　その　本を　下(くだ)さい。　= Please give me that book.

B- さん：　はい、この　本を　どうぞ。　= Yes, please take this book.

3. Pair Practice

Following the examples, use この、その、あの、どの as well as the particle の to indicate who possesses various objects in the classroom. Use the list of classroom objects in Appendix 4 if necessary.

A- さん：　あの　電話(でんわ)は　先生(せんせい)の　です。= That telephone over there is the teacher's.

B- さん：　そう　ですか。　この　電話(でんわ)は　私の　です。

= Is that right? This telephone is mine.

文化箱 Culture Chest

おみやげ, Giving Gifts

Japan is a "gift giving" nation. Foreigners are sometimes unsure about what to bring for their hosts when visiting Japan for the first time. The following sorts of things might be good for a high school student to give to a Japanese host family:

- Picture books from home
- items with local place names or school/college names from your hometown
- items with your school logo on them
- T-shirts with English written on them
- famous products from your home region, handmade crafts or local foods

Items related to the interests and hobbies of your host family are good places to start.

Since giving very expensive presents might lead your Japanese hosts to feel obligated to buy an expensive gift for you in return, the best gift is something unique but not necessarily expensive.

Be sure to think ahead when making or purchasing things to take or send to Japan, since there are many things that cannot legally be taken into or out of countries and other things that cannot be taken onto airplanes.

In Japan, おみやげ can be readily purchased at any tourist site.

第2課の4

その　えんぴつと　けしゴムを　二つ下さい。

Please give me that pencil and two erasers.

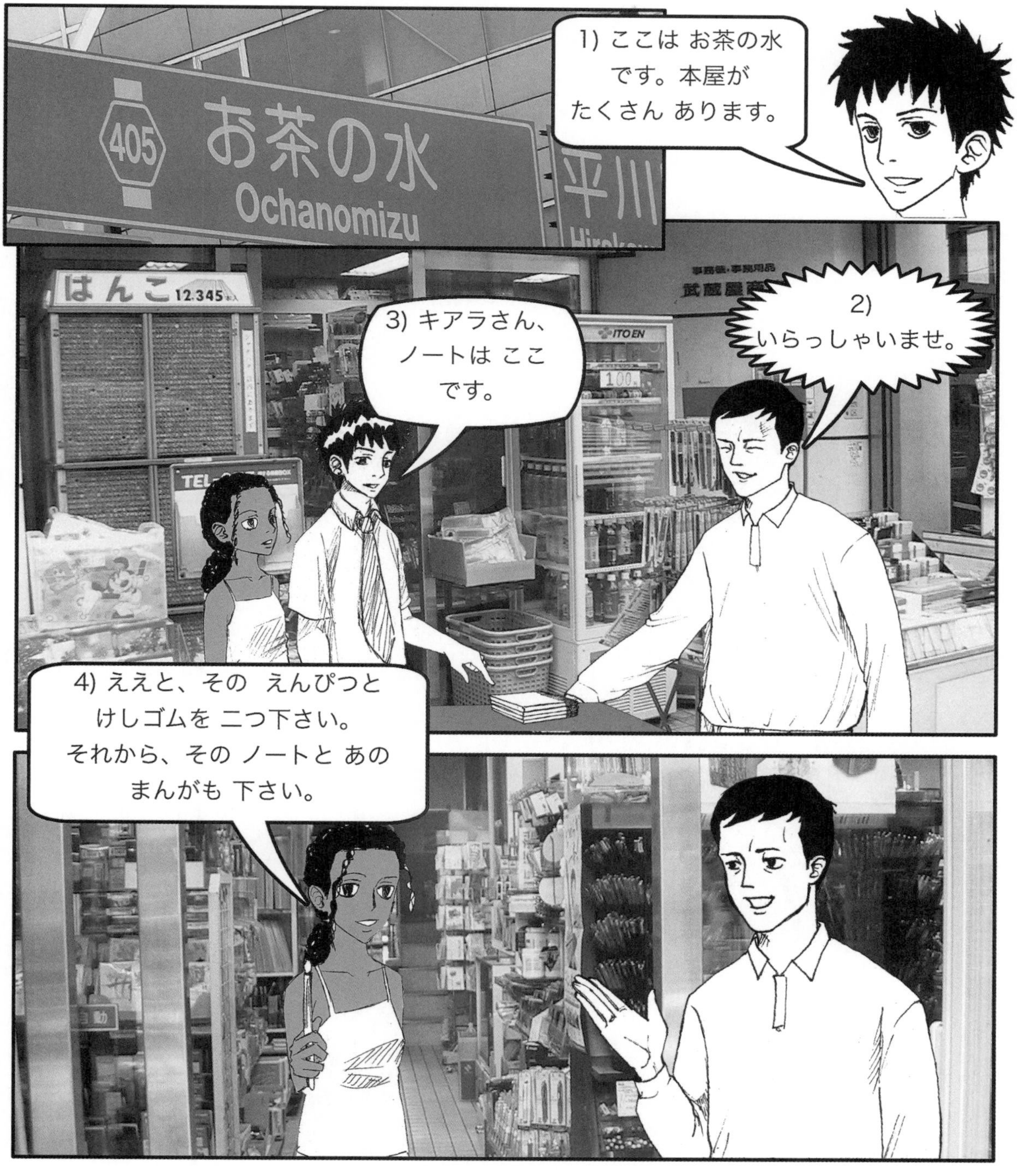

1) ここは お茶の水 です。本屋が たくさん あります。

2) いらっしゃいませ。

3) キアラさん、ノートは ここ です。

4) ええと、その えんぴつと けしゴムを 二つ下さい。それから、その ノートと あの まんがも 下さい。

■ 会話(かいわ) Dialogue

REMINDER: You may see some kanji / vocabulary you do not recognize. Use the context to try to understand the meanings of those parts of the dialogue.

1. じゅん　：　ここは　おちゃのみず　です。*本屋(ほんや)が　たくさん　あります。

2. 本屋(ほんや)の人(ひと)：　いらっしゃいませ。

3. じゅん　：　キアラさん、ノート(のーと)は　ここ　です。

4. キアラ(きあら)　：　ええと、その　えんぴつと　けしゴム(ごむ)を　二(ふた)つ　下(くだ)さい。
それから、その　ノート(のーと)と　あの　まんがも　下(くだ)さい。

*本屋(ほんや) – bookstore

■ 単語(たんご) New Words

1. えんぴつ (*n*)
2. こくばん (*n*)
3. ボールペン(ぼーるぺん) (*n*)
4. チョーク(ちょーく) (*n*)
5. ペン(ぺん) (*n*)
6. まんが (*n*)
7. けしゴム(ごむ) (*n*)
8. 水(みず) (*n*)
9. ノート(のーと) (*n*)
10. かばん (*n*)
11. バックパック(ばっくぱっく) (*n*)
12. したじき (*n*)
13. かみ (*n*)

ここ (*pron.*) – here

そこ (*pron.*) – there

あそこ (*pron.*) – over there

どこ (*inter.*) – where?

一(ひと)つ – 1 thing/object

二(ふた)つ – 2 things/objects

三(みっ)つ – 3 things/objects

四(よっ)つ – 4 things/objects

五(いつ)つ – 5 things/objects

六(むっ)つ – 6 things/objects

七(なな)つ – 7 things/objects

八(やっ)つ – 8 things/objects

九(ここの)つ – 9 things/objects

十(とお) – 10 things/objects

いくつ (*inter.*) – How many things/objects?

To help you remember how to count objects, listen to and learn the counting song on **TimeForJapanese.com**

■ 言葉の探索 Language Detection

1. General counters

一つ, 二つ, etc. are the counters for:

a. objects that do not have a particular shape (like erasers and bags)

b. objects that do not fit into any of the categories for counters (see the chart of counters in Appendix 1).

例 EXAMPLE

A) かばんを　二つ　下さい。 = Please give me two bags.

B) この　けしゴムを　三つ　どうぞ。 = Please have these three erasers.

While it is more common for the counter to follow the noun and the particle, as in the above two examples, the following pattern is also acceptable:

四つの　りんごを　下さい。　Please give me four apples.

2. ここ、そこ、あそこ、どこ

These words follow the same pattern as これ, それ, あれ, どれ but refer only to location (and not physical objects) and do not need to precede a noun.

ここ = here

そこ = there near the listener

あそこ = over there

どこ = Where?

A) けしゴムは　ここ　です。 = The eraser is here.

B) 本は　あそこ　です。 = The book is over there.

C) ベン君は　どこ　ですか。 = Where is Ben?

D) 妹さんは　そこ　ですか。 = Is your younger sister there?

3. も

も is a particle that means "also" or "too."

A) じゅん君は　日本人　です。 = Jun is Japanese.

B) 愛子さんも　日本人　です。 = Aiko is also Japanese.

C) 森本さんは　英語の　先生　です。 = Mr./Ms. Morimoto is an English teacher.

D) ブラウンさんも　英語の　先生　です。 = Mr./Ms. Brown is also an English teacher.

While "too" and "also" can fit many different places in an English sentence, in Japanese sentences the も will always come after the person or thing that it is modifying. For instance, in the first example above, 愛子 is being added from the first sentence to the second sentence, so the name 愛子 is followed by the particle も. In the second example above, Ms. Brown is being added to the first sentence and consequently is followed by particle も. Particle も **replaces** the particles は, が, and を.

■ 自習(じしゅう) Self Check

1. Fill in the blanks with Japanese according to the English translations.

えんぴつは ________________ です。 = The pencil is here.

________________ は ________________ です。 = The eraser is near you.

________________________________ = The notebook is over there.

________________________________ = The book is also over there. (use も)

________________________________ = Where is Tokyo?

■ 練習(れんしゅう)の時間(じかん) Time for Practice

1. Pair Practice

With a partner, count the number of backpacks in the classroom using 一(ひと)つ, 二(ふた)つ, etc. After you have done this, try to find other objects that do not have a particular shape and count them.

2. Pair Practice

Using the classroom object vocabulary in Appendix 4, ask your partner where objects or people are in the classroom. After you identify the location of one person or object, use the the new particle も to identify other things that are also in that location.

A- さん： 先生(せんせい)は どこ ですか。 = Where is the teacher?
B- さん： (*pointing*) 先生(せんせい)は あそこ です。 = The teacher is over there.
B- さん： じゅん君(くん)も あそこです。 = Jun is also over there.

3. Pair Practice

Using the list of Classroom Objects in Appendix 4 in the back of the book, practice asking your partner how to say things in Japanese and English as in the examples.

Asking for the Japanese:
A) Chair は 日本語(にほんご)で 何(なん)と 言(い)いますか。 = How do you say "chair" in Japanese?
B) Chair は 日本語(にほんご)で「いす」と 言(い)います。 = For "chair," in Japanese you say, "isu."

Asking for the English:
A) 鉛筆(えんぴつ)は 英語(えいご)で 何(なん)と 言(い)いますか。 = How do you say "enpitsu" in English?
B) 鉛筆(えんぴつ)は 英語(えいご)で「pencil」と 言(い)います。 = For "enpitsu," in English you say, "pencil."

■ キアラのジャーナル Kiara's Journal

Read the journal entry below, and then answer these questions.

❶ What means of transportation did Kiara and Jun use to get to Ocha-no-mizu?

❷ Why were they going there?

❸ Why did Jun want Kiara to try an Indian restaurant for dinner?

Dear Journal,

I went to a part of 東京 called お茶の水 today. We took the 山手 line and then transferred to the 総武 line to get there. Through the train windows we could see how different the various parts of 東京 are. It was much better than riding the subway and only seeing those ads on the station walls. One thing I realized is that 東京 is really crowded in some parts but not in others.

We headed to お茶の水 because Jun said there were lots of colleges and bookstores near there, and I needed to get supplies for school and a book about the history of 東京. I also wanted to get someまんが ^-^.

Later, we met up with じゅん君の 友達 Ben again for dinner in 六本木, an area of 東京 where many foreigners live. He and じゅん君 went to the same elementary school and he hopes to go to the same high school as じゅん君 next year. He seems like he's really smart and kind of cute too.

We went into an Indian restaurant where we each ordered a different kind of curry. It was really good but pretty spicy. I had to drink about five little glasses of 水 (water) to help cool my mouth down afterwards. For lunch, じゅん君 had taken me to a Japanese curry restaurant so that I could see the difference between the two types of curries.

■ 文化箱 Culture Chest

The Tokyo Subway

The map shows the Yamanote train line that circles Tokyo. The closest station to Jun's house is Ueno (上野).

How many stops did Kiara and Jun travel to get to Ochanomizu? Find the Shinjuku station on the map. It is one of the busiest stations in the world, with over 3 million people travelling through this station daily. It is a good place NOT to be during rush hour!

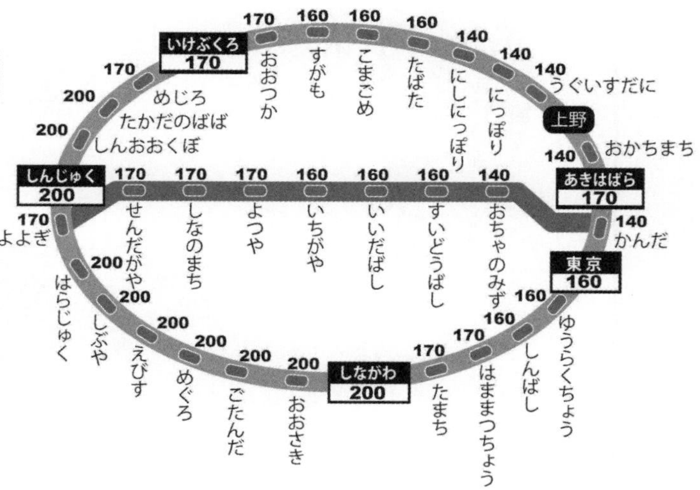

第2課の5

お母さん、晩ご飯は　何　ですか。
かあ　ばん　はん　なん

Mom, what's for dinner?

1.

1) ああ、私は おなかが、ぺこぺこ です。

2) 僕も ペコペコ です。お母さん、ばんごはんは 何 ですか。

2.

3) たこ ですよ～。

3.

4) たこ？！

4.

5) あいちゃん、お父さん、ばんごはんですよ！

6) はい！

5.

7) はい、たこ です。どうぞ。

8) これが たこ？

■ 会話(かいわ) Dialogue

REMINDER: You may see some kanji / vocabulary you do not recognize. Use the context to try to understand the meanings of those parts of the dialogue.

1. キアラ(きあら) ： ああ、私は　おなかが、ペコペコ(ぺこぺこ)　です。
2. じゅん ： 僕(ぼく)も　ペコペコ(ぺこぺこ)　です。お母さん、ばんごはんは　何(なん)　ですか。
3. まゆみ ： たこ　ですよ。
4. キアラ(きあら) ： たこ？！
5. まゆみ ： あいちゃん、お父(とう)さん、ばんごはん　ですよ！
6. 愛子(あいこ) & 太郎(たろう) ： はい！
7. まゆみ ： はい，たこ　です。どうぞ。
8. キアラ(きあら) ： これが　たこ？

■ 単語(たんご) New Words

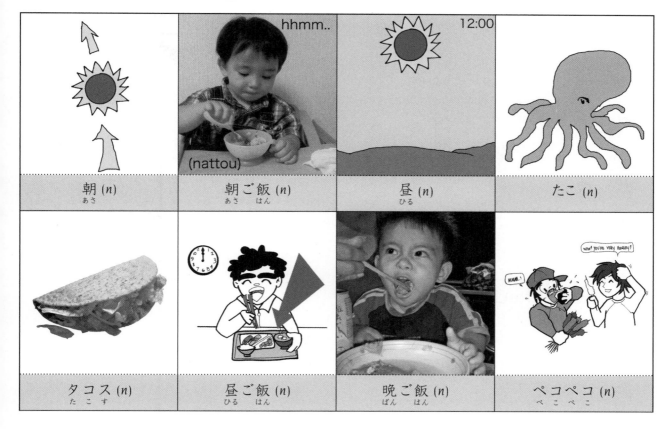

 朝(あさ) (*n*)	 朝(あさ)ご飯(はん) (*n*)	 昼(ひる) (*n*)	 たこ (*n*)
 タコス(たこす) (*n*)	 昼(ひる)ご飯(はん) (*n*)	 晩(ばん)ご飯(はん) (*n*)	 ペコペコ(ぺこぺこ) (*n*)

仕事(しごと) (*n*) – job, occupation　　ああ (*interj.*) – Ah!, Oh!

■ 言葉(ことば)の探索(たんさく) Language Detection

1. Homonyms

The Japanese language contains fewer sounds than English. This results in many more homonyms, words that sound the same but have different meanings. Some examples of English homonyms are *too–two–to, which–witch, read–red*, etc. Homonyms in Japanese may have the same pronunciation but will use different kanji. For example, 箸(はし) - chopsticks, 橋(はし) - bridge, and 端(はし) - edge; another example is 紙(かみ) - paper, 髪(かみ) - hair, and 神(かみ) - gods.

Many Japanese homonyms have subtle differences in intonation such as raised or lowered pitch and therefore are not pure homonyms in the English sense. The best way to distinguish between homonyms in spoken Japanese is to pay attention to the context, both by listening to and watching the situation closely. In written Japanese, the different meanings for homonyms are made clear through the different kanji and/or context.

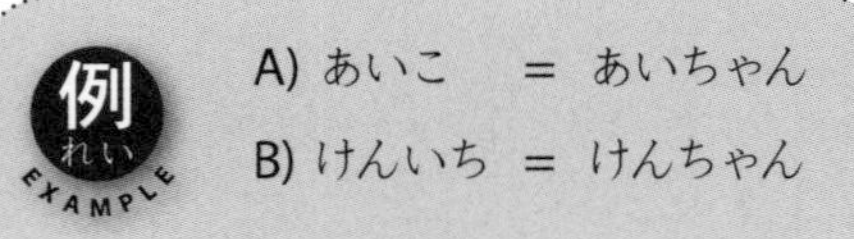

例
れい
EXAMPLE
A) あいこ = あいちゃん
B) けんいち = けんちゃん

2. Abbreviating names in Japanese

Japanese people often shorten the names of small children, family members, and friends to indicate familiarity. The suffix ~ちゃん(~CHAN) can replace the more polite suffix ~さん(~SAN). ~ちゃん(~CHAN) is used often with females younger than the speaker and for very young boys, but it can be used with the name of anybody you are very close to.

3. Mimetic or onomatopoeic words - ぎたい語(ご)

Expressions or words that mimic sounds associated with a thing or action are called onomatopoeia. Japanese has many such expressions.

A) ペコペコ (ぺこぺこ) = your stomach growling

B) ゴロゴロ (ごろごろ) = the sound of something rolling; this also refers to the action (or lack there of) of being a "couch potato."

C) ペラペラ (ぺらぺら) = to speak fluently

■ 自習(じしゅう) Self Check

1. Homonyms

Can you guess which of these two kanji for AME means *rain* and which means *candy*?

a. 飴(あめ)　　　b. 雨(あめ)

If at the beginning of your class your teacher says, 「かみを 出(だ)して 下(くだ)さい。」, which of the three meanings of かみ is meant?

a. god　　　b. paper　　　c. hair

2. Abbreviating names

Pretend that the following are family members or close friends. Think of a pet name to show that you are close to them.

a. 真一 (しんいち)　b. 祥子 (しょうこ)　c. 健一 (けんいち)　d. 大輔 (だいすけ)　e. 祐介 (ゆうすけ)

3. Mimetic or onomatopoeic words - ぎたい語 (ご)

Can you match the ぎたい語 expression with its meaning?

1. プンプン (ぷんぷん)	3. ピカピカ (ぴかぴか)	a. shining	c. smiling
2. ツルツル (つるつる)	4. ニコニコ (にこにこ)	b. being angry	d. slippery

■ 練習の時間 (れんしゅうのじかん) Time for Practice

1. Pair Practice

With a partner, shorten and add ちゃん to the names of the students in your class to come up with "cute" new names for everyone.

2. Small Group Practice

Practice asking who your partner's friends are. Take turns asking in Japanese. In your answers, try to shorten your friends' names and add ちゃん.

A- さん：友達 (ともだち) は　だれ　ですか。 = Who are your friends?

B- さん：友達 (ともだち) は　マー (まー) ちゃんと　ジェイ君 (じぇいくん)　です。 = My friends are Maa and Jei.

■ 文化箱 (ぶんかばこ) Culture Chest

Tokyo Neighborhoods

Tokyo is a city of neighborhoods. You have already read a little about Hiroo, Ochanomizu, and Roppongi. These are just a few of the many neighborhoods in Tokyo. Each neighborhood has a different feel. Here are some other famous areas of Tokyo:

- Ginza is a chic and trendy part of the city with top quality shops and the city's Kabuki theater.
- Akihabara has a high concentration of electronic stores. One of the few places in Japan where it's OK to bargain for what you buy!
- Harajuku is the place to watch crazy modern fashion trends of the young, especially on Sundays.

Many foreigners find Tokyo to be a comfortable city in which to live, despite its being one of the largest cities in the world. Perhaps this is because with so many neighborhoods to choose from, most people can find something to their liking.

Dear お母さん、

I arrived in 東京 a few days ago in the late afternoon. I've had a fantastic time so far! じゅん君 is a really nice guy. He's a year younger in school so he won't be in any of my classes when I start in two days, but he's introducing me to a lot of other kids who will be. Last night we met an Australian named Ben. Ben's been living here since he was six.

His お母さん works for the Australian Embassy here and his お父さん works for an export company. His Japanese is amazing and he knows a lot about Japanese history. I haven't learned that much about Japanese history yet, but I want to. And I don't know if I'll be as fluent in Japanese as he is after my year here, but I'm going to try!

I went with my new 友達(ともだち) to a part of the city called 六本木(ろっぽんぎ). There are a lot of international restaurants there. Ben wanted to take us to his favorite Indian restaurant. I had Japanese curry for lunch and they wanted to take me to an Indian restaurant for dinner, so I could compare the two types of curry. Both were good, in very different ways. Have you had both? Which is your favorite?

Schools here in 日本 are getting ready to start their second trimester of the school year, which is why everyone already knows their classmates. My first day is coming up soon, so while we were out today, we stopped by a stationery shop. I bought 鉛筆(えんぴつ)、下敷き(したじき)、ノート(のーと)、消しゴム(けしごむ)、and a 鞄(かばん). We also went to a clothing store so that I could buy my school 制服(せいふく). The 制服 that I have to wear is kind of cute, but I'm not sure how much I'll like wearing a uniform all of the time. The good thing is that it is versatile: the girls' uniforms come with a light jacket, as well as athletic clothes for gym class and for wearing after school. And it's kind of nice not to have to worry about what to wear every day.

Well お母さん、I have to go. E-mail 下(くだ)さい！Tell everyone else こんにちは！

Love, or as they would say in Japan, 大好(だいす)きです！

キアラ(きあら)

■ 単語チェックリスト New Word Checklist

たんごちぇっくりすと

2-1

かぞく・家族 *n* family (my)
なん/なに・何 *inter.* what
だれ *inter.* who
しゃしん・写真 *n* photograph
いぬ・犬 *n* dog
ねこ・猫 *n* cat
でんわ・電話 *n* telephone
ごかぞく・ご家族 *n* someone else's family
しょうかい・紹介 する *v* to introduce
しょうかい してください・紹介 して下さい *v* introduce (please)
あね・姉 *n* older sister (my)
あに・兄 *n* older brother (my)
おとうと・弟 *n* younger brother (my)
いもうと・妹 *n* younger sister (my)
きょうだい・兄弟 *n* siblings
そふ・祖父 *n* grandfather (my)
そぼ・祖母 *n* grandmother (my)
いる/います *v* to exist [animate beings]
ある/あります *v* to exist [inanimate things]
の *part.*
いちばんうえの あに/あね・一番上の兄/姉 *n* oldest brother/sister (my)
にばんめの あに/あね・二番目の兄/姉 *n* second oldest brother/sister (my)
すぐしたの おとうと/いもうと・すぐ下の 弟/妹 *n* next youngest brother/sister (my)
いちばんしたの おとうと/いもうと・一番下の 弟/妹 *n* youngest brother/sister (my)
ぎりの〜 step-
いち 一 *count.* one
に・二 *count.* two
さん・三 *count.* three
よん/し・四 *count.* four
ご・五 *count.* five
ろく・六 *count.* six
しち/なな・七 *count.* seven
はち・八 *count.* eight
く/きゅう・九 *count.* nine
じゅう・十 *count.* ten
いくつ *inter.* how many (things)?
ひとり・一人 *count.* one person
ふたり・二人 *count.* two people
さんにん・三人 *count.* three people
よにん・四人 *count.* four people
ごにん・五人 *count.* five people
ろくにん・六人 *count.* six people
しち/ななにん・七人 *count.* seven people
はちにん・八人 *count.* eight people
きゅうにん・九人 *count.* nine people
じゅうにん・十人 *count.* ten people
なんにん・何人 *inter.* how many people

2-2

おとうさん・お父さん *n* father (someone else's)
おかあさん・お母さん *n* mother (someone else's)
おにいさん・お兄さん *n* older brother (someone else's)
おねえさん・お姉さん *n* older sister (someone else's)
おとうとさん・弟さん *n* younger brother (someone else's)
いもうとさん・妹さん *n* younger sister (someone else's)
おばあさん *n* grandmother (someone else's)
おばさん *n* aunt or woman quite a bit older than you
おじいさん *n* grandfather (someone else's)
おじさん *n* uncle or man quite a bit older than you
いえ/うち・家 *n* house, home
ひと・人 *n* person
と *part.*
しつれいします。・失礼します。 *exp.* excuse me; I'm sorry to bother you.
ともだち・友達 *n* friend
じゅういち・十一 *count.* eleven
じゅうに・十二 *count.* twelve
じゅうさん・十三 *count.* thirteen
じゅうよん/じゅうし・十四 *count.* fourteen
じゅうご・十五 *count.* fifteen
じゅうろく・十六 *count.* sixteen
じゅうなな/じゅうしち・十七 *count.* seventeen
じゅうはち・十八 *count.* eighteen
じゅうく/じゅうきゅう・十九 *count.* nineteen
にじゅう・二十 *count.* twenty
にじゅういち・二十一 *count.* twenty-one
さんじゅう・三十 *count.* thirty
よんじゅう・四十 *count.* forty
ごじゅう・五十 *count.* fifty
ろくじゅう・六十 *count.* sixty
ななじゅう・七十 *count.* seventy
はちじゅう・八十 *count.* eighty
きゅうじゅう・九十 *count.* ninety
ひゃく・百 *count.* one hundred

2-3

この this (thing)
その that (thing)
あの that (thing) over there

どの *inter.* which (thing)
ぼうし *n* hat/cap
てぃーしゃつ・Tシャツ *n* t-shirt
きゃんでぃ/あめ・キャンディ/飴 *n* candy/sweets
ありがとう *exp.* thanks
どうも ありがとう *exp.* thank you
どうも ありがとう ございます *exp.* thank you very much
どういたしまして *exp.* you are welcome
おみやげ・お土産 *n* souvenir(s)
あめ・飴 *n* candy/sweets
を *part.* used after the direct object
へ *part.* either of these can be used to mean "to" and comes after a place of destination
に *part.* particle after a place word to mean "to" before a verb of motion (similar to the particle へ)

2-4

えんぴつ 鉛筆 *n* pencil
こくばん・黒板 *n* blackboard
ぼーるぺん・ボールペン *n* ballpoint pen
ちょーく・チョーク *n* chalk
ぺん・ペン *n* pen
まんが・漫画 *n* Japanese comics
けしごむ・消しゴム *n* eraser
みず・水 *n* water
のーと・ノート *n* notebook
かばん・鞄 *n* briefcase, bag
ばっくぱっく・バックパック *n* backpack
したじき・下敷き *n* writing pad, mat
かみ・紙 *n* paper
ここ *pron.* here
そこ *pron.* there
あそこ *pron.* over there
どこ *inter.* where?
ひとつ・一つ *count.* one (thing)
ふたつ・二つ *count.* two (things)
みっつ・三つ *count.* three (things)
よっつ・四つ *count.* four (things)
いつつ・五つ *count.* five (things)
むっつ・六つ *count.* six (things)
ななつ・七つ *count.* seven (things)
やっつ・八つ *count.* eight (things)
ここのつ・九つ *count.* nine (things)
とお・十 *count.* ten (things)
いくつ *inter.* how many (things)?

2-5

あさ・朝 *n* morning
あさごはん・朝ご飯 *n* breakfast
ひる・昼 *n* daytime, noon
たこ *n* octopus
たこす・タコス *n* tacos (Mexican)
ひるごはん・昼ご飯 *n* lunch
ばんごはん・晩ご飯 *n* dinner, evening meal
ぺこぺこ・ペコペコ hunger, mimetic expression for
しごと・仕事 *n* job, occupation
ああ *interj.* Ah!, Oh!

The Ins and Outs of Schools in Japan

第3課

Learning and Performance Goals

This chapter will enable you to:

A) talk about your school, classes, and grades
B) talk about what happens in a typical Japanese school day
C) compare two situations using "but"
D) engage in basic small talk about the weather
E) say that things do or do not exist and talk about things that you have or do not have
F) use direct objects appropriately in statements and questions
G) use time words to talk about the past, present, and future
H) use 28 additional kanji
I) use the "can-do" chart found on **TimeForJapanese.com** to chart your progress for what you "can-do" for each chapter

第3課の1 いいえ、小学校(しょうがっこう)は　ありません。
No, there is no elementary school.

■ 会話(かいわ) Dialogue 

REMINDER: You may see some kanji / vocabulary you do not recognize. Use the context to try to understand the meanings of those parts of the dialogue.

1. じゅん： 中学校(ちゅうがっこう)は　ここ　です。高校(こうこう)は　あそこ　です。

2. キアラ(きあら)： 大学(だいがく)は　ありますか。

3. じゅん： はい、私の　友達の　お兄(にい)さんの　大学(だいがく)が　あります。

4. キアラ(きあら)： 小学校(しょうがっこう)は　ありますか。

5. じゅん： いいえ、小学校(しょうがっこう)は　ありません。

6. じゅん： キアラ(きあら)さんは　高校(こうこう)　二年生(ねんせい)　ですね。僕(ぼく)は　一年生(ねんせい)　です。
じゃあ、学校(がっこう)に　*はいりましょう。

7. キアラ(きあら)： はい、はいりましょう。

8. じゅん： あっ！くつは　だめ　です！

9. キアラ(きあら)： すみません！

10. キアラ(きあら)： きょうしつは　どこ　ですか。

11. じゅん： ２の３は　あそこ　です。先生(せんせい)も　あそこに　います。

12. じゅん： こちらは　山本先生(やまもとせんせい)　です。英語(えいご)の　先生(せんせい)　です。

13. キアラ(きあら)： 初(はじ)めまして。私は　キアラ(きあら)　です。どうぞ　よろしく　おねがいします。

14. 山本(やまもと)： ああ、キアラ(きあら)さん　ですか。初(はじ)めまして。どうぞ　よろしく。
ここに　すわって　下(くだ)さい。

*はいりましょう – let's enter/go into

■ 単語(たんご) New Words 

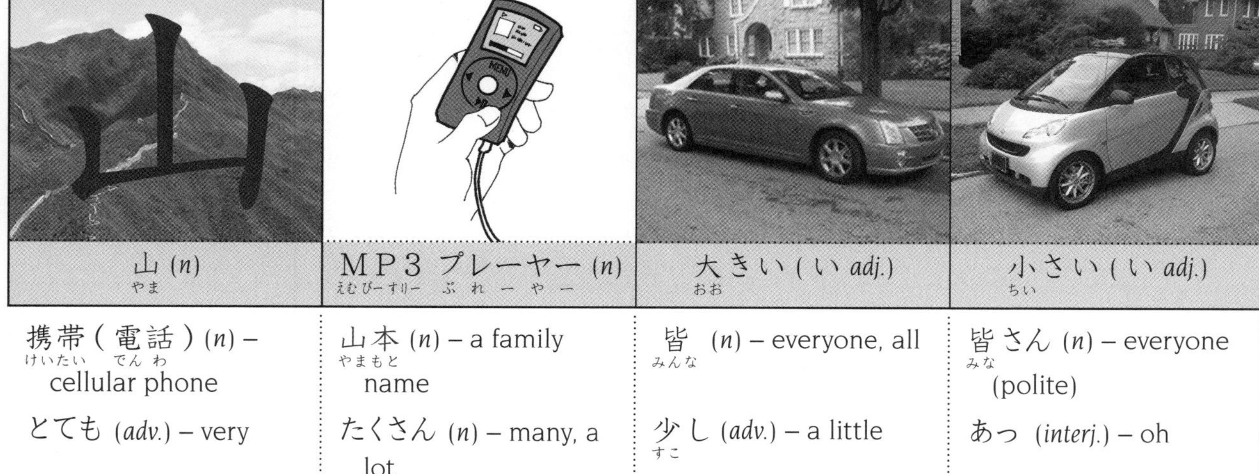

山(やま) (*n*)	MP3 プレーヤー(えむぴーすりー ぷれーやー) (*n*)	大(おお)きい (い *adj.*)	小(ちい)さい (い *adj.*)
携帯(けいたい) (電話(でんわ)) (*n*) – cellular phone	山本(やまもと) (*n*) – a family name	皆(みんな) (*n*) – everyone, all	皆(みな)さん (*n*) – everyone (polite)
とても (*adv.*) – very	たくさん (*n*) – many, a lot	少(すこ)し (*adv.*) – a little	あっ (*interj.*) – oh

何年生 (なんねんせい) (*inter.*) – What year/grade?

小学一年生 (しょうがくいちねんせい) (*n*) – elementary school first grader

小学二年生 (しょうがくにねんせい) (*n*) – elementary school second grader

小学三年生 (しょうがくさんねんせい) (*n*) – elementary school third grader

小学四年生 (しょうがくよんねんせい) (*n*) – elementary school fourth grader

小学五年生 (しょうがくごねんせい) (*n*) – elementary school fifth grader

小学六年生 (しょうがくろくねんせい) (*n*) – elementary school sixth grader

中学一年生 (ちゅうがくいちねんせい) (*n*) – middle school, first year student (7th grader)

中学二年生 (ちゅうがくにねんせい) (*n*) – middle school, second year student (8th grader)

中学三年生 (ちゅうがくさんねんせい) (*n*) – middle school, third year student (9th grader)

高校一年生 (こうこういちねんせい) (*n*) – high school, first year student (10th grader)

高校二年生 (こうこうにねんせい) (*n*) – high school, second year student (11th grader)

高校三年生 (こうこうさんねんせい) (*n*) – high school, third year student (12th grader)

大学一年生 (だいがくいちねんせい) (*n*) – first year college/university student

■ 漢字 (かんじ) Kanji

高 (10 strokes)	コウ (こう); たか(い) – tall, expensive, high	丶	亠	亠	宀	古	声	高
	高(校) (こうこう) – high school; 高(い) (たか) – tall, expensive, high	高	高	高				
	This looks like the TALL pagodas found all over East Asia. Many of these TALL pagodas would also be quite EXPENSIVE to build.							

小 (3 strokes)	ショウ (しょう); ちい(さい) – small	亅	小	小				
	小(学校) (しょうがっこう) – elementary school; 小(さい) (ちい) – small							
	This is a drawing of a person pulling his/her arms down and closer to his/her body, so as to appear SMALLer.							

中 4 strokes	チュウ；なか – middle, inside ちゅう	丨	冂	口	中			
	中(学校) – middle school; 中 – medium; ちゅう がっこう　　ちゅう 中 – middle, inside なか							
	One stroke divides this character right down the MIDDLE.							
大 3 strokes	ダイ；おお(きい) – big, large だい	一	ナ	大				
	大 – big, large; 大(きい) – big, large; だい　おお 大(学) – college, university だい がく							
	This is a drawing of a person with arms stretched out to appear BIG or LARGE.							
学 8 strokes	ガク – to learn がく	丶	丷	⺍	⺍	𭕄	𭕄	学
	学(校) – school; (中)学(生) – middle school student がく こう　ちゅう がく せい	学						
	This character is a child (子) under a roof with large drops of "LEARNing" pouring down into the child's head through the roof of the SCHOOL.							
校 10 strokes	コウ – school (related to the facilities of a school) こう	一	十	才	木	木'	杧	杧
	(学)校 – school; (高)校 – high school student がく こう　こう こう	杧	杪	校				
	Tree/wood (木) and a father (父) wearing a top hat (strokes 5 and 6). Years ago a SCHOOL was often no more than a wooden building where a father put on a top hat to teach. き　ちち							
年 6 strokes	ネン；とし – year ねん	ノ	𠂉	仁	午	𠆢	年	
	(何)年 – what year?; (何)年(生) – what grade?; (今)年 – this year なん ねん　なん ねん せい　こ とし							
	The best way to remember this is through repetition by writing the year on all homework and tests from now on. For example: 1492 年, 1967 年 ...							
先 6 strokes	セン – earlier, previous, future せん	ノ	𠂉	牛	生	𭃂	先	
	先(生) – teacher; 先(週) – last week せん せい　せん しゅう							
	This kanji is a picture of a very big pot of earth (土) with a small sprout planted EARLIER, growing on the left. It is being carried by a MASTER gardener whose legs can be seen below the tray.							

生 (5 strokes)	セイ (sei) – life; う（まれる）– to be born	ノ	𠂉	牛	牛	生		
	（先(せん)）生(せい) – teacher; （何年(なんねん)）生(せい) – what grade?							
	The earth/soil（ 土 ）is the basis of LIFE. This kanji has a new branch, just BORN, near the top.							

山 (3 strokes)	～サン(さん) – Mt. ~; やま – mountain	丨	山	山				
	（富士(ふじ)）山(さん) – Mt. Fuji;（大(おお)きい）山(やま) – big mountain							
	This is a primitive drawing of a MOUNTAIN.							

■ 言葉(ことば)の探索(たんさく) Language Detection

1. いません/ありません - does not exist

To change these verbs (います/あります) from the affirmative to the negative, change the ~ます ending to ~ません. When affirmative statements are made with ~います/あります where people or things exist or are possessed, you use the particle が after the subject. When you make negative statements with いません/ありません, you *often* use は after the subject.

あります - exists (for inanimate objects) ⇨ ありません - (does not exist)
います - exists (for animate objects) ⇨ いません - (does not exist)

A) あそこに　小学校(しょうがっこう)が　あります。でも　中学校(ちゅうがっこう)は　ありません。
= There is an elementary school over there. But there is no middle school over there.

B) 犬(いぬ)が　います。でも　ねこは　いません。= There is a dog. But there is no cat.

C) 中学校(ちゅうがっこう)が　あります。でも　高校(こうこう)は　ありません。
= There is a junior high school. But there is no high school.

2. 大(おお)きい / 小(ちい)さい (adjectives) and とても / 少(すこ)し (adverbs) - The basics of using them

Use the following pattern to use adjectives and/or adverbs to make basic A=B or A は B です sentences. The adjective or adverb quite often comes after the は. Adjectives and adverbs do not have particles which follow them. There are some special cases you will learn later, however this is generally the rule to follow. (その学校(がっこう)はとても大(おお)きいです。That school is very big.)

Topic (A) は + adverb + adjective (B) です。

A) 私の　学校(がっこう)は　大(おお)きい　です。 = My school is big.

B) 私の　ぼうしは　少(すこ)し　小(ちい)さい　です。 = My hat is a little small.

C) じゅん君(くん)の　バックパック(ばっくぱっく)は　とても　大(おお)きい　です。 = Jun's backpack is very big.

D) そのノート(のーと)は　大(おお)きいですね。 = That notebook is big, isn't it?

■ 自習(じしゅう) Self Check

1. Say the following out loud to yourself in Japanese. Use affirmative and negative variations of あります and います "to exist" as needed.

A) There is no junior high school. ⇨ 中学校(ちゅうがっこう)は ________________。

B) There are two second year students. ⇨ 二年生(ねんせい)が 二人(ふたり) ________________。

C) There is no high school. ⇨ ________________。

D) There are four siblings. ⇨ ________________。

E) I have 4 friends. ⇨ ________________。

F) There is no cat. ⇨ ________________。

G) There are a pencil and 2 erasers over there. ⇨ ________________。

2. Say the following out loud to yourself in Japanese. Include the words for *big*, *small*, *a little*, and *very* as needed.

A) My Japanese class is large. ⇨ 私の 日本語の クラス(くらす)は ________________ です。

B) My eraser is small. ⇨ 私の けしゴム(ごむ)は ________________ です。

C) Takeshi's dog is a little small. ⇨ ________________。

D) Miki's university is very large. ⇨ ________________。

E) My friend's school is very small. ⇨ ________________。

■ 練習(れんしゅう)の時間(じかん) Time for Practice

1. Pair Practice

Use objects on your desk, in the classroom, and in the pictures below for this activity. Take turns using Japanese to ask if each of the objects exists or not (on the desk or in the room). Answer the questions using あります／ありません or います/いません. (NOTE: Use the particle は in questions about existence.)

A- さん：ぼうしは ありますか。		= Do you have a hat?/Is there a hat?
B- さん：はい、ぼうしが あります。		= Yes, I have a hat./Yes, there is a hat.
-OR-	いいえ、ぼうしは ありません。	= No, I don't have a hat./No, there is no hat.

2. Pair Practice

Compare this list of people with the picture of Kiara's family. Using your Japanese, take turns stating whether these people are in the picture with Kiara's family or not. Use います/いません. (NOTE: は (wa) is the particle used in the question.)

A- さん： お父さんは　いますか？ = Is father here?
B- さん： はい、います。 = Yes, he is (here).
-OR- いいえ、いません。 = No, he is not (here).

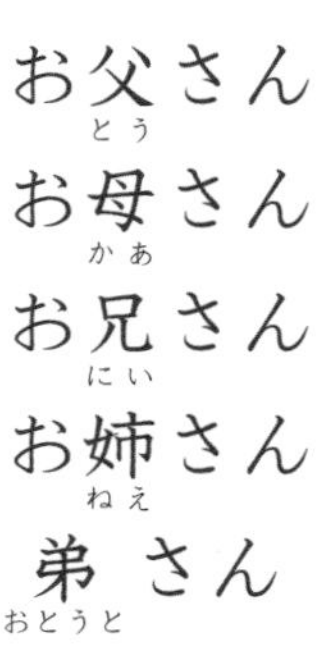

お父(とう)さん
お母(かあ)さん
お兄(にい)さん
お姉(ねえ)さん
弟(おとうと)さん

妹(いもうと)さん
おばあさん
おばさん
おじいさん
おじさん

3. Pair Practice

Following the examples below, use 小さい, 大きい, とても, and 少(すこ)し to talk about people's sizes starting first with Kiara's family above and then talking about your family members and friends. Be nice!

キアラ(きあら)さんの　妹(いもうと)さんは　とても　小(ちい)さい　です。 = Kiara's younger sister is very small.
父(ちち)は　少(すこ)し　大(おお)きい　です。 = My father is a little big (tall).

*NOTE: that when Japanese say that someone is 大きい、 they usually mean tall or large, not fat.

4. Interview Practice

Make a 2-column chart on a piece of scrap paper. Title the first column 名前(なまえ) and the other 年生(ねんせい). Interview at least five classmates. Ask each his/her name and what grade he/she is in and record that information on your chart, in English. When everyone has finished interviewing, use your Japanese to report the grade level of one of your interviewees to the class.

A: お名前(なまえ)は　何(なん)　ですか。 = What is your name?
B: Chelsea(ちぇるしー)　です。 = It is Chelsea.
A: Chelsea(ちぇるしー) さん、何年生(なんねんせい)　ですか。 = Chelsea, what year are you?
B: 高校二年生(こうこうにねんせい)　です。 = (I'm a) 2nd year high school student.
A: はい、分(わ)かりました。 = Oh, I understand.
-OR- ああ、そうですか。 = Oh, really?

■ 文化箱(ぶんかばこ) Culture Chest

School System

Japan has a variety of public and private schools. Students in Japan almost all go through twelve years of public or private education and most advance to some type of post-secondary education. Typical schools are organized as follows:

Elementary School: 6 years
Junior High School: 3 years
High School: 3 years

Most students also go to nursery school (保育園(ほいくえん)) and kindergarten (幼稚園(ようちえん)). During their ninth year of school (中学三年生(ちゅうがくさんねんせい)), students are busy studying for entrance examinations to get into the high school of their choice. Similarly, during their twelfth year of school (高校三年生(こうこうさんねんせい)), students must study for the college entrance exams. In their last year of junior high and in their last year of high school, students are often expected to focus their time on working to pass these exams. This is why it is rare for high school students to have part-time jobs, or even to be involved in other activities outside of schoolwork during their last year of high school. Students even eliminate their club activities during their final year of high school to provide more time for exam preparation. Parents generally feel that the student's main "job" is to successfully pass the entrance exams for high school and then for college or university.

Many Japanese students go to じゅく (cram schools) for extra study and practice for these entrance exams. Some students even start attending じゅく as early as elementary school. Many families feel that the amount of time and money spent preparing for entrance exams is worth it, since Japanese society places much social status on the high school and college one attends. One benefit of this system for students is that their parents care so much about this exam that many high schoolers have almost no chores to do at home while they are preparing for the exams!

■ キアラ(きあら)のジャーナル(じゃーなる) Kiara's Journal 

Read the journal entry below, and then answer these questions.

❶ What grade levels are in high schools in Japan?
❷ Where did Kiara's teacher study English?
❸ Describe Kiara's school.

Dear Journal,

We had our first day of school today. To get to our 学校(がっこう), we had to change trains twice, and then walk about five blocks. It took about thirty minutes. At home, I usually ride the school bus, but じゅん君(くん) said that they don't use school buses in Japan.

小学校(しょうがっこう) consists of 一年生(ねんせい)から 六年生(ねんせい)、中学校(ちゅうがっこう)は grades 7-9 or 中学(ちゅうがく)一年生(ねんせい)から 中学三年生(ねんせい), as they are called. 高校(こうこう) is grades 10-12 or 高校一年生から 高校(こうこう)三年生(ねんせい). Since 高校 is not mandatory, everyone who attends 高校 in Japan has to pass an entrance exam in order to be accepted. Nearly everyone in the entire country goes to 高校. It's a lot different from home, where it is easy to enter 高校. ベン君 is still a 中学生. ベン君は 中学三年生です。じゅん君(くん)は 高校一年生です。私は 高校二年生です。

My homeroom teacher, 山本先生(やまもとせんせい), is really kind. He's from 横浜(よこはま) and travels almost an hour every day to get to this 高校. He is one of the English teachers here. He studied at 東京大学(とうきょうだいがく), one of the best and oldest universities in Japan. Right after college, he lived in New Zealand for one year, so he speaks English with a New Zealand accent. I never really thought about how many different kinds of accents there are just in my own language.

この 高校は とても 大きい です。It's three stories tall, like most schools, complete with a こい pond in the middle of the courtyard. I think I'm going to like going out there to draw. My homeroom's on the first floor, and I stay in that one room most of the day. In Japan, teachers move from classroom to classroom more than the students do. Each teacher has a desk in the large faculty room next to the principal's office, and they usually carry their things around with them from classroom to classroom like students do in the U.S.

After classes, we all had to clean the floors, blackboard, and the hallway outside of our room, empty the trash can, and clean up part of the schoolyard. My 先生 in the U.S. told me about this, but I thought that it was a joke! It wasn't too bad, though; I actually enjoyed getting a bit of exercise in the afternoon.

社会(しゃかい)と　音楽(おんがく)と　英語(えいご)が　あります。

You will have social studies, music and English.

1

2)おはよう。

1)先生、おはようございます。

2

3) 今日の スケジュールを おしえて下さい。

3

4)はい。学校は 八時から です。今日は、社会と 国語と 体育と 美術と 音楽と 英語が あります。しつもんは ありますか。

4

5) はい、あります。明日の　スケジュールと 今日の スケジュールは ちがいますね。スケジュールは 毎日 ちがいますか。

5

6) 時間割 ですか。ええ、毎日ちがいます。

■ 会話(かいわ) Dialogue

REMINDER: You may see some kanji / vocabulary you do not recognize. Use the context to try to understand the meanings of those parts of the dialogue.

1. キアラ(きあら)　：　先生、おはよう　ございます。
2. 山本(やまもと)先生：　おはよう。
3. キアラ(きあら)　：　今日(きょう)の　スケジュール(すけじゅーる)を　*おしえて　下(くだ)さい。
4. 山本(やまもと)先生：　はい。学校は　八時(はちじ)　から　です。今日(きょう)は、社会(しゃかい)と　国語(こくご)と　体育(たいいく)と　美術(びじゅつ)と　音楽(おんがく)と　英語(えいご)が　あります。しつもんは　ありますか。
5. キアラ(きあら)　：　はい、あります。明日(あした)の　スケジュール(すけじゅーる)と　今日(きょう)の　スケジュール(すけじゅーる)は　違(ちが)いますね。スケジュール(すけじゅーる)は　毎日(まいにち)　違(ちが)いますか。
6. 山本(やまもと)先生：　時間割(じかんわり)　ですか。ええ、毎日(まいにち)　違(ちが)います。

* おしえて　下(くだ)さい – please teach (tell) me

■ 単語(たんご) New Words

スケジュール(すけじゅーる) (*n*)	 授業(じゅぎょう) or クラス(くらす) (*n*)	 教室(きょうしつ) (*n*)	英語(えいご) (*n*)	国語(こくご) (*n*)
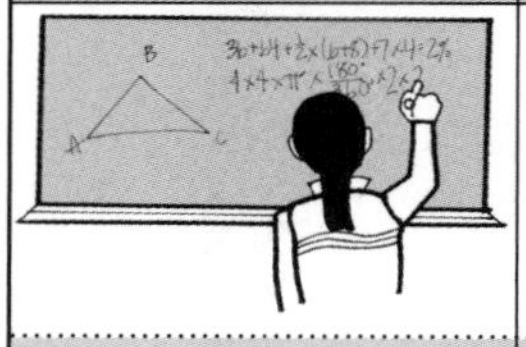 数学(すうがく) (*n*)	 科学(かがく) (*n*)	 体育(たいいく) (*n*)	 美術(びじゅつ) (*n*)	 音楽(おんがく) (*n*)
 ホームルーム(ほーむるーむ) (*n*)	 昼休(ひるやす)み (*n*) (昼(ひる)ご飯(はん))	 宿題(しゅくだい) (*n*)	小(しょう)テスト(てすと) (*n*)	 テスト(てすと) (*n*)
 試験(しけん) (*n*)	作文(さくぶん) (*n*)	 楽(たの)しい (い *adj.*)	 難(むずか)しい (い *adj.*)	科目(かもく) (*n*) – subject, course 社会(しゃかい) (*n*) – social studies

Hours and Minutes

一時	いちじ	1:00
二時	にじ	2:00
三時	さんじ	3:00
四時	よじ	4:00
五時	ごじ	5:00
六時	ろくじ	6:00
七時*	しちじ or ななじ (if clarifying)	7:00
八時*	はちじ	8:00
九時*	くじ	9:00
十時	じゅうじ	10:00
十一時	じゅういちじ	11:00
十二時	じゅうにじ	12:00
何時 (*inter.*)	なんじ	what time?

一分	いっぷん	: 01
二分	にふん	: 02
三分	さんぷん	: 03
四分	よんぷん	: 04
五分	ごふん	: 05
六分	ろっぷん	: 06
七分	ななふん	: 07
八分	はっぷん	: 08
九分	きゅうふん	: 09
十分	じゅっぷん	: 10
十一分	じゅういっぷん	: 11
十二分	じゅうにふん	: 12
十三分	じゅうさんぷん	: 13
二十分	にじゅっぷん	: 20
二十一分	にじゅういっぷん	: 21
四十三分	よんじゅうさんぷん	: 43
何分 (*inter.*)	なんぷん	how many minutes?

* Note the pronunciations for 4 o'clock, 9 o'clock, and 7 minutes as well as the special note for 7 o'clock.

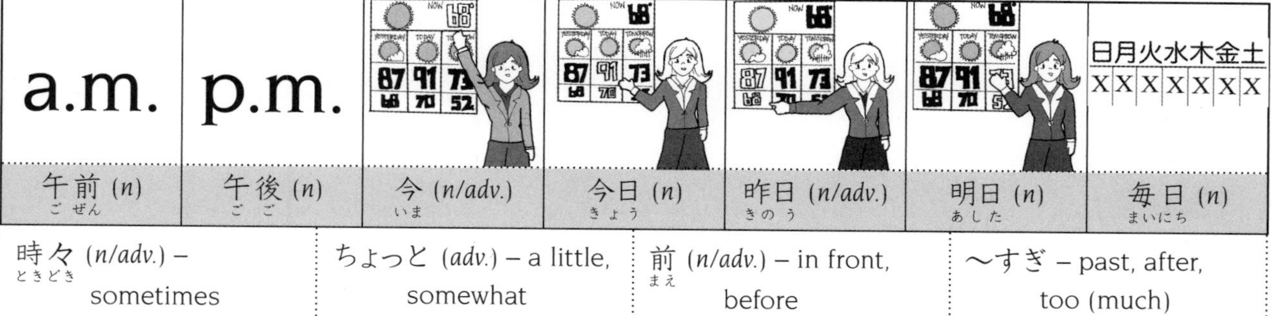

午前 (*n*) ごぜん	午後 (*n*) ごご	今 (*n/adv.*) いま	今日 (*n*) きょう	昨日 (*n/adv.*) きのう	明日 (*n*) あした	毎日 (*n*) まいにち

時々 ときどき (*n/adv.*) – sometimes

〜ごろ / ころ – about

ちょっと (*adv.*) – a little, somewhat

から (*part.*) – from

前 まえ (*n/adv.*) – in front, before

〜はん (*n*) – half hour

〜すぎ – past, after, too (much)

Other words you might like to use:

生物学 (*n*)	せいぶつがく	biology
保健体育 (*n*)	ほけんたいいく	health (class)
家庭科 (*n*)	かていか	family consumer science
歴史 (*n*)	れきし	history
アメリカ史 (*n*)	あめりかし	American history
日本史 (*n*)	し	Japanese history
世界史 (*n*)	せかいし	world history
経済学 (*n*)	けいざいがく	economics
心理学 (*n*)	しんりがく	psychology
物理学 (*n*)	ぶつりがく	physics
事務所 (*n*)	じむしょ	office
時間割 (*n*)	じかんわり	schedule, timetable

一秒 (*n*)	いちびょう	1 second
二秒 (*n*)	にびょう	2 seconds
三秒 (*n*)	さんびょう	3 seconds
四秒 (*n*)	よんびょう	4 seconds
五秒 (*n*)	ごびょう	5 seconds
六秒 (*n*)	ろくびょう	6 seconds
七秒 (*n*)	ななびょう	7 seconds
八秒 (*n*)	はちびょう	8 seconds
九秒 (*n*)	きゅうびょう	9 seconds
十秒 (*n*)	じゅうびょう	10 seconds
何秒 (*inter.*)	なんびょう	how many seconds?

■ 漢字 (かんじ) Kanji

英 8 strokes	エイ (えい) – gifted, talented	英(語) (えいご) – English	The first three strokes are the plant radical, while the rest looks like a flower box on the big (大) stand of a TALENTED ENGLISH gardener who speaks ENGLISH to the plants to make them grow.
国 8 strokes	～コク (こく), ～ゴク (ごく), くに – country, nation	(中)国 (ちゅうごく) – China; (韓)国 (かんこく) – Korea; (母)国 (ぼこく) – mother country	This shows a king (王 (おう)), bouncing a ball (玉 (ぎょく)) in his four-walled kingdom (country). It shows that it is easy to have a ball in your own COUNTRY, but cool things can also happen in other COUNTRIES.
音 9 strokes	オン (おん), おと – sound	音(楽) (おんがく) – music; 音 (おと) – sound	This kanji consists of two parts. To stand (立) is on top of the sun (日). Imagine the SOUND someone would want to make standing on the sun!
楽 13 strokes	ガク (がく), たの(しい) – fun, enjoyable	音(楽) (おんがく) – music; 楽(しい) (たの) – fun, enjoyable	This kanji looks like a white (白) bird chirping HAPPILY and with great JOY on top of a short tree (木).
今 4 strokes	コン (こん) – this, いま – now	今(日は) (こんにち) – hello; 今(何時) (いまなんじ) – What time is it now?	This shows a two-story house with a roof held up by only one wall: the house leans to the right under the weight. The owner needs to fix it NOW!
分 4 strokes	ブン (ぶん), フン (ふん), プン (ぷん) – minute, portion; わ(かる) – to understand	(一)分 (いっぷん), (二)分 (にふん), (三)分 (さんぷん) – one minute, two minutes, three minutes; 分(かります) (わ) – to understand	This kanji has an eight (八) on top of a sword (刀). When you use a sword to cut something into eight small parts, like reducing an hour down to MINUTES, you can more easily UNDERSTAND it.

■ 言葉(ことば)の探索(たんさく) Language Detection

1. The direct object particle – を

The direct object is the object or person that receives the action of a verb. The particle を, the direct object indicator, is pronounced *"o,"* just like the hiragana お. It is found in the "w" column on the hiragana chart, and is typed "wo" on a keyboard. The particle を comes after the direct object.

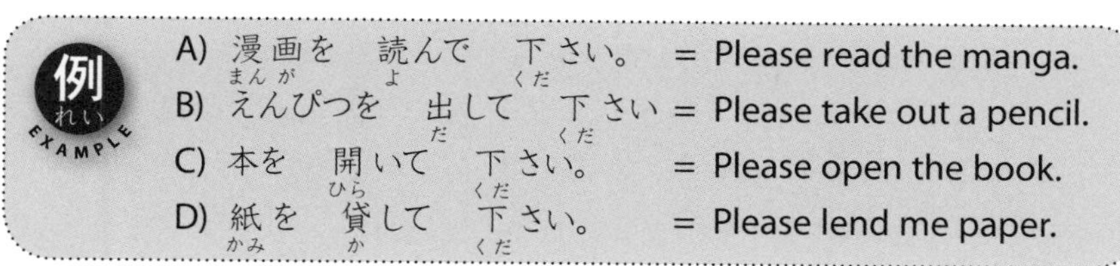

例(れい) EXAMPLE
A) 漫画(まんが)を 読(よ)んで 下(くだ)さい。 = Please read the manga.
B) えんぴつを 出(だ)して 下(くだ)さい = Please take out a pencil.
C) 本を 開(ひら)いて 下(くだ)さい。 = Please open the book.
D) 紙(かみ)を 貸(か)して 下(くだ)さい。 = Please lend me paper.

In the first example, the 漫画(まんが) is receiving the action of the verb (what is being read). In the second example, the えんぴつ is receiving the action of the verb (it is what is being taken out). Therefore, 漫画(まんが) and えんぴつ are direct objects and are followed by the particle を.

2. Telling time

A. **Hours:** 時(じ) is the counter for hours. It is used like "o'clock" in English, following the number. Unlike *o'clock*, 時 cannot be cut when telling time. For instance, for 5:00 it is OK to say "It is five" in English but incorrect to say「五(ご)です」in Japanese. You must say「五時(ごじ) です」.

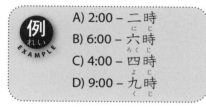

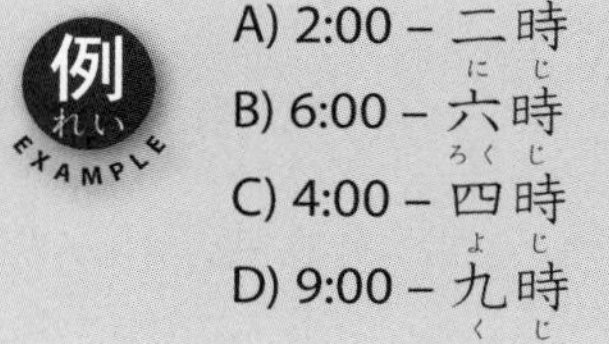

例(れい) EXAMPLE
A) 2:00 – 二時(にじ)
B) 6:00 – 六時(ろくじ)
C) 4:00 – 四時(よじ)
D) 9:00 – 九時(くじ)

Use 前(まえ) or すぎ to talk about "before # o'clock" or "after # o'clock." If used, these words always follow the time expression and never precede it.

A.	九時前(くじまえ)	before 9
B.	十一時(じゅういちじ)すぎ	after 11
C.	五時十分前(ごじじゅっぷんまえ)	ten minutes before 5
D.	八時二十分(はちじにじゅっぷん)すぎ	twenty minutes after 8

Use the particle から (*from*) after the time expression to talk about when something starts.

A.	学校(がっこう)は 七時半(しちじはん)から です。	School starts (is from) 7:30.
B.	英語(えいご)の 授業(じゅぎょう)は 九時十五分(くじじゅうごふん)から です。	English class starts at (is from) 9:15.
C.	ばんごはんは、まいにち 六時四十五分(ろくじよんじゅうごふん)から です。	Every day, dinner starts at (is from) 6:45.

B. **Minutes:** 分(ふん) or 分(ぷん) is the counter for minutes. The pronunciation of 分(ふん) or 分(ぷん) changes slightly depending on the number that precedes it.

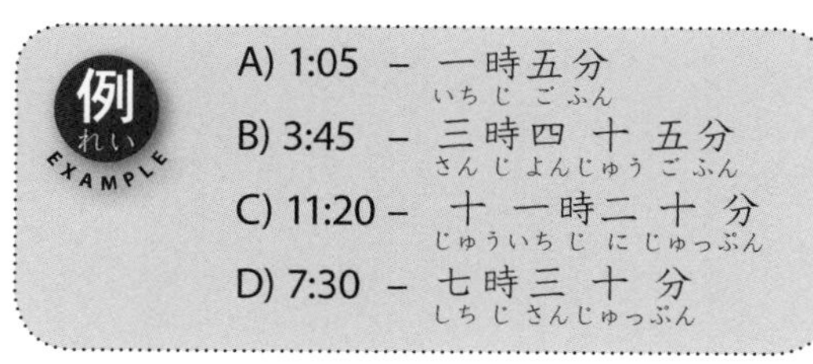

例(れい) EXAMPLE
A) 1:05 – 一時五分(いちじごふん)
B) 3:45 – 三時四十五分(さんじよんじゅうごふん)
C) 11:20 – 十一時二十分(じゅういちじにじゅっぷん)
D) 7:30 – 七時三十分(しちじさんじゅっぷん)

3. Time words

There are two types of time words in Japanese, GENERAL and SPECIFIC.

A. General time words used as adverbs do not need any particle after them. General time words include:

今(いま)	毎日(まいにち)	明日(あした)	今日(きょう)	午後(ごご)	昼(ひる)
(now)	(every day)	(tomorrow)	(today)	(P.M.)	(noon)

General time words may be followed by the particle は, to indicate emphasis or that the time is the actual topic. Time words can appear in many different places in a sentence, but they usually come toward the beginning.

B. The particle に follows immediately after specific time words (when we would use the prepositions *on*, *in*, or *at* in English). Some time words are:

二時三十分(にじさんじゅっぷん)に at 2:30　　六時(ろくじ)に at 6 o'clock　　２０５８年(にせんごじゅうはちねん)に in the year 2058

Below are some example sentences showing how to use both general and specific time words and expressions.

A) 明日(あした)　この本を　貸(か)して　下(くだ)さい。 = Tomorrow, please lend me this book.

B) 今(いま)　紙(かみ)を　出(だ)して　下(くだ)さい。 = Now, please take out some paper.

C) 八時半(はちじはん)に　黒板(こくばん)を　見(み)て　下(くだ)さい。 = Please look at the blackboard at 8:30.

Notice which time words are followed by the particle に.

■ 自習(じしゅう) Self Check

1. Say the following in Japanese, inserting particles as needed.

- ➲ その漢字(かんじ) _____ 読(よ)んで　下(くだ)さい。 (Please read that kanji.)
- ➲ お水(みず) _____ 飲(の)んでもいいですか。 (May I please have a drink of water?)
- ➲ 八時(はちじ) _____ 宿題(しゅくだい) _____ 出(だ)して　下(くだ)さい。 (At 8:00, please take out your homework.)
- ➲ 毎日(まいにち) _____ Eメール(めーる) _____ 書(か)いて　下(くだ)さい。 (Please write an e-mail every day.)
- ➲ Please read your kanji every day. ⇨ ____________________。
- ➲ Please close your book at 3:00. ⇨ ____________________。

2. Cover up the right column with your hand or a piece of paper as you say the times in the left column out loud to yourself in Japanese. Check yourself by looking at the right column.

a.	7:00	しちじ
b.	1:30	いちじ　はん
c.	before 3:00	さんじ　まえ
d.	after 9:15	くじ　じゅうごふん　すぎ
e.	5:20	ごじ　にじゅっぷん
f.	12:33	じゅうにじ　さんじゅうさんぷん
g.	after 6:00	ろくじ　すぎ

■ 練習(れんしゅう)の時間(じかん) Time for Practice

1. Small Group Practice

Take turns giving each other commands. If A-さん is speaking, B-さん should act out the command. A-さん should pay close attention to the particles in the commands.

A) この本を　開(ひら)いて　下(くだ)さい。

B) あの　漢字(かんじ)を　読(よ)んで　下(くだ)さい。

C) 漢字(かんじ)を　書(か)いて　下(くだ)さい。

D) えんぴつを　出(だ)して　下(くだ)さい。

E) 紙(かみ)を　見(み)て　下(くだ)さい。

F) この　ひらがなを　読(よ)んで　下(くだ)さい。

G) 先生(せんせい)を　見(み)て　下(くだ)さい。

H) 日本の　音楽(おんがく)を　聞(き)いて　下(くだ)さい。

2. Pair Practice

What time is it?

Without showing your partner, quickly write down six times of increasing difficulty (including AM or PM for the last four). Take turns asking and answering your partner and record their responses. At the end of the pair practice, check your answers.

A-さん：すみません。今(いま)、何時(なんじ)ですか。 = Excuse me. What time is it now?

B-さん：午前(ごぜん)　１１(じゅういち)時(じ)　２０(にじゅっ)分(ぷん)です。 = It is 11:20 AM.

3. Pair Practice

Ask your partner if they have the following school subjects and if they do, follow up by asking the name of their teacher and what time the class meets. Then fill in your answers in the spaces below each subject.

A-さん：英語(えいご)の　授業(じゅぎょう)は　ありますか。 = Do you have an English class?

B-さん：はい、あります。 = Yes, I do.

A-さん：英語(えいご)の　先生(せんせい)の　名前(なまえ)は　何(なん)　ですか。 = What is the name of your English teacher?

B-さん：ジョンソン先生(じょんそんせんせい)です。 = Mr./Ms. Johnson.

A-さん：英語(えいご)の　授業(じゅぎょう)は　何時(なんじ)　ですか。 = What time is your English class?

B-さん：午後(ごご)　一時(いちじ)　三十分(さんじゅっぷん)　です。 = 1:30 PM.

Subject	英語(えいご)	数学(すうがく)	科学(かがく)	体育(たいいく)	美術(びじゅつ)	日本語(にほんご)	歴史(れきし)	音楽(おんがく)	生物学(せいぶつがく)
Teacher									
Time									

■ 文化箱 Culture Chest

High School Courses

Most courses offered in a Japanese high school can be found in other countries as well. However, some Japanese high schools offer classes you might not see in a typical non-Japanese high school, such as calligraphy, classical Japanese and ethics. English classes are required study beginning in middle school.

■ キアラのジャーナル Kiara's Journal 

Read the journal entry below, and then answer these questions.

❶ List three of Kiara's six classes.

❷ What is Kiara's favorite class? Which will be her most difficult class? Why?

❸ Give a specific example of how Kiara's language skills have improved.

❹ Make a sentence in Japanese using a specific time expression about your own daily schedule.

Dear Journal,

I had my second day of 高校 today. 毎日 六つの クラスが あります。社会と 国語と 数学と 美術と 音楽と 英語が あります。 美術が とても 楽しい です。日本の 学校 の 国語の クラスは 日本語 です。私の 数学の 先生は とても いい人です。 先生は この 高校に 九年間 います。Most teachers are transferred to other schools every five years or so. It's not that common to have a 先生 at the same school for as long as 私の 数学の 先生。山本先生は この 高校に 三年間 います。

クラスは ちょっと 大きい です。生徒が 四十一人 います。The rest of my classes are about the same size. 高校は 一年生から 三年生まで です。私の 社会の 先生は とてもいい 先生 です。She lived in the U.S. for two years right after college as an assistant Japanese teacher in a high school in Seattle. She really liked it there. She said that the weather there was similar to the weather where she grew up, in 金沢.

私の 国語の 先生も いい 先生 です。It's still going to be my hardest 授業 by far. I only know a little Japanese and I'm going to have to find a lot of ways to help myself remember new 単語 and 漢字 as I go through the year. I should be able to learn a lot this year, as long as I remember to review my 単語 and 漢字 毎日。

国語、which of course is what we would call 日本語 in America, is an interesting term. It makes sense. "Nation's language." While there are Koreans, Chinese, English, Australians, Americans, and other people from all over the world living here, Japan is basically a country where the vast majority of people are ethnic Japanese and Japanese is the official language.

美術 is still my favorite class. We are starting out this year drawing from a still life, but we're also keeping a sketchbook where we can draw whatever we like, after we finish our assignment.

私の 日本語 is improving a little more each day. One of the things that I realized today was how to use the particle を。 For example, じゅん君 asked me, "漫画(まんが)を 読(よ)みますか。" 後(あと)で, he said "ドアを 開(あ)けて下(くだ)さい。" So when I wanted to ask him for a pencil, I knew that pencil is "えんぴつ" and that "貸(か)して下さい" means "please lend." And after listening to じゅん君の requests, I realized which particle I need to use between "pencil" and "please lend me." じゅん君 said that if the "pencil" is what is borrowed, or the " 漫画 " is what is read, or if the "door" is what is to be opened, the object (or sometimes it is a person) that has the action done to it must be followed by " を ." That's the direct object.

The other language point I picked up today was about time. It seems that whenever anyone refers to a specific time to do something, like 一時に (*at one o'clock*) or 2051 年に (*in the year 2051*), the time is followed by the particle に . If you are using words that don't talk about specific times but are more general like 今年(ことし) (*this year*) or 毎日 (*every day*) you don't use に after the word. I was excited — my language skills are growing so quickly!

第3課の3 次は　何時間目ですか。 What period is next?

つぎ　なんじかんめ

1
1)ここは コンピューターラボ です。あそこは 体育館 です。

2
2)そう です か。図書館は どこ ですか。

3
3) あそこ です。
4) この 高校は とても 大きい ですね。次は 何時間目 ですか。

4

5) ええと。次は 四時間目 です。四時間目は 数学 です。

6)五時間目は 何 ですか。

5
7)五時間目は 英語 です。六時間目は 美術 です。授業の 後、 部活が あります。私の クラブは 柔道部 です。

6

8) そう ですか。私は、茶色 帯 三だん です。

9) ええっ！ 三だん ですか。すごい ですね。

■ 会話(かいわ) Dialogue

REMINDER: You may see some kanji / vocabulary you do not recognize. Use the context to try to understand the meanings of those parts of the dialogue.

1. じゅん：ここは　コンピューターラボ(こんぴゅーたーらぼ)　です。あそこは　体育館(たいいくかん)　です。
2. キアラ(きあら)：そう　ですか。　図書館(としょかん)は　どこ　ですか。
3. じゅん：あそこ　です。
4. キアラ(きあら)：この　高校(こうこう)は　とても　大(おお)きい　ですね。次(つぎ)は　何時間目(なんじかんめ)　ですか。
5. じゅん：ええと。次(つぎ)は　*四時間目(よじかんめ)　です。四時間目(よじかんめ)は　数学(すうがく)　です。
6. キアラ(きあら)：五時間目(ごじかんめ)は　何(なん)　ですか。
7. じゅん：五時間目(ごじかんめ)は　英語(えいご)　です。六時間目(ろくじかんめ)は　美術(びじゅつ)　です。
   授業(じゅぎょう)の　後(あと)、部活(ぶかつ)が　あります。私　の　クラブ(くらぶ)は　柔道部(じゅうどうぶ)　です。
8. キアラ(きあら)：そう　ですか。私は、*茶色帯三(ちゃいろおびさん)だん　です。
9. じゅん：ええっ！三(さん)だん　ですか。すごい　ですね。

* Notice this is pronounced <u>YO</u>JIKANME, *dropping the "N" sound of* YON.

* 茶色帯三段(ちゃいろおびさんだん) – third degree brown belt

■ 単語(たんご) New Words

一時間目(いちじかんめ) (*n*) – 1st period
二時間目(にじかんめ) (*n*) – 2nd period
三時間目(さんじかんめ) (*n*) – 3rd period
四時間目(よじかんめ) * (*n*) –4th period

五時間目(ごじかんめ) (*n*) – 5th period
六時間目(ろくじかんめ) (*n*) – 6th period
何時間目(なんじかんめ) (*inter.*) – what period?
放課後(ほうかご) (*n/adv.*) – after school

後(あと) – after
後(あと)で – afterwards
次(つぎ) (*adv.*) – next
部活(ぶかつ) (*n*)– school clubs/activities

* To refer to the club (部活(ぶかつ)) of a sport or group, put 部(ぶ) after the sport or group. For example バスケ(ばすけ) is *basketball* while バスケ部 is *basketball team* or *club*.

図書館(としょかん) (n)
体育館(たいいくかん) (n)
コンピューターラボ(こんぴゅーたーらぼ) (n)
成績(せいせき) (n)
野球(やきゅう) or ベースボール(べーすぼーる) (n)
バスケ(ばすけ) (n)
柔道(じゅうどう) (n)
合唱(がっしょう) (n)
(お)寺(てら) (n)
神社(じんじゃ) (n)

Other words you might like to use:

ブラスバンド部 (ぶらすばんどぶ) (n)

陸上部 (りくじょうぶ) (n)

卓球部 (たっきゅうぶ) (n)

剣道部 (けんどうぶ) (n)

バスケ部 (ばすけぶ) (n)

バレーボール部 (ばれーぼーるぶ) (n)

■ 漢字 (かんじ) Kanji

書 10 strokes	ショ (しょ), か(く) – write	㇆	⺕	⺕	亖	亖	聿	聿
	書 (か) (きます) – to write; (図 (と)) 書 (しょ) (館 (かん)) – library	書	書	書				
	This is a large hand with all four fingers gripping a brush moving forward and backward WRITING the character for sun (日).							

寺 6 strokes	ジ (じ), てら – temple	一	十	土	圭	寺	寺	
	(東大 (とうだい)) 寺 (じ) – Todaiji Temple in Nara; (お) 寺 (てら) – temple							
	The upper part of this character is "ground" (土), while the lower part means "an inch," or a "little bit." In general, TEMPLES are built on ground that is a little bit more peaceful.							

時 10 strokes	ジ (じ), とき – time	丨	冂	日	日	日一	日十	日土
	(一 (いち)) 時 (じ) – 1:00; 時 (とき) (々 (どき)) – sometimes	𠮷	時	時				
	The left side of this kanji is the kanji for sun (日) while the right is the kanji for temple (寺). Long ago, temple bells rang to tell the TIME which was measured in the temple by the position of the sun.							

門 8 strokes	モン (もん) – gate	丨	𠃍	戸	戸	門	門	門
	(寺 (てら) の) 門 (もん) – gate of the temple	門						
	This is a drawing of a GATE. It looks like swinging doors or a swinging GATE.							

間 12 strokes	カン (かん), あいだ – interval, space	丨	𠃍	戸	戸	門	門	門
	(時 (じ)) 間 (かん) – hour (interval) of time; 間 (あいだ) – space between	門	門	間	間	間		
	This is a drawing of a GATE with the sun poking through the SPACE for an INTERVAL of time.							

下 3 strokes	カ(か), した – below, under; くだ(る) – descend, give	一	丅	下				
	下(くだ)さい – please; 下(した) – below, under							
	The second stroke of this kanji is pointing DOWN, indicating something BELOW or UNDERNEATH. Point at some money on the ground and ask your friend to GIVE it to you.							

■ 言葉(ことば)の探索(たんさく) Language Detection

Class periods

The Japanese words for class periods are formed from several root words. Here is an example for 2nd period, 二時間目(にじかんめ).

二(に) = two ⇨ 二時(にじ) = two o'clock ⇨ 二時間(にじかん) = a two hour period of time
⇨ 二時間目(にじかんめ) = second period

■ 自習(じしゅう) Self Check

- ➲ Count from 1st period to 7th period in Japanese.
- ➲ Now count backwards from 7th period to 1st period.
- ➲ Count odd periods only.
- ➲ What are your three best/favorite periods?

■ 練習(れんしゅう)の時間(じかん) Time for Practice

1. Pair Practice

The class schedule below is Jun's schedule for today. Use this schedule to ask your partner what period Jun has which class. Take turns asking and answering.

A- さん：英語(えいご)は　何時間目(なんじかんめ)　ですか。 = What period is English?
B- さん：英語(えいご)は　四時間目(よじかんめ)　です。 = English is 4th period.

今日(きょう)の　時間割(じかんわり)

時間目	じゅぎょう
一時間目	びじゅつ
二時間目	かがく
三時間目	しゃかい
四時間目	英語(えいご)
ひる休み	
五時間目	たいいく
六時間目	すうがく
ほうかご	ぶかつどう

2. Class Practice

Copy the chart below on a piece of scrap paper. Fill in the 授業(じゅぎょう) column with the following classes. Be sure to mix up the order:

英語(えいご)　美術(びじゅつ)　数学(すうがく)　音楽(おんがく)　社会(しゃかい)　日本語(にほんご)　自習(じしゅう)

今日(きょう)の 時間割(じかんわり)

時間目(じかんめ)	授業(じゅぎょう)	生徒(せいと)の名前(なまえ)	時間目(じかんめ)	授業(じゅぎょう)	生徒(せいと)の名前(なまえ)
一時間目(いちじかんめ)			四時間目(よじかんめ)		
二時間目(にじかんめ)			五時間目(ごじかんめ)		
三時間目(さんじかんめ)			六時間目(ろくじかんめ)		

Use Japanese to survey your classmates, one at a time, until you find a person with one of the exact classes you have on your schedule at the exact same period. Use Japanese to ask that student to sign their name in the box on your form. Begin when your teacher says "HAI, HAJIMEMASHOU." Once your survey form is completely signed or when your teacher tells you to stop, sit down. Be prepared to report some of your survey results to the class. You may ask each student you interview what class they have each period.

A- さん： 二時間目(にじかんめ)は　何(なん)ですか。 = What class do you have second period?

B- さん： 美術(びじゅつ) です。 = I have art.

If this is the same class that A- さん has second period, A- さん then says:

名前(なまえ)を　書(か)いて　下(くだ)さい。 = Please write your name.

■ 文化箱(ぶんかばこ) Culture Chest

部活(ぶかつ) School Clubs

In Japan, sports teams are considered to be after-school clubs just like the various culture- and music-related groups are. Students in Japan join one club or sport when they enter high school, rather than many. They usually practice with this club, or 部活(ぶかつ), every day after school for the entire school year and stay with the same group until they graduate. There is often a wide range of sports 部活 such as 柔道部(じゅうどうぶ), 空手部(からてぶ), 剣道部(けんどうぶ), バスケ部(ばすけぶ), 野球部(やきゅうぶ), and バレーボール部(ばれーぼーるぶ). Other clubs might include the broadcasting club, art club, tea ceremony club, and English club. The members of clubs often become very close and this bond can be an important part of a student's school life.

■ キアラのジャーナル(きあらのじゃーなる) Kiara's Journal 

Read the journal entry below, and then answer these questions.

❶ What adjective does Kiara use to describe the sport of kendo?

❷ What are some differences between Shinto shrines and Buddhist temples?

❸ What is a good thing to do if you miss your stop on the Tokyo subway?

Dear Journal,

Today was so busy. We had our first full day of 学校の クラス(くらす)。これは 今日(きょう)の クラス(くらす)の スケジュール(すけじゅーる) です。始(はじ)めは ホームルーム(ほーむるーむ) です。一時間目(いちじかんめ)は 国語(こくご) です。次(つぎ)は 音楽(おんがく) です。三時間目(さじかんめ)は 社会(しゃかい) です。明日(あした)、社会の 授業(じゅぎょう)は 図書館(としょかん)で あります。 午後(ごご)の クラス(くらす)の 後(あと)で、じゅん君(くん)と私 met in the 体育館(たいいくかん)。I wanted to see the 剣道部(けんどうぶ)。剣道(けんどう)は とても 難(むずか)しい です。

昨日(きのう)、on our way home, we passed by an amazing 神社(じんじゃ)、a Shinto shrine. Shinto is one of Japan's major religions; Buddhism is the other. Buddhism originated in India, and spread from China to Korea, and then to Japan. Buddhist temples are called お寺(てら)。You can easily tell the difference between shrines and temples, because the entrance to the grounds of 神社 are set off by a large gate, usually orange, called a 鳥居(とりい)。Often there is a straw rope hung across the top. White paper zigzag cutouts hang from the rope, letting us know that the space inside this 鳥居 is purified and sacred. In front of a 寺(てら), you can usually find a large elaborate wooden 門(もん), with two huge and ferocious guardian deities keeping watch from either side of the gate.

The 鳥居(とりい) in front of the shrine on the way home looked really familiar, like I'd seen it someplace before. Jun, Ben, and I go most of the way home from school together, so I asked Jun if we could stop and walk up to the 神社 sometime. He sent a text message to his お母さん, asking if we had time before 晩(ばん)ご飯(はん)。お母さん said OK です。Up close, the 鳥居(とりい)は とても 大(おお)きいです。Some 鳥居 are made from 木(き), some are made of stone or concrete, but this one seemed to be made of some sort of metal, which Jun said is not as common. すごい です。Inside the shrine grounds, a long row of lanterns (in the shape of the 東京の 京) led up the hill to the big red 神社 building. The path had large stone fox statues on both sides. These foxes had an intense stare; they were actually a little freaky. It was as if they wanted to speak, but had been frozen in time. Beyond the fox statues, at the base of the staircase up to another, higher, 神社 building, something big and hairy scurried through the bushes. I only caught a glimpse of it out of the corner of my eye; and neither じゅん君 nor ベン(べん)君 saw it. It really made me nervous, so I asked them if we could go home and come back 明日(あした)。

We finally made it back to the subway station, just in time for the next train to 銀座(ぎんざ)。That was where we had to transfer to catch 次(つぎ)の train home. I was tired, and not really paying attention, so before I knew it, the others had walked off the train, onto the platform, and the doors were closing, with me still sitting there inside the train. This just wasn't turning out to be my day! じゅん君 had already told me, though, that if I got lost or separated like this, I should just get out at the 次の station and wait for him. So I did, and sure enough, he and ベン(べん)君 showed up about five minutes later, with とても 大(おお)きい grins on their faces.

第3課の4 今日、宿題は　ありません。 There is no homework today.

1) 先生、すみません。ちょっと暑いです。まどを開けてもいいですか。

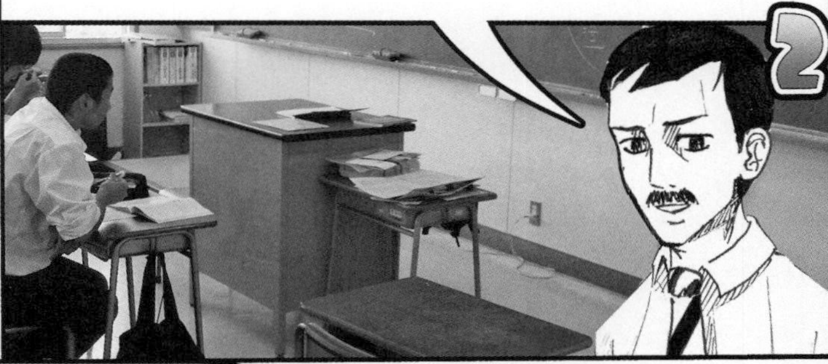

2) いいですよ。その　まどと　あのまどを　開けて下さい。皆さん、今日、宿題は　ありません。でも、小テストが　あります。それでは、教科書と紙一枚を出して下さい。えんぴつも　出して下さい。

3) 先生、すみません。ペンで書いても　いい ですか。
4) ペンは　だめです。 えんぴつで書いて　下さい。皆さん　えんぴつはありますか。
5) はい、あります。
6)はい、じゃあ始めましょう。

■ 会話 Dialogue

REMINDER: You may see some kanji / vocabulary you do not recognize. Use the context to try to understand the meanings of those parts of the dialogue.

1. キアラ　：先生、すみません。　ちょっと　暑い　です。　まどを　開けても いい ですか。
2. 山本先生：いい　ですよ。その　まどと　あの　まどを　開けて　下さい。皆さん、今日、しゅくだいは　ありません。でも、小テストが あります。それでは、教科書と　紙　*一枚を　出して　下さい。えんぴつも　出して　下さい。
3. キアラ　：先生、すみません。ペンで　書いても　いい　ですか。

4. 山本先生(やまもとせんせい)：ペン(ぺん)は　だめ　です。えんぴつで　書(か)いて　下(くだ)さい。
皆(みな)さん　えんぴつは　ありますか。

5. 皆(みんな)　　　：はい、あります。

6. 山本先生(やまもとせんせい)：はい、じゃあ　始(はじ)めましょう。　　* 一枚 - one piece

■ 単語(たんご) New Words

だめ (な *adj.*)	暑(あつ)い (い *adj.*)	寒(さむ)い (い *adj.*)	涼(すず)しい (い *adj.*)	蒸(む)し暑(あつ)い (い *adj.*)

ドア(どあ) (*n*) – door
窓(まど) (*n*) – window

でも (*part./conj.*) – but

開(あ)ける／開(あ)けます (*v*) – to open (doors/windows)

閉(し)める／閉(し)めます (*v*) – to close (doors, windows)

■ 漢字(かんじ) Kanji

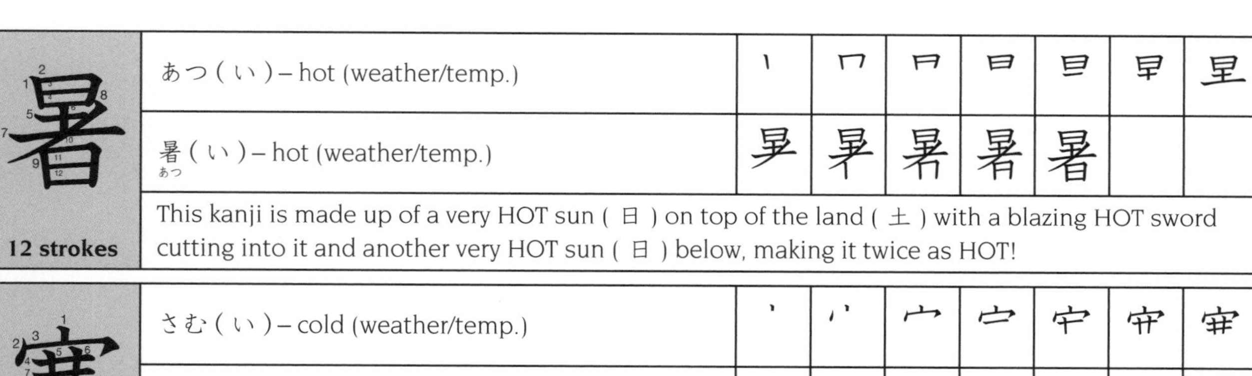

暑 12 strokes	
あつ(い) – hot (weather/temp.)	
暑(あつ)(い) – hot (weather/temp.)	暑
This kanji is made up of a very HOT sun (日) on top of the land (土) with a blazing HOT sword cutting into it and another very HOT sun (日) below, making it twice as HOT!	

寒 12 strokes	
さむ(い) – cold (weather/temp.)	
寒(さむ)(い) – cold (weather/temp.)	寒
Under the roof of this kanji is a grid shape of a radiator trying to heat up a very COLD room. At the bottom of the kanji are two snowflakes representing winter (冬) which makes things even COLDER!	

神 9 strokes	
シン(しん), ジン(じん), かみ – God/god, spirits	
神(じん)(社(じゃ)) – Shinto shrine; 神(しん)(道(とう)) – Shinto religion, literally "the way of the gods"; 神(かみ)(様(さま)) – god(s)	神
The left side is a version of the radical that means "to show" (示); the right side is a rice field (田) with a long line extending from ground to the heavens. It is very important to show the GODS how hard you are trying to grow a good crop.	

社 7 strokes	シャ，ジャ – association, company	丶	ラ	ネ	ネ	ネ一	社	社
	(神)社 – Shinto shrine; (会)社 – company or corporation; 社(会) – society; social studies							
	The right side is the earth (土), which shows (示) the solid foundation upon which SOCIETY is based! 神 is the character for god while 社 implies ASSOCIATION. So 神社 is an association of gods and the SHRINE where they all gather.							

■ 言葉の探索 Language Detection

1. でも、. . .

でも means "but" or "however," and is often used to link two sentences. The first sentence ends with a period. でも, followed by a comma, comes at the beginning of the second sentence.

A) 中学校 と 高校が あります。 でも、 小学校は ありません。
= There is junior high school and a high school. However, there is no elementary school.

B) 今日は 暑い です。 でも、 エアコンは ありません。
= Today is hot. But there isn't any air conditioning.

2. で **(by means of)**

The particle で, when it follows a noun, can mean to do something "by means of" X, or to use X as a tool/instrument.

A) ボールペンで 書いて 下さい。 = Please write by (means of) pen.

B) 漢字で 書いて 下さい。 = Please write (using) kanji.

C) 英語で 言って 下さい。 = Please say it in (by means of) English.

■ 自習 Self Check

1. Link each of the two sentences using でも.

今日は 暑いです。 明日は 寒い です。 (Today is hot. Tomorrow will be cold.)

じゅん君が います。 かずひさ君は いません。 (Jun is here. Kazuhisa is not here.)

明日、英語の 授業が あります。 数学の 授業は ありません。
(Tomorrow, I have English class. I do not have math class.)

2. Using で, "by means of," translate these phrases into 日本語.

by means of paper ____________________ by means of a pencil ____________________

by means of chopsticks ____________________ by means of computer ____________________

■ 練習の時間 Time for Practice
れんしゅう　じかん

1. Pair Practice

With a partner, link each of the two sentences using でも.

A) 今日は　涼しい　です。　明日は　蒸し暑い　です。
B) これは　えんぴつ　です。　それは　えんぴつ　では　ありません。
C) 六時間目が　あります。　七時間目は　ありません。
D) 猫が　います。　犬は　いません。
E) 兄が　います。　弟は　いません。

2. Pair Practice

Add a second sentence beginning with でも to each of the sentences below. Make sure the information in the second sentence is different enough that the use of でも is appropriate. Take turns.

A) 今日は　寒い　です。
B) あれは　本　です。
C) 姉が　います。
D) 三時間目に　数学が　あります。

3. Pair Practice

Following the example, use で (by means of) to ask for permission to write using the following. Your partner, in the role of teacher, will grant permission for you to use two of these and deny permission for you to use three of these.

1. えんぴつ　2. ボールペン (ぼーるぺん)　3. チョーク (ちょーく)　4. ペン (ぺん)　5. コンピューター (こんぴゅーたー)

A-さん：えんぴつで　書いても　いいですか。 = May I write with a pencil?
B-さん：はい、えんぴつで　書いても　いいです。 = Yes, you may write with a pencil.
OR-　いいえ、えんぴつで　書いては　だめです。 = No, you may not write with a pencil.

■ 文化箱 Culture Chest
ぶんかばこ

School Calendar

The Japanese school year begins in April and ends in March. It is usually divided into three terms. Summer vacation lasts for a month, from late July through much of August, when the second term begins. Winter vacation, which lasts a month or less, centers around the New Year's holiday, and separates the second and third terms. College entrance exams begin in January for the national standardized test and continue into February and early March, for individual university tests. The graduation ceremony (卒業式 (そつぎょうしき)) is held in March. The opening ceremony marking the new school year (入学式 (にゅうがくしき)) happens in early or mid-April.

There are many seasonal events on the school calendar. These include school trips called 修学旅行 (しゅうがくりょこう) that last for one or more days, school sports festivals often held in early fall, and school cultural festivals or 文化祭 (ぶんかさい) in late fall. These events entail a great deal of planning and group work and are considered part of a young person's education.

第3課の5

むし暑い　ですね。
It's muggy, isn't it.

■ 会話(かいわ) Dialogue

REMINDER: You may see some kanji / vocabulary you do not recognize. Use the context to try to understand the meanings of those parts of the dialogue.

(After school)

1. じゅん：ベン君(くん)、こんにちは。
2. ベン(べん)：こんにちは。暑(あつ)い　ですねえ。キアラ(きあら)さん、日本の　学校(がっこう)は　どう　ですか。
3. キアラ(きあら)：楽(たの)しい　です。でもむし暑(あつ)い　ですね。私達(たち)の　学校(がっこう)には　エアコン(えあこん)が　ありません。中学校(ちゅうがっこう)は　どう　ですか。
4. ベン(べん)：涼(すず)しい　です。私の　中学校(ちゅうがっこう)は　エアコン(えあこん)が　ありますよ。

(a very strong wind comes out of nowhere)

5. ベン(べん)：わっ！　すごい風(かぜ)　ですね。
6. じゅん：あの　神社(じんじゃ)の　鳥居(とりい)に　*行(い)きましょう。
7. キアラ(きあら)：ええ！　ここは　どこ　ですか。

* 行(い)きましょう – Let's go.

■ 単語(たんご) New Words

エアコン(えあこん) (*n*) | 風(かぜ) (*n*) | 行(い)きましょう (*v*) | 速(はや)く (*adv.*)

鳥居(とりい) (*n*) – shrine gate	わっ! (*interj.*) – wow!
どう (*interj.*) – how	さあ (*interj.*) – well...
すごい (い *adj.*) – amazing, great, terrible, to a great extent	ねえ (*part.*) – sentence ending that can be exclamatory or express surprise
ね (*part.*) – sentence ending for a rhetorical question or when seeking agreement	よ (part.) – sentence ending for a strong declarative statement or for emphasis

■ 漢字(かんじ) Kanji

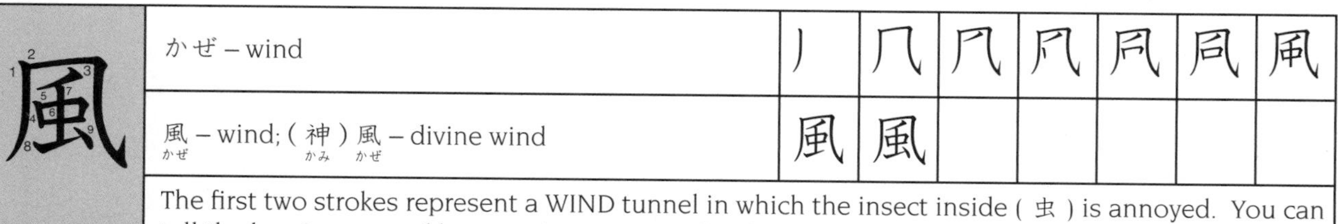

風 (9 strokes)								
かぜ – wind	ノ	几	凡	凧	凬	凮	風
風(かぜ) – wind; (神(かみ)) 風(かぜ) – divine wind	風	風					
The first two strokes represent a WIND tunnel in which the insect inside (虫) is annoyed. You can tell the bug is annoyed because its antenna (the third stroke) is bent and tilted.							

友 4 strokes	ユウ(ゆう), とも – friend	一	ナ	方	友			
	友(とも)(達(だち)), 友人(ゆうじん) – friend							
	The first two strokes of this kanji for FRIEND are a person, reaching an arm across a table (又) to shake hands with a new FRIEND.							

■ 言葉(ことば)の探索(たんさく) Language Detection

1. ね/ねえ

When using these two, inflection is everything. Think about how, in English, the phrase "It's cold" can have several different meanings, depending on your inflection: "It's cold." "It's cold!" or "It's cold?" The same is true with the use of ね and ねえ, particles that come at the end of the Japanese sentence to express a range of emotions or intensities. ね generally is used in a statement where the speaker is hoping for/expecting agreement. ねえ is generally used where an exclamation mark would be used in English. They can be used:

A. to confirm something in the form of a rhetorical question, or when seeking agreement from the person listening, as in "... right?"

明日(あした)は　寒(さむ)い　ですね。 = Tomorrow will be cold, won't it?

B. as an exclamation mark.

寒(さむ)い　ですねえ。 = It's cold!

It is common in Japan to repeat a question before giving the answer. Often the repeated part will have the particle ね at the end to confirm that the question was understood. You can also use ね after you repeat directions or new information to confirm that you accurately understood what the speaker said. This is a great communication strategy, so try to use it when you get new information from your pair practice partners.

2. よ

よ comes at the end of the sentence and is used to make a definite statement that the listener should agree with such as "I am telling you ..." or "Hey ..." In some contexts, it acts like an exclamation mark in English. よ should be used sparingly, especially when speaking to superiors, as it can easily be construed as a bit too direct, even rude.

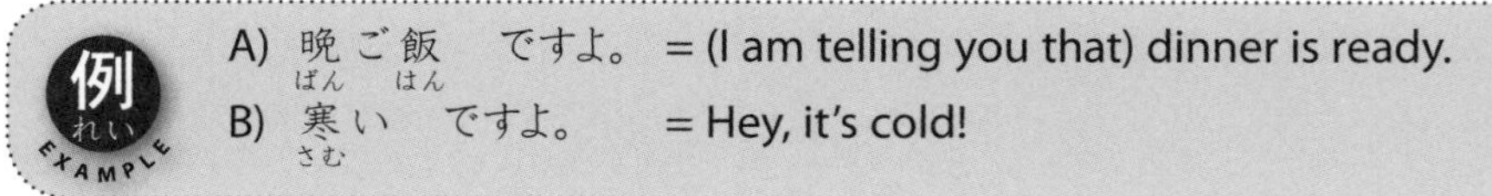

例 れい EXAMPLE
A) 晩(ばん)ご飯(はん)　ですよ。 = (I am telling you that) dinner is ready.
B) 寒(さむ)い　ですよ。 = Hey, it's cold!

■ 自習(じしゅう) Self Check

1. Say the following, using ね:

It's cool, isn't it? = 涼(すず)しい　です____。

It's hot, isn't it? = ______________________。

2. Say the following, using よ:
I'm telling you, it's muggy. = むし暑い　です__。
I'm telling you, this is sushi. = ____________________。

■ 練習の時間 Time for Practice

1. Pair Practice

Pointing out as many objects as you can (refer to Appendix 4 for names of classroom objects as needed), confirm that you are using the correct Japanese word by asking a confirmation question with ね. Your partner will answer authoritatively using よ.

A-さん：(*Points to a desk*) あれは　つくえ　ですね。= That over there is a desk, isn't it?
B-さん：はい、あれは　つくえ　ですよ。 = Yes, that over there is a desk!

2. Pair Practice

For this information gap activity, your teacher has asked your class to find out information about pen pals. Assume you and your partner have had many pen pals, and that you have much information to share. Use the two tables for this exercise on TimeforJapanese for this activity. One person should have Table A, the other, Table B. Decide who will use Table A and who will use Table B, then take turns asking/answering questions to fill in the gaps. Use ね, ねえ, and よ in your answers as appropriate. When all the blanks on your questionnaire are filled in, say「できました」. You may be asked to share some of your information with your class.

(*location*)
B-さん：Maria は　どこに　いますか。 = Where is Maria?
A-さん：Maria は Barcelona に　いますよ。 = Maria is in Barcelona, you know.

(*weather — both are in same city*)
B-さん：Barcelona は　涼しい　ですね。 = Barcelona's weather is cool, isn't it?
A-さん：そうですね。Barcelona は　とても 涼しい　ですねえ。
= Yes (I agree). The weather in Barcelona is very cool!

Other questions might include:
・何年生ですか。　・部活は何ですか。　・ご家族は何人ですか。

■ 文化箱 Culture Chest

1. 鳥居 Shinto Shrine Gate

The literal meaning of 鳥居, the red gates at the entrances to sacred places, often Shinto shrines, is 鳥の居るところ or 鳥が居ます which could be translated as "place where the bird is." Some birds are thought of as very powerful. This may mean actual power, like birds of prey (eagles, hawks, or owls), or a

"powerful presence," such as great blue herons or white cranes or storks. Other powerful birds are mythological, such as the thunderbird or the phoenix in Western tales or the garuda of Indonesian legends. Large cranes and other birds often perch on high places to scout for prey or to sun themselves. Japanese hope that these birds will land on a 鳥居 and stay there for as long as possible. What grander perch could a special bird have than a 鳥居 at the entrance of a 神社? Shinto 鳥居 are often painted a vermilion (red-orange) color, but are also unpainted stone, concrete, wood, or other materials. They are often adorned with しめなわ, "enclosing rope." These are often made of straw and are braided or twisted and are used for ritual purification in Shintoism. Zigzag shaped papers called しで usually hang from these ropes and mark the boundary between the sacred and non-sacred when they are attached to しめなわ, and Shinto practitioners believe these help purify things they touch or pass over.

2. 制服 Uniforms

Most high school students in Japan wear school uniforms. Rules about wearing proper uniforms differ from school to school and can be quite specific. Wearing a uniform outside of school identifies students as part of a particular school and shows school pride. Some students push the limits of what is acceptable within the school rules just as they do in many other places. Rules related to makeup, piercing, and hair also differ from high school to high school, although few Japanese high schools allow their students to wear jewelry or even makeup at school.

What are some good arguments for and against having school uniforms?

■ キアラのジャーナル Kiara's Journal 

Read the journal entry below, and then answer these questions.

❶ Where did the students run to seek shelter from the storm?

❷ What kind of animal did Jun think the hairy beast was?

❸ What is a 時の門?

❹ Ben compared the hairy animal to what other creature?

❺ Make a prediction about the content of Kiara's next journal entry.

ジャーナルへ

This was such a bizarre day! No one's ever going to believe what happened, but here goes.

The three of us had just left our 部活、heading toward the subway station. We stopped in to get some あめ at our favorite Seven-Eleven, but as soon as we left the store, winds blew up, whipping everything around. The closest building was the 神社, so we ran toward it, dodging papers and cardboard and plastic bags. A bicycle, knocked over by the wind, almost hit じゅん君。At the 鳥居 gate, that same hairy animal I saw the other day darted out of the bushes and ran through the 鳥居 with us.

Suddenly, everything stopped! The wind vanished, the garden and 神社 vanished too! Instead, we were in some sort of tunnel. Right in front of us, flying forward, was that same hairy animal!

I screamed at じゅん君と ベン君 to see if they knew where we were and what was going on.

じゅん君 yelled back "分かりません！ But that looks like the 狸 we saw earlier!"

ベン君 said "I didn't think 狸 were real! And even if they are real, what's it doing here? And where are we going?"

All that I could contribute was, "What's a 狸?"

At this point, the animal ... he, ... it, turned and stared at us in surprise. He spoke. "How did you get here? Who are you?"

ベン君 whimpered, "We don't know. We were just trying to get out of the storm, and now we're in this wind tunnel or something. We headed for the 神社, and the next thing we knew, we were, umm, here."

じゅん君 interjected, "Speaking of here, where is here? And who, or what, are you?"

The 狸 replied, "私は 友 です。これは 私の 時の門 です。"

"時の門?" じゅん君 repeated, "それは 何 ですか。"

友さん replied, "It's not a word commonly used in 日本語 yet since few creatures know that these gates can be used for time travel. でも、百年後 (in 100 years), it will be a very common word! 僕は 2125 年 から 来ました。Something must have gone wrong, though, because you are not supposed to be here! That 風 must have affected the gate, but there's nothing that I can do now. We're on our way!"

I was starting to freak out, with all this talk about the past and the future and mistakes. I had to ask, "How can we be talking to a little fur ball? Animals aren't supposed to talk!"

Ben answered, "Japanese folk tales mention 狸 and 狐 (foxes) as having supernatural powers. They're supposed to be shape-shifters, animals that can change their appearance at will. Normally, they're portrayed as being quite tricky, but these are just stories. It's not real, of course."

"That may be," 友 sniffed, "but could one of you go over there to that switch please. We're coming in for a landing, and with your extra weight, we're descending much faster than we should be. I need help slowing us down. Hang on. We're almost there!"

■ 単語チェックリスト New Word Checklist
たんごちぇっくりすと

3-1

やま・山 *n* mountain
えむぴーすりー ぷれーやー・MP3 プレーヤー *n* MP3 player
おおきい・大きい い *adj.* big, large
ちいさい・小さい い *adj.* small
けいたい（でんわ）・携帯（電話） *n* cellular phone
やまもと・山本 *pn* Yamamoto (family name)
みんな・皆 *pron.* everyone, all
みなさん・皆さん *n* everyone (polite)
とても *adv.* very
たくさん *n* many, a lot
あっ *interj.* oh
すこし・少し *adv.* little
がっこう・学校 *n* school
がくせい；せいと・学生；生徒 *n* student
こうこう・高校 *n* high school
こうこうせい・高校生 *n* high school student
ちゅうがくせい・中学生 *n* middle school student
しょうがっこう・小学校 *n* elementary school
しょうがくせい・小学生 *n* elementary school student
ちゅうがっこう・中学校 *n* middle school
だいがく・大学 *n* college/university
だいがくせい・大学生 *n* college/university student
ほいくえん・保育園 *n* nursery school
ようちえん・幼稚園 *n* kindergarten
なんねんせい・何年生 *inter.* what grade/year
しょうがく いちねんせい・小学 一年生 *n* elementary school first grader
しょうがく にねんせい・小学 二年生 *n* elementary school second grader
しょうがく さんねんせい・小学 三年生 *n* elementary school third grader
しょうがく よねんせい・小学 四年生 *n* elementary school fourth grader
しょうがく ごねんせい・小学 五年生 *n* elementary school fifth grader
しょうがく ろくねんせい・小学 六年生 *n* elementary school sixth grader
ちゅうがく いちねんせい・中学 一年生 *count.* seventh grader
ちゅうがく にねんせい・中学 二年生 *count.* eighth grader
ちゅうがく さんねんせい・中学 三年生 *count.* ninth grader
こうこう いちねんせい・高校一年生 *count.* tenth grader
こうこう にねんせい・高校二年生 *count.* eleventh grader
こうこう さんねんせい・高校三年生 *count.* twelfth grader
だいがく いちねんせい・大学 一年生 *n* first year college/university student

3-2

すけじゅーる・スケジュール *n* schedule
じゅぎょう・授業 *n* class
くらす・クラス *n* class
きょうしつ・教室 *n* classroom
えいご・英語 *n* English language
こくご・国語 *n* national language (Japanese language)
すうがく・数学 *n* math
かがく・科学 *n* science
たいいく・体育 *n* physical education
びじゅつ・美術 *n* art, fine arts
おんがく・音楽 *n* music
ほーむるーむ・ホームルーム *n* homeroom
ひるやすみ・昼休み *n* lunch break
しゅくだい・宿題 *n* homework
しょうてすと・小テスト *n* small test, quiz
てすと・テスト *n* test
しけん・試験 *n* test, exam
さくぶん・作文 *n* essay
たのしい・楽しい い *adj.* fun, enjoyable
むずかしい・難しい い *adj.* difficult
かもく・科目 *n* school subject
しゃかい・社会 *n* social studies
いちじ・一時 *count.* one o'clock
にじ・二時 *count.* two o'clock
さんじ・三時 *count.* three o'clock
よじ・四時 *count.* four o'clock
ごじ・五時 *count.* five o'clock
ろくじ・六時 *count.* six o'clock
しちじ／ななじ・七時 *count.* seven o'clock
はちじ・八時 *count.* eight o'clock
くじ・九時 *count.* nine o'clock
じゅうじ・十時 *count.* ten o'clock
じゅういちじ・十一時 *count.* eleven o'clock
じゅうにじ・十二時 *count.* twelve o'clock
なんじ・何時 *inter.* what time
いっぷん・一分 *count.* one minute
にふん・二分 *count.* two minutes
さんぷん・三分 *count.* three minutes
よんぷん・四分 *count.* four minutes
ごふん・五分 *count.* five minutes
ろっぷん・六分 *count.* six minutes
ななふん・七分 *count.* seven minutes
はちふん／はっぷん・八分 *count.* eight minutes
きゅうふん・九分 *count.* nine minutes
じゅっぷん／じっぷん・十分 *count.* ten minutes
じゅういっぷん・十一分 *count.* eleven minutes
じゅうにふん・十二分 *count.* twelve minutes
じゅうさんぷん・十三分 *count.* thirteen minutes

にじゅっぷん・二十分 *count.* twenty minutes
にじゅういっぷん・二十一分 *count.* twenty-one minutes
よんじゅうさんぷん・四十三分 *count.* forty-three minutes
なんぷん・何分 *inter.* how many minutes
ごぜん・午前 *n* A.M.
ごご・午後 *n* P.M.
いま・今 *n/adv.* now
きょう・今日 *n* today
きのう・昨日 *n/adv.* yesterday
あした・明日 *n* tomorrow
まいにち・毎日 *n* every day
ときどき・時々 *n/adv.* sometimes
ちょっと *adv.* little, somewhat
まえ・前 *adv.* front, in front, before
すぎ／～すぎ past, after
ごろ／ころ about
から *part.* from (used with spec. times or locations)
はん・～半 *n* half hour
せいぶつがく・生物学 *n* biology
ほけんたいいく・保健体育 *n* health (class)
かていか・家庭科 *n* family consumer science
れきし・歴史 *n* history
あめりかし・アメリカ史 *n* American history
にほんし・日本史 *n* Japanese history
せかいし・世界史 *n* world history
けいざいがく・経済学 *n* economics
しんりがく・心理学 *n* psychology
ぶつりがく・物理学 *n* physics
じむしょ・事務所 *n* office
じかんわり・時間割 *n* schedule, timetable
いちびょう・一秒 *count.* one second
にびょう・二秒 *count.* two seconds
さんびょう・三秒 *count.* three seconds
よんびょう・四秒 *count.* four seconds
ごびょう・五秒 *count.* five seconds
ろくびょう・六秒 *count.* six seconds
ななびょう・七秒 *count.* seven seconds
はちびょう・八秒 *count.* eight seconds
きょうびょう・九秒 *count.* nine seconds
じゅうびょう・十秒 *count.* ten seconds
なんびょう・何秒 *inter.* How many seconds?

3-3

いちじかんめ・一時間目 *count.* first period
にじかんめ・二時間目 *count.* second period
さんじかんめ・三間館目 *count.* third period
よじかんめ・四時間目 *count.* fourth period
ごじかんめ・五時間目 *count.* fifth period
ろくじかんめ・六時間目 *count.* sixth period
なんじかんめ・何時間目 *inter.* what period
ほうかご・放課後 *n/adv.* time after school
あと・後 after
あとで・後で *adv.* afterwards
つぎ・次 *n/adv.* next
ぶかつ・部活 *n* club activity
としょかん・図書館 *n* library
たいいくかん・体育館 *n* gymnasium
こんぴゅーたーらぼ・コンピューターラボ *n* computer lab
せいせき・成績 *n* score, grade
やきゅう；べーすぼーる・野球；ベースボール *n* baseball
ばすけ；ばすけっとぼーる・バスケ；バスケットボール *n* basketball
じゅうどう・柔道 *n* judo
がっしょう・合唱 *n* chorus, choir
（お）てら・（お）寺 *n* temple
じんじゃ・神社 *n* shrine
ぶらすばんど・ブラスバンド *n* brass band
りくじょうぶ・陸上部 *n* track and field club
たっきゅうぶ・卓球部 *n* Ping-Pong club
けんどうぶ・剣道部 *n* kendo club
ばすけぶ・バスケ部 *n* basketball club (team)
ばれーぼーるぶ・バレーボール部 *n* volleyball club (team)

3-4

だめ な *adj* is bad
あつい・暑い い *adj.* hot (weather)
さむい・寒い い *adj.* cold (weather)
すずしい・涼しい い *adj.* cool (weather)
むしあつい・蒸し暑い い *adj.* humid (weather)
どあ・ドア *n* door
まど・窓 *n* window
でも *part.* "but" or "however" at the beginning of a sentence
あける・開ける／あけます・開けます *v* to open [door/window]
しめる・閉める／しめます・閉めます *v* to close; to shut (doors/windows)

3–5

えあこん・エアコン *n* air conditioning
かぜ・風 *n* wind
いきましょう・行きましょう *exp.* let's go
はやく・速く *adv.* quickly
とりい・鳥居 *n* torii (Shinto shrine gate)
どう *inter.* how
わっ！ *interj.* wow!
さあ *inter.* well...
すごい い *adj.* amazing, great, terrible, to a great extent
ね *part.* sentence ending for a rhetorical question or when seeking agreement
ねえ *part.* sentence ending that can be exclamatory or express surprise
よ *part.* sentence ending for a strong declarative statement or for emphasis

People and Places of Nagasaki

第4課

Learning and Performance Goals

This chapter will enable you to:

A) learn a little about trade in Japan in during the Tokugawa period (1603–1868)
B) learn the location of Kyushu (one of Japan's four main islands) and some of its geographical features
C) interview someone about what country she/he is from, what language is spoken there, and what sorts of food are eaten there
D) use three directional verbs (行きます to go, 来ます to come, and 帰ります to return home) in asking and answering questions about coming to school, going to a friend's house, or returning home
E) learn about the origins of some Japanese foods and other goods
F) create simple non-past and non-past negative sentences. For instance, if your friend invites you to a party, you will be able to say whether or not you are going
G) use 12 new kanji
H) use the "can-do" chart found on **TimeForJapanese.com** to chart your progress for what you "can-do" for each chapter

Hakata Port, Kyushu

第4課の1 何人(なにじん)　ですか。 Where are you from?

■ 会話(かいわ) Dialogue 

REMINDER: You may see some kanji / vocabulary you do not recognize. Use the context to try to understand the meanings of those parts of the dialogue.

1. ベン(べん)　：あなたは、だれ　ですか。
2. じゅん　：それは　何(なん)　ですか。
3. キアラ(きあら)　：あの風(かぜ)は　どこから　ですか。
4. 友(とも)　：皆(みな)さん、ちょっと　待(ま)って　下さい。僕(ぼく)の　名前(なまえ)は　友(とも)　です。あの風(かぜ)は　あの　鳥居(とりい)から　です。あの　鳥居(とりい)は　時(とき)の門(もん)　です。
5. じゅん　：時(とき)の門(もん)？
6. ベン(べん)&キアラ(きあら)：それは　何(なん)　ですか。
   (the sound of footsteps of many samurai)
7. 友(とも)　：ちょっと、静(しず)かにして　下さい。ところで、あなた達(たち)は、何人(なにじん)　ですか。

■ 単語(たんご) New Words 

アメリカ(あめりか) (*n*)	 アメリカ人(あめりかじん) (*n*)	 カナダ(かなだ) (*n*)	 カナダ人(かなだじん) (*n*)
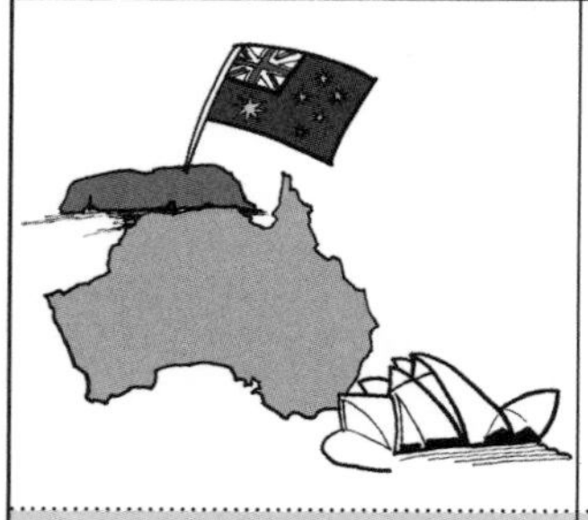 オーストラリア(おーすとらりあ) (*n*)	 オーストラリア人(おーすとらりあじん) (*n*)	ニュージーランド(にゅーじーらんど) (*n*)	 ニュージーランド人(にゅーじーらんどじん) (*n*)

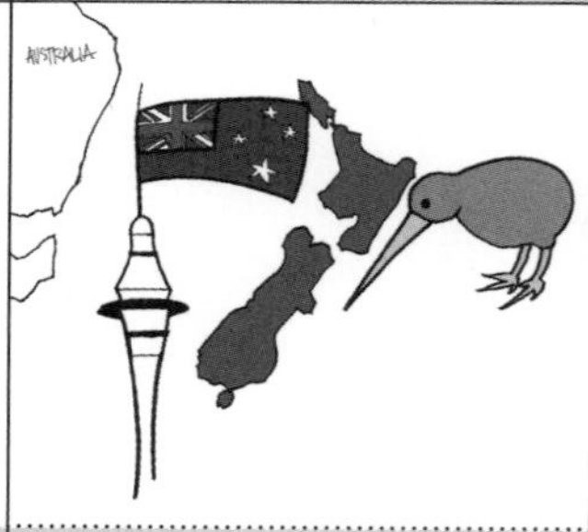

For nationalities such as the ones next page, you may designate that the person is of that country's descent/ancestry rather than a "citizen of" by replacing "人(じん)" with "系(けい)." In the examples below, the first word means England, and イギリス人(いぎりすじん) = English/British citizen while イギリス系(いぎりすけい) = a person of English/British descent/ancestry.

イギリス (*n*) いぎりす	イギリス人 (*n*) いぎりすじん イギリス系 (*n*) いぎりすけい	オランダ (*n*) おらんだ	オランダ人 (*n*) おらんだじん	ロシア (*n*) ろしあ	ロシア人 (*n*) ろしあじん
ポルトガル (*n*) ぽるとがる	ポルトガル人 (*n*) ぽるとがるじん	スペイン (*n*) すぺいん	スペイン人 (*n*) すぺいんじん	フランス (*n*) ふらんす	フランス人 (*n*) ふらんすじん
ドイツ (*n*) どいつ	ドイツ人 (*n*) どいつじん	中国 (*n*) ちゅうごく	中国人 (*n*) ちゅうごくじん	韓国 (*n*) かんこく	韓国人 (*n*) かんこくじん
インドネシア (*n*) いんどねしあ	インドネシア人 (*n*) いんどねしあじん	イタリア (*n*) いたりあ	イタリア人 (*n*) いたりあじん	メキシコ (*n*) めきしこ	メキシコ人 (*n*) めきしこじん
* 何人 (*inter.*) なにじん	ところで (*exp./conj.*)				

ケニア / ケニア人 (*n*) – Kenya/Kenyan (person) けにあ / けにあ

南アフリカ人 (*n*) – South African (person) みなみあふりか

ブラジル人 (*n*) – Brazilian (person) ぶらじる

ペルー人 (*n*) – Peruvian (person) ぺるー

プエルトリコ人 (*n*) – Puerto Rican (person) ぷえるとりこ

イラン人 (*n*) – Iranian (person) いらん

メキシコ系 (*n*) – of Mexican descent めきしこけい

日系人 (*n*) – of Japanese descent にっけいじん

何系 (*inter.*) – what ethnicity/heritage? なにけい

外国 (*n*) – foreign country がいこく

外国人 (*n*) – foreigner がいこくじん

から (*part.*) – from (prev. intro.)

(手伝う) 手伝います (*v*) – to help, assist (てつだ)

(言う) 言います (*v*) – to say (い)

Go to **TimeForJapanese.com** to learn more nationalities in Japanese.

* You were previously introduced to this kanji compound read as なんにん. Depending upon the context, you should be able to tell whether the kanji compound means "how many people?" (なんにんですか) or "what nationality?" (なにじんですか).

■ 漢字(かんじ) Kanji

言 (7 strokes)	ゲン(げん); い(う), こと – to speak	丶	亠	亠	亖	言	言	言
	言(げん)(語(ご)) – language; 言(い)(う) – to say; 言(こと)(葉(ば)) – words, language							
	This kanji shows a face. The first stroke is the forehead and is often drawn vertically. The second stroke is a "unibrow." Subsequent strokes form the eyes, then the nose, and finally the open mouth that is SPEAKING.							

外 (5 strokes)	ガイ(がい); そと – outside	ノ	ク	タ	夕	外		
	外(そと) – outside; 外(がい)(国(こく)) – foreign country; 外(がい)(国人(こくじん)) – foreigner, foreign person							
	This kanji combines the katakana タ(た) and ト(と). How to put タ + ト together for a memorization hint lies OUTSIDE my creative abilities.							

■ 言葉(ことば)の探索(たんさく) Language Detection

1. 何人(なにじん)ですか。/ 何系(なにけい)ですか。

When asking about someone's nationality or heritage, you can use these two questions.

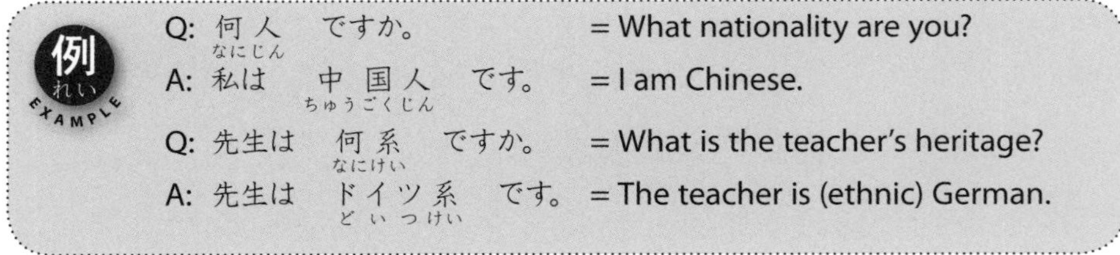
例(れい) EXAMPLE

Q: 何人(なにじん) ですか。 = What nationality are you?
A: 私は 中国人(ちゅうごくじん) です。 = I am Chinese.
Q: 先生は 何系(なにけい) ですか。 = What is the teacher's heritage?
A: 先生は ドイツ系(どいつけい) です。 = The teacher is (ethnic) German.

2. 友(とも)さんは、「__________。」と 言(い)いました。 - **Tomo said, "__________."**

The most common way to quote someone is to say the person's name, followed by は to show that he or she is the topic, followed by the quote, then the quotation particle と, and finally the verb "said" 言(い)いました。

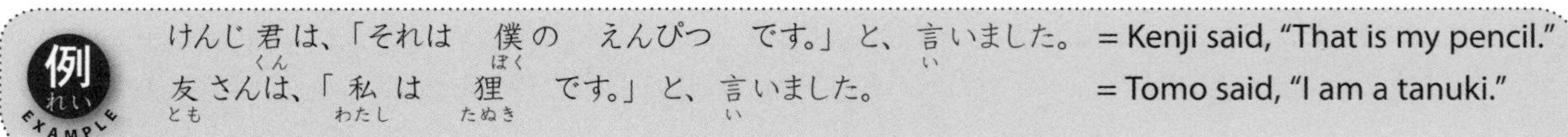
例(れい) EXAMPLE

けんじ君(くん)は、「それは 僕(ぼく)の えんぴつ です。」と、言(い)いました。 = Kenji said, "That is my pencil."
友(とも)さんは、「私(わたし)は 狸(たぬき) です。」と、言(い)いました。 = Tomo said, "I am a tanuki."

3. あなた **- you**

The pronoun あなた means *you* but it is generally not polite to use it unless you absolutely have to. Most people would not use this pronoun when referring to someone older, as it can be considered rude in this case. It is not as commonly used as "you" in English. Always try to address the person you are talking to by his or her name or title when possible or not at all if he/she is understood. あなた can be useful, however, when you do not know the name of the person you are talking to.

■ 自習 Self Check

1.　何人 or 何系 - what nationality/heritage

Practice asking what country someone is from or what heritage they are, using 何人 or 何系.

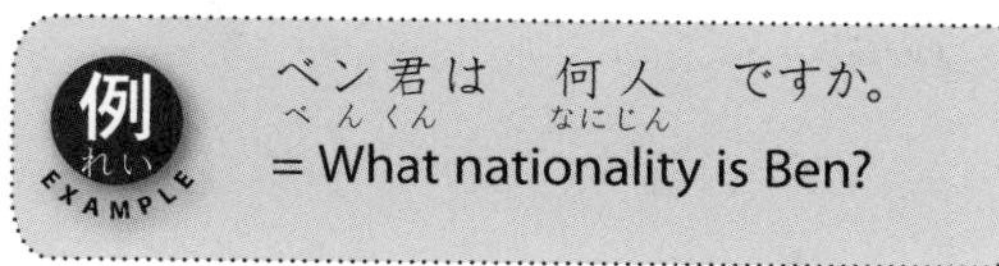
例
れい
EXAMPLE
ベン君は　何人　ですか。
= What nationality is Ben?

A) What nationality is the teacher?
B) What nationality is (my friend's) mother?
C) What nationality is the English teacher?
D) What nationality is Tomo?
E) What is the heritage of that person over there?

2.　～と　言いました。

Translate sentences A and B into English and sentences C and D into Japanese.

A) キアラさん　は、「これは　本　です。」と　言いました。
B) 母は、「座って　下さい。」と　言いました。
C) The teacher said, "It is three o'clock."
D) I said, "My school is very big."

3.　あなた

With which of the following could you use あなた?

your teacher	your younger sister	your friend	your dog	Mr. Smith	Mrs. Miyazaki

■ 練習の時間 Time for Practice

1. Pair Practice

Ask three classmates about the national origin or heritage of their families. Be prepared to report your findings. (Take turns.)

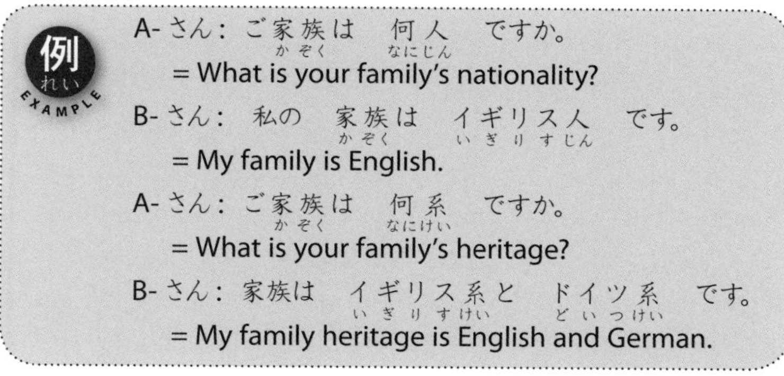
例
れい
EXAMPLE
A-さん: ご家族は　何人　ですか。
= What is your family's nationality?
B-さん: 私の　家族は　イギリス人　です。
= My family is English.
A-さん: ご家族は　何系　ですか。
= What is your family's heritage?
B-さん: 家族は　イギリス系と　ドイツ系　です。
= My family heritage is English and German.

2. Pair Practice

Use the picture to talk about where each student is from.

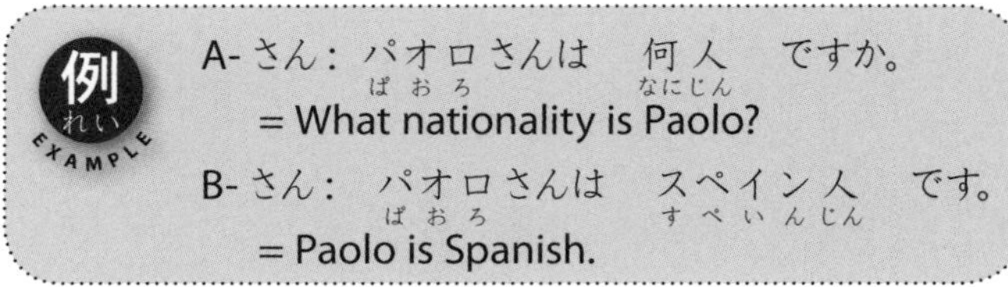
例(れい) EXAMPLE

A- さん：パオロ(ぱおろ)さんは 何人(なにじん) ですか。
= What nationality is Paolo?

B- さん：パオロ(ぱおろ)さんは スペイン人(すぺいんじん) です。
= Paolo is Spanish.

3. Group Practice

Survey six classmates. Ask them where their grandparents came from. If you don't know the answer when you are asked, say 知(し)りません. Report your results to the class.

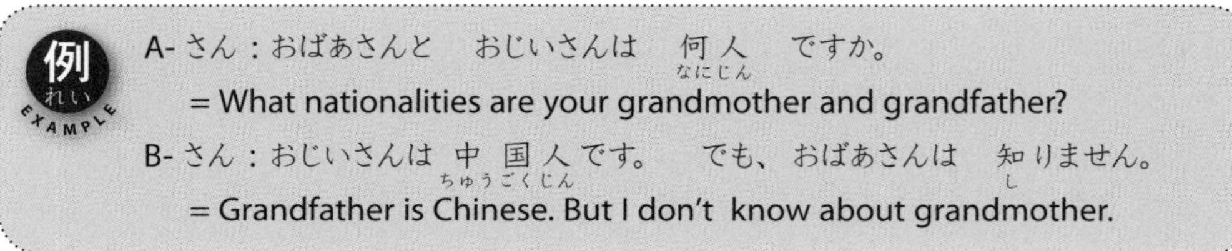
例(れい) EXAMPLE

A- さん：おばあさんと おじいさんは 何人(なにじん) ですか。
= What nationalities are your grandmother and grandfather?

B- さん：おじいさんは 中国人(ちゅうごくじん)です。 でも、おばあさんは 知(し)りません。
= Grandfather is Chinese. But I don't know about grandmother.

■ 文化箱(ぶんかばこ) Culture Chest

九州(きゅうしゅう)

One of the largest and most famous cities on the southern island of 九州(きゅうしゅう) is 長崎(ながさき). The name 九州 was given to the island for the nine feudal states that made up this island. On this island exists some of the oldest evidence of Japanese civilization. On the eastern coast of the island, clay funerary statues called はにわ, dating from 1,500 to 1,800 years ago, have been unearthed. These statues of houses, warriors, horses, and other animals were placed around the graves of important people.

Much of the Tom Cruise movie *The Last Samurai* centers around rebels in southern 九州. Far away from the power of the Imperial Court, this part of Japan had always been one of the least controlled by feudal governments. The samurai of さつま, what is now the western half of Kagoshima Province in southern 九州, and 長州(ちょうしゅう) in far western 本州(ほんしゅう) (Japan's largest island), were instrumental in the overthrow of the shogun-dominated 徳川(とくがわ) government (1603–1868). These rebels were also interested in the restoration of power to the Emperor, just after the Tokugawa Period. Eventually, though, some of these same samurai came to disagree with Japan's path toward westernization and trade with the outside, and they attempted the second rebellion that lies at the heart of the film *The Last Samurai*.

■ キアラのジャーナル (きあら じゃーなる) Kiara's Journal

Read the journal entry below, and then answer these questions.

❶ What is a tanuki? See if you can find a picture of one.
❷ What is the time tunnel called in Japanese?
❸ Where did the travelers arrive?
❹ In what year did they arrive?
❺ Describe or draw a picture of the people and clothing Kiara and her friends might have seen in their new location.

ジャーナル(じゃーなる)へ

You're never going to believe what happened today. We were running for cover from a sudden windstorm toward the nearest shelter, a Shinto 神社(じんじゃ)。As we ducked under the 鳥居(とりい) gate, lights flashed and the next thing we knew, we were inside some sort of room, or tunnel, but there were no walls! It was very strange. The furry little animal we had seen the day before, rustling around in the bushes near the 神社、ran through the 鳥居 with us, and that must have triggered the "door" to this place. Ben said that the creature was a 狸(たぬき) or a "raccoon dog." We have raccoons at home, but they don't look anything like this. The creature could talk too!「私(わたし)の 名前(なまえ)は 友(とも) です。」と、言いました。He was sort of cute, but seemed to be a bit cranky. Here's what happened next ...

じゅん君(くん)は、「それは いい です けど… ここは どこ ですか!」と、言いました。We seemed to be flying through this tunnel of darkness lit only by small glowing lights. 友さんは、「これは タイムトンネル(たいむとんねる)、時(とき)の門(もん) です。今(いま)から 日本の 1601 年へ 行(い)きます。」と、言いました。じゅん君は、「ええ? 1601 年 ですか。うそ!」と、言いました。"How is that possible?" 友さんは、「それは 後(あと)で。長崎(ながさき)へ ようこそ。」と、言いました。ベン(べん)君は、「1601 年の 長崎(ながさき)には 色々(いろいろ)な 外国人(がいこくじん)が います。ポルトガル人(ぽるとがるじん)と スペイン人(すぺいんじん)と フィリピン人(ふぃりぴんじん)と 中国人(ちゅうごくじん)と 韓国人(かんこくじん)が います。」と、言いました。

As we walked out the gate, I turned around to look at it. We were right in front of yet another, different 神社! I'm not sure how this whole 時(とき)の門(もん) thing works yet, but walking into this live history lesson, set over 四百年前(まえ)、is very strange indeed! From our hillside, we could see the deep blue-green of the 海(うみ) below us, with a few large sailing ships anchored in the bay. People walked here and there, many carrying baskets. We started down the hill on a hard-packed dirt road, lined on both sides with shops and houses. People were wearing clothes that looked like the pictures in 私の 高校の 世界史(せかいし)の 教科書(きょうかしょ). Some had on traditional 日本の 着物(きもの)、others were wearing 大きい ぼうし with feathers, big baggy pants, and funny shoes.

友さんは、「その 人達(ひとたち)は スペイン(すぺいん)から 来(き)た人達(ひとたち) です。あの人は イギリス人(いぎりすじん) です。」と、言いました。「はい、あそこへ 行(い)きましょう。」

And with that, 友さん led us off in the other direction.

第4課の2 何語(なにご)を　話(はな)しますか。 What language do you speak?

■ 会話(かいわ) Dialogue

REMINDER: You may see some kanji / vocabulary you do not recognize. Use the context to try to understand the meanings of those parts of the dialogue.

1. ベン(べん)　：ええ〜っ！あの　歴史(れきし)の　教科書(きょうかしょ)の　中(なか)の　ウィリアム・アダムズ(うぃりあむ・あだむず)？
2. じゅん　：サイン(さいん)　お願(ねが)いします！
3. キアラ(きあら)　：写真(しゃしん)　お願(ねが)いします！
4. ベン(べん)　：あくしゅも　お願(ねが)いします。
5. アダムズ(あだむず)：写真(しゃしん)　ですか。　それは　何　ですか。あなた達(たち)は　だれ　ですか。
どこから　ですか。なぜ　私の　名前(なまえ)が　分(わ)かりますか。

■ 単語 New Words
たんご

Hallo!
Zdrav stvuyte!
Boas Tardes!
Hola!
Bonjour!
オランダ語 (n) おらんだご
ロシア語 (n) ろしあご
ポルトガル語 (n) ぽるとがるご
スペイン語 (n) すぺいんご
フランス語 (n) ふらんすご
Ni Hao!
Ahn nyeong ha se yo!
Selemat Siang!
Ciao!
Guten tag!
中国語 (n) ちゅうごくご
韓国語 (n) かんこくご
インドネシア語 (n) いんどねしあご
イタリア語 (n) いたりあご
ドイツ語 (n) どいつご
サイン (n) さいん
あくしゅ (n)
写真を撮ります (v) しゃしん と
写真を撮ってもいいですか。(しゃしん と) – May I take a photo?
(話す) 話します (v) – to speak (はな はな)
(知る) 知ります (v) – to know something/someone (し し)

手話 (しゅわ) (n) – sign language.　スワヒリ語 (すわひりご) (n) – Swahili　なぜ or どうして (inter.) – why

sheets of.../ flat things	number/ quantity	pages	sheets of.../ flat things	number/ quantity	pages
一枚 (いちまい)	one	一ページ (いちぺーじ)	七枚 (ななまい)	seven	七ページ (ななぺーじ)
二枚 (にまい)	two	二ページ (にぺーじ)	八枚 (はちまい)	eight	八ページ (はちぺーじ)
三枚 (さんまい)	three	三ページ (さんぺーじ)	九枚 (きゅうまい)	nine	九ページ (きゅうぺーじ)
四枚 (よんまい)	four	四ページ (よんぺーじ)	十枚 (じゅうまい)	ten	十ページ (じゅうぺーじ)
五枚 (ごまい)	five	五ページ (ごぺーじ)	十一枚 (じゅういちまい)	eleven	十一ページ (じゅういちぺーじ)
六枚 (ろくまい)	six	六ページ (ぺーじ)	何枚 (なんまい)	how many?	何ページ (なんぺーじ)

■ 漢字 Kanji
かんじ

話 (13 strokes)							
ワ (わ); はなし, はな(す) – to speak, conversation	丶	亠	亡	言	言	言	言
話(す) (はな) – to talk (to someone/something else); (電)話 (でんわ) – telephone (literally, electric talking)	訁	訐	訐	話	話	話	

The left seven strokes of this kanji form a radical, 言, that is in many words related to speaking. The right side has a tongue (舌) which is 1,000 (千) on top of a mouth (口). Imagine 1,000 mouths forming one tongue in order to SPEAK.

■ 言葉(ことば)の探索(たんさく) Language Detection

～ます

The ～ます form of Japanese verbs is used for the polite non-past tense. The non-past tense can have one of two meanings. It can be present or future tense depending on the context:

a. Present or continuous action.

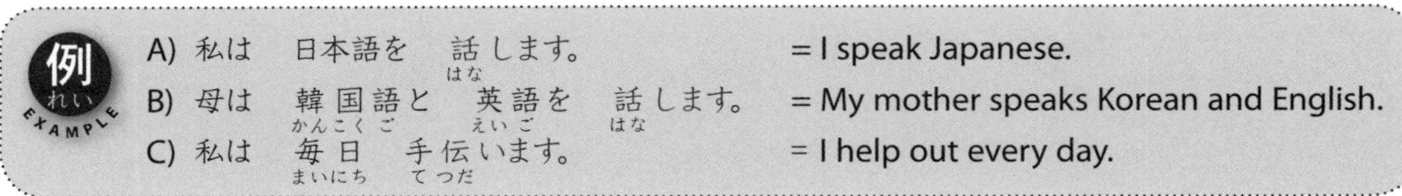

例 れい EXAMPLE
A) 私は　日本語を　話(はな)します。 = I speak Japanese.
B) 母は　韓国語(かんこくご)と　英語(えいご)を　話(はな)します。 = My mother speaks Korean and English.
C) 私は　毎日(まいにち)　手伝(てつだ)います。 = I help out every day.

b. Future tense.

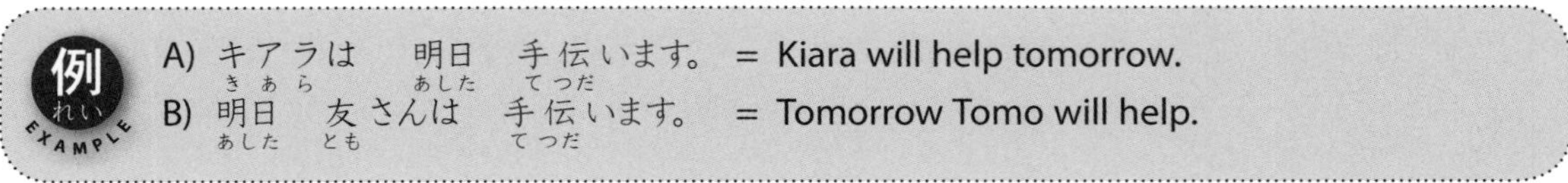

例 れい EXAMPLE
A) キアラ(きあら)は　明日(あした)　手伝(てつだ)います。 = Kiara will help tomorrow.
B) 明日(あした)　友(とも)さんは　手伝(てつだ)います。 = Tomorrow Tomo will help.

NOTE: the ～ます form is NOT used to say that someone "is doing" something right at that moment. You will learn how to say that in chapter 6.

■ 自習(じしゅう) Self Check

～ます　話(はな)します

Give the two possible translations, continuous action and future tense, for the following:

A) ベン君(べんくん)は　日本語を　話(はな)します。

B) 愛子(あいこ)さんは　手伝(てつだ)います。

C) 毎日(まいにち)、友(とも)さんが　います。

D) ゆみさんは　写真(しゃしん)を　とります。

■ 練習(れんしゅう)の時間(じかん) Time for Practice

1. Small Group Practice

Bring a picture of a famous person from another country to class, or draw a picture of a real or imaginary foreign friend. Introduce this person to your classmates, including their name, nationality, and what language(s) they speak. Trade pictures and introduce your newest foreign friend to classmates.

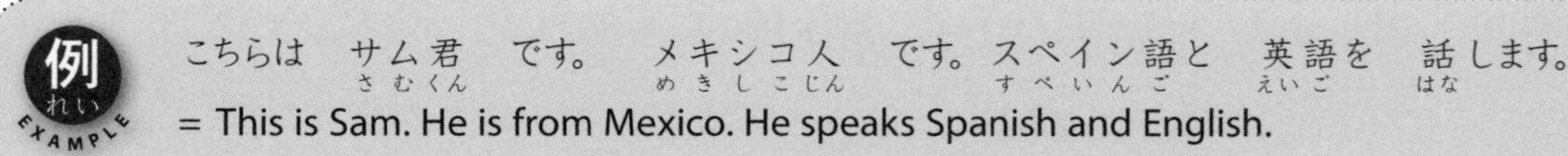

例 れい EXAMPLE
こちらは　サム君(さむくん)　です。　メキシコ人(めきしこじん)　です。スペイン語(すぺいんご)と　英語(えいご)を　話(はな)します。
= This is Sam. He is from Mexico. He speaks Spanish and English.

2. Pair Practice

何ページ

Take turns giving each other a page number to find in your textbook. See how quickly you can locate the correct page. Use the counter ページ.

A-さん：四十三ページを　開いて　下さい。 = Please open your book to page 43.
B-さん：(*opens the textbook to page 43*)
A-さん：よく　できました。 = Good job! (if B-さん opens to the correct page)
A-さん：だめ　です。 = Wrong. (if B-さん opens to wrong page)

■ 文化箱 Culture Chest

サイン　お願いします！

サイン is one of the many foreign "loan" words that have become integrated into the Japanese language. You will learn many other such "loan" words in the course of your study of Japanese. サイン　お願いします！ "Please give me your signature!" is a phrase that you might often hear when visiting Japanese schools or famous sites in Japan, especially in the popular tourist cities of Nara or Kyoto. This might make you feel like a rock star, but it is often an assignment for timid, yet eager Japanese school children. Japanese students from all over Japan visit these famous sites on school field trips, and one aspect of going to these sites is the opportunity to practice their English language speaking skills with foreign tourists. Taking photos with visitors and getting signatures in another language is a highlight for many school children in Japan.

■ キアラのジャーナル Kiara's Journal

Read the journal entry below, and then answer these questions.

❶ What did Tomo want to show Kiara, Ben, and Jun at the fruit and vegetable store?
❷ Where did this object originally come from? How did it get to Japan?
❸ Near the end of the journal entry, Ben gasps. Why is he so surprised?

ジャーナルへ

友さんと じゅん君と ベン君 walked farther into the town down the narrow dirt street. This was totally weird on so many levels! I mean, what seems like only a few hours ago, we were deciding what club to visit after school, and now we're wandering around dirt streets in medieval Nagasaki. My friends are never going to believe this. I knew that I was embarking on an adventure when I came to Japan, but I never imagined...

友さん stopped us in front of a fruit and vegetable store. そして 友さんは、「これを 見て下さい。」と、言いました。He held up a small brown round object.「これは スペインからです。」私は、「What's special about その potato? 」と、言いました。友さんは、「これは ジャガイモです。ジャガイモは オランダ人が 持って来ました (brought)。」と、言いました。「First, スペイン人は 南米 (South America) から ヨーロッパ (Europe) へ 持って行きました (took)。And then, オランダ人は インドネシアの ジャカルタ (Jakarta) へ持って行きました。そしてオランダ人は ジャカルタから ここに 持って来ました。」と、言いました。ベン君は とても surprised でした。そして、「そう ですか。That must be why they are called ジャガイモ。イモ means potato, and the fact that they came from Jakarta, Indonesia is why this particular kind of potato is called ジャガイモ。 ジャガ is short for Jakarta! なるほど!」と、言いました。The store owner smiled widely, leaned forward, and asked,「何人 ですか。」じゅん君は、「この人は アメリカ人 です。その人は オーストラリア人 です。僕は日本人 です。」と、言いました。

The おじさん asked,「そう ですか。アメリカは オランダに ありますか。」Realizing that America had not even become a country yet, all that I could say was「それは ちょっと 違います (a little different)。」おじさん asked,「何語を 話しますか。スペイン語を 話しますか。」私は、「いいえ、英語を 話します。日本語も ちょっと 話します。」と、言いました。He then looked at ベン君 and said「何語を 話しますか。」ベン君は、「僕も 英語を 話します。」と言いました。He stared again at me, then at ベン君、and then glanced at the tall, thin Caucasian man waiting next door at the calligrapher's stall. He mumbled something to himself, then smiled and said,「あの人も 英語を 話しますよ。」Surprised, we turned toward the tall man wearing an old British sailor's uniform. I asked,「何語を 話しますか。」He answered,「私は オランダ語と 英語と 日本語も 話します。なぜ ですか。」I said,「私と この人も 英語を話します。あなたは、何人 ですか。」「僕は イギリス人 です。でも オランダから 来ました。僕の 名前は ウィリアム・アダムズ です。」the man replied in good 日本語、but with a pretty serious accent.

"THE William Adams?" ベン君 gasped. "You're the one who was shipwrecked here and later met..." Before he could finish his sentence, 友さん jumped into the conversation. "That vegetable store owner, over there, that's who you met. And that's how these kids heard about you." 友さん then turned to us with,「はい、アダムズさんは very busy でしょう。」友さん bowed to アダムズさん、「すみません。」と言いました。Then he turned back to us. 友さんは、「あそこに とても いい 寿司屋が ありますよ。」と、言いました。

I realized that my stomach was actually a bit ペコペコ、and I also realized that it was probably good that ベン君 was not able to finish his sentence to Mr. Adams. If he had, he would have told Mr. Adams about the future. From all of the sci-fi books and 漫画 that I've read, I know that this would definitely not have been a good thing to do.

第4課の3 私は ここで 食べません。
I won't eat here.

1

1) いらっしゃいませ！ ようこそ！あ、すみません。狸は、ちょっと・・・。

2) この狸は 私達の 友達 です。

3) 日本語も 分かります。

4) すみません。狸は、ちょっと・・・。

5) はい、分かりました。私は ここで 食べません。ちょっと 待って下さい。

2.

6) 大丈夫 ですよ・・・。

3.

7) こんにちは。

8)いらっしゃいませ！

9) アダムズさん、ここで 私達は ラーメンを 食べます。一緒に どうぞ。

10) ありがとう ございます。

4.

11) お飲み物は？

SHE DOESN'T REALIZE I'M TOMO ! TRICKED HER. HEHEHE...

5.

12) お茶を お願いします。

■ 会話(かいわ) Dialogue 

REMINDER: You may see some kanji / vocabulary you do not recognize. Use the context to try to understand the meanings of those parts of the dialogue.

【ラーメン屋(や)　で】

1. 店員(てんいん)　：　いらっしゃいませ！　ようこそ！　あ、すみません。狸(たぬき)は、ちょっと…。
2. キアラ　：　この　狸(たぬき)は　私達(たち)の　友達(ともだち)　です。
3. ベン　：　日本語も　分(わ)かります。
4. 店員(てんいん)　：　すみません。狸(たぬき)は、ちょっと…。
5. 友(とも)　：　はい、分(わ)かりました。私は　ここで　食(た)べません。ちょっと　待(ま)って下さい。
6. 友(とも)　：　大丈夫(だいじょうぶ)ですよ…。
7. 友(とも)　：　こんにちは。
8. 店員(てんいん)　：　いらっしゃいませ！
9. ベン　：　アダムズさん、ここで　私達(たち)は　ラーメンを　食(た)べます。一緒(いっしょ)に　どうぞ。
10. 友(とも)　：　ありがとう　ございます。
11. 店員(てんいん)　：　お飲(の)み物(もの)は？
12. 友(とも)　：　お茶(ちゃ)を　お願(ねが)いします。

* 大丈夫(だいじょうぶ) - all right (introduced in chapter 6)

■ 単語(たんご) New Words 

 パン (*n*)	 パン屋(や) (*n*)	 本屋(ほんや) (*n*)	 物(もの) (*n*)	 食(た)べ物(もの) (*n*)
飲(の)み物(もの) (*n*)	レストラン (*n*)	(食(た)べる) 食(た)べます (*v*)	まだ (*adv.*) – not yet (something) は、ちょっと・・・ – (something) is a little... コーラ (*n*) – cola	
(飲(の)む) 飲(の)みます (*v*)	いらっしゃいませ (*exp.*)	車(くるま) (*n*)	チキン / 鶏肉(とりにく) (*n*) – chicken (meat) ハンバーガー (*n*) – hamburger	

漢字(かんじ) Kanji

食 (9 strokes)							
ショク;た(べる) – food, eat	ノ	人	𠆢	今	今	今	食
食(た)(べる) – to eat; 食(た)(べ物(もの)) – food/foods; 食(しょく)(事(じ)) – to dine	食	食					
The top two strokes here represent a roof, and below the roof is the kanji for good (良). It is always good to EAT under a roof.							

飲 (12 strokes)							
の(む) – drink	ノ	人	𠆢	今	今	今	食
飲(の)(む) – to drink; 飲(の)(み物(もの)) – drink/drinks	食	飠	飲	飲	飲		
The left side of this kanji is the radical for "to eat" (食) and the right side means lacking (欠). It is fine to live with a lack of food as long as you have something to DRINK.							

物 (8 strokes)							
ブツ(ぶつ), もの – thing, object	ノ	ᅩ	牛	牛	牛	物	物
物(もの) – thing, object; (本(ほん))物(もの) – the real thing, genuine object; (動(どう))物(ぶつ) – animal, lit. a moving thing	物						
The left side of this kanji is the radical for "cow" (牛). The right side looks like it could be long hair on a cow or some THING. We don't know what it is, but it is a THING.							

車 (7 strokes)							
シャ(しゃ), くるま – car, cart	一	𠂆	冂	日	目	亘	車
車(くるま) – car, cart; 自動車(じどうしゃ) – automobile; 自転車(じてんしゃ) – bicycle; (電(でん))車(しゃ) – electric train							
Think of viewing this kanji as you would a horse cart from above with the first and last horizontal strokes as the wheels, the center as the cart body, and the last stroke as the axle.							

言葉(ことば)の探索(たんさく) Language Detection

1. 食(た)べません **– negative of ～ます verbs**

To change a ～ます verb to its negative form, simply change the ～ます ending to ～ません. (Note that as in the examples below, the particle after the direct object usually changes from を to は for negative sentences.)

A) 寿司(すし)を　食(た)べます。 = I eat sushi.
B) いもは　食(た)べません。 = I do not eat potatoes.

Q: スペイン語(すぺいんご)を　話(はな)しますか。 = Do you speak Spanish?
A: スペイン語(すぺいんご)は　話(はな)しません。 = (I) do not speak Spanish.
Q: お父さんは　日本語を　話(はな)しますか。 = Does your father speak Japanese?
A: いいえ、日本語は　話(はな)しません。 = No, he does not speak Japanese.

2. 日本で　寿司(すし)を　食(た)べます。

We learned earlier that the particle で can mean "by means of." で also indicates the place of action. In the sentence above, 日本 is the place of action (where the sushi is being eaten) and therefore is followed by で.

A) レストラン(れすとらん)で　お茶(ちゃ)を　飲(の)みます。 = At the restaurant, I will drink green tea.
B) 妹は　家で　手伝(てつだ)います。 = My younger sister helps out at home.
C) 学校で　お昼(ひる)ご飯(はん)を　食(た)べません。 = I don't eat lunch at school.

3. ちょっと・・・・

ちょっと can be used to say "no thank you" to someone without giving a specific reason why. ちょっと literally means "a little."

A-さん：　この寿司(すし)を　どうぞ。 = Here, try this sushi.
B-さん：　すみません。寿司(すし)は　ちょっと・・・ = I'm sorry, but sushi is a little . . .

■ 自習(じしゅう) Self Check

1. 〜ません

Change the following into the negative:

A) 話(はな)します
B) います
C) あります
D) 言(い)います
E) 食(た)べます
F) 飲(の)みます

2. で

Practice using で in Japanese for the place of action. The places where the actions take place are written in gray. Use this pattern: (topic) は (place) で (direct object) を (verb).

けいた君(くん)は　図書館(としょかん)で　本(ほん)を　読(よ)みます。
= Keita reads books in the library.

A) I will speak Japanese in Japan.
B) I will not speak English in Japan.
C) My mother speaks Korean at home.
D) My younger sister eats lunch in the cafeteria. (カフェテリア(かふぇてりあ) = cafeteria)
E) Please read manga at home.
F) My teacher helped in the computer lab.

■ 練習(れんしゅう)の時間(じかん) Time for Practice

1. Pair Practice

With a partner, take turns asking what you would eat and drink at the following places in Japanese. Use the list of foods and drinks below to help you with your answers. After you finish talking about the restaurants below, talk about restaurants in your area where you or your partners frequent.

例(れい) EXAMPLE

A- さん： お寿司屋(すしや)で 何(なに)を 食(た)べますか。あそこで 何(なに)を 飲(の)みますか。
= What do you eat at the sushi restaurant? What do you drink?

B- さん： お寿司屋(すしや)で 巻(ま)き寿司(ずし)を 食(た)べます。あそこで お茶(ちゃ)を 飲(の)みます。
= At the sushi restaurant, I eat rolled sushi. I drink green tea.

ラーメン屋
らーめんや

イタリアンレストラン
いたりあんれすとらん

ケンタッキー
けんたっきー
(フライドチキン)
ふらいどちきん

マクドナルド
まくどなると

メキシカン
めきしかん
レストラン
れすとらん

お寿司屋
すしや

食(た)べ物(もの)		飲(の)み物(もの)	
ハンバーガー (はんばーがー)	たこ	コーラ (こーら)	お茶(ちゃ)
チキン (ちきん)	スパゲッティ (すぱげってぃ)	オレンジジュース (おれんじじゅーす)	お水(みず)
ピザ (ぴざ)	みそラーメン (らーめん)	ミルク (みるく)	
タコス (たこす)			

2. Pair Practice

With a partner, read through the words listed below. Then take turns using one word from each column to make questions and answers. Add direct objects, particles, and/or conjunctions as necessary. Make sure you include at least some questions that will be answered in the negative to help your partner practice the negative 〜ません pattern.

例(れい) EXAMPLE

(母 and 話(はな)します)

A- さん： お母さんは 日本語を 話(はな)しますか。 = Does your mother speak Japanese?

B- さん： はい、母は 日本語を 話(はな)します。 = Yes, my mother speaks Japanese.

-OR- いいえ、日本語は 話(はな)しません。 = No, my mother doesn't speak Japanese.

妹さん	お父さん	食(た)べます	話(はな)します
お兄さん	おばあさん	飲(の)みます	見(み)ます
お母さん	先生		

■ 文化箱 Culture Chest

狸

What's a 狸？狸 is the Japanese name for a "raccoon-dog," an animal that lives throughout Japan. It is somewhat larger than a North American raccoon. 狸 are mischievous creatures with the reputation of being tricksters. They are said to have the ability to "shape-shift," or turn into other beings. According to Japanese folklore, when a 狸 places a large leaf on its head, it can change shape, often becoming a Buddhist monk or priest.

■ キアラのジャーナル Kiara's Journal 

Read the journal entry below, and then answer these questions.

❶ What nationalities might you find in 17th-century Nagasaki?
❷ Nagasaki is famous (有名) for two types of food. What are they?
❸ To find a traditional-style restaurant in Japan today, what sign would you look for?

ジャーナルへ

We've been in Nagasaki only a few hours, but I wanted to update you on what I've done so far. I'm learning a lot about Japanese food!

友さんは、「ここには 韓国の 食べ物と 中国の 食べ物と スペインの 食べ物と 日本の 食べ物が あります。オランダ人は 二年前 日本へ 来ました。 だから、オランダの 食べ物は まだ ありません。長崎は とても いい ところ です。 あそこの お寿司屋さんに たこが あります。ポルトガルでは、たこを たくさん 食べます。長崎は、ラーメンと *ぎょうざも *有名 です。何を 食べますか。」と、言いました。

ベン君は、「中国人が たくさん いますね。 ここは ラーメンが とても おいしいです。ラーメンと ぎょうざを 食べませんか。アダムズさんも ラーメン屋さんへ 行きました。」

「いい ですよ。 何でも いい ですよ。」と、友さんは、言いました。

友さんは sure gets excited about his food. He's really quite chunky for a たぬき of only about 三 feet. Eating seems to be a top priority for the little guy. In fact, he doesn't want to stop.

そして 友さんは、「後で あの寿司屋へも 行きませんか。とても いい レストラン ですよ！」と、言いました。

At the entrance to the ラーメン屋 hung a long のれん curtain. You see these outside Japanese restaurants even in the 21st century, covering the door. That was とても 小さな レストラン でした。ラーメン屋の人 took our order. ベン君は、「私は みそラーメンを 食べます。」と、言いました。わたしは、とんこつラーメンを 食べました。とんこつラーメン is pork broth noodle soup. 友さんは、5 dishes を 食べました。He eats a lot!

また 後で。

* ぎょうざ - fried wontons, often called pot stickers in the West * 有名 - famous

第4課の4 私は　江戸(えど)に　行(い)きます。

I will go to Edo.

1.

1)　明日 私は
江戸に 行きます。

2) え、東京 ですか?
私達も 一緒に 行きます！

3) 私達は 東京から
です。だから、
アダムズさんと 一緒に
東京に帰ります！

2.

4) いいえ、東京では　ありません。
私は、江戸に 行きます。

5) 江戸と
東京は 同じ
です。

3.

6)よく
分かりません
？？？？

7) とにかく、江戸に
私達も、一緒に
行っても いい ですか。

8) だめ です。あ！人が 来ます。
静かにして下さい。旅館へ
行きましょう。

■ 会話(かいわ) Dialogue

REMINDER: You may see some kanji / vocabulary you do not recognize. Use the context to try to understand the meanings of those parts of the dialogue.

1. アダムズ(あだむず)： 明日(あした)　私は　江戸(えど)に　行(い)きます。
2. ベン(べん)　：　え、東京　ですか？　私達(わたしたち)も　一緒(いっしょ)に　行(い)きます！
3. じゅん　：　私達(わたしたち)は　東京から　です。だから、アダムズ(あだむず)さんと　一緒(いっしょ)に　東京に　帰(かえ)ります！
4. アダムズ(あだむず)：　いいえ、東京では　ありません。私は、江戸(えど)に　行(い)きます。
5. じゅん　：　江戸(えど)と東京は　同(おな)じ　です。
6. アダムズ(あだむず)：　よく　分(わ)かりません ????
7. キアラ(きあら)　：　とにかく、江戸(えど)に　私達(わたしたち)も、一緒(いっしょ)に　行(い)っても　いい　ですか。
8. 友(とも)　：　だめ　です。あ！人が　来(き)ます。静(しず)かに　して下さい。*旅館(りょかん)へ　行(い)きましょう。

* 旅館(りょかん) - ryokan, Japanese inn/hotel

■ 単語(たんご) New Words

			(する) します (v) – to do
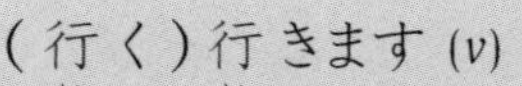 (行(い)く) 行(い)きます (v)	(来(く)る) 来(き)ます (v)	(帰(かえ)る) 帰(かえ)ります (v)	だから (conj.) – so, therefore

■ 漢字(かんじ) Kanji

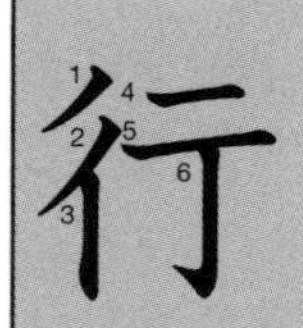 行 6 strokes	コウ(こう) – journey; い(く) – to go	ノ	彡	彳	彳一	行	行	
	行(い)(く) – go; (旅(りょ))行(こう) – a trip, travel							
	The left three strokes show a person with a hat about to GO to the crossroads, represented by the three strokes on the right.							

来 7 strokes	ライ(らい) – next/coming; く(る) – to come	一	丆	冖	立	平	来	来
	来(く)(る) – to come; 来(らい)(週(しゅう)) – next week							
	This kanji consists of one (一) and rice (米). One COMES to rice, one grain at a time, to get food in Japan.							

帰 (10 strokes)	かえ(る) – return (home)	丨	刂	刂	刂	刂	刂	刂
	帰(る) – return (home)	帰	帰	帰				
	The katakana for リ and ヨ in this kanji show that one has traveled (RYOKOU), but the upside down 出る (to exit, or to go out) shows that this person has turned around and COME BACK or RETURNED.							

■ 言葉の探索 Language Detection

1. へ/に direction particles

Three verbs of movement you have just learned are 行きます 来ます 帰ります (go, come, return). Verbs of movement often have a goal of movement (a destination) which takes either the particle へ or に. In this case, these two particles are interchangeable. Note that when へ is a particle, it is always pronounced "E". Use this pattern: (topic) は (place) に or へ (direction verb).

A) ベン君は 日本へ 帰ります。 = Ben will return to Japan.
B) キアラさんは イタリアに 行ます。 = Kiara will go to Italy.
C) じゅん君は 僕の 家に 来ません。 = Jun will not come to my house.
D) 明日、アメリカへ 行きますか。 = Tomorrow, are you going to the U.S.?

NOTE: Remember to use へ or に after places where you go, and to use で after places where something is done.

2. The point of view of the speaker determines which direction verb is used in Japanese.

*A- さん: 私の 家へ 来ますか。 = Will you come to my house?
B- さん: はい、行きます。 = Yes, I will go.
A- さん (*at school*): 放課後、部活に 行きますか。 = After school, are you going to club?
B- さん (*at school*): 今日は 行きません。家へ 帰ります。 = Today I'm not going. I'm going home.

*NOTE: In English, Person B can say that he/she will "come" to the house. In Japanese, Person B must say he/she will "go" to the house since from B's point of view the house is away from him/her. That is, he/she will actually be "going" to the house from somewhere else.

■ 自習 Self Check

1. 私は東京に/へ 行きます。 (I will go to Tokyo.)
Now try to say these in Japanese:

A) Kiara will go to school.
B) Jun will return to Japan.
C) Keita goes to the gymnasium.
D) Keiko will go to the cafeteria*.
*(カフェテリア = cafeteria)
E) Keita will go to the computer lab.
F) My older brother will go to the bakery.
G) My teacher returns to Japan.
H) My mother will go to Japan tomorrow.
I) I go to school at 7:30.

2. Direction words based on speaker's point of view

Say the following in Japanese:

A) Will you come to Japan? (Asked by your friend in Japan)
B) Yes, I will go to Japan. (You are currently not in Japan.)
C) No. I will not go to Japan. (You are currently not in Japan.)

■ 練習(れんしゅう)の時間(じかん) Time for Practice

1. Pair Practice

Ask your partner questions in Japanese about places where you might come, go, or return to. Take turns and alternate between affirmative and negative answers. After you have finished asking about the places below, ask about local places.

A- さん：	数学(すうがく)の 教室(きょうしつ)へ 行(い)きます／来(き)ますか。	= Will you go/come to the math classroom?
B- さん：	はい、 行(い)きます／来(き)ます。	= Yes, I will go/come.
-OR-	いいえ、 行(い)きません／来(き)ません。	= No, I will not go/come.

- school
- library
- gymnasium
- friend's house
- restaurant

■ 文化箱(ぶんかばこ) Culture Chest

中国(ちゅうごく) と 日本

China and Japan have a long history of interaction, dating back at least 1,800 years. Many traditions, customs, and foods from China made their way to Japan and took on a uniquely Japanese shape. One aspect of Chinese culture that remains much the same is Chinese food. Though slightly tempered for Japanese tastes, Chinese restaurants all around Japan serve up large bowls of ラーメン(らーめん) (ramen noodles), served with a side of steaming hot ぎょうざ (pot-stickers). ぎょうざ are pan-fried wonton wrappers that have usually been stuffed with a pork and vegetable filling.

■ キアラのジャーナル Kiara's Journal 

Read the journal entry below, and then answer these questions.

❶ Where did they go and when?
❷ What does Kiara think she will do tomorrow (明日)?
❸ What are Kiara, Jun, and Ben going to drink later?
❹ What will they eat for dinner?

ジャーナルへ

今日は とても amazing です。東京から 長崎へ 来ました。長崎で ウィリアムアダムズさんに 会いました (met)。アダムズさんは イギリス人 です。でも、彼は オランダ人と 一緒に オランダから 日本へ 来ました。とても いい人 です。アダムズさんは very smart man. I heard from Ben that the main character in *Shogun* was based on William Adams. Ben told me that the book was a best-selling novel (and a popular TV mini-series) about the early contact between Westerners and Japanese. 明日、私達は 家へ 帰ります (I think)。その 前に、アダムズさんと もう 一度 会いたい (want to meet again) です。アダムズさんと 写真を 撮ります (at least I want to)。今、私達は 旅館 (a traditional inn) に います。後で お茶を すこし 飲みます。そして、晩ご飯を 食べます。晩ご飯に 天ぷらを 食べます。

また。

第4課の5

この 寿司(すし)を 食(た)べて 下さい。
Please eat this sushi.

■ 動詞(どうし)の復習(ふくしゅう) Verb Review

います	to exist (animate people and animals)
あります	to exist (inanimate objects)
分(わ)かります	to understand
*始(はじ)めます	to begin
*出(だ)します	to take out
*開(ひら)きます	to open
*閉(と)じます	to close
*書(か)きます	to write
*聞(き)きます	to listen
*読(よ)みます	to read
*飲(の)みます	to drink
*見(み)ます	to look
*言(い)います	to say
*行(い)きます	to go
*立(た)ちます	to stand
*座(すわ)ります	to sit
食(た)べます	to eat
話(はな)します	to speak
手伝(てつだ)います	to help
来(き)ます	to come
帰(かえ)ります	to return
します	to do

* Previously introduced as part of requests and commands.

■ 漢字(かんじ) Kanji

見 (7 strokes)	み(る) – see; み(える) – visible, can be seen	丨	冂	冃	月	目	貝	見
	見(み)(る) – see; 見(み)(える) – visible, can be seen							
	An eye (目) walking around on two legs (the last two strokes). Imagine SEEING that or even worse, being SEEN by it.							
聞 (14 strokes)	き(く) – to listen, to ask; き(こえる) – can be heard	丨	冂	冃	門	門	門	門
	聞(き)(く) – to hear, listen; 聞(き)(こえる) – can be heard	門	門	門	閂	閂	聞	聞
	When you LISTEN, you sometimes have to place your ear (耳) up against the temple gate (門). To be sure that you HEARD correctly, later you should ASK if you were HEARing correctly.							

■ 言葉(ことば)の探索(たんさく) Language Detection

Japanese verbs can be broken down into three main types. Understanding each type will help you understand how to conjugate verbs and use them in different ways.

The ~MASU form

Throughout this book, you have been introduced to verbs in the ~MASU forms. For example, 食(た)べます (I *eat*), or 中国語(ちゅうごく)を 話(はな)します (I *speak Chinese*). This form is generally referred to as the です/ます form in Japanese (and sometimes the "polite form" in English).

The dictionary form

Whenever a new verb is introduced in the New Words list, the dictionary form of that verb (which is shorter) is also provided. This form is used to look up verbs in dictionaries. Other uses will be introduced later.

The ~TE form

Early on in this text you learned a number of classroom phrases. Many of these expressions utilize the ~TE form. This is the form you can use when making a polite request or command. It is also one of the most useful of Japanese verb forms. In addition to the request or command, it can be used to say things in the present progressive tense, like お水(みず)を 飲(の)んで います。 (I *"am drinking" water*) rather than 水(みず)を 飲(の)みます。 (I *drink water*).

You will learn how to conjugate ~て -form verbs and use them in a number of different ways in Chapter 6.

These charts will help you to review the verbs you've learned up to this point and to clearly see how they are conjugated. Look for patterns in the verb conjugations below. Notice what is changed in the verb stem, the part of the verb which is left once you drop ます from the end. This change only happens in う verbs (verbs that end in an "う"sound other than る) and is consistent with them.

Type 1, or ～う, verbs through Chapter 4

non-past (～ます)	non-past negative (～ません)	～て-form	dictionary (infinitive) form	English meaning
飲(の)みます	飲(の)みません	飲(の)んで	飲(の)む	to drink
読(よ)みます	読(よ)みません	読(よ)んで	読(よ)む	to read
言(い)います	言(い)いません	言(い)って	言(い)う	to say
手伝(てつだ)います	手伝(てつだ)いません	手伝(てつだ)って	手伝(てつだ)う	to help, assist
立(た)ちます	立(た)ちません	立(た)って	立(た)つ	to stand
あります	ありません	あって	ある	to exist (inanimate)
帰(かえ)ります	帰(かえ)りません	帰(かえ)って	帰(かえ)る	to return
とります	とりません	とって	とる	to take (a photo)
座(すわ)ります	座(すわ)りません	座(すわ)って	座(すわ)る	to sit
分(わ)かります	分(わ)かりません	分(わ)かって	分(わ)かる	to understand
書(か)きます	書(か)きません	書(か)いて	書(か)く	to write
聞(き)きます	聞(き)きません	聞(き)いて	聞(き)く	to listen, hear
開(ひら)きます	開(ひら)きません	開(ひら)いて	開(ひら)く	to open (books, etc.)
出(だ)します	出(だ)しません	出(だ)して	出(だ)す	to get out, take out
話(はな)します	話(はな)しません	話(はな)して	話(はな)す	to speak

Type 2, or ～る, verbs through Chapter 4

non-past (～ます)	non-past negative (～ません)	～て-form	dictionary (infinitive) form	English meaning
開(あ)けます	開(あ)けません	開(あ)けて	開(あ)ける	to open
います	いません	いて	いる	to exist (animate)
食(た)べます	食(た)べません	食(た)べて	食(た)べる	to eat
閉(と)じます	閉(と)じません	閉(と)じて	閉(と)じる	to close
始(はじ)めます	始(はじ)めません	始(はじ)めて	始(はじ)める	to begin, start
見(み)ます	見(み)ません	見(み)て	見(み)る	to look
見(み)せます	見(み)せません	見(み)せて	見(み)せる	to show

Irregular verbs through Chapter 4

non-past (～ます)	non-past negative (～ません)	～て-form	dictionary (infinitive) form	English meaning
来(き)ます	来(き)ません	来(き)て	来(く)る	to come
します	しません	して	する	to do

Exception:

non-past (～ます)	non-past negative (～ません)	～て-form	dictionary (infinitive) form	English meaning
行(い)きます	行(い)きません	行(い)って	行(い)く	to go

■ 自習(じしゅう) Self Check

1. Change these verbs into the non-past negative. Try not to look at the chart:

A) 食(た)べます
B) 飲(の)みます
C) 手伝(てつだ)います
D) 分(わ)かります
E) 来(き)ます
F) 行(い)きます
G) 開(ひら)きます
H) 言(い)います

2. Restate these requests in 日本語:

A) Please write.
B) Please listen.
C) Please sit down.
D) Please open the window.
E) Please drink this cola. (コーラ(こーら) = cola)
F) Please go to the cafeteria. (カフェテリア(かふぇてりあ) = cafeteria)
G) Please read this kanji.
H) Please go home now.

■ 練習(れんしゅう)の時間(じかん) Time for Practice

1. Small Group Activity

In this book's Introduction, you learned several types of graphic organizers that might help you in your language learning. You've probably been using one frequently. As a small group activity, compare the graphic organizer that works best for you with those of your partners. Try to come to a consensus about a graphic organizer that is different than what you usually use but is also effective. Then, on a separate piece of paper, use this graphic organizer to group the ます form of the verbs in the charts on pages 143–144 into as many different categories as possible (e.g., verbs related to motion, actions that happen at home, verbs related to being bored). Be creative!

2. Small Group Activity

Play verb "pictionary." One group member silently selects one verb from the verb charts on the preceding pages. That person then has one minute to draw a picture so that the other group members can identify that verb. The first person to correctly say the NEGATIVE form of the verb becomes the next "artist."

3. Pair Practice

One student looks at the verb charts in this section to give as many commands as possible using the ~TE form of verbs in 30 seconds. Without looking at the chart, the partner acts out the commands. Try to be the pair to get the most commands given and acted out in 30 seconds.

■ 文化箱(ぶんかばこ) Culture Chest

Exploring 九州(きゅうしゅう)

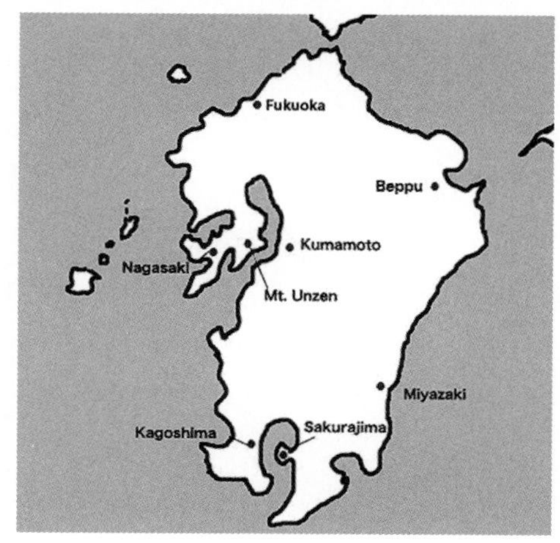

九州(きゅうしゅう) is a wonderful island to tour. You may want to start in Beppu, the hot spring mecca in Oita Prefecture which is home to over 4,000 natural hot springs. Next visitors can see the はにわ statues mentioned in section 1 of this chapter, in 宮崎(みやざき), after taking a break from the beaches there. For a different beach experience, you can head west to be buried up to your neck in naturally hot black sands on one of the beaches in Kagoshima. If this thermal energy is not enough for you, Kagoshima Prefecture is also home to Sakurajima, one of the most active volcanoes in the world. Next you might want to travel north to visit Kumamoto, home of beautiful Mt. Aso and 熊本(くまもと) City, a charming castle town in the central part of the island. You can head farther west, past Mt. Unzen, another active volcano, to the seaport of 長崎(ながさき) City. You may want to enjoy the northernmost part of the island, with its ancient ceramic kiln sites, by also stopping in dynamic 福岡(ふくおか) City, the largest city in Kyushu, before getting on a train that links 九州 with the main island of 本州(ほんしゅう).

■ キアラのジャーナル Kiara's Journal (A)

Read the journal entry below, and then answer these questions.

❶ What did Kiara do at the 本屋?
❷ While Kiara was writing in her journal, what was Ben doing?
❸ After Tomo made his startling announcement, what did he do?
❹ How did Ben respond to the announcement?

ジャーナルへ

After lunch we had a busy afternoon visiting different places. Here is the list of what we did:

1. 本屋へ 行きました。そこで 本を 買いました。
2. 私は ジャーナルを 書きました。ベン君は 漫画を 少し 読みました。
3. じゅん君は アダムズおじさんと ちょっと 話しました。友さんは また ラーメンを 食べました。
4. 後で みんな お茶を 少し 飲みました。そして 晩ご飯を 食べました。晩ご飯に 天ぷらを 食べました。（天ぷらは ポルトガルと スペインから 来ました。）

We had just about finished eating our tempura, and were getting ready to return to the 旅館 when 友さん said,「明日 東京へ 行きます。でも……」There was a really long pause.

じゅん君は、「でも……？」と 友さんに、聞きました。

そして、友さんは、「ちょっと、問題が あります。I've not yet perfected navigation to an exact time period.」と 言って、その後 quickly 外へ 出て 行きました。

私は、「ええっ！ What are we going to do? The time gate is the only way to get back!」

ベン君 stayed calm and said,「この 部屋は ちょっと 暑い ですね。その まどを 開けて 下さい。」

じゅん君も tried to make it sound as if it wasn't going to be too bad. Look on the bright side: my trip to 日本 is definitely going to be one no one else has ever experienced!

■ キアラのジャーナル Kiara's Journal (B)

Read the journal entry below, and then answer these questions.

❶ How many Portuguese sailors were staying at the inn?
❷ How long had these men been in Nagasaki?
❸ Name at least two things the Portuguese brought to Japan.
❹ Are the Portuguese the only foreigners to be trading with Japan? Support your answer.

ジャーナル(じゃーなる)へ

I'm actually really concerned about what 友(とも)さん said last night. If he can't control when we land, we might actually never get home! He did say that he's working on it and that he's almost got it fixed. I just hope that he's telling the truth.

Despite these worries, we went to sleep すこし early last night in the 旅館(りょかん)、after a terrific 晩(ばん)ご飯(はん)。ここの 天(てん)ぷらは とても delicious です。At the 旅館、四人の ポルトガル人(ぼるとがるじん)も いました。They were very friendly. We communicated in 日本語、although theirs was much better than ours, since they had lived here for several years. 私の 日本語は ちょっと improving. 晩ご飯の 後(あと)で 音楽の performance が ありました。ポルトガル人 really enjoyed it.

その ポルトガル人たちは 五年前に ここに 来ました。でも、ポルトガルと 日本は 1543 年から trade を 始(はじ)めました。 Everything had been going very well here for nearly 六十年間(かん)。その ポルトガル人 brought guns, which the 大名(だいみょう)、or feudal lords, really wanted. Ultimately, each 大名 wanted to gain control over the other small fiefdoms and eventually rule the entire archipelago. その ポルトガル人 also brought 食べ物、especially vegetables, from the various parts of the world they had visited in their travels. The king of ポルトガル人 was very interested in promoting Christianity and sent many Jesuit monks, including St. Francis Xavier, to East Asia. Xavier は スペイン(すぺいん)から です。In Japan, the ポルトガル人 had been quite successful at trade, until 1600, when this group of オランダ(おらんだ)人 arrived.

Last year, rumors abounded about a 船(ふね) shipwrecked off an island near Nagasaki. The sailors rescued in that wreck have been here for a few months. ポルトガル人は、「The first few months were とても horrible for the オランダ人。」と、言いました。Evidently the オランダ人 were trying to cut into the Portuguese trade, so the two nationalities didn't get along at all. でも、since they have gotten to know each other, they've become friendlier. ポルトガル人は、「アダムズさんは とても いい人 です。」と言いました。The オランダ人 seem to be recovering from this rough experience. 彼(かれ)は、「早(はや)く家(いえ)へ帰りたいです。」と、私達(わたしたち)に 言いました。

■ 単語チェックリスト New Word Checklist

4-1

あめりか・アメリカ *pn* United States of America (place name)
あめりかじん・アメリカ人 *n* American (person)
いう・言う / いいます・言います *v* to say
いぎりす・イギリス *pn* England (place name)
いぎりすけい・イギリス系 *n* English (descent)
いぎりすじん・イギリス人 *n* English (person)
いたりあ・イタリア *pn* Italy (country)
いたりあじん・イタリア人 *n* Italian (person)
いらんじん・イラン人 *n* Iranian (person)
いんどねしあ・インドネシア *pn* Indonesia (place name)
いんどねしあじん・インドネシア人 *n* Indonesian (person)
おーすとらりあ・オーストラリア *pn* Australia (place name)
おーすとらりあじん・オーストラリア人 *n* Australian (person)
おらんだ ・オランダ *pn* Holland (place name)
おらんだじん・オランダ人 *n* Dutch (person)
がいこく・外国 *n* foreign country
がいこくじん・外国人 *n* foreigner
かなだ・カナダ *pn* Canada (place name)
かなだじん・カナダ人 *n* Canadian (person)
から *part.* from (prev. intro)
かんこく・韓国 *pn* South Korea (place name)
かんこくじん・韓国人 *n* South Korean (person)
くに・国 *n* country
けにあ・ケニア *pn* Kenya (place name)
けにあじん・ケニア人 *n* Kenyan (person)
すぺいん・スペイン *pn* Spain (place name)
すぺいんじん・スペイン人 *n* Spaniard (person)
たいわん・台湾 *pn* Taiwan (place name)
たいわんじん・台湾人 *n* Taiwanese (person)
ちゅうごく・中国 *pn* China (place name)
ちゅうごくじん・中国人 *n* Chinese (person)
てつだう・手伝う / てつだいます・手伝います *v* to help, to assist
どいつ・ドイツ *pn* Germany (place name)
どいつじん・ドイツ人 *n* German (person)
ところで *exp.* by the way
なにけい・何系 *inter.* what ethnicity or heritage
なにじん・何人 *inter.* what nationality
にっけいじん・日系人 *n* of Japanese descent
にゅーじーらんど・ニュージーランド *pn* New Zealand (place name)
にゅーじーらんどじん・ニュージーランド人 *n* New Zealander (person)
ぷえるとりこじん・プエルトリコ人 *n* Puerto Rican (person)
ぶらじるじん・ブラジル人 *n* Brazilian (person)
ふらんす・フランス *pn* France (place name)
ふらんすじん・フランス人 *n* French (person)
ぺるーじん・ペルー人 *n* Peruvian (person)
ぽるとがる・ポルトガル *pn* Portugal (place name)
ぽるとがるじん・ポルトガル人 *n* Portuguese (person)
みなみあふりか・南アフリカ *n* South African (person)
めきしこ・メキシコ *pn* Mexico (place name)
めきしこじん・メキシコ人 *n* Mexican (person)
ろしあ・ロシア *pn* Russia (place name)
ろしあじん・ロシア人 *n* Russian (person)

4-2

あくしゅ・握手 *n* handshake
いたりあご・イタリア語 *n* Italian (language)
いちぺーじ / いっぺーじ・一ページ *count.* one page/page one
いちまい・一枚 *count.* one sheet/piece
いんどねしあご・インドネシア語 *n* Indonesian (language)
おらんだご・オランダ語 *n* Dutch (language)
かんこくご・韓国語 *n* Korean (language)
きゅうぺーじ・九ページ *count.* nine pages, page nine
きゅうまい・九枚 *count.* nine sheets
ごぺーじ・五ページ *count.* five pages, page five
ごまい・五枚 *count.* five sheets
さいん サイン *n* signature
さんぺーじ・三ページ *count.* three pages, page three
さんまい・三枚 *count.* three sheets
しゃしん(を)とる・写真(を)撮る / とります・撮ります *v* to take a photo
じゅうまい・十枚 *count.* ten sheets

じゅっぺーじ / じっぺーじ・十ページ *count.* ten pages, page ten
しゅわ・手話 *n* sign language
しる・知る / しります・知ります *v* to know something/someone
すぺいんご・スペイン語 *n* Spanish (language)
すわひりご・スワヒリ語 *n* Swahili (language)
ちゅごうくご・中国語 *n* Chinese (language)
どいつご・ドイツ語 *n* German (language)
なぜ; どうして *inter.* why
ななぺーじ / しちぺーじ・七ページ *count.* seven pages, page seven
ななまい / しちまい・七枚 *count.* seven sheets
なんぺーじ・何ページ *inter.* how many pages, what page
なんまい・何枚 *inter.* how many sheets
にぺーじ・二ページ *count.* two pages, page two
にまい・二枚 *count.* two sheets
はちぺーじ / はっぺーじ・八ページ *count.* eight pages, page eight
はちまい・八枚 *count.* eight sheets
はなす・話す / はなします・話します *v* to speak
ふらんすご・フランス語 *n* French (language)
ぽるとがるご・ポルトガル語 *n* Portuguese (language)
よんぺーじ・四ページ *count.* four pages, page four
よんまい・四枚 *count.* four sheets
ろくぺーじ・六ページ *count.* six pages, page six
ろくまい・六枚 *count.* six sheets
ろしあご・ロシア語 *n* Russian (language)

4-3

いらっしゃいませ *exp.* welcome (usually used at a place of business)
くるま・車 *n* car, vehicle
こーら・コーラ *n* cola
たべもの・食べ物 *n* food(s)
たべる・食べる / たべます・食べます *v* to eat
ちきん・チキン / とりにく・鶏肉 *n* chicken
(～は) ちょっと… *exp.* something is
(～は、) ちょっと… a little...
のみもの・飲み物 *n* drink(s)
のむ・飲む / のみます・飲みます *v* to drink
ぱん・パン *n* bread
はんばーがー・ハンバーガー *n* hamburger
ぱんや・パン屋 *n* bakery
ほんや・本屋 *n* bookstore
まだ *adv.* not yet (with negative verb)
もの 物 *n* thing
れすとらん・レストラン *n* restaurant

4-4

いく・行く / いきます・行きます *v* to go
かえる・帰る / かえります・帰ります *v* to return
くる・来る / きます・来ます *v* to come
する / します (して) *v* to do
だから *conj.* because of that

Time in Nara

第5課

Learning and Performance Goals

This chapter will enable you to:

A) form the past tense and the past negative tense of verbs
B) talk about past, future, and present schedules
C) learn basic details of the Nara period (710–794) and the traditional Japanese calendar
D) learn how to read basic schedules
E) use 17 additional kanji
F) use the "can-do" chart found on **TimeForJapanese.com** to chart your progress for what you "can-do" for each chapter

Daibutsu (Big Buddha) of Todaiji Temple, Nara

第5課の1

毎週(まいしゅう)　月曜日(げつようび)の　１２時(じゅうにじ)に　私に、電話(でんわ)して　下さい。

Please telephone me every Monday at 12:00.

1) 月、火、水、木、金、土、日。月,火、水、木、金、土、日。

2) キアラさん、それは 何 ですか。

3) 曜日の練習です。じゅん君から、聞きました。

4) 月は 月曜日、火は 火曜日 ですね。

5) よく出来ました！

あ！今、何時ですか。母は、「毎週月曜日１２時に私に、電話して下さい。」と言いました。今日は、月曜日ですね。

6) はい、今日は、月曜日です。今１１時５９分ですよ。

7) 後　一分！でも、今は７５１年 です。ここに　電話はありませんね。

8) 僕は、ここから 母に電子メールを　送りましたよ。キアラさんも、お母さんにメールを　送りますか。

9) それはいい アイディアですねえ！

■ 会話 Dialogue

REMINDER: You may see some kanji / vocabulary you do not recognize. Use the context to try to understand the meanings of those parts of the dialogue.

1. キアラ： 月*、火、水、木、金、土、日。月、火、水、木、金、土、日。
2. ベン　： キアラさん、それは　何　ですか。
3. キアラ： 曜日の　練習　です。じゅん君　から、聞きました。
4. ベン　： 月は、月曜日、火は　火曜日　ですね。
5. キアラ： よく　出来ました！
あ！今、何時　ですか。母は、「毎週　月曜日　12時に　私に、電話して下さい。」と　言いました。今日は、月曜日　ですね。
6. じゅん： はい、今日は、月曜日　です。今　11時59分　ですよ。
7. キアラ： 後　一分！でも、今は751年です。ここに　電話は　ありませんね。
8. ベン　： 僕は、ここから　母に　電子メールを　送りましたよ。
キアラさんも、お母さんに　メールを　送りますか。
9. キアラ： それは　いい　アイディア　ですねえ！

* **Note** about counting days of the week: The readings of the kanji for days of the week are normally different when they stand alone (not in conjunction with other kanji), but do not change when referring to days of the week.

■ 単語 New Words

祭り (*n*)	電子メール (*n*)	(送る)/ 送ります (*v*)	日月火水木金土 (X under 月) 月曜日 (*n*)	日月火水木金土 (X under 火) 火曜日 (*n*)
日月火水木金土 (X under 水) 水曜日 (*n*)	日月火水木金土 (X under 木) 木曜日 (*n*)	日月火水木金土 (X under 金) 金曜日 (*n*)	日月火水木金土 (X under 土) 土曜日 (*n*)	日月火水木金土 (X under 日) 日曜日 (*n*)
日月火水木金土 ? 何曜日 (*inter.*)	(起きる) 起きます (*v*)	(寝る) 寝ます (*v*)	大事 (な *adj.*) – important 練習 します (*v*) – to practice 前 (*n/adv.*) – before, front, in front	

■ 漢字 Kanji

前 (9 strokes)	ゼン；まえ，〜まえ – in front, before	丶	丷	䒑	广	广	肖	前
	(名)前 – name; (午)前 – A.M., morning	前	前					
	The top of this kanji looks like two seeds popping up above the ground, while the bottom includes a moon and a knife, both objects important to have BEFORE planting seeds.							
午 (4 strokes)	ゴ – noon	ノ	𠂉	二	午			
	午(前) – morning, A.M.; 午(後) – afternoon, P.M.							
	Noon is when the clock is at 12. The last two strokes of this kanji mean 10 (十). Add 2 (the first two strokes) to the ten and you have 12, which represents NOON.							
後 (9 strokes)	ゴ；あと – after, afterward; うし(ろ) – behind, back	ノ	彳	彳	彳	彳	彳	後
	後 – after; (午)後 – P.M., afternoon	後	後					
	The FIRST three strokes are also in the left side in the kanji for the verb "to go" (行). The next three strokes are the top part of thread (糸). The last three strokes are the top part of winter (冬). Imagine someone going out with a piece of thread in the winter to measure the snow AFTER a snowfall.							
良 (7 strokes)	よ(い) – good	丶	㇆	ヨ	ヨ	良	良	良
	良(い) – good							
	良 or GOOD is the same as what is below the roof in "to eat" — 食 . We all know that eating is very GOOD!							
月 (4 strokes)	ゲツ；がつ – month; つき – moon	ノ	冂	月	月			
	(今)月 – this month; 月(曜日) – Monday							
	This is a stylized picture of a MOON with clouds moving across it. "Moon-day" sounds just like MONDAY.							
火 (4 strokes)	カ；ひ – fire	丶	丷	火	火			
	火(曜日) – Tuesday							
	See the person standing in the middle, surrounded on each side by FLAMES and FIRE? This kanji also looks like some sticks standing against each other with sparks or FIRE coming out. TUESDAY is FIRE day.							

水 4 strokes	スイ(すい)；みず – water	亅	刁	水	水			
	水(すい) – water; 水(すい)（曜日(ようび)）– Wednesday							
	The first stroke is the fishhook breaking into the smooth WATER represented by the remaining three strokes. WEDNESDAY is WATER day.							

金 8 strokes	キン(きん) – gold; かね – money	ノ	人	亼	今	仐	全	金
	金(きん) – gold;（お）金(かね) – money; 金(きん)（曜日(ようび)）– Friday	金						
	This kanji is a king（王）under his roof with two large pieces of gold at his feet. That is some serious GOLD! FRIDAY is usually payday or GOLD day.							

土 3 strokes	ド(ど)；つち – soil, ground	一	十	土				
	土(つち) – earth, soil; 土(ど)（曜日(ようび)）– Saturday							
	"DIRT Day" is SATURDAY, when you have free time to dig in the DIRT in your garden.							

曜 18 strokes	ヨウ(よう) – day of the week	丨	冂	月	日	日ヿ	日ヨ	日ヨ	日ヨ	日ヨヨ
	（何(なん)）曜(よう)（日(び)）– what day of the week?	日ヨヨ	日ヨヨ	日ヨヨ	日ヨヨ	日ヨヨ	日ヨヨ	日ヨヨ	曜	曜
	This kanji has the radical for DAY on the left. Two katakana ヨ(よ) on top of a short-tailed bird (strokes 11–18) gives this character its pronunciation. Every day（日）that you can hear birds chirping is a good day ですヨ(よ)！									

Note that you already know the first kanji for Thursday（木曜日(もくようび)）.

■ 言葉(ことば)の探索(たんさく) Language Detection

1. Review of the time particle に

You learned in Chapter 3 that the particle に is used after specific time words and not after general time words. Specific time words include hours and minutes, and *occasionally* the days of the week or month, and months themselves. General time words, such as 毎日(まいにち) (every day) or 明日(あした) (tomorrow), are NOT followed by any particle.

A) 一時に　宿題(しゅくだい)を　します。 = At one o'clock I will do homework.
B) 午後(ごご)　六時三十五分に　寿司(すし)を　食(た)べます。 = At 6:35 P.M. I eat sushi.
C) 火曜日(かようび)に　バスケ(ばすけ)を　します。 = On Tuesday I play basketball.
D) 毎日(まいにち)　午前(ごぜん)七時三十分に　学校へ　行きます。 = Every day I go to school at 7:30 A.M.
E) 明日(あした)　部活(ぶかつ)は　何時に　ありますか。 = What time do you have club tomorrow?

■ 自習(じしゅう) Self Check

1. Which time words can be followed by に?

a. 五時
b. 毎日(まいにち)
c. 木曜日(もくようび)
d. 土曜日(どようび)
e. 明日(あした)
f. きのう

2. Review the following by covering up the right column with your hand or a piece of paper as you say the words in the left column out loud to yourself in Japanese. Check yourself by looking at the right column.

a. 5:00	ごじ
b. after 9:00	くじ　すぎ
c. before 8:00	はちじ　まえ
d. 1:02	いちじにふん
e. 10:25	じゅうじにじゅうごふん
f. 11:38	じゅういちじさんじゅうはっぷん

3. Say the seven days of the week out loud to yourself in Japanese:

a. Monday 月曜日(げつようび)
b. Tuesday ____________
c. Wednesday ____________
d. Thursday ____________
e. Friday ____________
f. Saturday ____________
g. Sunday ____________

■ 練習(れんしゅう)の時間(じかん) Time for Practice

1. Pair Practice

Ask your partner the following questions:

1. 何時(なんじ)に　起(お)きますか。
2. 何時(なんじ)に　寝(ね)ますか。
3. 何曜日(なんようび)に　学校(がっこう)に　来(き)ますか。
4. 何曜日(なんようび)に　学校(がっこう)に　来(き)ませんか。
5. 何時(なんじ)に　学校(がっこう)に　来(き)ますか。
6. 何時(なんじ)に　学校(がっこう)から　家(うち)へ　帰(かえ)りますか。
7. 何時(なんじ)に　朝(あさ)ごはんを　食(た)べますか。
8. 何時(なんじ)に　昼(ひる)ごはんを　食(た)べますか。
9. 何時(なんじ)に　晩(ばん)ごはんを　食(た)べますか。

2. Pair Practice

Schedule Information Gap

Tetsuya's family has some communication gaps. His mother and father did not talk to each other about what he should do on Sunday before heading out for the day, and therefore each parent left him a different schedule for chores to do for the day. Go to **TimeForJapanese.com** for this chapter and section to download what you will need for this activity.

■ 文化箱(ぶんかばこ) Culture Chest

Nara (奈良(なら))

The city of 奈良(なら) is a wonderful place to explore, full of ancient temples and shrines. The huge Buddhist temple of 東大寺(とうだいじ), one of the great architectural treasures of Japan, is located here. Can you tell the meaning of this temple's name from its kanji? The temple, and the "big" Buddha inside, were completed and the temple officially opened in 752. At the time of construction, 東大寺(とうだいじ) was the largest wooden structure in the world, and it is said to still hold that title. The Buddhist statue inside is also the largest gilt bronze Buddha in the world at 15 meters. The building has burned down twice, and the current structure, rebuilt in the early 1700s, is actually 30% smaller than the original!

Originally called 平城京(へいじょうきょう), 奈良(なら) was the earliest established capital of Japan. During what became known as the Nara Period (奈良時代(ならじだい), 710–794), the burgeoning court and nobles enjoyed writing poetry in Chinese and studying popular Buddhist scriptures imported from China and Korea. Chinese influence was so strong at the time that the city, with its north-south orientation and straight-line streets, was modeled after the Chinese capital of Chang-an (present-day Xian). 奈良(なら) remains famous today for its many temples (including 東大寺(とうだいじ)) and parks, some of which are now part of a UNESCO World Heritage Site.* Every year millions of tourists visit Nara to see these attractions and its other main feature, the 1,200 tame deer that roam freely, looking for tourists to feed them しかせんべい (deer crackers). The deer are considered sacred and are protected by law.

*UNESCO: United Nations Educational, Scientific, and Cultural Organization

■ キアラのジャーナル(きあら じゃーなる) Kiara's Journal

Read the journal entry below, and then answer these questions.

❶ What day of the week did Kiara mention having school?
❷ What day of the week did the strong winds come?
❸ What city are they in as Kiara writes this journal entry?
❹ What did Ben tell Kiara to look at?

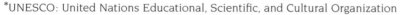

ジャーナルへ

先週 (last week) の 木曜日に 学校が ありました。そして、金曜日に 大風が あって、時の門を 通りました。It must have taken all night to get to 長崎、since we arrived on 土曜日。今日は、月曜日です。月曜日 is usually considered the first day of the week in Japan. 今日の朝、we activated the 時の門 again and we are off on another adventure ending up in 奈良。I was hoping that we would luck out and get home, but this is really pretty exciting.

When we go through the 時の門、for some reason, ベン君 is able to send text messages using his cell phone. I don't know why, but he received a message from his mother about doing something 昨日の晩。 I'm going to try to send a message to my family on my laptop the next time we go through the 時の門。I hope it will work.

今朝、as we were about to leave 長崎、アダムズさんを 見ました。徳川家康、the future 将軍 of 日本、was in town, and アダムズさんと 徳川家康 were supposed to have a meeting. 友さんは「早く 時の門に 行きましょう。ここは ちょっと 危ない ですよ。」と、言いました。As we reached the 鳥居、友さん took the dipper from the fountain in front of the gate. Then he grabbed a pinch of salt from his かばん and sprinkled the salt in the 水。The 門 glazed over and 友さん told us to jump through. 三時間後 we walked out. じゅん君は、「ここは どこですか。」と、言いました。

ベン君は、「あれを 見て 下さい！」と、言いました。私は、「あの寺は 東大寺 ですか。」と、聞きました。A Buddhist monk overheard us and replied「はい、そうです。あの お寺は 世界で 一番 大きい 木の 建物 です。」と、言いました。東大寺は、21st century の 今でも、世界で 一番 大きい 木で 作った 建物 です。すばらしい ですね。

私は、「友さん、私は ちょっと 東大寺へ 行きます。私は 美術 が 大好き (really like) です。あそこを 見に行きます。」と、言いました。

でも、友さん was nowhere to be found。じゅん君 は、「友さんは どこに いますか。一分前 ここに いました。でも、今は どこですか。」と、言いました。

第5課の2 私も、アメリカで、漢字を ちょっと 勉強しました。

あめりか かんじ べんきょう

I also studied some kanji in the U.S.

1.
1) 先週の 水曜日、奈良で 中国語の 授業を 始めました。皆さん、次の 授業に 来て下さい。
2.
2) どこ ですか。
3) 東大寺です。東大寺は 分かりますか。
4) はい、分かります。
3.
5) 女性も、中国語を 勉強しますか。
6)いいえ、女性は 中国語を 勉強しません。でも、キアラさん、来て 下さいね。
4.
7) はい、分かりました。
8) 僕は、漢字が 好きです。
5.
9) 私も、アメリカで、漢字を ちょっと 勉強しました。
6.
10) ええっ？！

会話 Dialogue

REMINDER: You may see some kanji / vocabulary you do not recognize. Use the context to try to understand the meanings of those parts of the dialogue.

1. 中国語の先生 ： 先週の　水曜日、奈良で　中国語の　授業を　始めました。皆さん、次の　授業に来て　下さい。
2. ベン ： どこ　ですか。
3. 中国語の先生 ： 東大寺　です。東大寺は　分かりますか。
4. じゅん ： はい、分かります。
5. キアラ ： 女性も、中国語を　勉強しますか。
6. 中国語の先生 ： いいえ、女性は　中国語を　勉強しません。でも、キアラさん、来て　下さいね。
7. キアラ ： はい、分かりました。
8. ベン ： 僕は、漢字が　*好き　です。
9. キアラ ： 私も、アメリカで、漢字を　ちょっと　勉強しました。
10. 中国語の先生 ： ええっ？！

*好き – to like (introduced in Chapter 7)

単語 New Words

誕生日 (*n*)	（生まれる） 生まれます (*v*)	（始める） 始めます (*v*)	（勉強（を）する） 勉強（を）します (*v*)

Months

一月 (*n*) – January
二月 (*n*) – February
三月 (*n*) – March
四月 (*n*) – April
五月 (*n*) – May
六月 (*n*) – June
七月 (*n*) – July
八月 (*n*) – August
九月 (*n*) – September
十月 (*n*) – October
十一月 (*n*) – November
十二月 (*n*) – December
何月 (*inter.*) – what month?
（終わる）終わります (*v*) – to finish
いつ (*inter.*) – when?

Ages

一歳 – 1 year old
二歳 – 2 years old
三歳 – 3 years old
四歳 – 4 years old
五歳 – 5 years old
六歳 – 6 years old
七歳 – 7 years old
八歳 – 8 years old
九歳 – 9 years old
十歳 – 10 years old
十一歳 – 11 years old
十二歳 – 12 years old
十三歳 – 13 years old
十四歳 – 14 years old
二十歳 – 20 years old

Thousands

千 (せん) – 1,000
二千 (に せん) – 2,000
三千 (さんぜん) – 3,000
四千 (よんせん) – 4,000
五千 (ご せん) – 5,000
六千 (ろくせん) – 6,000
七千 (ななせん) – 7,000
八千 (はっせん) – 8,000
九千 (きゅうせん) – 9,000
何千 (なんせん) – how many thousands
一万 (いちまん) – 10,000
二万 (に まん) – 20,000
三万 (さんまん) – 30,000
四万 (よんまん) – 40,000
五万 (ご まん) – 50,000
六万 (ろくまん) – 60,000
七万 (ななまん) – 70,000
八万 (はちまん) – 80,000
九万 (きゅうまん) – 90,000
十万 (じゅうまん) – 100,000
十一万 (じゅういちまん) – 110,000
十二万 (じゅう に まん) – 120,000
十三万 (じゅうさんまん) – 130,000
十四万 (じゅうよんまん) – 140,000
十五万 (じゅう ご まん) – 150,000
十六万 (じゅうろくまん) – 160,000
十七万 (じゅうななまん) – 170,000
十八万 (じゅうはちまん) – 180,000
十九万 (じゅうきゅうまん) – 190,000
二十万 (に じゅうまん) – 200,000
二十一万 (に じゅういちまん) – 210,000

■ 漢字 (かんじ) Kanji

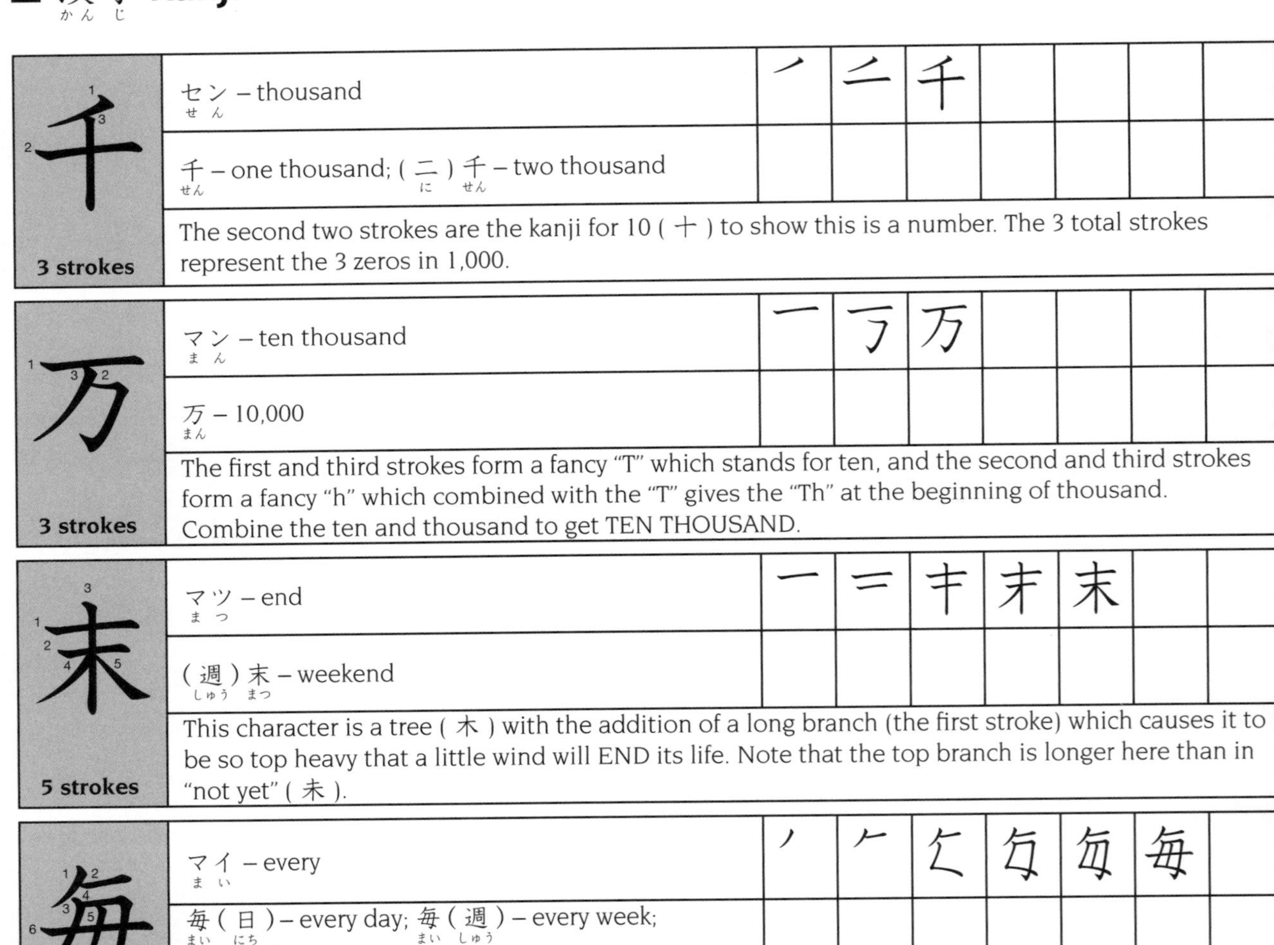

千 — 3 strokes

センー thousand (せん)

千 (せん) – one thousand; (二) (に) 千 (せん) – two thousand

The second two strokes are the kanji for 10 (十) to show this is a number. The 3 total strokes represent the 3 zeros in 1,000.

万 — 3 strokes

マン – ten thousand (まん)

万 (まん) – 10,000

The first and third strokes form a fancy "T" which stands for ten, and the second and third strokes form a fancy "h" which combined with the "T" gives the "Th" at the beginning of thousand. Combine the ten and thousand to get TEN THOUSAND.

末 — 5 strokes

マツ – end (まつ)

(週) (しゅう) 末 (まつ) – weekend

This character is a tree (木) with the addition of a long branch (the first stroke) which causes it to be so top heavy that a little wind will END its life. Note that the top branch is longer here than in "not yet" (未).

毎 — 6 strokes

マイ – every (まい)

毎 (まい) (日) (にち) – every day; 毎 (まい) (週) (しゅう) – every week;
毎 (まい) (年) (ねん/とし) – every year

The grid part of this kanji looks like a calendar. Think of the top two strokes as a hand pulling sheets of the calendar across EVERY day.

週 (11 strokes)							
シュウ (しゅう) – week	丿	冂	月	円	円	用	周
(今)週 (こんしゅう) – this week; (来)週 (らいしゅう) – next week	周	㒼周	调	週			
The first two strokes show the walls surrounding many working people, who have to follow the path (the last 3 strokes) and work in the dirt (土) to feed their mouths (口) all WEEK.							

■ 言葉(ことば)の探索(たんさく) Language Detection

1. Past tense of 〜ます verbs

To form the past tense of a ~ます verb, change the ~ます ending to ~ました.

私は　食(た)べます。	= I eat.
私は　食(た)べました。	= I ate.
一月に　愛子さんは　中国に　行きます。	= Aiko will go to China in January.
八月に　愛子さんは　中国に　行きました。	= Aiko went to China in August.
明日(あした)　先生と　話します。	= I will speak to the teacher tomorrow.
キアラさんは　友さんと　日本語で　話しました。	= Kiara spoke to Tomo in Japanese.

2. Negative past tense of 〜ます verbs

To form the negative past tense of a ます verb, add でした to the negative tense.

ベン君(べんくん)は　手伝(てつだ)いません。	= Ben does not help.
キアラ(きあら)さんは　手伝(てつだ)いません　でした。	= Kiara did not help.
僕(ぼく)は　飲(の)みません。	= I will not drink.
太郎(たろう)さんは　飲(の)みません　でした。	= Tarou did not drink.

Verb tense overview

〜ます non-past	〜ました past	〜ません negative non-past	〜ませんでした negative past	(英語)
話します	話しました	話しません	話しませんでした	to speak
来ます	来ました	来ません	来ませんでした	to come
あります	ありました	ありません	ありませんでした	to exist (inanimate)
勉強(べんきょう)します	勉強(べんきょう)しました	勉強(べんきょう)しません	勉強(べんきょう)しませんでした	to study

■ 自習(じしゅう) Self Check

1. Past

Say the following out loud to yourself in Japanese.

A) Mayumi talked.
B) Daisuke went to Canada.
C) I ate rice.
D) Ken came to school.
E) Tomoko ate sushi at lunch.
F) Mayumi studied Japanese.

2. Past negative

Say the following out loud to yourself in Japanese.

A) Kenji did not eat.
B) Kiara did not go.
C) Jun did not play basketball.
D) Ben did not drink water.
E) Yesterday, Tomo didn't go to Shikoku.
F) Wednesday, I did not eat bread.

3. Say the following in Japanese:

A) Tuesday
B) Friday
C) January
D) October
E) Monday
F) June
G) April
H) Saturday
I) Thursday
J) March
K) June
L) November

■ 練習(れんしゅう)の時間(じかん) Time for Practice

1. Class Practice

何月(なんがつ) 生(う)まれ ですか。

You are trying to convince your teacher to throw a class birthday party, but you will need to pick the month with the most birthdays and have it that month. Survey your classmates in Japanese about when their birthdays are, asking as many students as you can.

Q 何月(なんがつ) 生(う)まれ ですか。 = What month were you born?
A 一月(いちがつ) 生(う)まれ です。 = I was born in January.

2. Pair Practice

Emiko's schedule of activities

Emiko has had a busy year. Take turns with your partner restating these activities into 日本語. Remember to use the past tense and the particle after the time word.

A) In April, Emiko went to Kyoto.
B) In February, Emiko went to a Shinto shrine.
C) In August, Emiko returned home.
D) In September, Emiko helped out at home.
E) In October, Emiko went to the middle school.
F) In January, Emiko went to Sapporo.
G) In July, Emiko went to Okinawa.
H) In December, Emiko did not eat ice cream.
I) In June, Emiko ate ice cream.
J) In May, Emiko did not go to a party.

3. Pair Practice

Yesterday's schedule

Use the vocabulary words below to ask your partner whether or not she/he studied each subject yesterday. Answer based upon fact.

歴史 (れきし)	体育 (たいいく)	数学 (すうがく)	音楽 (おんがく)
英語 (えい)	日本語	美術 (びじゅつ)	ドイツ語 (どいつ)

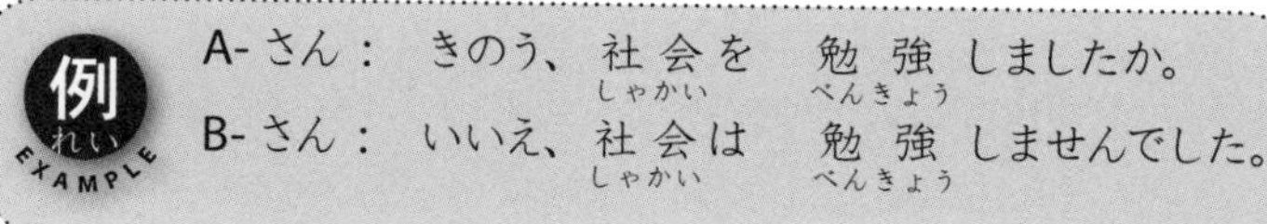

例 れい EXAMPLE
A- さん： きのう、社会を 勉強しましたか。
B- さん： いいえ、社会は 勉強しませんでした。

■ 文化箱 Culture Chest

Chinese Influence during the Nara Period

During the Nara Period (奈良時代, 710–794), Nara was the capital of all that was unified Japan (from Kyushu in the south to near present-day Tokyo in the northeast). At this time, China was undergoing a "golden age" that resulted in its culture being admired and imitated around Asia. The Japanese emperors were very interested in Chinese philosophy and culture, including Buddhism, Confucianism, Daoism, art, architecture, and literature. They sent teachers and scholars to China to study and bring back what they learned. Once they reached Japan, these new Chinese ideas began to take on a Japanese style that deeply influenced subsequent development of Japanese art, architecture, writing, and even martial arts and fashion. Can you think of an example of how another culture has influenced the one where you live?

■ キアラのジャーナル Kiara's Journal

Read the journal entry below, and then answer these questions.

❶ What time was the music going to start?
❷ Who was the Emperor during the early Nara Period?
❸ What were some of the Chinese things that the Emperor had seen and heard?
❹ What religion did early spiritual religions and practice in Japan come to be known as?
❺ Where did Kiara, Ben, and Jun speak to the Chinese teacher?

ジャーナルへ

今日は 七百五十一年 です。奈良の 人達は とても 忙しい です。 七百五十二年に この寺の dedication ceremony が あります。毎日、十二時半に construction workers は 一緒に お昼ご飯を 食べます。そして 一時半から また 仕事をします。今日、午後六時二十分から 音楽会が ありました。奈良時代 (Nara Period) の 音楽は 私達の 音楽と すごく 違います。At first the music was pretty painful to listen to, since the beat and tones are totally different from music in the 21st century. But now I'm a bit more used to the different sound. 午後七時四十五分から 晩ご飯を 食べました。

しょうむ天皇 (Emperor) は、中国の 美術が 大好きでした。中国の 音楽も たくさん 聞きました。食べ物は 日本と 中国の 食べ物が ありました。今まで 日本の 宗教 (religion) は mainly indigenous religions which later became known as 神道 でした。でも、奈良時代から 仏教 (Buddhism) も 入りました (entered)。今、奈良は 日本の 首都 (capital) です。天皇 (Emperor) は 奈良に います。中国人と 韓国人も たくさん います。The Korean Peninsula から、奈良時代に たくさんの 人が 日本に 来ました。Nara seems like quite an international place right now for me.

At the 音楽の コンサート、中国語の 先生と 話しました。その 先生は、「先週の 水曜日に 奈良で 中国語の 授業を 始めました。」と、言いました。「次の 授業に来て 下さい。先週は 三十五人 来ました。仏教 (Buddhism) の お経 (scriptures) は 中国語です。今は、まだ 日本に、there is no other writing system. 中国語を copying them is how writing is practiced and taught here.」と、言いました。

ベン君は、「僕は 漢字が 好き です。でも 中国語は 分かりません。」と、言いました。

友さんは私に、「こうぼう だいしさんを 知っていますか。」と、言いました。

私は、「知りません。奈良の 人 ですか。」と、言いました。

友さんは、「僕の 友達の 友達 です。」と、言いました。それから、友さんは 私に、「空海は (otherwise known as Koubou Daishi) 七百七十四年に 生まれました。Some people say that 彼 (he) は 高野山で ひらがなと かたかなを 作りました。」と、言いました。

奈良は とても すばらしい です。本当に いい 所 です。

第5課の3 朝から、晩まで、ずっと 食べます。
あさ ばん

I eat from morning all the way until night.

1.

1）友さんは、本当に たくさん食べますね。

2）はい、朝から 晩まで ずっと 食べます。

2.

3) 日本の 食べ物から、中国の 食べ物まで、何でも 食べますね。

3.

4）それは、いつから ですか。

5) 生まれた時から、今日まで ずっと です。ここから、ここ まで、食べ物です。あ、この寿司は、だれも 食べませんね。

4.

6) だれも 何も 食べませんよ。

7）じゃ、私が、全部 食べます。

■ 会話 Dialogue

REMINDER: You may see some kanji / vocabulary you do not recognize. Use the context to try to understand the meanings of those parts of the dialogue.

1. キアラ： 友さんは、本当に　たくさん　食べますね。
2. 友　　： はい、朝から　晩まで　ずっと　食べます。
3. ベン　： 日本の　食べ物から、中国の　食べ物まで、何でも * 食べますね。
4. じゅん： それは、いつから　ですか。
5. 友　　： 生まれた時から、今日まで、ずっと　です。ここから、ここまで、食べ物です。あ、この　寿司は、だれも　食べませんね。
6. じゅん： だれも　何も　食べませんよ。
7. 友　　： じゃ、私が、全部　食べます。

* 何でも (*adv.*) – anything, everything

■ 単語 New Words

から (*part.*) – from
まで (*part.*) – until (used with spec. locations or times)
何日 (*inter.*) – what day of the month?
何も (*pron*) – nothing

Calendar

月	火	水	木	金	土	日
	1 一日 ついたち	2 二日 ふつか	3 三日 みっか	4 四日 よっか	5 五日 いつか	6 六日 むいか
7 七日 なのか	8 八日 ようか	9 九日 ここのか	10 十日 とおか	11 十一日 じゅういちにち	12 十二日 じゅうににち	13 十三日 じゅうさんにち
14 十四日 じゅうよっか	15 十五日 じゅうごにち	16 十六日 じゅうろくにち	17 十七日 じゅうしちにち	18 十八日 じゅうはちにち	19 十九日 じゅうくにち	20 二十日 はつか
21 二十一日 にじゅういちにち	22 二十二日 にじゅうににち	23 二十三日 にじゅうさんにち	24 二十四日 にじゅうよっか	25 二十五日 にじゅうごにち	26 二十六日 にじゅうろくにち	27 二十七日 にじゅうしちにち
28 二十八日 にじゅうはちにち	29 二十九日 にじゅうくにち	30 三十日 さんじゅうにち	31 三十一日 さんじゅういちにち			

■ 言葉の探索 Language Detection

1. から . . . まで

These two words are used to mean “from” and “until.” Together with specific times or places, they mean “from this time until that time” or “from this place until that place.” Both から and まで come after the time or place words they modify.

A) けん君(くん)は　一時から　二時まで　寝(ね)ました。 = Ken slept from 1:00 until 2:00.
B) 英語の授業(じゅぎょう)は　九時十分から　十時まで　です。 = English class is from 9:10 until 10:00.
C) 学校は　四月から　三月まで　です。 = School is from April until March.
D) 学校は　月曜日から　金曜日まで　です。 = School is from Monday until Friday.
E) 家から　学校まで　来ました。 = I came from home to school.
F) アメリカ(あめりか)から　日本まで　行きます。 = I will go from the U.S. to Japan.

2. だれも、何(なに)も

A question word followed by も generates a negative expression. A few examples are だれも "nobody," and 何も "nothing." These words are followed by the NEGATIVE form of the verb.

A) 日曜日(にちようび)は、だれも　学校に　いません。 = Nobody is at school on Sunday.
B) 昨日(きのう)　だれも　ベースボール(べーすぼーる)を　しません　でした。 = No one played baseball yesterday.
C) 私は　何(なに)も　知(し)りません。 = I don't know anything.
D) 昨日(きのう)、キアラ(きあら)さんは　何(なに)も　しません　でした。 = Kiara didn't do anything yesterday.

3. Years and addresses

When time and addresses are given, larger units such as years, months, countries, or states come before smaller units such as hours, minutes, street addresses, or apartment numbers. Basically the order goes from largest to smallest unit.

In Example C, 〒106-0047 is the postal code which is the first thing you write for Japanese mailing addresses. (The 〒 mark appears with postal codes. It stands for "Japan Post.") 東京 is the city, 港区(みなとく) = Minato Ward, 南麻布(みなみあざぶ) = South Azabu (the neighborhood within the district), and 4–23–2 is the block, building, and house number. Tarou Satou is a person the mail is going to. 様(さま) is typically used as an honorific suffix at the end of names when writing letters. Other suffixes such as さん, 先生, ちゃん, etc. are used when speaking.

例 (れい) EXAMPLE

A) 1918 年 11 月 11 日　火曜日　午前(ごぜん) 11 時
B) 平成(へいせい) 14 年1月 20 日
= Heisei year 14, January, 20th
C) 〒106-0047
東京都(とうきょうと)　港区(みなとく)
南麻布(みなみあざぶ)　4–23–2
佐藤太郎様(さとうたろうさま)

■ 自習(じしゅう) Self Check

Say the following out loud to yourself in Japanese:

1. ________________から . . . ________________まで

A) I played volleyball from 8:00 until 9:30.
B) I helped from September until December.
C) I went from Tokyo to Kyoto.
D) I ate dinner from 5:00 until 5:30.
E) Mayumi talked to her friend from 6:00 until 8:00.

2. だれも/何も

A) Nobody will go to Tokyo.
B) Kiara did not drink anything.
C) My father did not eat anything.
D) My friend didn't study anything.
E) No one is in the room.
F) My older sister did not eat anything for breakfast.
G) Michio will not study anything on Sunday.

3. Dates

A) November 6
B) Say your birthday (including the year)
C) July 1
D) January 20
E) March 14
F) May 2

■ 練習(れんしゅう)の時間(じかん) Time for Practice

1. Pair Practice

だれも **and** 何も

Using the verbs in the charts on pages 143 and 144 and others you have learned, ask as many questions as you can using だれ and 何(なに). Your partner must answer negatively using だれ and 何(なに)も properly as in the examples.

例(れい) EXAMPLE

A) A-さん： 何(なに)を 飲(の)みますか。 = What will you drink?
B-さん： 何(なに)も 飲(の)みません。 = I will not drink anything.

B) A-さん： だれが 分(わ)かりましたか。 = Who understood?
B-さん： だれも 分(わ)かりませんでした。 = Nobody understood.

C) A-さん： だれが 何(なに)を しますか。 = Who will do what?
B-さん： だれも 何(なに)も しません。 = Nobody will do anything.

2. Pair Practice

いつ から、 いつ まで ですか。

Using the particles から and まで, make sentences with your partner in Japanese about when the following activities begin and end. Use the tense indicated.

私の 日本語の クラス(くらす)は 九時十五分から 十時五分まで です。
= My Japanese class is from 9:15 until 10:05.

A) Jun	1:17	2:30	studies	math
B) Kiara	June 18	July 2	Japan	will go
C) Jun's mother	Dec. 14	Dec. 17	Tokyo	went
D) My father	Friday	Sunday	Chicago	will go
E) My friend	10 P.M.	11 P.M.	party	was there
F) My teacher	today	tomorrow	Nara	goes/visits

3. Pair Practice

いつ　ですか。

Use Japanese to ask your partner the dates below. Take turns asking and answering.

A) A-さん：地球(ちきゅう)の　日は　いつ　ですか。 = When is Earth Day?

B-さん：4月22日です。 = It's April 22.

B) A-さん：お母さんの　誕生日(たんじょうび)は　何月何日(なんがつなんにち)　ですか。

= What month and date is your mother's birthday?

B-さん：母の　誕生日(たんじょうび)は　八月六日(むいか)　です = My mother's birthday is August 6th.

A) New Year's Eve – おおみそか (December 31)

B) New Year's Day – 元日(がんじつ) (January 1)

C) Halloween – ハロウィーン(はろうぃーん) (October 31)

D) spring equinox – 春分の日(しゅんぶんのひ) (March 21)

E) Greenery Day – みどりの日(ひ) (May 4)

F) Boxing Day – クリスマスの翌日(くりすますのよくじつ) (December 26)

G) your birthday

H) your 先生 's birthday

I) a holiday of your choice

■ 文化箱(ぶんかばこ) Culture Chest

Imperial Years and Dates

Kasuga Taisha gate, Nara

The Japanese system of using era names, or 年号(ねんごう) for dating has been in use since the 7th century and is still in use today.

An example of this system is using the term 平成(へいせい) 20年 for the year 2008. A literal translation would be "in the year of (the Emperor) Heisei 20. Adopted from the Chinese tradition, these Imperial reign period names are closely linked to the imperial family and were originally chosen by court officials when a new emperor was installed or if something auspicious, or disastrous, happened. The reign period of Heisei 平成(へいせい) began in 1989 when the previous emperor passed away. The first year of his reign was the year one. What reign year is it now, based upon this system?

Japan also uses the Western system for counting years so a Japanese person is just as likely to say 1998年 as 平成(へいせい) 10年. This is a good example of how Japan adapts elements from ancient China and other modern cultures into its own unique ways of doing things.

■ キアラのジャーナル Kiara's Journal

Read the journal entry below, and then answer these questions.

❶ What is the name of the building that Kiara entered?
❷ What does Tomo eat in this entry?
❸ What did he eat yesterday?
❹ How many pages of notes has Tomo written about important food items?
❺ What was special about Kouken?

ジャーナルへ

今日 東大寺の 中に 入りました (went into). 金曜日から 今日まで 友さんと 一緒に いました。友さんは 毎日 たくさんの 食べ物を 食べました。彼は 何でも 食べます！ 友さんは お魚 (fish) と 芋（ポテト）と 漬け物を 食べました。昨日は、晩ご飯に 中国の 食べ物を たくさん 食べました。お酒も いっぱい 飲みました。友さんは 食べ物の事を ノートに 三ページぐらい 書きました。その ノートに 天平勝宝 三年と 書きました。私は、「むずかしい！ 友さん、それは 何ですか。」と、聞きました。友さんは、「孝謙天皇の 年号です。今年は、孝謙天皇の 三年目 です。」と、言いました。孝謙天皇は one of very few female emperors in Japanese 歴史。今、私達は、その very unusual era にいます。面白い ですね。

ああ、今は とても 眠い です。We've been so busy every day. I just have to take a break now and get some sleep.

お休み。

第5課の4

先週も、 あちこちに 行きました。

Last week too, we went here and there.

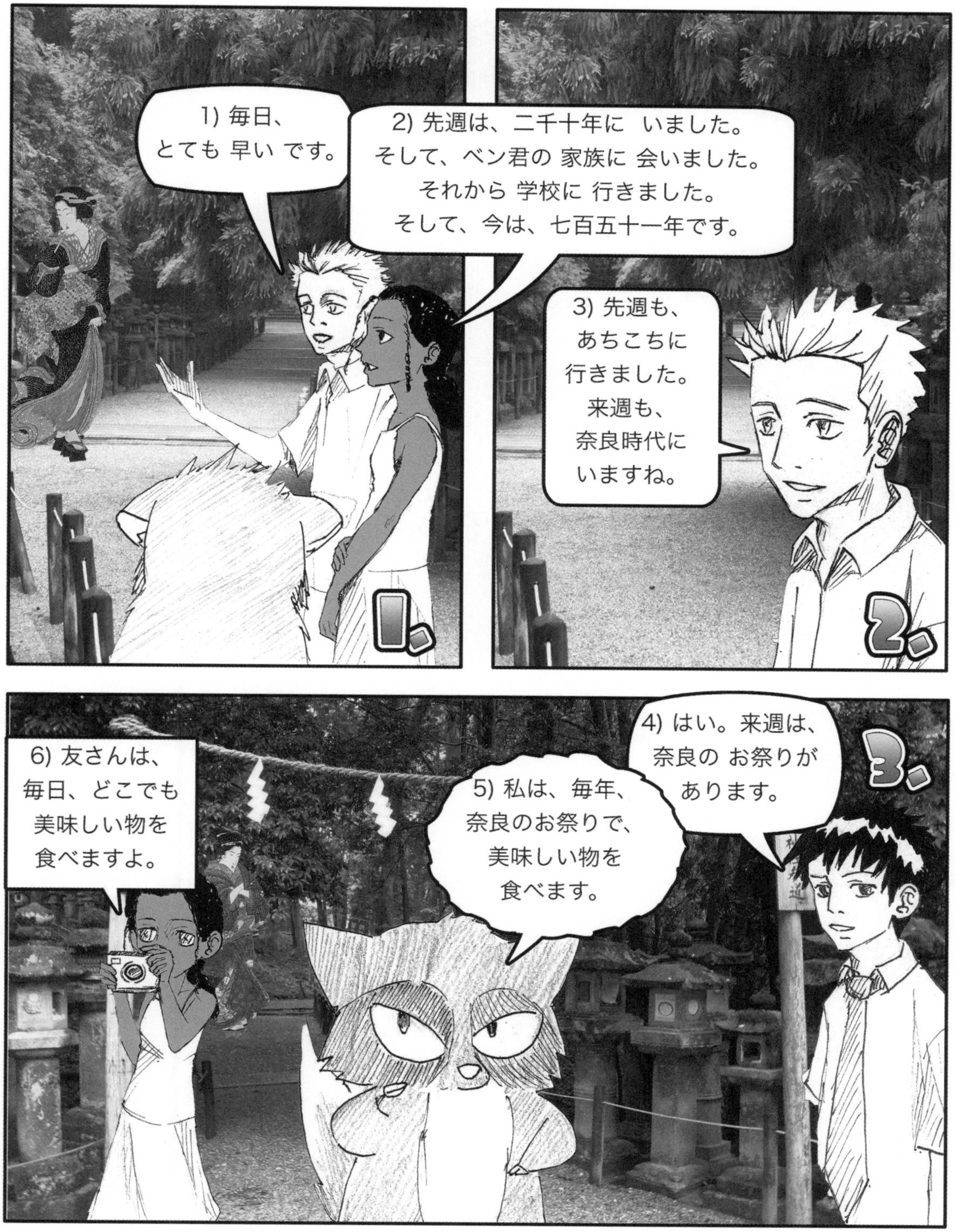

1) 毎日、
とても 早い です。

2) 先週は、二千十年に いました。
そして、ベン君の 家族に 会いました。
それから 学校に 行きました。
そして、今は、七百五十一年です。

1.

3) 先週も、
あちこちに
行きました。
来週も、
奈良時代に
いますね。

2.

■ 会話 Dialogue

REMINDER: You may see some kanji / vocabulary you do not recognize. Use the context to try to understand the meanings of those parts of the dialogue.

1. ベン　：毎日、とても　早い　です。
2. キアラ：先週は、二千十年に　いました。そして、ベン君の　家族に　会いました。それから、学校に　行きました。そして、今は、七百五十一年　です。
3. ベン　：先週も、あちこちに　行きました。来週も、奈良時代に　いますね。
4. じゅん：はい。来週は、奈良の　お祭りが　あります。
5. 友　　：私は、毎年、奈良の　お祭りで、美味しい物を　食べます。
6. キアラ：友さんは、毎日、どこでも　美味しい物を　食べますよ。

■ 単語 New Words

散歩 (*n*)	去年 (*n*)	今年 (*n*)	来年 (*n*)	毎年 (*n*)	忙しい (*exp./conj.*)

散歩(を)する / します (*v*) – to take a walk

先週 (*n*) – last week

今週 (*n*) – this week

来週 (*n*) – next week

週末 (*n*) – weekend

毎週 (*n*) – every week

先月 (*n*) – last month

今月 (*n*) – this month

来月 (*n*) – next month

毎月 (*n*) – every month

先週の火曜日 (*n*) – Tuesday of last week

何年 (*inter.*) – what year?

* Note that at this point you have learned three different pronunciations for the kanji 月. They are in the words 月曜日, 毎月, and 一月.

■ 漢字 Kanji

電 (13 strokes)								
デン – electricity	一	𠂆	戸	帀	帀	雨	雨	
電(気) – electricity; 電(話) – telephone	雨	雨	雨	雨	雷	電		
The top half of this kanji is the radical for rain (雨). The last strokes look like a kite with a long tail. Imagine Benjamin Franklin flying that kite under the rain in his famous experiment to discover ELECTRICITY.								

達 (12 strokes)								
ダツ, タチ, ダチ – to reach or arrive at; pluralizes some words	一	十	土	土	圭	幸	幸	
(友)達 – friend; (私)達 – we; (先生)達 – teachers; 達します – to arrive	幸	幸	丶幸	達	達			
The dirt (土), sheep (羊), and a road (the last 3 strokes) here show how a GROUP (the pluralization part) of sheep can follow a long dirt road to REACH their destination.								

■ 言葉の探索 (ことば たんさく) Language Detection

1. This week, next week, last week, every week/month/year

The prefixes 先 (せん) (before), 今 (こん) (now/present), and 来 (らい) (next) are placed in front of some time expressions:

先週 (せんしゅう)	last week	今週 (こんしゅう)	this week	来週 (らいしゅう)	next week
先月 (せんげつ)	last month	今月 (こんげつ)	this month	来月 (らいげつ)	next month

Years are slightly different:

去年 (きょねん)	last year	今年 (ことし)	this year	来年 (らいねん)	next year

2. Every day/week/month/year

The prefix 毎 (まい) (every) can be used in front of many time expressions.

毎日 (まいにち)	every day	毎週 (まいしゅう)	every week	毎月 (まいつき)	every month	毎年 (まいとし) or 毎年 (まいねん)	every year

■ 自習 (じしゅう) Self Check

1. Without looking at the above section, try to say each of the following out loud in Japanese:

A) last week
B) next week
C) this month
D) every day
E) every month
F) this week
G) last month
H) next month
I) every week
J) every year

■ 練習の時間 (れんしゅう じかん) Time for Practice

1. Tic-Tac-Toe

Place your marker on a spot and say the phrase for that square out loud to your partner in Japanese. If your partner feels that you are correct, you get to keep the square. If they challenge you, they may take the square. If they challenge you and are wrong, they lose a turn. Take turns. Try to get three in a row. An answer key has been provided at the end of the pair practices of this section.

(a)

this week	every year	next year
next week	yesterday	today
Tuesday of last week	this year	next month

(b)

this month	last year	every week
this Friday	tomorrow	last week
every day	next Saturday	last month

2. Pair Practice

Take turns asking and answering the following questions with your partner in Japanese.

		Partner's answers
A)	来年(らいねん)は　何年(なんねん)　ですか。	A) ________
B)	今月(こんげつ)は　何月(なんがつ)　ですか。	B) ________
C)	来週(らいしゅう)の　月曜日(げつようび)は　何日(なんにち)　ですか。	C) ________
D)	明日(あした)は　何曜日(なんようび)　ですか。	D) ________
E)	今日(きょう)は　何曜日(なんようび)　ですか。	E) ________
F)	今日(きょう)は　何日(なんにち)　ですか。	F) ________
G)	先週(せんしゅう)の　金曜(きんよう)は　何日(なんにち)　でしたか。	G) ________
H)	去年(きょねん)は　何年(なんねん)　でしたか。	H) ________
I)	来週(らいしゅう)の　水曜日(すいようび)　は　何日(なんにち)　ですか。	I) ________
J)	先月(せんげつ)は　何月(なんがつ)　でしたか。	J) ________
K)	あなたの　誕生日(たんじょうび)は　いつ　ですか。	K) ________
L)	お母さんの　誕生日(たんじょうび)は　いつ　ですか。	L) ________

3. Pair Practice

Information gap

You and two friends are trying to compile a three-month schedule. A-さん and B-さん should write the activities below on paper giving each a date from the calendar before having a conversation with each other and C-さん about when each activity happens. C-さん should write and ask questions. Notice the date for today. If the activity happened before "today," be sure to use the past tense of the verb.

A-さん：　いつ　日本語を　勉強(べんきょう)　しますか。
B-さん：　六月三日(ろくがつみっか)に　勉強(べんきょう)　しました。
B-さん：　いつ　寿司(すし)を　食べましたか。
A-さん：　五月二十四日(ごがつにじゅうよっか)に　食べました。

私たちの　スケジュール(すけじゅーる)

五月					
月	火	水	木	金	土/日
	1	2	3	4	5-6
7	8	9	10	11	12-13
14	15	16	17	18	19-20
21	22	23	24	25	26-27
28	29	30	31		

六月					
月	火	水	木	金	土/日
				1	2-3
4	5	6	7	8	9-10
11	12	13	14 今日	15	16-17
18	19	20	21	22	23-24
25	26	27	28	29	30-31

七月					
月	火	水	木	金	土/日
1	2	3	4	5	6-7
8	9	10	11	12	13-14
15	16	17	18	19	20-21
22	23	24	25	26	27-28
29	30	31			

A
1. basketball
2. study Japanese
3. math test
4. judo club
5. (free choice)

B
6. tennis
7. sushi restaurant
8. friend's birthday
9. English test
10. (free choice)

Tic-Tac-Toe answer key:

(a) 今週(こんしゅう)／毎年(まいとし)／来年(らいねん)
来週(らいしゅう)／きのう／今日(きょう)
先週(せんしゅう)の火曜日(かようび)／今年(ことし)／来月(らいげつ)

(b) 今月(こんげつ)／去年(きょねん)／毎週(まいしゅう)
今週(こんしゅう)の金曜日(きんようび)／あした／先週(せんしゅう)
毎日(まいにち)／来週(らいしゅう)の土曜日(どようび)／先月(せんげつ)

■ 文化箱(ぶんかばこ) Culture Chest

Cross-Cultural Holidays

People migrate from place to place and from country to country. As they do, they carry their celebrations and holidays with them. For instance, people of Mexican heritage celebrate Dia de los Muertos (Day of the Dead) in November to honor the deceased, Irish celebrate St. Patrick's Day, and Chinese all over the world celebrate Chinese New Year. Japan is culturally more homogeneous, but other cultures and economics have influenced its holiday celebrations as well. For instance, Christmas and Valentine's Day (two Western holidays) are celebrated in Japan, but not exactly as they might be celebrated in the West. In Japan, Valentine's Day has become a day when women give chocolate to their male friends and colleagues. Chocolate companies in Japan created a second commercial holiday related to Valentine's Day called White Day. This is a holiday observed on March 14. Do a web search to find pictures of how these holidays are celebrated in Japan. What strikes you as different? Does your family honor a holiday special to your cultural heritage?

■ キアラ(きあら)のジャーナル(じゃーなる) Kiara's Journal

Read the journal entry below, and then answer these questions.

❶ When did Kiara meet Jun's family?
❷ To whom is Kiara going to try to write an email tomorrow?
❸ What is Kiara going to do at Todaiji Temple?

ジャーナル(じゃーなる)へ

先週 じゅん君の ご家族に 会(あ)いました。それから 学校へ 行きました。今週 友さんに会いました。アメリカの 友達の 学校は 来週から です。They are never going to believe the trip I'm having. 来週 私は どこで だれと 会うでしょう？この experience は 毎日(まいにち) surprising です。

明日(あした) 母に 電子メール(でんしめーる)を 書きます。Maybe it will go through. 友さんと じゅん君と ベン君と 私は、毎日 忙(いそが)しい です。私達は たくさん いい 人達と 会いましたが、ちょっと 休みたい です。奈良(なら)で 来週 大きな 祭(まつ)りが あります。その 前(まえ)に 東大寺(とうだいじ)でちょっと お手伝(てつだ)いします。東大寺で 絵(え)を 描(か)きます (drawing). 私は、絵が 好(す)き です。その 絵を 電子メール(でんしめーる)で 母に 送(おく)ります。

第5課の5 Verb Review

■ ベンの話(はなし)

Answer the following based upon Ben's story below.

❶ Where was Ben born?

❷ What is Ben's Birthday?

❸ How old was Ben when his family moved to Tokyo?

❹ What school subject does Ben really like?

❺ What century are Ben and his friends in as he is writing?

Ben's Story

僕(ぼく)は　オーストラリア(おーすとらりあ)で　生(う)まれました。誕生日(たんじょうび)は　七月八日(しちがつようか)　です。家族は　六人です。父と　母と　兄と　妹が　二人います。キャンベラ(きゃんべら)の　幼稚園(ようちえん)に　行きました。九年前、6才(さい)の時、東京へ　来ました。その四月、日本の　小学校に　入(はい)りました。4年生の　時(とき)に、じゅん君と　会(あ)いました。じゅん君は　今も　とても　いい　友達(ともだち)　です。そして、13才(さい)で、中学一年生に　なりました。今は、15才(さい)で、中学三年生　です。今、中学校で　日本語と英語と　数学(すうがく)と　科学(かがく)を　勉強(べんきょう)　しています。歴史(れきし)も　勉強しています。歴史はとてもおもしろいです。僕(ぼく)は、歴史が　大好(だいす)きです。先週、友達と　時の門に　入りました。今日(きょう)は、751年1月20日　です。21世紀(せいき)から　8世紀まで　来ました。

■ 練習(れんしゅう)の時間(じかん) Time for Practice

1. Pair Practice

Say the following dates in Japanese. (Hint: Information in dates in Japanese flows from general to specific, so the year will come first and the exact time last.)

After you have practiced saying the dates out loud, match them with the events in the box. .

1. November 1, 1974
2. March 3, every year
3. May 5, every year
4. December 3, every year
5. March 24, 1603
6. September 30, 1998
7. March 14, every year
8. August 6, 1954
9. April 16, 1600

a. Godzilla was born	f. William Adams landed in Japan
b. Tokugawa period begins	g. First Pokémon release in the US
c. Hello Kitty was born	h. Hina Matsuri (girl's festival)
d. Children's Day	i. White Day
e. Emperor's Birthday	

2. Pair Practice

Use the "Verbs by Chapter" in Appendix 1. One student gives the non-past (ます) form of verbs introduced up through chapter 5, then the partner has to give the other three forms of the same verb:

a) Negative non-past

b) Past

c) Negative past

A- さん：　あります。

B- さん：　ありません。 ありました。
ありませんでした。

NOTE: switch roles often so that both partners become really smooth at saying all three forms.

■ 単語チェックリスト New Word Checklist

たんごちぇっくりすと

5-1

おきる・起きる / おきます・起きます（おきて・起きて） *v* to wake (up)
おくる・送る / おくります・送ります *v* to send
かようび・火曜日 *n* Tuesday
きんようび・金曜日 *n* Friday
げつようび・月曜日 *n* Monday
すいようび・水曜日 *n* Wednesday
だいじ・大事 な *adj.* important
でんしめーる・電子メール / めーる・メール *n* e-mail
どようび・土曜日 *n* Saturday
なんようび・何曜日 *inter.* what day of the week?
にちようび・日曜日 *n* Sunday
ねる・寝る / ねます・寝ます *v* to sleep
まえ・前 *n/adv.* before, front, in front
まつり・祭り *n* festival
もくようび・木曜日 *n* Thursday
れんしゅう（を）・練習（を）する / します *v* to practice

5-2

いちがつ・一月 *n* January
いつ *inter.* when?
いっさい・一歳 *count.* one year old
うまれる・生まれる / うまれます・生まれます *v* to be born
おわる・終わる / おわります・終わります *v* to finish
きゅうさい・九歳 *count.* nine years old
きゅうせん・九千 *count.* nine thousand
くがつ・九月 *n* September
ごがつ・五月 *n* May
ごさい・五歳 *count.* five years old
ごせん・五千 *count.* five thousand
さんがつ・三月 *n* March
さんさい・三歳 *count.* three years old
さんぜん・三千 *count.* three thousand
しがつ・四月 *n* April
しちがつ / なながつ・七月 *n* July
じゅういちがつ・十一月 *n* November
じゅういっさい・十一歳 *count.* eleven years old
じゅうがつ・十月 *n* October
じゅうさんさい・十三歳 *count.* thirteen years old
じゅうにがつ・十二月 *n* December
じゅうにさい・十二歳 *count.* twelve years old
じゅうよんさい・十四歳 *count.* fourteen years old
じゅっさい / じっさい・十歳 *count.* ten years old
せん・千 *count.* one thousand
たんじょうび・誕生日 *n* birthday
ななさい・七歳 *count.* seven years old
ななせん・七千 *count.* seven thousand
なんがつ・何月 *inter.* what month?
なんぜん・何千 *inter.* how many thousands?
にがつ・二月 *n* February
にさい・二歳 *count.* two years old
にせん・二千 *count.* two thousand
はじめる・始める / はじめます・始めます *v* to begin
はたち・二十歳 *count.* twenty years old
はちがつ・八月 *n* August
はっさい・八歳 *count.* eight years old
はっせん 八千 *count.* eight thousand
べんきょう（を）・勉強（を）する / します *v* to study
よんさい・四歳 *count.* four years old
よんせん・四千 *count.* four thousand
ろくがつ・六月 *n* June
ろくさい・六歳 *count.* six years old
ろくせん・六千 *count.* six thousand

5-3

から *part.* from
なんにち・何日 *inter.* what day of the month
いつか・五日 *count.* fifth (day of the month)
ここのか・九日 *count.* ninth (day of the month)
さんじゅういちにち・三十一日 *count.* thirty-first (day of the month)
さんじゅうにち・三十日 *count.* thirtieth (day of the month)
じゅういちにち・十一日 *count.* eleventh (day of the month)
じゅうくにち・十九日 *count.* nineteenth (day of the month)
じゅうごにち・十五日 *count.* fifteenth (day of the month)
じゅうさんにち・十三日 *count.* thirteenth (day of the month)
じゅうしちにち・十七日 *count.* seventeenth (day of the month)
じゅうににち・十二日 *count.* twelfth (day of the month)
じゅうはちにち・十八日 *count.* eighteenth (day of the month)
じゅうよっか・十四日 *count.* fourteenth (day of the month)
じゅうろくにち・十六日 *count.* sixteenth (day of the month)
ついたち・一日 *count.* first (day of the month)
とおか・十日 *count.* tenth (day of the month)
なにも・何も *pron.* nothing

なのか・七日 *count.* seventh (day of the month)

にじゅういちにち・二十一日 *count.* twenty-first (day of the month)

にじゅうくにち・二十九日 *count.* twenty-ninth (day of the month)

にじゅうごにち・二十五日 *count.* twenty-fifth (day of the month)

にじゅうさんにち・二十三日 *count.* twenty-third (day of the month)

にじゅうしちにち・二十七日 *count.* twenty-seventh (day of the month)

にじゅうににち・二十二日 *count.* twenty-second (day of the month)

にじゅうはちにち・二十八日 *count.* twenty-eighth (day of the month)

にじゅうよっか・二十四日 *count.* twenty-fourth (day of the month)

にじゅうろくにち・二十六日 *count.* twenty-sixth (day of the month)

はつか・二十日 *count.* twentieth (day of the month)

ふつか・二日 *count.* second (day of the month)

みっか・三日 *count.* third (day of the month)

むいか・六日 *count.* sixth (day of the month)

ようか・八日 *count.* eighth (day of the month)

よっか・四日 *count.* fourth (day of the month)

5-4

いそがしい・忙しい *adj.* busy

きょねん・去年 *n* last year

ことし・今年 *n* this year

こんげつ・今月 *n* this month

こんしゅう・今週 *n* this week

さんぽ・散歩 *n* walk

さんぽ・散歩(を)する/します *v* to take a walk

しゅうまつ・週末 *n* weekend

せんげつ・先月 *n* last month

せんしゅう・先週 *n* last week

せんしゅうのかようび・先週の火曜日 *n* Tuesday of last week

なんねん・何年 *inter.* what year?

まいしゅう・毎週 *n* every week

まいつき・毎月 *n* every month

まいとし/まいねん・毎年 *n* every year

らいげつ・来月 *n* next month

らいしゅう・来週 *n* next week

らいねん・来年 *n* next year

Body Parts and Clothing in Hiraizumi

第 6 課

Learning and Performance Goals

This chapter will enable you to:

A) use the names of basic body parts
B) talk about and use expressions to describe physical attributes
C) talk about wearing clothing and accessories
D) ask, give, and deny permission for activities
E) answer questions about actions that are taking place
F) use adverbs in the present positive and present negative tenses
G) use 18 additional kanji
H) use the "can-do" chart found on **TimeForJapanese.com** to chart your progress for what you "can-do" for each chapter

* The expectation is that you will have learned katakana by the time you finish this chapter. You can find the Kana Book on **TimeForJapanese.com**.

Steps leading to the Konjikido, Hiraizumi, Iwate

第6課の1 頭が　とても　いい　です。

あたま

You are very smart.

■ 会話(かいわ) Dialogue

REMINDER: You may see some kanji / vocabulary you do not recognize. Use the context to try to understand the meanings of those parts of the dialogue.

1. ベン(べん)　：あなたが、あの　弁慶(べんけい)さん　ですか。
2. 弁慶(べんけい)　：そう　です。私は　弁慶(べんけい)　です。
3. ベン(べん)　：あなたは　とても　有名(ゆうめい)　ですね！
4. キアラ(きあら)：とても　強(つよ)い　侍(さむらい)　ですね。心(こころ)も　強(つよ)い　ですね。
   それに　頭(あたま)が　とても　いいですね。
5. 友　：そして、いい　人(ひと)　ですね。
6. ベン(べん)　：目(め)も、鼻(はな)も、口(くち)も、耳(みみ)も、頭(あたま)も、顔(かお)も足(あし)も、皆(みんな)　大きい　ですね！

■ 単語(たんご) New Words

 侍(さむらい) (*n*)	 強(つよ)い (い *adj.*)	 弱(よわ)い (い *adj.*)	 低(ひく)い (い *adj.*)	 長(なが)い (い *adj.*)	 短(みじか)い (い *adj.*)
 悲(かな)しい (い *adj.*)	 高(たか)い (い *adj.*)	 静(しず)か (な *adj.*)	 有名(ゆうめい) (な *adj.*)	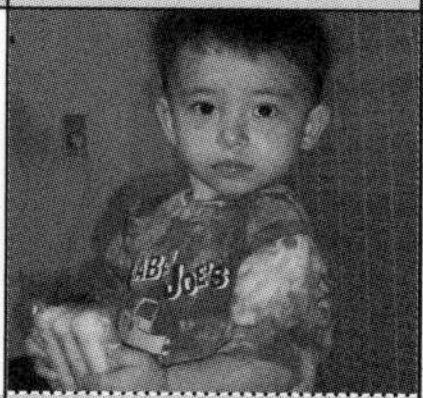 (持(も)つ) 持(も)ちます (*v*)	 (待(ま)つ) 待(ま)ちます (*v*)
	(入(い)れる) 入(い)れます (*v*)	(入(はい)る) 入(はい)ります (*v*)	(出(で)る) 出(で)ます (*v*)	遠(とお)い (い *adj.*)	

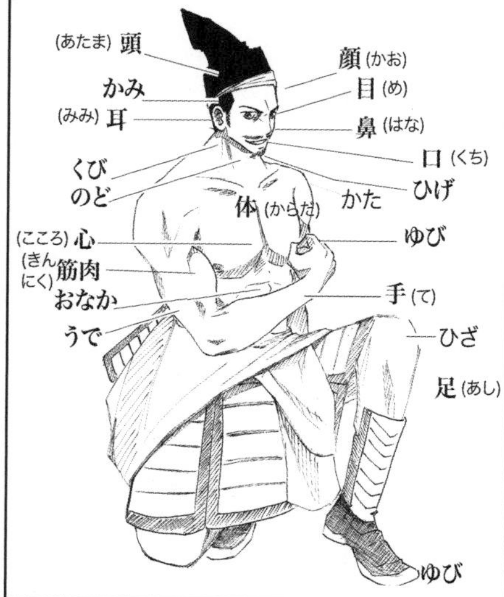

近(ちか)い (い *adj.*) – close, near	ひみつ (*n*) – secret
いつも (*n/adv.*) – always	声(こえ) (*n*) – voice
背(せ) or 背(せい) (*n*) – stature, height	

■ 漢字(かんじ) Kanji

体 (7 strokes)							
タイ(たい); からだ – body	ノ	亻	仁	什	休	休	体
体(からだ) – body; 体(たい)(育館(いくかん)) – gymnasium							
The left two strokes are a person (人) leaning his BODY on the world's largest book (本)!							

目 (5 strokes)							
モク(もく); め – eye	丨	冂	月	月	目		
目(め) – eye; (科(か))目(もく) – subject							
This is a picture of an EYEBALL turned 90 degrees. The 3rd and 4th strokes represent the pupil in the middle.							

口 (3 strokes)							
くち / ぐち – mouth	丨	冂	口				
口(くち) – mouth; (入(いり))口(ぐち) – entrance; (出(で))口(ぐち) – exit							
This kanji is a picture of a MOUTH opened really wide.							

耳 (6 strokes)							
みみ – ear	一	丅	下	下	三	耳	
耳(みみ) – ear							
Starting with your eye (目), go over a little to your left and right, then down a little (represented by the lines that extend to the left and right and down) to get to your EARS (耳).							

手 (4 strokes)							
シュ(しゅ); ズ(ず); て – hand	ノ	二	三	手			
手(て) – hand; (上(じょう))手(ず) – skillful; (下(へ))手(た) – unskillful							
Think of the first stroke as the thumb and the second stroke as the main part of the HAND, with two fingers to the right and two fingers to the left. You can imagine how this HAND (手) got so disfigured!							

足 (7 strokes)							
ソク(そく); あし – foot, leg; た(りる) – to be enough, sufficient	丨	冂	口	早	早	𠯁	足
足(あし) – leg, foot; (一(いっ))足(そく) – a pair of socks/shoes							
The top of this character is the mouth (口) on the body of a runner who is showing off his really big FEET at the end of his LEGS.							

4 strokes

シン；こころ – heart, spirit	
心(しん)(臓(ぞう)) – the heart (organ); 心(こころ) – heart, spirit	

This kanji (心) has four strokes, one representing each chamber of the HEART. They are drawn best when the calligrapher uses a lot of strong SPIRIT.

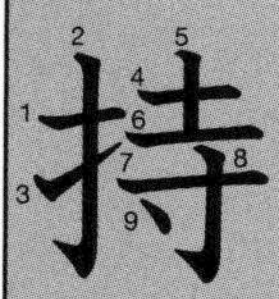

9 strokes

も(つ) – to hold, to have	
持(も)つ – to hold, to have	持 持

The first three strokes represent the hand (手) radical. The right side of this kanji is a Buddhist temple (寺). Think of something you HAVE or HOLD in your hand as you visit a Buddhist temple.

9 strokes

ま(つ) – to wait	
待(ま)(つ) – to wait	待 待

The first three strokes are the left side of the character "to go" (行), while the right side is a Buddhist temple (寺). Think of how annoying it would be to go to a Buddhist temple only to have TO WAIT for a long time.

11 strokes

キョウ；つよ(い) – to be strong	
強(つよ)(い) – to be strong; 勉強(べんきょう)する – to study (i.e., to exert strong effort even against your natural inclination)	強 強

The left side of this kanji (弓) is a Japanese bow while the right side is 虫 (MUSHI), or bug, with a katakana ム (MU) on top. If a bug is STRONG enough to pull this bow, he must be a very STRONG bug indeed!

■ 言葉(ことば)の探索(たんさく) Language Detection

1. 強(つよ)い / 弱(よわ)い

強(つよ)い and 弱(よわ)い literally mean "strong" and "weak."

A) じゅん君(くん)の　体(からだ)は　強(つよ)い　です。 = Jun('s body) is strong.
B) 私の　足(あし)は　弱(よわ)い　です。 = My legs are weak.
C) 一郎(いちろう)の　心(こころ)は　強(つよ)い　です。 = Ichirou has a lot of heart. (Ichirou has a strong heart.)

強(つよ)い and 弱(よわ)い can also be used to talk about being good or bad at something.

A) この　高校の　サッカー部は　強(つよ)い　です。 = This high school's soccer club (team) is strong.
B) その　学校の　野球部(やきゅうぶ)は　弱(よわ)い　です。 = That school's baseball club is weak.

2. When describing someone's physical features in Japanese, the person is followed by the particle は (wa), the body part by the particle が, then an adjective descriptor..

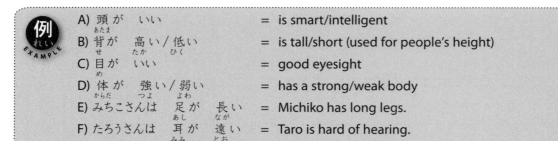

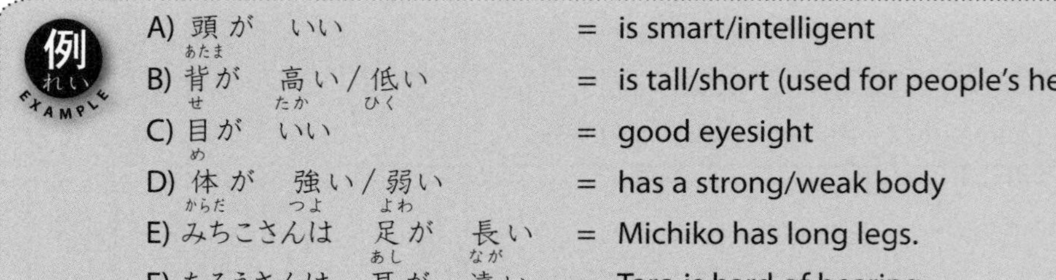

A) 頭(あたま)が いい = is smart/intelligent
B) 背(せ)が 高(たか)い／低(ひく)い = is tall/short (used for people's height)
C) 目(め)が いい = good eyesight
D) 体(からだ)が 強(つよ)い／弱(よわ)い = has a strong/weak body
E) みちこさんは 足(あし)が 長(なが)い = Michiko has long legs.
F) たろうさんは 耳(みみ)が 遠(とお)い = Taro is hard of hearing.
G) たかひろさんは 鼻(はな)が 高(たか)い = Takahiro has a tall/high nose.

* NOTE: When describing facial features of people of European descent, Japanese often use the term "high" nose when describing an aquiline nose or classical "Greek" nose. This term can have a complimentary meaning. As an idiom, this phrase implies that someone is proud of something. When used to refer to someone else's excessive pride it can be a negative term. Take care in using it.

■ 自習(じしゅう) Self Check

1. 強(つよ)い／弱(よわ)い

How would you say the following in Japanese?

A) The kendo club is strong.
B) This school's basketball team is weak.
C) (insert team) is strong.
D) (insert team) is weak.

2. Body parts and adjectives

Try to say the following in Japanese using the names of people you know. Start each sentence with: (*person's name*) は ______。

A) __________ is tall.
B) __________ is smart.
C) __________ has long legs.
D) __________ has good eyesight.

■ 練習(れんしゅう)の時間(じかん) Time for Practice

1. Pair Practice

Parts of the body

Point to a body part and ask your partner what it is. Your partner will say the name of that body part in Japanese. If correct, switch. If incorrect, teach your partner what the correct word is until he or she can say it, then switch roles. Keep speaking until both partners can smoothly say all the body parts introduced in this section.

A-さん： (*point to your eye*) これは 何(なん)ですか。
B-さん： それは 目(め)です。

2. Whole Class Activity

Here are the words for "Head, Shoulders, Knees and Toes" in Japanese. Practice singing with your class. Once you have mastered it, sing it faster, double-time!

3. Pair Practice

Kanji slapjack

Spread out your kanji cards for body parts on the table, face up. You will also need a picture of Benkei; draw one or enlarge the one on page 181. To play, choose one of the versions below, or come up with your own version.

- Version 1: Spread out your kanji cards for body parts on the table, face up. Your teacher, or another friend, calls out a Japanese vocabulary word. You and your partner see who can be the first to slap the correct kanji. The quickest "slapper" gets to keep the card.
- Version 2: You and your partner take turns picking up a kanji card and placing it in the correct place on the picture of Benkei. You must say the name of the body part as you set it in place. See how quickly you can move all the cards onto the picture of Benkei. Try to beat your time in the second round.
- Version 3: With the kanji cards already in place on the picture of Benkei, take turns saying a body part in Japanese. Your partner has two seconds to slap the correct card. If your partner slaps the correct card, that card belongs to him/her and is removed from play. If your partner slaps the wrong card, the card stays in play. Play ends when all the cards have been removed from Benkei. The player holding the most cards wins.

4. Group Practice

先生 Says

One person, the "leader," calls out a body part and then the verb "to touch" (*さわって下さい), with or without "先生 says" in front. When the "leader" uses " 先生 says," everyone touches that body part, just like "Simon says. . ." When the leader omits this and only gives the command, no action should be taken. The last one standing gets to lead the next round.

Leader: 先生 says " 耳(みみ) " を さわって下さい。 (Please touch your ear.)
(Action: Everyone in the class should touch their ears.)
Leader: 足(あし)を さわって下さい。
(Action: No one in the class should touch their leg.)

* SAWATTE KUDASAI means "Please touch."

■ 文化箱(ぶんかばこ) Culture Chest

平泉(ひらいずみ)

Hiraizumi, with a population of about 9,000, is a small town in Iwate Prefecture in northern 本州(ほんしゅう). Around 1100, it served as the northern capital for the ruling Fujiwara Clan, and rivaled Kyoto in wealth and power for the next 100 years. Estimates vary, but at its peak the city's population may have reached one million, making Hiraizumi one of the largest cities in the world at the time.

Tourists posing behind a faceless cutout of Benkei. Hiraizumi, Iwate.

The glory of Hiraizumi crashed in 1189 when Minamoto no Yoritomo destroyed the city as part of his plan to unite all Japan.

Two victims of the destruction of Hiraizumi are legendary today: Yoshitsune and Benkei. Yoshitsune, younger brother of the 将軍(しょうぐん) (military ruler of all of Japan) Yoritomo, had helped his older brother in his rise to power. Mistrust and intrigue led Yoritomo to turn on his younger brother, forcing Yoshitsune to commit 切腹(せっぷく) (ritual suicide).

Benkei, Yoshitsune's samurai retainer (家来(けらい) in Japanese; a retainer is a type of servant or attendant), is legendary throughout Japan for his size, physical strength, and steadfast loyalty to his master. Saito Musashibō Benkei (1155–1189), known simply as Benkei, was a 僧兵(そうへい) (Buddhist monk warrior). There are so many legends about Benkei that it is impossible to distinguish between fact and fiction. He is reported to have been over two meters tall at age seventeen. Legend has it that Benkei remained standing even after he died in Hiraizumi defending a bridge as he continued to fight to the end against all odds to save his master Yoshitsune from an invading army.

■ キアラのジャーナル **Kiara's Journal**

Read the journal entry below, and then answer these questions.

❶ What time of day did the TOKI no MON arrive at its next stop?

❷ What was the first thing Ben saw when he went outside?

❸ Who do Jun, Ben, and Kiara meet? What does this person invite them to do?

ジャーナルへ

今朝、奈良の 友達に さようならと、言いました。そして、また 時の門に 入りました。今、私は ちょっと 悲しいです。でも この **adventure** は 楽しい です。それと、時々 ちょっと 危ない です。**The way that** 友さん **activates the** 時の門は まだ ひみつです。時の門を 出た時は、午後四時 でした。友さんは、「ええっ… ここ ですか。」と、言いました。

ベン君は、「どこですか。」と、聞きました。そして、「わあ！あの 家は とても 大きい ですね。あの 人達は 侍 ですか。」と、言いました。

じゅん君は、「そう です。でも、ちょっと、静かに して下さい。」と、言いました。

一人の 侍 が 近くに 来ました。そして、「あなた達は、だれ ですか。」と、言いました。

友さんは、「私は 友です。あなたの 敵 **(enemy)** では ありません。こちらは じゅんと ベンと キアラ です。私達は、あの 神社から 来ました。」と、言いました。

その侍さんは、「僕は 弁慶 です。 源 義経の 家来 **(servant)** です。」と、言いました。そして、「敵は 明日、**will attack** と、思います。」と、言いました。

ベン君は、「弁慶さん ですか。あなたは とても 有名 です。強い 侍で、心も 広い ですね。」と、言いました。そして、「ここは 平泉ですか。」と、聞きました。

友さんは、「そう です。今は **1181** 年 です。弁慶さんは とても いい人 です。」と、言いました。

ベン君 **was excited and whispered,** 「弁慶は 昔話 **(legend)** の 中 だけの 人だと 思って いました！」

友さんは、「今、ベン君の 目の前 **(front)** に いる 人は、本物 **(real)** の 弁慶さん ですよ。」と、小さい 声で 言って、**wink** しました。

弁慶さんは、「私の 家に 来ませんか。八時半から 晩ご飯を 食べます。今晩は 友達が、美味しい **(tasty)** 米 **(uncooked rice)** を 持って来ます。どうぞ 来て下さい。」と、言いました。

第6課の2 弁慶(べんけい)さんは、 とても 背(せ)が 高(たか)い ですね。

Benkei is very tall, isn't he!

1.
1) 弁慶さんは、 とても 背が 高い ですね。 かっこいい です。
2.
2) 父も、 背が 高い です。
3) へえ。 キアラさんの お父さんは、どんな 人 ですか。
4) 父は目が大きい です。ちょっと 太っています。足が 長いです。手が とても大きいです。 そしてバスケが とても上手です。 ベン君のお父さんは、 背が高いですか。
5) 父ですか。ええ、まあまあ 高い です。 鼻も 高い です。足は ちょっと 短い です。 友さんの お父さんは どんな 狸 ですか。
6) 僕の父は、とても 背が 低いです。顔と頭が 大きい です。おなかも 大きい です。太って います。 そして、手と 足が短い です。
7) 写真を 見せて下さい。
3.
8) ほら、これが お父さんの 写真 です。見て下さい。とても かっこ いい 狸 です。

■ 会話 Dialogue 

REMINDER: You may see some kanji / vocabulary you do not recognize. Use the context to try to understand the meanings of those parts of the dialogue.

1. ベン　：弁慶さんは、とても　背が　高い　ですね。　かっこいい　です。
2. キアラ：父も、背が　高い　です。
3. じゅん：へえ。キアラさんのお父さんは、どんな　人　ですか。
4. キアラ：父は、目が　大きい　です。ちょっと　太っています。　足が　長い　です。手が　とても　大きい　です。そして　*バスケが　とても　上手　です。ベン君の　お父さんは、背が　高い　ですか。
5. ベン　：父　ですか。ええ、まあまあ　高い　です。鼻も　高い　です。足は　ちょっと　短いです。友さんの　お父さんは、どんな　狸　ですか。
6. 友　　：僕の　父は、とても　背が　低い　です。顔と　頭が　大きい　です。おなかも　大きいです。太っています。そして、手と　足が　短い　です。
7. ベンと　キアラと　じゅん：写真を　見せて下さい。
8. 友　　：ほら、これが　お父さんの　写真　です。見て下さい。　とても　かっこいい　狸です。

■ 単語 New Words 

かっこいい（い *adj.*）	スマート（な *adj.*）	やせています (*v*)	太っています (*v*)

上手（な *adj.*）– skillful

まあまあ (*adv.*) – so so

どんな (*inter.*) – what/which kind of?

（やめる）やめます (*v*) – to stop, to quit

やせる / やせます (*v*) – thin (to become)

（ふとる）ふとります (*v*) – fat (to become)

Other words you might like to use:

渋い（い *adj.*）– tasteful, subtle

おしゃれ（な *adj.*）– fashionable

■ 漢字(かんじ) Kanji

平 (5 strokes)								
	ヘイ(へい)；たいら – even, flat	一	〒	㇒	亚	平		
	平安時代(へいあんじだい) – the Heian Period; 平(たいら) – Taira (family name); 平(たい)ら flat							
	This KANJI has a post firmly planted in the ground (the vertical stroke). Two strong horizontal supports keep the top roof EVEN and FLAT.							

和 (8 strokes)								
	ワ(わ) – peace and harmony; ancient name for Japan	ノ	二	千	禾	禾	禾	和
	(平)和(へいわ) – peace; 和(食)(わしょく) – Japanese meal; 和(室)(わしつ) – Japanese-style room; 和(服)(わふく) – Japanese-style clothing	和						
	The right side is mouth (口). We would have more PEACE AND HARMONY if everyone sat quietly under a tree (strokes 2–5), silently meditating without using their mouths.							

低 (7 strokes)								
	ひく(い) – short, low	ノ	イ	亻	化	任	低	低
	低(ひく)い – short, low (height)							
	The left part of this kanji is a standing person (人). The right side is 氏(し), which means "clan" or "family" with the kanji for one (一) as the final stroke. Think of this as one entire clan of very SHORT (vertically-challenged) people with the final stroke representing a floor that the clan can barely rise above.							

太 (4 strokes)								
	タイ(たい)；ふと(い) – large, deep (voice); ふと(る) – to become fat	一	ナ	大	太			
	太(ふと)る – to become large or fat; 太(鼓)(たいこ) – large (fat) Japanese drum; (太平洋)(たいへいよう) – Pacific Ocean							
	This is the KANJI for a big (大) dog (犬) that has just caught one too many biscuits and is beginning to get FAT.							

■ 言葉(ことば)の探索(たんさく) Language Detection

1. て-form of verbs

Another conjugation for verbs in Japanese is the て-form. You were introduced to this form in Chapter 1, when you practiced classroom commands. The て-form has several uses:

A. to give commands (section 6-2)
B. to ask and give permission (or) to deny permission (6-3)
C. to show the present progressive tense (i.e., "is doing something") (6-4)
D. to connect two or more verbs (in the same sentence) (6-5)

For conjugation purposes, Japanese has three types of verbs. It is useful to know the rules that determine which of the three types any given verb belongs to. It is also useful to know the rules for how each of the three types of verbs can be put into the て-form.

How to form the て-form:

Type 1 or う verbs

The て-form conjugation for Type 1 or う verbs varies depending on the "verb stem" (the part of the verb that comes just before the ます ending).

Type 1 or う verbs have two main characteristics: 1. they are verbs with more than one character in the verb stem AND 2. the ending sound of the verb stem ends in み, に, び, い, ち, り, き, ぎ, or し. For example, the verb 飲みます IS a Type 1 or う verb because it has more than one character in the verb stem (のみ) AND the verb stem ends in a い sound (み). The verb み(ます) ends in one of the い sounds, but has only one character in the verb stem (み), and therefore is NOT a Type 1 or う verb. To determine if a verb is Type 1 or う verb, do this two-step test: first, check whether the verb stem has more than one syllable. Then, determine whether the verb stem ends in one these hiragana: み, に, び, い, ち, り, き, ぎ, or し. If it does, it is probably a Type 1 or う verb. If not, it is probably one of the other types. The chart below shows how to conjugate MASU-forms of う verbs into the て-form.

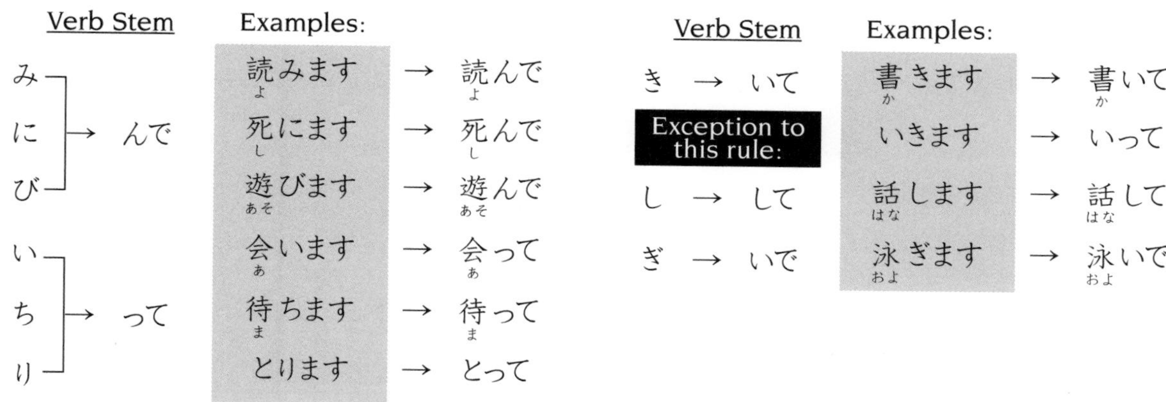

To remember how to convert Type 1 or う verbs to the て-form, sing the song below to the tune of "Three Blind Mice."

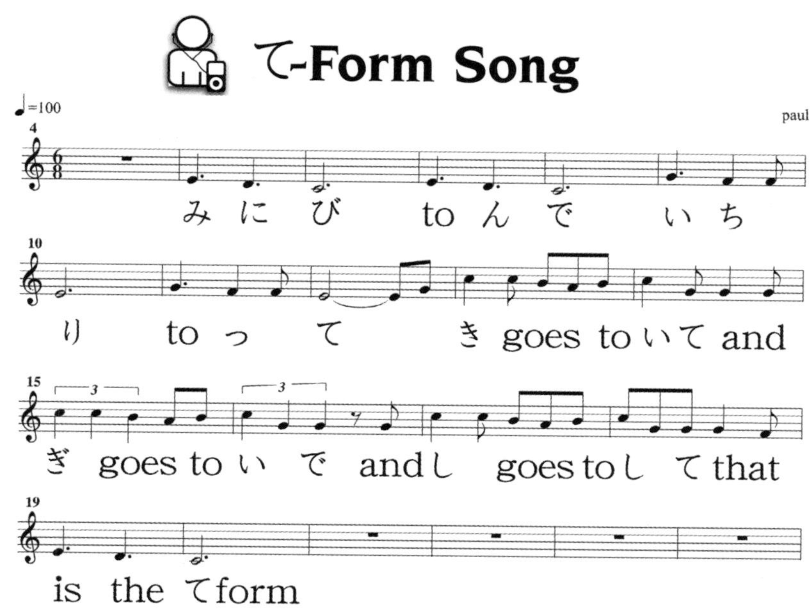

Type 1 Verbs (Chapters 1–6)

	non-past (～ます)	non-past negative (～ません)	～て-form	dictionary form (infinitive form)	English meaning
みにび	飲(の)みます	飲(の)みません	飲(の)んで	飲(の)む	to drink
	読(よ)みます	読(よ)みません	読(よ)んで	読(よ)む	to read
いちり	言(い)います	言(い)いません	言(い)って	言(い)う	to say
	手伝(てつだ)います	手伝(てつだ)いません	手伝(てつだ)って	手伝(てつだ)う	to help
	待(ま)ちます	待(ま)ちません	待(ま)って	待(ま)つ	to wait
	帰(かえ)ります	帰(かえ)りません	帰(かえ)って	帰(かえ)る	to return home
	座(すわ)ります	座(すわ)りません	座(すわ)って	座(すわ)る	to sit
	知(し)ります	知(し)りません	知(し)って	知(し)る	to know
	とります	とりません	とって	とる	to take
	入(はい)ります	入(はい)りません	入(はい)って	入(はい)る	to enter, go into
	あります	ありません	あって	ある	to exist (inanimate)
	太(ふと)ります	太(ふと)りません	太(ふと)って	太(ふと)る	to become fat
	分(わ)かります	分(わ)かりません	分(わ)かって	分(わ)かる	to understand
き	聞(き)きます	聞(き)きません	聞(き)いて	聞(き)く	to listen, to hear
	開(ひら)きます	開(ひら)きません	開(ひら)いて	開(ひら)く	to open books
*	行(い)きます	行(い)きません	行(い)って	行(い)く	to go
ぎ	泳(およ)ぎます	泳(およ)ぎません	泳(およ)いで	泳(およ)ぐ	to swim
し	話(はな)します	話(はな)しません	話(はな)して	話(はな)す	to speak

* 行きます is an exception to the song above because the き does not become いて but instead って。

Type 2 or る verbs

Verb stems in the Type 2 or る verb group generally end in an え sound rather than an い sound or only have one hiragana. To create the て-form from the ます form of Type 2 verbs, simply drop the ます and add て to the verb stem.

A) 食べます → 食べて (the dictionary form is 食べる)

B) 開(あ)けます → 開けて (the dictionary form is 開ける)

Type 2 Verbs (Chapters 1–6)

non-past (〜ます)	non-past negative (〜ません)	〜て -form	dictionary form (infinitive form)	English meaning
開(あ)けます	開(あ)けません	開(あ)けて	開(あ)ける	to open (doors/windows)
います	いません	いて	いる	to exist (animate)
閉(し)めます	閉(し)めません	閉(し)めて	閉(し)める	to close (doors/windows)
食(た)べます	食(た)べません	食(た)べて	食(た)べる	to eat
閉(と)じます	閉(と)じません	閉(と)じて	閉(と)じる	to close
始(はじ)めます	始(はじ)めません	始(はじ)めて	始(はじ)める	to begin, start
見(み)ます	見(み)ません	見(み)て	見(み)る	to look or to see
見(み)せます	見(み)せません	見(み)せて	見(み)せる	to show

NOTE: You will eventually learn more about the dictionary forms of verbs in Intermediate Japanese. Most verbs that end in "eru" or "iru" (in the dictionary form) are "ru verbs" but there are few cases in which a verb ends in one of these two sounds and is not a "ru verb" such as かえる (to return) which is an "u verb." You just have to memorize the few cases like かえる when a verb ends in "eru" or "iru" but is not a "ru verb."

Irregular verbs (します and 来(き)ます)

します (to do) and 来(き)ます (to come) are exceptions because they are irregular verbs. Their て-forms are:

します → して (the dictionary form is する)
来(き)ます → 来(き)て (the dictionary form is 来(く)る)

Irregular Verbs

non-past (〜ます)	non-past negative (〜ません)	〜て-form	dictionary form (infinitive form)	English meaning
来(き)ます	来(き)ません	来(き)て	来(く)る	to come
します	しません	して	する	to do

2. Commands/requests

You can make familiar (informal) commands in Japanese simply by using verbs in their て-form conjugations.

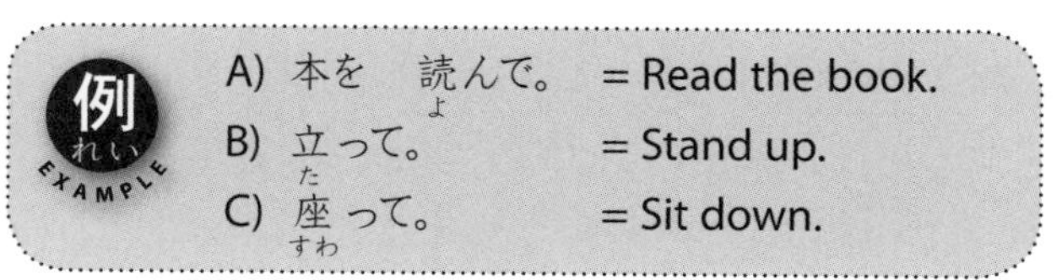

例 れい EXAMPLE
A) 本を 読(よ)んで。 = Read the book.
B) 立(た)って。 = Stand up.
C) 座(すわ)って。 = Sit down.

Polite requests can be made by adding 下さい (*please*) after the て-form verb:

A) 食べて　下さい。 = Please eat.
B) 手伝って　下さい。 = Please help.
C) 学校に　来て　下さい。 = Please come to school.

3. すこし、とても、ちょっと、まあまあ

Adverbs are words that modify adjectives, verbs, or other adverbs. As with English, in Japanese adverbs generally come before the words they modify. Notice the use of は (topic marker) and が (subject marker).

A) 久美子さんは　頭 が　とても　いい　です。 = Kumiko is really smart.
B) ゆみさんは　体 が　ちょっと　弱い　です。 = Yumi's body is a little weak.
C) 先生は　少し　ハンサム　です。 = The teacher is a little good looking.

■ 自習 Self Check

1. て-form

Restate the following out loud to yourself in Japanese using verbs in their て-form conjugations. What is the verb type for each?

A) 言います
B) 飲みます
C) 食べます
D) 来ます
E) 帰ります

2. Polite commands

Try to say the following in Japanese, changing the verbs into their て-form conjugations.

A) Please do it. (します)
B) Please return home. (帰ります)
C) Please go to the library. (行きます)

3. すこし、ちょっと、まあまあ, とても **adverbs**

Use one of these adverbs to say the following in Japanese:

Ichiro's eyes are a little weak. → 一郎さんは　目が　ちょっと　弱い　です。

A) Emi has very good vision.
B) Mr. Yamamoto is kind of long legged.
C) ____________________ is a little smart.

■ 練習の時間 Time for Practice
れんしゅう　じかん

1. Pair Practice

Use the verbs in the verb charts on pages 192 and 193 to practice making the て-form. A-さん should read the verbs in the left column and B-さん should say the て-form (looking at the chart as little as possible). Take turns.

2. Small Group Practice

Take turns being the group leader. As group leader, give three polite commands to the group (refer to the lists of commands on pages 28 and 44). Without looking at the textbook, group members act out each command. After finishing these, give new creative commands to your partners using your new knowledge of how to put verbs in the て-form. HINT: Adding direct objects, goals of movement, etc. can make your commands more fun!

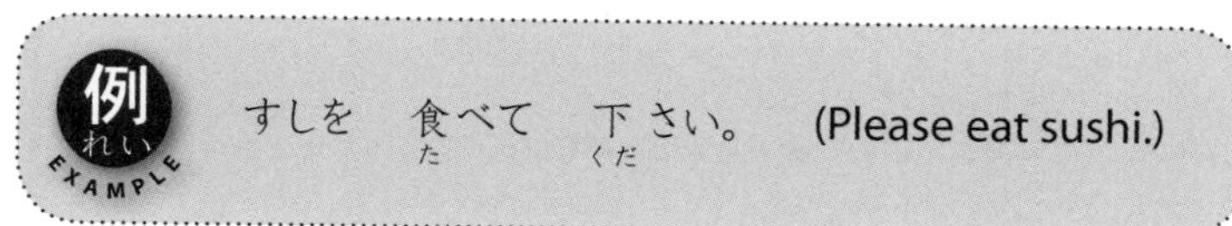

例 れい EXAMPLE
すしを　食(た)べて　下(くだ)さい。　(Please eat sushi.)

3. Group Practice

Play "Sensei Says (て-form of verb) 下さい." The "leader" calls out commands including both those you learned in Chapter 1-6 and those that use a body part plus さわって下さい from Chapter 6-1.

4. Group Practice

Play Add-on in a group with the first person saying something that someone else has. Person B must repeat the same words, but add onto it an adjective (長(なが)い , 小(ちい)さい , etc.). Person C then repeats everything but adds an adverb (すこし , まあまあ , etc.). Person D adds to the sentence by saying そして or でも , and then saying something about another attribute.

A- さん：　手(て)が　あります。
B- さん：　小(ちい)さい ＋ 手(て)が　あります。
C- さん：　とても ＋ 小(ちい)さい　手(て)が　あります。
D- さん：　とても　小(ちい)さい　手(て)が　あります。 ＋ そして、　目(め)が　あります。

■ 文化箱 Culture Chest
ぶんかばこ

松尾芭蕉
まつおばしょう

Matsuo Basho, Japan's most famous haiku poet, is forever linked with Hiraizumi. He was famous for traveling the countryside to find inspiration for his haiku poems. In one work, 奥(おく)の細道(ほそみち) "The Narrow Road to the Back Country," Basho traveled to and around northern Japan. In 1689, Basho gazed upon the abandoned fields of the former great city of Hiraizumi as he wrote:

夏草(なつくさ)や　*Ah, summer grass!*
兵(つわもの)　どもが　*All that remains*
夢(ゆめ)の跡(あと)　*Of the warriors' dreams.*

The 5-7-5 syllable pattern haiku is probably the most well known among the various types of Japanese poems. Can you make your own haiku in English and Japanese?

Here is one for inspiration with the 5-7-5 syllable pattern in both English and Japanese:

Time for Japanese　この本(ほん)を
If you study hard each day　毎日(まいにち)読(よ)んで
You will learn a lot!　よく学(まな)ぶ

■ キアラ(きあら)のジャーナル(じゃーなる)　Kiara's Journal 

Read the journal entry below, and then answer these questions.

❶ What does Kiara say about Benkei's hair?
❷ What has been happening between Yoshitsune and his older brother?
❸ Where did Kiara see Benkei and Yoshitsune?

ジャーナル(じゃーなる)へ

昨日、弁慶(べんけい)さんに 会(あ)いました。そして、晩(ばん)ご飯(はん)を いっしょに (together) 食べました。弁慶(べんけい)さんは 目が ちょっと 大きい です。それから、髪(かみ)の 毛(け)が とても 長(なが)いです。ちょっと 太(ふと)っています。とても 強い です。そして、弁慶さんは とても いい人です。

でも、ここは ちょっと こわい です。ベン君(べんくん)は、「源 義経(みなもとのよしつね)と 彼の お兄さんは 前から けんか していました (have been fighting).」と、言いました。

今朝(けさ)、私達は お寺(てら)で、弁慶さんと 義経(よしつね)さんを 見ました。二人は、大きい 桜(さくら)の 木の下 (under) に いました。義経(よしつね)さんには、ひげが ありました。とても かっこいい scenery でした。そして、私は それを 見(み)て びっくり しました (was very surprised).「皆さん、これを 見てください！」と言って、私は 友さんと、じゅん君と、ベン君に、スケッチブックを 見せました。皆、「あっ！」と、びっくり しました。私は「去年(きょねん)、アメリカの 学校の 図書館(としょかん)で この絵(え)を 描(か)きました。」と、言いました。友さんが、「義経(よしつね)さんと 弁慶さんの 浮世絵(うきよえ) (woodblock print) ですね。」と、言いました。「はい、色鉛筆(いろえんぴつ) (colored pencils) で 描(か)きました。」と、私は 言いました。

It was really interesting to see in real life what I had seen in an art book from my library last year!

Just like in the picture, 義経(よしつね)さんは ハンサムです。彼(かれ)は、渋(しぶ)いです。弁慶さんは、目がとても いいです。それに、背(せ)が 高(たか)い です。そして、二人(ふたり)は、とても かっこいいです。

第6課の3

お茶を　飲んでも　いい　ですか。

May I drink some green tea?

1.

1) キアラさん、大丈夫 ですか。

2) ちょっと、頭が 痛いです。

3) 少し 熱が ありますね。

2.

4) 風邪 ですね。無理を しては いけません。この お茶を　飲んで 下さい。体に いい ですよ。

3.

5) ありがとう。ちょっと 布団で 昼寝しても いい ですか。

4.

6) 僕も、その お茶を 飲んでも いいですか。それと、僕も、昼寝してもいい ですか。

7) 友さんも、風邪 ですか。

5.

8) いいえ。すみません、美味しい 飲み物と 昼寝が とても 好き ですから・・・・。

9) 友さん、キアラさんは、病気 ですよ！

■ 会話(かいわ) Dialogue 

REMINDER: You may see some kanji / vocabulary you do not recognize. Use the context to try to understand the meanings of those parts of the dialogue.

1. じゅん ： キアラ(きあら)さん、大丈夫(だいじょうぶ) ですか。
2. キアラ(きあら) ： ちょっと、頭(あたま)が 痛(いた)い です。
3. 弁慶(べんけい) ： 少(すこ)し 熱(ねつ)が ありますね。
4. ベン(べん) ： 風邪(かぜ) ですね。無理(むり)を しては いけません。この お茶(ちゃ)を 飲んで 下さい。 体(からだ)に いい ですよ。
5. キアラ(きあら) ： ありがとう。ちょっと 布団(ふとん)で 昼寝(ひるね)しても いい ですか。
6. 友 ： 僕(ぼく)も、そのお茶(ちゃ)を 飲んでも いい ですか。それと、僕(ぼく)も、昼寝(ひるね) しても いい ですか。
7. 弁慶(べんけい) ： 友さんも、風邪(かぜ) ですか。
8. 友 ： いいえ。すみません、美味(おい)しい 飲み物と 昼寝(ひるね)が とても *好(す)きです から....。
9. ベン(べん) ： 友さん、キアラ(きあら)さんは、病気(びょうき)ですよ！

* 好(す)き – to like

■ 単語(たんご) New Words 

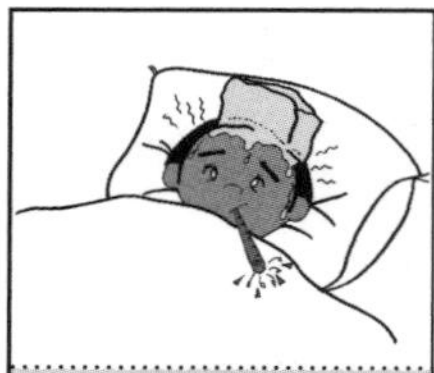 熱(ねつ) (n)	 風邪(かぜ) (n)	 ジュース(じゅーす) (n)	 布団(ふとん) (n)	 昼寝(ひるね) (n)	 医者(いしゃ) (n)
病気(びょうき) (n) – illness, sickness	病院(びょういん) (n)	薬(くすり) (n)	無理(むり) (な adj.)	大丈夫(だいじょうぶ) (な adj.)	痛(いた)い (い adj.)
心配(しんぱい)(を)する / します (v)	けが(を)する / します (v)	無理(むり)しないで 下さい (exp.)	昼寝(ひるね)(を) する / します (v) – to take a nap * 薬(くすり)(を)飲(の)む / 飲(の)みます (v) – to take medicine *Note: when medicine is consumed, the verb for "to drink" is used. 具合(ぐあい)が悪(わる)い (exp.) – sick, feel bad 風邪(かぜ)(を) 引(ひ)く / 引(ひ)きます (v) – to catch a cold		

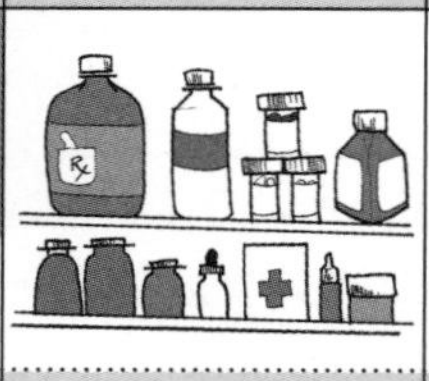

Other useful health related expressions you might like to know:

救急車(きゅうきゅうしゃ)(を) 呼(よ)んで下さい。 (*exp.*) – Please call an ambulance.
看護婦(かんごふ) (*n*) – nurse　　健康(けんこう) (*n*) – health
健康(けんこう)に いい です (*exp.*) – It is good for your health.

■ 漢字(かんじ) Kanji

Kanji	Readings / Words	Stroke order
医 7 strokes	イ(い) – related to medicine or the medical field	一 丆 … 医
	医(い)(者(しゃ)) – doctor; 医(い)(学(がく)) – study of medicine	
	矢(や) is an arrow and this one is enclosed on three sides in a shelter. If this arrow were to puncture the outer surface, a lot of MEDICINE would surely be needed!	
者 8 strokes	シャ(しゃ); もの – person	一 十 土 耂 … 者 者
	(医(い))者(しゃ) – doctor; (学(がく))者(しゃ) – scholar	者
	The top of this kanji is soil (土) or earth, while the bottom is sun (日). A PERSON has started tying these two together with one large stitch of the needle and thread.	
薬 16 strokes	くすり – medicine	一 …
	薬(くすり) – medicine; 薬(くすり)(屋(や)) – drugstore, apothecary	… 薬 薬
	A leafy plant (the first three strokes, 艹 , appear in kanji related to plants) is growing up a tree (木), but it is sickly and white (白), with drops of sap shooting out all over (the 4 strokes to the side of white). It seems in need of some tender loving care and some MEDICINE.	

■ 言葉(ことば)の探索(たんさく) Language Detection

1.　・・・てもいい　です。 You may . . .

You learned several phrases using this pattern in the Classroom Expressions section of Chapter 1. Here, you will learn how to create more phrases that grant permission. This pattern uses a verb in the て-form followed by もいい です. To ask permission, add a か to the end.

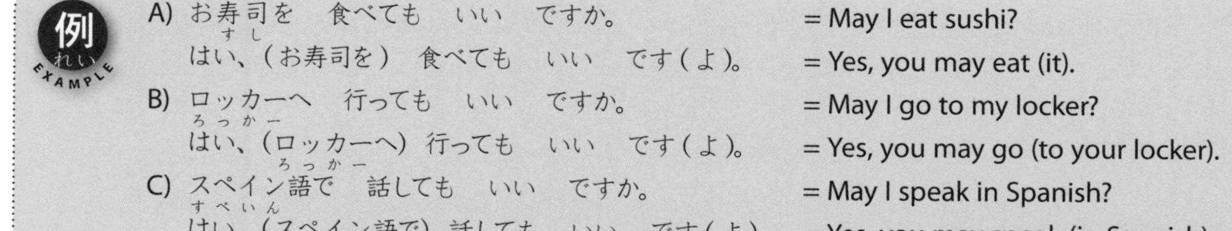
例(れい) EXAMPLE

A) お寿司(すし)を　食べても　いい　ですか。 = May I eat sushi?
はい、(お寿司を)　食べても　いい　です(よ)。 = Yes, you may eat (it).
B) ロッカー(ろっかー)へ　行っても　いい　ですか。 = May I go to my locker?
はい、(ロッカー(ろっかー)へ)　行っても　いい　です(よ)。 = Yes, you may go (to your locker).
C) スペイン(すぺいん)語で　話しても　いい　ですか。 = May I speak in Spanish?
はい、(スペイン(すぺいん)語で)　話しても　いい　です(よ)。 = Yes, you may speak (in Spanish).

NOTE that putting よ at the end of a sentence in which you are giving someone permission can sometimes be perceived as being slightly condescending if used toward equals. It should never be used when speaking to people older than you or of higher status.

2. ・・・ては　だめです／いけません

To deny someone permission to do something, use the て-form of a verb followed by は いけません (the は here is the particle は, using the "wa" sound).

この　まどを　開(あ)けても　いい　ですか。 = May I open this window?
いいえ、(まどを)　開(あ)けては　いけません。 = No, you may not open it.

その　薬(くすり)を　飲んでも　いい　ですか。 = May I take that medicine?
いいえ、この　薬(くすり)を　飲んでは　いけません。 = No, you may not take this medicine.

けん君(くん)の　家(うち)へ　行っても　いいですか。 = May I go to Ken's house?
いいえ、　行っては　いけません。 = No, you may not.

A more casual way to deny permission is to use だめ in place of いけません。

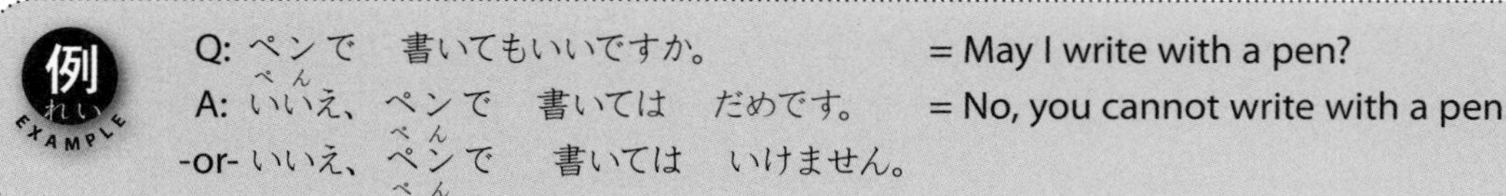

例 れい EXAMPLE
Q: ペン(ぺん)で　書いてもいいですか。 = May I write with a pen?
A: いいえ、ペン(ぺん)で　書いては　だめです。 = No, you cannot write with a pen.
-or- いいえ、ペン(ぺん)で　書いては　いけません。

3. Review of で meaning "by means of" or "using such and such"

The particle で can mean "by means of" or "using such and such" as you learned in Chapter 3 section 4.

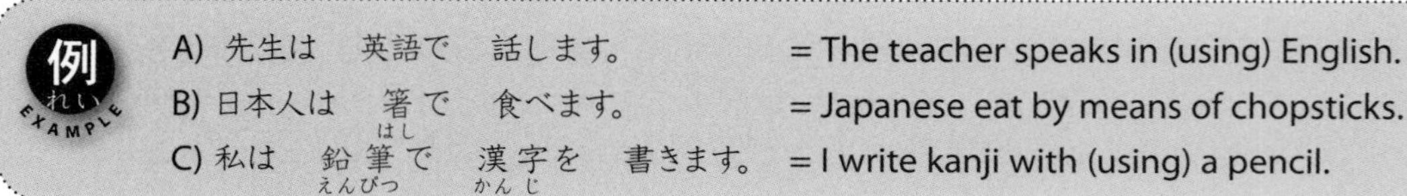

例 れい EXAMPLE
A) 先生は　英語で　話します。 = The teacher speaks in (using) English.
B) 日本人は　箸(はし)で　食べます。 = Japanese eat by means of chopsticks.
C) 私は　鉛筆(えんぴつ)で　漢字(かんじ)を　書きます。 = I write kanji with (using) a pencil.

As introduced in Chapter 4 section 3, the particle で can also indicate the place of action (for example, 学校で 昼(ひる)ご飯(はん) を食べました。= At school I ate lunch).

■ 自習(じしゅう) Self Check

1. Use the ～ても いい ですか pattern to ask permission to do the following.
   A) May I stand up? 立(た)って________________ですか。
   B) May I sit down? ______________も　いい　ですか。
   C) May I write?
   D) May I read the book?

2. Use the ～てもいい です pattern to give permission to do the following:
   A) You may look.
   B) You may eat.
   C) You may return home.
   D) You may go to the cafeteria.
   E) On Saturday, you may go to Tokyo.
   F) In March you may go to your grandmother's house.
   G) On Tuesday you may eat pizza.

3. Use Japanese to tell someone they may not do the following:

A) You may not drink. 飲(の)んで ______いけません。

B) You may not go. 行(い)って ____________。

C) You may not go to the restroom.

D) You may not go to your locker.

E) You may not eat.

4. Use the particle で after the word (tool), which is the "means" by which something is done. Say the following in Japanese:

A) May I write with a pen? ____________ 書(か)いても いい ですか。

B) You may eat sushi with chopsticks.

C) You may not speak in English.

■ 練習(れんしゅう)の時間(じかん) Time for Practice

1. Pair Practice

Politely request each of the following. Your partner can grant or deny your request as he/she sees fit. Take turns.

You want to write in hiragana.

You : ひらがなで 書いてもいいですか。

Your partner: いいえ、ひらがなで 書いてはいけません。

-OR- はい、ひらがなで 書いてもいいです。

A) You are thirsty.

B) You want to eat cake.

C) You want to sit down.

D) You want to take a nap.

E) You want to go to the library.

F) You want to return home at 11 P.M.

G) You want to play tennis today.

H) You want to eat dinner at 9:30 P.M.

2. Pair Practice

Use the cues below to create questions using the particle で. Your partner should answer according to his/her own circumstances. Take turns.

(Do you) come to school by bus?

You : バス(ばす)で 学校へ 来ますか。

Your partner : いいえ、私は、バスで 学校へ 来ません。

-OR- はい、私は、毎日 バス(ばす)で 学校へ 来ます。

A) eat spaghetti with chopsticks

B) do homework with a pencil

C) go to the bookstore by taxi (タクシー(たくしー))

D) go to France by boat (ふね)

E) play tennis using a racquet (ラケット(らけっと))

F) type (タイプ(たいぷ)を します) a letter (手紙(てがみ)) on a computer (コンピューター(こんぴゅーたー))

3. Charades

Take a slip of paper from your teacher. Your job is to silently act out the illness or physical problem. Your classmates will try to guess what your problem is.

Class: どう しましたか。 = What happened?

熱(ねつ)が ありますか。 = Do you have a fever?

■ 文化箱 Culture Chest

Chinese and Japanese Medicine

Did you know that Japanese men and women often live to be among the oldest people in the world? Credit for this longevity goes partly to Japan's modern medical care and national health insurance system, but no doubt in large measure to the extremely healthy traditional Japanese diet.

If you get sick while in Japan, you are likely to be taken to a hospital since Japanese tend to use hospitals, clinics, and doctor's offices more often than in some other cultures. As modern as Japan's medical system is, traditional Chinese herbs, remedies, and medical practices are also widely available in Japan and have been used to some extent since the Nara Period in the 700s.

The 20th century saw a tremendous increase in the import of Western foods and drinks into Japan. While the traditional Japanese diet is heavily based upon fish products and rice, the influx of sugars and meats is affecting the height and weight of many Japanese. It will be interesting to see what impact Western foods and drinks such as cheeseburgers and colas will have on the health and lifespan of Japanese people in the future.

■ キアラのジャーナル Kiara's Journal 

Read the journal entry below, and then answer these questions.

❶ What was the weather like in Hiraizumi at the time that Kiara and her friends were there?
❷ What did Benkei loan Kiara?
❸ How was Kiara feeling?
❹ What changed how Kiara was feeling?

ジャーナルへ

今、平泉は ちょっと 寒い です。弁慶さんは、いい ジャケット (jacket) を 着ていました。私は 弁慶さんに、「ジャケットを 借りても いい ですか。」と、言いました。He didn't really understand the word "jacket," but through my gestures, he caught on.

弁慶さんは、「いい ですよ。」と、言いました。彼は、やさしい人です。

私は ちょっと 風邪を 引きました。ここには、ティッシュは、ありません。お医者さんも いません。薬も ありません。弁慶さんは 私の 事を 心配しました。(The rest were a little worried too.) そして、「キアラさん、大丈夫 ですか。少し 熱が ありますね。」と、言いました。

私は、「はい、少し あります。でも、大丈夫 です。もう ちょっと 寝ます。」と、言いました。

ベン君は、「キアラさん、この お茶を 飲んで下さい。体に いいですよ。」と、言いました。私は、「いただきます。どうも ありがとう。」と、言いました。その後、六時間ぐらい 昼寝 しました。そして、元気に なりました。

第6課の4 私達は　洋服(ようふく)を　着(き)ています。

We are wearing Western clothing.

1.

1) あなた達の服は とてもかっこいいですね。

2) これは学校の制服です。

3) ２１世紀の学校の 服 です。

2.

4) 着物ではありませんね。

5) そう ですね。私達は 洋服を着ています。

6) 見て下さい。私達は、シャツとジャケットを 着ています。 そして、ズボンを はいています。靴下と 靴も、はいて います。

3.

4.

7) 私は、スカートをはいています。

8) それは 侍の 服 ですね。あなたは 侍 ですか。私も その スカートをはいても いい ですか。

5.

9) いいえ、私は 侍ではありません。このスカートは女の子の制服です。

10) ２１世紀はへんですね。

■ 会話 Dialogue

REMINDER: You may see some kanji / vocabulary you do not recognize. Use the context to try to understand the meanings of those parts of the dialogue.

1. 弁慶　：あなた達の　服は　とても　かっこいい　ですね。
2. じゅん：これは　学校の　制服　です。
3. ベン　：*21世紀の　学校の　服　です。
4. 弁慶　：着物では　ありませんね。
5. じゅん：そう　ですね。私達は　洋服を　着ています。
6. ベン　：見て下さい。私達は、シャツと　ジャケットを　着ています。
そして、ズボンを　はいています。靴下と　靴も、はいています。
7. キアラ：私は、スカートを　はいています。
8. 弁慶　：それは　侍の　服　ですね。あなたは　侍　ですか。
私も、その　スカート　を　はいても　いい　ですか。
9. キアラ：いいえ、私は　侍では　ありません。そして、これは、侍の　服では
ありません。この　スカートは　女の子の　制服　です。
10. 弁慶　：21世紀は　へん　ですね。

* 21世紀 – 21st century

■ 単語 New Words

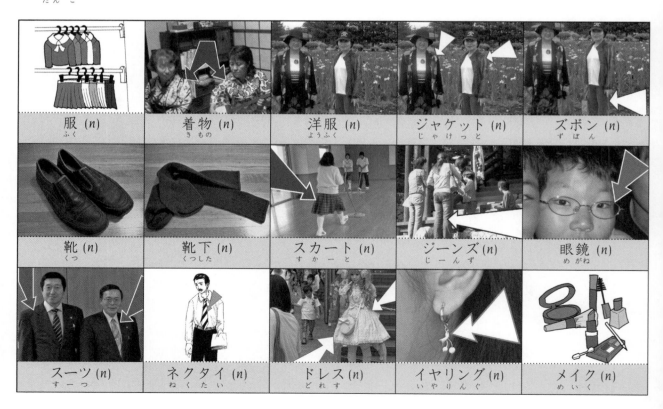

服（ふく）(n)	 着物（きもの）(n)	 洋服（ようふく）(n)	 ジャケット（じゃけっと）(n)	 ズボン（ずぼん）(n)
靴（くつ）(n)	 靴下（くつした）(n)	 スカート（すかーと）(n)	 ジーンズ（じーんず）(n)	 眼鏡（めがね）(n)
 スーツ（すーつ）(n)	 ネクタイ（ねくたい）(n)	 ドレス（どれす）(n)	 イヤリング（いやりんぐ）(n)	 メイク（めいく）(n)

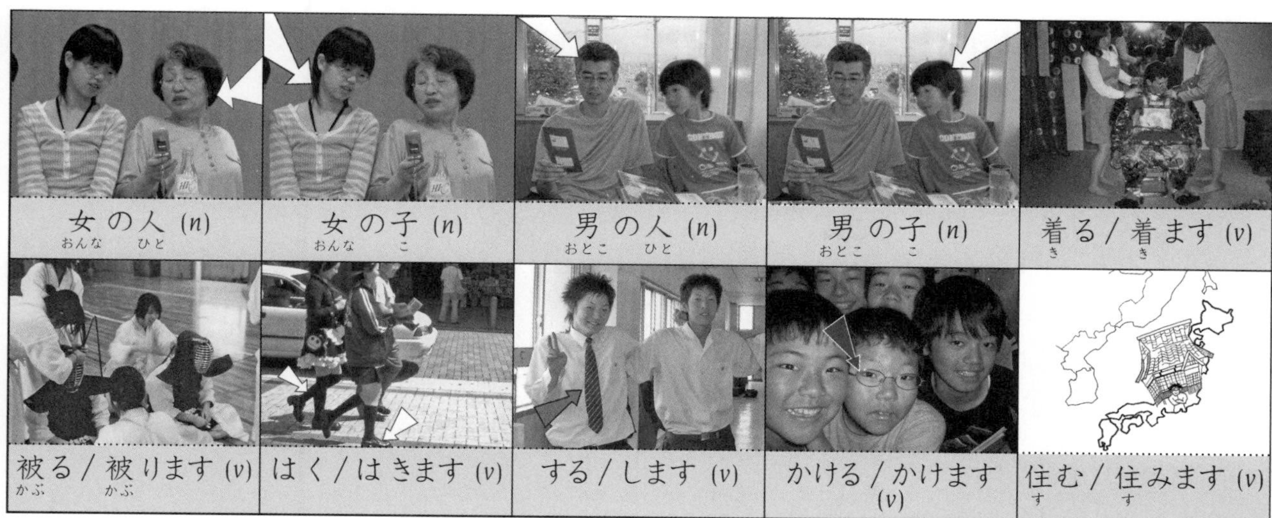

(お) 餅（もち） (*n*) – pounded rice cake

シャツ (*n*) – shirt

下着（したぎ） (*n*) – underwear

パンツ (*n*) – underwear

シンプル (な *adj.*) – simple

普通（ふつう） (な *adj./adv*) – usual, normal

すてき (な *adj.*) – wonderful, nice

人（ひと） (*n*) – person

ハンサム (な *adj.*) – handsome

* する or します means "to wear" (as in jewelry) and "to do." It can be used alone or in conjunction with some nouns to form a variety of verbs. Some examples of this usage include:

タイプ(を) する / します – to type	ハイキング(を) する / します – to hike
バスケを する / します – to play basketball	空手（からて）(を) する / します – to do karate

Colors

1. 白（しろ）い (い *adj.*) – white (-colored)
2. 黒（くろ）い (い *adj.*) – black (-colored)
3. 赤（あか）い (い *adj.*) – red (-colored)
4. 青（あお）い (い *adj.*) – blue (-colored)
5. 黄色（きいろ）い(い *adj.*) – yellow (-colored)
6. 紫（むらさき） (*n*) – purple (-colored)
7. 緑（みどり） (*n*) – green (-colored)
8. オレンジ(*n*) – orange (-colored)
9. ピンク (*n*) – pink (-colored)
10. グレイ (*n*) – gray (-colored)
11. はい色（いろ） (*n*) – gray (-colored)

■ 漢字（かんじ） Kanji

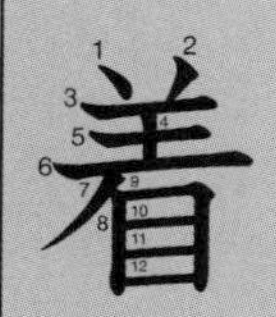 12 strokes	き (る) – to wear	丶	丷	䒑	𦍌	𦍌	𦍋	𦍋
	着（き） (る) – to wear (above the waist); 着（き） (物（もの）) – traditional Japanese dress	着	着	着	着	着		
	The top section of this kanji looks like 羊（ひつじ） or "sheep." And the bottom half is 目 or "eye." What sort of outfit could you WEAR to catch the sheep's eye? Another way that you might remember it is that the eye that you see is WEARing a really nice wool sweater.							

■ 言葉の探索 Language Detection

1. The present progressive tense: て-form + います。

To say that someone is in the process of doing something, use the て-form of a verb plus います。

A) キアラさんは　せんべいを　食べて　います。 = Kiara is eating senbei.
B) 山口先生は　平泉に　住んで　います。 = Mr. Yamaguchi lives in Hiraizumi.
C) 花子さんは　ながいスカーフを　して　います。 = Hanako is wearing a long scarf.

2. Verbs for "to wear"

Japanese uses many verbs for the English word "wear." To say someone is wearing an article of clothing or an accessory, use the correct verb in the ています form.

A) 着て　います (wearing something from the waist up or something like a robe or a kimono)
B) はいて　います (wearing something below the waist, such as pants, shoes, or socks)
C) 被って　います (wearing something on the head, such as a hat or helmet)
D) して　います (wearing jewelry or other accessories such as a scarf)
E) かけて　います (wearing glasses or sunglasses)

3. The negative present progressive: て-form + いません。

To say someone is NOT in the process of doing something, use the verb in the て-form plus いません。

A) キアラさんは　靴下を　はいて　いません。 = Kiara is not wearing any socks.
B) 花子さんは　日本に　住んで　いません。 = Hanako is not living in Japan.
C) けい子さんは　メガネを　かけていません。 = Keiko is not wearing glasses.

4. The blue shirt is mine. The red hat is Mom's.

Go to the Web Activities on **www.TimeForJapanese**.com for this chapter and section to download this Bonus Sheet.

■ 自習 Self Check

1. The present progressive tense, positive and negative: て-form + います／いません

Try to say the following in Japanese:

A) I am reading a good book. 私は　いい　本を ______________。
B) I live in Nagoya.
C) The first year students are eating with chopsticks.
D) The third year high school students are not living here. 高校三年生は ______________。
E) Grandmother is not drinking green tea.

2. Verbs for wearing

Try to say the following in Japanese:

A) Tomo is wearing a hat. 友さんは　ぼうしを ______________。

B) Kenji's older sister is wearing a kimono.

C) Ben's younger brother is not wearing any pants!

■ 練習(れんしゅう)の時間(じかん) Time for Practice

1. Pair Practice

Use a photograph from a magazine with people wearing a variety of clothing and accessories and doing various activities. Person A should use the ています form to describe what the figures in the picture are wearing and doing. Person B draws a picture of what he/she hears described.

A) 森山君(もりやまくん)は　ズボン(ずぼん)を　はいて　います。 = Moriyama is wearing slacks.

B) 高橋(たかはし)先生は　帽子(ぼうし)を　被(かぶ)って　います。 = Ms. Takahashi is wearing a hat.

C) けい子(こ)さんは　ネックレス(ねっくれす)を　して　います。 = Keiko is wearing a necklace.

2. Pair Practice

With verbs of wearing using the ～ています and ～ていません ending forms, describe someone in the photo here or someone near you. Your partner should try to guess whom you are describing. Keep adding clues until your partner guesses correctly. Take turns, and alternate between the positive and negative tenses.

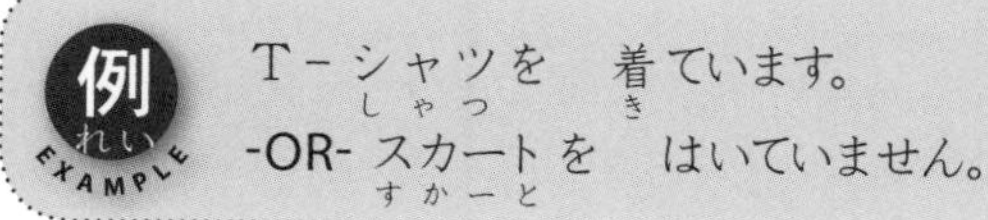

例 T－シャツ(しゃつ)を　着(き)ています。

-OR- スカート(すかーと)を　はいていません。

3. Pair Practice

Use the pictures below and the actions of the people around you to practice saying what others are doing. Use the て います pattern with verbs of action to make your statements.

A) 本を　読んでいます。

B) タコスを　食べています。

■ 文化箱 Culture Chest

岩手県 Iwate Prefecture

Hiraizumi lies in Iwate Prefecture in northern Japan. The name 岩手 comes from a legend in which a demon was driven out of the prefecture and forced to put his hand (手) print in a rock (岩) to symbolize his promise to never come back.

Iwate is the home of the beloved Japanese children's story writer Kenji Miyazawa (1896–1933), beautiful Mt. Iwate, saw-toothed coastline, and a number of good ski resorts. One of the most famous foods in Morioka, the capital of Iwate, is 煎餅, a snack that is a combination of a cracker and cookie. There are a wide variety of types and flavors of senbei and they can be found all over Japan.

Hiraizumi is famous for 餅, a type of sticky rice cake. Perhaps Hiraizumi became famous for mochi due to the name of one type of mochi sold in Hiraizumi, 弁慶の力餅. The name is a pun since "chikaramochi" usually means someone who has strength (力餅), so the name of the Hiraizumi treat can also mean "Benkei the Strongman." Mochi is extremely popular throughout Japan, especially during the New Year's holidays.

■ キアラのジャーナル Kiara's Journal

Read the journal entry below, and then answer these questions.

❶ What are traditional pants called in Japanese?

❷ What did Tomo do when he was away from the group?

❸ Who does Kiara want to give mochi to?

ジャーナルへ

弁慶さんは、侍の服を 着ています。かっこいい です。とても ハンサム です。

ベン君は、弁慶さんの 侍の服を 着たかったです。じゅん君は、「その ぼうしを かぶっても いい ですか。」と、弁慶さんに 聞きました。

弁慶さんは、「いい ですよ。この はかま (traditional pants) も 履きますか。ジャケットも着ますか。」と、言いました。

じゅん君は、「すごい！ どうも ありがとう ございます。」と言って、「ベン君、侍のぼうしを かぶりませんか。」と、ベン君に 聞きました。

ベン君は、「侍の ぼうしを かぶっても いい ですか。」と、弁慶さんに 聞きました。

弁慶さんは、「ええ、大丈夫 ですよ。かぶってみて 下さい。あれ、ところで (by the way) 友さんは どこ ですか。」と、言いました。

その時 (at that time)、友さんが 来ました。彼は、「僕は お餅を 少し 食べて来ました。ここの お餅は とても おいしいですよ！」と、言いました。

私は、「わ！ 私達に、お餅の おみやげを 持って来ましたか。昨日 その お餅を 見ました。」と、言いました。友さんは、「ア…ア… ごめんなさい。忘れました。でも、あちこちに (here & there) たくさん ありますよ。」と、言いました。

後でみんなで、お餅を 食べに 行きました。平泉の お餅は とても 美味しい です。母にも あげたいです。

第6課の5

弁慶(べんけい)さんに　会(あ)って、　たくさん 話(はな)して、　歴史(れきし)を　勉強(べんきょう)しました。

We met Benkei, talked a lot, and studied history.

1.

1) 平泉は、どう でしたか。

2) とても きれい でした。

3) 弁慶さんに 会って、たくさん 話して，歴史を 勉強して，文化も 勉強して、・・・

2.

4) 日本語もたくさん 勉強して、病気も して・・・

5) キアラさん、ここで じょうだんを言っては いけません。

6) 美味しい 食べ物を 食べて 美味しい 飲み物も 飲みました。

3.

7) キアラさん、どんな 単語を 勉強 しましたか。

4.

8) これは 目、これは 鼻、これは 口、これは 耳、これは 頭、そして、これは 手、これは 足 です。もっと 言っても いい ですか。

9) もう時間 です。みなさん、行きますよ！弁慶さん、さようなら。

5.

10) さようなら。２１世紀の、弁慶の ファンに よろしく。

11) 分かりました。では、さようなら。ありがとう。

■ 会話 Dialogue

REMINDER: You may see some kanji / vocabulary you do not recognize. Use the context to try to understand the meanings of those parts of the dialogue.

1. 弁慶　：　平泉は、どう　でしたか。
2. ベン　：　とても　きれい　でした。
3. じゅん：　弁慶さんに　会って、たくさん　話して、歴史を　勉強して、文化も　勉強して…
4. キアラ：　日本語も　たくさん　勉強して、病気もして…
5. ベン　：　キアラ さん、ここで　*じょうだんを　言っては　いけません。
6. 友　　：　おいしい　食べ物を　食べて、おいしい　飲み物も　飲みました。
7. 弁慶　：　キアラさん、どんな　単語を　勉強しましたか。
8. キアラ：　これは　目、これは　鼻、これは　口、これは　耳、これは　頭、そして、これは　手、これは　足です。もっと　言っても　いい　ですか。
9. 友　　：　もう時間　です。皆さん、行きますよ！　弁慶さん、さようなら。
10. 弁慶　：　さようなら。*２１世紀の、弁慶の　ファンに　よろしく。
11. 皆　　：　分かりました。では、さようなら。ありがとう。

* じょうだん – joke　　　* ２１世紀 – 21st century　　　* 弁慶　の　ファン – Benkei's fans

■ 単語 New Words

		経験 (*n*) – (an) experience
		素晴しい (い *adj.*) – wonderful
		. . .　に　よろしく (*exp.*) – say hello to... (for me)
文化 (*n*)	どう　でしたか。(*inter.*)	習う / 習います (*v*) – to learn

■ 言葉の探索 Language Detection

1. Multiple verbs using the て-form

To list a series of actions in one sentence, change all of the verbs to their て-form conjugations except for the last verb. The tense of the entire sentence is determined by the tense of the final verb.

A) 私は　朝ご飯を　食べて、音楽を　聞いて、学校へ　行きました。
　　= I ate breakfast, listened to music, and went to school.

B) 友は　ラーメンを　食べて、ジュースを　飲んで　寝ます。
　　= Tomo eats ramen, drinks juice, and then sleeps.

■ 自習 Self Check

1. Multiple verbs using the て-form

How would you say the following in Japanese?

A) Ben put on his shirt, ate breakfast, and then came to the high school.
B) I will eat ramen (noodles), take a nap, and then go to the library.
C) I read the book, did homework, and then went to sleep.

■ 練習の時間 Time for Practice

1. Pair Practice

Translate the following sentences into Japanese. Take turns, remembering to use the て-form to link the actions. Also remember that the tense of the sentence is determined by the final verb.

A) I woke up, ate breakfast, and came to school.
B) I will go home, eat some mochi, and study.
C) I ate lunch, went to English class, and talked with my friend.
D) I studied, did/practiced judo, and returned home.
E) I talked with my friend, ate dinner, and read a book.
F) I caught a cold, took some medicine, and took a nap.
G) I will go to baseball practice, eat dinner, and watch TV.

2. Pair Practice

Using the verbs in the verb charts in section 6-2, think of a short story with lots of action (use at least five verbs). Tell your story to your partner, who will try to illustrate it. Do not look at the drawing until it is finished! Use the past tense. Take turns, trying to use multiple verbs in each sentence by including the て-form of all but the last verb.

You might say: 私は、朝ご飯を 食べて、学校へ 行って、友だちと 話して 音楽のクラスに 行きました。勉強 して、それから、部活を しました。テストの 成績は だめ でした。

Your partner draws a picture showing you eating breakfast, going to school, talking to your friends, and going to music class. Then he/she draws you studying, participating in a club activity, and not doing very well on a test.

3. Group Practice

Take turns going to the front of the classroom and miming an action (without speaking). The class has to call out the action in Japanese, using the ています form.

■ 文化箱 Culture Chest

東北

The northern six prefectures, or provinces, of 本州 are referred to collectively as 東北. The characters for east (東) and north (北) are used in this order. (In English the reverse, "northeast," is normally used.) This is one of the more rural parts of the country. 東北 had a reputation in Japan as being a remote and distant countryside long before Basho wandered through in the 1600s looking for poetic inspiration.

Some of the extraordinary sites of 東北 include famous destinations such as 松島 (Pine Islands) near 仙台; the 雪国 skiing region in the west-central area; 田沢湖, the deepest lake in Japan; and the snow monkeys of northern 青森.

Thousands of people visit 東北 every summer for its festivals. They include the 青森ねぶた祭り every August, with its brilliantly illuminated floats and colorfully-dressed participants, the 竿燈祭り in 秋田市, with its long poles with dozens of hanging lanterns balanced by participants, and the 七夕祭り of 仙台, where streets are almost flooded with brightly colored streamers seemingly hanging from the stars.

■ キアラのジャーナル Kiara's Journal 

Read the journal entry below, and then answer these questions.

❶ Kiara's Japanese language skills are getting better. List three areas of Japanese language where she improved quite a bit while in Hiraizumi.

❷ Retell what you know about Benkei.

❸ When you travel to Tohoku, what will you want to see and do first?

ジャーナルへ

平泉は とても いい 所 です。昔、ここで 大きい war が ありました。弁慶さんの story は とても sad です。東京へ 帰って インターネット リサーチを します。ベン君は、「この story は 面白い。」と、言いました。

私は 平泉で 日本語を たくさん 勉強しました。体の parts の 名前を 習いました。手と 目と 耳などの 名前を 習いました。And now I can describe what people look like. For example, ベン君は 背が 高い ですから、バスケが 上手です。I learned how to use adverbs like 少し、ちょっと、とても. . . . And now I can talk about health, too. Things like おなかが 痛い、とか、かぜを 引きました。Good thing, too. I'm feeling a bit sick! Oh, and if we had a fashion show here on this side of the 時の門、I could be the M.C. For instance, ベン君は 今、とても ステキな 侍の ぼうしを かぶっています。

Even though my body feels a bit weak, I'm feeling good about how my language is progressing. Being able to use my language in context really helps, of course, and I have a great time with it.

■ 単語チェックリスト New Word Checklist

たんごちぇっくりすと

6-1

あし・足 *n* leg, foot
あたま・頭 *n* head
いつも *n/adv.* always
いれる・入れる／いれます・入れます *v* to put into
うで・腕 *n* arm
おなか・お腹 *n* stomach
かお・顔 *n* face
かた・肩 *n* shoulder
かなしい・悲しい い *adj.* sad
かみ（のけ）・髪（の毛） *n* hair
からだ・体 *n* body
きんにく・筋肉 *n* muscle
くち・口 *n* mouth
くび・首 *n* neck
こえ・声 *n* voice
こころ・心 *n* heart (not one's physical heart); soul
さむらい・侍 *n* samurai
しずか・静か な *adj.* quiet
せ／せい・背 *n* height, stature
たかい・高い い *adj.* high, tall, expensive
ちかい・近い い *adj.* close, near
つよい・強い い *adj.* strong
て・手 *n* hand
でる・出る／でます・出ます *v* to go out, to leave, to get out
とおい・遠い い *adj.* far, distant
ながい・長い い *adj.* long
のど・咽喉 *n* throat
はいる・入る／はいります・入ります *v* to come in, to go in, to enter
はな・鼻 *n* nose
ひくい・低い い *adj.* low, short (height)
ひげ・髭 *n* mustache, beard
ひざ・膝 *n* knee
ひみつ・秘密 *n* secret
まつ・待つ／まちます・待ちます *v* to wait
みじかい・短い い *adj.* short(length)
みみ・耳 *n* ear
め・目 *n* eye
もつ・持つ／もちます・持ちます *v* to have, to hold, to carry
ゆうめい・有名 な *adj.* famous
ゆび・指 *n* finger(s)
よわい・弱い い *adj.* weak

6-2

かっこいい い *adj.* cool (look/appearance)
しぶい・渋い い *adj.* tasteful, subtle
じょうず・上手 な *adj.* skillful
すまーと・スマート な adj. slim, stylish
どんな *inter.* what/which kind of?
ふとっています・太っています fat/plump (is)
ふとる・太る／ふとります・太ります *v* fat (to become)
まあまあ *adv.* so so, not bad, moderate
やせています slim/skinny (is)
やせる／やせます *v* thin (to become)
おしゃれ な *adj.* fashionable

6-3

いしゃ・医者 *n* doctor
いたい・痛い い *adj.* painful
かぜ・風邪 *n* cold (a)
かぜ（を）・風邪（を） ひく・引く／ひきます・引きます *v* to catch a cold
かんごふ・看護婦 *n* nurse
きゅうきゅうしゃ をよんで・救急車を呼んで *n* Call an ambulance!
ぐあいが わるい・具合が 悪い *exp.* sick, feel bad
くすり 薬 *n* medicine
くすり（を）・薬（を） のむ・飲む／のみます・飲みます *v* to take medicine
けが（を）・怪我（を） する／します *v* to injure, to hurt
けんこう・健康 *n* health
けんこうに・健康に いいです *exp.* good for your health
じゅーす・ジュース *n* juice
しんぱい（を）・心配（を） する／します *v* to worry
だいじょうぶ・大丈夫 な *adj.* all right, safe, OK
ねつ・熱 *n* fever
びょういん・病院 *n* hospital
びょうき・病気 *n* illness, sickness
ひるね・昼寝 *n* nap
ひるね（を）・昼寝（を） する／します *v* to nap
ふとん・布団 *n* futon
むり・無理 な *adj.* impossible, overdoing
むりしないで ください・無理しないで下さい *exp.* Don't overexert.

6-4

あおい・青い い *adj.* blue (-colored)
あかい・赤い い *adj.* red (-colored)
いやりんぐ・イヤリング *n* earring
おとこのこ・男の子 *n* boy
おとこのひと・男の人 *n* man, male
おれんじ・オレンジ *n* orange (-colored)
おんなのこ・女の子 *n* girl
おんなのひと・女の人 *n* woman, female
おんなのひと・女の人 *n* woman, female
かける／かけます *v* to wear (glasses or sunglasses)
かぶる・被る／かぶります・被ります *v* to wear, on the head
きいろい・黄色い い *adj.* yellow (-colored)
きもの・着物 *n* kimono (Japanese traditional clothing)

きる・着る / きます・着ます *v* to wear, above the waist or dresses
くつ・靴 *n* shoes
くつした・靴下 *n* socks
ぐれい・グレイ *n* gray (-colored)
くろい・黒い い *adj.* black (-colored)
じーんず・ジーンズ *n* jeans
したぎ・下着，ぱんつ・パンツ *n* underwear
じゃけっと・ジャケット *n* jacket
しゃつ・シャツ *n* shirt
しろい・白い い *adj.* white (-colored)
しんぷる・シンプル な *adj.* simple
すーつ・スーツ *n* suit
すかーと・スカート *n* skirt
すてき・素敵 な *adj.* wonderful, nice
ずぼん・ズボン *n* pants, trousers
すむ・住む / すみます・住みます *v* to live/reside
する / します（して）*v* to wear; to do
どれす・ドレス *n* dress (a)
ねくたい・ネクタイ *n* necktie
はいいろ・はい色 *n* gray (-colored)
はく・履く / はきます・履きます *v* to wear, below the waist
はんさむ・ハンサム な *adj.* handsome, good-looking
ひと・人 *n* person
ぴんく・ピンク *n* pink (-colored)
ふく・服 *n* clothes
ふつう・普通 *adj./adv.* usual, normal
みどり・緑 *n* green (-colored)
むらさき・紫 *n* purple (-colored)
めいく・メイク *n* makeup (facial)
めがね・眼鏡 *n* eyeglasses
（お）もち・餅 *n* sticky rice cake
ようふく・洋服 *n* clothes, Western clothes

6-5

けいけん・経験 *n* experience
すばらしい・素晴らしい い *adj.* wonderful
どう でしたか。 *exp.* How was it?
ならう・習う / ならいます・習います *v* to learn
…に よろしく *exp.* Say hello to…
ぶんか・文化 *n* culture

Hobbies in the Ancient City of Heian-kyou

第 7 課

Learning and Performance Goals

This chapter will enable you to:

A) state and talk about your hobbies and to ask others about theirs
B) combine two sentences using conjunctions
C) talk about foods, drinks, music, etc., and state your likes, dislikes, and the sorts of things you are good or bad at
D) use color words to describe things
E) learn about the Heian period (794–1185) and a little about some of the well-known literary styles from that period
F) use 14 additional kanji
G) use the "can-do" chart found on **TimeForJapanese.com** to chart your progress for what you "can-do" for each chapter

Fountain at Ryoanji Temple, Kyoto

第7課の1

僕の　趣味は　食べる事　です。

ぼく　しゅみ　た　こと

My hobby is eating.

1) 友さん、あなたの趣味は 何ですか。

2) 僕の 趣味は食べる事 です。キアラさんの趣味は、何ですか。

3) 私の 趣味は、絵を 描く事です。それから、歌を 歌う事と、柔道を する事 です。ベン君の 趣味は、何 ですか。

1.

2.

4) そう ですね。僕の 趣味は、歴史と 読書です。そして、ビデオゲームも 趣味です。

5) じゅん君、あなたの 趣味は、何 ですか。

3.

4.

6) え？ 僕の 趣味 ですか。ひみつ です。

7)じゅん君の 趣味は寝る事 ですよ。

＊#
@X（＊&＊
#@！

5.

6.

■ 会話(かいわ) Dialogue

REMINDER: You may see some kanji / vocabulary you do not recognize. Use the context to try to understand the meanings of those parts of the dialogue.

1. キアラ： 友さん、あなたの 趣味(しゅみ)は 何(なん) ですか。

2. 友　： 僕(ぼく)の 趣味(しゅみ)は 食(た)べる事(こと) です。キアラ(きあら)さんの 趣味(しゅみ)は、何(なん) ですか。

3. キアラ： 私の 趣味(しゅみ)は、*絵(え)を描(か)く事(こと) です。それから、歌(うた)を 歌(うた)う事(こと)と、柔道(じゅうどう)を する事(こと) です。ベン君(べんくん)の 趣味(しゅみ)は、何(なん) ですか。

4. ベン： そう ですね。僕(ぼく)の 趣味(しゅみ)は、歴史(れきし)と 読書(どくしょ) です。そして、ビデオゲームも 趣味(しゅみ)です。

5. キアラ： じゅん君(くん)、あなたの 趣味(しゅみ)は、何(なん) ですか。

6. じゅん： え？ 僕(ぼく)の 趣味(しゅみ) ですか。*ひみつ です。

7. 友　： じゅん君(くん)の 趣味(しゅみ)は、寝(ね)る事(こと) ですよ。

* 絵を 描く事 – drawing/painting pictures　　* ひみつ – secret

■ 単語(たんご) New Words

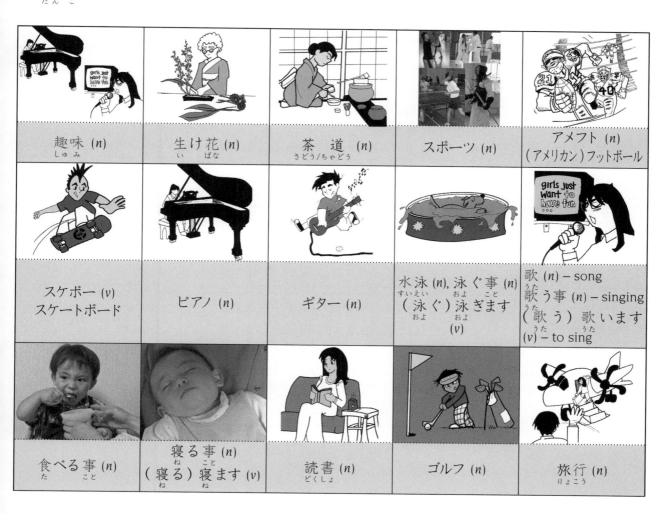

 趣味(しゅみ) (*n*)	 生け花(いけばな) (*n*)	 茶道(さどう/ちゃどう) (*n*)	 スポーツ (*n*)	 アメフト (*n*) (アメリカン)フットボール
 スケボー (*v*) スケートボード	 ピアノ (*n*)	 ギター (*n*)	 水泳(すいえい) (*n*), 泳(およ)ぐ事(こと) (*n*) (泳(およ)ぐ) 泳(およ)ぎます (*v*)	 歌(うた) (*n*) – song 歌(うた)う事 (*n*) – singing (歌(うた)う) 歌(うた)います (*v*) – to sing
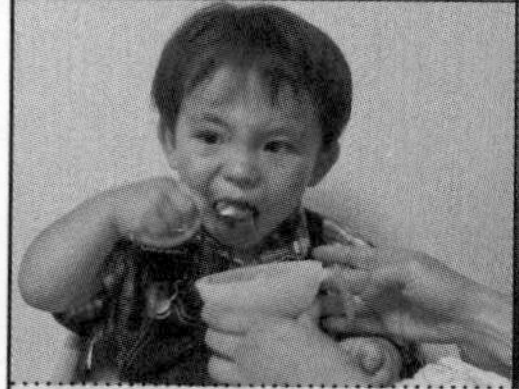 食(た)べる事(こと) (*n*)	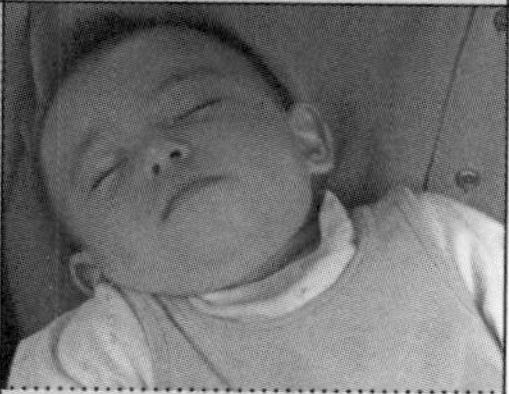 寝(ね)る事(こと) (*n*) (寝(ね)る) 寝(ね)ます (*v*)	 読書(どくしょ) (*n*)	 ゴルフ (*n*)	 旅行(りょこう) (*n*)

		それに (*conj.*) – moreover, furthermore
		それから (*conj.*) – then; and then
		そして (*conj.*) – then; and then
		事(こと) (*n*) – thing (intangible)
トランプ (*n*)	(弾(ひ)く) 弾(ひ)きます (*v*)	ジョギング (*n*) – jogging

Other vocabulary you might like to know:

乗馬(じょうば) (*n*)

踊(おど)り (*n*)

スキー (*n*)

料理(りょうり) (*n*)

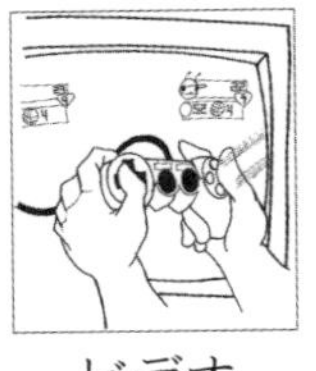
ビデオゲーム (*n*)

え (*n*) painting, drawing

買物(かいもの) (*n*) shopping

■ 漢字(かんじ) Kanji

花 (7 strokes)	はな – flower	一	十	艹	艹	䒑	芢	花
	花(はな) – flower; 花(はな)(子(こ)) – a girl's name; (生(い)け)花(ばな) – Japanese flower arranging; 花(はな)(火(び)) – fireworks							
	The first three strokes here make up a radical related to plants (艹). The final 4 strokes mean change (化). When FLOWERS bloom, plants change their appearance.							

池 (6 strokes)	チ(ち), いけ – pond	丶	冫	氵	氵	汈	池	
	池(いけ) – pond							
	The first three strokes are the water radical (氵, a simplified form of 水), and the right side of this kanji means "to be." A POND is rainwater becoming another kind of water.							

趣 (15 strokes)	シュ(しゅ) – gist, tend (to), become	一	十	土	牛	丰	走	走	走
	趣(しゅ)(味(み)) – hobby	走	走	走	赶	趄	趣	趣	
	The radical for run (走) is on the left side of this kanji. To get the GIST of someone using this kanji, you should run to it and put your ear (耳) closer, and BECOME better at things by practicing them again (又) and again (又).								

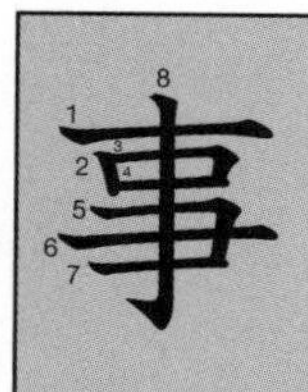

味 8 strokes	ミ；あじ – taste/flavor, to taste or appreciate	丨	ㄇ	口	口一	口二	吘	味
	味(あじ) – taste or flavor; 味(あじ)(わう) – to taste or appreciate; 趣味(しゅみ) – hobby	味						
	The mouth (口) has not yet (未) savored the TASTE or FLAVOR of the delicious food.							

事 8 strokes	ジ；こと – intangible thing	一	丅	冖	𠮛	亘	亘	亘
	事(こと) – intangible thing; (大)事(だいじ) – important	事						
	The THING about this kanji is that it starts with one (一) mouth (口) and a backwards capital E (ヨ which is also the katakana for YO) with the middle line longer than the other horizontal lines. This kanji ends with a hooked line through the middle of the entire THING.							

■ 言葉(ことば)の探索(たんさく) Language Detection

1. (私の) 趣味(しゅみ)は、読書(どくしょ) です。 **= (My) hobby is reading.**

A) 私の 趣味(しゅみ)は、音楽(おんがく) です。 = My hobby is music.
B) キアラの 趣味(しゅみ)は、柔道(じゅうどう) です。 = Kiara's hobby is judo.
C) 母の 趣味(しゅみ)は、ピアノ(びあの)です。 = My mother's hobby is the piano.
D) 友達の 趣味(しゅみ)は、読書(どくしょ)では ありません。 = My friend's hobby is not reading.

2. が **used for new information**

A second way to talk about hobbies uses the particle が. This is a common pattern in Japanese.

(私は) 読書(どくしょ)が 趣味(しゅみ) です。 = Reading is my hobby.

The topic of this sentence is 私, followed by は. The actual "hobby" is followed by the "new information marker" が. In this pattern, the word for *hobby*, 趣味(しゅみ), is not followed by a particle.

A) 私は 音楽が 趣味(しゅみ) です。 = As for me, music is a hobby.
B) キアラさんは 柔道が 趣味(しゅみ) です。 = As for Kiara, judo is a hobby.
C) 母は ピアノ(びあの)が 趣味(しゅみ) です。 = As for my mother, piano is a hobby.
D) 友達は 読書(どくしょ)が 趣味(しゅみ)です。 = As for my friend, reading is a hobby.

3. The dictionary form, sometimes called the "plain" form of verbs, is very useful for talking about hobbies.

書く事(こと)が 趣味(しゅみ) です。 = Writing is my hobby.

Since the beginning of this book, you've seen references to the dictionary form of the verb. You may have not really understood what that meant, but basically the "dictionary form" is exactly what it sounds like: it is the form used to look up a verb in the dictionary. Here is where you will start learning other uses for the dictionary form. To say that your hobby is writing, eating, sleeping, etc., add 事 to the end of the dictionary form of the verb. This changes the verb into a gerund, a type of noun. To check and review the dictionary forms of verbs you have learned, refer to Appendix 1. Some examples are:

書く事 (writing), 話す事 (conversing), 食べる事 (eating), 寝る事 (sleeping). Can you think of more?

This form can be used to say things like:

書く事が　上手　です。	= I/he/she am/is good at writing.
話す事が　下手　です。	= I/he/she am/is bad at talking.
日本語を　勉強する事が　趣味　です。	= Studying Japanese is my/his/her hobby.
姉の　趣味は　ゴルフを　する事　です。	= My older sister's hobby is golf.
歌う事は　母の　趣味　です。	= Singing is my mother's hobby.

物 is also translated as "thing" or "object." But it is only used for tangible things. 事 can be translated as an intangible "thing." The particle の can be substituted for 事.

4.　それから = after that, and そして = and/and then

Both それから and そして are transitional words. They can be used as conjunctions to tie the content of two sentences together. Using transitional words helps make your language clearer and more interesting.

A) 私は　朝ご飯を　食べました。それから、学校へ　行きました。
= I ate breakfast. After that, I went to school.

B) うちへ　帰りました。それから、スナックを　食べました。
= I returned home. Then, I ate a snack.

C) 本を　読みました。そして、テレビを　見ました。
= I read a book. And then I watched TV.

D) サラさんの　趣味は　テニスです。そして、お姉さんの　趣味も　テニスです。
= Sara's hobby is tennis. And her older sister's hobby is also tennis.

■ 自習 Self Check

1.　私の趣味は＿＿＿＿＿です。

Use this pattern to say the following out loud to yourself in Japanese.

A) My hobby is skateboarding.
B) ＿＿＿＿＿＿＿＿＿'s hobby is volleyball.
C) Jun's mother's hobbies are tea ceremony and karate.
D) Tom's little sister's hobby is reading.
E) The math teacher's hobby is golf.
F) (make your own sentence)

2.　Dictionary form + 事

Using the dictionary form of a verb as a gerund (a form of a noun) try to say the following out loud to yourself in Japanese.

A) My hobby is singing.

B) Ben's friend's hobby is swimming.

C) Tomo's hobbies are eating and sleeping.

D) Playing guitar is Sara's hobby.

E) My grandfather's hobby is jogging.

F) (make your own sentence)

3. それから and そして

Combine these sentences using first それから and then again using そして and say them out loud to yourself in Japanese.

A) I came to school. I studied English.

B) I ate sushi. I drank tea.

C) (Make another sentence combination of your own choosing.)

■ 練習(れんしゅう)の時間(じかん) Time for Practice

1. Group Practice

Make a two-column chart on a piece of scrap paper, with the headings 名前(なまえ) on the left and 趣味(しゅみ) on the right. Interview at least six classmates in Japanese about their hobbies. Follow the sample dialogue provided here. Review your findings and be prepared to report them in Japanese to the class.

A-さん： お名前(なまえ)は　何ですか。
B-さん： 私は　Alicia です。
A-さん： Alicia さんの　趣味(しゅみ)は　何ですか。
B-さん： 私の　趣味(しゅみ)は　ギターです。それから、読書です。

2. Pair Practice

Use Japanese to interview your partner about his/her family members' hobbies. Follow the sample dialogue here. Write down the answers (in English) on a piece of scrap paper. Be prepared to report your results to the class.

A-さん：ご家族(かぞく)は　何人(なんにん)　ですか。
B-さん：僕(ぼく)と　父と　母と　兄(あに)の　四人(よにん)です。
A-さん：お父さんの　趣味(しゅみ)は　何　ですか。
B-さん：父の　趣味(しゅみ)は　ゴルフ　です。

3. Pair Practice

Starting with the time you woke up yesterday, and alternatively using それから and そして at the beginning of sentences, tell your partner at least eight things you did yesterday. After you have finished, join another set of partners and tell them what your partner did yesterday.

■ 文化箱(ぶんかばこ) Culture Chest

Heian Period (794–1185)

In 794, at the beginning of the Heian period, Emperor Kanmu moved the capital of Japan to the site of modern-day Kyoto. The stability this move lent to Japanese society led to a flourishing of Japanese culture, including the Buddhist religion, literature, and the arts. The invention of hiragana and katakana allowed for the writing of literature in Japanese for the first time. Hiragana and katakana were largely considered writing systems for the less educated, so, while the more educated male elite still wrote in classical Chinese, early pioneers of truly "Japanese" literature were court women who had not been trained in Chinese literary techniques.

Activities enjoyed by the aristocracy during the Heian Period included writing poetry, relaxing while enjoying views of the moon or cherry blossoms, and participating in Buddhist practices and rituals. This cultural period is revered in Japan as a high point in Japanese history by many; however, it is also considered a time when the influence of China dominated Japanese society. To some, a more truly Japanese culture developed later.

■ キアラのジャーナル Kiara's Journal 

Read the journal entry below, and then answer these questions.

❶ **Where does Tomo want to go and why is he anxious about going there?**
❷ **Where did they exit the gate?**
❸ **What do you think is meant by "紫式部さんの時代"?**
❹ **What was 紫式部's hobby?**
❺ **Tomo said to Ben and Jun,「けんかしないで下さい。」Given the context, what do you think that means?**

ジャーナルへ

弁慶さんは いい人 でした。彼の 体が とても 大きかったので、being around him I felt とても 安全。However, this morning we overheard an old man talking about hearing rumors that a group of soldiers loyal to 頼朝 were planning something bad. 友さんは、「早く 時の門へ 行きましょう！ 危ない です。」と、言いました。私達は、いそいで 静かに 時の門に 行きました。

The next thing we know, 時の門から 大きな お寺の 前に 出ました。ベン君は、「ここは どこ ですか！ わあ！ あれは 清水寺 ですか。すばらしい ですね。」と、言いました。

じゅん君は、「あれが 清水寺なら、ここは 京都ですね。」と、言いました。

友さんは、「そう ですね。でも、今の 時代、ここは 京都と いいません。ここは 今、平安京、と、言います。多分 1010 C.E. ぐらい です。」と、言いました。

私は、「うそ でしょう！じゃあ、ここは、今、 紫式部の 時代ですか。彼女の (her) 趣味は 本を 書く事でした。とても すてきな 女の人 です。」と、言いました。

じゅん君は、「そうですね。彼女の 本の 名前は 何でしたか。」と、聞きました。

ベン君 was surprised and,「本当に 知りませんか！とても 有名 ですよ！」と、言いました。

じゅん君は、「うるさいな。友さん、教えて下さい。」と、言いました。

友さんは、「ベン君、じゅん君、だめ ですよ。けんかしないで 下さい。 紫式部さんの 本

の 名前は『源氏物語』ですよ。とても 有名な 本 です。」と、言いました。そして、「紫式部さんと 会いましょうか。紫さんは 僕の 友達 ですよ。」と、言いました！

私は、「ええーっ！?」と、大きい声で いいました。でも、友さんは already walking past the great temple 清水寺、そして、「今日は 水曜日 ですね。紫さんは いつも 水曜日に 和歌を 習っています (is learning)。紫さんの 趣味は 本を 書く事と 和歌を 詠むことです。」と、言いました。

This was the second time that I had heard the word 趣味. I felt like I understood what it meant, so I tried to use it in a sentence to see if it worked the way I thought it would. 私は、「友さん、あなたの 趣味は何 ですか。」と 聞きました。

友さんは、「僕の 趣味は 食べる事 です。キアラさんの 趣味は 何ですか。」と、言いました。

「私の 趣味は 絵を 描く事と 歌を 歌う事と 生け花と 柔道です。ベン君の 趣味は 何 ですか。」と、私は、次に (next)、ベン君に、聞きました。

ベン君は、「そう ですねえ。僕の 趣味は 歴史と 読書 です。」と、言いました。

第7課の2

キアラさんは、日本が 大好き ですね。
だいす

Kiara, you really love Japan, don't you?

1) 私は、この『時の門』の旅行が、大好きです。

2) 学校は好きですか。

3) はい、日本の学校も大好きです。友達も、家族も、食べ物も大好き です。

4) キアラさんは、日本が 大好きですね。

5)はい。それに、アメリカも 大好きですよ。

6)キアラさんはどんな 物が 嫌いですか。

7) そう です ねえ・・・・。蛙が 嫌いですね。

8)え？かえるですか？

9) ごめん、ごめん。冗談 ですよ。私は、冗談が、大好き です。

10) 面白くないです！ もう、帰る！

11) はい、これが蛙。

■ 会話(かいわ) Dialogue

REMINDER: You may see some kanji / vocabulary you do not recognize. Use the context to try to understand the meanings of those parts of the dialogue.

1. キアラ：　私は、この　『時の門』の　旅行(りょこう)が、大好(だいす)き　です。
2. じゅん：　学校は、好(す)き　ですか。
3. キアラ：　はい、日本の　学校も　大好(だいす)き　です。
   友達も、家族(かぞく)も、食べ物も　大好(だいす)き　です。
4. ベン　：　キアラさんは、日本が　大好(だいす)き　ですね。
5. キアラ：　はい。それに、アメリカも　大好(だいす)き　ですよ。
6. 友　　：　キアラさんは、どんな物が、嫌(きら)い　ですか。
7. キアラ：　そう　ですねえ…。　蛙(かえる)が　嫌(きら)い　ですね。
8. 友　　：　え？　蛙(かえる)ですか？
9. 友　　：　ごめん、ごめん。冗談(じょうだん)　ですよ。私は、冗談(じょうだん)が、大好(だいす)き　です。
10. キアラ：　*面白(おもしろ)くない　です！もう、帰る！
11. 友　　：　はい、これが　蛙(かえる)。

*面白(おもしろ)くない – not fun or amusing

■ 単語(たんご) New Words

たいてい (*adv.*) – usually

動物(どうぶつ) (*n*) – animal

■ 漢字 Kanji

好 (6 strokes)								
す（き）– like	く	女	女	女	好	好	
好（き）– to like							
This character combines woman 女 and child 子 to make something that everyone LIKES—a mother hugging a child.							

■ 言葉の探索 Language Detection

1. 好き、大好き、嫌い、大嫌い - like, love, dislike, dislike a lot

Whatever or whomever is liked or disliked is almost always followed by the particle が. Note: All of these words are な adjectives. (You will learn more about な adjectives in Chapter 8.)

私は ________ が 好き です。 = I like . . .
大好き です。 = I love (really like) . . .
嫌い です。 = I dislike . . .
大嫌い です。 = I hate (really dislike). . .

Contrast can be shown by using は instead of が.

天ぷらが 好き です。 = I like tempura.
天ぷらが 好き です。 でも お寿司は 嫌いです。
= I like tempura. But I don't like sushi.

Both statements above mean "I like tempura." However, in the example using は, the emphasis is slightly different. This statement could be restated as "I like tempura. But as for sushi, I dislike it."

(for affirmative statements:)

A) 私は ダンスをする事が 好き です。 = I like dancing.
B) 弟は 食べる事が 好き です。 = My little brother likes to eat.
C) 友達は 旅行が きらい です。 = My friend dislikes travelling.

To say "I don't like something", change the ending from です to では ありません or じゃ ありません.

A) 私は お寿司が 好きでは ありません。 = I don't like sushi.
B) 犬は 豆腐が 好きでは ありません。 = Dogs don't like tofu.
C) 友さんは 歌う事が 好きじゃ ありません。 = Tomo does not like to sing.

2. どんな (what kind of / what sort of) + noun

The question word どんな means "what kind" or "what sort" and precedes the noun in question.

*Note: When you ask a preference or for new, specific information which you do not know, the particle following that subject is が.

例(れい) EXAMPLE

Q: どんな　動物(どうぶつ)が　好き　ですか。 = What sort of animals do you like?
A: 犬(いぬ)と　猫(ねこ)が　大好き　です。 = I love dogs and cats.
Q: どんな　科目(かもく)が　好き　ですか。 = What sort of subjects do you like?
A: そう　ですね。科学(かがく)が　好き　です。それから、数学(すうがく)も　好き　です。
= Let me see. I like science. And I also like math.
Q: お母さんは　どんな　スポーツ(すぽーつ)が　好き　ですか。
= What kind of sports does your mother like?
A: 母は　スポーツ(すぽーつ)が　好きでは　ありません。でも、料理(りょうり)は　好き　です。
= My mother does not like sports. But she likes cooking.

■ 自習(じしゅう) Self Check

1. Talking about things you like and don't like

Say the following out loud to yourself in Japanese.

A) I like (the art of) flower arranging.
B) Yuki dislikes American football.
C) Ben really likes swimming.
D) Ken really dislikes playing the guitar.
E) My mother doesn't like tennis (テニス).
F) My grandmother really likes ramen (noodles).
G) My friends really like Japan.

2. Asking what kind of...

Say the following out loud to yourself in Japanese.

A) What kind of food do you like?
B) What kind of animals does your mother like?
C) What kind of drink does your little brother like?
D) What country (国(くに)) does your grandmother like?
E) What kind of class do you like?
F) What kind of car (くるま) do you like?
G) What kind of music does your mother like?

■ 練習(れんしゅう)の時間(じかん) Time for Practice

1. Pair Practice

Ask your partner if he/she likes the following things. Partners should use 大好き, 好き, きらい, or 大きらい in their answers. After you have asked about all of the things in the chart, ask and answer questions about other objects and activities until you are told to stop.

A-さん：お寿司(すし)は　好き　ですか。
B-さん：はい、私は、お寿司(すし)が　好き　です。
-OR- いいえ、私は、寿司(すし)が　嫌い(きらい)　です。

サッカー	アイスクリーム	読書(どくしょ)	猫(ねこ)	蛙(かえる)
さしみ	テニス	チョコレート	野球(やきゅう)	花(はな)
コーラ	フットボール	犬(いぬ)	お茶(ちゃ)	

2. Pair Practice

Ask your partner to identify a specific thing he or she likes, and one he or she dislikes, from each category below. Then switch.

A-さん： どんな 動物(どうぶつ)が 好きですか。
B-さん： 狸(たぬき)が 好きです。
A-さん： そう ですか。どんな 動物(どうぶつ)が 嫌(きら)いいですか。
B-さん： ＿＿＿＿＿が 嫌いです。

A) 動物(どうぶつ)
B) 食べ物
C) 飲み物
D) 科目(かもく)
E) 音楽(おんがく)
F) 本
G) 映画(えいが) (movie)
H) 車(くるま) (car)
I) (other objects or things you can think of)

■ 文化箱(ぶんかばこ) Culture Chest

紫式部(むらさきしきぶ)

紫式部(むらさきしきぶ) is the name of the author of 源氏物語(げんじものがたり), or *The Tale of Genji*, a story about the relations between aristocratic men and women in the capital city of Kyoto, then called 平安京(へいあんきょう). It is sometimes called the world's first novel.

Murasaki Shikibu was born about 973 C.E. and died either in 1014 C.E. or 1025 C.E.; the records are unclear. Murasaki was not her real name—she served Empress Shoshi and Murasaki (referring to purple wisteria flowers) may have been a nickname. She is considered one of the great writers in Japanese history and her portrait and a scene from *The Tale of Genji* appear on the two thousand yen note.

■ キアラ(きあら)のジャーナル(じゃーなる) Kiara's Journal 

Read the journal entry below, and then answer these questions.

❶ Where did they first go when they arrived in Heian-kyou, current-day Kyoto?
❷ Why did Tomo want to introduce the trio to Lady Murasaki?
❸ What secret did Lady Murasaki share?
❹ Why was Lady Murasaki a little sad at the restaurant?
❺ Why does Kiara think that Lady Murasaki is a great author?

ジャーナル(じゃーなる)へ

1010年(ねん)、平安京(へいあんきょう)は 日本の capital でした。中国から たくさんの ideas が 日本に 来ました。紫式部(むらさきしきぶ)さんは この時 平安京に いました。

紫さんの 家へ 皆(みんな)で 行きました。友さんは、「紫さん、ひさしぶり です！ お元気 ですか。」と、言いました。

「まあ、友さん ですか。ようこそ。いつ ここに 来ましたか。この 人達は だれですか。」と、言いました。

友さんは、「昨日 来ました。それから、こちらは キアラさんと じゅん君と ベン君です。この 人達は 読書が 好き です。 ですから、紫さんに introduce したいと 思いました。(thought)」と、言いました。

紫さんは、「そうですか。初めまして。 よろしく お願いします。私も 読書が 好き です。詩を 書く事も 好き です。」と、言いました。

私達は、「どうぞ よろしく お願いします。」 と、言いました。

紫さんは、「キアラさんは 平安京が 好き ですか。」 と、聞きました。

私は、「ええ、大好き です。特に 清水寺が 大好き です。紫さんの 趣味は 和歌を 作ることですね。」 と、言いました。

「はい、私は 毎週 和歌の 勉強を しています。でも、ひみつ ですが、読書や 和歌を 作ること より、物を 食べることが もっと (more) 大好きです。」 と、言いました。

友さんは、「だから、紫さんと、私は、友達なんです!」 と、私達に smile しました。そして、「紫さん、晩ご飯を食べましたか。僕は おなかが ペコペコ です。食事を しましょう。」 と、言いました。

じゅん君は、「僕も ペコペコです。僕は 豆腐 (tofu) が 好き です。美味しい *湯豆腐屋さんは ありますか。」 と、言いました。

紫さんは、「ええ、川の そばに (river side) いい 湯豆腐屋さんが ありますよ。」 と、言いました。「こちらへ どうぞ」。

それから、a really cute little 湯豆腐屋に 入りました。There was no signage at all outside, but inside, 人が たくさん いました。すばらしい 畳の部屋 (tatami room) が いっぱい ありました。友さんは 私に、「ここで いい ですか。」 と、言いました。そして、「僕は 何年か 前に ここに 来た事が あると 思いますが…。」 と、紫さんに 言いました。

紫さんは、「そう ですよ。わたしと 一緒に 来ましたよ。」 と、言いました。友さんが、一緒に 来たことを 忘れていたので、紫さんは ちょっと さびしそう でした。Actually, it seemed like it did not matter for her, but I thought to myself that she probably will write about her slight sadness in her next poem or book. I think Lady Murasaki is skilled at observing details and commenting on people's emotions. She also has a very good imagination. だから、紫さんは、素晴らしい作家 (author) です。

食べ物は とても 美味しかったです。それに、私は 紫さんが 本当に 好き です。 いい 友だちに なりたいです。

あ、もう 遅い (late) 時間 です。

お休み。

* 湯豆腐屋: Restaurant specializing in tofu boiled in broth. Kyoto has many ゆどうふや。

第7課の3 キアラさんは、日本語が とても 上手(じょうず) です。

Kiara's Japanese is very good.

1.

1) 今日は、紫式部さんのパーティー です。
皆で 和歌を 詠む パーティー です。

2) キアラさんは、日本語が とても 上手 です。いい和歌を 作って下さいね。

3) ありがとう！がんばります！

2.

4) 友さんは、食べる事が 得意 ですね。

3.

5) ありがとう。がんばります！

4.

6) 友さん、和歌も がんばりますか。

5.

7) いいえ、和歌は ちょっと・・・。和歌は 苦手 ですから、がんばりません。でも、食べる事は 得意ですから、がんばりますよ～！

■ 会話(かいわ) Dialogue

REMINDER: You may see some kanji / vocabulary you do not recognize. Use the context to try to understand the meanings of those parts of the dialogue.

1. ベン　：今日(きょう)は、紫式部(むらさきしきぶ)さんの　パーティー　です。*皆(みんな)で　和歌(わか)を　詠(よ)む　パーティー　です。
2. じゅん：キアラさんは、日本語が　とても　上手(じょうず)　です。いい　和歌(わか)を　作(つく)って　下さいね。
3. キアラ：ありがとう！　がんばります！
4. ベン　：友さんは、食べる事が　得意(とくい)　ですね。
5. 友　　：ありがとう！がんばります！
6. ベン　：友さん、和歌(わか)も　がんばりますか。
7. 友　　：いいえ、和歌(わか)は　ちょっと…。和歌(わか)は　苦手(にがて)　ですから、がんばりません。でも、食べる事は　得意(とくい)　ですから、　がんばりますよ～！

* 和歌(わか) – to compose waka, traditional Japanese poems

■ 単語(たんご) New Words

(やる) やります (v) – to do (informal)

(やってみる) やってみます (v) – try to do

■ 漢字(かんじ) Kanji

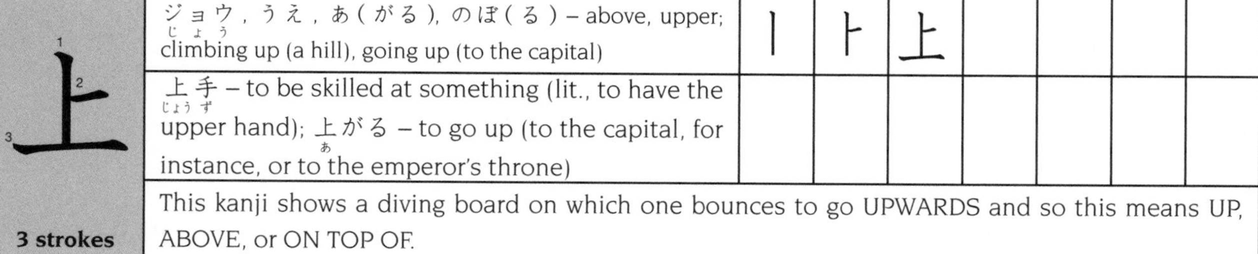

上 (3 strokes)	ジョウ, うえ, あ(がる), のぼ(る) – above, upper; climbing up (a hill), going up (to the capital)	丨	⺊	上				
	上手(じょうず) – to be skilled at something (lit., to have the upper hand); 上(あ)がる – to go up (to the capital, for instance, or to the emperor's throne)							
	This kanji shows a diving board on which one bounces to go UPWARDS and so this means UP, ABOVE, or ON TOP OF.							

■ 言葉（ことば）の探索（たんさく） Language Detection

1. 上手（じょうず）、下手（へた）

The words 上手 (*to be good at something*) and its opposite 下手 (*to be bad at something*) are used in the same way as 好（す）き and 嫌（きら）い. All of these words are な adjectives.

A) 由美子（ゆみこ）さんは　バスケが　上手（じょうず）　です。 = Yumiko is good at basketball.

B) 私は　サッカーが　下手（へた）　です。 = I am bad at soccer.

2. 得意（とくい）、苦手（にがて）

得意（とくい） (*skilled*) and 苦手（にがて） (*unskilled*) are similar to 上手 and 下手, but 得意（とくい） implies that someone specializes in the activity he/she is skilled at, and that he/she enjoys it. Similarly, 苦手（にがて） implies that he/she dislikes whatever they are unskilled at and would like to avoid it if possible. All of these words are な adjectives.

A) 山田先生（やまだせんせい）は　柔道（じゅうどう）が　得意（とくい）　ですよ。 = Mr./Ms. Yamada is good (specializes) at judo (you know).

B) 山本（やまもと）先生は　英語が　得意（とくい）　ですね。 = Mr. Yamamoto is skilled at English, isn't he?

C) 私は　数学（すうがく）が　苦手（にがて）　です。 = I am not good at (and I dislike) math.

3. The particle が can function as a conjunction that means "but," joining two contrasting sentences. Note that が comes at the end of the first part of the sentence.

A) キアラさんは　柔道（じゅうどう）が　得意（とくい）　ですが、水泳（すいえい）は　苦手（にがて）　です。
= Kiara is skilled at judo, but she is not skilled at swimming.

B) 母は　ゴルフが　上手（じょうず）　ですが、父は　下手（へた）　です。
= My mother is good at golf, but my father is poor at it.

C) ハンバーガーが　嫌（きら）い　ですが、ステーキは　大好き　です。
= I dislike hamburgers, but I love steak.

NOTE: that が can be used more than once in a sentence, each time for a different purpose. Also note how は is used in some of the examples to provide contrast.

■ 自習（じしゅう） Self Check

1. 上手（じょうず）、下手（へた）

Try to say the following in Japanese.

A) Junko is good at tea ceremony.
B) Junkichi is bad at cards.
C) I am bad at drawing manga.
D) Keiko's younger sister is good at playing the guitar.
E) (compose your own example)
F) (compose your own example)

2. 得意(とくい)、苦手(にがて)

Try to say the following in Japanese.

A) Keiko is good (specializes) at music.

B) My friends are not good at skateboarding.

C) My father is good (specializes) at kendo.

D) My friend is not good at Korean. But he is good at French.

3. Combine these sentences using が.

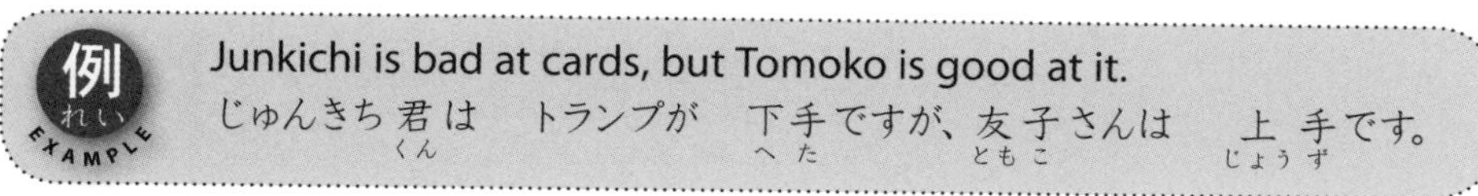

例 れい EXAMPLE
Junkichi is bad at cards, but Tomoko is good at it.
じゅんきち君(くん)は　トランプが　下手(へた)ですが、友子(ともこ)さんは　上手(じょうず)です。

A) I hate sushi. I love tempura.

B) My older sister is good at math. My little brother is good at history.

C) Tomohisa specializes in golf. He is not skilled at tennis.

■ 練習(れんしゅう)の時間(じかん) Time for Practice

1. Pair Practice

Point to one of the illustrations below and ask your partner in Japanese if he or she is good at the activity. Answer according to your own personal situation. Take turns.

A- さん (*pointing to soccer*): サッカーが　上手(じょうず)　ですか。

B- さん：　いいえ、サッカーは　下手(へた)　です。嫌い(きらい)　です。

A- さん：　そう　ですか。私も　サッカーが　苦手(にがて)　です。

2. Pair Practice

Ask your partner if he or she is skilled or unskilled at each of these activities. You can use a chart like the one on next page to record the answers. Then switch.

例 (れい) EXAMPLE

A-さん： 料理は　得意　ですか。
B-さん：はい、得意　です。料理を　する事が　好き　です。
A-さん：そう　ですか。
-OR-
A-さん： スキーは　得意　ですか。
B-さん：いいえ、苦手　です。
A-さん：そう　ですか。私も　スキーが　苦手　です。

Activity	得意／苦手	Activity	得意／苦手	Activity	得意／苦手
cooking		playing piano		music	
baseball		math		drawing	
playing guitar		skiing		other activities of your choice	

■ 文化箱 Culture Chest

Paying Compliments

Japanese tend not to brag, so they rarely use the expression 上手 when talking about their own abilities or those of their family members. They are usually quite complimentary of others, however, and often compliment even the simplest things, even if the compliment is not necessarily one hundred percent true. For example, Japanese will often tell 外国人 (foreigners in Japan) the following:

お箸を使うのが　（お）上手　ですね。 = You are good at using chopsticks.
日本語が　（お）上手　ですね。 = You are very good at Japanese.

A proper reply to most compliments (rather than どうも　ありがとう) would be いいえ、いいえ , implying that you are not so good at that and that there is no need to pay such a compliment in the first place.

和歌

The kanji for WA in WAKA means "Japanese" and the KA means "songs." 和歌 are poems that have been written in Japan for centuries. Various types of long and short 和歌 were composed on special occasions (such as the new year, or when viewing the full moon), at parties, or as letters between lovers. 紫式部 included nearly 800 和歌 in her 源氏物語 novel.

■ キアラのジャーナル Kiara's Journal

Read the journal entry below, and then answer these questions.

❶ How does Lady Murasaki feel about making waka?
❷ How skillful is Lady Murasaki at waka?
❸ What does Kiara like now that she did not like before coming to Japan?
❹ At the end of this journal entry, how does Kiara feel about her waka experience?

ジャーナルへ

今日、紫式部さんが 和歌の 勉強しているのを 少し 見ました。紫さんは「和歌を 作る事が 大好き です。」と、言いました。和歌を 作る事を、和歌を 詠むと、いいます。本を 読む、とは、違う 漢字です。

紫さんは 和歌が とても 上手 です。ベン君も 和歌を 少し がんばりました。でも、ベン君は 和歌を 詠む事が ちょっと 下手 です。

友さんは また **disappeared**。彼は 食べる事が 得意 です。じゅん君は どこでも 寝る事が 得意 です。ベン君も、寝る事が 好き ですが、歴史も 好き です。彼はスポーツが 下手 です。日本へ 来る前、私は 勉強が あまり 好きではありませんでしたが、今は 好きです。明日、紫式部さんと 友達と 和歌を 作ってみます **(make and see how it sounds)**.

私は、高校の 日本語の クラスで、俳句を 作りました。でも、和歌の事が ちょっと 分かりません。**The number of syllables for a** 俳句 **is 5-7-5, while the waka is longer, 5-7-5-7-7.** 長いですね。私は 俳句が ちょっと 上手 ですが、和歌が あまり 上手では ありません。紫式部さんは、「私は 友達と いつも パーティーで 和歌を 作ります。とても楽しいです。」と、言いました。

じゅん君は、「パーティーで 和歌を 作るんですか。それは 楽しい ですか。 平安時代と **21th century** は とても 違いますね。」と、言いました。そして、「だから 紫さんは 和歌が 上手 なんですね。僕は下手です。」と、言いました。

そこへ、友さんが、帰って 来ました。ベン君は、「どこへ 行っていましたか。ご飯は、もう 食べましたか。」と、聞きました。

友さんは「ちょっとだけ 食べました。後で また 一緒に 食べますよ。大丈夫です。」と、言いました。私は、「友さんは、やっぱり 食べる事が、得意 ですね。」と、言いました。

晩ご飯は 紫さんの 友達と 一緒に 食べました。遅くまで 和歌を 詠みました。私は あまり 上手では ありませんでしたが、和歌を詠む事が、とても 好きでした。**Believe it or not, it's a little like writing a rap song.**

お休みなさい。

第7課の4

友さんの　銀色(ぎんいろ)の　着物(きもの)も、かっこいいですよ。

Tomo's silver-colored kimono also looks great!

1.

1) 紫さん、おはよう ございます。

2) おはよう ございます、皆さん。

2.

3) わ！ 紫さん、きれいな 着物ですね！

4) ありがとう。紫は、私の色です。この 白い 花と もも色の 花は 友さんが 好きなので・・・。

5) ありがとう ございます。私は、ファッションは、あまり 得意では ありません。でも、紫さんの その 着物が 本当に 大好き です。

3.

6) ありがとう。友さんの 銀色の 着物も、とても かっこいい ですよ。ベン君と じゅん君の 黒の 着物も、いい ですね。キアラさんの、黄色と 青の 花も、とても かわいい です。さ、朝ご飯 ですよ。

■ 会話(かいわ) Dialogue

REMINDER: You may see some kanji / vocabulary you do not recognize. Use the context to try to understand the meanings of those parts of the dialogue.

1. 皆(みんな)　：紫(むらさき)さん、おはよう　ございます。
2. 紫(むらさき)　：おはよう　ございます、皆(みな)さん。
3. キアラ：わ！　紫(むらさき)さん、きれいな　着物(きもの)　ですね！
4. 紫　：ありがとう。紫(むらさき)は、私の　色(いろ)　です。この　白(しろ)い花(はな)と　もも色(いろ)の　花(はな)は　友さんが　好きなので…。
5. 友　：ありがとう　ございます。私は、ファッションは、あまり　得意(とくい)では　ありません。でも、紫(むらさき)さんの　その　着物(きもの)が　本当(ほんとう)に　大好き　です。
6. 紫　：ありがとう。友さんの　銀色(ぎんいろ)の　着物も、とても　かっこいい　ですよ。ベン君(くん)と　じゅん君の　黒(くろ)の　着物も、いい　ですね。キアラさんの、黄色(きいろ)と　青(あお)の　花(はな)も、とても　かわいい　です。さ、朝(あさ)ご飯(はん)　ですよ。

■ 単語(たんご) New Words

白(しろ)	赤(あか)	もも色(いろ)
黒(くろ)	ねずみ色(いろ)	紫(むらさき)
オレンジ(おれんじ)	グレイ(ぐれい)	青(あお)
黄色(いろ)	緑(みどり)	ピンク(ぴんく)

はい色(いろ) (*n*) or グレイ (*n*)	銀色(ぎんいろ) (*n*)	金色(きんいろ) (*n*)
色(いろ) (*n*) – color	色々(いろ) (な *adj.*) – various	何色(いろ) (*inter.*) – what color?
彼(かれ) (*pron.*) – he; boyfriend	彼女(かのじょ) (*pron.*) – her; girlfriend	全然(ぜんぜん) (*adv.*) – not at all
	あまり (*adv.*) – not very	

Other words you might like to know:

橙色(だいだいいろ) (*n*) – orange　金髪(きんぱつ) (*n*) – blond (hair)　茶色(いろ) (*n*) – brown　茶髪(ちゃぱつ) (*n*) – brown (hair)

■ 漢字(かんじ) Kanji

色 (6 strokes)	いろ – color	ノ	ク	⺈	𠂊	刍	色	
	色(いろ) – color; (黄(き))色(いろ) – yellow							
	The first two strokes are a cuckoo bird (the kind of bird you see in a cuckoo clock); ク is the katakana for KU on top of a two-COLOR flag (巴). The bottom of this kanji represents the shadow from the flag.							

白 (5 strokes)	ハク(はく); しろ、しろ(い) – white	ノ	丿	冂	白	白		
	白(しろ) – white; 白(しろ)い – white (*adj.*); 白(はく)(人(じん)) – Caucasian							
	Take the sun (日) and add a small flash of light (the first small stroke). The WHITE color is blindingly bright!							

黒 (11 strokes)	コク(こく); くろ、くろ(い) – black	丨	冂	日	日	甲	甲	里
	黒(くろ) – black; 黒(くろ)い – black (*adj.*); 黒(こく)(板(ばん)) – blackboard	里	里	黒	黒			
	The ground (土) of the rice field (田) is burnt BLACK by the fire (火) which you can see in the four strokes on the bottom (灬).							

赤 (7 strokes)	セキ(せき); あか、あか(い) – red, crimson, scarlet	一	十	土	土	赤	赤	赤
	赤(あか) – red; 赤(あか)い – red (adj.); 赤(あか)(ちゃん) – baby							
	The first three strokes are earth or soil (土). The bottom four strokes represent fiery RED lava pushing up on the earth.							

青 (8 strokes)	セイ(せい); あお、あお(い) – blue, green; inexperienced	一	十	丰	龶	青	青	青
	青(あお) – blue; 青(あお)い – blue (*adj.*); 青(せい)(年(ねん)) youth	青						
	One (一) way to remember this 漢字 is to think how BLUE the soil of earth (土) looks under the light of the 月 .							

■ 言葉(ことば)の探索(たんさく) Language Detection

1. 赤、赤色 - Colors (nouns)

Colors in Japanese can appear as nouns, as you can see below, or as adjectives, as you learned in chapter 6.

例 (れい) EXAMPLE

A) 私は　赤(あか)が　好(す)き　です。 = I like the color red.
B) この　Tシャツは　黒(くろ)では　ありません。 = This T-shirt is not black.
C) 僕(ぼく)の　ユニフォームの　色は　青(あお)と　赤(あか)　です。 = My uniform's colors are blue and red.

2. あまり、全然(ぜんぜん)

あまり and 全然(ぜんぜん) are both adverbs that are used ONLY with the negative form of the verb. あまり means "not very," while 全然(ぜんぜん) means "not at all." These adverbs generally precede the verb they modify.

A) ベン君(くん)は　数学(すうがく)が　あまり　好きでは　ありません。
= Ben does not like math very much.

B) 私は　お茶(ちゃ)を　全然(ぜんぜん)　飲みませんが、コーヒーは　時々(ときどき)　飲みます。
= I never drink green tea, but I sometimes drink coffee.

C) 花子(はなこ)さんは　絵(え)を　描(か)く事(こと)が　あまり　上手では　ありません。
= Hanako is not very good at drawing.

■ 自習(じしゅう) Self Check

1. Say the following out loud to yourself in Japanese.

A) Today my shirt is green.
B) The paper is white.
C) I love orange.
D) I do not like purple very much.
E) I like yellow a little bit.
F) My father does not like blue at all.

■ 練習(れんしゅう)の時間(じかん) Time for Practice

1. Pair Practice

1. Point to something on or near your partner. Ask what color it is in Japanese. Take turns.

A-さん：(*pointing*) それは　何色(なにいろ)　ですか。
B-さん：これは　赤(あか)　です。
A-さん：そう　ですね。

2. Ask your partner about his or her family members' favorite colors in Japanese. If you are unsure, either make up an answer or say that you don't know (しりません) in 日本語. Include an adverb (とても，まあまあ，少(すこ)し，あまり，全然(ぜんぜん)) in your statements showing their degrees of like/dislike. You will first have to find out who is in your partner's family, as in the sample dialogue below. Take turns.

A-さん：ご家族(かぞく)は　何人　ですか。
B-さん：父と　母と　おばあさんと　私の　四人です。
A-さん：お父さんは　何色(なにいろ)が　好(す)き　ですか。
B-さん：父は　黒(くろ)と白(しろ)が　とても　好(す)きです。
A-さん：そう　ですか。

2. Class Practice

だれ　ですか。

Write down five statements, using color words, in Japanese, on a piece of scrap paper. The statements should describe one of the other students in the class. Next, one person reads his/her statements to the class; after three clues, the class can guess which classmate is being described. The first person to guess correctly reads his/her clues next.

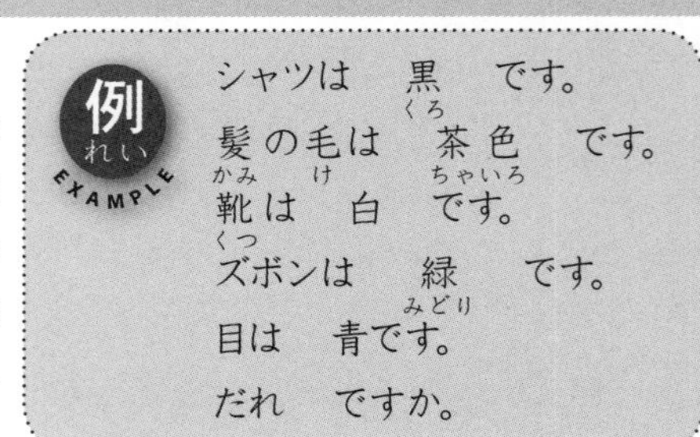

■ 文化箱(ぶんかばこ) Culture Chest

Fashion—Then and Now

Dress was very important to 10th- and 11th-century Japanese nobility, and they spent much time thinking about and planning what to wear. Elaborate layers of silk 着物(きもの) were time-consuming to weave and expensive to buy. Seasonal patterns were carefully considered by both the weavers and the wearers of 着物. Even something as simple as wearing an out-of-season under-kimono could be cause for gossip and comment at court. For instance, 清少納言(せいしょうなごん), a contemporary of 紫式部(むらさきしきぶ), wrote in her collection of anecdotes and commentary called 枕草子(まくらのそうし) or *Pillow Book*, something that may be translated as "A woman with bad hair wearing a white cloth robe is not a pretty thing"!

Presently, the wearing of 着物 is generally limited to formal occasions such as weddings, funerals, tea ceremony or flower arranging occasions, or trips to temples or shrines. Visit Kyoto today, however, and you will see many a kimono-robed woman walking down the street.

■ キアラ(きあら)のジャーナル(じゃーなる) Kiara's Journal 

Read the journal entry below, and then answer these questions.

❶ What colors were the flowers on Lady Murasaki's kimono?

❷ What color was Kiara's kimono?

❸ What was a little different?

❹ What was delicious?

ジャーナル(じゃーなる)へ

今朝(けさ)、朝(あさ)ご飯(はん)の 時に、紫(むらさき)さんは 着物を 着ました。とても いい 着物 でした。彼女(かのじょ)の着物に 花が たくさん ありました。その 花は 白と もも色 でした。とても きれいでした。私の部屋(へや)にも 着物が ありました。私の 着物は 黄(き)色と 青の 花がありました。きれい でした。じゅん君と ベン君も 黒(くろ)の 着物を 着ました。友さんは 銀(ぎん)色の着物を 着ました。男(おとこ)の子(こ)の 着物も とてもきれいでした。朝ご飯の 時、音楽も ありました。平安時代の 音楽は とても different でした。The tempo is quite slow and the scale is not anywhere near what I'm used to. ご飯は とても おいしかったです。白いご飯を たくさん 食べました。緑(みどり)の 漬(つ)け物と オレンジ色の魚(さかな) (fish) と 赤の ストロベリーも ありました。朝ご飯の 後で 色々な お寺(てら)と 神社(じんじゃ)を見に行きました。午後から 雅楽(ががく)のコンサートを 聞きました。紫さんは、「この 音楽の 皆(みな)さんは とても 上手 です。」と、言いました。

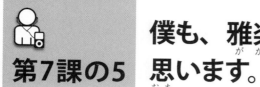

第7課の5

僕も、雅楽は　とてもかっこいいと思います。

I also think that gagaku is really cool!

1) 紫さん、この音楽は、何と言いますか。

2) 雅楽 です。ベン君と じゅん君と キアラさんは、雅楽が 好き ですか。

3) すみません、僕は、ちょっと. . . . あまり　好きでは ありません。

4) 私は好きです！格好いいです。

5) 僕も、雅楽は とても かっこいいと思います。僕は、色々な 音楽が 好きです。

6) 私は雅楽は、とても 好きですが、ベン君は、あまり 好きでは ありませんね。じゃあ、ベン君、私と　何か 食べに行きましょう。

■ 会話 Dialogue

REMINDER: You may see some kanji / vocabulary you do not recognize. Use the context to try to understand the meanings of those parts of the dialogue.

1. キアラ： 紫さん、この音楽は、何と　言いますか。
2. 紫　　： *雅楽　です。ベン君と　じゅん君と　キアラさんは、雅楽が　好き　ですか。
3. ベン　： すみません、僕は、ちょっと… あまり　好きでは　ありません。
4. キアラ： 私は好き　です！　かっこいい　です！
5. じゅん： 僕も、雅楽は　とても　かっこいいと　思います。僕は、色々な　音楽が好きです。
6. 友　　： 私は、雅楽が、とても　好き　ですが、ベン君は、あまり　好きでは　ありませんね。じゃあ、ベン君、私と　何か　*食べに　行きましょう。

* 雅楽 – court music during the Heian Period　* 食べに　行きましょう – let's go to eat

■ 単語 New Words

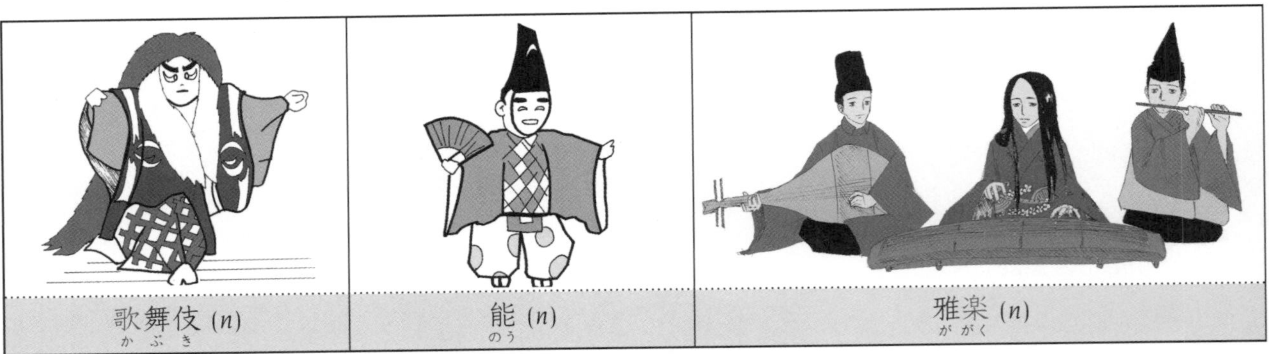

歌舞伎 (*n*)	能 (*n*)	雅楽 (*n*)

■ 漢字 Kanji

歌 (14 strokes)	
カ ; うた ; うた (う) – song, sing	
歌 – a song; 歌 (う) – to sing	
The left side of this (可) looks like mouths open and SINGING SONGS on risers of a chorus while the right side looks similar to "next" (次). The singers are ready to SING the next SONG!	

思 (9 strokes)	
シ , おも (う) think, believe	
思 (う) – to think, to believe	
When you are out working in the rice field (田), your heart (心) has nothing to do but THINK.	

■ 言葉の探索 Language Detection

～と思います。 - I think . . .

～と思います is used when you want to express your own opinion. What comes before the ～と思います must be in the plain form. The plain form of the verb is the dictionary form, which was introduced in the first section of this chapter. The plain form of です is だ. Note the difference below between the polite form and the plain form for the non-past affirmative tense for the following types of words.

	Polite	Plain		Polite	Plain
1. verbs	食べ ます	食べる	3. い adjectives	美味しい です	美味しい
2. nouns	すし です	すし だ	4. な adjectives	静か です	静か だ

A) 私は　6時に　帰ると　思います。 = I think that I will return at 6:00.
B) あの　人は　日本人だと　思います。 = I think that person over there is Japanese.
C) ハンバーガーは　美味しいと　思います。 = I think hamburgers are delicious.
D) あの　フランス人は　有名だと　思います。 = I think that the French person over there is famous.

■ 自習 Self Check

Say the following out loud to yourself in Japanese.

A) I think I will go to Japan.
B) I think Japanese is fun.
C) I think the first year students are quiet.
D) I think that this is a Chinese language book.
E) I think (finish this sentence based upon what you really think about something or someone).

■ 練習の時間 Time for Practice

1. Pair Practice

In groups of 3 or 4, make four statements about objects or people others can see or might be familiar with. Three of these should be factual, one should be an うそ (lie). Use the ～と思います pattern to say what you believe about the object or person. Try to use adjectives, verbs, and nouns in your statements. Be prepared to make your statements to the class who will then guess which one of your statements is an うそ.

Statement sample: (*pointing to a notebook*)
この　ノートは　先生の　だと　思います。 = I think that this notebook is the teacher's.
Class member response　違と　思います。 = I think (that) is false.

2. Pair Practice

Use the following cues to ask your partner questions about which of the following he/she likes or is skilled at. B-さん should always answer negatively, using the adverbs あまり or 全然. Take turns.

例 EXAMPLE

A- さん：アイスクリームは　好き　ですか。
B- さん：いいえ、アイスクリームは　全然好き　ではありません。
-OR- A- さん：ダンスは　とくいですか。
B- さん：いいえ、あまり　とくい　ではありません。

liver (レバー)	disco (ディスコ)	broccoli (ブロッコリー)	cactus (サボテン)
okra (オクラ)	spiders (くも)	grapefruit (グレープフルーツ)	mountain climbing (山のぼり)

■ 文化箱 Culture Chest

雅楽 Gagaku

雅楽, or "elegant music," is a style of court music that dates back to the Nara period (奈良時代) and combines influences from Tang-dynasty China, Korea, and Shinto. It is performed with traditional wind, string, and percussion instruments and is often accompanied by classical dance. Theater also developed in conjunction with 雅楽; 能 (Noh theater) became especially popular in the 14th century. 雅楽 uses a pentatonic scale, that is, a musical scale with five pitches per octave. Touru Takemitsu is one well-known modern Japanese composer (he wrote the soundtracks for the movies *Ran* and *Kwaidan*, among others) who has used traditional Japanese music in his compositions. See if you can find some of Touru's music to listen to online. Can you hear the influence of 雅楽 in any of his pieces?

■ キアラのジャーナル Kiara's Journal

Read the journal entry below, and then answer these questions.

1. What did Kiara and Murasaki spend the day doing?
2. What is your favorite color? Would you find it on a kimono?
3. Do you think Heian-kyou was a colorful town? Why or why not?

ジャーナルへ

今日は、紫式部さんと 九時から 三時まで いっしょに いました。とても 楽しかったです。いっしょに 平安京の お寺と 神社を 見ました。平安時代にも お寺と 神社は、たくさん ありました。

紫さんと よく 話しました。私は 色の 名前と 趣味の事を 勉強しました。Color words come in noun form and adjective form. I started off practicing with the noun form, like 赤 and 青 for red and blue. For example、「この着物は 赤と青です。とても きれいです。」じゅん君 told me there is another way to use color words as adjectives, but I decided to practice that later. それから、I learned that after hobby words, you use 'は' when the hobby is the topic. For example、「私の 趣味は 絵を 描く事 です。」is how I would say "My hobby is drawing pictures." もう少し がんばって 日本語の 勉強を しますね！

■ 単語チェックリスト New Word Checklist

たんごちぇっくりすと

7-1

あめふと，あめりかんふっとぼーる・アメフト，アメリカンフットボール *n* American football
いけばな・生け花 *n* flower arranging
うた・歌 *n* song
うたう・歌う / うたいます・歌います *v* to sing
うたうこと・歌う事 *n* singing
え・絵 *n* painting, drawing
おどり・踊り *n* dancing
およぐ・泳ぐ / およぎます・泳ぎます *v* to swim
およぐこと・泳ぐ事 *n* swimming
かいもの・買い物 *n* shopping
ぎたー・ギター *n* guitar
ごるふ・ゴルフ *n* golf
さどう / ちゃどう・茶道 *n* tea ceremony
しゅみ・趣味 *n* hobby
じょうば・乗馬 *n* horseback riding
じょぎんぐ・ジョギング *n* jogging
すいえい・水泳 *n* swimming
すきー・スキー *n* skiing
すけぼー・スケボー（を）する *v* to skateboard
すぽーつ・スポーツ *n* sports
そして *conj.* then; and then
それから *conj.* then; and then
それに *conj.* moreover; furthermore
たべること・食べる事 *n* eating
どくしょ・読書 *n* reading
とらんぷ・トランプ *n* playing cards; card game
ねること・寝る事 *n* sleeping
ぴあの・ピアノ *n* piano
ひく・弾く / ひきます・弾きます *v* to play [a stringed instrument]
びでおげーむ・ビデオゲーム *n* video games
りょうり・料理 *n* cooking
りょこう・旅行，たび・旅 *n* trip; travel

7-2

おもう・思う / おもいます・思います *v* to think
かえる・蛙 *n* frog
きらい・嫌い な *adj.* dislike
じょうだん・冗談 *n* joke
すき・好き な *adj.* like
だいきらい・大嫌い な *adj.* dislike a lot, hate
だいすき・大好き な *adj.* love, really like
たいてい *adv.* usually
どうぶつ・動物 *n* animal
ねずみ・鼠 *n* rat, mouse

7-3

がんばる・頑張る / がんばります・頑張ります *v* to do one's best
じょうず・上手 な *adj.* skillful
とくい・得意 な *adj.* skilled at
にがて・苦手 な *adj.* unskilled at
へた・下手 な *adj.* not good at
やってみる / やってみます（やってみて）*v* to see if you can do (something); try to do (something)
やる / やります（やって）*v* to do

7-4

あお・青 *n* blue
あか・赤 *n* red
あまり *adv.* not very
いろ・色 *n* color
いろいろ・色々 *adv.* various
おれんじ・オレンジ *n* orange
かのじょ・彼女 *pron.* she; girlfriend
かれ・彼 *pron.* he; boyfriend
きいろ・黄色 *n* yellow
きんいろ・金色 *n* gold
ぎんいろ・銀色 *n* silver
きんぱつ・金髪 *n* blond (hair)
ぐれい・グレイ *n* gray
くろ・黒 *n* black
しろ・白 *n* white
ぜんぜん・全然 *adv.* not at all
だいだいいろ・橙色 *n* orange (colored)
ちゃいろ・茶色 *n* brown
ちゃぱつ・茶髪 *n* brown (hair)
なにいろ・何色 *inter.* what color?
ねずみいろ・鼠色 *n* gray (mouse-colored)
はいいろ・灰色 *n* gray, ash-colored
ぴんく・ピンク *n* pink
みどり・緑 *n* green
むらさき・紫 *n* purple
ももいろ・もも色 *n* pink (peach) color

7-5

ががく・雅楽 *n* gagaku, ancient Japanese court music
かぶき・歌舞伎 *n* kabuki theater
のう・能 *n* Noh (a type of theater)

Adjectives in Amanohashidate

第 8 課

Learning and Performance Goals

This chapter will enable you to:

A) use a larger number of adjectives
B) learn how to use adjectives as well as their negative, past, and past negative tenses
C) learn about the folk tale of Urashima Tarou
D) use 16 additional kanji
E) use the "can-do" chart found on **TimeForJapanese.com** to chart your progress for what you "can-do" for each chapter

Amanohashidate, on the Sea of Japan, is said to be one of Japan's three most scenic views.

第8課の1 海が　きれい　ですね。
The ocean is beautiful, isn't it?

1) わあ・・・・
海が きれい ですね。
2) ビーチも
美しい ですね。
3) そう
ですね。ここは
天橋立 です。

4) ほら！あそこに
おじいさんが います。

5) わあ、ひげが とても 長い
ですね。そして、あの はこは
とても 不思議 ですね。

■ 会話(かいわ) Dialogue 

REMINDER: You may see some kanji / vocabulary you do not recognize. Use the context to try to understand the meanings of those parts of the dialogue.

1. キアラ： わあ…海(うみ)が　きれい　ですね。
2. ベン　： ビーチも　美(うつく)しい　ですね。
3. 友　　： そう　ですね。ここは　天橋立(あまのはしだて)　です。
4. ベン　： ほら！あそこに　おじいさんが　います。
5. キアラ： わあ、ひげがとても　長(なが)い　ですね。そして、あの　はこは　とても　不思議(ふしぎ)　ですね。

■ 単語(たんご) New Words

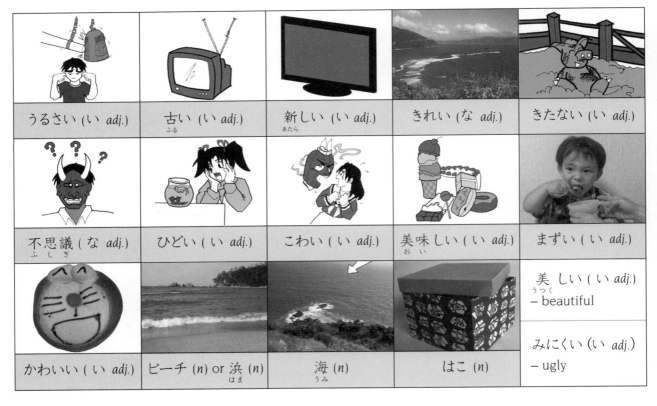

うるさい (い *adj.*)	古(ふる)い (い *adj.*)	新(あたら)しい (い *adj.*)	きれい (な *adj.*)	きたない (い *adj.*)
不思議(ふしぎ) (な *adj.*)	ひどい (い *adj.*)	こわい (い *adj.*)	美味(おい)しい (い *adj.*)	まずい (い *adj.*)
かわいい (い *adj.*)	ビーチ (*n*) or 浜(はま) (*n*)	海(うみ) (*n*)	はこ (*n*)	美(うつく)しい (い *adj.*) – beautiful みにくい (い *adj.*) – ugly

Other words you might like to use:

- 危(あぶ)ない (い *adj.*) – dangerous
- じれったい (い *adj.*) – irritating
- きびしい (い *adj.*) – strict
- やさしい (い *adj.*) – easy, kind, gentle
- ずるい (い *adj.*) – cunning
- ばかばかしい (い *adj.*) – foolish; silly
- かしこい (い *adj.*) – wise; bright
- 嬉(うれ)しい (い *adj.*) – glad; happy
- わがまま (な *adj.*) – selfish

■ 漢字 Kanji

Kanji	Readings and use	Stroke order
美 (9 strokes)	ビ；うつく(しい) – beautiful 美(しい) – beautiful; 美(人) – beautiful person (woman)	丶 丷 䒑 䒑 䒑 䒑 𦍌 美 美
	The upper half of this kanji is a sheep (羊) and the bottom part is the kanji for big (大). In ancient China, the sheep was an important domesticated animal. Big wool coats and large wool carpets are certainly BEAUTIFUL.	
長 (8 strokes)	チョウ – head, chief; なが(い) – long (length) 長(い) – long (adj.); 長(崎) – Nagasaki (city in Kyushu); (校)長(先生) – school principal; (班)長 – leader of the group, "head honcho."	丨 𠂉 ... 長
	This is a picture of an old man whose hair is streaming in the wind. This kanji implies LENGTH, including time and spatial length. It also looks like a LONG table with a stack of books on it.	
短 (12 strokes)	みじか(い) – short (length) 短(い) – short (length)	ノ ... 短
	The left half of this kanji is an arrow, though one could imagine it as an archer. The right side is a bean. An arrow must be a SHORT one to go through a bean.	
海 (9 strokes)	カイ；うみ – ocean, sea 海 – ocean, sea; (日本)海 – Sea of Japan	丶 ... 海
	The left three strokes of this kanji are the radical for water. Imagine water splashing on a beach every (毎) day, eventually creating an OCEAN of water.	

Notice that when kanji are used in compound words with other kanji (called 漢語 or 熟語), they are usually read with their Chinese reading (音読み). If the kanji is used on its own, it is usually read with the Japanese reading (訓読み). Some words, such as many verbs and adjectives, have kanji with hiragana endings called " おくりがな." Words with おくりがな endings usually use the Japanese reading (訓読み).

Previously introduced kanji:

Kanji	Previous Pronunciation and Use	New Pronunciation and Use
大	大(学)	大きい；大きい帽子 (large hat)
小	小(学校)	小さい；小さい部屋 (small room)

Notice that some kanji are in compounds of kanji called 漢語, while others are followed by hiragana and make stand-alone words.

■ 言葉(ことば)の探索(たんさく) Language Detection

1. い and な adjectives

An adjective is a word that describes a person, place, or thing. Notice that in Japanese there are two types of adjectives. They are classified as い adjectives or な adjectives as outlined below. Refer to the list of adjectives in Appendix 1 for more examples.

A) all い adjectives end in "い."

B) MOST な adjectives end in sounds other than "い" (two exceptions are 有名(ゆうめい) and きれい).

Using い adjectives:

Just like in English, い adjectives can come before or after the nouns that they modify. Notice how the adjectives are used in these examples.

(noun は *adj.*)

A) あの　映画(えいが)は　こわい　です。 = That movie is scary.

B) この　朝(あさ)ご飯(はん)は　美味(おい)しい　です。 = This breakfast is delicious.

(*adj.* + noun)

C) あれは　こわい　映画(えいが)　です。 = That is a scary movie.

D) これは　美味(おい)しい　朝(あさ)ご飯(はん)　です。 = This is a delicious breakfast.

Using な adjectives:

な adjectives can also come before or after the nouns that they modify. However, if they come before the noun, the adjective must be followed by a な.

(noun は *adj.*)

A) 教室(きょうしつ)は　静(しず)か　です。 = The classroom is quiet.

B) 私の　犬は　元気　です。 = My dog is lively.

(*adj.* な + noun)

C) 静(しず)かな　教室(きょうしつ)　です。 = It is a quiet classroom.

D) 私の　元気な　犬　です。 = It is my lively dog.

■ 自習(じしゅう) Self Check

1. Say each of the following out loud, and decide which are い adjectives and which are な adjectives.

- 大きい
- 小さい
- 短(みじか)い
- 美(うつく)しい
- 美味(おい)しい
- 不思議(ふしぎ)
- かわいい
- 長(なが)い
- うるさい
- きれい
- 静(しず)か
- こわい

2. Restate the following in Japanese.

A) The beach is dirty.

B) Koro is a scary dog.

C) The teacher is quiet

D) This is a lively/energetic cat.

■ 練習(れんしゅう)の時間(じかん) Time for Practice

1. Use the images below to ask and answer questions with your partner in Japanese.

A-さん：	どれが　長(なが)い　ですか。	= Which one is long?
B-さん：	これが　長(なが)い　です。	= (*Point to the correct image.*) This one is long.
A-さん：	はい、そう　です。	= Yes, that's right.

2. Use the adjectives below to ask your partner questions about people you both know. If the answer is negative, use a different adjective in the answer.

A-さん：	とも子(こ)さんは　足が　小さい　ですか。	= Are Tomoko's feet small?
B-さん：	はい、小(ちい)さい　です。	= Yes, they are small.
-OR-	いいえ、大(おお)きい　です。	= No, they are big.

A) 静(しず)か　　C) うるさい　　E) 強(つよ)い

B) 大きい　　D) つまらない　　F) 面白(おもしろ)い

3. First, factually describe a picture below with an adjective AFTER the noun. Then your partner should restate what you said, changing the word order, placing the adjective BEFORE the noun. For な adjectives, be sure to insert な after the adjectives when the adjective comes BEFORE the nouns. (Note: deer – しか)

A-さん：	この猫(ねこ)は　静(しず)か　です。	= This cat is quiet.
B-さん：	そう　ですね。　静(しず)かな　猫(ねこ)　ですね。	= That's right. It is a quiet cat, isn't it?

■ 文化箱 Culture Chest

The Tale of 浦島太郎

The folk story of 浦島太郎 is well known to all Japanese children. As with many folktales, there are several different versions. Here is one.

One day, the fisherman 浦島太郎 rescued a turtle on the beach. It was being tormented by a group of young boys, who were hitting it with a stick. In gratitude, the turtle returned the next day to invite 太郎 to visit the 竜宮城, the Dragon King's splendid palace at the bottom of the sea. The Princess 乙姫 welcomed 太郎 with delicious food and singing and dancing, and 太郎 spent much happy time there. Eventually, though, 太郎 began to miss his family and friends and decided to return to his home. As お土産, the Princess gave him a jewel-encrusted 玉手箱, or treasure chest, with the stern warning never to open the box. Again riding on the turtle's back, 太郎 returned to the beach near his home. To his surprise, 太郎 recognized not a soul. Desolate, he sat down on the beach and, forgetting the Princess's words, opened the treasure chest. Immediately, a puff of white smoke [some versions say "purple smoke"] emerged to envelop 太郎. He was transformed into an old man with a long beard. The days 太郎 thought he had spent under the sea actually numbered almost 300 years!

■ キアラのジャーナル Kiara's Journal 

Read the journal entry below, and then answer these questions.

❶ What was the weather like in Amanohashidate?
❷ How did Kiara feel about the weather?
❸ What was the name of the person they met on their walk?
❹ What was the most outstanding physical feature of that person?

ジャーナルへ

今日は、朝ご飯の 後、紫 さんと 一緒に 清水寺の となりの 神社の 鳥居に 行きました。紫さんは、とても いい人でした。さようならを 言うのは、さびしかったですが、紫さんに さよならを 言って、時の門に 入りました。

After some time passed、私達は、時の門を 出ました。友さんが、「天橋立 という ところ に います。」と、言いました。天橋立の 漢字は '天橋' (heaven's bridge) と '立' (standing on or to stand) です。天橋立は、とても きれい です。

Not only are we not back in the 21st century, we're not even close. According to Tomo san, we're still only in the year 1388! I can't believe that we've been traveling together for about five months and now we're seeing things that happened in the 14th century! I'm thinking that I should learn to operate the 時の門 myself.

OK, it's time to get back to practicing my Japanese writing. I've been studying adjectives a lot lately so that I can better describe some of the things that I'm seeing. Here goes...

天橋立に 来ました。ここは 少し あたたかい (warm) です。私は、あたたかいのが 好きです。海の 真ん中に、まっすぐな 長い道(みち)が あります。It looks like a bridge floating in the water, or if you look at it upside down, you could say, it looks like a bridge to heaven. 海(うみ)も 空(そら)も、とても きれい です。母も、ここが 大好きだろうと 思います。

私達は、皆(みんな)で climbed up to the top of the hill. We could see 遠(とお)い 島(しま)。すばらしかった です。その 後(あと)、天橋立の ビーチで 散歩(さんぽ)しました。そこで、おじいさんに *会いました。その おじいさんの 名前は 浦島太郎(うらしまたろう)でした。かれの ひげは、とても 長かったです。

* 会(あ)いました – met

第8課の2 この海は　もっと　きれいでした。

This ocean used to be prettier.

1\.

1) こんにちは。

2\.

2)こんにちは。

3\.

3) おじいさん、ひげが とても 長い ですね。 おじいさんは 何才 ですか。

4\.

4) 僕は 三百才 です。昔々、この海は もっと きれい でした。そして かわいい 亀が いました。五人の 子供達も いました。でも 彼らは 悪いことを しました。

5) ええっ・・・ 何を しましたか。

5\.

やめなさい！

6) 子供達は 亀を いじめました。僕は、「やめなさい！」と、言いました。すると、すぐに 子供達は、家に 帰りました。

6\.

7) わあ。亀は こわかった でしょうね。

■ 会話(かいわ) Dialogue

REMINDER: You may see some kanji / vocabulary you do not recognize. Use the context to try to understand the meanings of those parts of the dialogue.

1. キアラ：こんにちは。
2. 太郎　：こんにちは。
3. キアラ：おじいさん、ひげが　とても　長(なが)い　ですね。おじいさんは　何才(なんさい)　ですか。
4. 太郎　：僕(ぼく)は　三百才(さんびゃくさい)　です。昔々(むかしむかし)、この　海は　もっと　きれい　でした。
   そして　かわいい　亀(かめ)が　いました。五人の　子供達(こどもたち)も　いました。
   でも　彼(かれ)らは　悪(わる)い　ことを　しました。
5. ベン　：ええっ . . . 何を　しましたか。
6. 太郎　：子供達(こどもたち)は　亀(かめ)を　*いじめました。僕(ぼく)は、「やめなさい！」と、言(い)いました。
   *すると、すぐに　子供達(こどもたち)は、家(いえ)に　帰(かえ)りました。
7. じゅん：わあ。亀(かめ)は　こわかった　でしょうね。

* いじめました – (to) badger/torment　* すると – and then

■ 単語(たんご) New Words

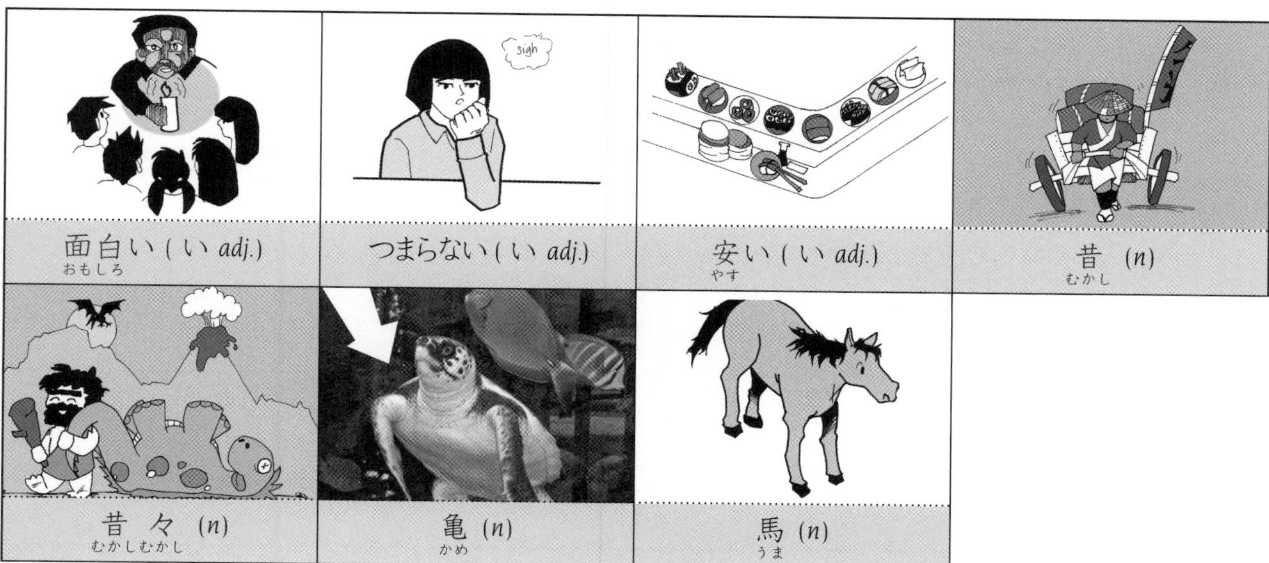

天橋立(あまのはしだて) (pn) – place name
彼(かれ)ら (pron.) – they (boys)
子供(こども) (n) – child
子供達(こどもたち) (n) – children

悪(わる)い (い adj.) – bad
高(たか)い (い adj.) – expensive, tall (prev. introduced)
良(よ)い (い adj.) – well, good (same as いい but can be conjugated)
すぐ – immediately, at once

■ 漢字(かんじ) Kanji

安	
	アン(あん) – safe; やす(い) – cheap
	安(全)(あんぜん) – safe; 安(い)(やすい) – cheap
6 strokes	The top half of this kanji is a roof, and the lower half represents a woman. You can think of this particular woman as someone who is CHEAP and paranoid so she is staying under her own roof to stay SAFE and to save money.

悪	
	わる(い) – bad
	悪(い)(わるい) – bad
11 strokes	The top half of this kanji (亜) is the kanji for Asia; the bottom part (心) is the kanji for heart or spirit. Just think, if all of Asia (あ) were pressing down on your heart, it would be very 悪い or BAD!

面	
	メン(めん); おも – face, mask
	面(白い)(おもしろい) – interesting, enjoyable
9 strokes	Here is a FACE or a MASK with one huge eye (目(め)) in the middle and a wig blowing off held on by only one thread of hair (the second stroke). Is this a funny MASK or a scary one?

天	
	テン(てん); あま – heaven
	天(皇)(てんのう) – emperor; 天(ぷら)(てん) – Japanese batter fried vegetables, shrimp, and fish; 天(橋立)(あまのはしだて) – place name
4 strokes	The kanji for big (大) is based on a person holding out his/her arms and legs to appear bigger. Here, the additional horizontal line above that person represents the space above humans, that is, the SKY or HEAVEN.

立	
	た(つ) – to stand; リツ(りつ) – to stand
	立(つ)(た) – to stand; 立って下さい(たってください) – please stand; (起)立(きりつ) – stand (at attention)
5 strokes	This kanji shows a person STANDing tall on the ground (bottom stroke) with a very wide brimmed hat on his head.

昔	
	むかし – long ago
	昔(むかし) – long ago; 昔(々)(むかしむかし) – long, long ago
8 strokes	The top part of this kanji symbolizes "accumulation," with the kanji for ten (十) added to another 十. More and more "days" 日 accumulate and are multiplied by ten, making our story take place LONG, LONG AGO.

々 (3 strokes)

Stroke order: ノ ク 々

人々(ひとびと) – people; 木々(きぎ) – trees; 昔々(むかしむかし) – long, long ago

This mark has no pronunciation by itself and is not technically a kanji, but is rather a "kanji mark" or pluralizer.

■ 言葉(ことば)の探索(たんさく) Language Detection

1. Past tense of い adjectives

The past tense of い adjectives is created by dropping the "い" and adding "かった" to the adjective stem and keeping です at the end of the sentence. The affirmative past tense of an い adjective is followed by です, not でした.

A) 大きい です。 ⇨ 大き~~い~~+かった です。 ⇨ 大きかった です。 = It was big.

B) 涼(すず)しい です。 ⇨ 涼(すず)し~~い~~+かった です。 ⇨ 涼(すず)しかった です。 = It was cool (weather).

2. Past tense of な adjectives

The past tense of な adjectives is created by adding でした after the adjective without any other changes.

A) その人は 元気 です。 ⇨ 元気 でした。 = He/she was fine (energetic/healthy).

B) 不思議(ふしぎ)な はこ です。 ⇨ 不思議(ふしぎ)な はこ でした。 = It was a mysterious box.

Adjective conjugation chart: non-past and past

い adjectives	Non-past tense ～いです	Past tense ～かったです	英語
青(あお)い	青(あお)いです	青(あお)かったです	blue
面白(おもしろ)い	面白(おもしろ)いです	面白(おもしろ)かったです	interesting

な adjectives	Non-past tense	Past tense	英語
静(しず)か	静(しず)かです	静(しず)かでした	quiet
ふしぎ	ふしぎです	ふしぎでした	strange

Irregular adjective	Non-past tense	Past tense	英語
いい or 良(よ)い	いいです，良(よ)いです	良(よ)かったです	good

■ 自習(じしゅう) Self Check

Say the words in the left column, followed by the past form.

1. い adjective conjugation

is ~	⇨	was ~
A) 大きい	⇨	大きかった　です
B) 小さい	⇨	______________
C) 美しい	⇨	______________
D) 長い	⇨	長かった　です
E) 短い	⇨	______________
F) こわい	⇨	______________
G) 赤(あか)い	⇨	______________
H) みにくい	⇨	______________
I) おいしい	⇨	______________
J) つまらない	⇨	______________
K) 高(たか)い	⇨	______________
L) 安(やす)い	⇨	______________

2. な adjective conjugation

is ~	⇨	was ~
A) きれい	⇨	きれい　でした
B) 静(しず)か	⇨	______________
C) すてき	⇨	______________
D) 好(す)き	⇨	______________
E) 嫌(きら)い	⇨	______________
F) 上手(じょうず)	⇨	______________
G) 元気	⇨	______________

3. Irregular いい adjective conjugation

is ~	⇨	was ~
A) いい／良(よ)い	⇨	良(よ)かった　です
B) かっこいい	⇨	______________

4. Imagine that you saw this shrine last week. Use as many adjectives as you can in the past tense to describe it.

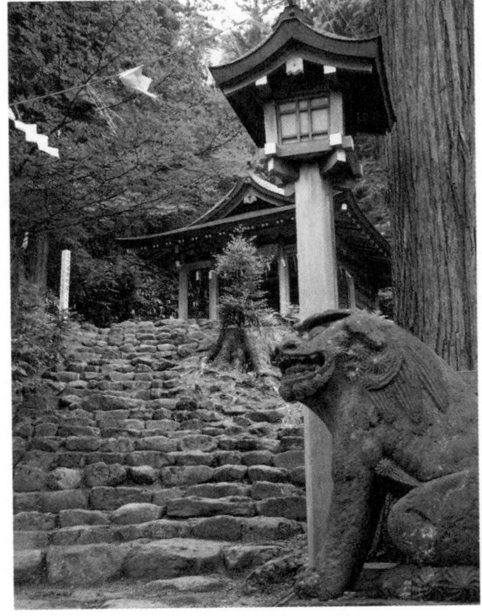

Oga Peninsula, Akita

■ 練習(れんしゅう)の時間(じかん) Time for Practice

1. Pair Practice

Pretend that you have just participated in the activities below. Ask and answer questions about how they were. Use as many adjectives as you can in your answers. Be sure to use both い and な adjectives as well as the irregular adjective いい.

例(れい) EXAMPLE

A-さん： 宿題(しゅくだい)は　どう　でしたか。 = How was the homework?
B-さん： つまらなかった　です。 そして、 長かった　です。 = It was boring. And it was long.
A-さん： 本当(ほんとう)。 = Really?

playing basketball	playing video games	reading manga
doing homework	swimming	doing karate

2. Pair Practice

With your partner, use as many Japanese adjectives in sentences to describe the following as you can until your teacher tells you to stop. Be sure to use both い and な adjectives as well as the irregular adjective いい.

A-さん　映画(えいが)は　どう　でしたか。 = How was the movie?
B-さん：(映画(えいが)は)　面白(おもしろ)かった　です。 = The movie was interesting.
A-さん：そうですか。 = Is it/that so?

NOTE: If you do not know the vocabulary in the left-hand column, you can simply say something like 「5番(ばん)は　どうでしたか。」(How was number 5?)

1. movie you saw		6. a high school class	
2. elementary teacher		7. a school event	
3. middle school (building)		8. a singer/band you heard	
4. a present		9. (your choice)	
5. something you did last night		10. (your choice)	

■ 文化箱 Culture Chest

昔々 (Long, Long Ago...)

Two common types of Japanese folklore are 昔々 (tales of long ago) and 伝説 (legends). Japanese and Western folk tales have many similarities: both often contain important lessons and both are used to transmit morals and social customs to children. Unlike most Western folk tales, though, Japanese folk tales do not always have happy endings (a tradition you can see continuing on in today's Japanese TV shows and movies). Japanese of all ages have long enjoyed listening to these stories about 動物 (animals), 神 (spirits and gods), 鬼 (demons and ogres), and お化け (monsters and ghosts). In fact, the Japanese word for "interesting", 面白い, reflects a time when families would sit at home, around the fire pit, and listen to stories. As the plot grew more interesting, the audience would draw closer to the fire, with the white 白い light from the fire reflecting on their faces 面. 面白いですね！

■ キアラ のジャーナル Kiara's Journal

Read the journal entry below, and then answer these questions.

❶ Where did Urashima Taro first see the turtle?
❷ Why did the turtle thank Urashima Taro?
❸ What sort of present did Urashima Taro receive from the princess?
❹ Did Urashima Taro follow the princess' advice about this present?
❺ How old is Urashima Taro now?

ジャーナルへ

天橋立に 来て すぐ、ある おじいさんと 会いました。その おじいさんの 名前は 浦島太郎 でした。太郎さんは 三百才 だと、言いました。(How it could be?!) 彼は とても 優しかったです。若い 時に ビーチで 亀を rescue しました。その 亀は ビーチで 寝ていましたが、意地悪な 五人の 男の子達に、teased with sticks and rocks. 太郎さんは その亀を rescued from the 意地悪な 男の子達。その 亀は、「どうも 有り難う ございました。」と、言いました。

次の日、太郎さんは また ビーチへ 行きました。木の 下に 座って、昼ご飯を 食べていました。そこへ、その 亀が 来ました。亀さんは、「きのうは、とても うれしかった です。」と、言いました。そして、「私と 一緒に 海の中に 行きませんか。」と、言いました。

太郎さんは、「いい ですね。でも、私は 海の中に 行くと 死にますよ。」と、言いました。

亀さんは、「大丈夫です。さあ、どうぞ。」と、言いました。

太郎さんは rode on the back of 亀さん、and 海の中に 行きました。There was a beautiful castle under the sea。It was called『りゅうぐうじょう』。太郎さんは、「そこは、とても すばらしかった です。」と、いいました。金と 銀の treasures が たくさん ありました。大きい 部屋に 入りました。そこに、とても きれいな 女の人が、来ました。She was a princess of the castle, and she was called『おとひめさま』。おとひめさまは、「私の 亀を 助けて

(saved) 下さって、本当に ありがとう ございました。今日は、美味しい物を たくさん 食べて下さい。」と、言いました。太郎さんは、寿司や 色々な 美味しい物を たくさん 食べました。それは、とても 楽しい 時間でした。ご飯の 後で おとひめさまは 太郎さんに プレゼントを あげました。プレゼントは とても きれいな箱でした。おとひめさまは、「これは とても 大事な 物 です。この 箱を never あけては いけません。」と、言いました。その後、亀さんと 太郎さんは ビーチに 帰りました。そして、太郎さんは 家へ 帰りました。でも、彼の お母さんと お父さんは、どこにも いませんでした。友達も いませんでした。There was nobody who knew Taro. それは、とても 不思議な 事でした。太郎さんは very confused で ビーチへ 行って、プレゼントの 箱を 開けました。すると (And then), とつぜん (suddenly) 太郎さんは 三百才の おじいさんに なりました！太郎さんは、海の中で、一日、楽しい時間を enjoy したと 思っていました。でも、それは 一日では ありませんでした。About 三百年間でした！だから、今、太郎さんは 三百才の おじいさん です。かわいそう ですね。

時の門は、すごいです！(awesome!) 私達を、昔話 (legend) の 世界 (world) に、連れて 来てくれました！(brought)

第8課の3

これは　美味しくありません。

This is not delicious.

1) 友さん、ここに
いましたか・・・・。

2) おっと・・・　ごめんなさい。おなかが
ペコペコ でした。このかには とても
美味しかった です。でも、この 漬け物は
美味しく ありません。

3) あれ、全部
食べましたか。
ひどいなあ・・・。私達は
ずっと 友さんを 待って
いましたよ。

1.

2.

3.

■ 会話(かいわ) Dialogue

REMINDER: You may see some kanji / vocabulary you do not recognize. Use the context to try to understand the meanings of those parts of the dialogue.

1. キアラ： 友さん、ここに　いましたか…。
2. 友　　： おっと…　ごめんなさい。おなかが　ペコペコ　でした。この　かには　とても　美味(おい)しかった　です。でも、この　漬け物(つもの)は　美味(おい)しく　ありません。
3. ベン　： あれ、全部(ぜんぶ)　食べましたか。ひどいなあ…。私達は　ずっと　友さんを待っていましたよ。

■ 単語(たんご) New Words

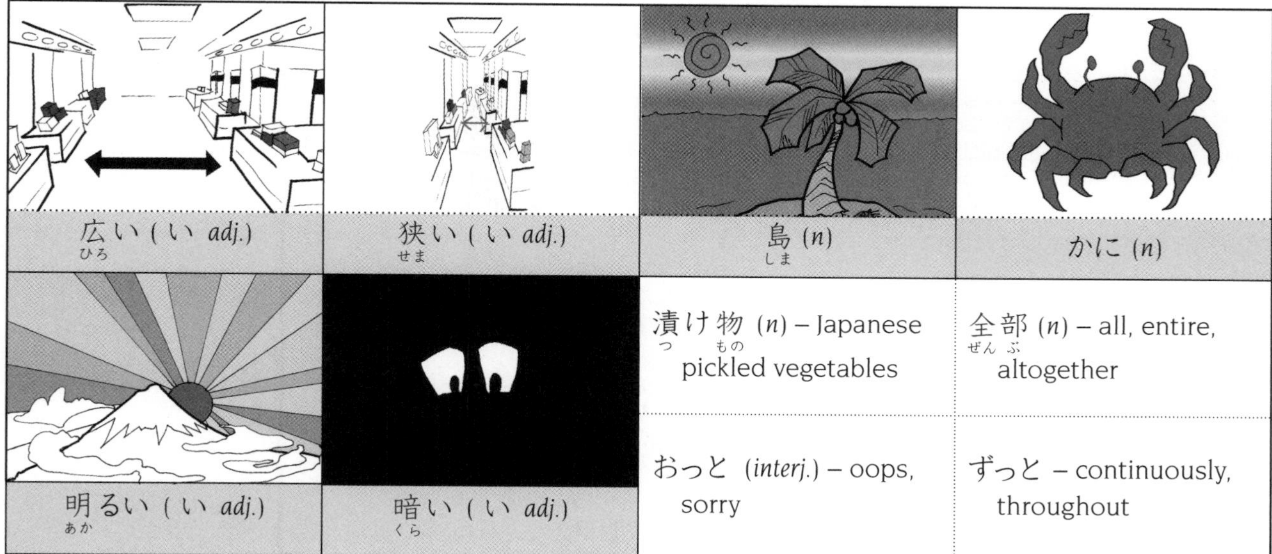

広(ひろ)い（い adj.）
狭(せま)い（い adj.）
島(しま)（n）
かに（n）
明(あか)るい（い adj.）
暗(くら)い（い adj.）
漬け物(つもの)（n）– Japanese pickled vegetables
全部(ぜんぶ)（n）– all, entire, altogether
おっと（interj.）– oops, sorry
ずっと – continuously, throughout

■ 漢字(かんじ) Kanji

有 6 strokes	ユウ(ゆう)；あ（る）– to exist, to be	一	ナ	冇	有	有	有	
	有（名）(ゆうめい) – famous							
	Imagine that the man in the moon (月) really EXISTS. Now imagine him spreading his arms out as he tries to jump over the moon (the first 2 strokes of this kanji).							

広 5 strokes	ひろ（い）– wide, spacious	丶	亠	广	広	広		
	広(ひろ)（い）– wide, spacious; 広（島）(ひろしま) – (city of) Hiroshima							
	Under a canopy (the first three strokes) it is easier to move ム (katakana MU) around if it is WIDE and SPACIOUS. Let the "mu-ving" around remind you of the katakana ム .							

島	
10 strokes	トウ(とう); しま – island
	(広(ひろ))島(しま) – (city of) Hiroshima; (バリ(ばり))島(とう) – the island of Bali; (半(はん))島(とう) – peninsula
	This kanji resembles the kanji for bird 鳥(とり), except there is a mountain 山 on the bottom. Just like a bird flies, an ISLAND, too, is a bit of the mainland that has flown off.

暗	
13 strokes	くら(い) – dark, dim
	暗(くら)い – dark
	Picture the sun (日(ひ)) going down until there is not a single sound (音) to be heard. Then everything will look and feel very DARK!

明	
8 strokes	メイ(めい) – light; あか(るい) – light, bright
	明(あか)るい – bright; 明(めい)(治時代(じじだい)) – reign period from 1868–1912
	Picture the sun (日(ひ)) about to peek out from behind the moon (月(つき)) after an eclipse. Everything will quickly become very BRIGHT!

■ 言葉(ことば)の探索(たんさく) Language Detection

1. Negating adjectives in present/future and past tenses

A. To change an い adjective to the negative non-past tense, drop the "い" and add "く　ないです" or "く　ありません" to the adjective stem. To put it into the negative past, drop the "い" and add "く　なかった　です" or "く　ありませんでした" to the adjective stem.

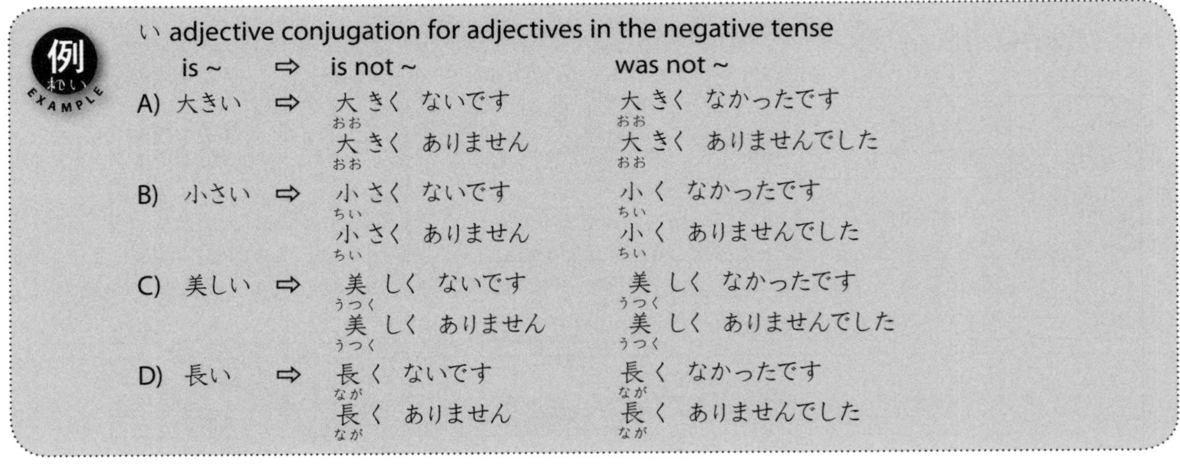

例 (れい) EXAMPLE

い adjective conjugation for adjectives in the negative tense

	is ~	⇨	is not ~	was not ~
A)	大きい	⇨	大(おお)きく　ないです	大(おお)きく　なかったです
			大(おお)きく　ありません	大(おお)きく　ありませんでした
B)	小さい	⇨	小(ちい)さく　ないです	小(ちい)く　なかったです
			小(ちい)さく　ありません	小(ちい)く　ありませんでした
C)	美しい	⇨	美(うつく)しく　ないです	美(うつく)しく　なかったです
			美(うつく)しく　ありません	美(うつく)しく　ありませんでした
D)	長い	⇨	長(なが)く　ないです	長(なが)く　なかったです
			長(なが)く　ありません	長(なが)く　ありませんでした

B. To put a な adjective in the negative non-past tense, simply add では　ありません/じゃ　ありません or では　ないです/じゃ　ないです to the end of the adjective. To change it to the negative past tense, change the ない ending to なかったです, or ありません to ありませんでした. See the examples below.

例(れい) EXAMPLE

A) きれい ⇨

	negative	negative past
A) きれい ⇨	きれいでは　ないです。	きれいでは　なかったです。
	きれいじゃ　ないです。	きれいじゃ　なかったです。
	きれいでは　ありません。	きれいでは　ありませんでした。
	きれいじゃ　ありません。	きれいじゃ　ありませんでした。
B) 静(しず)か ⇨	静(しず)かでは　ないです。	静(しず)かでは　なかったです。
	静(しず)かじゃ　ないです。	静(しず)かじゃ　なかったです。
	静(しず)かでは　ありません。	静(しず)かでは　ありませんでした。
	静(しず)かじゃ　ありません。	静(しず)かじゃ　ありませんでした。

IMPORTANT NOTES

The negative form of いい or 良(よ)い is 良(よ)く　ありません / 良(よ)く　ないです.

The negative past tense of いい or 良(よ)い becomes 良(よ)く　ありませんでした or 良(よ)く　なかったです.

Adjective conjugation chart: Non-past and negative

い adjectives	Non-past 〜い　です	Negative 〜く　ありません 〜く　ないです	Negative past 〜く　ありませんでした 〜く　なかったです	英語
面白(おもしろ)い	面白(おもしろ)い　です	面白(おもしろ)く　ありません 面白(おもしろ)く　ないです	面白(おもしろ)く　ありませんでした 面白(おもしろ)く　なかったです	interesting
まずい	まずい　です	まずく　ありません まずく　ないです	まずく　ありませんでした まずく　なかったです	tastes bad
ひどい	ひどい　です	ひどく　ありません ひどく　ないです	ひどく　ありませんでした ひどく　なかったです	terrible
な adjectives	**Non-past**	**Negative**	**Negative past**	**英語**
有名(ゆうめい)	有名(ゆうめい)です	有名(ゆうめい)では　ありません 〜じゃ　ありません 〜では　ないです 〜じゃ　ないです	有名(ゆうめい)では　ありませんでした 〜じゃ　ありませんでした 〜では　なかったです 〜じゃ　なかったです	famous
すてき	すてき　です	すてきでは　ありません 〜じゃ　ありません 〜では　ないです 〜じゃ　ないです	すてきでは　ありませんでした 〜じゃ　ありませんでした 〜では　なかったです 〜じゃ　なかったです	cool, nice

Irregular adjective		Negative	Negative past	英語
いい or 良(よ)い	いい　です 良(よ)い　です	良(よ)よく　ありません 良(よ)よく　ないです	良(よ)よく　ありませんでした 良(よ)よく　なかったです	good

■ 自習(じしゅう) Self Check

Say the words in the left column, followed by the negative form.

1. adjective conjugation practice

			is not ~	was not ~
A)	is ~	⇨		
B)	大きい	⇨	________	________
C)	小さい	⇨	________	________
D)	高い	⇨	________	________
E)	長い	⇨	________	________
F)	短い	⇨	________	________
G)	有名(ゆうめい)	⇨	________	________
H)	大好(だいす)き	⇨	________	________
I)	得意(とくい)	⇨	________	________
J)	ひま	⇨	________	________
K)	いい	⇨	________	________
L)	静(しず)か	⇨	________	________

■ 練習(れんしゅう)の時間(じかん) Time for Practice

1. Pair Practice

Play tic-tac-toe with your partner. In the first round, each player must state the NEGATIVE form of the adjective to mark and claim a square. In the next rounds, each player must state the NEGATIVE PAST form of the adjective, then the PAST, and then repeat the NEGATIVE form if necessary. If you disagree with your partner's conjugation of the adjective, say "違(ちが)います!" ("That's incorrect") and check the correct answer. If you are proven wrong, you forfeit your turn. After you have finished, find a new partner and play the game again. Time yourself, and good luck!

美味(おい)しい	こわい	高(たか)い
面白(おもしろ)い	元気(げんき)	短(みじか)い
小(ちい)さい	きれい	安(やす)い

つまらない	不思議(ふしぎ)	うるさい
長(なが)い	まずい	静(しず)か
かわいい	みにくい	大きい

すてき	いい／良(よ)い	美(うつく)しい
わるい	きたない	美味(おい)しい
静(しず)か	きれい	新(あたら)しい

2. Pair Practice

A-さん picks one picture and makes comments using the adjective supplied. B-さん disagrees, and responds with a comment using the negative or negative past form of the same adjective. Use the non-past for the first round and the past tense for the second.

Round 1: 面白(おもしろ)い interesting

A) （この）映画(えいが)は 面白(おもしろ)い ですね。 = This movie is interesting, isn't it.

B) いいえ、面白(おもしろ)くない です。 = No, it isn't interesting.

-OR- いいえ、面白(おもしろ)くありません。

Round 2:

A) 映画(えいが)は 面白(おもしろ)かったですね。 = The movie was interesting, wasn't it.

B) いいえ、面白(おもしろ)くなかったです。 = No, it wasn't interesting.

-OR- いいえ、面白(おもしろ)くありません でした。

1. きれい

2. 大きい

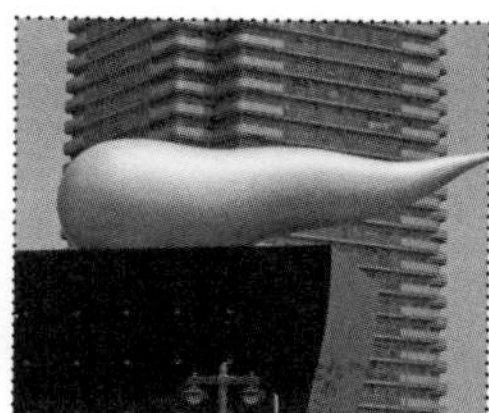
3. 長い

4. みじかい

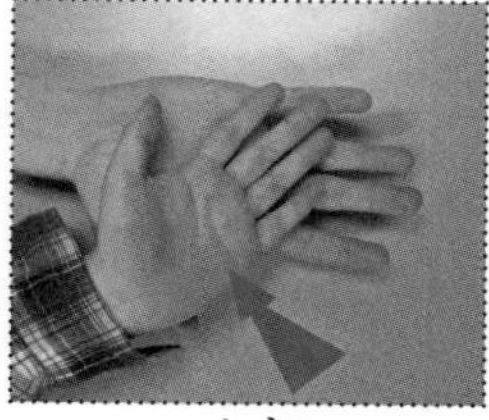
5. 小さい

6. 新しい

7. 静(しず)か

8. じゃま

■ 文化箱(ぶんかばこ) Culture Chest

擬音語(ぎおんご)・擬態語(ぎたいご)

As you learned in Chapter 2, 擬音語(ぎおんご) are onomatopoeic words that mimic or imitate sounds such as ワンワン (the sound a dog makes) and ニャーニャー (the sound a cat makes), and 擬態語(ぎたいご) are mimetic words such as the rumbling of a stomach (ペコペコ), the sound of a couch potato (ゴロゴロ), and the sound of someone speaking fluently (ペラペラ). 擬態語 and 擬音語 are used in Japanese quite often and understanding and being able to use them can be very useful for Japanese learners. Some of these sounds represent a state or an emotion and are repeated. Here are some other examples to broaden your repertoire.

ドキドキ – a nervousness or a rapidly beating heart

トントン – a light repetitive drum beat or sound of knocking on a door

ドンドン – drumming (noise), or something done rapidly

ニコニコ – what smiling might "sound" like

カアカア – a crow's cry

ワンワン – a dog's bark

ニャーニャー – a cat's meow

■ キアラのジャーナル Kiara's Journal 

Read the journal entry below, and then answer these questions.

❶ What word does Kiara use to describe what Amanohashidate was like?

❷ Both Osaka and Hiroshima are famous for what food?

❸ What food item is Amanohashidate famous for?

ジャーナルへ

天橋立は とても 面白かった です。I was hoping to get here sometime, but didn't think that it would be this way! I am still having a hard time believing that we're able to go back and forth in time. It's like something I've only seen on TV.

This Tomo character is a bit crazy! He keeps slipping away from the rest of us to find something to eat. 友さんは いつも 食べ物の メモを 書いています。I knew that Japan had some places that were more famous than others for certain types of foods. There's so much more to Japanese cuisine than I had realized. 例えば (a new word I just learned, that means "for example") 大阪は お好み焼き で 有名です。広島も、お好み焼きで 有名です。でも、大阪の お好み焼きと 広島の お好み焼きは とても 違います。天橋立は かにで 有名 です。ここの かには 本当に 美味しい です。母は かにが 大好き です。母に この かにの 料理を 作ってあげたい です。

*お好み焼き A type of Japanese food that resembles pancakes. Customers can choose which ingredients to put in it. お好み焼き literally means "fried or cooked as you like it."

第8課の4

漬け物は、美味しくありませんでした。

The pickles were not tasty!

友の日記

そばは とても 美味しかった です。
漬け物は 美味しく ありません でした。
かには とても 美味しかった です。
レストランの ウェイトレスは あまり
やさしく ありません でした。
浦島太郎さんは とても おだやかな 人 でした。

友の日記(にっき)

そばは　とても　美味(おい)しかった　です。

漬(つ)け物は　美味(おい)しく　ありません　でした。

かには　とても　美味(おい)しかった　です。

レストランの　ウェイトレスは　あまり　やさしく　ありませんでした。

浦島太郎(うらしまたろう)さんは　とても　おだやかな　人　でした。

■ 単語(たんご) New Words

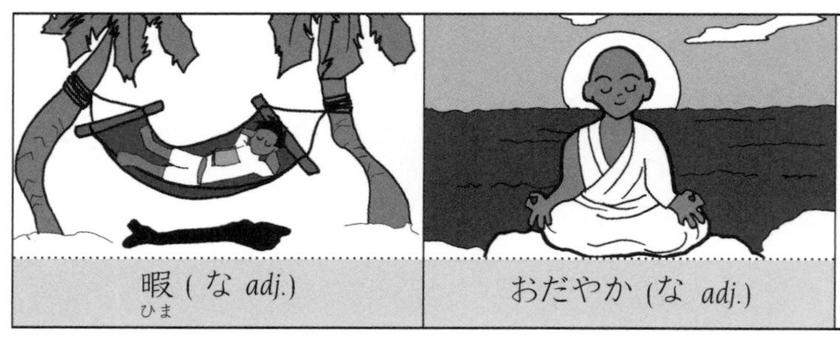

まったく (*adv.*) – really, indeed, truly

■ 言葉(ことば)の探索(たんさく) Language Detection

Adjective Conjugation Chart: Overview

い adjectives	Non-past tense ～い です	Past tense ～かった です	Negative ～く ありません ～く ないです	Negative past ～く ありませんでした ～く なかったです	英語
まずい	まずい です	まずかった です	まずく ありません まずく ないです	まずく ありませんでした まずく なかったです	tastes disgusting
ひどい	ひどい です	ひどかった です	ひどく ありません ひどく ないです	ひどく ありませんでした ひどく なかったです	terrible
忙(いそが)しい	忙(いそが)しい です	忙(いそが)しかった です	忙(いそが)しく ありません 忙(いそが)しく ないです	忙(いそが)しく ありませんでした 忙(いそが)しく なかったです	busy
な adjectives	～です	～でした	～では ありません ～では ないです (or じゃ in place of では)	～では ありませんでした ～では なかったです (or じゃ in place of では)	英語
暇(ひま)	暇(ひま) です	暇(ひま) でした	暇(ひま) では ありません 暇(ひま) では ないです	暇(ひま) では ありませんでした 暇(ひま) では なかったです	free time
おだやか	おだやか です	おだやか でした	おだやかで はありません おだやかでは ないです	おだやかでは ありませんでした おだやかでは なかったです	calm, peaceful

Irregular adjective	Non-past tense ～です	Past tense ～かった です	Negative ～く ありません ～く ないです	Negative past ～く ありませんでした ～く なかったです	英語
いい or 良(よ)い	いいです 良(よ)いです	良(よ)かった です	良(よ)く ありません 良(よ)く ないです	良(よ)く ありませんでした 良(よ)く なかったです	good

■ 練習(れんしゅう)の時間(じかん) Time for Practice

1. Pair Practice

With a partner, try to complete each row in the chart above from left to right after looking only at the English. Keep the answers covered until after you say them. Take turns.

(looking at "tastes disgusting")
A- さん： まずいです。
B- さん： まずかったです。

2. Pair Practice

Take turns stating out loud the words that should go in the blanks below.

A) Was not big ⇨ ______________________

B) ______________________ ⇨ 忙(いそが)しく ありません でした

C) ______________________ ⇨ 美しく なかった です。

D) Was not good ⇨ ______________________

E) ______________________ ⇨ かわいく なかった です。

F) Was not clean ⇨ ______________________

G) Did not have free time ⇨ ______________________

3. Self Practice

Here's your chance to see how well you've learned how to conjugate adjectives. Try to fill in all the blanks on your own.

Time Reference	Positive +/Negative –	Adjective (英語)	日本語
present/future	+	pretty	きれいです。
	–		大きく ありませんでした。
present/future	–	busy	
present/future	+		暇(ひま)です。
present/future			まずく ありません。
past	–	terrible	
present/future	+	cute	
present/future	–		不思議(ふしぎ)では ありません。
present/future			すてきでは ありません。

Time Reference	Positive +/Negative –	Adjective (英語)	日本語
past	+	interesting	
past	–		良(よ)く　ありませんでした。

4. Small Group Activity

Adjective conjugation review activity

Directions: Look at the following calendar. Ask the person to your left about a specific activity. Make sure to use the past tense if the activity has already occurred. The group members decide if the question is grammatically correct. If your question is correctly conjugated and makes sense, you win one point. If one of your partners can prove it doesn't, they get the point. Keep going around the circle until all the activities have been discussed. Begin with finding "今日" (today) on the calendar.

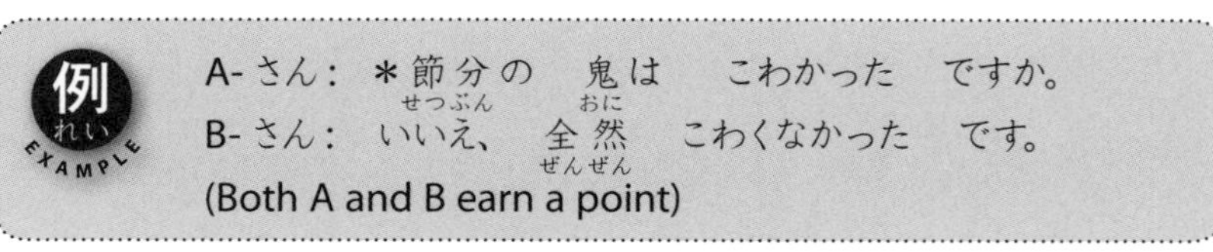

例 れい EXAMPLE
A-さん：＊節分(せつぶん)の　鬼(おに)は　こわかった　ですか。
B-さん：いいえ、　全然(ぜんぜん)　こわくなかった　です。
(Both A and B earn a point)

* 節分(せつぶん) is traditionally the day before each season. Nowadays, Setsubun is celebrated by children throwing beans at someone dressed as a goblin (typically the father of the house) while shouting「鬼はそと。 福はうち。」= "Out with the goblin. In with the good luck." The goblin represents bad luck so when he runs away he removes any bad luck from the household for the coming year. For most small children, it is a fun holiday that permits pelting your father with beans!

二月

土・日	月	火	水	木	金
	1	2	3 節分(せつぶん)	4	5 日本語のテスト
6/7 学校の ピクニック	8	9	10	11	12 買い物： チョコレート
13/14	15	16 今日	17 バンドの練習(れんしゅう)	18	19 イタリアン レストラン
20/21 カラオケ	22	23	24 数学(すうがく)のテスト	25	26
27/28	29 母の誕生日				

■ 単語チェックリスト New Word Checklist

たんごちぇっくりすと

8-1

あたらしい・新しい い *adj.* new
あぶない・危ない い *adj.* dangerous
うつくしい・美しい い *adj.* beautiful
うみ・海 *n* ocean, sea
うるさい い *adj.* noisy, loud
うれしい・嬉しい い *adj.* glad; happy
おいしい・美味しい い *adj.* delicious
かしこい い *adj.* wise; bright
かわいい い *adj.* cute
きたない い *adj.* dirty, messy
きびしい い *adj.* strict
きれい な *adj.* clean or pretty
こわい い *adj.* scary
じれったい い *adj.* irritating
ずるい い *adj.* cunning
ばかばかしい い *adj.* foolish; silly
はこ・箱 *n* box
びーち・ビーチ, はま ・浜 *n* beach
ひどい い *adj.* terrible
ふしぎ・不思議 な *adj.* mysterious
ふるい・古い い *adj.* old (used for things)
まずい い *adj.* not tasty, not good
みにくい い *adj.* ugly
やさしい・優しい い *adj.* easy, simple, kind, gentle
わがまま な *adj.* selfish

8-2

あまのはしだて・天橋立 *pn* Amanohashidate (place name)
うま・馬 *n* horse
おもしろい・面白い い *adj.* interesting
かめ・亀 *n* turtle
かれら・彼ら *pron.* they, them
こども・子供 *n* child, children
こどもたち・子供達 *n* children
すぐ *adv.* immediately, at once
たかい・高い い *adj.* expensive, high, tall
つまらない い *adj.* boring
むかし・昔 *n* long ago
むかしむかし・昔々 *n* long long ago
やすい・安い い *adj.* cheap
よい・良い い *adj.* well
わるい・悪い い *adj.* bad

8-3

あかるい・明るい い *adj.* light, bright
おっと *interj.* oops, sorry
かに *n* crab
くらい・暗い い *adj.* dark, dim
しま・島 *n* island
ずっと continuously, throughout
せまい・狭い い *adj.* narrow
ぜんぶ・全部 *n* all, entire, altogether
つけもの・漬け物 *n* pickled vegetables
ひろい・広い い *adj.* wide, spacious

8-4

おだやか な *adj.* calm, peaceful
ひま な *adj.* free (time)
まったく・全く *adv.* really, indeed, truly

Purchasing and Giving Gifts in Edo

第 9 課

Learning and Performance Goals

This chapter will enable you to

A) use the verb する after a noun to create new verbal expressions
B) use expressions useful when shopping, including making some comparisons
C) ask the price of something in a store, and ask for something bigger or cheaper
D) talk about presents you received for your last birthday and what presents you plan to give family members and friends for their birthdays
E) use the particle の to replace a noun
F) use verbs for giving and receiving
G) use 6 additional kanji
H) use the "can-do" chart found on **TimeForJapanese.com** to chart your progress for what you "can-do" for each chapter

Zoujouji Temple Gate, Tokyo

第9課の1 買い物を　します。
かもの
I'm going shopping.

1) ここは、２００年前の 東京 ですか。
2) はい。江戸時代 です。１６０３年から１８６７年まで、東京の名前は 江戸 でした。
3) 本物の江戸ですね。かっこいいですね！
4) さて、皆さん、今日のスケジュールです。始めに朝ご飯を食べます。次に、ちょっと散歩をします。それに、買い物をします。
5) 何を買いますか。
6) 浮世絵です。それから、食事をします。
7) 何を食べますか。
8) おでんです。さ、行きますよ。

■ 会話(かいわ) Dialogue 

REMINDER: You may see some kanji / vocabulary you do not recognize. Use the context to try to understand the meanings of those parts of the dialogue.

1. じゅん：　ここは、200年前(まえ)の　東京　ですか。

2. 友　　：　はい。江戸時代(えどじだい)　です。1603年から　1867年まで、東京の　名前(なまえ)は　江戸(えど)　でした。

3. ベン　：　本物(ほんもの)の　江戸(えど)　ですね。かっこいい　ですね！

4. 友　　：　さて、皆(みな)さん、今日(きょう)の　スケジュール　です。始(はじ)めに　朝(あさ)ご飯(はん)を　食べます。次(つぎ)に、ちょっと　散歩(さんぽ)をします。それに、買(か)い物(もの)を　します。

5. キアラ：　何を　買いますか。

6. 友　　：　浮世絵(うきよえ)　です。それから、食事(しょくじ)を　します。

7. ベン　：　何を　食べますか。

8. 友　　：　*おでん　です。さ、行きますよ。

* おでん – a Japanese dish boiled in a soy flavored *dashi* (broth).

■ 単語(たんご) New Words 

(買(か)う)/ 買(か)います (v)

買(か)い物(もの) (n)

(売(う)る)/ 売(う)ります (v)

店(みせ) (n)

絵(え) (n)

映画(えいが) (n)

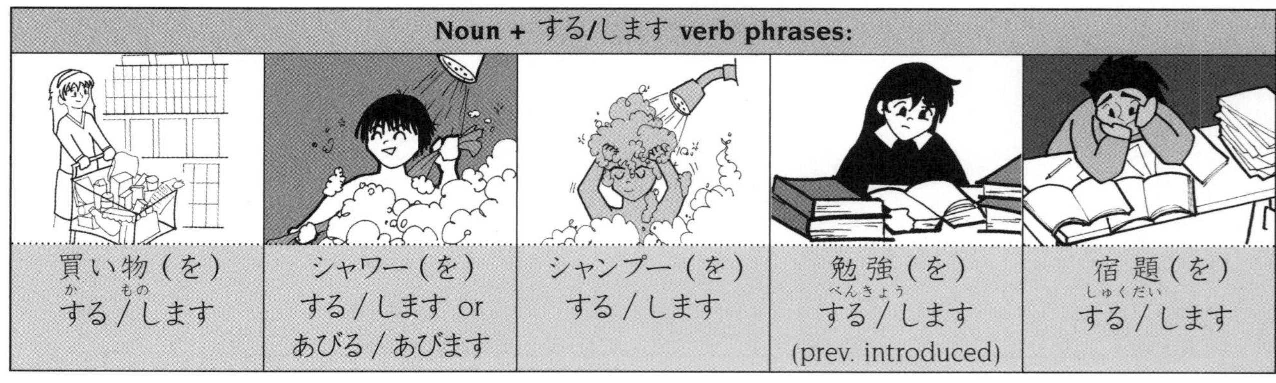

Noun + する/します verb phrases:

買(か)い物(もの)(を) する / します

シャワー (を) する / します or あびる / あびます

シャンプー (を) する / します

勉強(べんきょう) (を) する / します (prev. introduced)

宿題(しゅくだい) (を) する / します

けんか(を)する/します	電話[でんわ](を)する/します	デート(を)する/します

仲直[なかなお]り(を)する/します – reconcile, to make up/forgive

本物[ほんもの] (*n*) – real thing, genuine article

食事[しょくじ](を)する/します (*v*) – to eat/have a meal

ビデオゲーム(を)する/します (*v*) – to play video/computer games

バスケ(を)する/します (*v*) – to play basketball

旅行[りょこう](を)する/します (*v*) – to travel

カラオケ(を)する/します (*v*) – to do karaoke

サッカー(を)する/します (*v*) – to play soccer

Other words you might like to know:

浮世絵[うきよえ] (*n*) – traditional Japanese woodblock print (lit. *visions of the floating world*)

版画[はんが] (*n*) – woodblock print, art print

新版画[しんはんが] (*n*) – new woodblock print, new art print

■ 漢字[かんじ] Kanji

買 (12 strokes)

バイ[ばい]; か(う) – to buy; purchase

買[か]います – to buy, purchase; 買[か](い物[もの]) – shopping; (売[ばい])買[ばい] – selling and buying

The bottom of this character is the KANJI for shellfish (貝[かい]). In early societies, shells (貝[かい]) were used for currency to PURCHASE things. This character looks like an eye (目[め]) with two little legs under it reaching up to some shelves above to BUY something.

売 (7 strokes)

バイ[ばい]; う(る) – to sell

売[う]ります – to sell; 売[う](り物[もの]) – an item for sale

We see a samurai (士[し]) standing on a primitive table trying TO SELL the table. The problem is, the top of the table has come loose from its two legs (to the point where there is a gap between the legs and the top of the table), so it is difficult to sell.

店 (8 strokes)

テン[てん], みせ – store, shop

店[みせ] – store, shop; (売[ばい])店[てん] – shop

The first three strokes are an awning with a chimney in the middle to let out all the hot air produced by the fortune teller (占[うらない]) who claims her business is a perfectly legitimate STORE or SHOP.

■ 言葉(ことば)の探索(たんさく) Language Detection

1. (Noun) + (を) します

Many verb phrases in Japanese consist of a noun followed by します or をします. Use of the particle を is optional if there is no direct object, but is incorrect when the sentence does have a direct object. In other words, it is OK to say:

________ (noun) + optional を + します

勉強(べんきょう)を　します。

OR:

日本語を　勉強(べんきょう)　します。

but it is NOT OK to say:

日本語を　勉強(べんきょう)を　します. The particle を can only appear in a sentence once.

A) 私は　毎日(まいにち)　買い物(かもの)(を)　します。 = I shop every day.
B) ベン君は　サッカー(を)　しません。 = Ben does not play soccer.
C) きのう、私は 宿題(しゅくだい)(を)　しました。 = I did homework yesterday.
D) 八時に　食事(しょくじ)(を)　しました。 = I had a meal at 8:00.

Examples that include a direct object:

A) 私は、昨日(きのう)　レポートを　タイプしました。 = Yesterday I typed a report.
B) 日本語と　数学(すうがく)を　勉強(べんきょう)しています。 = I am studying Japanese and math.

2. Quotation marks for a quote within a quote

This pattern is used in the Journal entries from Kiara. Refer to this example as needed to help you understand this pattern.

____________ (person quoted) は、「____________ (quotation)」と、言いました。

母は、「私は、『宿題(しゅくだい)を　して　下さい 。』と、言いましたよ。」と、言いました。

Mother said, "I told you, 'Please do the homework.'"

■ 自習(じしゅう) Self Check

1. (Noun) + (を) します

Practice saying the following to yourself out loud in Japanese.

A) I wash my hair every day.
B) Ben played video games yesterday.
C) Telephone your mother.
D) I study science every day.
E) Every year I travel to Kyushu.

■ 練習の時間 Time for Practice

れんしゅう　じかん

1. Pair Practice

Ask your partner how often he or she does the following activities. Use time words such as 毎日 (まいにち) (every day), よく (often), or 時々 (ときどき) (sometimes) in your question. Draw the table below on a piece of scrap paper and record your partner's answers. Your teacher may ask you to report your results to the class.

例 (れい) EXAMPLE

A- さん： 毎日　テレビを　見ますか。
B- さん： はい、毎日　見ます。
-OR-　　いいえ、全然 (ぜんぜん)　見ません。

Remember: For あまり (not very much) and 全然 (ぜんぜん) (not at all) you must use the negative form of the verb.

する事	毎日	よく	時々	あまり	ぜんぜん
1. go to the library					
2. play video games					
3. shampoo your hair					
4. go shopping					
5. get into a fight					
6. listen to music					
7. walk with a dog					
8. take a shower					
9. eat cereal (シリアル)					
10. do homework					
11. study Japanese					
12. talk on the phone					
13. play soccer					
14. watch TV					
15. (an activity of your choice)					

2. Whole Class Activity

Using 〜しています。

Charades: Choose a slip of paper from among those your teacher will hand out. Your job is to go to the front of the classroom and act out the activity you selected. Once your classmates call out「何を　していますか。」do your best to act out the activity as your classmates try to guess what it is.

■ 文化箱(ぶんかばこ) Culture Chest

The First Posters of the Stars!

Eishousai Chouki, "Catching Fireflies", c.1795

The art of 版画(はんが), or woodblock printing, became popular in Japan during the 江戸 period (1603–1867), particularly a type of 版画(はんが) called 浮世絵(うきよえ), which literally means "scenes from the floating world." 浮世絵(うきよえ) included depictions of famous actors and actresses, travel scenes from some of the most beautiful places in Japan, and records of current events. The word "floating" may be a reference to the "floating" social position and activities of the common people depicted in 浮世絵(うきよえ) as opposed to the rigid social status of the nobility. 浮世絵(うきよえ) can also imply "images of the here and now," a favorite theme of Japanese art. Because of highly advanced printing techniques, these prints were among the first in the world to be mass-produced cheaply and purchased by the common people. Prior to this time, it was quite unthinkable for commoners to own artwork. One famous series of woodblock prints is Hiroshige's 53 Stations on the 東海道(とうかいどう) (the main road leading to Edo).

During the early years of the Meiji Restoration (1870s), Japanese ceramics and other artwork, including 浮世絵(うきよえ), poured out of Japan and into Europe for the first time. These prints, though purchased cheaply in Japan, had a tremendous impact on the work of many European artists such as Van Gogh, Gauguin, and Toulouse-Lautrec.

Today, artists in Japan still create woodblock prints; their works are known as 新版画(しんはんが) or "new woodblock prints."

■ キアラのジャーナル(きあら じゃーなる) Kiara's Journal 

Read the journal entry below, and then answer these questions.

❶ What was Tokyo called in 1837?
❷ What are ukiyoe?
❸ Kiara mentions artistic techniques that set ukiyoe apart. What are they?
❹ List three of Hokusai's traits that Kiara mentions.
❺ Why do they decide to only go window shopping rather than buying an ukiyoe?

ジャーナルへ

今日、東京へ 帰(かえ)りました！でも、1837 年の 東京 です！それに、東京の 名前は 東京では ありません。今、ここの 名前は 江戸(えど)です。1837 年の 江戸は とても 面白(おもしろ)い です。有名(ゆうめい)な アーティストが たくさん います。私は 美術(びじゅつ)が 大好き ですから、よく 勉強(べんきょう)を しました。

北斎と 広重と 歌麿の 事を 勉強しました。彼らは 江戸時代、浮世絵という アートを 作りました。その浮世絵は 21c.、all over the world で 有名です。ヨーロッパの ゴッホ (Vincent Van Gogh) と ゴーギャン (Paul Gauguin) と other Impressionist artists も received influence from those 浮世絵。One thing that makes 浮世絵 so interesting is the strong black outlining。それに , the use of space is also very different。

友さんは、「こちらへ 来て下さい。とてもいい おでんの 屋台 (food cart vendor) が あります！」と、言いました。ベン君は、「また 食べ物の 事ですか。ちょっと前に 食べたでしょう！」と、言いました。友さんは、「それは そう ですけど、少し おでんを 食べてから 北斎さんの 絵と 広重さんの 絵を 見に 行きましょう。」と、言いました。私は、「友さん、本当に 北斎さんを 知っているんですか。有名な人を 良く 知っていますね。」と、言いました。

友さんは、「この前、北斎さんと 広重さんは 店で すごい けんかを しました。僕は その 二人の 間に 入りました。そして、『ちょっと やめて下さい。あなた達は 二人とも 素晴らしい アーティスト (artist) ですよ！』と、言いました。それから、北斎さんと 僕は、一緒に 北斎さんの家に ご飯を 食べに 行きました。彼はちょっと 年を 取っています。それから とても laid back artist です。彼は 料理を するのが 上手 です。」と、言いました。

ベン君は、「そう ですか。この 辺に (around here) 浮世絵の 店は ありますか。母に おみやげを 買って 帰ります。母は 日本の 絵が 大好き です。でも、21c. の 東京の店で 買うと、それは とても 高い です。」と、言いました。

友さんは、「そう ですね。でも、時の門に 新しい 物を 持って行くのは だめ です。ここに 持って 来た物 だけ、持って 帰る事が できます。北斎さんの 絵を 持って 帰る事は 出来ません。だから、店で 浮世絵を ウィンドウショッピング しましょう。その前に おでんを 食べましょう！この店は 江戸で 一番 美味しい おでんの 店 です。」と、言いました。

第9課の2 はい、一冊 1,025円* です。
いっさつ　えん

Yes, one volume is 1,025 yen.

1.
1) ごめん 下さ〜い！

2.
2) は〜い。いらっしゃいませ。
3) この 本は、いくら ですか。

3.
4) はい、一冊 1,025円 です。

4.
5) じゃあ、二冊下さい。
6)はい、二冊で 2,050円 です。
7) すみません、筆も 三本 下さい。

5.
8) はい、一本1,500円 ですから、三本で 4,500円です。全部で 6,550円です。
9)じゃあ、10,000円から お願いします。

6.
10) はい、10,000円 から ですね。
11) では、3,450円の おつりです。どうも、ありがとう ございました。また どうぞ。

■ 会話(かいわ) Dialogue

REMINDER: You may see some kanji / vocabulary you do not recognize. Use the context to try to understand the meanings of those parts of the dialogue.

1. じゅん　：ごめん下さ～い！
2. 店員　：は～い。いらっしゃいませ。
3. ベン　：この本は、いくら　ですか。
4. 店員　：はい、一冊(いっさつ)　1,025 円*　です。
5. ベン　：じゃあ、二冊(にさつ)　下さい。
6. 店員　：はい、二冊で　2,050 円　です。
7. キアラ：すみません、筆(ふで)も　三本(さんぼん)　下(くだ)さい。
8. 店員　：はい、一本(いっぽん)　1,500 円　ですから、三本で　4,500 円　です。全部(ぜんぶ)で　6,550 円　です。
9. 友　：じゃあ、10,000 円から　お願いします。
10. 店員　：はい、10,000 円から　ですね。
11. 店員　：では、3,450 円の　おつり　です。どうも、ありがとう　ございました。またどうぞ。

* NOTE: Even though conversations in this chapter use the modern Japanese currency term 円(えん), the Japanese actually did not start using 円(えん) as their official currency until around 1870 at the beginning of the Meiji Restoration.

■ 単語(たんご) New Words

どう (exp.) – how about it?

全部で(ぜんぶで) (exp.) – in all; total; all together

特別(とくべつ) (n/ な adj.) – special

別(べつ) (n/ な adj.) – separate

別々(べつべつ) (n/ な adj.) – separately; individually

(いただく) いただきます (v) – (polite) to receive, I will receive

Counter for bound objects (books, magazines, notebooks, etc.)		Counter for long cylindrical objects such as pencils, straws, bottles, etc.		Counter for cupfuls	
一冊 いっさつ 二冊 にさつ 三冊 さんさつ 四冊 よんさつ 五冊 ごさつ 六冊 ろくさつ	七冊 ななさつ 八冊 はっさつ 九冊 きゅうさつ 十冊 じゅっ/じっさつ 何冊 なんさつ	一本 いっぽん 二本 ほん 三本 さんぼん 四本 よんほん 五本 ごほん 六本 ろくぽん	七本 ななほん 八本 はっぽん 九本 きゅうほん 十本 じゅっ/じっぽん 何本 なんぼん	一杯 いっぱい 二杯 にはい 三杯 さんばい 四杯 よんはい 五杯 ごはい 六杯 ろくはい	七杯 ななはい 八杯 はっぱい 九杯 きゅうはい 十杯 じゅっ/じっぱい 何杯 なんばい

■ 漢字(かんじ) Kanji

全 6 strokes	ゼン(ぜん) – all, entirely	全
	全(部)(ぜんぶ) – all things, everything; 全(然)(ぜんぜん) – not at all; 全(国)(ぜんこく) – the entire country	
	The first 2 strokes look like a roof. The final four strokes are the kanji for king (王(おう)). We all like to think we are kings who rule over ALL things under our roof ENTIRELY.	

部 11 strokes	ブ(ぶ) – section, group of, part	立 音
	(剣道)部(けんどうぶ) – kendo club; (全)部(ぜんぶ) – all things, everything	音 部
	The left side of this character shows someone standing (立) on a mouth (口), while waving a banner (the last three strokes). You can be sure that you do not want to be a PART of that crazy scene.	

円 4 strokes	エン(えん), まる(い) – circle, yen, round	円
	円(えん) – yen; 円い(まるい) – round	
	This kanji has two boxes on top to write in the cost in YEN of each item you are buying, and a space at the bottom to write in the total cost of your order in YEN.	

■ 言葉(ことば)の探索(たんさく) Language Detection

1. Useful shopping expressions

ごめん 下(くだ)さい! = Excuse me! (Said as you enter someone's house or a store.)

いらっしゃいませ! = Welcome! (Said by the store or restaurant employees as customers enter.)

これは　いくら　ですか。	=	How much is this?
五千円(ごせんえん)　です。	=	It is 5,000 yen.
あの辞書(じしょ)を　下(くだ)さい。	=	I'll take that dictionary/Please give me that dictionary.
このＳサイズの　シャツを　下(くだ)さい。	=	I'll take this small shirt/Please give me this small shirt.
10,000 円から、お願(ねが)いします。	=	Here is 10,000 yen. (*lit*. Please take it out of a 10,000 yen [bill].)

NOTE: This phrase is optional since it is very common for customers to silently hand their money over.

5,000 円の　おつりです。	=	Your change is 5,000 yen.

2. Using the particle で to mean "for . . ."

三つで… For three, it's . . .

The particle で comes after the counter word indicating the quantity of the items in question. This use of で occurs mainly when buying things in stores or restaurants.

quantity + で followed by the cost

A) 二つで　5ドル　= for 2 it is $5

B) 三枚(まい)で　300 円(えん)　= for 3 sheets, it is 300 yen

C) 十本で　1,000 円(えん)　= for 10, it is 1,000 yen

NOTE: で is not necessary when you are referring to one item.

一つ　1,500 円　です。 = One is 1,500 yen.

（カフェテリアで）

A- さん：　このハンバーガーは　一つ　いくら　ですか。
= How much is this hamburger?

B- さん：　200 円です。　= ¥200.

A- さん：　じゃあ、四つで、800 円　ですね。四つ、　下さい。
= Well then, for 4, it's ¥800 (right). 4 please.

（店で）

A- さん：　この　黒いシャツは　三枚(まい)で　いくら　ですか。
= This black shirt, how much for three?

B- さん：　それ　ですか。　それは　三枚で　5000 円　です。
= That (one)? That (one) is 3 for ¥5,000.

A- さん：　安い　ですね。　じゃあ、　それを　三枚　下さい。
= That's cheap! Well then, three of those please.

3. Counters

As you learned in Chapter 2, different word endings are used to count people and things in Japanese. For objects, the counter usually depends on the shape. For instance, long cylindrical objects such as pencils, pens, tubes, or bottles use the counter 本.

NOTE: The counter usually follows the object that is being counted. For a complete list of counters, see the chart in Appendix 1. If you don't know the exact counter for something, you can usually use the generic counters 一つ、二つ、三つ、etc. However, knowing the correct counter and using it properly makes you a much more fluent speaker of Japanese.

■ 自習(じしゅう) Self Check

1. Useful shopping expressions

Practice saying the following out loud to yourself in Japanese.

A) How much do those pants near you cost?
B) They are 6,500 yen.
C) Here is 7,000 yen.
D) Your change is 500 yen.

2. Practice with counters

Practice asking for various numbers of classroom objects using these counters:

- generic counters (一つ、二つ、…)
- ～枚(まい)
- ～人
- ～本
- ～冊(さつ)
- ～ページ

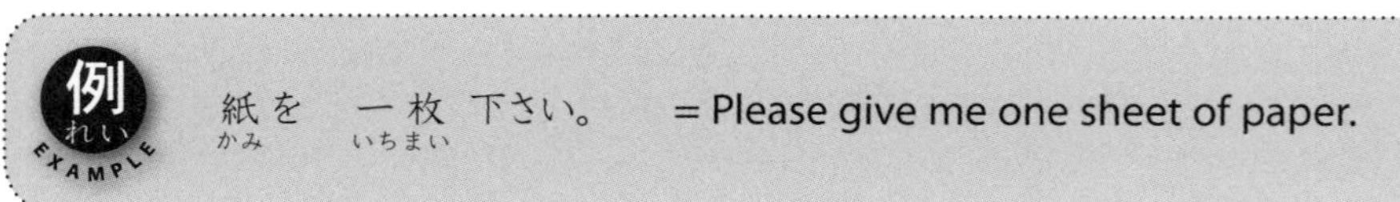

例 れい EXAMPLE
紙(かみ)を 一枚(いちまい) 下さい。 = Please give me one sheet of paper.

3. Review your counting skills. Count from 1,000 to 10,000, by thousands. Then practice asking for these items:

- 1,000 sheets of paper
- 2,000 sheets of paper
- 3,000 pencils
- 4,000 pencils
- 5,000 people
- 6,000 people
- 7,000 books
- 8,000 books
- 9,000 trees
- 10,000 trees
- 11,000 men
- 12,000 women
- 13,000 (your choice of item)
- 14,000 (your choice of item)
- 15,000 (your choice of item)
- 20,000 (your choice of item)
- 30,000 people
- 40,000 people
- 52,000 people
- 61,000 people
- 75,000 people
- 88,000 people
- 93,000 people
- 100,000 people
- 999,999 people

■ 練習の時間 Time for Practice

1. Pair Practice

Choose three of the stores below and develop a skit by acting out the roles of customer (客) and store employee (店員). You must buy at least one thing from each of the three stores. Use the dialogue below as a model. Then switch roles. Your teacher may ask you to present one of your skits to the class.

本　一冊　¥300

花　一本　¥150

コーラ　Mサイズ　¥140

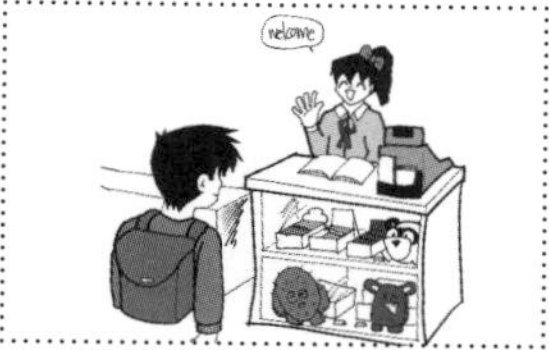

鉛筆　一本　¥55

ノート　一冊　¥150

消しゴム　一つ　¥57

スパゲッティー　一つ　¥520

ガーリックパン　三枚　¥100

Lサイズの　赤い

タンクトップ　一枚　¥1,225

(ケーキ屋で)

店員　：いらっしゃいませ。

客　：こんにちは。この　ケーキは　一つ　いくら　ですか。

店員　：その　ケーキ　ですか。一つ、350円　です。

客　：じゃ、二つ　下さい。

店員　：はい。二つで　700円　です。1,000円　から　ですね。はい、300円の　おつりです。ありがとうございました。また、どうぞ。

(clerk hands over cakes and the change)

客　：どうも。

2. Pair Practice

You are the customer and your partner is the waiter/waitress at a new Italian restaurant. Use the menu below to order the following items. The waiter/waitress then tells you how much your meal will cost.

One slice of cheese pizza and two bottles of orange juice.

Customer :　チーズの　ピザを　一枚と　オレンジジュースを　二本　下さい。

Waiter/waitress :　全部で　1,400円です。

a. two pepperoni pizzas and one iced coffee
b. one green salad, one vegetarian pizza, and one cola
c. one Caesar salad, one cheese pizza, and one ice cream
d. one pepperoni pizza and one cheese pizza
e. one green salad, two vegetarian pizzas, and two orange juices

イタリアンレストラン・ナポリ
メニュー

サラダ		デザート	
グリーンサラダ	300	アイスクリーム	350
シーザーサラダ	400		
ピザ		飲み物	
ペパローニ	650	コーラ	250
チーズ	600	オレンジジュース	400
ベジタリアン	650	アイスコーヒー	300

■ 文化箱(ぶんかばこ) Culture Chest

Innovating and Conserving

Japanese have long been creative innovators of technology. Did you know, for instance, that the original Space Invaders スペースインベーダー video game came out in Japan in 1978? Many are equally enthusiastic consumers of new technological products. Stores are often busy with shoppers purchasing the latest new devices. Examples include utensils for the kitchen, televisions and electronics for the living room, and even heated toilet seats for the bathroom! Cell phones and handheld devices for playing games and watching movies are often developed and released in Japan long before they appear in other international markets.

Even though consumerism is alive and well in Japan, the Japanese also lead much of the world in environmentally friendly technology in a number of fields. Many individuals recognize the need to balance economic growth with environmental conservation. Beginning in the late 1990s, purchases in stores that previously had been elaborately wrapped now receive only a small piece of decorative tape, and many consumers bring their own shopping bags.

Recycling in cities is now largely mandated by the Japanese government and strictly enforced. Everyone must carefully sort glass, paper, metals, and other trash before putting it out for garbage pickup. How does your community work toward promoting good environmental standards?

■ キアラのジャーナル　Kiara's Journal

Read the journal entry below, and then answer these questions.

❶ Where exactly did they meet Hokusai?

❷ Why did they change their plan from window shopping to real shopping?

❸ What did Kiara and Ben buy? How much did their purchases cost?

ジャーナルへ

江戸の おでんは とても おいしかった です。おでんを食べた後、買い物を しました。江戸の 銀座に たくさんの kabuki theater が あります。北斎さんと、彼の 好きな kabuki theater の 前で 会いました。そして、一緒に 店に 浮世絵を 見に 行きました。私は富士山の 絵が 大好き です。その店に 色々な 富士山の 絵が ありました。ベン君は 歌舞伎役者 (kabuki actor) の絵が 好き でした。

Even though 友さん had said we could not take anything home (through the 時の門), we decided to buy some things anyway. While we were eating おでん、友さん also mentioned that we may be able to transfer things from our 時の門 trip to the 21st century if we bury a time capsule and then dig it up when we get back to our modern 東京. 友さんは、「まだ、はっきり 分かりませんが ... if we really can do it or not。」と、言いました。 We will have to find out the right place and right time to bury the time capsule, but all of us were excited about buying real 浮世絵 at the 店.

私は、「すみません、この北斎の 絵は いくら ですか。」と、聞きました。

店員さんは、「それですか。それは とてもいい 北斎の 版画 ですよ。特別、安くしますよ。千二百円で どうですか。」と、言いました。

北斎さんは、「千二百円！私は あなたに 三百円で 売りましたよ！ この人達は 僕の友達です。安くして下さい。」と、言いました。

ベン君は、「じゃあ、これも 買います。二枚で いくら ですか。」と、聞きました。

店員さんは、「北斎さんの 友達 ですから 二枚で 二千円で どうでしょう。」と、言いました。

北斎さんは、「いい でしょう。ベン君の 目は この絵の 中の 色と 同じ ですね。」と、言いました。

ベン君は、「あ、そう ですね。では、その絵を 下さい。」と、言いました。

店員さんは、「はい、いい 買い物 ですね。」と、言いました。

As we went out the door、友さん bowed to the storekeeper and said「どうも、すみませんでした。」

とても きれいな 浮世絵を 買って 楽しかった です。持って 帰れたら よかったですけど。

お休み。

第9課の3 もっと 大きい スリッパは ありますか。

Are there bigger slippers?

1.
1) すみません。もっと 大きい スリッパは ありますか。
2) すみません。スリッパは、その 大きさだけ です。大丈夫 ですか。
3) 大丈夫 です。ありがとう ございます。
2.
4) 私は、もっと 小さい スリッパが いい です。もっと 小さいのは、ありますか。
5) すみません。本当に、その サイズ だけ です。もっと 小さいのも もっと 大きいのも、ありません。
3.
4.
6) 残念 です。
7) 大丈夫 ですか。
5.
8) はい、大丈夫 です。
9) さ、部屋に 行って 休みましょう。
10) そう ですね。僕は、お風呂に 入ります。
6.

■ 会話(かいわ) Dialogue

REMINDER: You may see some kanji / vocabulary you do not recognize. Use the context to try to understand the meanings of those parts of the dialogue.

1. ベン　：　すみません。もっと　大きい　スリッパは　ありますか。
2. 旅館(りょかん)の人：　すみません。スリッパは、その　大きさ　だけです。大丈夫(だいじょうぶ)　ですか。
3. ベン　：　大丈夫(だいじょうぶ)　です。ありがとう　ございます。
4. 友　：　私は、もっと　小さい　スリッパが　いい　です。もっと　小さいのは、ありますか。
5. 旅館の人：　すみません。本当(ほんとう)に、その　サイズ　だけ　です。もっと　小さいのも　もっと　大きいのも、ありません。
6. 友　：　残念(ざんねん)　です。
7. 旅館の人：　大丈夫(だいじょうぶ)　ですか。
8. 友　：　はい、大丈夫(だいじょうぶ)　です。
9. キアラ　：　さ、部屋(へや)に　行って　休みましょう。
10. じゅん　：　そう　ですね。僕(ぼく)は、*お風呂(ふろ)に　入(はい)ります。

* お風呂(ふろ) – a traditional Japanese bath which is deep and usually rectangular.

■ 単語(たんご) New Words

	もっと (*adv.*) – more
(探(さが)す)/ 探(さが)します (*v*)	残念(ざんねん) (*n*/ な *adj.*) – regrettably, unluckily

■ 言葉(ことば)の探索(たんさく) Language Detection

1. もっと　安(やす)い　靴(くつ)は　ありますか。 **Do you have any cheaper shoes?**

To ask for something cheaper, bigger, smaller, etc., use this pattern:

もっと ADJECTIVE + NOUN は　ありますか。

A) もっと　明(あか)るい　部屋(へや)は　ありますか。 = Is there a brighter room?
B) もっと　小さい　自転車(じてんしゃ)は　ありますか。 = Is there a smaller bicycle?
C) もっと　短(みじ)かい　靴下(くつした)は　ありますか。 = Do you have any shorter socks?
D) もっと　静(しず)かな　犬は　いますか。 = Is there a quieter dog?

2. Using の to replace nouns

もっと　大きいのは　ありますか。 = Do you have a bigger one?

With the "もっと ADJECTIVE + NOUN は　ありますか。" pattern, the NOUN can be dropped and replaced by の if the NOUN is understood by context. Though this looks as though you have both the particles の and は here, remember that the の is used in place of a noun in this situation.

NOTE: For な adjectives, you MUST include な after this type of adjective whether it is followed by a noun or by の.

A) もっと　美味しいのは　ありますか。 = Is there a more delicious one?
B) もっと　明るいのは　ありますか。 = Is there a brighter one?
C) もっと　すてきなのは　ありますか。 = Is there a nicer one?
D) もっと　きれいなのは　ありますか。 = Is there a prettier one?

■ 自習 Self Check

1. もっと ADJECTIVE + NOUN は　ありますか。

Practice saying the following in Japanese out loud to yourself.

A) Do you have any larger shirts?
B) Do you have any cheaper shoes?
C) Are there any more delicious restaurants?
D) Are there any brighter classrooms?
E) Do you have any darker T-shirts?
F) Are there any smaller jeans?
G) Are there any taller buildings? (たてもの)
H) Is there any more expensive sushi?

2. もっと ADJECTIVE + のは　ありますか。

Practice saying the following in Japanese out loud to yourself.

A) Are there any more difficult ones?
B) Are there any scarier ones?
C) Are there any wider ones?
D) Are there any darker ones?
E) Are there any quieter ones?
F) Are there any cleaner ones?
G) Do you have any shorter ones?
H) Do you have any blacker ones?

■ 練習の時間 Time for Practice

1. Small Group Practice

Adjective review

Place a complete set of adjective vocabulary cards in a pile in the middle of a desk or the floor, face down. Then make another set of flashcards with four of each of the following: *present*, *past*, *negative*, and *negative past*. Mix this set of cards and place them in a separate pile, face down. The first person turns over one card in each pile and makes a sentence according to the cards. For instance, if the cards are "小さい" and "negative," your sentence would use the negative form of 小さい. It might be something like: その人の　かばんは　小さくない　です。 (*That person's bag is not small.*) Keep going through both piles until everyone has had a chance to make several sentences. Help your group members if they get stuck.

2. Small Group Practice

Make two sets of cards, at least ten cards in each set. One set should have a different noun written (or drawn) on each card, while the other set should have an adjective written on each card. Place each pile face down and take turns turning over the top card in each pile. Once you know the two words, make a comparative sentence. Shuffle the cards and repeat. Some of your sentences might be silly!

You have the cards 本 *and* 高い.
もっと　高い本は　ありますか。 = Do you have any more expensive books?

3. Pair Practice

Use the menu in section 2 of this chapter. Take turns being the picky customer. This time, when you order, ask for something bigger, smaller, tastier, or in some way different than what is on the menu. Take turns.

4. Pair Practice

You are going clothing shopping in Shinjuku in Tokyo with your friend who is quite picky. Help your friend find something to buy. Here are several items that you both look at. Your friend makes a negative comment about each item, and then asks for a different one. Use the example dialogue below as a model.

You　：この　赤(あか)いTシャツは　どう　ですか。
友だち：小さいです。　もっと　大きい　サイズは　ありませんか。

A) red T-shirt
B) blue shoes
C) black pants
D) white jacket
E) purple socks

■ 文化箱(ぶんかばこ) Culture Chest

Taking a Bath, Japanese Style

In Japan, bathing is a time-honored social ritual, in part due to the large number of natural hot springs there. Oita Prefecture alone has over 4,000 natural hot springs, and, in the winter, even Japanese monkeys have been known to enjoy a hot dip.

Japanese お風呂(ふろ) (baths) include natural outdoor 温泉(おんせん), or hot springs, often found in scenic mountain locations; public baths known as 銭湯(せんとう); and simple baths at home. Regardless of which sort of bath is being used, the bather first washes with soap and shampoo and then uses the shower or water faucet outside the tub to thoroughly rinse off. The bather then carefully steps into the deep hot water in the tub for a long relaxing soak. Guests staying with a family are often honored with the first bath. Remember not to drain the water when you are done, though, since everyone

Hotel onsen, Izu Peninsula

in the family uses the same hot water. Traditional Japanese inns, or 旅館 have large bathing areas for their guests. Today, these baths are segregated into male baths, 男風呂, and female baths, 女風呂, and are sometimes quite elaborate, including waterfalls and multiple bathing pools of different temperatures.

■ キアラのジャーナル **Kiara's Journal** 

Read the journal entry below, and then answer these questions.

❶ What did Kiara, Ben, and Tomo do after they bought the ukiyoe?
❷ Did the slippers at the inn fit Ben?
❸ Describe the men's bath.
❹ Describe the women's bath.

ジャーナルへ

浮世絵を 買って 旅館を 探しました。下町に かわいい 旅館が ありました。ベン君には その旅館の スリッパは ちょっと 小さかった です。ベン君は、「もっと 大きいのは ありますか。」と、聞きました。

旅館の人は、「ああ、すみません。それだけ です。もっと 大きいのは ありません。」と、言いました。

ベン君は、「大丈夫 です。ありがとう ございます。」と、言いました。その後、部屋へ行きました。

私の 部屋は とても きれい でした。後で、お風呂に 入りました。お風呂は ちょっと 小さかった ですが、**soaking in a hot bath** で、とても リラックス しました。

お風呂の 後、旅館で 皆で 一緒に 晩ご飯を 食べました。ベン君と じゅん君は とても 元気に 話しました。ベン君は、「この旅館の 男の人の お風呂には、四つの お風呂が ありました。それに 高い 滝 **(waterfall)** も ありました。すばらしかったです。」と、言いました。

私は「嘘でしょう。女の人の お風呂は もっと 小さかった です。熱くて、リラックス しましたが、ちょっと 暗かった です。」と、言いました。

友さんは、「残念 ですが、昔の 日本には、そういう 事が 良く ありました。江戸時代、**guests** は だいたい 男の人 でした。**In the 20th and 21st centuries, of course, this changes.** でも 今は、江戸時代 で、侍 が いる時代 ですからね。」と、言いました。

じゅん君は、「そう ですね。去年、家族と 一緒に 山へ 行った時に、女風呂 **(women's bath)** も、男風呂 **(men's bath)** も、同じくらいの サイズ でした。」と、言いました。

第9課の4 私は　ベン君に、おせんべいと漫画(まんが)を　あげます。

I will give senbei and a comic book to Ben.

1) はい、私は
ベン君に、
おせんべいと
漫画を あげます。

2) ありがとう！
いただきます。

3)
これは、
僕達から
友さんに
です。
どうぞ。

1

4) 富士山の
浮世絵 ですか。
すばらしい！
ありがとう。

2.

5) 私は、
じゅん君に
この筆を
もらいました。
じゅん君、
ありがとう。

3.

6) キアラさん、それで、
漢字を 練習して下さいね。

4.

7)
じゃ、僕は
キアラさんに、
漢字の 名前を
あげます。

8) すてき！漢字の 名前を
もらう事は、とても うれしい
です。ありがとう。

5.

■ 会話(かいわ) Dialogue 

REMINDER: You may see some kanji / vocabulary you do not recognize. Use the context to try to understand the meanings of those parts of the dialogue.

1. キアラ　：　はい、私は　ベン君(くん)に、おせんべいと　漫画(まんが)を　あげます。
2. ベン　　：　ありがとう！いただきます。
3. じゅん　：　これは、僕達(ぼくたち)から　友さんに　です。どうぞ。
4. 友　　　：　富士山(ふじさん)の　浮世絵(うきよえ)　ですか。すばらしい！ありがとう。
5. キアラ　：　私は、じゅん君に　この筆(ふで)を　もらいました。じゅん君、ありがとう。
6. じゅん　：　キアラさん、それで、漢字(かんじ)を　練習(れんしゅう)して　下(くだ)さいね。
7. 友　　　：　じゃ、僕(ぼく)は、キアラさんに、漢字(かんじ)の　名前(なまえ)を　あげます。
8. キアラ　：　すてき！漢字(かんじ)の　名前を　もらう事は、とても　うれしい　です。ありがとう。

■ 単語(たんご) New Words 

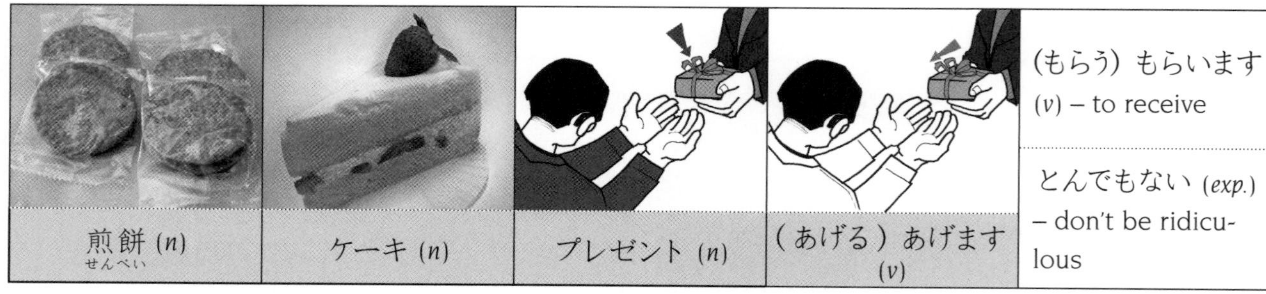

煎餅(せんべい) (*n*)	ケーキ (*n*)	プレゼント (*n*)	(あげる) あげます (*v*)	(もらう) もらいます (*v*) – to receive とんでもない (*exp.*) – don't be ridiculous

■ 言葉(ことば)の探索(たんさく) Language Detection

1. Verbs for giving: やります/あげます

These verbs mean "to give."

a. やります is very informal. Use it to talk about giving something to people younger than you or giving food to animals.

b. あげます is used in most circumstances. It means you are giving something to someone of equal or greater status. Now it is becoming more common to use あげます in situations where it would be OK to use やります.

Use the particle に after the name of the person who is given something; に indicates the recipient of the action.

A) 私は　あなたに　本を　あげます。 = I will give you a book.

B) じゅん君は　お母さんに　帽子(ぼうし)を　あげました。 = Jun gave his mom a hat.

C) キアラさんは　先生に　日本の　おみやげを　あげました。
= Kiara gave her teacher a souvenir from Japan.

D) ベン君は　犬に　水を　やりました。 = Ben gave some water to the dog.

2. **Verbs of receiving:** もらいます/いただきます

もらいます and the more polite いただきます both mean "to receive." いただきます generally implies that something was received from a superior and もらいます is more commonly used between family and friends. Note that the giver can be followed by either particle に or particle から.

A) 私は　愛子(あいこ)さんに　箱(はこ)を　もらいました。
= I received a box from Aiko.

B) 花子さんは　ともき君から　ネックレスを　もらいます。
= Hanako will receive a necklace from Tomoki.

C) 母の日(ひ)に、お母さんは　じゅんさんに　ばらを　三本　もらいました。
= On Mother's Day, Jun's mother received three roses from him.

D) 私は　山本先生から　とても　きれいな　絵(え)を　いただきました。
= I received a very pretty painting from Mr. Yamamoto (a teacher).

NOTE: Before Japanese begin a meal, everyone says "いただきます," literally "I will receive," as a way of thanking all who have had a hand in preparing the food. Japanese also say "ごちそうさまでした" after a meal to show their appreciation.

■ 自習(じしゅう) Self Check

1. あげます/やります **– to give**

Try to say the following out loud to yourself in Japanese.

A) Mr. Suzuki will give juice to the first year students.
B) I gave cookies (クッキー) to the Russian teacher.
C) Mary gave some money (お金(かね)) to her friend.
D) Ichirou gave rice to the koi (こい [fish]).
E) Jun's mother did not give Ben a birthday present.
F) (compose a sentence of your own)

2. もらいます/いただきます **– to receive**

A) I got an eraser from the teacher.
B) Please get paper from your friend.
C) Yes, I have received the present.
D) My little brother received a CD from my uncle.
E) Aiko received some chocolates (チョコレート) from Ben.
F) (compose a sentence of your own)

3. Try to say the following in Japanese. Use やります.

A) I gave the cat a new toy. (おもちゃ)
B) The teacher gave the flowers some water.
C) My grandfather gave the dog some milk.
D) Please give the horse some senbei.
E) I gave my little sister a new dress.
F) (compose a sentence of your own)

■ 練習の時間 Time for Practice

1. Pair Practice

This year for their birthdays, the people shown below received presents from each other. Following the pattern in the example, use as many different combinations of people and presents as possible to ask and state who might have received what from whom.

(talking about the people pictured below are A- さん and B- さん)
A- さん ： お兄さんは　お父さんから　何を　もらいましたか。
B- さん ： お父さんに　ネクタイを　一本　もらいました。

father

uncle

younger sister

older brother

Kiara

mother

2. Pair Practice

Use Japanese to ask your partner what he/she received from family members on his/her last birthday. Take turns.

You　： 誕生日プレゼントに　お母さんに　何を　もらいましたか。
B- さん ： 母から　このブレスレットを　もらいました。

3. Pair Practice

A-さん should ask B-さん in Japanese what kind of presents B-さん will give each of the family members and friends listed here. Use the sample dialogue below to get started.

A- さん ： お父さんの　誕生日プレゼントに　何を　あげますか。
B- さん ： そうですね。　父に　靴下を　あげます。

A) ➲ father for Father's Day (父の日) – 3 books
B) ➲ mother for Mother's Day (母の日) – 2,000 円
C) ➲ friend Keiko for her birthday – a blue t-shirt
D) ➲ younger brother for his birthday – 5 pencils and a notebook
E) ➲ English teacher for birthday – cake
F) ➲ pet hamster (ハムスター) – a ball (玉)
G) ➲ the school principal (校長先生) – trip souvenir (おみやげ)
H) ➲ your grandfather/grandmother's birthday present

■ 文化箱 Culture Chest

Gift Giving in Japan

Gift-giving practices in Japan are elaborate and complex. It is customary for most people to send beautifully-wrapped presents called お中元 (from the beginning to middle of July) and お歳暮 (around Dec. 20-28) to people with whom they have a relationship: their family doctor, children's teachers, mentors, bosses and so on. Department stores take full economic advantage of these customs with fancy displays of boxed gifts during those seasons, things like perfectly-ripe fruits or nicely-presented gift sets of coffee or tea.

Japanese also give and receive gifts in many other situations. For instance, it is customary to take a gift when you visit someone's house or when you come back from a trip. When in doubt about gift giving in Japan, it is safest to consult with your 先生 or a Japanese person.

■ キアラのジャーナル Kiara's Journal

Read the journal entry below, and then answer these questions.

❶ What did they decide to do in Asakusa?
❷ What did Kiara give Ben?
❸ What did Kiara receive from Jun?
❹ What did Tomo receive from Jun?
❺ What was Tomo's present to Kiara?
❻ How do the group members feel about each other now, after having travelled together for quite a while?

ジャーナルへ

今日 私は 遅くまで 寝ました。とても 疲れて いました。ゆっくり 朝ご飯を 食べてから、皆で 浅草神社へ 行きました。じゅん君の 家は その神社の 近くなので、江戸時代の その場所 (place) が 見たかったから です。それに、そこが、the right place for the time capsule だから です！

浅草神社は 古くて とても 有名 です。そこで ベン君は、「じゅん君の 家と 同じ (same) 場所を 探しますよ！そして、let's each buy some kind of おみやげ as presents for each other! それをタイムカプセルに 入れて、うめて (bury)、僕達の 時代に 帰って、その タイムカプセルを 開けましょう！」と、言いました。

じゅん君は、「それは いい アイディア ですね。ベン君は あたまが いい ですね。」と、言いました。I imagined us opening the time capsule in the 21st century in the garden of Jun's house in Tokyo and seeing the ukiyoe and other presents from the Edo era! From there, we split up to go shopping.

昼に、ラーメン屋で みんなと 会いました。そのラーメン屋は、ちょっと まずかったですが、そこの おばあさんは とても かわいかった です。食べてから、また ショッピングをしました。私は 煎餅と 魚と お箸を 買って、それから、浴衣と 北斎さんの 浮世絵も 買いました。

その晩、旅館で 皆に おみやげを あげました。私は ベン君に 美味しい煎餅と 漫画の 本を あげました。じゅん君は 友さんに 富士山の 浮世絵を あげました。私は、じゅん君に いい筆を もらいました。本当に 楽しかった です。

プレゼントを 皆で exchange してから、私は 筆で 漢字を 書く 練習を 始めました。友さんは 私の 名前を 漢字で 書きました。「気新」と 書きました。「気」の 意味は "energy、spirit。"「新」の 意味は "new"。 So Tomo said my new name means something like "new/revitalized energy/spirit" in English.

じゅん君は、「かっこいい ですね！私の 名前は ひらがな だけ ですよ！」と、言いました。私は、「友さん、すてきな 漢字を、どうも 有り難う ございます。」と、言いました。友さんは、「いやいや、どういたしまして (You are welcome)。あなた達と 一緒にいるのは 本当に 楽しい です。ありがとうね。」と、言って、and at that point、友さん started to tear up! But he managed to say、「皆 いい友達に なりましたね。ありがとう…。じゃ、食べましょう！」

What happened tonight was really sweet. 私は やっぱり じゅん君の 家へ 帰りたい (I want to...)… ですが、この 旅行も 楽しい です。

第9課の5 これは、私の 妹(ももうと)が くれました。
My younger sister gave me this.

1.

1) キアラさん、
いつも その
ブレスレットを
していますね。
かわいい ですね。

2) あ、これ ですか。
これは、私の 妹が
くれました。誕生日
プレゼント です。

2.

3) へえ、僕も
誕生日に この
シャツを
兄から
もらいました。

3.

4) 7月4日は、妹の 誕生日
です。私も すてきな
プレゼントを 妹に あげます。

4.

5) 何を
あげますか。

6) 着物と、たくさんの 日本の おかしと
漢字の 名前も あげます！

■ 会話 Dialogue

REMINDER: You may see some kanji / vocabulary you do not recognize. Use the context to try to understand the meanings of those parts of the dialogue.

1. ベン　：キアラさん、いつも　そのブレスレットを　していますね。かわいい　ですね。
2. キアラ：あ、これ　ですか。これは、私の　妹が　くれました。誕生日プレゼントです。
3. ベン　：へえ、僕も、誕生日に　この　シャツを、兄から　もらいました。
4. キアラ：7月4日は、妹の　誕生日　です。私も　すてきな　プレゼントを　妹に　あげます。
5. じゅん：何を　あげますか。
6. キアラ：着物と、たくさんの　日本の　お菓子と　漢字の　名前も　あげます！

■ 単語 New Words

くれる/くれます (*v*) – (to) give [to me or someone in my family]

(お) 菓子 (*n*) – Japanese traditional candy/sweets

■ 言葉の探索 Language Detection

くれます = something is given to you or to someone else in your family or group

When くれます is used, the name of the giver is the subject and is followed by が or sometimes は. Just remember that in most cases you can use が (<u>G</u>a) for the <u>G</u>iver. The recipient is followed by the particle に. You can think of the person receiving something as getting down on "bended <u>knee</u>" to receive something if he/she is extremely grateful.

A) 友達が　私に　この　ブレスレットを　くれました。
= My friend gave me this bracelet.

B) 数学の　先生が　私に　いい本を　くれました。
= The math teacher gave me a good book.

C) キャシーさんは　私に　新しいCDを　二枚　くれました。
= Kathy gave me two new CDs.

■ 自習 Self Check

Try to say the following out loud to yourself in Japanese. Use くれます.

A) My father gave me money.
B) My friend gave me a purple shirt.
C) My grandfather will give me new clothes.
D) Our mother gave my little brother an expensive backpack.
E) My mother gave me three beautiful pencils.
F) (compose a sentence of your own)

■ 練習の時間 Time for Practice

1. Group Practice

Use a piece of scrap paper to draw the certificate below, writing your name on the blank that says 名前. Your teacher will re-distribute the forms to the class. On the new certificate that you receive, draw a picture of a present appropriate to give to the person whose name is at the top (be nice ☺). Sign the paper, and return the form to your teacher. Once you have received your new "present," be prepared to tell the class who gave you what, using the appropriate verb for giving/receiving. Use the sample statement below as a model.

名前：____________________

プレゼント：

サイン：____________________

A) トム君は　私に　すごい車を　くれました。 = Tom gave me a cool car.
-OR- ぼくは　トム君に　すごい車を　もらいました。 = I received a cool car from Tom.

B) アリシアさんは　私に　赤いドレスを　くれました。 = Alicia gave me a red dress.
-OR- 私は　アリシアさんに　赤いドレスを　もらいました。 = I received a red dress from Alicia.

■ 文化箱 Culture Chest

Celebrations

How do you celebrate your birthday, or a holiday like Independence Day or Thanksgiving? Do you have a party, and get together with your family? Or do you go out to dinner with friends? Many traditional holidays, such as 雛祭り (Girl's Day, on March 3) or 子供の日 (Children's Day, on May 5), are celebrated by decorating the house. Other holidays, such as お正月 (the New Year's holiday), involve getting together with relatives and making visits to the local shrine or temple. During お盆, in August, many people travel back to their hometown, to visit and clean the graves of their ancestors.

■ キアラのジャーナル Kiara's Journal

Read the journal entry below, and then answer these questions.

❶ How does Kiara feel about leaving Edo?

❷ Why do they plan to leave through the gate at the Asakusa Shrine?

❸ Who does Kiara say she wants to travel with again?

> ジャーナルへ
>
> 江戸は とても 楽しかった です。We've had an incredible time: 北斎さんと 会って、買い物をして、お土産を 交換 (exchange) しました。でも、I miss being able to talk to my 父や 母や 友達など。明日は、浅草神社から 私達の 時代に 帰ります。浅草神社は じゅん君の 家と 近いから です。あ！ところで、私達は、とうとう (at last)、found the location of Jun's house in the 江戸時代！ We put the presents in the time capsule and buried them there. Will the time capsule be able to transfer from Edo to our era? If we go into the 時の門 there, we've got a pretty good chance of getting back into our own time. また、いつか、友さんと 旅行 (to travel) を したい ですね。
>
> おやすみ。

■ 単語チェックリスト New Word Checklist

9-1

いちまん・一万 *count.* ten thousand
うきよえ・浮世絵 *n* woodblock print (prior to and through the Edo Period)
うる・売る / うります・売ります *v* to sell
え・絵 *n* painting, drawing
えいが・映画 *n* movie
かいもの・買い物 *n* shopping
かいもの（を）・買い物（を）する / します *v* to go shopping
かう・買う / かいます・買います *v* to buy
からおけ（を）・カラオケ（を）する / します *v* to(sing/do) karaoke
きゅうまん・九万 *count.* ninety thousand
けんか（を）・喧嘩（を）する / します *v* to fight
ごまん・五万 *count.* fifty thousand
さっかー（を）・サッカー（を）する / します *v* to play soccer
さんまん・三万 *count.* thirty thousand
しゃわー（を）・シャワー（を）する / します *v* to take a shower
しゃんぷー（を）・シャンプー（を）する / します *v* to shampoo
じゅういちまん・十一万 *count.* one hundred ten thousand
じゅうきゅうまん・十九万 *count.* one hundred ninety thousand
じゅうごまん・十五万 *count.* one hundred fifty thousand
じゅうさんまん・十三万 *count.* one hundred thirty thousand
じゅうななまん・十七万 *count.* one hundred seventy thousand
じゅうにまん・十二万 *count.* one hundred twenty thousand
じゅうはちまん・十八万 *count.* one hundred eighty thousand
じゅうまん・十万 *count.* one hundred thousand
じゅうよんまん・十四万 *count.* one hundred forty thousand
じゅうろくまん・十六万 *count.* one hundred sixty thousand
しゅくだい（を）・宿題（を）する / します *v* to do homework
しょくじ（を）・食事（を）する / します *v* to have a meal; to dine
しんはんが・新版画 *n* woodblock print (new), art print (new)
でーと（を）・デート（を）する / します *v* to (go on a) date
でんわ（を）・電話（を）・する / します *v* to telephone
なかなおり（を）仲直り（を）する / します *v* to make up; to reconcile
ななまん・七万 *count.* seventy thousand
なんまん・何万 *inter.* how many ten-thousands?
にじゅういちまん・二十一万 *count.* two hundred ten thousand
にじゅうまん・二十万 *count.* two hundred thousand
にまん・二万 *count.* twenty thousand
ばすけ（を）・バスケ（を）する / します *v* to play basketball
はちまん・八万 *count.* eighty thousand
はんが・版画 *n* woodblock print
びでおげーむ（を）・ビデオゲーム（を）する / します *v* to play video games
べんきょう（を）・勉強（を）する / します *v* to study
ほんもの・本物 *n* real thing, genuine article
みせ・店 *n* shop; store
よんまん・四万 *count.* forty thousand
りょこう（を）・旅行（を）する / します *v* to take a trip; to travel
ろくまん・六万 *count.* sixty thousand

9-2

いくら *inter.* how much?
いただく / いただきます *v* to receive (very polite), lit.: I will receive.
いっさつ・一冊 *count.* one volume
いっぱい・一杯 *count.* one cupful
いっぽん・一本 *count.* one cylindrical object
えす (S) さいず・S サイズ *n* small (S) size
えむ (M) さいず・M サイズ *n* medium (M) size
える (L) さいず・L サイズ *n* large (L) size
おつり・お釣り *n* change (cash)
きゅうさつ・九冊 *count.* nine volumes
きゅうはい・九杯 *count.* nine cupfuls
きゅうほん・九本 *count.* nine cylindrical objects
ごさつ・五冊 *count.* five volumes
ごはい・五杯 *count.* five cupfuls
ごほん・五本 *count.* five cylindrical objects
さんさつ・三冊 *count.* three volumes
さんばい・三杯 *count.* three cupfuls
さんぼん・三本 *count.* three cylindrical objects
じゅっさつ / じっさつ・十冊 *count.* ten volumes
じゅっぱい / じっぱい・十杯 *count.* ten cupfuls
じゅっぽん / じっぽん・十本 *count.* ten cylindrical objects
ぜんぶで・全部で *exp.* in all; total; all together

てんいん・店員 *n* shopkeeper; clerk
どう・ですか *exp.* how about it?
とくべつ・特別 *n/* な *adj.* special
ななさつ・七冊 *count.* seven volumes
ななはい・七杯 *count.* seven cupfuls
ななほん・七本 *count.* seven cylindrical objects
なんさつ 何冊 *inter.* how many volumes?
なんばい 何杯 *inter.* how many cupfuls?
なんぼん・何本 *inter.* how many cylindrical objects?
にさつ・二冊 *count.* two volumes
にはい・二杯 *count.* two cupfuls
にほん・二本 *count.* two cylindrical objects
はちほん / はっぽん・八本 *count.* eight cylindrical objects
はっさつ・八冊 *count.* eight volumes
はっぱい・八杯 *count.* eight cupfuls
べつ・別 *n/* な *adj.* separate
べつべつ・別々 *n/* な *adj.* separately; individually
よんさつ・四冊 *count.* four volumes
よんはい・四杯 *count.* four cupfuls
よんほん・四本 *count.* four cylin-dri-cal objects
ろくさつ・六冊 *count.* six volumes
ろっぱい・六杯 *count.* six cupfuls
ろっぽん・六本 *count.* six cylindrical objects

9-3

さがす・探す / さがし・探します *v* to search
ざんねん・残念 *n/* な *adj.* regrettably, unluckily
もっと *adv.* more

9-4

あげる・上げる / あげます・上げます *v* to give [to equals or superiors]
けーき・ケーキ *n* cake
せんべい・煎餅 *n* rice crackers
とんでもない *exp.* Don't be ridiculous! Not a chance! My pleasure
ぷれぜんと・プレゼント *n* present; a gift
もらう / もらいます *v* to receive (very polite), lit.: I will receive.

9-5

(お)かし・(お)菓子 *n* Japanese traditional sweets
くれる / くれます (くれて) *v* to give [to me or a family member]

Meeting Basho in Kanazawa

第 10 課

Learning and Performance Goals

This chapter will enable you to:

A) say what the weather might do
B) politely invite someone to do something
C) accept or decline invitations
D) say that you want or do not want to do something
E) learn about the famous haiku poet, Matsuo Basho
F) use 9 additional kanji
G) use the "can-do" chart found on **TimeForJapanese.com** to chart your progress for what you "can-do" for each chapter

Geta at a temple on Koyasan

第10課の1 明日も　晴れ　でしょう。

Probably tomorrow will also be sunny.

1.
1) 私は、春が好き です。
2) 僕も、この季節が好きです。

2.
3) 僕は、夏が 大好きです。
4) 私は、秋が 好きです。食べ物が、美味しい ですから。

5) 春も、夏も、秋も、冬も 皆 きれい です。私は、全部の 季節が好き です。それが、俳句の 心 です。
6) ほら！お城の 夕焼けが、きれい ですね！
3.

7) そうですね。明日も、晴れでしょう。
4.

■ 会話(かいわ) Dialogue

REMINDER: You may see some kanji / vocabulary you do not recognize. Use the context to try to understand the meanings of those parts of the dialogue.

1. キアラ： 私は、春(はる)が　好(す)き　です。
2. じゅん： 僕も、この　季節(きせつ)が　好(す)き　です。
3. ベン　： 僕は、夏(なつ)が　大好き　です。
4. 友　　： 私は、秋(あき)が　好き　です。食べ物が、美味(おい)しい　ですから。
5. 芭蕉(ばしょう)　： 春(はる)も、夏(なつ)も、秋(あき)も、冬(ふゆ)も、皆(みんな)　きれい　です。私は、全部(ぜんぶ)の季節(きせつ)が好き　です。それが、俳句(はいく)の　心　です。
6. キアラ： ほら！お城(しろ)の　*夕焼(ゆうや)けが、きれいですね！
7. 芭蕉(ばしょう)　： そう　ですね。明日(あした)も、晴(は)れ　でしょう。

* 夕焼(ゆうや)け – sunset. *Lit.*: burning (sun) of the evening (sky)

■ 単語(たんご) New Words

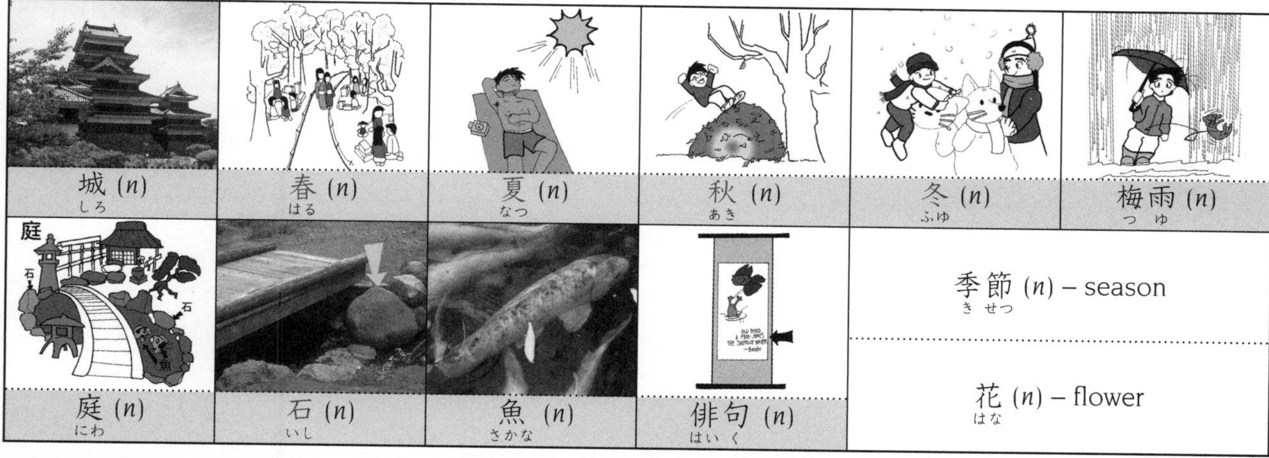

城(しろ) (n)
春(はる) (n)
夏(なつ) (n)
秋(あき) (n)
冬(ふゆ) (n)
梅雨(つゆ) (n)
庭
石
石
庭(にわ) (n)
石(いし) (n)
魚(さかな) (n)
俳句(はいく) (n)
季節(きせつ) (n) – season
花(はな) (n) – flower

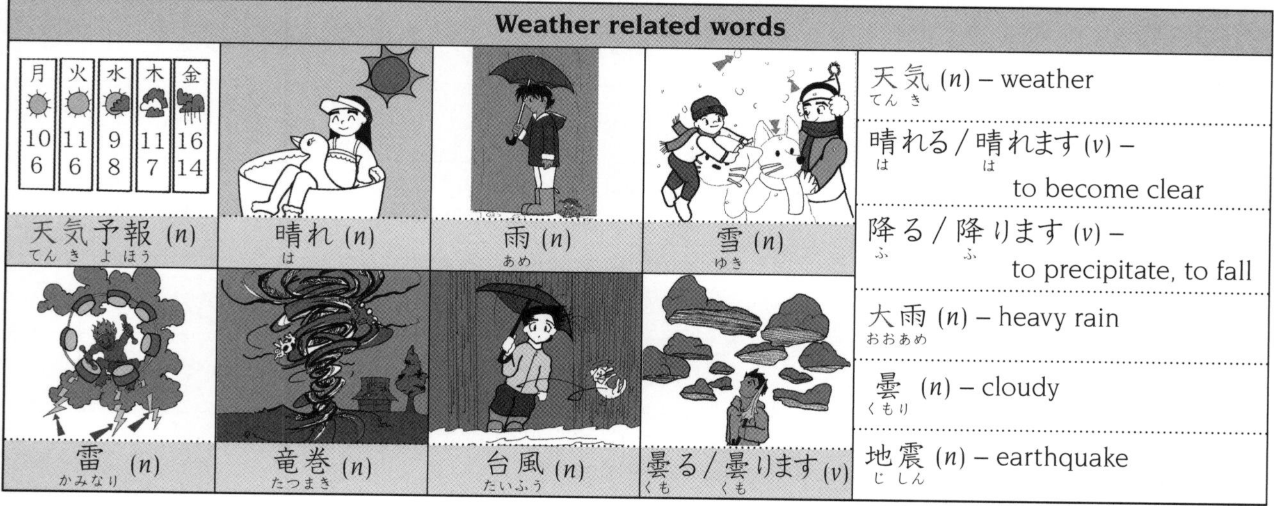

Weather related words
月
火
水
木
金
10 6
11 6
9 8
11 7
16 14
天気予報(てんきよほう) (n)
晴(は)れ (n)
雨(あめ) (n)
雪(ゆき) (n)
天気(てんき) (n) – weather
晴(は)れる / 晴(は)れます (v) – to become clear
降(ふ)る / 降(ふ)ります (v) – to precipitate, to fall
大雨(おおあめ) (n) – heavy rain
曇(くもり) (n) – cloudy
地震(じしん) (n) – earthquake
雷(かみなり) (n)
竜巻(たつまき) (n)
台風(たいふう) (n)
曇(くも)る / 曇(くも)ります (v)

一度(いちど) – 1 time, 1 degree
二度(にど) (*n*) – 2 times, 2 degrees
三度(さんど) (*n*) – 3 times, 3 degrees
四度(よんど) (*n*) – 4 times, 4 degrees
五度(ごど) (*n*) – 5 times, 5 degrees
六度(ろくど) (*n*) – 6 times, 6 degrees
七度(ななど) (*n*) – 7 times, 7 degrees
八度(はちど) (*n*) – 8 times, 8 degrees
九度(きゅうど)*(*n*) – 9 times, 9 degrees
十度(じゅうど) (*n*) – 10 times, 10 degrees
何度(なんど) (*inter.*) – How many times/ degrees?
温度(おんど) (*n*) – temperature

* *9 degrees* can alternatively be pronounced as くど, but not *9 times.*

NOTE: There is a slightly different intonation between the pronunciation of times and degrees. This can be heard in the audio file for this section.

■ 漢字(かんじ) Kanji

春 (9 strokes)	
はる – spring	
春(はる) – spring	春 春
SPRING includes two (二) big (大) days (日) for children in Japan, the first day of school in April and Children's Day in May.	

夏 (10 strokes)	
なつ – summer	一
夏(なつ) – summer	夏 夏 夏
The top two strokes are a shady umbrella (丁) over a large watchful eye (目) of a person sitting cross legged on a lawn chair at the beach in SUMMER.	

秋 (9 strokes)	
あき – autumn, fall	千 禾
秋(あき) – autumn, fall	秋 秋
The first stroke of this kanji looks like the blade of an axe used to cut up trees (木) to make a fire (火) to keep warm on a cold AUTUMN night.	

冬 (5 strokes)	
ふゆ – winter	ノ ク 夂 冬 冬
冬(ふゆ) – winter	
Now that it is WINTER, the long tear (the first stroke) from the hint for the kanji for summer above, again (又) and again (又) is turning into two pieces of ice (the last two strokes) due to the WINTER cold.	

石 (5 strokes)	
セキ；いし – stone, rock	一 ア 石 石
石(いし) – stone, rock	
Imagine the final 3 strokes (ロ) as a STONE so hard that any attempt to drive a nail (丁) into the STONE results in the nail simply being bent to the left.	

■ 言葉の探索 Language Detection

1. 暑い　でしょう。

A. でしょう is derived from です and implies little doubt in the statement. It is best translated as meaning "probably." It is used often in Japanese in weather forecasts and in other circumstances where one is assuming something will happen in the future. When asking a question in Japanese, the last syllable has a raised inflection, similar to what happens in English. With statements, the tone is flat or the inflection goes down as in these examples. でしょう can be preceded by nouns, adjectives, or the dictionary forms of verbs.

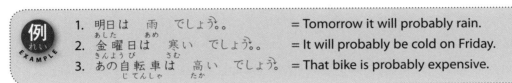

1. 明日は　雨　でしょう。 = Tomorrow it will probably rain.
2. 金曜日は　寒い　でしょう。 = It will probably be cold on Friday.
3. あの自転車は　高い　でしょう。 = That bike is probably expensive.

B. でしょう can also mean "right?" when you are trying to confirm something. As in English, when making a statement, the last syllable has a lowered inflection, however when there is some doubt in the statement or if it is an outright question, the intonation is raised.

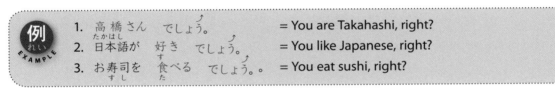

1. 高橋さん　でしょう。 = You are Takahashi, right?
2. 日本語が　好き　でしょう。 = You like Japanese, right?
3. お寿司を　食べる　でしょう。 = You eat sushi, right?

2. 天気予報 – **Weather forecasts**

Below is an example of a typical weather forecast you might hear in Japan. Notice the use of でしょう.

天気予報を　お伝えします。明日の　東京地方は、晴れ、時々　曇り　でしょう。
予想最低気温は　12度、予想最高気温は　25度、降水確率は、20%です。

English Translation:
Now for the weather forecast. Tomorrow the Tokyo region will be sunny with periods of clouds. The expected low temperature will be 12 degrees (Celsius) with a high temperature of 25 degrees, and a 20% chance of precipitation.

■ 自習 Self Check

1. でしょう

Can you say the following in Japanese?

A) Russia's winter probably is cold.
B) Kyushu's summer probably is hot.
C) It will probably snow tomorrow.
D) It will probably rain Saturday.
E) Indonesia's trees are probably very big.
F) Kyoto's weather is probably cool in April.
G) It will probably a little cold in the morning.
H) My father will probably give me money for my birthday.

2. Weather forecast

Refer to the example weather forecast in the 探索(たんさく) above to say the following things in Japanese:

A) Now for the weather forecast.
B) Tomorrow the Kyoto region will be rainy with periods of clouds.
C) The expected low temperature will probably be 15 degrees.
D) The expected high temperature will probably be 23 degrees.
E) The chance of precipitation is 80%.

■ 練習(れんしゅう)の時間(じかん) Time for Practice

1. Pair Practice

Take out your set of flash cards for weather-related vocabulary from this section. First, flash your cards briefly to your partner. See if she/he can correctly provide the English and/or Japanese. Take turns. Then, lay nine of these cards out on a piece of scrap paper on the table between you (English or picture side up) in a tic-tac-toe format and play tic-tac-toe with your partner. Play paper-rock-scissors to see who goes first. The winner selects a square that they wish to take and says the Japanese word for the English card that's in the square. For example, for *winter* you would say "これは 冬(ふゆ) です。" If you're correct, pick up the card and place either an X or an O on the square. If you're wrong, lay it back down and it's your partner's turn. After three games, switch languages and play by translating from Japanese to English.

* Alternatively, use a weather forecast from a Japanese website or newspaper and make sentences about current weather predictions to mark squares on your game boards.

2. Small Group Practice

Use a piece of scrap paper to copy the chart below. Interview two classmates about the seasonal weather in the place they were born. Then report your results to your partner or to the class.

例(れい) EXAMPLE

You : どこで 生(う)まれましたか。 = Where were you born?
B- さん : (the place you were born) で 生(う)まれました。 = I was born in ____________.
You : (that same place) の 春(はる)の 天気(てんき)は どうですか。
= How is _____'s spring weather?
B-(ー)さん : 春(はる)は、少(すこ)し寒いです。 そして、時々(ときどき) 雪(ゆき)が 降(ふ)ります。
= Spring is a little cold. And furthermore, sometimes snow falls.

名前 ____________	春の天気	夏の天気	秋の天気	冬の天気
場所(ばしょ) (place) ____________				
場所(ばしょ) (place) ____________				

■ 文化箱 Culture Chest

金沢

Medieval 金沢 was ruled by the 前田藩 (clan). In Japan each clan was ruled by a 大名 or regional feudal lord. The kanji 大名 literally means "big name" and if you were the ruler of an area, you would be the most important name in the region.

Between 1185 and 1600, Japan saw the rise of the 侍 or military class and the decline of power of the nobility, the ruling class that had controlled the country up until the end of the 平安時代 (794–1185). By the late 16th century, the 大名 had gained firm political control over their domains and most swore loyalty to the 将軍, Japan's most powerful military leader. By the late 1500s, under the strong hands of successive 将軍, Japan gradually became more and more politically stable.

During this more peaceful era, samurai had to justify their privileged existence, since their role as warrior was no longer important. This is when ideals of loyalty and preserving honor on the battlefield became codified for the first time, and when many of the "traditional" Japanese arts, such as the tea ceremony, began to flourish.

By the time Basho traveled the country, the Tokugawa clan had brought a measure of unification and peace to much of Japan. However, bandits and other hardships still made it dangerous for Basho to travel to the northern rural regions. By being able to cover so much ground so quickly without being injured or killed, legends grew that he may have had ninja skills.

Incense and offerings, Kyoto

■ キアラのジャーナル Kiara's Journal 

Read the journal entry below, and then answer these questions.

❶ Where and in what time period are Kiara, Ben, and Jun now?

❷ Had Tomo ever met Matsuo Basho prior to this experience?

❸ Write down what you learned about haiku from this diary entry.

Note: There are no spaces in between words in the Journal entries for this chapter. Japanese does not normally use spaces between words (although this book has used them, for ease of understanding for beginning learners).

ジャーナルへ

今度は、私達は、石川県の金沢に来ました。今は 1690年の春です。近くの店の人は、「今、金沢に松尾芭蕉さんが来ています。」と、言いました。うれしかったです！芭蕉さんは俳句で世界一有名な人です。

私は、学校で英語の俳句を作りました。私は俳句が好きです。短くて面白いと思います。

俳句は 5 ― 7 ― 5 の syllable lines です。いつも季語（季節の言葉）を入れます。季語を入れると、もっと 面白くなります。For example, 春の季語は、桜、青い leaves、動物の babies などです。

Here is a poem by 芭蕉 that shows how 季語 can add a deeper meaning to a 俳句。

『さまざまな事	various things
思い出す	remembered
桜かな』	the cherry blossoms

芭蕉さんは、Mie prefecture の伊賀上野というところで、この句を作りました。芭蕉さんの生まれた所です。Seeing the beautiful cherry blossoms in his hometown probably brought back a lot of memories for 芭蕉 .

The spring is a time of change in Japan (the new school year starts on April 1st, and many workers are transferred to new jobs in new locations around this time as well) so for the Japanese the image of cherry blossoms could trigger a flood of memories of many of the changes in their life. You add 季語 to indicate something you feel very deeply. The 季語 offer an image of a season, and bring you closer to understanding the poet's thoughts. Therefore, Japanese say that 俳句 are very 深い (deep)、高い (high) and 広い (wide) despite being very 短い short poems.

Anyway, back to our time in Kanazawa... 私達は、始めに金沢のお城 (castle) に行きました。森の池の近くに、年取ったおじいさんがいました。私は友さんに、「あの人は、だれですか。」と聞きました。

友さんは、「あの人は松尾芭蕉です。彼はいつも俳句を、森や池など、きれいな所で作ります。僕は、今まで芭蕉さんと、まだ会ったことがありませんでした。」と、言いました。He suggested that we go up and introduce ourselves。

ベン君は芭蕉さんに、「すみません。僕達は日本を旅行しています。今、金沢へ花見に来ました。ここの春はとてもきれいですね。」と、言いました。He did not want to come right out and ask Basho's name, but wanted to make sure that it was him.

芭蕉さんは、「そうですか。僕も風のようにこの国をあちこち回って、ここに花を見に来ました。このお城の桜はとてもきれいですね。」と、言いました。

第10課の2 「ここで一緒に、食事をしませんか。」

"Won't you have a meal here with us?"

1.

1) 芭蕉さんは、
本当に 素敵な人
ですね。

2) 芭蕉さんに、
「僕達と 一緒に、
時の門の旅を
しませんか。」と
言いませんか。

2.

3) そして、「一緒に、たくさんの
俳句を 作りませんか。」と
言いましょう。

3.

4) 彼は、
「はい。いい ですよ。」
と言うでしょう！

4.

5) 残念 ですが
それは
ちょっと・・・・。
それが 時の門の
ルール です。
だれも、私達と
一緒に 時の門に
入る 事は
出来ません。

5.

6) でも、芭蕉さんに、「ここで 一緒に、
食事を しませんか。」と 言いましょう！

■ 会話(かいわ) Dialogue 

REMINDER: You may see some kanji / vocabulary you do not recognize. Use the context to try to understand the meanings of those parts of the dialogue.

1. じゅん ： 芭蕉(ばしょう)さんは、本当に　素敵(すてき)な　人ですね。

2. ベン ： 芭蕉(ばしょう)さんに、「僕達(ぼくたち)と一緒(いっしょ)に、時の　門の　*旅(たび)を　しませんか。」と、言いませんか。

3. キアラ ： そして、「一緒(いっしょ)に、たくさんの　俳句(はいく)を　作りませんか。」と、言いましょう。

4. じゅん ： 彼(かれ)は、「はい。いいですよ。」と、言うでしょう！

5. 友 ： 残念(ざんねん)　ですが　それは　ちょっと…。それが　時の門の　ルール　です。だれも、私達と　一緒(いっしょ)に　時の門に　入(はい)る事は　出来(でき)ません。でも、芭蕉(ばしょう)さんに、「ここで　一緒(いっしょ)に、食事(しょくじ)をしませんか。」と、言いましょう！

* 旅(たび) – travel, take a trip

■ 単語(たんご) New Words 

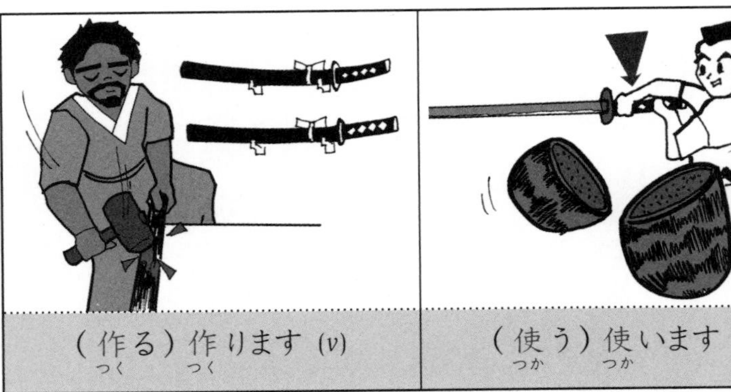

（作(つく)る）作(つく)ります (*v*)	（使(つか)う）使(つか)います (*v*)

だれも (*exp.*) – no one	
一昨日(おととい) – day before yesterday	
明後日(あさって) – day after tomorrow	
どこも (*adv.*)– nowhere (with negative verb); everywhere (with positive verb)	
どこへも (*adv.*) – not (going) anywhere	
どこにも (*adv.*) – not (going) anywhere	

■ 漢字(かんじ) Kanji

使 (8 strokes)								
つか（う）– to use	ノ	イ	亻	仁	佇	佰	佶	使
使(つか)（う）– to use	使							
People (the radical on the left, 亻) like to think there is only one (一) "correct" view of history (史) but the truth is that everyone (一) USES his or her personal bias when trying to understand history. These three radicals USED together make up the character 使 – "to use."								

作	サク，つく（る）– to make	ノ	イ	イ'	化	作	作	作
	作(つく)（る）– to make; 作(さく)（文(ぶん)）– essay							
7 strokes	The person (the radical on the left side, イ) is MAKING a set of bookshelves with three shelves already in place. He's using a hammer (the third stroke) to nail the top corner together.							

■ 言葉(ことば)の探索(たんさく) Language Detection

1. 食べませんか。= Won't you eat (with me)?

This polite form of an invitation in Japanese can be described as a negative invitation or an invitation in the negative. Similar to the English "Won't you please...," in Japanese you can extend a polite invitation by making a negative question. It is implied that you mean "with me." To use this form, take the verb that you want to use, drop the ～ます ending and add ～ませんか.

A) 飲みませんか。 = Won't you drink (with me)?
B) 英語で　話しませんか。 = Won't you speak English (with me)?
C) テレビゲームを　しませんか。 = Won't you play video games?

2. 食べましょう。 = Let's eat.

To say "Let's do such and such" in Japanese, change the ～ます ending to ～ましょう.

A) 庭(にわ)で　お茶(ちゃ)を　飲みましょう。 = Let's drink tea in the garden.
B) 六月(がつ)に　日本へ　行きましょう。 = Let's go to Japan in June.
C) 散歩(さんぽ)を　しましょう。 = Let's go for a walk.

3. 食べましょうか。 = Shall we eat?

Placing a か after ましょう softens the invitation a little. It is a slightly more polite way to offer an invitation by making the invitation more of a question.

A) 海で　泳(およ)ぎましょうか。 = Shall we swim in the ocean?
B) 昼寝(ひるね)を　しましょうか。 = Shall we take a nap?
C) 一緒(いっしょ)に　日本語を　勉強(べんきょう)　しましょうか。 = Shall we study Japanese together?

4. どこも, どこへも and どこにも…

These three are used similarly to the expressions だれも and 何も, which were introduced in Chapter 5-3. だれも (no one) and 何も (nothing) are used to mean that someone or something does not exist in a place or time. どこも, どこへも, and どこにも are likewise used for negative expressions in which case どこも often translates as "nowhere" and どこへも and どこにも often translate as "not going anywhere." Note that どこも can also mean "everywhere" as in どこも　きれい　ですね。(Everywhere is clean), or "nowhere" as in どこも　きれい　ではありません。(Nowhere is clean).

A) その　生徒の　宿題は　どこにも　ありません。
= That student's homework isn't any place.

B) この近くに　お寿司屋さんは　どこにも　ありません。
= In this vicinity, there is no sushi restaurant anywhere.

C) 私は　どこも　好き　では　ありません。 = I do not like anywhere.

D) 学校は　どこも　楽しい　です。 = At school, everywhere is fun.

5. ちょっと …

This expression, which you learned earlier, literally means something is "a little. . . ." This expression can also be a very good way to decline a request in Japanese without giving a reason. If you have something else going on but would rather not give a reason, or if you just don't want to accept an invitation, this often works. It would be rude in most cases to ask for a further elaboration of ちょっと if someone turns down your request.

さとし： えみさん、土曜日に　映画に　行きませんか。
= Emi, won't you go to a movie (with me) on Saturday?

えみ　： ええと、土曜日は　ちょっと… = Umm, Saturday is a little . . .

サラ　： まりこさん、あした、ダンスパーティーへ　行きませんか。
= Mariko, won't you go to a dance party with me tomorrow?

まりこ： すみません、ダンスは　ちょっと… = I'm sorry, dancing is a little . . .

■ 自習 Self Check

1. … ませんか。 **– Polite invitation**

Can you say the following, out loud, in Japanese?

A) Won't you come to my house?

B) Would you like to play basketball (with me)?

2. Verb stem + ましょう (ましょうか)

A) Let's eat at that restaurant over there.

B) Shall we return (home)?

C) Let's drink water.

D) Shall we sing?

3. どこも、どこにも、どこへも

A) I will not go anywhere tomorrow..

B) It is not cold anywhere.

C) Everywhere is hot

■ 練習(れんしゅう)の時間(じかん) Time for Practice

1. Pair Practice

Politely invite your partner to do the following activities, using the negative invitation pattern. Your partner will either accept or decline. Switch roles.

You　：バスケを　しませんか。
友だち：はい、しましょう。
-OR-　いいえ、バスケは　ちょっと…
-OR-　ちょっと…

A) バスケを する
B) 宿題(しゅくだい)を する
C) 図書館(としょかん)へ　行く
D) お昼(ひる)ご飯(はん)を　食べる
E) 音楽(おんがく)を 聞(き)く
F) 料理(りょうり)を する
G) メキシコ 料理(りょうり)を 食べる
H) 映画(えいが)を　見る
I) 犬の　散歩(さんぽ)を する
J) 買い物を する
K) 私の家へ　来る
L) チェスを する

2. Pair Practice

You and your partner will each choose two of the activities listed above (or two of your own). Invite your partner to do these activities with you. Set up a time and a place to meet. Use the question words いつ and どこ. Remember to reconfirm the time and date.

A-さん：一緒に　宿題(しゅくだい)を　しませんか。
B-さん：はい、しましょう。いつ　しますか。
A-さん：あしたの　八時半(はん)は　どう　ですか。
B-さん：いいですね。どこで　しましょうか。
A-さん：スターバックスで　しましょう。
B-さん：じゃ、明日(あした)の　八時半(はん)に　スターバックスで　会(あ)いましょう。

3. Pair Practice

Choose two of the scenarios below and create a short (5–6 line) dialogue for each with your partner. Use the grammar patterns you have been practicing above. After you have rehearsed both dialogues, present one to your class.

A) Your friend suggests a movie on Tuesday night. You have to study and suggest Saturday instead.
B) Your mother wants to take you shopping for black shoes with her friends.
C) Your Japanese pen pal wants you to visit Japan in October.
D) Your friends are going to go to Mexico for spring vacation/holiday and invite you to go along.
E) Your friend invites you to meet after school but you have a headache. Your friend suggests you take medicine, but you hate to take medicine.
F) Your friend invites you to write a 40-page paper (作文(さくぶん)) with her.

■ 文化箱(ぶんかばこ) Culture Chest

松尾芭蕉(まつおばしょう)

Turtles in a pond in Kyoto

芭蕉(ばしょう) is the pen name of 松尾宗房(まつおむねふさ) (1644–1694). He is one of the most famous Japanese poets and is widely claimed to have popularized the 俳句(はいく) (5 – 7 – 5) poetic format. Arriving in 江戸(えど) in 1672, he was immediately popular and spent much of the rest of his life either at his banana leaf hut "芭蕉庵(ばしょうあん)" near the capital or traveling, seeking inspiration from nature for his poems. In the West, one of his most famous haiku is about a frog:

古(ふる)池や	*old pond*
蛙(かわず) とびこむ	*a frog jumps*
水の 音(おと)	*the sound of water*

■ キアラ(きあら)のジャーナル(じゃーなる) Kiara's Journal 

Read the journal entry below, and then answer these questions.

❶ How does Kiara describe the poet Basho?
❷ Where did Kiara go with Basho?
❸ What sort of place was it?
❹ What did Tomo want to do?
❺ Why couldn't they do what Tomo wanted to do immediately?

ジャーナルへ

芭蕉(ばしょう)さんはとても静(しず)かな人です。そして、ちょっと背(せ)が低(ひく)いです。やさしい顔(かお)をしていて、心が大きいです。

芭蕉さんは、「兼六園(けんろくえん)へ一緒(いっしょ)に行きませんか。あそこは、日本の、one of the three most beautiful gardens。木や 花や 石の 橋(はし)や 水などが すばらしい です。」と、言いました。

兼六園(けんろくえん)の名前の意味(いみ)は面白いです。It literally means the garden that combines the six characteristics that make up an excellent garden、according to ancient garden design techniques from China. The six characteristics are that a garden should be spacious and yet intimate, have some man-made elements but still should look natural and not tacky, and finally should have water elements and a nice view. I suppose it is hard to find a garden that can combine all 6 characteristics in a balanced fashion. でも、the cool thing about 兼六園(けんろくえん) is that それを全部(ぜんぶ)持っています！

兼六園の中を、あちこち歩きました。とても静かな所です。十一時に、友さんは、「じゃ、焼きそばを食べませんか。近くのレストランの焼きそばはとても美味しいです。」と、言いました。じゅん君は、「おととい焼きそばを食べましたよ。ここは海の近くですから、お寿司を 食べませんか。」と、言いました。友さんは、「お寿司ですか。それもいいですね。では、今すぐ、行きませんか。」と、言いました。芭蕉さんは石の上に座って、俳句を作り始めました。友さんは、「芭蕉さんが、俳句を作り終わってから行きましょう。」と、言いました。

第10課の3

日本語を、もっと勉強(べんきょう)したいです。
I want to study Japanese more.

1) 私は、
したい事が たくさん
あります。
2)
どんな事
ですか。
1.

2.
3)日本語を、もっと 勉強したい
です。時の門の 旅も たくさん
したいです。友達と 遊びたい
です。もっと柔道も したい
です。買い物も したい です。
4) メールも
したい です。
テレビも 映画も 見たい
です。
5) 僕は、
芭蕉さんと
俳句を
作りたい！
6) 私は、
何かを
食べたい
です！

■ 会話(かいわ) Dialogue

REMINDER: You may see some kanji / vocabulary you do not recognize. Use the context to try to understand the meanings of those parts of the dialogue.

1. キアラ： 私は、したい事が　たくさん　あります。
2. ベン　： どんな事ですか。
3. キアラ： 日本語を、もっと勉強したいです。時の門の　*旅(たび)も　たくさん　したい　です。友達と遊(あそ)びたい　です。もっと　柔道(じゅうどう)も　したい　です。買い物も　したい　です。
4. じゅん： *メールも　したいです。テレビも　映画(えいが)も　見たい　です。
5. ベン　： 僕は、芭蕉(ばしょう)さんと　俳句(はいく)を　作りたい！
6. 友　　： 私は、何かを　食べたい　です！

* 旅(たび) – travel, take a trip　　* メール – e-mail

■ 単語(たんご) New Words

何か(なに) – something	遊ぶ(あそ) / 遊びます(あそ) (v) – to play

■ 言葉(ことば)の探索(たんさく) Language Detection

1. 食べたいです。 **= I want to eat.**

To say you want to do something, you drop the ～ます and add ～たいです to the verb stem (the part of the verb that comes before the ます). Use this pattern only to express your own desires, not those of someone else.

NOTE: With the "verb stem + たい　です" pattern, it is OK to use the direct object particle from を or the subject particle が.

A) 私は　寿司(すし)が　食べたい　です。 = I want to eat sushi.
B) 私は　お茶(ちゃ)が　飲みたい　です。 = I want to drink green tea.
C) 私は　7月に　日本へ　行きたい　です。 = I want to go to Japan in July.
D) 私は　写真(しゃしん)を　撮(と)りたい　です。 = I want to take photographs.

■ 自習(じしゅう) Self Check

1. Using the ～たい-form (want to . . .)

Try to say the following out loud, to yourself, in Japanese.

A) I want to sell my book.
B) I want to wake up at 7:00.
C) I want go on a date with (name someone famous). (デートをします)
D) I want to dance. (ダンスをします)

2. しりとり

しりとり is a game played in many places under different names. By now, you have been exposed to quite a few vocabulary words and kanji. In Japanese しりとり, you try to see how many words you can string together by using the last syllable of the previous word as the first sound of the next word. For instance, わたし – しち – ちいさい... In this case the first word ends with し, and the next begins with し and then ends with ち. Then ち starts the third word, and so on. Use the kanji and vocabulary that you have been taught. Hint: Try not to use too many words that end in い. しり means *bottom/end* and とり is the noun form of とる which means *take*, so a rough direct translation of しりとり could be "taking from the end." Traditionally if you say a word which ends in "ん", you lose the game!

■ 練習(れんしゅう)の時間(じかん) Time for Practice

1. Small Group Practice

Put all your "verb" flash cards into one pile. Take turns flipping over a card and creating a sentence in the たい-form. Your group members will help you make sure your grammar is correct.

(*a card is turned over that reads* 勉強(べんきょう)する)

You might say : 私は 毎日 日本語を 勉強(べんきょう)したいです。 = I want to study Japanese every day.

(*turn over a card that reads* 行きます)

You might say : あのコンサートに 行きたいです。 = I want to go to that concert.

2. Pair Practice

Get out a sheet of scrap paper and something to write with. Flip a coin to see who goes first. When the teacher says 始(はじ)めましょう, Student A begins speaking sentences using the たい-form. Student B writes down what Student A says. Once your teacher says はい、終(お)りです, trade roles. When you are both finished, exchange papers and check for accuracy.

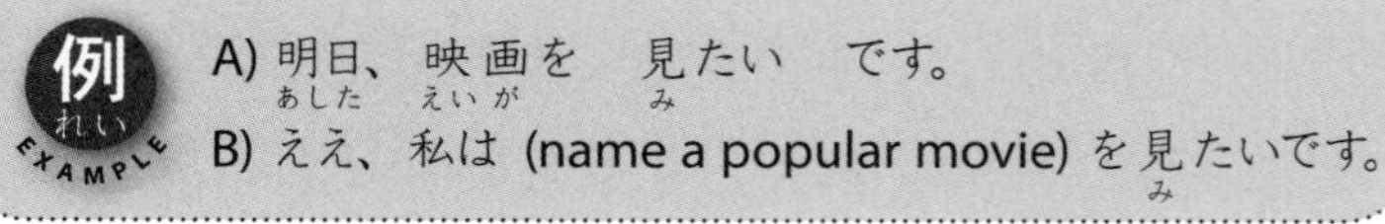

例(れい) EXAMPLE

A) 明日(あした)、映画(えいが)を 見(み)たい です。

B) ええ、私は (name a popular movie) を見(み)たいです。

■ キアラ(きあら)のジャーナル(じゃーなる) Kiara's Journal

Read the journal entry below, and then answer these questions.

1. What sort of restaurant did they enter?
2. What did Kiara decide to have to drink?
3. What did Jun decide to eat?
4. What did Tomo want to eat that he could not get?
5. What does Kiara want to do someday?

ジャーナルへ

お寿司屋(すしや)さんの人は、「いらっしゃいませ。何名様(なんめいさま)ですか。」と、言いました。友さんは、「五人です。」と、言いました。

ウェイトレスさんは、「こちらへどうぞ。」と、言いました。

芭蕉さんは、「キアラさんは何がいいですか。私は、このセットが食べたいです。」と、言いました。

私は、「いいですね。私もそれが食べたいです。それと、麦茶(むぎちゃ)が飲みたいです。ベン君は何を食べますか。」と聞きました。

ベン君は、「そうですね。僕はいなり寿司(すし)が食べたいです。それとお水も飲みたいです。じゅん君は食べますか。」と、じゅん君に聞きました。

じゅん君は、「そうですね。僕は、ええと、手巻き(てま)寿司(すし)が食べたいです。それから、ジュースが飲みたいです。」と、言いました。

友さんは、「皆さん、あまり食べませんね。私は、ちらし寿司(すし)と、寿司セットと、いなり寿司が食べたいです。お茶も飲みたいですね。あ！それと、私は、狸(たぬき)ですが、狸そばも食べたいです。」と、言いました。ウェイトレスさんは、「ここは、寿司屋(や)ですから、そばはありません。」と、言いました。私は、「友さん、狸そばって何ですか。」と聞きました。狸そばは、狸が入ったそばではありませんでした。友さんは「東京では、天ぷらの flake が入ったそばを、狸そばと言います。」と、言いました。お寿司屋さんにおそばはありませんでしたが、私も someday 狸そばが食べたいです。

第10課の4

まだ　起(お)きたくないです。
I do not want to wake up yet.

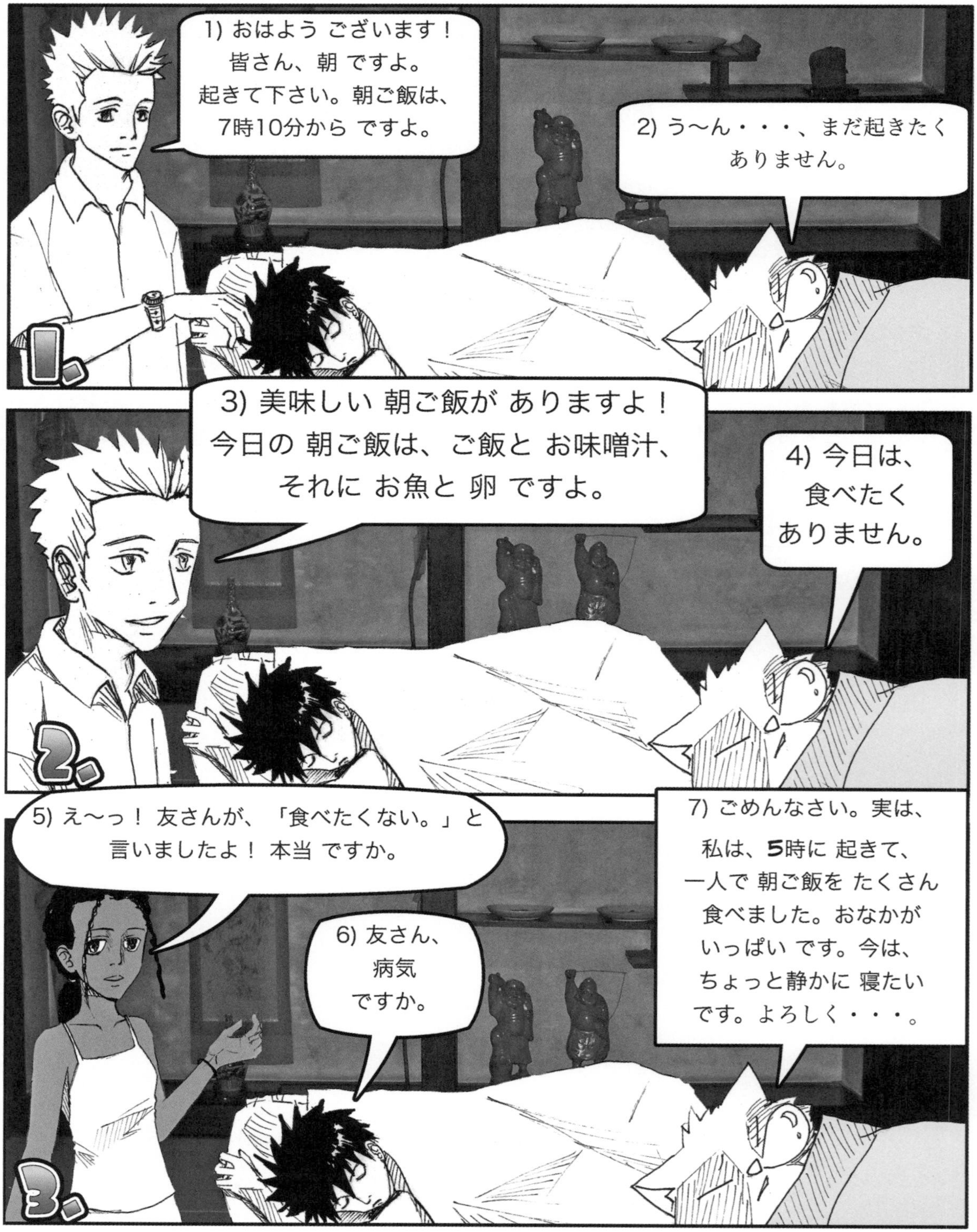

1.

1) おはよう ございます！ 皆さん、朝 ですよ。 起きて下さい。朝ご飯は、 7時10分から ですよ。

2) う～ん・・・、まだ起きたく ありません。

2.

3) 美味しい 朝ご飯が ありますよ！ 今日の 朝ご飯は、ご飯と お味噌汁、 それに お魚と 卵 ですよ。

4) 今日は、 食べたく ありません。

3.

5) え～っ！ 友さんが、「食べたくない。」と 言いましたよ！ 本当 ですか。

6) 友さん、 病気 ですか。

7) ごめんなさい。実は、 私は、5時に 起きて、 一人で 朝ご飯を たくさん 食べました。おなかが いっぱい です。今は、 ちょっと静かに 寝たい です。よろしく・・・。

■ 会話(かいわ) Dialogue

REMINDER: You may see some kanji / vocabulary you do not recognize. Use the context to try to understand the meanings of those parts of the dialogue.

1. ベン　：おはよう　ございます！　皆(みな)さん、　朝(あさ)　ですよ。起(お)きて　下さい。
朝(あさ)ご飯(はん)は、7時10分からですよ。

2. 友　：う～ん…、まだ　起(お)きたく　ありません。

3. ベン　：美味(おい)しい　朝ご飯が　ありますよ！今日の　朝ご飯は、ご飯と　お味噌汁(みそしる)、
それに　お魚(さかな)と　卵(たまご)　ですよ。

4. 友　：今日は、食べたく　ありません。

5. キアラ：え～っ！　友(とも)さんが、「食べたくない。」と、言いましたよ！　本当(ほんとう)　ですか。

6. じゅん：友さん、病気(びょうき)　ですか。

7. 友　：ごめんなさい。実(じつ)は、私は、5時に　起(お)きて、一人で　朝ご飯を
たくさん　食べました。お腹が　いっぱい　です。今は、ちょっと
静(しず)かに　寝(ね)たい　です。　よろしく…。

■ 単語(たんご) New Words

本当(ほんとう) (*n*)

お腹(なか)が　いっぱい (*exp.*)

うそ (*n*) – a lie

実(じつ)は (*adv.*) – by the way, actually

一人(ひとり)で (*exp.*) – by oneself, alone

まだ (*adv.*) – not yet, still

もう (*part.*) – already

■ 漢字(かんじ) Kanji

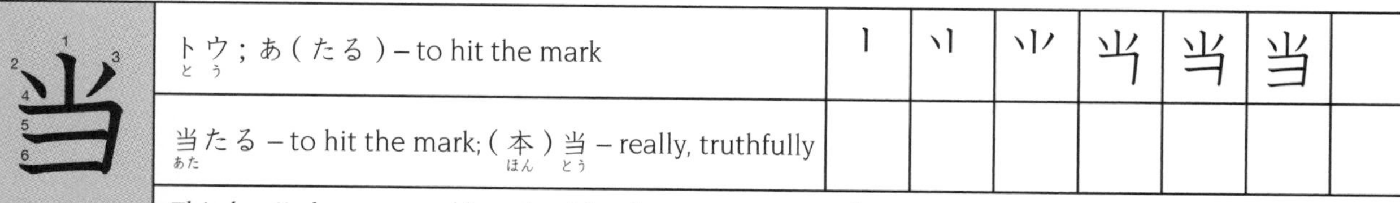

当 (6 strokes)	トウ(とう); あ(たる) – to hit the mark	丨	丨丶	丨丶丿	当	当	当	
	当(あた)る – to hit the mark; (本)当(ほんとう) – really, truthfully							
	This kanji shows a workbench with a hammer coming down, HITTING THE MARK causing sparks to fly out.							

■ 言葉(ことば)の探索(たんさく) Language Detection

1. 食べたく　ありません。 OR 食べたく　ないです。 = I don't want to eat.

To say that you do NOT want to do something, drop the い from the end of the たい-form of a verb and add 〜くありません. This is the same pattern used to negate an い adjective such as 美味(おい)しい (i.e., 美味(おい)しくありません, or 美味(おい)しくないです). The 〜たい pattern, meaning "want to...," also conjugates like an い adjective for the past tense (〜たかった).

NOTE: With the negative pattern, it is more common to use を instead of が for the direct object.

A) 私は　カラオケを　したく　ありません。 = I do not want to do karaoke.
B) 私は　散歩(さんぽ)を　したく　ありません。 = I do not want to take a walk.
C) 私は　昨日(きのう)　写真(しゃしん)を　撮(と)りたく　ありません　でした。
= I did not want to take pictures yesterday.
D) 来年(らいねん)も　日本語(にほんご)を　勉強(べんきょう)　したい　です。 = I want to study Japanese next year too.

Conjugation of the 〜たい form is exactly the same as it is for い adjectives. The stem of the い adjective is what is left after dropping the final い in the adjective. Similarly, drop only the final い in the 〜たい form of the verb. Compare these two examples:

Present/future:	白(しろ)い　です	食べたい　です
Past:	白かった　です	食べたかった　です
Present negative:	白くない　です	食べたくなかった　です
	白く　ありません	食べたく　ありません
Past negative:	白くなかった　です	食べたくない　です
	白く　ありません　でした	食べたく　ありません　でした

2. まだ – not yet or still

Used with a negative verb, まだ indicates that the action of the verb hasn't happened yet. It is used with です or before the verb (negative form) that it modifies.

A) 友さんは　まだ　食べていませんでした。 = Tomo had not eaten yet.
B) あなたの　家に　まだ　行きたくありません。 = I don't want to go to your house yet.
C) 雨は　まだ　降(ふ)って　いません。 = It's not raining yet.
D) キアラさん、まだ　宿題(しゅくだい)を　して　いませんか。
= Kiara, haven't you done your homework yet?
E) 明日(あした)の　数学(すうがく)の　テストの　勉強(べんきょう)は　もう　しましたか。
= Have you already studied for tomorrow's math test?
F) いいえ、まだです。 = No, not yet.
G) お姉(あね)さんは　まだ　独身(どくしん) (single)　ですか。 = Is your older sister still single?
H) はい、まだ　独身(どくしん)　です。 = Yes, she is still single.

3. もう **– already**

This adverb もう in conjunction with a verb indicates that the action has already happened.

A) 朝(あさ)ご飯(はん)を　もう　食べました。 = I have already eaten breakfast.
B) 友達と　もう　話しました。 = I have already spoken with my friend.
C) もう　コーラを　飲みました。 = I already drank the cola.
D) 宿題(しゅくだい)は　もう　しました。 = I have already done my homework.

■ 自習(じしゅう) Self Check

1. Say the following, out loud to yourself, in Japanese.

A) I want to drink milk.
B) I do not want to go surfing.
C) I wanted to take a shower at 7:00 A.M.
D) I did not want to sleep.
E) I want to eat gyoza and ramen.
F) I do not want to go to the garden.
G) Yesterday, I wanted to see a movie.
H) Tuesday, I did not want to study science.

2. Say the following in Japanese.

A) I don't want to study yet.
B) Have you eaten lunch? No, not yet.
C) Yamamoto-sensei hasn't come here yet.
D) I haven't watched (name a popular movie) yet.

■ 練習(れんしゅう)の時間(じかん) Time for Practice

I. Pair Practice

Play tic-tac-toe. Do じゃんけんぽん (paper/rock/scissors) to see who goes first. The first player chooses a space and changes that word from the dictionary form to the たい です form out loud. Play the game again, this time changing each into the たくありません or ～たくない です form. If you have time, play this game again using the past affirmative (～たかったです) and past negative (～たくなかったです).

手伝(てつだ)う	来る	練習(れんしゅう)する
起(お)きる	寝(ね)る	勉強(べんきょう)する
買い物する	開(あ)ける	聞く

話す	書く	立つ
座(すわ)る	閉(と)じる	終(お)わる
飲む	料理(りょうり)をする	テニスをする

はじめる	見る	出(だ)す
着る	売(う)る	言う
食べる	待つ	入(はい)る

2. Whole Class Practice

Your teacher will give you a slip of paper with two activities on it: one that you "want to do" and one that you "will do." Circulate among your classmates, politely inviting them to join you in the activity that you "want to do," until you find someone who "will do" that activity with you. (Note: You must agree to "do" at least one activity that you "will do" and find someone else willing to agree to do what you "want to do", in order to sit down.)

A- さん： 土曜日に (*name a film*) を　みませんか。
B- さん： いいえ、その　映画(えいが)は　見(み)たくありません。
-OR- すみません、土曜日は　ちょっと・・・・
-OR- はい、いいですよ。私も　その　映画(えいが)が　見(み)たいです。

3. Pair Practice

まだ and もう

Following the example, ask you partner if he or she still has not done the various things below. Your partner should answer honestly.

朝(あさ)ご飯(はん)を　食(た)べる
Question：まだ　朝(あさ)ご飯(はん)を　食(た)べて　いませんか。
Answer　：はい、まだ　食(た)べて　いません。
-OR- いいえ、もう　食(た)べました。

A) 昼(ひる)ご飯(はん)を　食べる
B) 晩(ばん)ご飯(はん)を　食べる
C) 友達(ともだち)と　話す
D) 宿題(しゅくだい)を　する
E) 家(うち)に　帰(かえ)る
F) Create as many additional questions as you can in the remaining time.)

■ 文化箱(ぶんかばこ) Culture Chest

Cherry Blossoms

Springtime in Japan always makes the television news headlines. Daily weather reports map and track the exact date and location the cherry blossoms will be in full bloom (満開(まんかい)). Coworkers, friends, and families gather in parks for spring parties. Everyone brings food and drinks, and sits on "portable" tatami mats under the blooming trees, eating, drinking, and singing. Cherry petals gently waft to and fro before lightly falling on the visitors below. If you've never seen dozens of cherry trees in full bloom, you might be overwhelmed the first time you visit a Japanese park or garden in spring. During this season, nightly news reports show people enjoying the blossoms around the country, beginning with Kyushu in the south, and, as the weather warms, moving up to Sapporo, in Hokkaido. These news and weather reports demonstrate how the Japanese are fascinated with this display of natural beauty. The fascination is even greater because the 満開(まんかい) season is so short. Do you know if there are any cherry trees near you?

■ キアラのジャーナル Kiara's Journal 

Answer the following questions based upon the diary entry below.

❶ What happened in the garden at 4:50 P.M.?
❷ Was Basho ready to return to the ryokan?
❸ What did Ben suggest doing?
❹ Why did Tomo agree to do what Ben suggested?

ジャーナルへ

今日は、兼六園に 六時間ぐらい いました。朝から晩までよい天気でした。少し風がありましたが、それがとても **comfortable** でした。午後五時十分前に、とつぜん、うるさい声が聞こえました。その声は、「皆さん、4時50分です。あと10分で、お庭が閉まります。今日は、どうもありがとうございました。お気をつけて、お帰り下さい。」と、言いました。

芭蕉さんはまだ石の上に座っていました。「私はこの庭が大好きです。旅館へ帰りたくありません。」と、言いました。

ベン君は、「僕も帰りたくないです。どうしましょうか。ビーチで散歩をしませんか。」と、言いました。友さんは、「散歩ですか。いいですね。ビーチにたこ焼き屋がありますね。」と、言いました。

私は、たこ焼きはあまり食べたくありませんでしたが、ビーチが、好きですから、いっしょに行きました。私は、ピザとメキシコの料理と中国の料理が、食べたかったです。でも、残念ですが、ここにそれはありません。

本当に、きれいなサンセットで、明日も晴れると思いましたが、友さんが、海の風をよくかいだ **(smelled)** 後、「明日は、大雨になりますよ。」と、言いました。

第10課の5

食べ物も、飲み物も、たくさん 持って行きましょう。

Let's take a lot of food and drinks.

1.

1) 桜は、来週、一番 きれい でしょう。

2.

2) 皆で、お花見を しませんか！

3) いい ですね！ しましょう、しましょう！

3.

4) 芭蕉さんも、一緒に 行きませんか。

5) それは いい ですね。

4.

6) 美味しい 物も、食べたい です。

7) もちろん です！食べ物も、飲み物も、たくさん 持って 行きましょう。でも、カラオケは したくありませんね。

5.

8) 僕は、カラオケを したい です。芭蕉さんの 俳句を ロックンロールで 歌いたい です！

6.

9) かっこいい・・・。

■ 会話 Dialogue

REMINDER: You may see some kanji / vocabulary you do not recognize. Use the context to try to understand the meanings of those parts of the dialogue.

1. 友　　：桜は、来週、一番　きれい　でしょう。
2. キアラ：皆で、お花見を　しませんか！
3. ベン　：いい　ですね！　しましょう、しましょう！
4. じゅん：芭蕉さんも、一緒に　行きませんか。
5. 芭蕉　：それは　いい　ですね。
6. キアラ：美味しい　物も、食べたい　です。
7. 友　　：もちろん　です！　食べ物も、飲み物も、たくさん　持って　行きましょう。でも、カラオケは　したくありませんね。
8. ベン　：僕は、カラオケを　したい　です。芭蕉さんの　俳句を　ロックンロールで　歌いたい　です！
9. キアラ：かっこいい…。

■ 単語 New Words

桜 (n)
花見 (n)
ロックンロール (n)
持って 行く / 行きます (v)
持って 来る / 来ます (v)
持って 帰る / 帰ります (v)
連れて 行く / 行きます (v)
もちろん (exp.) – of course
連れて 来る / 来ます (v) – to bring (person)
連れて 帰る / 帰ります (v) – to take (person) back (home)

■ 漢字 Kanji

桜 (10 strokes)	さくら – cherry blossoms, cherry tree	一	十	オ	木	木'	木''	木'''
	桜 – cherry blossoms, cherry tree	栥	桜	桜				
	This KANJI is quite easy to remember. There is a large tree (木) on the left with three petals falling on a woman (女) sitting under the CHERRY tree during 花見 .							

■ 言葉の探索 Language Detection

1. 持って行く – take (something)

As you learned in Chapter 6, you can combine verb phrases by putting all but the last verb in the TE form.

There are also many cases where two verbs are combined into one phrase with the first verb being in the TE form. A common example is with 持って行く, which combines the verbs "to hold" and "to go." If you hold (something) and go somewhere with it, the new verb you have made becomes *to take* (something).

If the second verb is 来る the phrase becomes *to bring* (持って来る) because you are coming somewhere with something.

If the second verb is 帰る the phrase becomes *to bring back* (持って帰る) because you are returning somewhere with something.

Note that this term is only used for taking or bringing a THING or an OBJECT.

A) 私は　かさを　持って行きます。 = I will take an umbrella.

B) お水を　持って来て　下さい。 = Please bring water.

C) 私は　毎日　家へ　日本語の本を　持って帰ります。
= I bring my Japanese book back home every day.

2. 連れて行く – to take somebody somewhere

To talk about taking or bringing people somewhere, use the て-form of the verb 連れる and attach it to a verb of direction.

連れて行きます = to take somebody somewhere
連れて来ます = to bring somebody somewhere
連れて帰ります = to return somewhere with someone

A) 私は　ゆみさん　と　私の犬を　連れて行きます。
= I will take Yumi and my dog (with me).

B) けんじのお父さんは　けんじを　アメリカへ　連れて来ます。
= Kenji's dad will bring Kenji to the U.S.

C) 妹さんを　パーティーから　連れて帰って下さい。
= Please take your younger sister back home from the party.

■ 自習 Self Check

1. 持って行く、持って来る、持って帰る

Try to say the following in Japanese:

A) I will bring money.

B) Kiara did not take a jacket to school.

C) I returned home with my homework.

2. 連(つ)れて行く、連(つ)れて来る、連(つ)れて帰る

Try to say the following in Japanese:

A) I will take Jun (with me).

B) Ben brought a cute first year student to my house.

C) I did not return home with my younger brother.

D) My teacher brought a friend to the classroom.

■ 練習(れんしゅう)の時間(じかん) Time for Practice

1. Small Group Practice

Create a sentence

Your teacher will give you a grid similar to the one below. Write your name (in katakana) in Space #1 and write verbs of your choice (use the dictionary form) in each of the remaining spaces. Take turns rolling the dice.

The first roll (of two dice) determines which verb you will use in your sentence. For instance, if you roll a "5," move your marker to space 5. Your second roll (with one die) determines what verb form you use in your sentence based on the choices below:

1 = non past (〜ます)
2 = negative non past (〜ません)
3 = past tense (〜ました)
4 = past negative (〜ませんでした)
5 = want to ~ (〜たい)
6 = do not want to ~ (〜たくないです or 〜たくありません)

Once you have rolled twice, make a sentence using the indicated form of the verb. If your group agrees that your sentence makes sense, put your name in Space 5 and pass the dice to your neighbor. You may write on your partners' papers (for instance, if you roll another "5"). Continue until all grids are filled. The person whose name is in the most spaces is the winner.

1 名前	2	3	4	5	6
7	8	9	10	11	12

2. Small Group Practice

Plan a flower-viewing party or some other appropriate party of your choice.

Step 1 – Prepare an invitation in Japanese that includes the reason for the party/picnic, time, place, what to bring, who can come, etc.

Step 2 – Announce the invitation to your class.

Step 3 – Make a list in Japanese of all the things that each person will take to the party. Use 持(も)って行きます.

A) まさ君は　寿司を　持って行きます。　= Masa will take sushi.

B) 友子さんは　飲み物を　持って行きます。　= Tomoko will take drinks.

Also, since many people will need rides to the party, make a separate list of who will bring which people to the party. Use 連れて行きます。

A) 私は　健太郎を　連れて行きます。　= I'll take Kentarou.

B) トム君は　ケンくんと　ナオミさんを　連れて行きます。　= Tom will take Ken and Naomi.

■ 文化箱 Culture Chest

花よりだんご

花よりだんご is a Japanese proverb which can be translated as "food and drink before flowers." A dango is a somewhat sweet Japanese snack that comes in a wide range of varieties and is a popular treat for 花見 (cherry blossom viewing) picnics and festivals. Although viewing transient cherry blossoms fluttering to the ground and picnicking below them is an ancient tradition in Japan, this expression might insinuate that the real attraction is the food and drink that accompanies the flowers!

The larger meaning of 花よりだんご can be the idea that the here and now concerns of people win out over more high-minded pursuits, or that substance often wins out over style.

Sakura Song

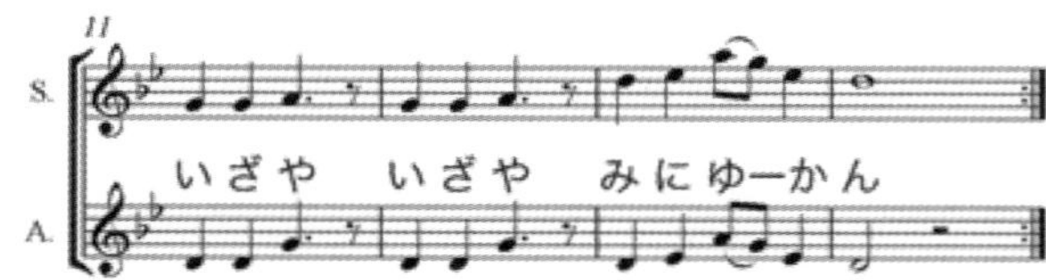

■ キアラのジャーナル Kiara's Journal 

Read the journal entry below, and then answer these questions.

❶ Describe three activities Kiara did in the park today.
❷ What did Tomo say after dinner?
❸ What does Basho do in response?
❹ Write down one possible English translation for the poem that Basho wrote.
❺ What is the last thing that Kiara says to Basho?

ジャーナルへ

今日、お花見をしました。兼六園には、桜がたくさんあります。その桜の木の下まで、たくさんの食べ物とジュースを持って行きました。桜はとても美しくて、おにぎりと焼きそばとだんごはとても美味しかったです。そして、琴の音楽もとてもきれいでした。

じゅん君は、「もう少し、ジュースを飲みたいです。もっとありますか。焼きそばも下さい。」と、言いました。ベン君は、「ありますよ。どうぞ。友さん、そこの焼きそばを取って下さい。」と、言いました。そして、「ねえ、この音楽はとてもいいですね。」と、言いました。

芭蕉さんは、「ええ、そうですね。あの人は三十年間琴をひいていますから、とても上手です。僕は毎年春に、琴が聞きたくなります。琴は春の声だと思います。」と、言いました。

『琴が春の声…』、その言葉は、いつまでも (forever) 私の心にあるでしょう。私達は、時の門の旅から、何も持って行けないし、誰も連れて行けません。でも、旅でもらったすてきな言葉は、どこへでも自由に (freely) 持って行くことが出来ます。それは、一番すてきなプレゼントですね。

友さんは、「このまま　ここに　いたいですが、私達は、行かなくては　なりません。(must go)」と、言いました。芭蕉さんは、「そうですか。」と言って、

『鐘消えて
花の香は撞く
夕哉』

という俳句を詠みました。その意味は：お寺の鐘の音が消えて (As the sound of the temple bell fades)、静かな春の夕ぐれ (evening) に、花の香 (scents) が lingers (like the fading tone).

本当にきれいな俳句だと思いました。

友さんが静かに、「じゃ、皆さん、行きますよ。芭蕉さん、本当にありがとうございました。」と、言いました。そして私は、「芭蕉さん、私は、日本語の勉強をもっとがんばります。」と、言いました。芭蕉さんは、「*約束ですよ、キアラさん。さようなら。」と、言いました。「さようなら、芭蕉さん。あなたを　忘れません。」

* 約束 – promise, appointment / 約束する (to promise)

■ 単語チェックリスト New Word Checklist

たんごちぇっくりすと

10-1

あき・秋 *n* fall/autumn
あめ・雨 *n* rain
いし・石 *n* stone, rock
いちど・一度 *count.* one time, one degree
おおあめ・大雨 *n* heavy rain
おんど・温度 *n* temperature
かみなり・雷 *n* lightning
きせつ・季節 *n* season
きゅうど・九度 *count.* nine times, nine degrees
くもり・曇り *n* cloudy
くもる・曇る / くもります・曇ります *v* become cloudy
ごど・五度 *count.* five times, five degrees
さかな・魚 *n* fish
さんど・三度 *count.* three times, three degrees
じしん・地震 *n* earthquake
じゅうど・十度 *count.* ten times, ten degrees
しろ・城 *n* castle
たいふう・台風 *n* typhoon
たつまき・竜巻 *n* tornado
つゆ・梅雨 *n* rainy season
てんき・天気 *n* weather
てんきよほう・天気予報 *n* weather report
なつ・夏 *n* summer
ななど・七度 *count.* seven times, seven degrees
なんど・何度 *inter.* how many times/degrees?
にど・二度 *count.* two times, two degrees
にわ・庭 *n* garden
はいく・俳句 *n* haiku (poem)
はちど・八度 *count.* eight times, eight degrees
はな・花 *n* flower
はる・春 *n* spring
はれ・晴れ *n* clear (skies)
はれる・晴れる / はれます・晴れます *v* become clear (weather)
ふゆ・冬 *n* winter
ふる・降る / ふります・降ります *v* to precipitate
ゆき 雪 *n* snow
よんど・四度 *count.* four times, four degrees
ろくど・六度 *count.* six times, six degrees

10-2

あさって・明後日 *n* day after tomorrow
おととい・一昨日 *n* day before yesterday
だれも *exp.* no one
どこにも *adv.* nowhere (w. neg. verb); everywhere, anywhere, anyplace
どこへも *adv.* nowhere, not anywhere, not any place (w. neg. verb) (ex: どこへも行きません。 = He is not going any place.)
どこも *adv.* everywhere, wherever
つかう・使う / つかいます・使います *v* to use
つくる・作る / つくります・作ります *v* to make

10-3

あそぶ・遊ぶ / あそびます・遊びます *v* to play
なにか・何か something

10-4

うそ・嘘 *n* lie
おなかが いっぱい・お腹が 一杯 *exp.* have a full stomach
じつは・実は *adv.* by the way, actually
ひとりで・一人で *exp.* alone, by oneself
ほんとう・本当 *n* truth, reality
まだ *adv.* not yet (with negative verb)
もう *adv./interj.* already

10-5

さくら・桜 *n* cherry tree/blossom
つれて・連れて いく・行く / いきます・行きます *v* to take someone
つれて・連れて かえる・帰る / かえります ・帰ります *v* to return with someone
つれて・連れて くる・来る / きます・来ます *v* to bring someone
はなみ・花見 *n* cherry blossom viewing, flower viewing
もちろん *exp.* of course
もって・持って いく・行く / いきます・行きます *v* to take something
もって・持って かえる・帰る / かえります・帰ります *v* to return with something
もって ・持って くる・来る / きます・来ます *v* to bring something
ろっくんろーる・ロックンロール *n* rock and roll (music)

Kanji List

Kanji	Ch/ sect.	Pronunciation	Meaning	Example usage
木	1-2	モク (もく); き	tree	木曜日 (もくようび) – Thursday
日	1-2	ニ (に); ひ; び; か	day; sun	日本 (にほん) – Japan
本	1-2	ホン (ほん); もと	book; origin	本当 (ほんとう) – really?
東	1-3	トウ (とう); ひがし	east	東北 (とうほく) – northeastern part
京	1-3	キョウ (きょう)	capital	東京 (とうきょう) – Tokyo
語	1-3	ゴ (ご)	language	日本語 (にほんご) – Japanese language
私	1-4	わたくし; わたし	I, me	私達 (わたしたち) – we/us
父	1-4	フ (ふ); ちち; (お)とう(さん)	father	祖父 (そふ) – grandfather
母	1-4	ボ (ぼ); はは; (お)かあ(さん)	mother	祖母 (そぼ) – grandmother
気	1-5	き	spirit; energy	元気 (げんき) – healthy, energetic
元	1-5	ゲン (げん); もと	an ancient currency; origin	地元 (じもと) – hometown
人	1-5	ジン (じん); ニン (にん); ひと	person	日本人 (にほんじん) – Japanese person
休	1-5	やす(む)	to rest, take a break, a vacation	春休み (はるやす) – spring break
何	2-1	なに; なん	what	何人 (なんにん) – how many people?, 何人 (なにじん) – what nationality?
家	2-1	カ; いえ; うち	home	家族 (かぞく) – family
兄	2-1	キョウ (きょう); あに; (お)にい(さん)	older brother	従兄 (いとこ) – older male cousin
姉	2-1	あね; (お)ねえ(さん)	older sister	従姉 (いとこ) – older female cousin
弟	2-1	ダイ (だい); おとうと	younger brother	兄弟 (きょうだい) – siblings
妹	2-1	いもうと	younger sister	妹さん (いもうと) – someone else's younger sister
一	2-2	イチ (いち); ひと(つ)	one	一つ (ひと) – one (thing)
二	2-2	ニ (に); ふた(つ)	two	二枚 (にまい) – two sheets
三	2-2	サン (さん); みっ(つ)	three	三本 (さんぼん) – 3 cylindrical object
四	2-2	シ (し); よん; よっ(つ)	four	四人 (よにん) – four people
五	2-2	ゴ (ご); いつ(つ)	five	五枚 (ごまい) – five flat objects
六	2-2	ロク (ろく); むっ(つ)	six	六ページ (ろく) – page 6
七	2-2	シチ (しち); なな; なな(つ)	seven	七月 (しちがつ) – July
八	2-2	ハチ (はち); やっ(つ)	eight	八つ (やっ) – eight things
九	2-2	キュウ (きゅう); く; ここの(つ)	nine	九時 (くじ) – nine o'clock
十	2-2	ジュウ (じゅう); とう	ten	十分 (じゅうぶん/じっぷん) – ten minutes
百	2-2	ヒャク (ひゃく)	hundred	三百 (さんびゃく) – three hundred
犬	2-3	いぬ	dog	子犬 (こいぬ) – a small dog
高	3-1	コウ (こう); たか(い)	tall, expensive	高校 (こうこう) – high school
小	3-1	ショウ (しょう)	small	小学校 (しょうがっこう) – elementary school
中	3-1	チュウ (ちゅう); なか	middle	中学校 (ちゅうがっこう) – middle school
大	3-1	ダイ (だい); おお(きい)	big; large	大学 (だいがく) – college/university
学	3-1	ガク (がく)	to learn	学生 (がくせい) – student
校	3-1	コウ (こう)	school	高校 (こうこう) – high school
年	3-1	ネン (ねん); とし	year	五年間 (ごねんかん) – five years (period)
先	3-1	セン (せん); さき	earlier, previous, future	先生 (せんせい) – teacher
生	3-1	セイ (せい)	to be born	生徒 (せいと) – student
山	3-1	サン (さん); やま	mountain	富士山 (ふじさん) – Mt. Fuji
英	3-2	エイ (えい)	gifted, talented	英語 (えいご) – English
国	3-2	コク (こく); ゴク (ごく); くに	country, nation	中国 (ちゅうごく) – China
音	3-2	オン (おん); おと	sound	音楽 (おんがく) – music
楽	3-2	ガク (がく); たの(しい)	fun, enjoyable	文楽 (ぶんらく) – puppet theater
今	3-2	コン (こん); いま	now	今月 (こんげつ) – this month
分	3-2	ブン (ぶん); フン (ふん); プン (ぷん); わ(かる)	minute, portion; to understand	六分 (ろっぷん) – six minutes
書	3-3	ショ (しょ); か(く)	write	図書館 (としょかん) – library

Kanji	Ch/ sect.	Pronunciation	Meaning	Example usage
寺	3-3	ジ;てら	temple	東大寺 (とうだいじ) – Todaiji Temple
時	3-3	ジ;とき	time	1時 (いちじ) – one o'clock
門	3-3	モン	gate	寺の門 (てら　もん) – temple's gate
間	3-3	カン;あいだ	interval, space	時間 (じかん) – time, hour, interval of time
下	3-3	カ;した;くだ(る)	below, descend, give, under	下さい (くだ) – please descend, give
暑	3-4	あつ(い)	hot (weather/temp.)	暑い (あつ) – is hot
寒	3-4	さむ(い)	cold (weather/temp.)	寒い (さむ) – is cold
神	3-4	シン;ジン;かみ	God/god, spirits	神様 (かみさま) – God, gods
社	3-4	シャ;ジャ	company, association	社会 (しゃかい) – social studies
風	3-5	フウ;かぜ	wind	台風 (たいふう) – typhoon
友	3-5	ユウ;とも	friend	友達 (ともだち) – friend
言	4-1	ゲン;い(う)	to speak	言語 (げんご) – language
外	4-1	ガイ;そと	outside	外国人 (がいこくじん) – foreign person
話	4-2	ワ;はなし;はな(す)	to speak, conversation	昔話 (むかしばなし) – folk tales
食	4-3	ショク;た(べる)	food, eat	食べ物 (た　もの) – foods
飲	4-3	の(む)	drink	飲み物 (の　もの) – drinks
物	4-3	ブツ;もの	tangible thing, object	買い物 (か　もの) – shopping (purchases)
車	4-3	シャ;くるま	car, cart	電車 (でんしゃ) – electric train; 自動車 (じどうしゃ) – automobile
行	4-4	い(く);コウ	go	旅行 (りょこう) – travel, a trip
来	4-4	ライ;く(る)	next, coming, to come	来週 (らいしゅう) – next week
帰	4-4	かえ(る)	return (home)	帰ります (かえ) – to return
見	4-5	み(る);み(える)	to see, visible, can be seen	花見 (はなみ) – flower viewing
聞	4-5	ブン;き(く);き(こえる)	to listen, to ask	聞きます (き) – to listen
前	5-1	ゼン;まえ;〜まえ	in front, before	名前 (なまえ) – name
午	5-1	ゴ	noon	午前 (ごぜん) – morning, A.M.
後	5-1	ゴ;あと	after, afterward	午後 (ごご) – afternoon, P.M.
良	5-1	よ(い);い(い)	good	良い (よ) – good, excellent
月	5-1	ゲツ;がつ;つき	month, moon	先月 (せんげつ) – last month
火	5-1	カ;ひ	fire	火曜日 (かようび) – Tuesday
水	5-1	スイ;みず	water	水曜日 (すいようび) – Wednesday
金	5-1	キン;かね	gold, money	金持ち (かねも) – rich man
土	5-1	ド;つち	soil, ground	土曜日 (どようび) – Saturday
曜	5-1	ヨウ	day of the week	何曜日 (なんようび) – what day of the week?
千	5-2	セン	thousand	千円 (せんえん) – 1,000 yen
万	5-2	マン	ten thousand	一万 (いちまん) – 10,000
末	5-2	マツ	end	週末 (しゅうまつ) – weekend
毎	5-2	マイ	every	毎日 (まいにち) – every day
週	5-2	シュウ	week	先週 (せんしゅう) – last week
電	5-4	デン	electricity	電気 (でんき) – electricity
達	5-4	タチ;たち;だち	to reach or arrive at; pluralizes some words	私達 (わたしたち) – us, we
体	6-1	タイ;からだ	body	体育館 (たいいくかん) – gymnasium
目	6-1	モク;め	eye	二つ目 (ふた　め) – one after next, second
口	6-1	くち;ぐち	mouth	入り口 (いり　ぐち) – entrance
耳	6-1	みみ	ear	耳 (みみ) – ear
手	6-1	シュ;た;て	hand	下手 (へた) – unskillful
足	6-1	ソク;あし	foot, leg; to be enough, sufficient	足首 (あしくび) – ankle
心	6-1	シン;こころ	heart, spirit, soul	安心 (あんしん) – relief, peace of mind
持	6-1	も(つ)	to hold, to have	持って来る (も　く) – to bring
待	6-1	ま(つ)	to wait	待つ (ま) – to wait
強	6-1	キョウ;つよ(い)	to be strong	強い (つよ) – strong
平	6-2	ヘイ	even, flat	平和 (へいわ) – peace
和	6-2	ワ	peace and harmony; ancient name for Japan	和食 (わしょく) – Japanese style meal

Kanji	Ch/ sect.	Pronunciation	Meaning	Example usage
低	6-2	ひく(い)	short, low	低い(ひく) – is short (stature)
太	6-2	タイ(たい);ふと(い); ふと(る)	plump, thick	太っています(ふと) – is fat
医	6-3	イ(い)	related to medicine/ medical field	医者(いしゃ) – doctor
者	6-3	シャ(しゃ);もの	person	学者(がくしゃ) – scholar
薬	6-3	くすり	medicine	薬屋(くすりや) – pharmacy
着	6-4	き(る)	to wear	着物(きもの) – traditional Japanese clothing
花	7-1	はな	flower	花火(はなび) – fireworks
池	7-1	チ(ち);いけ	pond	電池(でんち) – battery
趣	7-1	シュ(しゅ)	gist, to tend, become	趣味(しゅみ) – hobby
味	7-1	ミ(み);あじ;あじ(わう)	taste, flavor, to appreciate	味見(あじみ) – sampling, tasting
事	7-1	ジ(じ);こと	thing	仕事(しごと) – work, job
好	7-2	す(き)	like	好き(す) – to like
上	7-3	ジョウ(じょう);うえ; かみ;あ(がる)	above, upper; climb; go up (a hill)	上手(じょうず) – skillful
色	7-4	いろ	color	色々(いろいろ) – various
白	7-4	ハク(はく);しろ;しろ(い)	white	白い(しろ) – white
黒	7-4	コク(こく);くろ;くろ(い)	black	黒板(こくばん) – blackboard
赤	7-4	セキ(せき);あか;あか(い)	red, crimson, scarlet	赤ちゃん(あか) – baby
青	7-4	セイ(せい);あお;あお(い)	blue, green; young	青葉(あおば) – spring leaves
歌	7-5	カ(か);うた;うた(う)	song, sing	歌舞伎(かぶき) – kabuki theater
思	7-5	シ(し);おも(う)	to think, believe	思います(おも) – to think
美	8-1	ビ(び);うつく(しい)	beautiful	美人(びじん) – beautiful person
長	8-1	チョウ(ちょう);なが(い)	head, chief; long (in length)	校長(こうちょう) – school principal
短	8-1	みじか(い)	short (length)	短い(みじか) – is short (length)
海	8-1	カイ(かい);うみ	ocean, sea	日本海(にほんかい) – Sea of Japan
安	8-2	アン(あん);やす(い)	safe; cheap	安全(あんぜん) – safe
悪	8-2	わる(い)	bad	悪い(わる) – is bad, evil
面	8-2	メン(めん);おも	face, mask	面(めん) – mask
天	8-2	テン(てん);あま	heaven	天ぷら(てん) – deep fried fish and vegetables
立	8-2	た(つ)	to stand	立ちます(た) – to stand
昔	8-2	むかし	long ago	昔々(むかしむかし) – long long ago
々	8-2		(reduplicating mark)	人々(ひとびと) – people
有	8-3	ユウ(ゆう);あ(る)	to exist, to be	有名(ゆうめい) – famous
広	8-3	ひろ(い)	wide, spacious	広島(ひろしま) – city name
島	8-3	トウ(とう);しま	island	大島(おおしま) – large island, family name
暗	8-3	くら(い)	dark, dim	暗い(くら) – dark
明	8-3	メイ(めい);あか(るい)	light, bright	明るい(あか) – bright
買	9-1	バイ(ばい);か(う)	to buy, purchase	買います(か) – to buy
売	9-1	バイ(ばい);う(る)	to sell	売ります(う) – to sell
店	9-1	テン(てん);みせ	store, shop	本店(ほんてん) – head office
全	9-2	ゼン(ぜん)	all, entirely	全国(ぜんこく) – the entire country
部	9-2	ブ(ぶ)	section, group of	部活(ぶかつ) – club activities
円	9-2	エン(えん);まる(い)	yen, round	百円(ひゃくえん) – 100 yen
春	10-1	はる	spring	春(はる) – spring
夏	10-1	なつ	summer	夏休み(なつやす) – summer vacation
秋	10-1	あき	autumn, fall	秋田(あきた) – city/prefecture in northern Japan
冬	10-1	ふゆ	winter	冬(ふゆ) – winter
石	10-1	セキ(せき);いし	stone, rock	石山(いしやま) – family name
使	10-2	つか(う)	to use	使う(つか) – to use
作	10-2	つく(る)	to make	作る(つく) – to make
当	10-4	トウ(とう);あ(たる)	really, truthfully	本当(ほんとう) – really?
桜	10-5	さくら	cherry blossoms/tree	桜んぼう(さくら) – (edible) cherry

Appendix 1
Grammar References

Verb Conjugation Summary

Type 1 Verbs

non-past (～ます)	non-past negative (～ません)	～て-form	past (～ました)	past negative (～ませんでした)	dictionary (infinitive) form	English meaning
あります	ありません	あって	ありました	ありませんでした	ある	to exist (inanimate)
言(い)います	言(い)いません	言(い)って	言(い)いました	言(い)いませんでした	言(い)う	to say
読(よ)みます	読(よ)みません	読(よ)んで	読(よ)みました	読(よ)みませんでした	読(よ)む	to read
書(か)きます	書(か)きません	書(か)いて	書(か)きました	書(か)きませんでした	書(か)く	to write

Type 2 Verbs

non-past (～ます)	non-past negative (～ません)	～て-form	past (～ました)	past negative (～ませんでした)	dictionary (infinitive) form	English meaning
開(あ)けます	開(あ)けません	開(あ)けて	開(あ)けました	開(あ)けませんでした	開(あ)ける	to open (doors/windows)
食(た)べます	食(た)べません	食(た)べて	食(た)べました	食(た)べませんでした	食(た)べる	to eat
見(み)ます	見(み)ません	見(み)て	見(み)ました	見(み)ませんでした	見(み)る	to look

Irregular Verbs

non-past (～ます)	non-past negative (～ません)	～て-form	past (～ました)	past negative (～ませんでした)	dictionary (infinitive) form	English meaning
来(き)ます	来(き)ません	来(き)て	来(き)ました	来(き)ませんでした	来(く)る	to come
します	しません	して	しました	しませんでした	する	to do

Verbs by Chapter

ある / あります	2-1	to exist (inanimate things)
いる / います	2-1	to exist (animate beings)
言(い)う / 言(い)います	4-1	to say
手伝(てつだ)う / 手伝(てつだ)います	4-1	to help, to assist
話(はな)す / 話(はな)します	4-2	to speak
撮(と)る / 撮(と)ります	4-2	to take (a photo)
知(し)る / 知(し)ります	4-2	to know something/someone
食(た)べる / 食(た)べます	4-3	to eat
飲(の)む / 飲(の)みます	4-3	to drink
行(い)く / 行(い)きます	4-4	to go
帰(かえ)る / 帰(かえ)ります	4-4	to return
来(く)る / 来(き)ます	4-4	to come
寝(ね)る / 寝(ね)ます	5-1	to sleep
起(お)きる / 起(お)きます	5-1	to wake (up)
生(う)まれる / 生(う)まれます	5-2	to be born
終(お)わる / 終(お)わります	5-2	to finish, to end
始(はじ)める / 始(はじ)めます	5-2	to begin
勉強(べんきょう)(を)する / します	5-2	to study
散歩(さんぽ)(を)する / します	5-4	to take a walk

Verbs by Chapter

Verb	Chapter	Meaning
入(い)れる / 入(い)れます	6-1	to put into
出(で)る / 出(で)ます	6-1	to go out, to leave, to get out
入(はい)る / 入(はい)ります	6-1	to come in, to go in, enter
待(ま)つ / 待(ま)ちます	6-1	to wait
持(も)つ / 持(も)ちます	6-1	to have, to hold, to carry
太(ふと)って いる / います	6-2	to be fat
太(ふと)る / 太(ふと)ります	6-2	to get fat
やせて いる / います	6-2	to be skinny
呼(よ)ぶ / 呼(よ)びます	6-3	to call out (to), to call
(薬(くすり)を)飲(の)む / 飲(の)みます	6-3	to take medicine
怪我(けが)(を)する / します	6-3	to get wounded
心配(しんぱい)(を)する / します	6-3	to worry
昼寝(ひるね)(を)する / します	6-3	to nap
かける / かけます	6-4	to wear glasses or sun-glasses
被(かぶ)る / 被(かぶ)ります	6-4	to wear on your head
着(き)る / 着(き)ます	6-4	to wear (above waist; dress-es)
住(す)む / 住(す)みます	6-4	to live/reside
する / します	6-4	to wear (accessories); to do
履(は)く / 履(は)きます	6-4	to wear below the waist
歌(うた)う / 歌(うた)います	7-1	to sing
泳(およ)ぐ / 泳(およ)ぎます	7-1	to swim
弾(ひ)く / 弾(ひ)きます	7-1	to play (a stringed instrument)
思(おも)う / 思(おも)います	7-2	to think
頑張(がんば)る / 頑張(がんば)ります	7-3	to do one's best
やってみる / やってみます	7-3	to try (to do something)
やる / やります	7-3	to do
やめる / やめます	8-2	to stop
売(う)る / 売(う)ります	9-1	to sell
買(か)い物(もの)(を)する / します	9-1	to go shopping
買(か)う / 買(か)います	9-1	to buy
カラオケ(からおけ)(を)する / します	9-1	to (sing) karaoke
けんか(を)する / します	9-1	to argue, to fight
シャワー(しゃわー)(を)する / します	9-1	to take a shower
シャンプー(しゃんぷー)(を)する / します	9-1	to shampoo
宿題(しゅくだい)(を)する / します	9-1	to do homework
食事(しょくじ)(を)する / します	9-1	to have a meal
デート(でーと)(を)する / します	9-1	to go on a date
電話(でんわ)(を)する / します	9-1	to telephone
仲直(なかな)り(を)する / します	9-1	to make up; to reconcile
旅行(りょこう)(を)する / します	9-1	to take a trip; to travel
いただく / いただきます	9-2	to receive [very polite]
探(さが)す / 探(さが)します	9-3	to search
上(あ)げる / 上(あ)げます	9-4	to give
もらう / もらいます	9-4	to receive
くれる / くれます	9-5	to give [to me or a family member]
遊(あそ)ぶ / 遊(あそ)びます	10-3	to play; to amuse; to hang out
曇(くも)る / 曇(くも)ります	10-1	to be cloudy
晴(は)れる / 晴(は)れます	10-1	to be clear (skies)
降(ふ)る / 降(ふ)ます	10-1	to precipitate
使(つか)う / 使(つか)います	10-2	to use
作(つく)る / 作(つく)ります	10-2	to make
持(も)って 行(い)く / 行(い)ます	10-3	to take something
連(つ)れて 行(い)く / 行(い)きます	10-5	to take someone
連(つ)れて 帰(かえ)る / 帰(かえ)ります	10-5	to return with someone
連(つ)れて 来(く)る / 来(き)ます	10-5	to bring
持(も)って 帰(かえ)る / 帰(かえ)ります	10-5	to take back or to return back with something
持(も)って 来(く)る / 来(き)ます	10-5	to bring something

Counting Basic Numbers

I-10 (2-1)		11-20 (2-2)		Above 20 (2-2)		Hundreds (2-2)		Thousands (5-2)		Ten Thousands (5-2)	
1	一 いち	11	十一 じゅういち	21	二十一 にじゅういち	100	百 ひゃく	1,000	千 せん	10,000	一万 いちまん
2	二 に	12	十二 じゅうに			200	二百 にひゃく	2,000	二千 にせん	20,000	二万 にまん
3	三 さん	13	十三 じゅうさん	30	三十 さんじゅう	300	三百 さんびゃく	3,000	三千 さんぜん	30,000	三万 さんまん
4	四 よん/し	14	十四 じゅうよん/し	40	四十 よんじゅう	400	四百 よんひゃく	4,000	四千 よんせん	40,000	四万 よんまん
5	五 ご	15	十五 じゅうご	50	五十 ごじゅう	500	五百 ごひゃく	5,000	五千 ごせん	50,000	五万 ごまん
6	六 ろく	16	十六 じゅうろく	60	六十 ろくじゅう	600	六百 ろくひゃく	6,000	六千 ろくせん	60,000	六万 ろくまん
7	七 なな/しち	17	十七 じゅうなな/しち	70	七十 ななじゅう	700	七百 ななひゃく	7,000	七千 ななせん	70,000	七万 ななまん
8	八 はち	18	十八 じゅうはち	80	八十 はちじゅう	800	八百 はちひゃく	8,000	八千 はちせん	80,000	八万 はちまん
9	九 く/きゅう	19	十九 じゅうく/きゅう	90	九十 きゅうじゅう	900	九百 きゅうひゃく	9,000	九千 きゅうせん	90,000	九万 きゅうまん
10	十 じゅう	20	二十 にじゅう							100,000	十万 じゅうまん

Counters

	Hours (3-2)	Minutes (3-2)	Grade Levels (3-1)	Class Periods (3-3)	Times/ Temp. (10-1)	People (2-1)	Small Animals (2-1)	Ages (2-2)	Generic Count.s (2-4)	Flat Objects (4-2)	Pages (4-2)
1	一時 いちじ	一分 いっぷん	Elem./Primary 小学一年生 しょうがくいちねんせい	一時間目 いちじかんめ	一度 いちど	一人 ひとり	一匹 いっぴき	一歳 いっさい	一つ ひとつ	一枚 いちまい	一ページ いち/いっぺーじ
2	二時 にじ	二分 にふん	小学二年生 しょうがくにねんせい	二時間目 にじかんめ	二度 にど	二人 ふたり	二匹 にひき	二歳 にさい	二つ ふた	二枚 にまい	二ページ にぺーじ
3	三時 さんじ	三分 さんぷん	小学三年生 しょうがくさんねんせい	三時間目 さんじかんめ	三度 さんど	三人 さんにん	三匹 さんびき	三歳 さんさい	三つ みっ	三枚 さんまい	三ページ さんぺーじ
4	四時 よじ	四分 よんぷん	小学四年生 しょうがくよんねんせい	四時間目 よんじかんめ	四度 よんど	四人 よにん	四匹 よんひき	四歳 よんさい	四つ よっ	四枚 よんまい	四ページ よんぺーじ
5	五時 ごじ	五分 ごふん	小学五年生 しょうがくごねんせい	五時間目 ごじかんめ	五度 ごど	五人 ごにん	五匹 ごひき	五歳 ごさい	五つ いつ	五枚 ごまい	五ページ ごぺーじ
6	六時 ろくじ	六分 ろっぷん	小学六年生 しょうがくろくねんせい	六時間目 ろくじかんめ	六度 ろくど	六人 ろくにん	六匹 ろっぴき	六歳 ろくさい	六つ むっ	六枚 ろくまい	六ページ ろくぺーじ
7	七時 なな/しちじ	七分 ななふん	MS/Jr. High 中学一年生 ちゅうがくいちねんせい	七時間目 ななじかんめ	七度 ななど	七人 なな/しちにん	七匹 ななひき	七歳 ななさい	七つ なな	七枚 ななまい	七ページ ななぺーじ
8	八時 はちじ	八分 はっぷん	中学二年生 ちゅうがくにねんせい		八度 はちど	八人 はちにん	八匹 はっぴき	八歳 はっさい	八つ やっ	八枚 はちまい	八ページ はっぺーじ
9	九時 くじ	九分 きゅうふん	中学三年生 ちゅうがくさんねんせい		九度 きゅうど	九人 きゅうにん	九匹 きゅうひき	九歳 きゅうさい	九つ ここの	九枚 きゅうまい	九ページ きゅうぺーじ
10	十時 じゅうじ	十分 じゅっぷん	Senior High 高校一年生 こうこういちねんせい		十度 じゅうど	十人 じゅうにん	十匹 じゅっぴき	十歳 じゅっさい	十 じゅっ	十枚 じゅうまい	十ページ じゅっぺーじ
11	十一時 じゅういちじ	十一分 じゅういっぷん	高校二年生 こうこうにねんせい			十一人 じゅういっにん	十一匹 じゅういっぴき	十一歳 じゅういっさい	十一 じゅういち	十一枚 じゅういちまい	十一ページ じゅういっぺーじ
12	十二時 じゅうにじ	十二分 じゅうにふん	高校三年生 こうこうさんねんせい			十二人 じゅうににん	十二匹 じゅうにひき	十二歳 じゅうにさい	十二 じゅうに	十二枚 じゅうにまい	十二ページ じゅうにぺーじ

Dates (5-3)							Cylindrical Objects (9-2)	Cupfuls (9-2)	Bound Volumes (9-2)
1st	一日 ついたち	11th	十一日 じゅういちにち	21st	二十一日 にじゅういちにち	1	一本 いっぽん	一杯 いっぱい	一冊 いっさつ
2nd	二日 ふつか	12th	十二日 じゅうににち	22nd	二十二日 にじゅうににち	2	二本 にほん	二杯 にはい	二冊 にさつ
3rd	三日 みっか	13th	十三日 じゅうさんにち	23rd	二十三日 にじゅうさんにち	3	三本 さんぼん	三杯 さんばい	三冊 さんさつ
4th	四日 よっか	14th	十四日 じゅうよっか	24th	二十四日 にじゅうよっか	4	四本 よんほん	四杯 よんはい	四冊 よんさつ
5th	五日 いつか	15th	十五日 じゅうごにち	25th	二十五日 にじゅうごにち	5	五本 ごほん	五杯 ごはい	五冊 ごさつ
6th	六日 むいか	16th	十六日 じゅうろくにち	26th	二十六日 にじゅうろくにち	6	六本 ろっぽん	六杯 ろっぱい	六冊 ろくさつ
7th	七日 なのか	17th	十七日 じゅうしちにち	27th	二十七日 にじゅうしちにち	7	七本 ななほん	七杯 ななはい	七冊 ななさつ
8th	八日 ようか	18th	十八日 じゅうはちにち	28th	二十八日 にじゅうはちにち	8	八本 はっぽん	八杯 はっぱい	八冊 はっさつ
9th	九日 ここのか	19th	十九日 じゅうくにち	29th	二十九日 にじゅうくにち	9	九本 きゅうほん	九杯 きゅうはい	九冊 きゅうさつ
10th	十日 とおか	20th	二十日 はつか	30th	三十日 さんじゅうにち	10	十本 じゅっぽん	十杯 じゅっぱい	十冊 じゅっさつ
				31st	三十一日 さんじゅういちにち				

Question Words

どれ	1-5	which (one)?
何 (なん/なに)	2-1	what?
いくつ	2-4	how many (things)?
どこ	2-4	where?
どう	3-5	how?
どんな	6-2	what kind?
いくら	9-2	how much?
何時 (なんじ)	3-2	what time?
何分 (なんぷん)	3-2	how many minutes?
何曜日 (なんようび)	5-1	what day (of the week)?
何月 (なんがつ)	5-2	what month?
何日 (なんにち)	5-3	what day (of the month)?
何年 (なんねん)	5-4	what year?
何色 (なにいろ)	7-4	what color?
何千 (なんぜん)	9-1	how many thousands?
何冊 (なんさつ)	9-2	how many volumes?
何本 (なんぼん)	9-2	how many cylindrical objects?
何度 (なんど)	10-1	how many degrees (temp.)/ times?

い Adjectives

大きい (おお)	3-1	big, large
楽しい (たの)	3-2	fun, enjoyable
難しい (むずか)	3-2	difficult
暑い (あつ)	3-4	hot (weather)
寒い (さむ)	3-4	cold (weather)
涼しい (すず)	3-4	cool (weather)
蒸し暑い (む あつ)	3-4	humid (weather)
忙しい (いそが)	5-4	busy
低い (ひく)	6-1	low, short
弱い (よわ)	6-1	weak
悲しい (かな)	6-1	sad
高い (たか)	6-1	high, tall, expensive
強い (つよ)	6-1	strong
遠い (とお)	6-1	far, distant
長い (なが)	6-1	long
渋い (しぶ)	6-2	astringent, tasteful, low-key
痛い (いた)	6-3	painful
素晴らしい (す ば)	6-5	wonderful
かっこいい	7-5	cool
嬉しい (うれ)	8-1	glad; happy
美味しい (お い)	8-1	delicious
美しい (うつく)	8-1	beautiful
うるさい	8-1	noisy, loud
危ない (あぶ)	8-1	dangerous
かしこい	8-1	wise; bright
かわいい	8-1	cute
きたない	8-1	dirty, messy
きびしい	8-1	strict
こわい	8-1	scary
じれったい	8-1	irritating
ずるい	8-1	cunning
小さい (ちい)	8-1	small
つまらない	8-1	boring

い Adjectives

ばかばかしい	8-1	foolish; silly
ひどい	8-1	terrible
短い (みじか)	8-1	short
みにくい	8-1	ugly
青い (あお)	8-2	blue-colored
赤い (あか)	8-2	red-colored
面白い (おもしろ)	8-2	interesting
黄色い (きいろ)	8-2	yellow-colored
黒い (くろ)	8-2	black-colored
白い (しろ)	8-2	white-colored
安い (やす)	8-2	cheap
広い (ひろ)	8-3	wide, spacious
まずい	8-3	not tasty
狭い (せま)	8-3	narrow
明るい (あか)	9-3	bright; light

な Adjectives

大事 (だいじ)	5-1	important
静か (しず)	6-1	quiet
有名 (ゆうめい)	6-1	famous
おしゃれ	6-2	fashionable
上手 (じょうず)	6-2	skillful
スマート (すまーと)	6-2	slim, stylish
大丈夫 (だいじょうぶ)	6-3	all right
無理 (むり)	6-3	difficult
シンプル (しんぷる)	6-4	simple
素敵 (すてき)	6-4	wonderful, nice
ハンサム (はんさむ)	6-4	handsome, good-looking
嫌い (きら)	7-2	dislike
好き (す)	7-2	like
大嫌い (だいきら)	7-2	hate
大好き (だいす)	7-2	love
得意 (とくい)	7-3	skilled at
苦手 (にがて)	7-3	unskilled at
下手 (へた)	7-3	not good at
色々 (いろいろ)	7-4	various
きれい	8-1	pretty; clean
ふしぎ	8-1	mysterious
おだやか	8-4	calm, peaceful
ひま	8-4	free (time)
特別 (とくべつ)	9-2	special
残念 (ざんねん)	10-2	regrettable, unlucky

Adjective Conjugation Summary

い adjectives	Non-past tense ～い です	Past tense ～かった です	Negative ～くありません ～くないです	Negative past ～く ありませんでした ～く なかったです	英語
まずい	まずい です	まずかった です	まずく ありません まずく ないです	まずく ありませんでした まずく なかったです	tastes disgusting
ひどい	ひどい です	ひどかったで す	ひどく ありません ひどく ないです	ひどく ありませんでした ひどく なかったです	terrible
忙しい (いそが)	忙しい (いそが) です	忙しかった (いそが) です	忙しく (いそが) ありません 忙しく (いそが) ないです	忙しく (いそが) ありませんでした 忙しく (いそが) なかったです	busy
な adjectives	**～です**	**～でした**	**～では ありません ～では ないです (or じゃ in place of では)**	**～では ありませんでした ～では なかったです (or じゃ in place of では)**	**英語**
暇 (ひま)	暇 (ひま) です	暇 (ひま) でした	暇 (ひま) では ありません 暇 (ひま) では ないです	暇 (ひま) では ありませんでした 暇 (ひま) では なかったです	free time
おだやか	おだやか です	おだやか でした	おだやか では ありません おだやか では ないです	おだやか では ありません でした おだやか では なかった です	calm, peaceful
Irregular adjective	**～です**	**～かった です**	**～く ありません ～く ないです**	**～く ありませんでした ～く なかったです**	**英語**
いい or 良い (よ)	いい です or 良い (よ) です	良かった (よ) です	良く (よ) ありません 良く (よ) ないです	良く (よ) ありませんでした 良く (よ) なかったです	good

Adverbs & Time Words

Word	Lesson	Meaning
朝 (あさ)	2-5	morning
とても	3-1	very
少し (すこ)	3-1	a little, not much
明日 (あした)	3-2	tomorrow
今 (いま)	3-2	now
時々 (ときどき)	3-2	sometimes
昨日 (きのう)	3-2	yesterday
今日 (きょう)	3-2	today
ちょっと	3-2	a little, somewhat
次 (つぎ)	3-3	next
後で (あと)	3-3	afterwards
放課後 (ほうかご)	3-3	time after school
速く (はや)	3-5	quickly
まだ	4-3	not yet
来週 (らいしゅう)	5-4	next week
今年 (ことし)	5-4	this year
先月 (せんげつ)	5-4	last month
いつも	6-1	always
まあまあ	6-2	so so, not bad, moderate
たいてい	7-2	usually
あまり	7-4	not very
全然 (ぜんぜん)	7-4	not at all
まったく	8-4	really, indeed, truly
もっと	9-3	more

NOTE: This list offers a sampling of time words. More may be found in the Glossary, where they are listed as nouns, since many function as both adverbs and as nouns.

Particles

Particle	Reference	Usage
は	1013	denotes a sentence topic
か	1014	signifies a question
に	1015	in; at; used after a location or time word
の	1021, 1093	possession; replaces a noun
が	1021, 1071, 1073, 1095	new information marker; "but"; conjunction; used to combine two sentences
と	1022	used like English "and" when connecting two or more nouns; quotation particle used after quotation
を	1023	used after the direct object
も	1024	too; also; replaces particles は、が、and を
から	1031, 1032	from (a place or a time); from (used with spec. times or locations)
でも	1034	"but" or "however" at the beginning of a sentence
ね	1035	sentence ending for a rhetorical question or when seeking agreement
ねえ	1035	sentence ending that can be exclamatory or express surprise
よ	1035	sentence ending for a strong declarative statement or for emphasis
で	1043, 1063, 1092	by means of a "tool"; comes after the place of action; for (used for shopping or ordering food)
まで	1053	until (used with spec. locations or times)
など	1101	et cetera, and so forth
へ/に	1104	used with verbs of movement

Noun Categories

People

家族 (かぞく)	(my) family
ご家族 (かぞく)	someone else's family
おじさん	uncle or older man
おばさん	aunt or older woman
兄弟 (きょうだい)	siblings
先生 (せんせい)	teacher
友達 (ともだち)	friend
人 (ひと)	person
生徒 (せいと)	student
大学生 (だいがくせい)	college/university student
子供達 (こどもたち)	children

Activities

空手 (からて)	karate (martial art)
相撲 (すもう)	sumo wrestling
柔道 (じゅうどう)	judo
卓球 (たっきゅう)	Ping-Pong
歌舞伎 (かぶき)	kabuki drama
空手 (からて)	karate
茶道 (さどう) / 茶道 (ちゃどう)	tea ceremony
趣味 (しゅみ)	hobby
乗馬 (じょうば)	horseback riding
ジョギング (じょぎんぐ)	jogging
水泳 (すいえい)	swimming
スキー (すきー)	skiing
スポーツ (すぽーつ)	sports
寝る事 (ねること)	sleeping
能 (のう)	Noh drama theater
映画 (えいが)	movie
漫画 (まんが)	manga; comics
料理 (りょうり)	cooking
旅行 (りょこう)	a trip; travel

Objects/Things

(お)箸 (はし)	chopsticks
T シャツ (てぃー しゃつ)	T-shirt
写真 (しゃしん)	photograph
ぼうし	hat/cap
漫画 (まんが)	Japanese comics

Noun Categories

絵 (え)	painting, drawing
浮世絵 (うきよえ)	woodblock print
映画 (えいが)	movie
プレゼント (ぷれぜんと)	present

Places

海 (うみ)	ocean; sea
島 (しま)	island
ビーチ (びーち)	beach
城 (しろ)	castle
庭 (にわ)	garden
病院 (びょういん)	hospital
店 (みせ)	shop; store
神社 (じんじゃ)	shrine
寺 (てら)	temple
家 / 家 (いえ / うち)	house/home
本屋 (ほんや)	bookstore
パン屋 (ぱんや)	bakery
日本 / 日本 (にほん / にっぽん)	Japan
東京 (とうきょう)	capital of Japan
長崎 (ながさき)	(City of) Nagasaki
天橋立 (あまのはしだて)	(City of) Amanohashidate
平泉 (ひらいずみ)	(City of) Hiraizumi
金沢 (かなざわ)	(City of) Kanazawa
江戸 (えど)	(City of) Edo (now Tokyo)
平安京 (へいあんきょう)	(ancient City of) Heian-kyou (now Kyoto)
中学校 (ちゅうがっこう)	junior high school
高校 (こうこう)	high school
大学 (だいがく)	college/university

Appendix 2
Japanese Names

Girls' Names

花子 (はなこ)　友子 (ゆうこ)　明子 (あきこ)　えみ　さゆり　妙子 (たえこ)　まゆみ　恵美子 (えみこ)　操 (みさお)　素子 (もとこ)　かおり　美也子 (みやこ)　真澄 (ますみ)　絵里子 (えりこ)　浜子 (はまこ)

Boys' Names

健一 (けんいち)　道夫 (みちお)　一郎 (いちろう)　良和 (よしかず)　じゅん　友弘 (ともひろ)　友和 (ともかず)　ケン　けんじ　豊 (ゆたか)　友和 (ともかず)　明 (あきら)　潤吉 (じゅんきち)　友保 (ともやす)　秋宏 (あきひろ)　雅広 (まさひろ)

Family Names

石田 (いしだ)　石口 (いしぐち)　山口 (やまぐち)　山本 (やまもと)　山崎 (やまさき)　鈴木 (すずき)　高橋 (たかはし)　佐々木 (ささき)　松田 (まつだ)　上田 (うえだ)　木村 (きむら)　高村 (たかむら)

佐藤 (さとう)　田中 (たなか)　渡辺 (わたなべ)　吉田 (よしだ)　加藤 (かとう)　松本 (まつもと)　井上 (いのうえ)　斉藤 (さいとう)　池田 (いけだ)　本田 (ほんだ)　前田 (まえだ)　藤田 (ふじた)

Appendix 3
Food and Drinks (食べ物と飲み物 (たべものとのみもの))

Fruits (果物 (くだもの))

フルーツ (ふるーつ)	fruit
イチゴ (いちご)	strawberry
オレンジ (おれんじ)	orange
バナナ (ばなな)	banana
なし	Asian pear
メロン (めろん)	melon
りんご	apple
トマト (とまと)	tomato

Meals

朝ご飯 (あさごはん)	breakfast
昼ご飯 (ひるごはん)	lunch
晩ご飯 (ばんごはん)	dinner, evening meal
おやつ	snack

Condiments

砂糖 (さとう)	sugar
塩 (しお)	salt
醤油 (しょうゆ)	soy sauce
わさび	wasabi (Japanese horseradish)

Vegetables (野菜 (やさい))

人参 (にんじん)	carrot
大根 (だいこん)	daikon; white radish
キャベツ (きゃべつ)	cabbage
ほうれんそう	spinach

Main Dishes and Side Dishes

ご飯 (ごはん)	cooked rice, a meal
いか	squid
うどん	thick, white noodles
おこのみ焼き (おこのみやき)	savory Japanese lunch or dinner pancake

かに	crab
魚（さかな）	fish
寿司（すし）	food made with vinegared ice
のり	seaweed
ステーキ（すてーき）	steak
たこ	octopus
タコス（たこす）	Mexican tacos
たこ焼き（や）	breaded octopus balls
すきやき	sukiyaki; thinly-sliced meat and vegetables in hot broth
そば	thin buckwheat noodles
てり焼き（や）	teriyaki; grilled meat with sauce
豆腐（とうふ）	bean curd (tofu)
ハンバーガー（はんばーがー）	hamburger
ホットケーキ（ほっとけーき）	pancake; hotcake
巻き寿司（ま　ずし）	rolled sushi
ラーメン（らーめん）	ramen noodles
漬け物（つ　もの）	pickled vegetables
卵（たまご）	egg
パン（ぱん）	bread

Sweets and Snacks (甘い物とつまみ（あま　もの）)

アイスクリーム（あいすくりーむ）	ice cream
飴（あめ）	candy
(お)菓子（かし）	Japanese traditional sweets
カップケーキ（かっぷけーき）	cupcake
クッキー（くっきー）	cookie
ケーキ（けーき）	cake
煎餅（せんべい）	rice crackers
だんご	round sticky rice balls on a stick
チョコレート（ちょこれーと）	chocolate
餅（もち）	sticky rice cake

Drinks (飲み物（の　もの）)

(お)水（みず）	water
アイスコーヒー（あいすこーひー）	iced coffee
アイスティー（あいすてぃー）	iced tea
お茶（ちゃ）	green tea
牛乳／ミルク（ぎゅうにゅう　みるく）	milk
コーヒー（こーひー）	coffee
コーラ（こーら）	cola
ジュース（じゅーす）	juice
ミルクセーキ（みるくせーき）	milkshake
レモネード（れもねーど）	lemonade

Appendix 4
Classroom Objects

漢字	Romaji	英語
椅子（いす）	*isu*	chair
鉛筆（えんぴつ）	*enpitsu*	pencil
かばん	*kaban*	satchel, bag
紙（かみ）	*kami*	paper
ガム	*gamu*	gum
教科書（きょうかしょ）	*kyoukasho*	textbook
教室（きょうしつ）	*kyoushitsu*	classroom
消しゴム（け）	*keshigomu*	eraser
黒板（こくばん）	*kokuban*	blackboard
黒板消し（こくばん け）	*kokuban keshi*	blackboard eraser
コンピューター	*konpyu-ta-*	computer
作文（さくぶん）	*sakubun*	essay
宿題（しゅくだい）	*shukudai*	homework
辞書（じしょ）	*jisho*	dictionary

漢字	Romaji	英語
下敷き（したじ）	*shitajiki*	hard plastic sheet for writing on
生徒（せいと）	*seito*	student
先生（せんせい）	*sensei*	teacher
地図（ちず）	*chizu*	map
チョーク	*cho-ku*	chalk
机（つくえ）	*tsukue*	desk
ティッシュ	*tisshu*	tissue
テーブル	*te-buru*	table
テープ	*te-pu*	tape
電気（でんき）	*denki*	lights
電話（でん）	*denwa*	phone
ドア	*doa*	door
時計（とけい）	*tokei*	clock
ノート	*no-to*	notebook

漢字	Romaji	英語
ホワイトボード (ほわいとぼーど)	*howaitobo-do*	whiteboard
はさみ	*hasami*	scissors
旗 (はた)	*hata*	flag
バッグ	*baggu*	bag
プランナー	*puranna-*	planner, handbook
筆箱 (ふでばこ)	*fudebako*	pencil box
ホッチキス	*hotchikisu*	stapler
ボールペン	*bo-rupen*	ballpoint pen

漢字	Romaji	英語
本 (ほん)	*hon*	book
本棚 (ほんだな)	*hondana*	bookshelves
マジック	*majikku*	marker
窓 (まど)	*mado*	window
めがね	*megane*	glasses
定規 (じょうぎ)	*jougi*	ruler
お金 (かね)	*okane*	money

Japanese-English Glossary

This glossary has simplified abbreviations to make it easier to use. The following abbreviations are used for parts of speech:

い adj.	い adjective	*interj.*	interjection
な adj.	な adjective	*n*	noun
ir. adj.	irregular adjective	*part.*	particle
adv.	adverb	*pn*	person or place name
conj.	conjunction		
exp.	expression	*pron.*	pronoun
inter.	interrogative	*v*	verb

The numbering system for location of vocabulary words in the chapters is made up of the volume number (the first digit; 1 is this volume, *Beginning Japanese*); a two-digit chapter number; and the section number. An "s" indicates words that are supplemental: they are not on the New Words lists, but are also included in the book (in the Dialogues, Journal entries, etc.). For example:

Japanese	Location		English
ああ	1025	*interj.*	Ah!, Oh!
あい・愛	1022s	*n*	love
あいこ・愛子	1015s	*pn*	Aiko (female name)
あいすくりーむ・アイスクリーム	App.	*n*	ice cream
あいたい・会いたい	1044s	*v*	want to meet
あいでぃあ・アイディア	1051s	*n*	idea
あう・会う	1054s	*v*	meet (to)
あお・青	1074	*n*	blue
あおい・青い	1064	*い adj.*	blue-colored
あか・赤	1074	*n*	red
あかい・赤い	1064	*い adj.*	red-colored
あかるい・明るい	1083	*い adj.*	bright, light
あき・秋	1101	*n*	fall, autumn
あくしゅ	1042	*n*	handshake
あける・開ける/あけます・開けます	1034	*v*	open (to) [door/window]
あげる・上げる/あげます・上げます	1094	*v*	give (to) [to equals or superiors]

Japanese	Location		English
あさ・朝	1025	*n*	morning
あさごはん・朝ご飯	1025	*n*	breakfast
あさって・明後日	1102	*n*	day after tomorrow
あし・足	1061	*n*	leg, foot
あした・明日	1032	*n*	tomorrow
あそこ	1024	*pron.*	over there
あそぶ・遊ぶ/あそびます・遊びます	1103	*v*	play (to)
あたま・頭	1061	*n*	head
あたらしい・新しい	1081	い *adj.*	new
あちこち	1054s	*adv.*	here and there
あちら	1014s	*pn*	that (person) over there
あっ	1031	*interj.*	oh
あつい・暑い	1034	い *adj.*	hot (weather)
あと・後	1033		after
あとで・後で	1033	*adv.*	later, afterwards
あなた	1041s	*pron.*	you [best not used too often]
あに・兄	1021	*n*	older brother (my)
あにめ・アニメ	1011	*n*	animated cartoons/films
あね・姉	1021	*n*	older sister (my)
あの	1023		that (thing) over there
あぶない・危ない	1081	い *adj.*	dangerous
あまのはしだて・天橋立	1082	*pn*	Amanohashidate (place)
あまり	1074	*adv.*	not very
あめ・飴	1023	*n*	candy/sweets
あめ・雨	1101	*n*	rain
きゃんでぃ・キャンディ	1023s	*n*	candy/sweets
あめふと・アメフト, あめりかんふっとぼーる, アメリカンフットボール	1071	*n*	American football
あめりか・アメリカ	1041	*pn*	United States of America (place)
あめりかし・アメリカ史	1032	*n*	American history
あめりかじん・アメリカ人	1041	*n*	American (person)
ありがとう	1023	*exp.*	thanks
ある/あります	1021	*v*	exist (to) [inanimate things]
あるばいと・アルバイト	1025s	*n*	part time job
あれ	1015	*pron.*	that (over there)
いい/よい・良い	1041s	*ir. adj.*	good
いいえ	1014		no
いいえ、ちがいます。・違います。	1014	*exp.*	No, it is not/different.
いいえ、わかりません。・分かりません。	1016s	*exp.*	No, I don't understand
いう・言う/いいます・言います	1041	*v*	say (to)
いえ/うち・家	1022	*n*	house, home
いきましょう・行きましょう	1035	*exp.*	let's go
いぎりす・イギリス	1041	*pn*	England (place)
いぎりすけい・イギリス系	1041	*n*	English (descent)
いぎりすじん・イギリス人	1041	*n*	English (person)
いく・行く/いきます・行きます	1044	*v*	go (to)

Japanese	Location		English
いくつ	1021	*inter.*	how many (things)?
いくつ, (お)いくつ	1022s	*inter.*	how old (animate beings), how many
いくら	1092	*inter.*	how much?
いけ・池	1101s	*n*	pond
いけばな・生け花	1071	*n*	flower arranging
いし・石	1101	*n*	stone, rock
いしゃ・医者	1063	*n*	doctor
いす・椅子	App.	*n*	chair
いそがしい・忙しい	1054	い *adj.*	busy
いたい・痛い	1063	い *adj.*	painful
いただく/いただきます	1092	*v*	receive (to) (very polite), lit.: I will receive.
いたりあ・イタリア	1041	*pn*	Italy (place)
いたりあご・イタリア語	1042	*n*	Italian (language)
いたりあじん・イタリア人	1041	*n*	Italian (person)
いち・一	1021	*count.*	one
いちがつ・一月	1052	*n*	January
いちご・イチゴ	App.	*n*	strawberry
いちじ・一時	1032	*count.*	one o'clock
いちじかんめ・一時間目	1033	*count.*	first period
いちど・一度	1101	*count.*	one time
いちねんせい・一年生	1031s	*count.*	first year student
いちばんうえの あに/あね・一番上の 兄/姉	1021	*n*	oldest brother/sister (my)
いちばんしたの おとうと/いもうと・一番下の 弟/妹	1021	*n*	youngest brother/sister (my)
いちびょう・一秒	1032	*count.*	one second
いちぺーじ/いっぺーじ・一ページ	1042	*count.*	one page/page one
いちまい・一枚	1042	*count.*	one sheet/piece
いちまん・一万	1052	*count.*	ten thousand
いつ	1052	*inter.*	when?
いつか・五日	1053	*count.*	fifth (day of the month)
いっさい・一歳, 一才	1052	*count.*	one year old
いっさつ・一冊	1092	*count.*	one volume
いっしょ・一緒	1043s	*n*	together, at the same time, same
いっしょに・一緒に	1044s	*exp.*	together, at the same time, same
いつつ・五つ	1024	*count.*	five (things)
いっぱい・一杯	1092	*count.*	one cupful
いっぴき・一匹	1021	*count.*	one small animal
いっぷん・一分	1032	*count.*	one minute
いっぽん・一本	1092	*count.*	one cylindrical object
いつも	1061	*n/adv.*	always
いなりずし・稲荷寿司	1103s	*n*	sushi wrapped in fried tofu (*aburaage*)
いぬ・犬	1021	*n*	dog
いま・今	1032	*n/adv.*	now
いもうと・妹	1021	*n*	younger sister (my)
いもうとさん・妹さん	1022	*n*	younger sister (someone else's)
いやいや	1094s		by no means, reluctantly

Japanese	Location		English
いやりんぐ・イヤリング	1064	n	earring
いらっしゃいませ	1043	exp.	welcome (usually used at a place of business)
いらんじん・イラン人	1041	n	Iranian (person)
いる/います	1021	v	exist (to) [animate beings]
いれる・入れる/いれます・入れます	1061	v	put into (to)
いろ・色	1074	n	color
いろいろ・色々	1074	adv.	various
いんどねしあ・インドネシア	1041	pn	Indonesia (place)
いんどねしあご・インドネシア語	1042	n	Indonesian (language)
いんどねしあじん・インドネシア人	1041	n	Indonesian (person)
うぃんどうしょっぴんぐ(を)・ウィンドウショッピング(を) する/します	1091s	n	window-shop (to)
うぇいとれす・ウェイトレス	1084s	n	waitress
うきよえ・浮世絵	1091	n	woodblock print (prior to and through the Edo Period)
うそ・嘘	1104	n	lie
うた・歌	1071	n	song
うたう・歌う/うたいます・歌います	1071	v	sing (to)
うたうこと・歌う事	1071	n	singing
うち/いえ・家	1022s	n	home/house
うつくしい・美しい	1081	い adj.	beautiful
うで・腕	1061	n	arm
うま・馬	1082	n	horse
うまれる・生まれる/うまれます・生まれます	1052	v	born (to be)
うみ・海	1081	n	ocean, sea
うらしまたろう・浦島太郎	1084s	pn	Urashima Taro (folktale character)
うる・売る/うります・売ります	1091	v	sell (to)
うるさい	1081	い adj.	noisy, loud
うれしい・嬉しい	1081	い adj.	glad, happy
え・ 絵	1071	n	painting, drawing
えあこん・エアコン	1035	n	airconditioning
えいが・映画	1091	n	movie
えいご・英語	1032	n	English (language)
えいごで いって ください。・英語で 言って 下さい。	1016s	exp.	Please say it in English.
ええ/はい	1032s		yes
ええっ/え?	1033s	inter.	huh?
ええと	1033s	interj.	let me see, well...
えすさいず・ Sサイズ	1092	n	small (S) size
えど・江戸	1044s	pn	Edo, former name of Tokyo (place)
えむさいず・Mサイズ	1092	n	medium (M) size
えむぴーすりーぷれーやー・MP3プレーヤー	1031	n	MP3 player
えるさいず・Lサイズ	1092	n	large (L) size
えんぴつ・鉛筆	1024	n	pencil
おーすとらりあ・オーストラリア	1041	pn	Australia (place)
おーすとらりあじん・オーストラリア人	1041	n	Australian (person)
おいしい・美味しい	1081	い adj.	delicious
おおあめ・大雨	1101	n	heavy rain
おおきい・大きい	1031	い adj.	big, large
おおさか・大阪	1083s	pn	Osaka (place)
おかあさん・お母さん	1022	n	mother (someone else's)
おかえりなさい・お帰りなさい	1015	exp.	welcome home
おかし・(お)菓子	1095	n	Japanese traditional sweets
おきょう・お経	1052s	n	scriptures
おきる・起きる/おきます・起きます	1051	v	wake (up) (to)
おくる・送る/おくります・送ります	1051	v	send (to)
おじいさん	1022	n	grandfather (someone else's)
おしえて ください・教えて 下さい	1032s	exp.	tell me/teach me, please
おじさん	1022	n	uncle or man quite a bit older than you
おしゃれ	1062	な adj	fashionable
おだやか	1084	な adj	calm, peaceful
おちゃ・お茶	1024s	n	green tea
おちゃのみず・お茶の水	1024s	pn	Ochanomizu (section of Tokyo)
おっと	1083	interj.	oops, sorry
おつり	1092	n	change (cash)
おてあらいへ いっても いいですか。・お手洗いへ 行っても いいですか。	1016s	exp.	May I go to the restroom/W.C.?
おでん	1091s	n	oden (various ingredients stewed in soy-flavored dashi)
おとうさん・お父さん	1022	n	father (someone else's)
おとうと・弟	1021	n	younger brother (my)
おとうとさん・弟さん	1022	n	younger brother (someone else's)
おとこ・男	1064s	n	man, male
おとこのこ・男の子	1064	n	boy
おとこのひと・男の人	1064	n	man, male
おととい・一昨日	1102	n	day before yesterday
おどり・踊り	1071	n	dancing
おなか・お腹	1061	n	stomach
おなか(が) いっぱい・お腹(が)一杯	1104	exp.	have a full stomach
おなじ・同じ	1044s	n	same
おにいさん・お兄さん	1022	n	older brother (someone else's)

Japanese	Location		English
おにぎり	1105s	n	rice balls
おねえさん・お姉さん	1022	n	older sister (someone else's)
おねがい・お願い/おねがいします・お願いします	1013s	exp.	please
おばあさん	1022	n	grandmother (someone else's)
おばさん	1022	n	aunt or woman quite a bit older than you
おはよう	1015	exp.	good morning (informal)
おはよう　ございます	1015	exp.	good morning (formal)
おふろ・お風呂	1093s	n	bath
おみずを　のんでも　いいですか。・お水を飲んでも　いいですか。	1016s	exp.	May I drink (some) water?
おみやげ・お土産	1023	n	souvenir(s)
おもう・思う/おもいます・思います	1072	v	think (to)
おもしろい・面白い	1082	い adj.	interesting
おやすみ・お休み	1015	exp.	good night (informal)
おやすみなさい・お休みなさい	1015	exp.	good night (formal)
おやつ	App.	n	snack
およぐ・泳ぐ/およぎます・泳ぎます	1071	v	swim (to)
およぐこと・泳ぐ事	1071	n	swimming
おらんだ・オランダ	1041	pn	Holland (place)
おらんだご・オランダ語	1042	n	Dutch (language)
おらんだじん・オランダ人	1041	n	Dutch person
おれんじ・オレンジ	1064, 1074	n	orange
おれんじじゅーす・オレンジジュース	1043s	n	orange juice
おわる・終わる/おわります・終わります	1052	v	finish (to)
おんがく・音楽	1032	n	music
おんがくかい・音楽会	1052s	n	concert, recital
おんど・温度	1101	n	temperature
おんな・女	1064s	n	woman, female
おんなのこ・女の子	1064	n	girl
おんなのひと・女の人	1064	n	woman, female
か	1014	part.	signifies a question
が	1021s,	part.	new information marker, "but"
が	1071s	conj.	used to combine two sentences
がいこく・外国	1041	n	foreign country
がいこくじん・外国人	1041	n	foreigner
かいしゃいん・会社員	1025s	n	company employee
かいもの・買い物	1071	n	shopping
かいもの(を)・買い物(を)する/します	1091	v	go shopping (to)
かいわ・会話	1013s	n	dialogue

Japanese	Location		English
かう・買う/かいます・買います	1091	v	buy (to)
かえる・蛙	1072	n	frog
かえる・帰る/かえります・帰ります	1044	v	return (to)
かお・顔	1061	n	face
かがく・科学	1032	n	science
ががく・雅楽	1075	n	gagaku, ancient Japanese court music
かく・描く/かきます・描きます	1054s	v	draw (to)
かく・書く/かきます・書きます	1013	v	write (to)
がくせい・学生, せいと・生徒	1031	n	student
かける/かけます	1064	v	wear (glasses or sun glasses) (to)
かし (お)・(お)菓子	1095s	n	Japanese traditional sweets
かしこい	1081	い adj.	bright, wise
かぜ・風	1035	n	wind
かぜ・風邪	1063	n	cold (a)
かぜ(を)・風邪(を)ひく・引く/ひきます・引きます	1063	v	catch a cold
かぞく・家族	1021	n	family (my)
かた・肩	1061	n	shoulder
かっこいい	1062	い adj.	cool (look/appearance)
がっこう・学校	1031	n	school
がっしょう・合唱	1033	n	chorus, choir
かっぷけーき・カップケーキ	App.	n	cupcake
かていか・家庭科	1032	n	family consumer science
かなざわ・金沢	1101s	pn	Kanazawa (place)
かなしい・悲しい	1061	い adj.	sad
かなだ・カナダ	1041	pn	Canada (place)
かなだじん・カナダ人	1041	n	Canadian (person)
かに	1083	n	crab
かね (お)・(お)金	1092s	n	money
かのじょ・彼女	1074	pron.	she, girlfriend
かばん・鞄	1024	n	briefcase, bag
かぶき・歌舞伎	1075	n	kabuki theater
かぶる・被る/かぶります・被ります	1064	v	wear on the head (to)
かみ・紙	1024	n	paper
かみ(のけ)・髪(の毛)	1061	n	hair
かみなり・雷	1101	n	lightning
がむ・ガム	App.	n	gum
かめ・亀	1082	n	turtle
かもく・科目	1032	n	school subject
かようび・火曜日	1051	n	Tuesday
から	1032	part.	from (used with spec. times or locations)
からおけ・カラオケ	1105s	n	karaoke

Japanese	Location		English
からおけ(を)・カラオケ(を)する/します	1091	*v*	karaoke (to sing/do)
からだ・体	1061	*n*	body
からて・空手	1011	*n*	karate (martial art)
かりる・借りる/かります・借ります	1063s	*v*	borrow (to)
かれ・彼	1074	*pron.*	he, boyfriend
かれら・彼ら	1082	*pron.*	they, them
かわいい	1081	い *adj.*	cute
かんこく・韓国	1041	*pn*	South Korea (place)
かんこくけい・韓国系	1041s	*n*	Korean (descent)
かんこくご・韓国語	1042	*n*	Korean (language)
かんこくじん・韓国人	1041	*n*	Korean (person)
かんごし・看護師	1063	*n*	nurse
かんじ・漢字	1012s	*n*	Chinese characters (used in Japan)
がんばる・頑張る/ /がんばります・頑張ります	1073	*v*	do one's best (to)
き・木	1011s	*n*	tree
きいろ・黄色	1074	*n*	yellow
きいろい・黄色い	1064	い *adj.*	yellow-colored
きく・聞く/ききます・聞きます	1013	*v*	listen (to)
きこえる・聞こえる/きこえます・聞こえます	1104s	*v*	hear (can)
きせつ・季節	1101	*n*	season
ぎたー・ギター	1071	*n*	guitar
ぎたーを ひく/・ギターを弾く/ひきます・弾きます	1071	*v*	play guitar (to)
きたない	1081	い *adj.*	dirty, messy
きつね・狐	1035s	*n*	fox
きのう・昨日	1032	*n/adv.*	yesterday
きびしい	1081	い *adj.*	strict
きもの・着物	1011	*n*	kimono (Japanese traditional clothing)
きゃんでぃ・キャンディ	1023	*n*	candy/sweets
きゃんべら・キャンベラ	1021s	*pn*	Canberra (place)
きゅうきゅうしゃをよんで・救急車を 呼んで	1063	*n*	Call an ambulance!
きゅうさい・九歳	1052	*count.*	nine years old
きゅうさつ・九冊	1092	*count.*	nine volumes
きゅうしゅう・九州	1041s	*pn*	Kyushu (place)
きゅうじゅう・九十	1022	*count.*	ninety
きゅうせん・九千	1052	*count.*	nine thousand
きゅうど・九度	1101	*count.*	nine times/degrees
きゅうにん・九人	1021	*count.*	nine people
きゅうはい・九杯	1092	*count.*	nine cupfuls
きゅうひき・九匹	1021	*count.*	nine small animals
きゅうひゃく・九百	1023s	*count.*	nine hundred
きゅうびょう・九秒	1032	*count.*	nine seconds
きゅうふん・九分	1032	*count.*	nine minutes
きゅうぺーじ・九ページ	1042	*count.*	nine pages, page nine
きゅうほん・九本	1092	*count.*	nine cylindrical objects
きゅうまい・九枚	1042	*count.*	nine sheets
きゅうまん・九万	1052	*count.*	ninety thousand
きょう・今日	1032	*n*	today
きょうかしょ・教科書	1013	*n*	textbook
ぎょうざ	1043s	*n*	pot stickers
きょうしつ・教室	1032	*n*	classroom
きょうだい・兄弟	1021	*n*	siblings
きょうと・京都	1013s	*pn*	Kyoto (place)
きょねん・去年	1054	*n*	last year
きらい・嫌い	1072	な *adj*	dislike
きりつ。・起立。	1016s	*exp.*	stand up
ぎりの〜	1021		step-
きる・着る/きます・着ます	1064	*v*	wear above the waist (to)
きれい	1081	な *adj*	clean, pretty
きんいろ・金色	1074	*n*	gold
ぎんいろ・銀色	1074	*n*	silver
ぎんざ・銀座	1033s	*pn*	Ginza (place)
きんにく・筋肉	1061	*n*	muscle
きんぱつ・金髪	1074	*n*	blond (hair)
きんようび・金曜日	1051	*n*	Friday
く/きゅう・九	1021	*count.*	nine
ぐあいが わるい・具合が 悪い	1063	*exp.*	sick, feel bad
くうかい・空海	1052s	*pn*	Kukai (person's name)
くがつ・九月	1052	*n*	September
くじ・九時	1032	*count.*	nine o'clock
くすり・薬	1063	*n*	medicine
くすり(を) のむ・薬(を)飲む/のみます・飲みます	1063	*v*	take medicine (to)
くだもの・果物, ふるーつ・フルーツ	1075s	*n*	fruit
くち・口	1061	*n*	mouth
くつ・靴	1064	*n*	shoes
くっきー・クッキー	App.	*n*	cookie
くつした・靴下	1064	*n*	socks
くに・国	1041	*n*	country
くび・首	1061	*n*	neck
くもり・曇り	1101	*n*	cloudy
くもる・曇る/くもります・曇ります	1101	*n*	become cloudy
くらい・暗い	1083	い *adj.*	dark
くらす・クラス	1032	*n*	class
くる・来る/きます・来ます	1044	*v*	come (to)
くるま・車	1043	*n*	car, vehicle
ぐれい・グレイ	1064, 1074	*n*	gray
くれる/くれます	1095	*v*	give (to) [to me or a family member]
くろ・黒	1074	*n*	black
くろい・黒い	1064	い *adj.*	black-colored
くん (〜)・〜君	1013	*suffix*	suffix AFTER a boy's name
けーき・ケーキ	1094	*n*	cake
けいけん・経験	1065	*n*	experience
けいざい・経済	1032s	*n*	economy
けいざいがく・経済学	1032	*n*	economics
けいたい (でんわ)・携帯(電話)	1031	*n*	cellular phone

Japanese	Location		English
けが(を)・怪我(を) する/します	1063	v	injure, hurt oneself (to)
けさ・今朝	1051s	n/adv.	this morning
けしごむ・消しゴム	1024	n	eraser
げつようび・月曜日	1051	n	Monday
けど	1041s	conj.	but
けにあ・ケニア	1041	pn	Kenya (place)
けにあじん・ケニア人	1041	n	Kenyan (person)
けんか(を)・喧嘩(を) する/します	1091	v	fight (to)
げんき・元気	1015	n/な adj.	healthy, energetic
けんこう・健康	1063	n	health
けんこうに・健康に いい です	1063	exp.	good for your health
けんどう・剣道	1033s	n	kendo
けんどうぶ・剣道部	1033	n	kendo club
けんろくえん・兼六園	1102s	pn	Kenroku Park (place)
ご・五	1021	n	five
こーら・コーラ	1043	n	cola
こい・鯉	1031s	n	koi (carp)
こうけんてんのう・孝謙天皇	1053s	pn	Emperor Kouken
こうこう・高校	1031	n	high school
こうこういちねんせい・高校一年生	1031	count.	tenth grader
こうこうさんねんせい・高校三年生	1031	count.	twelfth grader
こうこうせい・高校生	1031	n	high school student
こうこうにねんせい・高校二年生	1031	count.	eleventh grader
こうぼうだいし・弘法大師	1052s	pn	Kobo Daishi (person's name)
こうやさん・高野山	1052s	pn	Mt. Koya (place)
こえ・声	1061	n	voice
ごかぞく・ご家族	1021	n	someone else's family
ごがつ・五月	1052	n	May
こくご・国語	1032	n	national language (Japanese language)
こくばん・黒板	1024	い adj.	blackboard
ここ	1024	pron.	here
ごご・午後	1032	n	P.M.
ここのか・九日	1053	count.	ninth (day of the month)
ここのつ・九つ	1024	count.	nine (things)
こころ・心	1061	n	heart (not one's physical heart), soul
ごさい・五歳	1052	count.	five years old
ごさつ・五冊	1092	count.	five volumes
ごじ・五時	1032	count.	five o'clock
ごじかんめ・五時間目	1033	count.	fifth period
ごじゅう・五十	1022	count.	fifty
ごせん・五千	1052	count.	five thousand
ごぜん・午前	1032	n	A.M.
こちら	1014	pron.	this person (polite)
こと・事	1071s	n	thing (tangible)
こと・琴	1105s	n	koto, Japanese zither/ harp

Japanese	Location		English
ごど・五度	1101	count.	five times/degrees
ことし・今年	1054	n	this year
ことば・言葉	1101s	n	language, dialect, words
こども・子供	1082	n	child, children
こどもたち・子供達	1082	n	children
ごにん・五人	1021	count.	five people
この	1023		this (thing)
ごはい・五杯	1092	count.	five cupfuls
ごはん・ご飯	1015	n	cooked rice, a meal
こぴー・コピー する/します	1062	v	copy, photocopy (to)
ごひき・五匹	1021	count.	five small animals
ごひゃく・五百	1023s	count.	five hundred
ごびょう・五秒	1032	count.	five seconds
ごふん・五分	1032	count.	five minutes
ごぺーじ・五ページ	1042	n	page five
ごほん・五本	1092	count.	five cylindrical objects
ごまい・五枚	1042	count.	five sheets, five pages
ごまん・五万	1052	count.	fifty thousand
ごめん (informal), ごめんなさい (formal)	1072s		excuse me, I'm sorry, beg your pardon
ごめんください・ごめん下さい	1092s	exp.	May I come in?, please forgive me
ごるふ・ゴルフ	1071	n	golf
これ	1015	pron.	this (one)
ころ, ごろ	1032		about
ごろ, ころ	1032		about
こわい	1081	い adj.	scary
こんげつ・今月	1054	n	this month
こんさーと・コンサート	1052s	n	concert
こんしゅう・今週	1054	n	this week
こんにちは・今日は	1015	exp.	hello
こんばんは・今晩は	1015	exp.	good evening
こんぴゅーたーらぼ・コンピューターラボ	1033	n	computer lab
さあ	1035	inter.	well...
さいん・サイン	1042	n	signature
さがす・探す/さがします 探します	1093	v	search (to)
さかな・魚	1101	n	fish
さくぶん・作文	1032	n	essay
さくら・桜	1105	n	cherry tree/blossom
さっかー(を)・サッカー(を) する/します	1091	v	play soccer (to)
さつま・薩摩	1041s	pn	Satsuma (place)
さて	1091s	interj.	well, now
さとう・砂糖	App.	n	sugar
さどう/ちゃどう・茶道	1071	n	tea ceremony
さびしい・寂しい	1061s	い adj.	lonely
さむい・寒い	1034	い adj.	cold (weather)
さむらい・侍	1061	n	samurai
さようなら	1015	exp.	goodbye
さん(〜), 〜さん	1013	suffix	suffix AFTER a name
さん・三	1021	count.	three
さんがつ・三月	1052	n	March

Japanese	Location		English
さんさい・三歳	1052	*count.*	three years old
さんさつ・三冊	1092	*count.*	three volumes
さんじ・三時	1032	*count.*	three o'clock
さんじかんめ・三時間目	1033	*count.*	third period
さんじゅう・三十	1022	*count.*	thirty
さんじゅういちにち・三十一日	1053	*count.*	thirty-first (day of the month)
さんじゅうにち・三十日	1053	*count.*	thirtieth (day of the month)
さんせっと・サンセット, ゆうやけ・夕焼け	1104s	*n*	sunset
さんぜん・三千	1052	*count.*	three thousand
さんだん・三段	1033s	*count.*	third degree (belt)
さんど・三度	1101	*count.*	three times; degrees
さんにん・三人	1021	*count.*	three people
ざんねん・残念	1093	*n/な adj.*	regrettably, unluckily
さんねんせい・三年生	1031s	*count.*	third year student
さんばい・三杯	1092	*count.*	three cupfuls
さんびき・三匹	1021	*count.*	three small animals
さんびゃく・三百	1023s	*count.*	three hundred
さんびょう・三秒	1032	*count.*	three seconds
さんぷん・三分	1032	*count.*	three minutes
さんぺーじ・三ページ	1042	*count.*	three pages, page three
さんぽ・散歩	1054	*n*	walk
さんぽ(を)・散歩(を) する/します	1054	*v*	take a walk (to)
さんぼん・三本	1092	*count.*	three cylindrical objects
さんまい・三枚	1042	*count.*	three sheets
さんまん・三万	1052	*count.*	thirty thousand
じーんず・ジーンズ	1064	*n*	jeans
しお・塩	App.	*n*	salt
しがつ・四月	1052	*n*	April
じかんわり・時間割	1032	*n*	schedule, time table
しけん・試験	1032	*n*	test, exam
しごと・仕事	1025	*n*	job, occupation
しごと(を)・仕事(を) する/します	1052s	*v*	work (to)
じしょ・辞書	App.	*n*	dictionary
じしん・地震	1101	*n*	earthquake
しずか・静か	1061	*な adj*	quiet
しずかに して ください。・静かに して 下さい。	1016s	*exp.*	Please be quiet.
じだい・時代	1071s	*n*	era, period, age
したぎ・下着, ぱんつ・パンツ	1064	*n*	underwear
したじき・下敷き	1024	*n*	writing pad, mat
しち/なな・七	1021	*count.*	seven
しちがつ/なながつ・七月	1052	*n*	July
しちじ/ななじ・七時	1032	*count.*	seven o'clock
しちにん/ななにん・七人	1021	*count.*	seven people
じつは・実は	1104	*adv.*	by the way, actually
しつもん・質問	1032s	*n*	question
しつれいします・失礼します	1022	*exp.*	excuse me, I'm sorry to bother you.
しぶい・渋い	1062	*い adj.*	tasteful, cool
しま・島	1083	*n*	island
じむしょ・事務所	1032	*n*	office
しめる・閉める/しめます・閉めます	1034	*v*	close (to), shut (to) [doors/windows]
じゃ/じゃあ	1033s		well then...
じゃーなる・ジャーナル	1011s	*n*	journal
じゃあ また	1015	*exp.*	see you later (in formal)
しゃかい・社会	1032	*n*	social studies, society
じゃがいも・ジャガイモ	1042s	*n*	potato
じゃかるた・ジャカルタ	1042s	*pn*	Jakarta (place)
じゃけっと・ジャケット	1064	*n*	jacket
しゃしん・写真	1021	*n*	photograph
しゃしん(を)・写真(を) とる・撮る/とります・撮ります	1042	*v*	take a photo (to)
しゃつ・シャツ	1064	*n*	shirt
しゃわー(を)・シャワー(を) する/します	1091	*v*	take a shower (to)
しゃんぷー(を)・シャンプー(を) する/します	1091	*v*	shampoo (to)
じゅーす・ジュース	1063	*n*	juice
じゅう・十	1021	*count.*	ten
じゆう・自由	1105s	*な adj.*	freedom, liberty
じゅういち・十一	1022	*count.*	eleven
じゅういちがつ・十一月	1052	*n*	November
じゅういちじ・十一時	1032	*count.*	eleven o'clock
じゅういちにち・十一日	1053	*count.*	eleventh (day of the month)
じゅういっさい・十一歳/十一才	1052	*count.*	eleven years old
じゅういっぷん・十一分	1032	*count.*	eleven minutes
じゅうがつ・十月	1052	*n*	October
じゅうきゅうまん・十九万	1052	*count.*	one hundred ninety thousand
しゅうきょう・宗教	1052s	*n*	religion
じゅうく/じゅうきゅう・十九	1022	*count.*	nineteen
じゅうくにち・十九日	1053	*count.*	nineteenth (day of the month)
じゅうご・十五	1022	*count.*	fifteen
じゅうごにち・十五日	1053	*count.*	fifteenth (day of the month)
じゅうごまん・十五万	1052	*count.*	one hundred fifty thousand
じゅうさん・十三	1022	*count.*	thirteen
じゅうさんさい・十三歳/十三才	1052	*count.*	thirteen years old
じゅうさんにち・十三日	1053	*count.*	thirteenth (day of the month)
じゅうさんぷん・十三分	1032	*count.*	thirteen minutes
じゅうさんまん・十三万	1052	*count.*	one hundred thirty thousand
じゅうじ・十時	1032	*count.*	ten o'clock
じゅうしちにち・十七日	1053	*count.*	seventeenth (day of the month)

Japanese	Location		English
じゅうど・十度	1101	count.	ten times/degrees
じゅうどう・柔道	1033	n	judo
じゅうなな/じゅうしち・十七	1022	count.	seventeen
じゅうななまん・十七万	1052	count.	one hundred seventy thousand
じゅうに・十二	1022	count.	twelve
じゅうにがつ・十二月	1052	n	December
じゅうにさい・十二歳	1052	count.	twelve years old
じゅうにじ・十二時	1032	count.	twelve o'clock
じゅうににち・十二日	1053	count.	twelfth (day of the month)
じゅうにふん・十二分	1032	count.	twelve minutes
じゅうにまん・十二万	1052	count.	one hundred twenty thousand
じゅうにん・十人	1021	count.	ten people
じゅうはち・十八	1022	count.	eighteen
じゅうはちにち・十八日	1053	count.	eighteenth (day of the month)
じゅうびょう・十秒	1032	count.	ten seconds
じゅうまい・十枚	1042	count.	ten sheets
しゅうまつ・週末	1054	n	weekend
じゅうまん・十万	1052	count.	one hundred thousand
じゅうよっか・十四日	1053	count.	fourteenth (day of the month)
じゅうよん/じゅうし・十四	1022	count.	fourteen
じゅうよんさい・十四歳/十四才	1052	count.	fourteen years old
じゅうよんまん・十四万	1052	count.	one hundred forty thousand
じゅうろく・十六	1022	count.	sixteen
じゅうろくにち・十六日	1053	count.	sixteenth (day of the month)
じゅうろくまん・十六万	1052	count.	one hundred sixty thousand
じゅぎょう・授業	1032	n	class
しゅくだい・宿題	1032	n	homework
しゅくだい(を)・宿題(を)する/します	1091	v	do homework (to)
じゅっさい/じっさい・十歳/十才	1052	count.	ten years old
じゅっさつ/じっさつ・十冊	1092	count.	ten volumes
じゅっぱい/じっぱい・十杯	1092	count.	ten cupfuls
じゅっぴき/じっぴき・十匹	1021	count.	ten small animals
じゅっぷん/じっぷん・十分	1032	count.	ten minutes
じゅっぺーじ/じっぺーじ・十ページ	1042	count.	ten pages, page ten
じゅっぽん/じっぽん・十本	1092	count.	ten cylindrical objects
しゅと・首都	1052s	n	capital
しゅみ・趣味	1071	n	hobby
しゅわ・手話	1042	n	sign language
しょーとぱんつ ショートパンツ	1064s	n	short pants, shorts
しょうかいしてください・紹介して 下さい	1021	v	introduce (please)
しょうかい・紹介する/します	1021	v	introduce (to)
しょうがくいちねんせい・小学一年生	1031	n	elementary school first grader
しょうがくさんねんせい・小学三年生	1031	n	elementary school third grader
しょうがくせい・小学生	1031	n	elementary school student
しょうがくにねんせい・小学二年生	1031	n	elementary school second grader
しょうがくよねんせい・小学四年生	1031	n	elementary school fourth grader
しょうがくろくねんせい・小学六年生	1031	n	elementary school sixth grader
しょうがっこう・小学校	1031	n	elementary school
じょうぎ・定規	App.	n	ruler
しょうぐん・将軍	1051s	n	military leader
じょうず・上手	1062	な adj	skillful
じょうだん・冗談	1072	n	joke
しょうてすと・小テスト	1032	n	small test, quiz
じょうば・乗馬	1071	n	horseback riding
しょうゆ・醤油	1015	n	soy sauce
じょぎんぐ・ジョギング	1071	n	jogging
しょくじ(を)・食事(を)する/します	1091	v	meal (to have a), dine (to)
しょうがくごねんせい・小学校五年生	1031	n	elementary school fifth grader
しりません・知りません	1016s	exp.	I don't know.
しる・知る/しります・知ります	1042	v	know something/someone (to)
じれったい	1081	い adj.	irritating
しろ・白	1074	n	white
しろ・城	1101	n	castle
しろい・白い	1064	い adj.	white-colored
じんじゃ・神社	1033	n	shrine
しんとう・神道	1052s	pn	Shinto (religion)
しんぱい(を)・心配(を)する/します	1063	v	worry (to)
しんはんが・新版画	1091	n	woodblock print (new), art print (new)
しんぷる・シンプル	1064	な adj	simple
しんりがく・心理学	1032	n	psychology
すーつ・スーツ	1064	n	suit
すいえい・水泳	1071	n	swimming
すいようび・水曜日	1051	n	Wednesday
すうがく・数学	1032	n	math
すかーと・スカート	1064	n	skirt
すき・好き	1072	な adj	like
すぎ (〜), 〜すぎ	1032		past, after

Japanese	Location		English
すきー・スキー	1071	*n*	skiing
すきやき・すき焼き	App.	*n*	thin slices of beef, cooked with vegetables
すぐ	1082		immediately, at once
すぐしたの・すぐ下の おとうと・弟/ いもうと ・妹	1021	*n*	next youngest brother/ sister (my)
すけじゅーる・ スケジュール	1032	*n*	schedule
すけっちぶっく・ スケッチブック	1062s	*n*	sketchbook
すけぼー(を)・スケボー (を) する/します	1071	*v*	skateboard (to)
すごい	1035	い *adj.*	amazing, great, terrible
すこし・少し	1031	*adv.*	little
すし・寿司	1011	*n*	sushi
すずしい・涼しい	1034	い *adj.*	cool (weather)
ずっと	1083		continuously, through- out
すてーき・ステーキ	App.	*n*	steak
すてき・素敵	1064	な *adj*	wonderful, nice
すぱげてぃ・スパゲティ	1043s	*n*	spaghetti
すばらしい・素晴らしい	1065	い *adj.*	wonderful
すぺいん・スペイン	1041	*pn*	Spain (place)
すぺいんご・スペイン語	1042	*n*	Spanish (language)
すぺいんじん・スペイン人	1041	*n*	Spaniard
すぽーつ・スポーツ	1071	*n*	sports
ずぼん・ズボン	1064	*n*	pants, trousers
すまーと・スマート	1062	な *adj*	slim, stylish
すみません	1033s	*interj.*	excuse me, I'm sorry
すむ・住む/すみます・ 住みます	1064	*v*	live/reside (to)
すもう・相撲	1011	*n*	Japanese sumo wresling
すりっぱ・スリッパ	1093s	*n*	slipper(s)
する/します (して)	1044	*v*	do (to), wear (to)
ずるい	1081	い *adj.*	cunning
すると	1082s	*conj.*	thereupon
すわひりご・スワヒリ語	1042	*n*	Swahili (language)
すわる・座る/ すわります・座ります	1013	*v*	sit (to)
せ/せい・背	1061	*n*	height, stature
せいき・世紀	1041s	*n*	century, era
せいせき・成績	1033	*n*	score, grade
せいと・生徒， がくせい・学生	1031	*n*	student
せいふく・制服	1025s	*n*	uniform (school)
せいぶつがく・生物学	1032	*n*	biology
せかい・世界	1032s	*n*	world (the), society
せかいし・世界史	1032	*n*	world history
せっと・セット	1103s	*n*	set
せまい・狭い	1083	い *adj.*	narrow
せん・千	1052	*count.*	one thousand
せんげつv先月	1054	*n*	last month
せんしゅう・先週	1054	*n*	last week
せんしゅうのかようび 先週の火曜日	1054	*n*	last week Tuesday
せんせい・先生, 〜せんせい・〜先生	1011	*n*	teacher, suffix AFTER a teacher's, lawyer's, or doctor's name
ぜんぜん・全然	1074	*adv.*	not at all
ぜんぶ・全部	1083	*n*	all, entire, altogether
ぜんぶで・全部で	1092	*exp.*	in all, total, all together
せんべい・煎餅	1094	*n*	rice crackers
そう	1033s	*adv.*	so, really, seeming
そうぶ・総武	1024s	*pn*	Soubu (train line)
そこ	1024	*pron.*	there
そして	1071	*conj.*	then, and then
そちら	1014s	*pron.*	that (person)
そと・外	1045s	*n*	outside
その	1023		that (thing)
そば	1103s	*n*	buckweat noodles
そふ・祖父	1021	*n*	grandfather (my)
そぼ・祖母	1021	*n*	grandmother (my)
それ	1015	*pron.*	that (one)
それから	1071	*conj.*	then, and then
それに	1071	*conj.*	moreover, furthermore
たいいく・体育	1032	*n*	physical education
たいいくかん・体育館	1033	*n*	gymnasium
だいがく・大学	1031	*n*	college/university
だいがくいちねんせい・ 大学一年生	1031		first year college/ university student
だいがくせい・大学生	1031	*n*	college/university student
だいきらい・大嫌い	1072	な *adj*	dislike a lot, hate
だいじ・大事	1051	な *adj*	important
たいしかん・大使館	1022s	*n*	embassy
だいじょうぶ・大丈夫	1063	な *adj.*	all right, safe, OK
だいすき・大好き	1072	な *adj*	love, really like
だいすきです。 ・大好きです	1025s	*exp.*	I love you
だいだいいろ・橙色	1074	*n*	orange
たいてい	1072	*adv.*	usually
たいふう・台風	1101	*n*	typhoon
だいみょう・大名	1045s	*n*	feudal lord
たいむかぷせる・ タイムカプセル	1094s	*n*	time capsule
たかい・高い	1061	い *adj.*	high, tall, expensive
だから	1044	*conj.*	because of that
たくさん・たくさん	1031	*n*	many, a lot
たこ	1025	*n*	octopus
たこす・タコス	1025	*n*	tacos (Mexican)
たこやき・たこ焼き	1104s	*n*	breaded octopus balls
だす・出す/だします・ 出します	1013	*v*	take (it) out (to)
ただいま	1015	*exp.*	I'm home
たつ・立つ/たちます・ 立ちます	1013	*v*	stand (to)

Japanese	Location		English
たっきゅうぶ・卓球部	1033	*n*	Ping-Pong club
たってください・立って下さい	1013	*exp.*	Stand please.
たつまき・竜巻	1101	*n*	tornado
たてもの・建物	1051s	*n*	building
たぬき・狸	1035s	*n*	raccoon dog, tanuki
たのしい・楽しい	1032	い *adj.*	fun, enjoyable
たび・旅, りょこう・旅行	1071s	*n*	trip, travel
たべもの・食べ物	1043	*n*	food(s)
たべる・食べる/たべます・食べます	1043	*v*	eat (to)
たべること・食べる事	1071	*n*	eating
たまご・卵	1015	*n*	egg
だめ	1034	な *adj*	is bad
だれ	1021	*inter.*	who
だれも	1102	*exp.*	no one
たろう・太郎	1014	*n*	Taro (male name)
たんご・単語	1013s	*n*	vocabulary
だんご	App.	*n*	dango (round sticky rice balls on a stick)
たんさく・探索	1013s	*n*	search, hunt
たんじょうび・誕生日	1052	*n*	birthday
ちいさい・小さい	1031	い *adj.*	small
ちかい・近い	1061	い *adj.*	close, near
ちがう・違う/ちがいます・違います	1016s	*v*	is not right, incorrect
ちきん・チキン, とりにく・鶏肉	1043	*n*	chicken
ちず・地図	App.	*n*	map
ちち・父	1014	*n*	father, dad
ちゃいろ・茶色	1074	*n*	brown
ちゃくせき。・着席。	1016s	*exp.*	sit down
ちゃぱつ・茶髪	1074	*n*	brown (hair)
ちゅうがくいちねんせい・中学一年生	1031	*count.*	seventh grader
ちゅうがくさんねんせい・中学三年生	1031	*count.*	ninth grader
ちゅうがくせい・中学生	1031	*n*	middle school student
ちゅうがくにねんせい・中学二年生	1031	*count.*	eighth grader
ちゅうがっこう・中学校	1031	*n*	middle school
ちゅうごく・中国	1041	*pn*	China (place)
ちゅうごくけい・中国系	1041s	*n*	Chinese (descent)
ちゅうごくご・中国語	1042	*n*	Chinese (language)
ちゅうごくじん・中国人	1041	*n*	Chinese (person)
ちょーく・チョーク	1024	*n*	chalk
ちょこれーと・チョコレート	App.	*n*	chocolate
ちょっと	1032	*adv.*	little, somewhat
ちょっと まって ください。・待って 下さい。	1016s	*exp.*	Wait a minute please.
ちょっと・・・	1043	*exp.*	a little ...
ちらしずし・散らし寿司	1103s	*n*	sushi in a box or bowl with a variety of ingredients

Japanese	Location		English
ついたち・一日	1053	*count.*	first (day of the month)
つかう・使う/つかいます・使います	1102	*v*	use (to)
つぎ・次	1033	*n/adv.*	next
つくる・作る/つくります・作ります	1102	*v*	make (to)
つけもの・漬け物	1083	*n*	pickled vegetables (Japanese)
つなみ・津波	1011	*n*	tsunami, exceptionally large ocean wave
つまらない	1082	い *adj.*	boring
つゆ・梅雨	1101	*n*	rainy season
つよい・強い	1061	い *adj.*	strong
つれて・連れて いく・行く/いきます・行きます	1105	*v*	take someone (to)
つれて・連れて かえる・帰る/かえります・帰ります	1105	*v*	return with someone (to)
つれて・連れて くる・来る/きます・来ます	1105	*v*	bring someone (to)
て・手	1061	*n*	hand
で	1043s, 1063s, 1092s	*part.*	by means of a "tool", at, for (used for shopping or ordering food)
でーと(を)・デート(を)する/します	1091	*v*	date (to go on a)
てーぷ・テープ	App.	*n*	tape
てーぶる・テーブル	App.	*n*	table
てぃーしゃつ・Tシャツ	1023	*n*	t-shirt
てぃっしゅ・ティッシュ	App.	*n*	tissue
できる・出来る/できます・出来ます	1016s	*v*	be able (to)
です	1013	*copula*	helping verb/linking verb used similarly to "is" or "am"
てすと・テスト	1032	*n*	test
てつだう・手伝う/てつだいます・手伝います	1041	*v*	help (to), assist (to)
では また	1015	*exp.*	see you later (formal)
てまきずし・手巻き寿司	1103s	*n*	sushi wrapped in nori
でも	1034	*part.*	"but" or "however" at the beginning of a sentence
てら・(お)寺	1033	*n*	temple (Buddhist)
てりやき・照り焼き	App.	*n*	teriyaki (meat or fish marinated in sweet soy sauce and broiled)
でる・出る/でます・出ます	1061	*v*	go out (to), leave (to), get out (to)
てれび・テレビ	1103s	*n*	television, TV
てんいん・店員	1092	*n*	shopkeeper, clerk
てんおう・天皇	1052s	*n*	emperor
てんき・天気	1101	*n*	weather
でんき・電気	App.	*n*	lights, electricity
てんきよほう・天気予報	1101	*n*	weather report

Japanese	Location		English
でんしめーる・電子メール/めーる・メール	1051	n	e-mail
てんぷら・天ぷら	1021s	n	tenpura (battered and deep fried fish or vegetable)
でんわ・電話	1021	n	telephone
でんわ(を)・電話(を)する/します	1091	v	telephone (to)
と	1022	part.	and (used to connect more than one noun, quotation particle, used after a direct quotation)
どあ・ドア	1034	n	door
どいつ・ドイツ	1041	pn	Germany (place)
どいつご・ドイツ語	1042	n	German (language)
どいつじん・ドイツ人	1041	n	German (person)
どう	1035	inter.	how
どう でしたか。	1065	exp.	How was it?
どう ですか	1092	exp.	how about it?
どういたしまして	1023	exp.	you are welcome
とうきょう・東京	1011	n	Tokyo (place)
とうきょうこくさいだいがく・東京国際大学	1022s	pn	Tokyo International University (place)
とうきょうだいがく・東京大学	1031s	pn	Tokyo University (place)
どうして, なぜ	1042	inter.	why
どうぞ	1015	adv.	please (here you go), by all means
どうぞ よろしく	1013	exp.	best regards, treat me favorably (same meaning as よろしく おねがいします)
どうぞ よろしく おねがいします・お願いします	1013	exp.	polite for よろしくお願いします
とうだいじ・東大寺	1051s	pn	Todaiji Temple (in Nara)
とうふ・豆腐	1011	n	tofu
どうぶつ・動物	1072	n	animal
どうも ありがとう	1023	exp.	thank you
どうも ありがとう ございます	1023	exp.	thank you very much (polite for どうも ありがとう)
とお・十	1024	count.	ten (things)
とおい・遠い	1061	い adj.	far, distant
とおか・十日	1053	count.	tenth (day of the month)
とおる・通る/とおります・通ります	1051s	v	pass through (to)
とき・時	1035s	n	time, hour
ときどき・時々	1032	n/adv.	sometimes
ときのもん・時の門	1041s	n	time gate
とくい・得意	1073	な adj	skilled at
とくがわ・徳川	1041s	pn	Tokugawa (family name)
どくしょ・読書	1071	n	reading
とくべつ・特別	1092	n/な adj.	special
とけい・時計	App.	n	clock
どこ	1024	inter.	where?
どこでも	1054s	n	anywhere
どこにも	1102	adv.	nowhere (w. neg. verb), everywhere, anywhere, anyplace
どこへも	1102	adv.	nowhere, not anywhere, not any place (w. neg. verb) (ex: どこへも 行きません。 = He is not going any place.)
どこも	1102	adv.	everywhere, wherever
ところ・所	1052s	n	place
ところで	1041	exp.	by the way
とし(を)とる・年(を)取る	1101s	v	grow old (to), age (to)
とじて ください・閉じて 下さい	1013	exp.	close/Shut (it) please.
としょかん・図書館	1033	n	library
とじる・閉じる/とじます・閉じます	1013	v	close (to), shut (to) [bound paper objects]
とつぜん・突然	1104s	adv.	abrupt, sudden, unexpected
とても	1031	adv.	very
とにかく	1044s	adv.	anyway, at any rate
どの	1023	inter.	which (thing)
とまと・トマト	App.	n	tomato
ともだち・友達	1022	n	friend
どようび・土曜日	1051	n	Saturday
とらんぷ・トランプ	1071	n	playing cards, card game
とりい・鳥居	1035	n	torii (Shinto shrine gate)
とりにく・鶏肉, ちきん・チキン	1043	n	chicken
どれ	1015	inter.	which (one)
どれす・ドレス	1064	n	dress (a)
とんこつらーめん・ラーメン	1043s	n	pork ramen
とんでもない	1094	exp.	Don't be ridiculous! Not a chance! My pleasure
どんな	1062	inter.	what/which kind of
とんねる・トンネル	1041s	n	tunnel
ながい・長い	1061	い adj.	long
ながさき・長崎	1041s	pn	Nagasaki (place)
なかなおり(を)・仲直り(を)する/します	1091	v	make up (to), reconcile (to)
なし・梨	App.	n	Asian pear
なぜ, どうして	1042	inter.	why
なつ・夏	1101	n	summer
など	1101s	part.	et cetera, and so forth
ななさい・七歳/七才	1052	count.	seven years old
ななさつ・七冊	1092	count.	seven volumes
ななじゅう・七十	1022	count.	seventy
ななせん・七千	1052	count.	seven thousand
ななつ・七つ	1024	count.	seven (things)
ななど・七度	1101	count.	seven times/degrees
ななはい・七杯	1092	count.	seven cupfuls
ななひき・七匹	1021	count.	seven small animals

Japanese	Location		English
ななひゃく・七百	1023s	*count.*	seven hundred
ななびょう・七秒	1032	*count.*	seven seconds
ななふん・七分	1032	*count.*	seven minutes
ななぺーじ/しちぺーじ・七ページ	1042	*count.*	seven pages, page seven
ななほん・七本	1092	*count.*	seven cylindrical objects
ななまい/しちまい・七枚	1042	*count.*	seven sheets
ななまん・七万	1052	*count.*	seventy thousand
なにいろ・何色	1074	*inter.*	what color
なにか・何か	1103		something
なにけい・何系	1041	*inter.*	what ethnicity or heritage
なにじん・何人	1041	*inter.*	what nationality
なにも・何も	1053	*pron.*	nothing
なのか・七日	1053	*count.*	seventh (day of the month)
なまえ・名前	1013	*n*	name
なら・奈良	1051s	*pn*	Nara (place)
ならう・習う/ならいます・習います	1065	*v*	learn (to)
ならじだい・奈良時代	1054s	*pn*	Nara Period
なりたくうこう・成田空港	1011s	*pn*	Narita International Airport (place)
なる/なります	1055	*v*	become (to)
なるほど	1042s	*exp.*	That makes sense.
なん/なに・何	1021	*inter.*	what
なんがつ・何月	1052	*inter.*	what month
なんさい・何歳/何才	1022s	*inter.*	how old (animate beings)
なんさつ・何冊	1092	*inter.*	how many volumes
なんじ・何時	1032	*inter.*	what time
なんじかんめ・何時間目	1033	*inter.*	what period
なんぜん・何千	1052	*inter.*	how many thousands
なんでも・何でも	1043s	*pn*	anything
なんど・何度	1101	*inter.*	how many times/degrees
なんにち・何日	1053	*inter.*	what day of the month
なんにん・何人	1021	*inter.*	how many people
なんねん・何年	1054	*inter.*	what year
なんねんせい・何年生	1031	*inter.*	what grade/year
なんばい・何杯	1092	*inter.*	how many cupfuls
なんびき・何匹	1021	*inter.*	how many small animals?
なんびょう・何秒	1032	*inter.*	How many seconds?
なんぷん・何分	1032	*inter.*	how many minutes
なんぺーじ・何ページ	1042	*inter.*	how many pages, what page
なんべい・南米	1042s	*pn*	South America (place)
なんぼん・何本	1092	*inter.*	how many cylindrical objects
なんまい・何枚	1042	*inter.*	how many sheets
なんまん・何万	1052	*inter.*	how many ten-thousands?
なんめいさま・何名様	1103s	*inter.*	how many people (polite)
なんようび・何曜日	1051	*inter.*	what day of the week
に	1015	*part.*	in, at, used after a location or time word
に	1023	*part.*	particle after a place word to mean "to" before a verb of motion (similar to the particle へ)
に・二	1021	*count.*	two
に よろしく, …に よろしく	1065	*exp.*	Say hello to . . .
にがつ・二月	1052	*n*	February
にがて・苦手	1073	*な adj*	unskilled at
にさい・二歳/二才	1052	*count.*	two years old
にさつ・二冊	1092	*count.*	two volumes
にじ・二時	1032	*count.*	two o'clock
にじかんめ・二時間目	1033	*count.*	second period
にじゅう・二十	1022	*count.*	twenty
にじゅういち・二十一	1022	*count.*	twenty-one
にじゅういちにち・二十一日	1053	*count.*	twenty-first (day of the month)
にじゅういちまん・二十一万	1052	*count.*	two hundred ten-thousand
にじゅういっぷん・二十一分	1032	*count.*	twenty-one minutes
にじゅうくにち・二十九日	1053	*count.*	twenty-ninth (of the month)
にじゅうごにち・二十五日	1053	*count.*	twenty-fifth (day of the month)
にじゅうさんにち・二十三日	1053	*count.*	twenty-third (day of the month)
にじゅうしちにち・二十七日	1053	*count.*	twenty-seventh (day of the month)
にじゅうににち・二十二日	1053	*count.*	twenty-second (day of the month)
にじゅうはちにち・二十八日	1053	*count.*	twenty-eighth (day of the month)
にじゅうまん・二十万	1052	*count.*	two hundred thousand
にじゅうよっか・二十四日	1053	*count.*	twenty-fourth (day of the month)
にじゅうろくにち・二十六日	1053	*count.*	twenty-sixth (day of the month)
にじゅっぷん・二十分	1032	*count.*	twenty minutes
にせん・二千	1052	*count.*	two thousand
にちようび・日曜日	1051	*n*	Sunday
にっけいじん・日系人	1041	*n*	Japanese descent
にど・二度	1101	*count.*	two times/degrees
にねんせい・二年生	1031s	*count.*	second year student
にはい・二杯	1092	*count.*	two cupfuls
にばんめの あに/あね・二番目の 兄/姉	1021	*n*	second oldest brother/sister (my)
にひき・二匹	1021	*count.*	two small animals
にひゃく・二百	1023s	*count.*	two hundred
にびょう・二秒	1032	*count.*	two seconds
にふん・二分	1032	*count.*	two minutes

Japanese	Location		English
にぺーじ・二ページ	1042	*count.*	two pages, page two
にほん・日本	1011	*pn*	Japan (place)
にほん・二本	1092	*count.*	two cylindrical objects
にほんご・日本語	1011	*n*	Japanese language
にほんし・日本史	1032	*n*	Japanese history
にほんじん・日本人	1014	*n*	Japanese person
にまい・二枚	1042	*count.*	two sheets
にまん・二万	1052	*count.*	twenty thousand
にゅーじーらんど・ニュージーランド	1041	*pn*	New Zealand (place)
にゅーじーらんどじん・ニュージーランド人	1041	*n*	New Zealander
にわ・庭	1101	*n*	garden
ね	1035	*part.*	sentence ending for a rhetorical question or when seeking agreement
ねえ	1035	*part.*	sentence ending that can be exclamatory or express surprise
ねくたい・ネクタイ	1064	*n*	necktie
ねこ・猫	1021	*n*	cat
ねずみ・鼠	1072	*n*	rat, mouse
ねずみいろ・鼠色	1074	*n*	gray (mouse colored)
ねつ・熱	1063	*n*	fever
ねむい・眠い	1053s	い *adj.*	sleepy
ねる・寝る/ねます・寝ます	1051	*v*	sleep (to)
ねること・寝る事	1071	*n*	sleeping
ねんかん・年間	1032s	*n*	period of years, duration
ねんごう・年号	1053s	*n*	reign year
の	1021	*part.*	possession, replaces a noun
のーと・ノート	1024	*n*	notebook
のう・能	1075	*n*	Noh (a type of theater)
のど・咽喉	1061	*n*	throat
のときに (〜)・〜の時に	1055s	*conj.*	when
のみもの・飲み物	1043	*n*	drink(s)
のむ・飲む/のみます・飲みます	1043	*v*	drink (to)
のり	App.	*n*	seaweed
のれん	1043s	*n*	noren curtain
は	1013	*part.*	denotes a sentence topic
ぱーてぃ・パーティ	1073s	*n*	party
はい	1014		yes, OK, here (roll call)
はい、そう です。	1014	*exp.*	yes it is
はい、わかります。・分かります。	1016s	*exp.*	Yes, I understand.
はいいろ・はい色	1064, 1074	*n*	gray, ash (color)
はいく・俳句	1101	*n*	haiku (poem)
ばいばい・バイバイ	1015		bye-bye
はいる・入る/はいります・入ります	1061		come in (to), go in (to), enter (to)
ばかばかしい	1081	い *adj.*	foolish, silly
はく・履く/はきます・履きます	1064	*v*	wear below the waist (to)

Japanese	Location		English
はこ・箱	1081	*n*	box
はさみ	App.	*n*	scissors
はし (お)・(お)箸	1015	*n*	chopsticks
はじめまして・初めまして	1013	*exp.*	How do you do?
はじめましょう・始めましょう	1011	*exp.*	Let's begin.
はじめる・始める/はじめます・始めます	1052	*v*	begin (to)
ばすけ・バスケ, ばすけっとぼーる・バスケットボール	1033	*n*	basketball
ばすけ(を)・バスケ(を)する/します	1091	*v*	play basketball (to)
ばすけぶ・バスケ部	1033	*n*	basketball club (team)
はた・旗	App.	*n*	flag
はたち・二十歳	1052	*count.*	twenty years old
はち・八	1021	*count.*	eight
はちがつ・八月	1052	*n*	August
はちじ・八時	1032	*count.*	eight o'clock
はちじゅう・八十	1022	*count.*	eighty
はちど・八度	1101	*count.*	eight times/degrees
はちにん・八人	1021	*count.*	eight people
はちびょう・八秒	1032	*count.*	eight seconds
はちふん/はっぷん・八分	1032	*count.*	eight minutes
はちぺーじ/はっぺーじ・八ページ	1042	*count.*	eight pages, page eight
はちほん/はっぽん・八本	1092	*count.*	eight cylindrical objects
はちまい・八枚	1042	*count.*	eight sheets
はちまん・八万	1052	*count.*	eighty thousand
はつか・二十日	1053	*count.*	twentieth (day of the month)
ばっぐ・バッグ	1023s	*n*	bag/sack
ばっくぱっく・バックパック	1024	*n*	backpack
はっさい・八歳, 八才	1052	*count.*	eight years old
はっさつ・八冊	1092	*count.*	eight volumes
はっせん・八千	1052	*count.*	eight thousand
はっぱい・八杯	1092	*count.*	eight cupfuls
はっぴき・八匹	1021	*count.*	eight small animals
はっぴゃく・八百	1023s	*count.*	eight hundred
はな・鼻	1061	*n*	nose
はな・花	1101	*n*	flower
はなす・話す/はなします・ 話します	1042	*v*	speak (to)
ばなな・バナナ	1023s	*n*	banana
はなみ・花見	1105	*n*	cherry blossom viewing, flower viewing
はにわ・埴輪	1041s	*n*	haniwa
はは・母	1014	*n*	mother, mom
はま・浜, びーち・ビーチ	1081	*n*	beach
はやい・早い	1054s	い *adj.*	early
はやく・速く	1035	*adv.*	quickly
はる・春	1101	*n*	spring
はれ・晴れ	1101	*n*	clear (skies)
ばれーぼーるぶ・バレーボール部	1033	*n*	volleyball club (team)
はれる・晴れる/はれます・晴れます	1101	*v*	become clear (weather)

Japanese	Location		English
はん・〜半	1032	*n*	half hour
ばん・晩	1021s	*n*	evening
ぱん・パン	1043	*n*	bread
はんが・版画	1091	*n*	woodblock print
ばんごはん・晩ご飯	1025	*n*	dinner, evening meal
はんさむ・ハンサム	1064	な *adj*	handsome, good looking
ぱんつ・パンツ, したぎ・下着	1064	*n*	underwear
はんばーがー・ハンバーガー	1043	*n*	hamburger
ぱんや・パン屋	1043	*n*	bakery
びーち・ビーチ, はま・浜	1081	*n*	beach
ぴあの・ピアノ	1071	*n*	piano
ひき (〜)・〜匹	1022s	*count.*	small animals count.
ひく・弾く/ひきます 弾きます	1071	*v*	play [a stringed instrument] (to)
ひくい・低い	1061	い *adj.*	low, short (height)
ひげ・髭	1061	*n*	mustache, beard
ひざ・膝	1061	*n*	knee
ぴざ・ピザ	1043s	*n*	pizza
びじゅつ・美術	1032	*n*	art, fine arts
びっくり・ビックリ する/します	1105s	*v*	be surprised (to), be amazed (to)
びでおげーむ・ビデオゲーム	1071	*n*	video games
びでおげーむ(を)・ビデオゲーム(を) する/します	1091	*v*	play video games (to)
ひと・人	1022	*n*	person
ひどい	1081	い *adj.*	terrible
ひとつ・一つ	1024	*count.*	one (thing)
ひとり・一人	1021	*count.*	one person
ひとりで・一人で	1104	*exp.*	alone, by oneself
ひま	1084	な *adj*	free (time)
ひみつ・秘密	1061	*n*	secret
ひゃく・百	1022	*count.*	one hundred
びょういん・病院	1063	*n*	hospital
びょうき・病気	1063	*n*	illness, sickness
ひらいずみ・平泉	1061s	*pn*	Hiraizumi (place)
ひらく・開く/ひらきます・開きます	1013	*v*	open (to) [book/bound object]
ひる・昼	1025	*n*	daytime, noon
ひるごはん・昼ご飯	1025	*n*	lunch
ひるね・昼寝	1063	*n*	nap
ひるね(を)・昼寝(を) する/します	1063	*v*	nap (to)
ひるやすみ・昼休み	1032	*n*	lunch break
ひろい・広い	1083	い *adj.*	wide, spacious
ひろお・広尾	1022s	*pn*	Hiroo (section of Tokyo)
ひろしま・広島	1083s	*pn*	Hiroshima (place)
ぴんく・ピンク	1064, 1074	*n*	pink
ふぁっしょん・ファッション	1074s	*n*	fashion
ふぁん・ファン	1065s	*n*	fan, supporter

Japanese	Location		English
ぷえるとりこじん・プエルトリコ人	1041	*n*	Puerto Rican (person)
ぶかつ・部活	1033	*n*	club activity
ふく・服	1064	*n*	clothes
ふしぎ・不思議	1081	な *adj*	mysterious
ふじさん・富士山	1094s	*pn*	Fuji (Mt.)
ふたご・双子	1022s	*n*	twins
ふたつ・二つ	1024	*count.*	two (things)
ふたり・二人	1021	*count.*	two people
ふつう・普通	1064	*adj./adv.*	usual, normal
ふつか・二日	1053	*count.*	second (day of the month)
ぶっきょう・仏教	1052s	*n*	Buddhism (religion)
ぶつりがく・物理学	1032	*n*	physics
ふで・筆	1033s	*n*	brush
ふでばこ・筆箱	App.	*n*	pencil box
ふとっています・太っています	1062		fat/plump (is)
ふとる・太る/ふとります 太ります	1062	*v*	fat (to get)
ふとん・布団	1063	*n*	futon
ふね・舟	1045s	*n*	ship, boat
ふゆ・冬	1101	*n*	winter
ぶらじるじん・ブラジル人	1041	*n*	Brazilian (person)
ぶらすばんど・ブラスバンド	1033	*n*	brass band
ふらんす・フランス	1041	*pn*	France
ふらんすご・フランス語	1042	*n*	French (language)
ふらんすじん・フランス人	1041	*n*	French (person)
ぷらんなー・プランナー	App.	*n*	planner, handbook
ふる・降る/ふります・降ります	1101	*v*	precipitate (to)
ふるーつ・フルーツ, くだもの・果物	1075s	*n*	fruit
ふるい・古い	1081	い *adj.*	old (used for things)
ぷれぜんと・プレゼント	1094	*n*	a gift, a present
ぶんか・文化	1065	*n*	culture
へ	1023	*part.*	particle after a place word to mean "to" before a verb of motion (similar to the particle に)
へ/に	1104	*part.*	used with verbs of movement after place of destination
べーすぼーる ベースボール, やきゅう・野球	1033	*n*	baseball
へいじょうきょう・平城京	1051s	*pn*	Heijoukyou (ancient name for Kyoto)
ぺこぺこ・ペコペコ	1025		hunger (mimetic expression for)
へた・下手	1073	な *adj*	not good at
べつ・別	1092	*n*/な *adj.*	separate
べつべつ・別々	1092	*n*/な *adj.*	separately, individually
へや 部屋	1015	*n*	room (a)

Japanese	Location		English
ぺるーじん・ペルー人	1041	n	Peruvian (person)
ぺん・ペン	1024	n	pen
べんきょう(を)・勉強(を) する/します	1052	v	study (to)
べんけい・弁慶	1061s	pn	Benkei (famous samurai name)
べんとう・弁当	1011	n	box lunch (Japanese), bento
ほーむるーむ ホームルーム	1032	n	homeroom
ぼーるぺん・ボールペン	1024	n	ballpoint pen
ほいくえん・保育園	1031	n	nursery school
ほうかご・放課後	1033	n/adv.	time after school
ぼうし	1023	n	hat/cap
ぼく・僕	1013	pron.	I, me (used by males only)
ほけんたいいく・保健体育	1032	n	health (class)
ほっちきす・ホッチキス	App.	n	stapler
ほら!	1081s	interj.	look, Look out!
ぽるとがる・ポルトガル	1041	pn	Portugal (place)
ぽるとがるご・ポルトガル語	1042	n	Portuguese (language)
ぽるとがるじん・ポルトガル人	1041	n	Portuguese (person)
ほわいとぼーど・ホワイトボード	App.	n	whiteboard
ほん・本	1011	n	book
ほんしゅう・本州	1041s	pn	Honshu (place)
ほんだな・本棚	App.	n	bookshelves
ほんとう・本当	1104	n	truth, reality
ほんもの・本物	1091	n	real thing, genuine article
ほんや・本屋	1043	n	bookstore
ほんやさん・本屋さん	1043	n	bookstore
まあまあ	1062	adv.	so so, not bad, moderate
まいしゅう・毎週	1054	n	every week
まいつき・毎月	1054	n	every month
まいとし/まいねん・毎年	1054	n	every year
まいにち・毎日	1032	n	every day
まいねん/まいとし・毎年	1054	n	every year
まえ・前	1032	n/adv.	front, in front, before
まきずし・巻き寿司	1043s	n	rolled sushi
まじっく・マジック	App.	n	marker
まずい	1081	い adj.	not tasty, not good
また	1092s	prefix	again, also, and
まだ	1043	adv.	not yet (with negative verb)
まつ・待つ/まちます・待ちます	1061	v	wait (to)
まつおばしょう・松尾芭蕉	1102s	pn	Basho Matsuo (Japanese poet)
まったく・全く	1084	adv.	really, indeed, truly
まつり・祭り	1051	n	festival
まで	1053	part.	until (used with spec. locations or times)

Japanese	Location		English
まど・窓	1034	n	window
まん・万	1052	count.	ten thousand
まんが・漫画	1011	n	Japanese comics
みぎ・右	1104s	n	right
みじかい・短い	1061	い adj.	short (length)
みず・水	1024	n	water
みせ・店	1091	n	shop, store
みせる・見せる	1045s	v	to show
みそしる・味噌汁	1104s	n	miso soup
みっか・三日	1053	count.	third (day of the month)
みっつ・三つ	1024	count.	three (things)
みてください。・見て下さい。	1013	exp.	Look/Watch please.
みどり・緑	1064, 1074	n	green
みなさん・皆さん	1031	n	everyone (polite)
みなみあふりか・南アフリカ	1041	pn	South Africa (place)
みにくい	1081	い adj.	ugly
みみ・耳	1061	n	ear
みる・見る/みます・見ます	1013	v	look/see (to)
ミルク	1043s	n	milk
みんな・皆	1031	pron.	everyone, all
むいか・六日	1053	count.	sixth (day of the month)
むかし・昔	1082	n	long ago
むかしむかし・昔々	1082	n	long long ago
むぎちゃ・麦茶	1103s	n	barley tea
むしあつい・蒸し暑い	1034	い adj.	humid (weather)
むずかしい・難しい	1032	い adj.	difficult
むっつ・六つ	1024	count.	six (things)
むらさき・紫	1064, 1074	n	purple
むらさきしきぶ・紫式部	1071s	pn	Murasaki Shikibu (Heian Period author)
むり・無理	1063	な adj.	impossible, overdoing
むり しないで ください・無理 しないで 下さい	1063	exp.	Don't overexert.
め・目	1061	n	eye
めいく・メイク	1064	n	make up (facial)
めがね・眼鏡	1064	n	eyeglasses
めきしこ・メキシコ	1041	pn	Mexico (place)
めきしこけい・メキシコ系	1041	n	Mexican descent
めきしこじん・メキシコ人	1041	n	Mexican (person)
めも・メモ	1083	n	memo, note
めろん・メロン	1023s	n	melon (honeydew)
も	1024	part.	too, also, replaces particles は、が、and を
もう	1104	adv./interj.	already
もういちど いって ください。・もう一度 言って 下さい。	1016s	exp.	Say it again please.
もくようび・木曜日	1051	n	Thursday
もち・餅	1064	n	sticky rice cake (mochi)
もち (お)・(お)餅	1064	n	sticky rice cake
もちろん	1105	exp.	of course

Japanese	Location		English
もつ・持つ/もちます・持ちます	1061	*v*	have (to), hold (to), carry (to)
もって・持って いく・行く/いきます・行きます	1105	*v*	take something (to)
もって・持って かえる/・帰る/かえります・帰ります	1105	*v*	return with something (to)
もって・持って くる・来る/きます・来ます	1105	*v*	bring something (to)
もっと	1093	*adv.*	more
もの・物	1043	*n*	thing
ももいろ・もも色	1074	*n*	pink (peach) color
もらう/もらいます	1094	*v*	receive (to) (very polite), lit.: I will receive.
もり・森	1101s	*n*	forest
もん・門	1033s	*n*	gate
もんだい・問題	1045s	*n*	problem
やきそば・焼きそば	1102s	*n*	fried noodles, yakisoba
やきゅう・野球, ベーすぼーる・ベースボール	1033	*n*	baseball
やくそく・約束	1105s	*n*	promise
やさしい・優しい	1081	い *adj.*	easy, simple, kind, gentle
やすい・安い	1082	い *adj.*	cheap
やすむ・休む	1015s	*v*	rest (to), take a break (to)
やせています	1062		slim/skinny (is)
やせる/やせます	1062	*v*	thin (to become)
やっつ・八つ	1024	*count.*	eight (things)
やってみる/やってみます	1073	*v*	see if you can do (something), try to do (something) (to)
やま・山	1031	*n*	mountain
やまのて・山の手	1024s	*pn*	Yamanote (train line)
やまもと・山本	1031	*pn*	Yamamoto (family name)
やる/やります	1073	*v*	do (to)
ゆうめい・有名	1061	な *adj*	famous
ゆうやけ・夕焼け, さんせっと・サンセット	1104s	*n*	sunset
ゆき・雪	1101	*n*	snow
ゆっくり	1016s	*adv.*	slowly, restful
ゆっくり おねがい します。・お願いします。	1016s	*exp.*	Please say it more slowly.
ゆび・指	1061	*n*	finger(s)
よ	1035	*part.*	sentence ending for a strong declarative statement or for emphasis
ヨーロッパ	1042s	*pn*	Europe (place)
よい・良い (よく・良く)	1082	い *adj.*	well
よい/いい・良い	1041s	*ir. adj.*	good
ようか・八日	1053	*count.*	eighth (day of the month)
ようこそ	1014	*exp.*	Welcome!, Nice to see you.
ようちえん・幼稚園	1031	*n*	kindergarten
ようふく・洋服	1064	*n*	clothes, Western clothes

Japanese	Location		English
よく	1103s	*adv.*	well, nicely
よくできました。・良く出来ました	1016s	*exp.*	Well done.
よこはま・横浜	1031s	*pn*	Yokohama (place)
よじ・四時	1032	*count.*	four o'clock
よじかんめ・四時間目	1033	*count.*	fourth period
よっか・四日	1053	*count.*	fourth (day of the month)
よっつ・四つ	1024	*count.*	four (things)
よにん・四人	1021	*count.*	four people
よむ・読む/よみます・読みます	1013	*v*	read (to)
よろしく	1013s	*adv.*	best regards, please remember me (favorably)
よろしく おねがいします・お願いします	1013	*exp.*	best regards, treat me favorably
よわい・弱い	1061	い *adj.*	weak
よん/し・四	1021	*count.*	four
よんさい・四歳/四才	1052	*count.*	four years old
よんさつ・四冊	1092	*count.*	four volumes
よんじゅう・四十	1022	*count.*	forty
よんじゅうさんぷん・四十三分	1032	*count.*	forty-three minutes
よんせん・四千	1052	*count.*	four thousand
よんど・四度	1101	*count.*	four times/degrees
よんはい・四杯	1092	*count.*	four cupfuls
よんひき・四匹	1021	*count.*	four small animals
よんひゃく・四百	1023s	*count.*	four hundred
よんびょう・四秒	1032	*count.*	four seconds
よんぷん・四分	1032	*count.*	four minutes
よんぺーじ・四ページ	1042	*count.*	four pages, page four
よんほん・四本	1092	*count.*	four cylindrical objects
よんまい・四枚	1042	*count.*	four sheets
よんまん・四万	1052	*count.*	forty thousand
らーめん・ラーメン	1043s	*n*	ramen
らいげつ・来月	1054	*n*	next month
らいしゅう・来週	1054	*n*	next week
らいねん・来年	1054	*n*	next year
りくじょうぶ・陸上部	1033	*n*	track and field club
りょうり・料理	1071	*n*	cooking
りょかん・旅館	1044s	*n*	ryokan, Japanese inn/hotel
りょこう・旅行, たび・旅	1071	*n*	trip, travel
りょこう(を)・旅行(を) する/します	1091	*v*	take a trip (to), travel (to)
りんご	1023s	*n*	apple
れい・礼	1016s	*exp.*	bow
れきし・歴史	1032	*n*	history
れすとらん・レストラン	1043	*n*	restaurant
れんしゅう(を)・練習(を) する/します	1051	*v*	practice (to)
ろく・六	1021	*count.*	six
ろくがつ・六月	1052	*n*	June
ろくさい・六歳	1052	*count.*	six years old

Japanese	Location		English
ろくさつ・六冊	1092	*count.*	six volumes
ろくじ・六時	1032	*count.*	six o'clock
ろくじかんめ・六時間目	1033	*count.*	sixth period
ろくじゅう・六十	1022	*count.*	sixty
ろくせん・六千	1052	*count.*	six thousand
ろくど・六度	1101	*count.*	six times/degrees
ろくにん・六人	1021	*count.*	six people
ろくびょう・六秒	1032	*count.*	six seconds
ろくぺーじ・六ページ	1042	*count.*	six pages, page six
ろくまい・六枚	1042	*count.*	six sheets
ろくまん・六万	1052	*count.*	sixty thousand
ろしあ・ロシア	1041	*pn*	Russia (place)
ろしあご・ロシア語	1042	*n*	Russian (language)
ろしあじん・ロシア人	1041	*n*	Russian (person)
ろっかーへ いっても いいですか。・ロッカーへ 行っても いいですか。	1016s	*exp.*	May I go to my locker?
ろっくんろーる・ロックンロール	1105	*n*	rock and roll (music)
ろっぱい・六杯	1092	*count.*	six cupfuls
ろっぴき・六匹	1021	*count.*	six small animals
ろっぴゃく・六百	1023s	*count.*	six hundred
ろっぷん・六分	1032	*count.*	six minutes
ろっぽん・六本	1092	*count.*	six cylindrical objects
ろっぽんぎ・六本木	1024s	*pn*	Roppongi section of Tokyo
わか・和歌	1072s	*n*	waka (classic Japanese poem)
わがまま	1081	な *adj.*	selfish
わかる・分かる/わかります・分かります	1016s	*v*	understand (to)
わさび	1015	*n*	wasabi, Japanese horseradish
わたし・私	1013	*pron.*	me, I
わたしたち・私達	1013	*pron.*	we, us
わっ!	1035	*interj.*	wow!
わるい・悪い	1082	い *adj.*	bad
を	1023	*part.*	used after the direct object

English-Japanese Glossary

This glossary has simplified abbreviations to make it easier to use. The following abbreviations are used for parts of speech:

い *adj.*	い adjective	*interj.*	interjection
な *adj.*	な adjective	*n*	noun
adv.	adverb	*part.*	particle
conj.	conjunction	*pn*	person or place name
exp.	expression	*pron.*	pronoun
inter.	interrogative	*v*	verb

The numbering system for location of vocabulary words in the chapters is made up of the volume number (the first digit; 1 is this volume, *Beginning Japanese*); a two-digit chapter number; and the section number. An "s" indicates words that are supplemental: they are not on the New Words lists, but are also included in the book (in the Dialogues, Journal entries, etc.). For example:

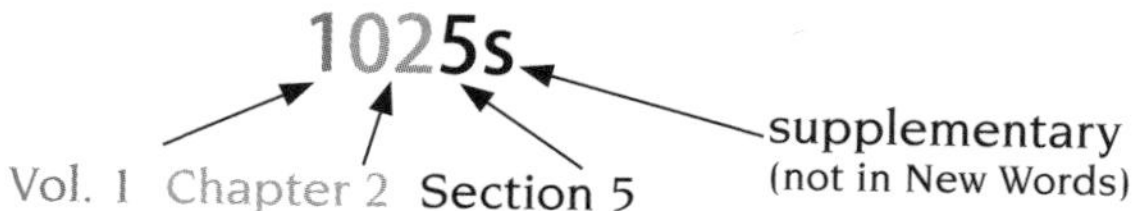

English	Location		Japanese
A.M.	1032	*n*	ごぜん・午前
about	1032		ごろ, ころ
abrupt, sudden, unexpected	1104s	*adv.*	とつぜん・突然
actually	1104	*adv.*	じつは・実は
after	1033		あと・後
after, past	1032		すぎ (～)・～過ぎ
afterwards, later	1033	*adv.*	あとで・後で
again, also, and	1092s	*prefix*	また
age, era, period	1071s	*n*	じだい・時代
age (to), grow old (to)	1101s	*v*	とし(を)とる・年(を)取る
Ah!, Oh!	1025	*interj.*	ああ
Aiko (female name)	1015s	*pn*	あいこ・愛子
airconditioning	1035	*n*	えあこん・エアコン
all, everyone	1031	*pron.*	みんな・皆
all, entire, altogether	1083	*n*	ぜんぶ・全部
all right, safe, OK	1063	な *adj.*	だいじょうぶ・大丈夫
all together, in all, total	1092	*exp.*	ぜんぶで・全部で
alone, by oneself	1104	*exp.*	ひとりで・一人で
a lot, many	1031	*n*	たくさん・たくさん
also, and, again	1092s	*prefix*	また
also, too; replaces particles, は, が, and を	1024	*part.*	も
already	1104	*adv./ interj.*	もう
altogether, all, entire	1083	*n*	ぜんぶ・全部
always	1061	*n/adv.*	いつも
Amanohashidate (place)	1082	*pn*	あまのはしだて・天橋立
amazing, great, terrible, to a great extent	1035	い *adj.*	すごい
American (person)	1041	*n*	あめりかじん・アメリカ人
American football	1071	*n*	あめふと・アメフト, あめりかんふっとぼーる・アメリカンフットボール
American history	1032	*n*	あめりかし・アメリカ史
ancient Japanese court music, gagaku	1075	*n*	ががく・雅楽
and, again, also	1092s	*prefix*	また
and so forth, et cetera	1101s	*part.*	など
and then, then	1071	*conj.*	そして, それから
animal	1072	*n*	どうぶつ・動物
animated cartoons/films	1011	*n*	あにめ・アニメ
anything	1043s	*pron.*	なんでも・何でも
anyway, at any rate	1044s	*adv.*	とにかく
anywhere	1054s	*n*	どこでも
anywhere, anyplace, everywhere, nowhere (w. neg. verb)	1102	*adv.*	どこにも
apple	1023s	*n*	りんご
April	1052	*n*	しがつ・四月
arm	1061	*n*	うで・腕
art, fine arts	1032	*n*	びじゅつ・美術
art print (new), woodblock print (new)	1091	*n*	しんはんが・新版画
Asian pear	App.	*n*	なし・梨
assist (to), help (to)	1041	*v*	てつだう・手伝う/てつだいます・手伝います

English	Location		Japanese
at, by means of a "tool", for (used for shopping or ordering food)	1043s	*part.*	で
at any rate, anyway	1044s	*adv.*	とにかく
at once, immediately	1082		すぐ
at the same time, same, together	1043s	*n*	いっしょ・一緒
at the same time, same, together	1044s	*exp.*	いっしょに・一緒に
August	1052	*n*	はちがつ・八月
aunt or woman quite a bit older than you	1022	*n*	おばさん
Australia (place)	1041	*pn*	おーすとらりあ・オーストラリア
Australian (person)	1041	*n*	おーすとらりあじん・オーストラリア人
autumn, fall	1101	*n*	あき・秋
backpack	1024	*n*	ばっくぱっく・バックパック
bad	1082	い *adj.*	わるい・悪い
bag, briefcase	1024	*n*	かばん・鞄
bag, sack	1023s	*n*	ばっぐ・バッグ
bakery	1043	*n*	ぱんや・パン屋
ballpoint pen	1024	*n*	ぼーるぺん・ボールペン
banana	1023s	*n*	ばなな・バナナ
barley tea	1103s	*n*	むぎちゃ・麦茶
baseball	1033	*n*	べーすぼーる・ベースボール, やきゅう・野球
Basho Matsuo (Japanese poet)	1102s	*pn*	まつおばしょう・松尾芭蕉
basketball	1033	*n*	ばすけ・バスケ, ばすけっとぼーる・バスケットボール
basketball club (team)	1033	*n*	ばすけぶ・バスケ部
bath	1093s	*n*	おふろ・お風呂
be able (to)	1016s	*v*	できる・出来る/できます・出来ます
beard, mustache	1061	*n*	ひげ・髭
be surprised (to), be amazed (to)	1105s	*v*	びっくり・ビックリする/します
beach	1081	*n*	はま・浜, びーち・ビーチ
beautiful	1081	い *adj.*	うつくしい・美しい
because of that	1044	*conj.*	だから
become (to)	1055	*v*	なる/なります
become clear (weather)	1101	*v*	はれる・晴れる/はれます・晴れます
become cloudy	1101	*v*	くもる・曇る/くもります・曇ります
before, front, in front	1032 1051	*n/adv.*	まえ・前
begin (to)	1052	*v*	はじめる・始める/はじめます・始めます
beg your pardon, excuse me, I'm sorry	1072s		ごめん (informal), ごめんなさい (formal)
Benkei (famous samurai name)	1061s	*pn*	べんけい・弁慶
bento, box lunch (Japanese)	1011	*n*	べんとう・弁当
best regards, please remember me (favorably)	1013s	*adv.*	よろしく
best regards, treat me favorably	1013	*exp.*	よろしく おねがいします・お願いします
best regards, treat me favorably (same meaning as よろしく おねがいします)	1013	*exp.*	どうぞ よろしく
big, large	1031	い *adj.*	おおきい・大きい
biology	1032	*n*	せいぶつがく・生物学
birthday	1052	*n*	たんじょうび・誕生日
black	1074	*n*	くろ・黒
black-colored	1064	い *adj.*	くろい・黒い
blackboard	1024	*n*	こくばん・黒板
blond (hair)	1074	*n*	きんぱつ・金髪
blue	1074	*n*	あお・青
blue-colored	1064	い *adj.*	あおい・青い
boat, ship	1045s	*n*	ふね・舟
body	1061	*n*	からだ・体
book	1011	*n*	ほん・本
bookshelves	App.	*n*	ほんだな・本棚
bookstore	1043	*n*	ほんや・本屋
bookstore	1043	*n*	ほんやさん・本屋さん
boring	1082	い *adj.*	つまらない
born (to be)	1052	*v*	うまれる・生まれる/うまれます・生まれます
borrow (to)	1063s	*v*	かりる・借りる/かります・借ります
bow	1016s	*exp.*	れい・礼
box	1081	*n*	はこ・箱
box lunch (Japanese), bento	1011	*n*	べんとう・弁当
boy	1064	*n*	おとこのこ・男の子
boyfriend, he	1074	*pron.*	かれ・彼
brass band	1033	*n*	ぶらすばんど・ブラスバンド
Brazilian (person)	1041	*n*	ぶらじるじん・ブラジル人
bread	1043	*n*	ぱん・パン
breaded octopus balls	1104s	*n*	たこやき・たこ焼き
breakfast	1025	*n*	あさごはん・朝ご飯
briefcase, bag	1024	*n*	かばん・鞄
bright, light	1083	い *adj.*	あかるい・明るい
bright, wise	1081	い *adj.*	かしこい
bring someone (to)	1105	*v*	つれて・連れて くる・来る/きます・来ます
bring something (to)	1105	*v*	もって・持って くる・来る/きます・来ます
brown	1074	*n*	ちゃいろ・茶色
brown (hair)	1074	*n*	ちゃぱつ・茶髪
brush	1033s	*n*	ふで・筆
buckweat noodles	1103s	*n*	そば
Buddhism (religion)	1052s	*n*	ぶっきょう・仏教
building	1051s	*n*	たてもの・建物

English	Location		Japanese
busy	1054	い adj.	いそがしい・忙しい
but	1041s	conj.	けど
but/however – at the beginning of a sentence	1034	part.	でも
buy (to)	1091	v	かう・買う/かいます・買います
by all means, please (here you go)	1015	adv.	どうぞ
by means of a "tool", at, for (used for shopping or ordering food)	1043s	part.	で
by no means, reluctantly	1094s		いやいや
by oneself, alone	1104	exp.	ひとりで・一人で
by the way	1041	exp.	ところで
bye-bye	1015		ばいばい・バイバイ
cake	1094	n	けーき・ケーキ
Call an ambulance!	1063	n	きゅうきゅうしゃをよんで・救急車を呼んで
calm, peaceful	1084	な adj.	おだやか
Canada (place)	1041	pn	かなだ・カナダ
Canadian (person)	1041	n	かなだじん・カナダ人
Canberra (place)	1021s	pn	きゃんべら・キャンベラ
candy, sweets	1023	n	あめ・飴, きゃんでぃ・キャンディ
cap, hat	1023	n	ぼうし・帽子
capital	1052s	n	しゅと・首都
car, vehicle	1043	n	くるま・車
card game; playing cards	1071	n	とらんぷ・トランプ
carry (to), have (to), hold (to)	1061	v	もつ・持つ/もちます・持ちます
castle	1101	n	しろ・城
cat	1021	n	ねこ・猫
catch a cold	1063	v	かぜ(を)・風邪(を)ひく・引く/ひきます・引きます
cellular phone	1031	n	けいたい (でんわ)・携帯(電話)
century, era	1041s	n	せいき・世紀
chair	App.	n	いす・椅子
chalk	1024	n	ちょーく・チョーク
change (cash)	1092	n	おつり
cheap	1082	い adj.	やすい・安い
cherry blossom viewing, flower viewing	1105	n	はなみ・花見
cherry tree/blossom	1105	n	さくら・桜
chicken	1043	n	ちきん・チキン, とりにく・鶏肉
child, children	1082	n	こども・子供
children	1082	n	こどもたち・子供達
China (place)	1041	pn	ちゅうごく・中国
Chinese (descent)	1041s	n	ちゅうごくけい・中国系
Chinese (language)	1042	n	ちゅうごくご・中国語
Chinese (person)	1041	n	ちゅうごくじん・中国人

English	Location		Japanese
Chinese characters (used in Japan)	1012s	n	かんじ・漢字
chocolate	App.	n	ちょこれーと・チョコレート
choir, chorus	1015	n	がっしょう・合唱
chopsticks	1015	n	はし (お)・(お)箸
chorus, choir	1033	n	がっしょう・合唱
class	1032	n	くらす・クラス
class	1032	n	じゅぎょう・授業
classroom	1032	n	きょうしつ・教室
clean; pretty	1081	な adj.	きれい
clear (skies)	1101	n	はれ・晴れ
clerk, shopkeeper	1092	n	てんいん・店員
clock	App.	n	とけい・時計
close (to), shut (to) [bound paper objects]	1013	v	とじる・閉じる/とじます・閉じます
close (to), shut (to) [doors/windows]	1034	v	しめる・閉める/しめます・閉めます
close, near	1061	い adj.	ちかい・近い
Close/Shut (it) please.	1013	exp.	とじて ください・閉じて 下さい
clothes	1064	n	ふく・服
clothes, Western clothes	1064	n	ようふく・洋服
cloudy	1101	n	くもり・曇り
club activity	1033	n	ぶかつ・部活
cola	1043	n	こーら・コーラ
cold (a)	1063	n	かぜ・風邪
cold (weather)	1034	い adj.	さむい・寒い
college, university	1031	n	だいがく・大学
college/university student	1031	n	だいがくせい・大学生
color	1074	n	いろ・色
come (to)	1044	v	くる・来る/きます・来ます
come in (to), go in (to), enter (to)	1061	v	はいる・入る/はいります・入ります
company employee	1025s	n	かいしゃいん・会社員
computer lab	1033	n	こんぴゅーたーらぼ・コンピューターラボ
concert	1052s	n	こんさーと・コンサート
concert, receital	1052s	n	おんがくかい・音楽会
continuously; throughout	1083		ずっと
cooked rice, a meal	1015	n	ごはん・ご飯
cookie	App.	n	くっきー・クッキー
cooking	1071	n	りょうり・料理
cool (look/appearance)	1062	ir. adj.	かっこいい
cool (weather)	1034	い adj.	すずしい・涼しい
cool, tasteful	1062	い adj.	しぶい・渋い
copy (to), photocopy (to)	1062	v	こぴー・コピー する/します
country	1041	n	くに・国
crab	1083	n	かに
culture	1065	n	ぶんか・文化
cunning	1081	い adj.	ずるい
cupcake	App.	n	かっぷけーき・カップケーキ
cute	1081	い adj.	かわいい

English	Location		Japanese
dad, father	1014	n	ちち・父
dancing	1071	n	おどり・踊り
dangerous	1081	い adj.	あぶない・危ない
dango (round sticky rice balls on a stick)	App.	n	だんご
dark	1083	い adj.	くらい・暗い
date (to go on a)	1091	v	でーと(を)・デート(を) する/します
day after tomorrow	1102	n	あさって・明後日
day before yesterday	1102	n	おととい・一昨日
daytime, noon	1025	n	ひる・昼
December	1052	n	じゅうにがつ・十二月
delicious	1081	い adj.	おいしい・美味しい
denotes a sentence topic	1013	part.	は
dialect, words, language	1101s	n	ことば・言葉
dialogue	1013s	n	かいわ・会話
dictionary	App.	n	じしょ・辞書
difficult	1032	い adj.	むずかしい・難しい
dine (to), have a meal (to)	1091	v	しょくじ(を)・食事(を) する/します
dinner, evening meal	1025	n	ばんごはん・晩ご飯
dirty, messy	1081	い adj.	きたない
dislike	1072	な adj.	きらい・嫌い
dislike a lot, hate	1072	な adj.	だいきらい・大嫌い
do (to)	1073	v	やる/やります
do (to)	1044	v	する/します (して)
do homework (to)	1091	v	しゅくだい(を)・宿題(を) する/します
do one's best (to)	1073	v	がんばる・頑張る/がんばります・頑張ります
doctor	1063	n	いしゃ・医者
dog	1021	n	いぬ・犬
Don't be ridiculous! Not a chance! My pleasure	1094	exp.	とんでもない
Don't overexert.	1063	exp.	むり しないでください・無理 しないで 下さい
door	1034	n	どあ・ドア
draw (to)	1054s	v	かく・描く/かきます・描きます
drawing, painting	1071	n	え・絵
dress (a)	1064	n	どれす・ドレス
drink (to)	1043	v	のむ・飲む/のみます・飲みます
drink(s)	1043	n	のみもの・飲み物
duration, period of years	1032s	n	ねんかん・年間
Dutch (language)	1042	n	おらんだご・オランダ語
Dutch (person)	1041	n	おらんだじん・オランダ人
e-mail	1051	n	でんしめーる/めーる・電子メール, ・メール
ear	1061	n	みみ・耳
early	1054s	い adj.	はやい・早い
earring	1064	n	いやりんぐ・イヤリング

English	Location		Japanese
earthquake	1101	n	じしん・地震
easy, simple, kind, gentle	1081	い adj.	やさしい・優しい
eat (to)	1043	v	たべる/たべます・食べる/食べます
eating	1071	n	たべること・食べる事
economics	1032	n	けいざいがく・経済学
economy	1032s	n	けいざい・経済
Edo (former name of Tokyo)	1044s	pn	えど・江戸
egg	1015	n	たまご・卵
eight	1021	count.	はち・八
eight (things)	1024	count.	やっつ・八つ
eight cupfuls	1092	count.	はっぱい・八杯
eight cylindrical objects	1092	count.	はちほん/はっぽん・八本
eight hundred	1023s	count.	はっぴゃく・八百
eight minutes	1032	count.	はちふん/はっぷん・八分
eight o'clock	1032	count.	はちじ・八時
eight pages, page eight	1042	count.	はちぺーじ/はっぺーじ・八ページ
eight people	1021	count.	はちにん・八人
eight seconds	1032	count.	はちびょう・八秒
eight sheets	1042	count.	はちまい・八枚
eight small animals	1021	count.	はっぴき・八匹
eight thousand	1052	count.	はっせん・八千
eight times/degrees	1101	count.	はちど・八度
eight volumes	1092	count.	はっさつ・八冊
eight years old	1052	count.	はっさい・八歳/八才
eighteen	1022	count.	じゅうはち・十八
eighteenth (day of the month)	1053	count.	じゅうはちにち・十八日
eighth (day of the month)	1053	count.	ようか・八日
eighth grader	1031	count.	ちゅうがくにねんせい・中学二年生
eighty	1022	count.	はちじゅう・八十
eighty thousand	1052	count.	はちまん・八万
either of these can be used to mean "to" and comes after a place of destination	1104	part.	へ/に
electricity, lights	App.	n	でんき・電気
elementary school	1031	n	しょうがっこう・小学校
elementary school fifth grader	1031	n	しょうがくごねんせい・小学校五年生
elementary school first grader	1031	n	しょうがくいちねんせい・小学一年生
elementary school fourth grader	1031	n	しょうがくよねんせい・小学四年生
elementary school second grader	1031	n	しょうがくにねんせい・小学二年生
elementary school sixth grader	1031	n	しょうがくろくねんせい・小学六年生
elementary school student	1031	n	しょうがくせい・小学生
elementary school third grader	1031	n	しょうがくさんねんせい・小学三年生
eleven	1022	count.	じゅういち・十一

English	Location		Japanese
eleven minutes	1032	count.	じゅういっぷん・十一分
eleven o'clock	1032	count.	じゅういちじ・十一時
eleven years old	1052	count.	じゅういっさい・十一歳/十一才
eleventh (day of the month)	1053	count.	じゅういちにち・十一日
eleventh grader	1031	count.	こうこうにねんせい・高校二年生
embassy	1022s	n	たいしかん・大使館
emperor	1052s	n	てんのう・天皇
Emperor Kouken	1053s	pn	こうけんてんのう・孝謙天皇
energetic, healthy	1015	n/な adj.	げんき・元気
England (place)	1041	pn	いぎりす・イギリス
English (descent)	1041	n	いぎりすけい・イギリス系
English (person)	1041	n	いぎりすじん・イギリス人
English language	1032	n	えいご・英語
enjoyable, fun	1032	い adj.	たのしい・楽しい
enter (to), come in (to), go in (to)	1061	v	はいる・入る/はいります・入ります
entire, altogether, all	1083	n	ぜんぶ・全部
era, century	1041s	n	せいき・世紀
era, period, age	1071s	n	じだい・時代
eraser	1024	n	けしごむ・消しゴム
essay	1032	n	さくぶん・作文
et cetera, and so forth	1101s	part.	など
Europe (place)	1042s	pn	よーろっぱ・ヨーロッパ
evening	1021s	n	ばん・晩
evening meal, dinner	1025	n	ばんごはん・晩ご飯
every day	1032	n	まいにち・毎日
every month	1054	n	まいつき・毎月
every week	1054	n	まいしゅう・毎週
every year	1054	n	まいとし/まいねん・毎年
everyone (polite)	1031	n	みなさん・皆さん
everyone, all	1031	pron.	みんな・皆
everywhere, wherever	1102	adv.	どこも
everywhere, nowhere (w. neg. verb), anywhere, anyplace	1102	adv.	どこにも
exam, test	1032	n	しけん・試験
exceptionally large ocean wave, tsunami	1011	n	つなみ・津波
excuse me, I'm sorry	1033s	interj.	すみません
excuse me, I'm sorry, beg your pardon	1072s		ごめん (informal), ごめんなさい (formal)
excuse me, I'm sorry to bother you.	1022	exp.	しつれいします・失礼します
excuse me; I'm sorry	1033s	inter.	すみません
exist (to) [animate beings]	1021	v	いる/います
exist (to) [inanimate things]	1021	v	ある/あります
expensive; high; tall	1082	い adj.	たかい・高い

English	Location		Japanese
experience	1065	n	けいけん・経験
eye	1061	n	め・目
eyeglasses	1064	n	めがね・眼鏡
face	1061	n	かお・顔
fall, autumn	1101	n	あき・秋
family (my)	1021	n	かぞく・家族
family consumer science	1032	n	かていか・家庭科
famous	1061	な adj.	ゆうめい・有名
fan, supporter	1065s	n	ふぁん・ファン
far, distant	1061	い adj.	とおい・遠い
fashion	1074s	n	ふぁっしょん・ファッション
fashionable	1062	な adj.	おしゃれ
fat (to get)	1062	v	ふとる・太る/ふとります・太ります
fat (is), plump (is)	1062		ふとっています・太っています
father (someone else's)	1022	n	おとうさん・お父さん
father, dad	1014	n	ちち・父
February	1052	n	にがつ・二月
feel bad, sick	1063	exp.	ぐあいが わるい・具合が 悪い
festival	1051	n	まつり・祭り
feudal lord	1045s	n	だいみょう・大名
fever	1063	n	ねつ・熱
fifteen	1022	count.	じゅうご・十五
fifteenth (day of the month)	1053	count.	じゅうごにち・十五日
fifth (day of the month)	1053	count.	いつか・五日
fifth period	1033	count.	ごじかんめ・五時間目
fifty	1022	count.	ごじゅう・五十
fifty thousand	1052	count.	ごまん・五万
fight (to)	1091	v	けんか(を)・喧嘩(を)する/します
fine arts, art	1032	n	びじゅつ・美術
finger(s)	1061	n	ゆび・指
finish (to)	1052	v	おわる・終わる/おわります・終わります
first (day of the month)	1053	count.	ついたち・一日
first period	1033	count.	いちじかんめ・一時間目
first year college/university student	1031	n	だいがくいちねんせい・大学一年生
first year student	1031s	count.	いちねんせい・一年生
fish	1101	n	さかな・魚
five	1021	n	ご・五
five (things)	1024	count.	いつつ・五つ
five cupfuls	1092	count.	ごはい・五杯
five cylindrical objects	1092	count.	ごほん・五本
five hundred	1023s	count.	ごひゃく・五百
five minutes	1032	count.	ごふん・五分
five o'clock	1032	count.	ごじ・五時
five pages, page five	1042	count.	ごぺーじ・五ページ
five people	1021	count.	ごにん・五人
five seconds	1032	count.	ごびょう・五秒
five sheets	1042	count.	ごまい・五枚
five small animals	1021	count.	ごひき・五匹

English	Location		Japanese
five thousand	1052	count.	ごせん・五千
five times/degrees	1101	count.	ごど・五度
five volumes	1092	count.	ごさつ・五冊
five years old	1052	count.	ごさい・五歳
flag	App.	n	はた・旗
flower	1101	n	はな・花
flower arranging	1071	n	いけばな・生け花
food(s)	1043	n	たべもの・食べ物
foolish, silly	1081	い adj.	ばかばかしい
foot, leg	1061	n	あし・足
foreign country	1041	n	がいこく・外国
foreigner	1041	n	がいこくじん・外国人
forest	1101s	n	もり・森
forty	1022	count.	よんじゅう・四十
forty thousand	1052	count.	よんまん・四万
forty-three minutes	1032	count.	よんじゅうさんぷん・四十三分
four	1021	count.	よん/し・四
four (things)	1024	count.	よっつ・四つ
four cupfuls	1092	count.	よんはい・四杯
four cylindrical objects	1092	count.	よんほん・四本
four hundred	1023s	count.	よんひゃく・四百
four minutes	1032	count.	よんぷん・四分
four o'clock	1032	count.	よじ・四時
four pages, page four	1042	count.	よんぺーじ・四ページ
four people	1021	count.	よにん・四人
four seconds	1032	count.	よんびょう・四秒
four sheets	1042	count.	よんまい・四枚
four small animals	1021	count.	よんひき・四匹
four thousand	1052	count.	よんせん・四千
four times/degrees	1101	count.	よんど・四度
four volumes	1092	count.	よんさつ・四冊
four years old	1052	count.	よんさい・四歳/四才
fourteen	1022	count.	じゅうよん/じゅうし・十四
fourteen years old	1052	count.	じゅうよんさい・十四歳/十四才
fourteenth (day of the month)	1053	count.	じゅうよっか・十四日
fourth (day of the month)	1053	count.	よっか・四日
fourth period	1033	count.	よじかんめ・四時間目
fox	1035s	n	きつね・狐
France (place)	1041	pn	ふらんす・フランス
free (time)	1084	な adj	ひま
freedom, liberty	1105s	な adj.	じゆう・自由
French (language)	1042	n	ふらんすご・フランス語
French (person)	1041	n	ふらんすじん・フランス人
Friday	1051	n	きんようび・金曜日
fried noodles, yakisoba	1102s	n	やきそば・焼きそば
friend	1022	n	ともだち・友達
frog	1072	n	かえる・蛙
from (used with spec. times or locations)	1032	part.	から
front, in front, before	1032 1051	n/adv.	まえ・前
fruit	1075s	n	くだもの・果物, ふるーつ・フルーツ

English	Location		Japanese
Fuji (Mt.)	1094s	pn	ふじさん・富士山
fun, enjoyable	1032	い adj.	たのしい・楽しい
furthermore, moreover	1071	conj.	それに
futon	1063	n	ふとん・布団
gagaku, ancient Japanese court music	1075	n	ががく・雅楽
garden	1101	n	にわ・庭
gate	1033s	n	もん・門
gentle, easy, simple, kind	1081	い adj.	やさしい・優しい
genuine article, real thing	1091	n	ほんもの・本物
German (language)	1042	n	どいつご・ドイツ語
German (person)	1041	n	どいつじん・ドイツ人
Germany (place)	1041	pn	どいつ・ドイツ
get out (to), go out (to), leave (to)	1061	v	でる・出る/でます・出ます
gift (a), present (a)	1094	n	ぷれぜんと・プレゼント
Ginza (place)	1033s	pn	ぎんざ・銀座
girl	1064	n	おんなのこ・女の子
girlfriend; she	1074	pron.	かのじょ・彼女
give (to) [to equals or superiors]	1094	v	あげる・上げる/あげます・/上げます
give (to) [to me or a family member]	1095	v	くれる/くれます
glad, happy	1081	い adj.	うれしい・嬉しい
go	1044	v	いく・行く/いきます・行きます
go in (to), come in (to), enter (to)	1061	v	はいる・入る/はいります・入ります
go out (to), leave (to), get out (to)	1061	v	でる・出る/でます・出ます
go shopping (to)	1091	v	かいもの(を)・買い物(を) する/します
gold	1074	n	きんいろ・金色
golf	1071	n	ごるふ・ゴルフ
good	1041s	ir. adj.	いい/よい・良い
good evening	1015	exp.	こんばんは・今晩は
good for your health	1063	exp.	けんこうに・健康にいいです
good morning (formal)	1015	exp.	おはよう ございます
good morning (informal)	1015	exp.	おはよう
good night (formal)	1015	exp.	おやすみなさい・お休みなさい
good night (informal)	1015	exp.	おやすみ・お休み
good-looking, handsome	1064	な adj	はんさむ・ハンサム
goodbye	1015	exp.	さようなら
grade, score	1033	n	せいせき・成績
grandfather (my)	1021	n	そふ・祖父
grandfather (someone else's)	1022	n	おじいさん
grandmother (my)	1021	n	そぼ 祖母
grandmother (someone else's)	1022	n	おばあさん
gray	1064, 1074	n	ぐれい・グレイ
gray (mouse colored)	1064, 1074	n	ねずみいろ・鼠色
gray (mouse colored)	1064, 1074	n	はいいろ・はい色
great, to a great extent, terrible, amazing	1035	い adj.	すごい
green	1064, 1074	n	みどり・緑

English	Location		Japanese
green tea	1024s	*n*	おちゃ・お茶
grow old (to), age (to)	1101s	*v*	とし(を)とる・年(を)取る
guitar	1071	*n*	ぎたー・ギター
gum	App.	*n*	がむ・ガム
gymnasium	1033	*n*	たいいくかん・体育館
haiku (poem)	1101	*n*	はいく・俳句
hair	1061	*n*	かみ(のけ)・髪(の毛)
half hour	1032	*n*	はん・〜半
hamburger	1043	*n*	はんばーがー・ハンバーガー
hand	1061	*n*	て・手
hand-book, planner	App.	*n*	ぷらんなー・プランナー
handshake	1042	*n*	あくしゅ・握手
handsome, good-looking	1064	な *adj*	はんさむ・ハンサム
haniwa	1041s	*n*	はにわ・埴輪
happy, glad	1081	い *adj.*	うれしい・嬉しい
hat, cap	1023	*n*	ぼうし・帽子
hate, dislike a lot	1072	な *adj.*	だいきらい・大嫌い
have (to), hold (to), carry (to)	1061	*v*	もつ・持つ/もちます・持ちます
have a full stomach	1104	*exp.*	おなか(が) いっぱい・お腹(が)一杯
have a meal (to), dine (to)	1091	*v*	しょくじ(を)・食事(を)する/します
he; boyfriend	1074	*pron.*	かれ・彼
head	1061	*n*	あたま・頭
health	1063	*n*	けんこう・健康
health (class)	1032	*n*	ほけんたいいく・保健体育
healthy, energetic	1015	*n*/な *adj.*	げんき・元気
hear (can)	1104s	*v*	きこえる・聞こえる/きこえます・聞こえます
heart (not one's physical heart), soul	1061	*n*	こころ・心
heavy rain	1101	*n*	おおあめ・大雨
height, stature	1061	*n*	せ/せい・背
Heijoukyou (ancient name for Kyoto)	1051s	*pn*	へいじょうきょう・平城京
hello	1015	*exp.*	こんにちは・今日は
help (to), assist (to)	1041	*v*	てつだう・手伝う/てつだいます・手伝います
helping verb/linking verb used similarly to "is" or "am"	1013	*copula*	です
here	1024	*pron.*	ここ
here (roll call), yes, OK	1014		はい
here and there	1054s	*adv.*	あちこち
high school	1031	*n*	こうこう・高校
high school student	1031	*n*	こうこうせい・高校生
high; tall; expensive	1061	い *adj.*	たかい・高い
Hiraizumi (place)	1061s	*pn*	ひらいずみ・平泉
Hiroo (section of Tokyo)	1022s	*pn*	ひろお・広尾
Hiroshima (place)	1083s	*pn*	ひろしま・広島
history	1032	*n*	れきし・歴史
hobby	1071	*n*	しゅみ・趣味
hold (to), carry (to), have (to)	1061	*v*	もつ・持つ/もちます・持ちます
Holland (place)	1041	*pn*	おらんだ・オランダ
home, house	1022	*n*	いえ/うち・家
homeroom	1032	*n*	ほーむるーむ・ホームルーム
homework	1032	*n*	しゅくだい・宿題
Honshu (place)	1041s	*pn*	ほんしゅう・本州
horse	1082	*n*	うま・馬
horseback riding	1071	*n*	じょうば・乗馬
hospital	1063	*n*	びょういん・病院
hot (weather)	1034	い *adj.*	あつい・暑い
hour, time	1035s	*n*	とき・時
house, home	1022	*n*	いえ/うち・家
how	1035	*inter.*	どう
how about it?	1092	*exp.*	どう ですか
how do you do?	1013	*exp.*	はじめまして・初めまして
however, but – at the beginning of a sentence	1034	*part.*	でも
how many (things)?	1021	*inter.*	いくつ
how many cupfuls	1092	*inter.*	なんばい・何杯
how many cylindrical objects	1092	*inter.*	なんぼん・何本
how many minutes	1032	*inter.*	なんぷん・何分
how many pages, what page	1042	*inter.*	なんぺーじ・何ページ
how many people	1021	*inter.*	なんにん・何人
how many people (polite)	1103s	*inter.*	なんめいさま・何名様
how many seconds?	1032	*inter.*	なんびょう・何秒
how many sheets	1042	*inter.*	なんまい・何枚
how many small animals?	1021	*inter.*	なんびき・何匹
how many ten-thousands?	1052	*inter.*	なんまん・何万
how many thousands	1052	*inter.*	なんぜん・何千
how many times/degrees	1101	*inter.*	なんど・何度
how many volumes	1092	*inter.*	なんさつ・何冊
how much?	1092	*inter.*	いくら
how old (animate beings)	1022s	*inter.*	なんさい・何歳, (お)いくつ (less formal)
How was it?	1065	*exp.*	どう でしたか。
huh?	1033s	*inter.*	ええっ/え?
humid (weather)	1034	い *adj.*	むしあつい・蒸し暑い
hunt, search	1013s	*n*	たんさく・探索
hunger (mimetic expression for)	1025		ぺこぺこ・ペコペコ
I don't know.	1016s	*exp.*	しりません・知りません
I love you	1025s	*exp.*	だいすきです。・大好きです
I, me (used by males only)	1013	*pron.*	ぼく・僕
I, me	1013	*pron.*	わたし・私
I'm sorry, excuse me	1033s	*inter.*	すみません
I'm sorry, beg your pardon, excuse me,	1072s		ごめん (informal), ごめんなさい (formal)
I'm home	1015	*exp.*	ただいま
ice cream	App.	*n*	あいすくりーむ・アイスクリーム

English	Location		Japanese
idea	1051s	*n*	あいでぃあ・アイディア
illness, sickness	1063	*n*	びょうき・病気
immediately, at once	1082		すぐ
important	1051	な *adj.*	だいじ・大事
impossible, overdoing	1063	な *adj.*	むり・無理
in all, total, all together	1092	*exp.*	ぜんぶで・全部で
in, at, used after a location or time word	1015	*part.*	に
incorrect, is not right	1016s	*v*	ちがう・違う/ちがいます・違います
indeed, truly, really	1084	*adv.*	まったく・全く
individually, separately	1092	*n*/な *adj.*	べつべつ・別々
Indonesia (place)	1041	*pn*	いんどねしあ・インドネシア
Indonesian (language)	1042	*n*	いんどねしあご・インドネシア語
Indonesian (person)	1041	*n*	いんどねしあじん・インドネシア人
in front, before, front	1032 1051	*n/adv.*	まえ・前
injure, hurt (oneself) (to)	1063	*v*	けが(を)・怪我(を)する/します
interesting	1082	い *adj.*	おもしろい・面白い
introduce (please)	1021	*v*	しょうかいして ください・紹介して下さい
introduce (to)	1021	*v*	しょうかい・紹介する/します
Iranian (person)	1041	*n*	いらんじん・イラン人
irritating	1081	い *adj.*	じれったい
is bad	1034	な *adj.*	だめ
is not right, incorrect	1016s	*v*	ちがう・違う/ちがいます・違います
island	1083	*n*	しま・島
Italian (language)	1042	*n*	いたりあご・イタリア語
Italian (person)	1041	*n*	いたりあじん・イタリア人
Italy (place)	1041	*pn*	いたりあ・イタリア
jacket	1064	*n*	じゃけっと・ジャケット
Jakarta (place)	1042s	*pn*	じゃかるた・ジャカルタ
January	1052	*n*	いちがつ・一月
Japan (place)	1011	*pn*	にほん・日本
Japanese comics	1011	*n*	まんが・漫画
Japanese descent	1041	*n*	にっけいじん・日系人
Japanese history	1032	*n*	にほんし・日本史
Japanese horseradish, wasabi	1015	*n*	わさび
Japanese inn/hotel, ryokan	1044s	*n*	りょかん・旅館
Japanese language	1011	*n*	にほんご・日本語
Japanese person	1014	*n*	にほんじん・日本人
Japanese sumo wrestling	1011	*n*	すもう・相撲
Japanese traditional sweets	1095	*n*	(お)かし・(お)菓子
Japanese zither/harp, koto	1105s	*n*	こと・琴
jeans	1064	*n*	じーんず・ジーンズ
job, occupation	1025	*n*	しごと・仕事

English	Location		Japanese
jogging	1071	*n*	じょぎんぐ・ジョギング
joke	1072	*n*	じょうだん・冗談
journal	1011s	*n*	じゃーなる・ジャーナル
judo	1033	*n*	じゅうどう・柔道
juice	1063	*n*	じゅーす・ジュース
July	1052	*n*	しちがつ/なながつ・七月
June	1052	*n*	ろくがつ・六月
kabuki theater	1075	*n*	かぶき・歌舞伎
Kanazawa (place)	1101s	*pn*	かなざわ・金沢
karaoke (to sing/do)	1091	*v*	からおけ(を)・カラオケ(を) する/します
karate (martial art)	1011	*n*	からて・空手
karaoke	1105s	*n*	からおけ・カラオケ
kendo	1033s	*n*	けんどう・剣道
kendo club	1033	*n*	けんどうぶ・剣道部
Kenroku Park (place)	1102s	*pn*	けんろくえん・兼六園
Kenya (place)	1041	*pn*	けにあ・ケニア
Kenyan (person)	1041	*n*	けにあじん・ケニア人
kimono (Japanese traditional clothing)	1011	*n*	きもの・着物
kind, gentle, easy, simple	1081	い *adj.*	やさしい・優しい
kindergarten	1031	*n*	ようちえん・幼稚園
knee	1061	*n*	ひざ・膝
know something/someone (to)	1042	*v*	しる・知る/しります・知ります
Kobo Daishi (person's name)	1052s	*pn*	こうぼうだいし・弘法大師
koi (carp)	1031s	*n*	こい・鯉
Korean (descent)	1041s	*n*	かんこくけい・韓国系
Korean (language)	1042	*n*	かんこくご・韓国語
Korean (person)	1041	*n*	かんこくじん・韓国人
koto, Japanese zither/harp	1105s	*n*	こと・琴
Kukai (person's name)	1052s	*pn*	くうかい・空海
Kyoto (place)	1013s	*pn*	きょうと・京都
Kyushu (place)	1041s	*pn*	きゅうしゅう・九州
language, dialect, words	1101s	*n*	ことば・言葉
large (L) size	1092	*n*	えるさいず・Lサイズ
large, big	1031	い *adj.*	おおきい・大きい
last month	1054	*n*	せんげつ・先月
last week	1054	*n*	せんしゅう・先週
last week Tuesday	1054	*n*	せんしゅうのかようび・先週の火曜日
last year	1054	*n*	きょねん・去年
later, afterwards	1033	*adv.*	あとで・後で
learn (to)	1065	*v*	ならう・習う/ならいます・習います
leave (to), get out (to), go out (to),	1061	*v*	でる・出る/でます・出ます
leg, foot	1061	*n*	あし・足
let me see, well...	1033s	*interj.*	ええと
let's go	1035	*exp.*	いきましょう・行きましょう
Let's begin.	1011	*exp.*	はじめましょう・始めましょう
liberty, freedom	1105s	な *adj.*	じゆう・自由

English	Location		Japanese
library	1033	n	としょかん・図書館
lie	1104	n	うそ・嘘
light, bright	1083	い adj.	あかるい・明るい
lights, electricity	App.	n	でんき・電気
like	1072	な adj.	すき・好き
linking verb, helping verb used similarly to "is" or "am"	1013	copula	です
listen (to)	1013	v	きく・聞く/ききます・聞きます
little	1031	adv.	すこし・少し
little, somewhat	1032	adv.	ちょっと
(something is) a little ...	1043	exp.	(～は) ちょっと…
live (to), reside (to)	1064	v	すむ・住む/すみます・住みます
lonely	1061s	い adj.	さびしい・寂しい
long	1061	い adj.	ながい・長い
long ago	1082	n	むかし・昔
long long ago	1082	n	むかしむかし・昔々
look, Look out!	1081s	interj.	ほら！
look (to), see (to)	1013	v	みる・見る/みます・見ます
Look/Watch please.	1013	exp.	みてください。・見て下さい。
loud, noisy	1081	い adj.	うるさい
love	1022s	n	あい・愛
love, really like	1072	な adj.	だいすき・大好き
low, short (height)	1061	い adj.	ひくい・低い
lunch	1025	n	ひるごはん・昼ご飯
lunch break	1032	n	ひるやすみ・昼休み
make (to)	1102	v	つくる・作る/つくります・作ります
make up (facial)	1064	n	めいく・メイク
make up (to), reconcile (to)	1091	v	なかなおり(を)・仲直り(を) する/します
male, man	1064	n	おとこのひと・男の人
male, man	1064s	n	おとこ・男
many, a lot	1031	n	たくさん・たくさん
map	App.	n	ちず・地図
March	1052	n	さんがつ・三月
marker	App.	n	まじっく・マジック
mat, writing pad	1024	n	したじき・下敷き
math	1032	n	すうがく・数学
May	1052	n	ごがつ・五月
May I come in?, please forgive me	1092s	exp.	ごめんください・ごめん下さい
May I drink (some) water?	1016s	exp.	おみずを・お水をのんでも・飲んでもいいですか。
May I go to my locker?	1016s	exp.	ろっかーへ・ロッカーへ いっても・行っても いいですか。
May I go to the restroom/W.C.?	1016s	exp.	おてあらいへ・お手洗いへ いっても・行っても いいですか。
meal (a), cooked rice	1015	n	ごはん・ご飯
me, I	1013	pron.	わたし・私

English	Location		Japanese
me, I (used by males only)	1013	pron.	ぼく・僕
medicine	1063	n	くすり・薬
medium (M) size	1092	n	えむさいず・Mサイズ
meet (to)	1054s	v	あう・会う
melon (honeydew)	1023s	n	めろん・メロン
memo, note	1083	n	めも・メモ
messy, dirty	1081	い adj.	きたない
Mexican (person)	1041	n	めきしこじん・メキシコ人
Mexican descent	1041s	n	めきしこけい・メキシコ系
Mexico (place)	1041	pn	めきしこ・メキシコ
middle school	1031	n	ちゅうがっこう・中学校
middle school student	1031	n	ちゅうがくせい・中学生
military leader	1051s	n	しょうぐん・将軍
milk	1043s	n	みるく・ミルク
miso soup	1104s	n	みそしる・味噌汁
mochi (sticky rice cake)	App.	n	もち・餅
moderate, so so, not bad	1062	adv.	まあまあ
mom, mother	1014	n	はは・母
Monday	1051	n	げつようび・月曜日
money	1092s	n	(お)かね・(お)金
more	1093	adv.	もっと
More slowly please.	1013	exp.	もっと ゆっくり おねがいします。・お願いします。
moreover, furthermore	1071	conj.	それに
morning	1025	n	あさ・朝
mother (someone else's)	1022	n	おかあさん・お母さん
mother, mom	1014	n	はは・母
mountain	1031	n	やま・山
mouse, rat	1072	n	ねずみ・鼠
mouth	1061	n	くち・口
movie	1091	n	えいが・映画
MP3 player	1031	n	えむぴーすりーぷれーやー・MP3 プレーヤー
Mt. Koya (place)	1052s	pn	こうやさん・高野山
Murasaki Shikibu (Heian Period author)	1071s	pn	むらさきしきぶ・紫式部
muscle	1061	n	きんにく・筋肉
music	1032	n	おんがく・音楽
mustache, beard	1061	n	ひげ・髭
mysterious	1081	な adj	ふしぎ・不思議
Nagasaki (place)	1041s	pn	ながさき・長崎
name	1013	n	なまえ・名前
nap	1063	n	ひるね・昼寝
nap (to)	1063	v	ひるね(を)・昼寝(を) する/します
Nara (place)	1051s	pn	なら・奈良
Nara Period	1054s	n	ならじだい・奈良時代
Narita International Airport (place)	1011s	pn	なりたくうこう・成田空港
narrow	1083	い adj.	せまい・狭い
national language (Japanese language)	1032	n	こくご・国語

English	Location		Japanese
near, close	1061	い *adj.*	ちかい・近い
neck	1061	*n*	くび・首
necktie	1064	*n*	ねくたい・ネクタイ
new	1081	い *adj.*	あたらしい・新しい
new information marker, "but", conjunction, used to combine two sentences	1021s, 1071s, 1073s, 1095s	*part.*	が
New Zealand (place)	1041	*pn*	にゅーじーらんど・ニュージーランド
New Zealander (person)	1041	*pn*	にゅーじーらんどじん・ニュージーランド人
next	1033	*n/adv.*	つぎ・次
next month	1054	*n*	らいげつ・来月
next week	1054	*n*	らいしゅう・来週
next year	1054	*n*	らいねん・来年
next youngest brother/sister (my)	1021	*n*	すぐしたの おとうと/いもうと・すぐ下の弟/妹
nice, wonderful	1064	な *adj.*	すてき・素敵
Nice to see you., Welcome!	1014	*exp.*	ようこそ
nicely, well	1103s	*adv.*	よく
nine	1021	*count.*	く/きゅう・九
nine (things)	1024	*count.*	ここのつ・九つ
nine cupfuls	1092	*count.*	きゅうはい・九杯
nine cylindrical objects	1092	*count.*	きゅうほん・九本
nine hundred	1023s	*count.*	きゅうひゃく・九百
nine minutes	1032	*count.*	きゅうふん・九分
nine o'clock	1032	*count.*	くじ・九時
nine pages, page nine	1042	*count.*	きゅうぺーじ・九ページ
nine people	1021	*count.*	きゅうにん・九人
nine seconds	1032	*count.*	きゅうびょう・九秒
nine sheets	1042	*count.*	きゅうまい・九枚
nine small animals	1021	*count.*	きゅうひき・九匹
nine thousand	1052	*count.*	きゅうせん・九千
nine times/degrees	1101	*count.*	きゅうど・九度
nine volumes	1092	*count.*	きゅうさつ・九冊
nine years old	1052	*count.*	きゅうさい・九歳
nineteen	1022	*count.*	じゅうく/じゅうきゅう・十九
nineteenth (day of the month)	1053	*count.*	じゅうくにち・十九日
ninety	1022	*count.*	きゅうじゅう・九十
ninety thousand	1052	*count.*	きゅうまん・九万
ninth (day of the month)	1053	*count.*	ここのか・九日
ninth grader	1031	*count.*	ちゅうがくさんねんせい・中学三年生
no	1014		いいえ
noon, daytime	1025	*n*	ひる・昼
no one	1102	*exp.*	だれも
No, I don't understand.	1016s	*exp.*	いいえ、わかりません。・分かりません。
No, it is not/different.	1014	*exp.*	いいえ、ちがいます。・違います。
Noh (a type of theater)	1075	*n*	のう・能
noisy, loud	1081	い *adj.*	うるさい
noon, daytime	1025	*n*	ひる・昼
noren curtain	1043s	*n*	のれん

English	Location		Japanese
normal, usual	1064	*adj./adv.*	ふつう・普通
nose	1061	*n*	はな・鼻
not anywhere, nowhere not any place (w. neg. verb)	1102	*adv.*	どこへも いきません。・行きません。
not at all	1074	*adv.*	ぜんぜん・全然
not bad, moderate, so so	1062	*adv.*	まあまあ
not good at	1073	な *adj.*	へた・下手
not tasty/good	1081	い *adj.*	まずい
not very	1074	*adv.*	あまり
not yet (with negative verb)	1043	*adv.*	まだ
notebook	1024	*n*	のーと・ノート
note, memo	1083	*n*	めも・メモ
nothing	1053	*pron.*	なにも・何も
November	1052	*n*	じゅういちがつ・十一月
now	1032	*n/adv.*	いま・今
now, well	1091s	*interj.*	さて
nowhere (w. neg. verb), everywhere, anywhere, anyplace	1102	*adv.*	どこにも
nowhere, not anywhere, not any place (w. neg. verb)	1102	*adv.*	どこへも いきません。・行きません。
nurse	1063	*n*	かんごし・看護師
nursery school	1031	*n*	ほいくえん・保育園
occupation, job	1025	*n*	しごと・仕事
ocean, sea	1081	*n*	うみ・海
Ochanomizu (section of Tokyo)	1024s	*pn*	おちゃのみず・お茶の水
October	1052	*n*	じゅうがつ・十月
octopus	1025	*n*	たこ
oden (various ingredients stewed in soy-flavored dashi)	1091s	*n*	おでん
of course	1105	*exp.*	もちろん
office	1032	*n*	じむしょ・事務所
oh	1031	*interj.*	あっ
Oh!, Ah!,	1025	*interj.*	ああ
OK, all right, safe,	1063	な *adj.*	だいじょうぶ・大丈夫
old (used for things)	1081	い *adj.*	ふるい・古い
older brother (my)	1021	*n*	あに・兄
older brother (someone else's)	1022	*n*	おにいさん・お兄さん
older sister (my)	1021	*n*	あね・姉
older sister (someone else's)	1022	*n*	おねえさん・お姉さん
oldest brother/sister (my)	1021	*n*	いちばんうえの あに/あね・一番上の兄/姉
one	1021	*count.*	いち・一
one (thing)	1024	*count.*	ひとつ・一つ
one cupful	1092	*count.*	いっぱい・一杯
one cylindrical object	1092	*count.*	いっぽん・一本
one hundred	1022	*count.*	ひゃく・百
one hundred thousand	1052	*count.*	じゅうまん・十万
one minute	1032	*count.*	いっぷん・一分
one o'clock	1032	*count.*	いちじ・一時
one page, page one	1042	*count.*	いちぺーじ/いっぺーじ・一ページ
one person	1021	*count.*	ひとり・一人
one second	1032	*count.*	いちびょう・一秒
one sheet/piece	1042	*count.*	いちまい・一枚

English	Location		Japanese
one small animal	1021	*count.*	いっぴき・一匹
one thousand	1052	*count.*	せん・千
one time	1101	*count.*	いちど・一度
one volume	1092	*count.*	いっさつ・一冊
one year old	1052	*count.*	いっさい・一歳/一才
oops, sorry	1083	*interj.*	おっと
open (to) [book/bound object]	1013	*v*	ひらく・開く/ひらきます・開きます
open (to) [door/window]	1034	*v*	あける・開ける/あけます・開けます
orange	1064 1074	*n*	おれんじ・オレンジ
orange juice	1043s	*n*	おれんじじゅーす・オレンジジュース
Osaka (place)	1083s	*pn*	おおさか・大阪
outside	1045s	*n*	そと・外
over there	1024	*pron.*	あそこ
overdoing, impossible	1063	な *adj.*	むり・無理
P.M.	1032	*n*	ごご・午後
page eight, eight pages	1042	*count.*	はちぺーじ/はっぺーじ・八ページ
page five, five pages	1042	*count.*	ごぺーじ・五ページ
page four, four pages	1042	*count.*	よんぺーじ・四ページ
page nine, nine pages	1042	*count.*	きゅうぺーじ・九ページ
page one, one page	1042	*count.*	いちぺーじ/いっぺーじ・一ページ
page seven, seven pages	1042	*count.*	ななぺーじ/しちぺーじ・七ページ
page six, six pages	1042	*count.*	ろくぺーじ・六ページ
page ten, ten pages	1042	*count.*	じゅっぺーじ/じっぺーじ・十ページ
page three, three pages	1042	*count.*	さんぺーじ・三ページ
page two, two pages	1042	*count.*	にぺーじ・二ページ
painful	1063	い *adj.*	いたい・痛い
painting, drawing	1071	*n*	え・絵
pants, trousers	1064	*n*	ずぼん・ズボン
paper	1024	*n*	かみ・紙
part time job	1025s	*n*	あるばいと・アルバイト
particle after a place word to mean "to" before a verb of motion (similar to the particle に)	1023	*part.*	へ
particle after a place word to mean "to" before a verb of motion (similar to the particle へ)	1023	*part.*	に
party	1073s	*n*	ぱーてぃ・パーティ
pass through (to)	1051s	*v*	とおる・通る/とおります・通ります
past, after	1032		すぎ (〜)・〜過ぎ
peaceful, calm	1084	な *adj.*	おだやか
pen	1024	*n*	ぺん・ペン
pencil	1024	*n*	えんぴつ・鉛筆
pencil box	App.	*n*	ふでばこ・筆箱
period, age, era	1071s	*n*	じだい・時代
period of years, duration	1032s	*n*	ねんかん・年間

English	Location		Japanese
person	1022	*n*	ひと・人
Peruvian (person)	1041	*n*	ぺるーじん・ペルー人
photocopy (to), copy (to)	1062	*v*	こぴー・コピーする/します
photograph	1021	*n*	しゃしん・写真
physical education	1032	*n*	たいいく・体育
physics	1032	*n*	ぶつりがく・物理学
piano	1071	*n*	ぴあの・ピアノ
pickled vegetables (Japanese)	1083	*n*	つけもの・漬け物
Ping-Pong club	1033	*n*	たっきゅうぶ・卓球部
pink	1074	*n*	ぴんく・ピンク
pink (peach) color	1074	*n*	ももいろ・もも色
pizza	1043s	*n*	ぴざ・ピザ
place	1052s	*n*	ところ・所
planner, hand-book	App.	*n*	ぷらんなー・プランナー
play (to)	1103	*v*	あそぶ・遊ぶ/あそびます・遊びます
play [a stringed instrument] (to)	1071	*v*	ひく・弾く/ひきます・弾きます
play basketball (to)	1091	*v*	ばすけ(を)・バスケ(を)する/します
play guitar (to)	1071	*v*	ぎたーを・ギターをひく・弾く/ひきます・弾きます
play soccer (to)	1091	*v*	さっかー(を)・サッカー (を) する/します
play video games (to)	1091	*v*	びでおげーむ(を)・ビデオゲーム(を)する/します
playing cards, card game	1071	*n*	とらんぷ・トランプ
please	1013s	*exp.*	おねがい・お願い/おねがいします・お願いします
please (here you go), by all means	1015	*adv.*	どうぞ
Please be quiet.	1016s	*exp.*	しずかに してください。・静かにして下さい。
please forgive me, May I come in?	1092s	*exp.*	ごめんください・ごめん下さい
please remember me (favorably), best regards	1013s	*adv.*	よろしく
Please say it in English.	1016s	*exp.*	えいごで いってください。・英語で 言って 下さい。
plump (is), fat (is)	1062		ふとっています・太っています
polite for よろしく お願いします	1013	*exp.*	どうぞ よろしく おねがいします・お願いします
pond	1101s	*n*	いけ・池
pork ramen	1043s	*n*	とんこつらーめん・とんこつラーメン
Portugal	1041	*pn*	ぽるとがる・ポルトガル
Portuguese (language)	1042	*n*	ぽるとがるご・ポルトガル語

English	Location		Japanese
Portuguese (person)	1041	*n*	ぽるとがるじん・ポルトガル人
possession, replaces a noun	1021	*part.*	の
pot stickers	1043s	*n*	ぎょうざ
potato	1042s	*n*	じゃがいも・ジャガイモ
practice (to)	1051	*v*	れんしゅう(を)・練習(を) する/します
precipitate (to)	1101	*v*	ふる・降る/ふります・降ります
present (a), gift (a)	1094	*n*	ぷれぜんと・プレゼント
pretty; clean	1081	な *adj.*	きれい
problem	1045s	*n*	もんだい・問題
promise	1105s	*n*	やくそく・約束
psychology	1032	*n*	しんりがく・心理学
Puerto Rican (person)	1041	*n*	ぷえるとりこじん・プエルトリコ人
purple	1064, 1074	*n*	むらさき・紫
put into (to)	1061	*v*	いれる・入れる/いれます・入れます
question	1032s	*n*	しつもん・質問
quickly	1035	*adv.*	はやく・速く
quiet	1061	な *adj.*	しずか・静か
quiz, small test	1032	*n*	しょうてすと・小テスト
raccoon dog, tanuki	1035s	*n*	たぬき・狸
rain	1101	*n*	あめ・雨
rainy season	1101	*n*	つゆ・梅雨
ramen	1043s	*n*	らーめん・ラーメン
rat, mouse	1072	*n*	ねずみ・鼠
read (to)	1013	*v*	よむ・読む/よみます・読みます
reading	1071	*n*	どくしょ・読書
real thing, genuine article	1091	*n*	ほんもの・本物
reality, truth	1104	*n*	ほんとう・本当
really, indeed, truly	1084	*adv.*	まったく・全く
really, seeming, so	1033s	*adv.*	そう
really like, love	1072	な *adj.*	だいすき・大好き
receive (to) (very polite)	1092	*v*	いただく/いただきます
receive (to)	1094	*v*	もらう/もらいます
receital, concert	1052s	*n*	おんがくかい・音楽会
reconcile (to), make up (to)	1091	*v*	なかなおり(を)・仲直り(を) する/します
red	1074	*n*	あか・赤
red-colored	1064	い *adj.*	あかい・赤い
regrettably, unluckily	1093	*n*/な *adj.*	ざんねん・残念
reign year	1053s	*n*	ねんごう・年号
religion	1052s	*n*	しゅうきょう・宗教
reluctantly, by no means	1094s		いやいや
replaces a noun, possession	1021	*part.*	の
replaces particles, は, が, and を, too, also	1024	*part.*	も
reside (to), live (to)	1064	*v*	すむ・住む/すみます・住みます
rest (to), take a break (to)	1015s	*v*	やすむ・休む
restful, slowly	1016s	*adv.*	ゆっくり
restaurant	1043	*n*	れすとらん・レストラン
return (to)	1044	*v*	かえる・帰る/かえります・帰ります
return with someone (to)	1105	*v*	つれて・連れて かえる・帰る/かえります・帰ります
return with something (to)	1105	*v*	もって・持って かえる・帰る/かえります・帰ります
rice balls	1105s	*n*	おにぎり
rice crackers	1094	*n*	せんべい・煎餅
right	1104s	*n*	みぎ・右
rock and roll (music)	1105	*n*	ろっくんろーる・ロックンロール
rock, stone	1101	*n*	いし・石
rolled sushi	1043s	*n*	まきずし・巻き寿司
room (a)	1015	*n*	へや・部屋
Roppongi (section of Tokyo)	1024s	*pn*	ろっぽんぎ・六本木
ruler	App.	*n*	じょうぎ・定規
Russia (place)	1041	*pn*	ろしあ・ロシア
Russian (language)	1042	*n*	ろしあご・ロシア語
Russian (person)	1041	*n*	ろしあじん・ロシア人
ryokan, Japanese inn/hotel	1044s	*n*	りょかん・旅館
sack, bag	1023s	*n*	ばっぐ・バッグ
sad	1061	い *adj.*	かなしい・悲しい
safe, OK,all right,	1063	な *adj.*	だいじょうぶ・大丈夫
salt	App.	*n*	しお・塩
same	1044s	*n*	おなじ・同じ
same, together, at the same	1043s	*n*	いっしょ・一緒
time	1044s	*exp.*	いっしょに・一緒に
samurai	1061	*n*	さむらい・侍
Satsuma (place)	1041s	*pn*	さつま・薩摩
Saturday	1051	*n*	どようび・土曜日
say (to)	1041	*v*	いう・言う/いいます・言います
Say hello to . . .	1065	*exp.*	… に よろしく
Say it again please.	1016s	*exp.*	もういちど いって ください。・もう一度 言って 下さい。
scary	1081	い *adj.*	こわい
schedule	1032	*n*	すけじゅーる・スケジュール
schedule, timetable	1032	*n*	じかんわり・時間割
school	1031	*n*	がっこう・学校
school subject	1032	*n*	かもく・科目
science	1032	*n*	かがく・科学
scissors	App.	*n*	はさみ
score, grade	1033	*n*	せいせき・成績
scriptures	1052s	*n*	おきょう・お経
sea, ocean	1081	*n*	うみ・海
search (to)	1093	*v*	さがす・探す/さがします・探します
search, hunt	1013s	*n*	たんさく・探索
season	1101	*n*	きせつ・季節
seaweed	App.	*n*	のり
second (day of the month)	1053	*count.*	ふつか・二日
second oldest brother/sister (my)	1021	*n*	にばんめの あに/あね・二番目の兄/姉

English	Location		Japanese
second period	1033	count.	にじかんめ・二時間目
second year student	1031s	count.	にねんせい・二年生
secret	1061	n	ひみつ・秘密
see (to), look (to)	1013	v	みる・見る/みます・見ます
see if you can do (something), try to do (something) (to)	1073	v	やってみる/やってみます
see you later (formal)	1015	exp.	では　また
see you later (informal)	1015	exp.	じゃあ　また
seeming, so, really	1033s	adv.	そう
selfish	1081	な adj.	わがまま
sell (to)	1091	v	うる・売る/うります・売ります
send (to)	1051	v	おくる・送る/おくります・送ります
sentence ending for a rhetorical question or when seeking agreement	1035	part.	ね
sentence ending for a strong declarative statement or for emphasis	1035	part.	よ
sentence ending that can be exclamatory or express surprise	1035	part.	ねえ
separate	1092	n/な adj.	べつ・別
separately, individually	1092	n/な adj.	べつべつ・別々
September	1052	n	くがつ・九月
set	1103s	n	せっと・セット
seven	1021	count.	しち/なな・七
seven (things)	1024	count.	ななつ・七つ
seven cupfuls	1092	count.	ななはい・七杯
seven cylindrical objects	1092	count.	ななほん・七本
seven hundred	1023s	count.	ななひゃく・七百
seven minutes	1032	count.	ななふん・七分
seven o'clock	1032	count.	しちじ/ななじ・七時
seven pages, page seven	1042	count.	ななぺーじ/しちぺーじ・七ページ
seven people	1021	count.	しちにん/ななにん・七人
seven seconds	1032	count.	ななびょう・七秒
seven sheets	1042	count.	ななまい/しちまい・七枚
seven small animals	1021	count.	ななひき・七匹
seven thousand	1052	count.	ななせん・七千
seven times/degrees	1101	count.	ななど・七度
seven volumes	1092	count.	ななさつ・七冊
seven years old	1052	count.	ななさい・七歳/七才
seventeen	1022	count.	じゅうなな/じゅうしち・十七
seventeenth (day of the month)	1053	count.	じゅうしちにち・十七日
seventh (day of the month)	1053	count.	なのか・七日
seventh grader	1031	count.	ちゅうがくいちねんせい・中学一年生
seventy	1022	count.	ななじゅう・七十
seventy thousand	1052	count.	ななまん・七万
shampoo (to)	1091	v	しゃんぷー(を)・シャンプー(を)する/します
she; girlfriend	1074	pron.	かのじょ・彼女
Shinto (religion)	1052s	n	しんとう・神道
ship, boat	1045s	n	ふね・舟
shirt	1064	n	しゃつ・シャツ
shoes	1064	n	くつ・靴
shop, store	1071	n	みせ・店
shopkeeper, clerk	1092	n	てんいん・店員
shopping	1091	n	かいもの・買い物
short (height), low	1061	い adj.	ひくい・低い
short (length)	1061	い adj.	みじかい・短い
short pants, shorts	1064s	n	しょーとぱんつ・ショートパンツ
shoulder	1061	n	かた・肩
show (to)	1045s	v	みせる・見せる
shrine	1033	n	じんじゃ・神社
shut (to), close (to) [bound paper objects]	1013	v	とじる・閉じる/とじます・閉じます
shut (to), close (to) [doors/windows]	1034	v	しめる・閉める/しめます・閉めます
Shut/Close (it) please.	1013	exp.	とじて　ください・閉じて　下さい
siblings	1021	n	きょうだい・兄弟
sick, feel bad	1063	exp.	ぐあいが　わるい・具合が　悪い
sickness, illness	1063	n	びょうき・病気
sign language	1042	n	しゅわ・手話
signature	1042	n	さいん・サイン
signifies a question	1014	part.	か
silly, foolish	1081	い adj.	ばかばかしい
silver	1074	n	ぎんいろ・銀色
simple	1064	な adj.	しんぷる・シンプル
simple, kind, gentle, easy	1081	い adj.	やさしい・優しい
sing (to)	1071	v	うたう・歌う/うたいます・歌います
singing	1071	n	うたうこと・歌う事
sit (to)	1013	v	すわる・座る/すわります・座ります
sit down	1016s	exp.	ちゃくせき。・着席。
six	1021	count.	ろく・六
six (things)	1024	count.	むっつ・六つ
six cupfuls	1092	count.	ろっぱい・六杯
six cylindrical objects	1092	count.	ろっぽん・六本
six hundred	1023s	count.	ろっぴゃく・六百
six minutes	1032	count.	ろっぷん・六分
six o'clock	1032	count.	ろくじ・六時
six pages, page six	1042	count.	ろくぺーじ・六ページ
six people	1021	count.	ろくにん・六人
six seconds	1032	count.	ろくびょう・六秒
six sheets	1042	count.	ろくまい・六枚
six small animals	1021	count.	ろっぴき・六匹
six thousand	1052	count.	ろくせん・六千
six times/degrees	1101	count.	ろくど・六度
six volumes	1092	count.	ろくさつ・六冊
six years old	1052	count.	ろくさい・六歳
sixteen	1022	count.	じゅうろく・十六

English	Location		Japanese
sixteenth (day of the month)	1053	count.	じゅうろくにち・十六日
sixth (day of the month)	1053	count.	むいか・六日
sixth period	1033	count.	ろくじかんめ・六時間目
sixty	1022	count.	ろくじゅう・六十
sixty thousand	1052	count.	ろくまん・六万
skateboard (to)	1071	v	すけぼー(を)・スケボー(を) する/します
sketchbook	1062s	n	すけっちぶっく・スケッチブック
skiing	1071	n	すきー・スキー
skilled at	1073	な adj.	とくい・得意
skillful	1062	な adj.	じょうず・上手
skinny (is), slim (is)	1062	v	やせる/やせています
skirt	1064	n	すかーと・スカート
sleep (to)	1051	v	ねる・寝る/ねます・寝ます
sleeping	1071	n	ねること・寝る事
sleepy	1053s	い adj.	ねむい・眠い
slim, stylish	1062	な adj.	すまーと・スマート
slim (is), skinny (is)	1062	v	やせる/やせています
slipper(s)	1093s	n	すりっぱ・スリッパ
slowly, restful	1016s	adv.	ゆっくり
small	1031	い adj.	ちいさい・小さい
small (S) size	1092	n	えすさいず・Sサイズ
small animals count.	1022s	count.	ひき (〜)・〜匹
small test, quiz	1032	n	しょうてすと・小テスト
snack	App.	n	おやつ
snow	1101	n	ゆき・雪
so so, not bad, moderate	1062	adv.	まあまあ
so, really, seeming	1033s	adv.	そう
social studies, society	1032	n	しゃかい・社会
society, world (the)	1032s	n	せかい・世界
socks	1064	n	くつした・靴下
someone else's family	1021	n	ごかぞく・ご家族
something	1103		なにか・何か
sometimes	1032	n/adv.	ときどき・時々
somewhat, little	1032	adv.	ちょっと
song	1071	n	うた・歌
Soubu (train line)	1024s	pn	そうぶ・総武
sorry, oops	1083	interj.	おっと
soul, heart (not one's physical heart)	1061	n	こころ・心
South Africa (place)	1041	pn	みなみあふりか・南アフリカ
South America (place)	1042s	pn	なんべい・南米
South Korea (place)	1041	pn	かんこく・韓国
souvenir(s)	1023	n	おみやげ・お土産
soy sauce	1015	n	しょうゆ・醤油
spacious, wide	1083	い adj.	ひろい・広い
spaghetti	1043s	n	すぱげてぃ・スパゲティ
Spain (place)	1041	pn	すぺいん・スペイン
Spaniard (person)	1041	n	すぺいんじん・スペイン人
Spanish (language)	1042	n	すぺいんご・スペイン語

English	Location		Japanese
speak (to)	1042	v	はなす・話す/はなします・話します
special	1092	n/な adj.	とくべつ・特別
sports	1071	n	すぽーつ・スポーツ
spring	1101	n	はる・春
stand (to)	1013	v	たつ・立つ/たちます・立ちます
Stand please.	1013	exp.	たってください・立って下さい
stand up	1016s	exp.	きりつ。・起立。
stapler	App.	n	ほっちきす・ホッチキス
stature, height	1061	n	せ/せい・背
steak	App.	n	すてーき・ステーキ
step-	1021		ぎりの〜・義理の
sticky rice cake	1064	n	もち・餅
stomach	1061	n	おなか・お腹
stone, rock	1101	n	いし・石
store, shop	1091	n	みせ・店
strawberry	App.	n	いちご・イチゴ
strict	1081	い adj.	きびしい
strong	1061	い adj.	つよい・強い
student	1031	n	がくせい・学生, せいと・生徒
study (to)	1052	v	べんきょう(を)・勉強(を) する/します
stylish, slim	1062	な adj.	すまーと・スマート
sudden, unexpected, abrupt	1104s	adv.	とつぜん・突然
suffix AFTER a boy's name	1013	suffix	くん (〜)・〜君
suffix AFTER a name	1013	suffix	さん・〜さん
sugar	App.	n	さとう・砂糖
suit	1064	n	すーつ・スーツ
summer	1101	n	なつ・夏
Sunday	1051	n	にちようび・日曜日
sunset	1104s	n	さんせっと・サンセット, ゆうやけ・夕焼け
supporter, fan	1065s	n	ふぁん・ファン
sushi	1011	n	すし・寿司
sushi in a box or bowl with a variety of ingredients	1103s	n	ちらしずし・散らし寿司
sushi wrapped in fried tofu (abura-age)	1103s	n	いなりずし・稲荷寿司
sushi wrapped in nori	1103s	n	てまきずし・手巻き寿司
Swahili (language)	1042	n	すわひりご・スワヒリ語
sweets, candy	1023	n	あめ・飴, きゃんでぃ・キャンディ
swim (to)	1071	v	およぐ・泳ぐ/およぎます・泳ぎます
swimming	1071	n	およぐこと・泳ぐ事, すいえい・水泳
t-shirt	1023	n	てぃーしゃつ・Tシャツ
table	App.	n	てーぶる・テーブル
tacos (Mexican)	1025	n	たこす・タコス

English	Location		Japanese
take (it) out (to)	1013	*v*	だす・出す/だします・出します
take a break (to), rest (to)	1015s	*v*	やすむ・休む
take a photo (to)	1042	*v*	しゃしん(を)・写真(を) とる・撮る/とります・撮ります
take a shower (to)	1091	*v*	しゃわー(を)・シャワー (を) する/します
take a trip (to), travel (to)	1091	*v*	りょこう(を)・旅行(を)する/します
take a walk (to)	1054	*v*	さんぽ(を)・散歩(を)する/します
take medicine (to)	1063	*v*	くすり(を)・薬(を) のむ・飲む/のみます・飲みます
take someone (to)	1105	*v*	つれて・連れて いく・行く/いきます・行きます
take something (to)	1105	*v*	もって・持って いく・行く/いきます・行きます
tall; expensive; high	1082	い *adj.*	たかい・高い
tanuki; raccoon dog	1035s	*n*	たぬき・狸
tape	App.	*n*	てーぷ・テープ
Taro (male name)	1014	*pn*	たろう・太郎
tasteful, cool	1062	い *adj.*	しぶい・渋い
tea ceremony	1071	*n*	さどう/ちゃどう・茶道
teacher, suffix AFTER a teacher's, lawyer's, or doctor's name	1011	*n*	せんせい・先生, 〜せんせい・〜先生
telephone	1021	*n*	でんわ・電話
telephone (to)	1091	*v*	でんわ(を)・電話(を)する/します
television, TV	1103s	*n*	てれび・テレビ
tell/teach me, please	1032s	*exp.*	おしえて ください・教えて 下さい
temperature	1101	*n*	おんど・温度
temple (Buddhist)	1033	*n*	(お)てら・(お)寺
ten	1021	*count.*	じゅう・十
ten (things)	1024	*count.*	とお・十
ten cupfuls	1092	*count.*	じゅっぱい/じっぱい・十杯
ten cylindrical objects	1092	*count.*	じゅっぽん/じっぽん・十本
ten minutes	1032	*count.*	じゅっぷん/じっぷん・十分
ten o'clock	1032	*count.*	じゅうじ・十時
ten pages, page ten	1042	*count.*	じゅっぺーじ/じっぺーじ・十ページ
ten people	1021	*count.*	じゅうにん・十人
ten seconds	1032	*count.*	じゅうびょう・十秒
ten sheets	1042	*count.*	じゅうまい・十枚
ten small animals	1021	*count.*	じゅっぴき/じっぴき・十匹
ten thousand	1052	*count.*	いちまん・一万
ten thousand	1052	*count.*	まん・万
ten times/degrees	1101	*count.*	じゅうど・十度
ten volumes	1092	*count.*	じゅっさつ/じっさつ・十冊
ten years old	1052	*count.*	じゅっさい/じっさい・十歳/十才
tenpura (battered and deep fried fish or vegetable)	1021s	*n*	てんぷら・天ぷら
tenth (day of the month)	1053	*count.*	とおか・十日
tenth grader	1031	*count.*	こうこういちねんせい・高校一年生
teriyaki (meat or fish marinated in sweet soy sauce and broiled)	App.	*n*	てりやき・照り焼き
terrible	1081	い *adj.*	ひどい
terrible, to a great extent, amazing, great	1035	い *adj.*	すごい
test	1032	*n*	てすと・テスト
test, exam	1032	*n*	しけん・試験
textbook	1013	*n*	きょうかしょ・教科書
thank you	1023	*exp.*	どうも ありがとう
thank you very much (polite for どうも ありがとう)	1023	*exp.*	どうも ありがとう ございます
thanks	1023	*exp.*	ありがとう
that (one)	1015	*pron.*	それ
that (over there)	1015	*pron.*	あれ
that (person)	1014s	*pron.*	そちら
that (person) over there	1014s	*pron.*	あちら
that (thing)	1023	*pron.*	その
that (thing) over there	1023	*pron.*	あの
That makes sense.	1042s	*exp.*	なるほど
then, and then	1071	*conj.*	そして, それから
there	1024	*pron.*	そこ
thereupon	1082s	*conj.*	すると
they, them	1082	*pron.*	かれら 彼ら
thin (to become)	1062	*v*	やせる/やせます
thin slices of beef, cooked with vegetables	App.	*n*	すきやき・すき焼き
thing	1043	*n*	もの・物
thing (in tangible)	1071s	*n*	こと・事
think (to)	1072	*v*	おもう・思う/おもいます・思います
third (day of the month)	1053	*count.*	みっか・三日
third degree (belt)	1033s	*count.*	さんだん・三段
third period	1033	*count.*	さんじかんめ・三時間目
third year student	1031s	*count.*	さんねんせい・三年生
thirteen	1022	*count.*	じゅうさん・十三
thirteen minutes	1032	*count.*	じゅうさんぷん・十三分
thirteen years old	1052	*count.*	じゅうさんさい・十三歳/十三才
thirteenth (day of the month)	1053	*count.*	じゅうさんにち・十三日
thirtieth (day of the month)	1053	*count.*	さんじゅうにち・三十日
thirty	1022	*count.*	さんじゅう・三十
thirty thousand	1052	*count.*	さんまん・三万
thirty-first (day of the month)	1053	*count.*	さんじゅういちにち・三十一日
this (one)	1015	*pron.*	これ

English	Location		Japanese
this (thing)	1023		この
this month	1054	*n*	こんげつ・今月
this morning	1051s	*n/adv.*	けさ・今朝
this (person [polite] or thing), here (place close to speaker)	1014	*pron.*	こちら
this week	1054	*n*	こんしゅう・今週
this year	1054	*n*	ことし・今年
three	1021	*count.*	さん・三
three (things)	1024	*count.*	みっつ・三つ
three cupfuls	1092	*count.*	さんばい・三杯
three cylindrical objects	1092	*count.*	さんぼん・三本
three hundred	1023s	*count.*	さんびゃく・三百
three minutes	1032	*count.*	さんぷん・三分
three o'clock	1032	*count.*	さんじ・三時
three pages, page three	1042	*count.*	さんぺーじ・三ページ
three people	1021	*count.*	さんにん・三人
three seconds	1032	*count.*	さんびょう・三秒
three sheets	1042	*count.*	さんまい・三枚
three small animals	1021	*count.*	さんびき・三匹
three thousand	1052	*count.*	さんぜん・三千
three times/degrees	1101	*count.*	さんど・三度
three volumes	1092	*count.*	さんさつ・三冊
three years old	1052	*count.*	さんさい・三歳
throat	1061	*n*	のど・咽喉
throughout, continuously	1083		ずっと
thunder	1101	*n*	かみなり・雷
Thursday	1051	*n*	もくようび・木曜日
time after school	1033	*n/adv.*	ほうかご・放課後
time capsule	1094s	*n*	たいむかぷせる・タイムカプセル
time gate	1041s	*n*	ときのもん・時の門
time, hour	1035s	*n*	とき・時
timetable, schedule	1032	*n*	じかんわり・時間割
tissue	App.	*n*	てぃっしゅ・ティッシュ
Todaiji Temple (in Nara)	1051s	*pn*	とうだいじ・東大寺
today	1032	*n*	きょう・今日
tofu	1011	*n*	とうふ・豆腐
together, at the same time, same	1043s	*n*	いっしょ・一緒
together, at the same time, same	1044s	*exp.*	いっしょに・一緒に
Tokugawa (family name)	1041s	*pn*	とくがわ・徳川
Tokyo (place)	1011	*pn*	とうきょう・東京
Tokyo International University (place)	1022s	*pn*	とうきょうこくさいだいがく・東京国際大学
Tokyo University (place)	1031s	*pn*	とうきょうだいがく・東京大学
tomato	App.	*n*	とまと・トマト
tomorrow	1032	*n*	あした・明日
too, also, replaces particles は, が, and を	1024	*part.*	も
torii (Shinto shrine gate)	1035	*n*	とりい・鳥居
tornado	1101	*n*	たつまき・竜巻
total, all together, in all	1092	*exp.*	ぜんぶで・全部で
track and field club	1033	*n*	りくじょうぶ・陸上部
travel, trip	1071	*n*	りょこう・旅行, たび・旅

English	Location		Japanese
travel (to), take a trip (to)	1091	*v*	りょこう(を)・旅行(を)する/します
treat me favorably, best regards	1013	*exp.*	よろしく おねがいします・お願いします
treat me favorably, best regards (same meaning as よろしく おねがいします)	1013	*exp.*	どうぞ よろしく
tree	1011s	*n*	き・木
trip, travel	1071	*n*	りょこう・旅行, たび・旅
trousers, pants	1064	*n*	ずぼん・ズボン
truth, reality	1104	*n*	ほんとう・本当
truly, really, indeed,	1084	*adv.*	まったく・全く
try to do (something) (to), see if you can do(something)	1073	*v*	やってみる/やってみます
tsunami, exceptionally large ocean wave	1011	*n*	つなみ・津波
Tuesday	1051	*n*	かようび・火曜日
tunnel	1041s	*n*	とんねる・トンネル
turtle	1082	*n*	かめ・亀
twelfth (day of the month)	1053	*count.*	じゅうににち・十二日
twelfth grader	1031	*count.*	こうこうさんねんせい・高校三年生
twelve	1022	*count.*	じゅうに・十二
twelve minutes	1032	*count.*	じゅうにふん・十二分
twelve o'clock	1032	*count.*	じゅうにじ・十二時
twelve years old	1052	*count.*	じゅうにさい・十二歳
twentieth (day of the month)	1053	*count.*	はつか・二十日
twenty	1022	*count.*	にじゅう・二十
twenty minutes	1032	*count.*	にじゅっぷん・二十分
twenty thousand	1052	*count.*	にまん・二万
twenty years old	1052	*count.*	はたち・二十歳
twenty-eighth (day of the month)	1053	*count.*	にじゅうはちにち・二十八日
twenty-fifth (day of the month)	1053	*count.*	にじゅうごにち・二十五日
twenty-first (day of the month)	1053	*count.*	にじゅういちにち・二十一日
twenty-fourth (day of the month)	1053	*count.*	にじゅうよっか・二十四日
twenty-ninth (of the month)	1053	*count.*	にじゅうくにち・二十九日
twenty-one	1022	*count.*	にじゅういち・二十一
twenty-one minutes	1032	*count.*	にじゅういっぷん・二十一分
twenty-second (day of the month)	1053	*count.*	にじゅうににち・二十二日
twenty-seventh (day of the month)	1053	*count.*	にじゅうしちにち・二十七日
twenty-sixth (day of the month)	1053	*count.*	にじゅうろくにち・二十六日
twenty-third (day of the month)	1053	*count.*	にじゅうさんにち・二十三日
twins	1022s	*n*	ふたご・双子
two	1021	*count.*	に・二
two (things)	1024	*count.*	ふたつ・二つ
two cupfuls	1092	*count.*	にはい・二杯

English	Location		Japanese
two cylindrical objects	1092	*count.*	にほん・二本
two hundred	1023s	*count.*	にひゃく・二百
two hundred ten thousand	1052	*count.*	にじゅういちまん・二十一万
two hundred thousand	1052	*count.*	にじゅうまん・二十万
two minutes	1032	*count.*	にふん・二分
two o'clock	1032	*count.*	にじ・二時
two pages, page two	1042	*count.*	にぺーじ・二ページ
two people	1021	*count.*	ふたり・二人
two seconds	1032	*count.*	にびょう・二秒
two sheets	1042	*count.*	にまい・二枚
two small animals	1021	*count.*	にひき・二匹
two thousand	1052	*count.*	にせん・二千
two times/degrees	1101	*count.*	にど・二度
two volumes	1092	*count.*	にさつ・二冊
two years old	1052	*count.*	にさい・二歳/二才
typhoon	1101	*n*	たいふう・台風
ugly	1081	い *adj.*	みにくい
uncle or man quite a bit older than you	1022	*n*	おじさん
understand (to)	1016s	*v*	わかる・分かる/わかります・分かります
underwear	1064	*n*	したぎ・下着, ぱんつ・パンツ
unexpected, abrupt, sudden	1104s	*adv.*	とつぜん・突然
uniform (school)	1025s	*n*	せいふく・制服
United States of America (place)	1041	*pn*	あめりか・アメリカ
university, college	1031	*n*	だいがく・大学
university/college student	1031	*n*	だいがくせい・大学生
unluckily, regrettably	1093	*n*/な *adj.*	ざんねん・残念
unskilled at	1073	な *adj.*	にがて・苦手
until (used with spec. locations or times)	1053	*part.*	まで
Urashima Taro (folktale character)	1084s	*pn*	うらしまたろう・浦島太郎
us, we	1013	*pron.*	わたしたち・私達
use (to)	1102	*v*	つかう・使う/つかいます・使います
used after a location or time word, in, at	1015	*part.*	に
used after the direct object	1023	*part.*	を
used like "and" or "with" to connect nouns, used imm. after a direct quotation	1022	*part.*	と
usual, normal	1064	*adj./adv.*	ふつう・普通
usually	1072	*adv.*	たいてい
various	1074	*adv.*	いろいろ・色々
vehicle, car	1043	*n*	くるま・車
very	1031	*adv.*	とても
video games	1071	*n*	びでおげーむ・ビデオゲーム
vocabulary	1013s	*n*	たんご・単語
voice	1061	*n*	こえ・声
volleyball club (team)	1033	*n*	ばれーぼーるぶ・バレーボール部
wait (to)	1061	*v*	まつ・/まちます・待つ/待ちます
Wait a minute please.	1016s	*exp.*	ちょっと まって ください。・待って 下さい。
waitress	1084s	*n*	うぇいとれす・ウェイトレス
waka (classic Japanese poem)	1072s	*n*	わか・和歌
wake (up) (to)	1051	*v*	おきる・/おきます・起きる/起きます
walk	1054	*n*	さんぽ・散歩
want to meet (to)	1044s	*v*	あいたい・会いたい
wasabi, Japanese horseradish	1015	*n*	わさび
water	1024	*n*	みず・水
we, us	1013	*pron.*	わたしたち・私達
weak	1061	い *adj.*	よわい・弱い
wear above the waist (to)	1064	*v*	きる・着る/きます・着ます
wear below the waist (to)	1064	*v*	はく・履く/はきます・履きます
wear glasses or sunglasses (to)	1064	*v*	かける/かけます
wear on the head (to)	1064	*v*	かぶる・被る/かぶります・被ります
weather	1101	*n*	てんき・天気
weather report	1101	*n*	てんきよほう・天気予報
Wednesday	1051	*n*	すいようび・水曜日
weekend	1054	*n*	しゅうまつ・週末
welcome (usually used at a place of business)	1043	*exp.*	いらっしゃいませ
welcome home	1015	*exp.*	おかえりなさい・お帰りなさい
Welcome!, Nice to see you.	1014	*exp.*	ようこそ
well	1082	い *adj.*	よい・良い (よく)
well, nicely	1103s	*adv.*	よく
well, now	1091s	*interj.*	さて
well...	1035	*inter.*	さあ
well..., let me see	1033s	*interj.*	ええと
Well done.	1016s	*exp.*	よくできました。・良く出来ました。
well then...	1033s		じゃ/じゃあ
Western clothes, clothes	1064	*n*	ようふく・洋服
what	1021	*inter.*	なん/なに・何
what color	1074	*inter.*	なにいろ・何色
what day of the month	1053	*inter.*	なんにち・何日
what day of the week	1051	*inter.*	なんようび・何曜日
what ethnicity or heritage	1041	*inter.*	なにけい・何系
what grade/year	1031	*inter.*	なんねんせい・何年生
what month	1052	*inter.*	なんがつ・何月
what nationality	1041	*inter.*	なにじん・何人
what page, how many pages	1042	*inter.*	なんぺーじ・何ページ
what period	1033	*inter.*	なんじかんめ・何時間目
what time	1032	*inter.*	なんじ・何時
what year	1054	*inter.*	なんねん・何年
what/which kind of	1062	*inter.*	どんな
Watch/Look please.	1013	*exp.*	みてください。・見て下さい。

English	Location		Japanese
when	1055s	*conj.*	のときに・〜の時に
when?	1052	*inter.*	いつ
where?	1024	*inter.*	どこ
wherever, everywhere	1102	*adv.*	どこも
which (one)	1015	*inter.*	どれ
which (thing)	1023	*inter.*	どの
which/what kind of	1062	*inter.*	どんな
white	1074	*n*	しろ・白
white-colored	1064	い *adj.*	しろい・白い
whiteboard	App.	*n*	ほわいとぼーど・ホワイトボード
who	1021	*inter.*	だれ
why	1042	*inter.*	どうして, なぜ
wide, spacious	1083	い *adj.*	ひろい・広い
wind	1035	*n*	かぜ・風
window	1034	*n*	まど・窓
window-shop (to)	1091s	*n*	うぃんどうしょっぴんぐ(を)・ウィンドウショッピング(を)する/します
winter	1101	*n*	ふゆ・冬
wise, bright	1081	い *adj.*	かしこい
woman, female	1064s	*n*	おんな・女
woman, female	1064	*n*	おんなのひと・女の人
wonderful	1065	い *adj.*	すばらしい・素晴らしい
wonderful, nice	1064	な *adj.*	すてき・素敵
woodblock print	1091	*n*	はんが・版画
woodblock print (new), art print (new)	1091	*n*	しんはんが・新版画
woodblock print (prior to and through the Edo Period)	1091	*n*	うきよえ・浮世絵
words, language, dialect	1101s	*n*	ことば・言葉

English	Location		Japanese
work (to)	1052s	*v*	しごと(を)・仕事(を)する/します
world (the), society	1032s	*n*	せかい・世界
world history	1032	*n*	せかいし・世界史
worry (to)	1063	*v*	しんぱい(を)・心配(を) する/します
wow!	1035	*interj.*	わっ！
write (to)	1013	*v*	かく・書く/かきます・書きます
writing pad, mat	1024	*n*	したじき・下敷き
yakisoba, fried noodles	1102s	*n*	やきそば・焼きそば
Yamamoto (family name)	1031	*pn*	やまもと・山本
Yamanote (train line)	1024s	*pn*	やまのて・山の手
yellow	1074	*n*	きいろ・黄色
yellow-colored	1064	い *adj.*	きいろい・黄色い
yes	1032s		ええ/はい
yes it is	1014	*exp.*	はい、そう です。
Yes, I understand.	1016s	*exp.*	はい、わかります。・分かります。
yes, OK, here (roll call)	1014		はい
yesterday	1032	*n/adv.*	きのう・昨日
Yokohama (place)	1031s	*pn*	よこはま・横浜
you [best not used too often]	1041s	*pron.*	あなた
you are welcome	1023	*exp.*	どういたしまして
younger brother (my)	1021	*n*	おとうと・弟
younger brother (someone else's)	1022	*n*	おとうとさん・弟さん
younger sister (my)	1021	*n*	いもうと・妹
younger sister (someone else's)	1022	*n*	いもうとさん・妹さん
youngest brother/sister (my)	1021	*n*	いちばんしたのおとうと/いもうと・一番下の 弟/妹

The materials in the disc may be Downloaded.

1. You must have an internet connection.
2. Type the URL below into your web browser.

   http://www.tuttlepublishing.com/beginning-japanese-downloadable-cd-content

For support email us at info@tuttlepublishing.com.